Coal Processing and Utilization

T0320226

Coal Processing and Utilization

D.V. Subba Rao

*Formerly Head of the Department of Mineral
Beneficiation, S.D.S Autonomous College,
Andhra Pradesh, India*

T. Gouricharan

*Senior Principal Scientist and Head, Coal Preparation,
Central Institute of Mining and Fuel Research,
Dhanbad, Jharkhand, India*

CRC Press
Taylor & Francis Group
Boca Raton London New York

CRC Press is an imprint of the
Taylor & Francis Group, an **informa** business

A BALKEMA BOOK

Cover images credits: Coal particles taken from Shutterstock, left bottom image; Heavy media cyclone obtained from Diester, right bottom image; Coal burning taken from Shutterstock.

CRC Press
Taylor & Francis Group
6000 Broken Sound Parkway NW, Suite 300
Boca Raton, FL 33487-2742

First issued in paperback 2019

ISBN-13: 978-1-138-02959-0 (hbk)
ISBN-13: 978-0-367-87887-0 (pbk)

Typeset by V Publishing Solutions Pvt Ltd., Chennai, India

Published by: CRC Press/Balkema
P.O. Box 11320, 2301 EH Leiden, The Netherlands
e-mail: Pub.NL@taylorandfrancis.com
www.crcpress.com – www.taylorandfrancis.com

Library of Congress Cataloging-in-Publication Data

Visit the Taylor & Francis Web site at
http://www.taylorandfrancis.com

and the CRC Press Web site at
http://www.crcpress.com

Dedication

Dr. S. Krishna Murthy & Smt. Siva Nagendramma
For their Care with Love and Affection
D.V. Subba Rao
Author

Contents

Preface

Coal remains the predominant source of fossil fuel and this scenario is likely to remain in the foreseeable future. The quality of coal is gradually deteriorating and affecting its utilization for all the downstream processes. Efficient utilization of the available resources requires its upgradation and coal beneficiation/washing is the most accepted method for upgradation of coal quality.

An attempt has been made to provide a book on coal processing and utilization for all the undergraduate and postgraduate students of Mineral, Mining and Metallurgical Engineering. This book gives an integrated picture of coal processing and utilization along with clean coal technology, while highlighting the presentation of all the basic principles, theory and practice in a systematic way.

This book is designed keeping in view the freshers who enter in the field of coal and its utilization. All the topics covered are dealt with in a self explanatory manner so that any new reader may find this book interesting and understand it easily. The contents of this book have been divided into three parts.

The first part of the book deals with the theories of origin and formation of coal, constituents of coal, sampling and analysis of coal, properties of coal and coking tests.

In the second part, unit operations viz., screening, size reduction, and dewatering are discussed. Prominence is given to describing the construction of washability curves by taking a hypothetical example. The beneficiation processes viz., heavy medium separation, jigging, flowing film concentration, cyclone separation, froth flotation, centrifugal separation and dry beneficiation, are dealt with in depth. The chapter "coal washing efficiency" is devoted exclusively to describing different criteria used for the evaluation of processing plant performance. Coal washing practices and recent developments in coal processing are added for the benefit of researchers. Illustrative examples and problems for practice are incorporated wherever necessary which may help the readers to use them in teaching, research and operating plants. A topic on applications of computers in coal processing plants is given in Annexure-I.

The third part, coal utilization, includes considerable details of carbonization, combustion, gasification and liquefaction.

Special emphasis is given to Indian coals by incorporating three separate chapters viz., classification of Indian coals, Indian coal resources and coal washing practice in India. Selected international and national standards used in coal and coke analysis and evaluation are given in annexure-II for the benefit of readers.

D.V. Subba Rao
Retired Associate Professor
Formerly Head, Department of Mineral Beneficiation
S.D.S Autonomous College, Garividi,
Vizianagaram District, Andhra Pradesh, India
dvsubbarao3@rediffmail.com
dvsubbarao3@gmail.com

Dr. T. Gouricharan
Senior Principal Scientist & Head, Coal Preparation
Professor, Academy of Scientific & Innovative Research
Central Institute of Mining & Fuel Research (Digwadih Campus),
Dhanbad, Jharkhand, India
gouricharancimfr@gmail.com
gouricharan@yahoo.com

Foreword

I have great pleasure to write the foreword to this book **"Coal Processing and Utilization"** authored by Mr. D.V. Subba Rao and Dr. T. Gouricharan. Mr. D.V. Subba Rao taught mineral and coal processing courses to undergraduates and guided many postgraduate students for more than 35 years. Dr. T. Gouricharan, student of D.V. Subba Rao, had more than 25 years of experience in coal preparation at Central Institute of Mining and Fuel Research (CIMFR), Dhanbad and published more than 80 papers in national and international journals.

In this book, the authors present the subject in a very simple manner and also include quite a few illustrative examples and problems for practice in order to have thorough understanding of the concepts. Keeping in view the undergraduate and post-graduate students, this book is very well articulated for ease of understanding with the broad classification of the contents into three parts.

The first part of the book deals with the geology, properties, analyses and tests of coal. The second part of the book comprises of washability characteristics, unit operations, and beneficiation processes of coal. Illustrative examples and problems for practice included will help the plant engineers, designers and researchers. The third part covers coal utilization and is of immense importance for the readers to have a good idea of carbonization, combustion, gasification and liquefaction in order to assess to what extent the coal has to be upgraded. For this, the authors are to be complimented for covering these aspects in the light of increased environmental awareness.

I am sure that the readers dealing with any aspect of coal, right from its geology to its utilization, would be benefited by this book written in the simplest possible way.

Dr. T.C. Rao
Formerly Director, Regional Research Laboratory, Bhopal
Professor & Head of the Department of Fuel and Mineral Engineering,
Indian School of Mines, Dhanbad, India

Acknowledgements

We are grateful to Dr. T.C. Rao, former Director, Regional Research Laboratory, Bhopal, and Professor and Head of the department of Fuel and Mineral Engineering, Indian School of Mines, Dhanbad for his valuable foreword. His constant encouragement helped us to prepare this book.

We have been inspired by Sri A.L. Mohan, former Principal of SDS Autonomous College, Garividi, and his initiation in attempting to write this book and make it a reality.

We are grateful to the Director, CSIR-Central Institute of Mining & Fuel Research, Dhanbad for his constant support and encouragement for preparing this book. The support extended by the staff members of the Coal Preparation Division CSIR-Central Institute of Mining & Fuel Research, Dhanbad is highly acknowledged.

We express our gratitude to Sri Y. Ramachandra Rao and Sri K. Satyanarayana, faculty of SDS Autonomous College, Garividi, for the discussions we had with them which helped to assess the needs of the students, extent of coverage of each topic and presentation of the topics.

We thank Dr. C. Raghu Kumar, Head, Minerals & Ferro Alloys Technology, Dr. Y. Ramamurthy, Principal Researcher, and Mr. Ch. Gopikrishna, Sr. Manager, Coal Characterization and Assessment, Process Technology, Tata Steel Ltd., Jamshedpur, Mr. B. Ratnakar, Junior Manager, JSW Steel Plant, Tornagallu, for providing useful literature and patiently going through the script for assessment and necessary modifications. Help extended by Mr. A. Janakiram, Associate GM, Hindustan Zinc Ltd., Mr. Kirtee Sunder Bhoi, Manager – Process Engineering, Metso India Pvt. Ltd., Mr. S.Siba Sankar Patra, Dy. Manager – Mineral processing, Mineral Technologies, Mr. G. Satish Kumar, Dy. Manager, Wear Minerals, Mr. R. Satyanarayana, Senior Engineer (Process), Metso India Pvt. Ltd. in completing this book successfully is thankfully acknowledged.

We were glad to work with the Taylor & Francis group and the cooperation of the editorial and production staff is quite comfortable and enjoyable.

Our deepest gratitude is expressed to Mrs. Krishna Veni, wife of D.V. Subba Rao and Mrs. T. Shanti Latha, wife of Dr. T. Gouricharan, for their emotional support throughout the period of preparation of this book and Mrs. Radha Rani and Mrs. Lalitha Rani, daughters of D.V. Subba Rao, and Mr. Aditya Shivcharan and Mr. Lalit Vidya Sagar, sons of Dr. T. Gouricharan, for extending all their help in preparing the manuscript.

Matter relating to basic principles of coal processing operations has been taken from the books "Mineral Beneficiation – A Concise Basic Course" and "Chapter 12 of Coal Production and Processing Technology" written by us and used in this book.

We thankfully acknowledge www.geologydata.info from which the description of the major coal fields of India has been taken and used in this book.

The tables in Annexure-II have been compiled in part with reference to the book Coal Geology by Larry Thomas, Second Edition, John Wiley Sons Ltd., 2013.

We gratefully acknowledge the following organizations for permitting us to use respective photographs:

Deister Concentrator, LLC Piper Drive, Fort Wayne, USA	Heavy Medium Cyclone Figure on cover page
Jayant Scientific Industries, Mumbai Maharashtra, India	Table Model Sieve Shaker Ro-tap Sieve shaker
Pennsylvania Crusher Corporation, USA	Bradford Breaker
aimehq.org	Sectional view of single toothed roll crusher
Great Wall Company, Zhengzhou, China	Double toothed roll crusher
TerraSource Global, St. Louis, Missouri, USA	Sizer
MBE Coal & Mineral Technology India Pvt. Ltd., Kolkata	Baum jig, Batac jig, Feldspar jig, ROM jig
mine-engineer.com	Spiral concentrator
Sepro Mineral Systems Corp., Canada	Falcon Concentrator
Downer Mineral Technologies, Australia	Kelsey jig
FLSmidth	Knelson Concentrator
Allmineral.asia	All-Air jig
Ardee Hi-Tech Pvt. Ltd., Visakhapatnam	Ramdars plant, Ardee Sort plant
Metso Minerals	High frequency vibrating screen
Westech Process Equipment India Pvt. Ltd.	Rotary vacuum disc filter
Andritz separation	Hyperbaric disc filter
Elgin Separation Solutions, St.Louis, Missouri, USA	CMI screen scroll centrifuge

List of tables

List of figures

Part A

Coal

Chapter 1

Introduction

It is not use of coal,
but how coal is used
that must be the focus of action
　　　　　　　　　　　—World Coal Institute

Coal plays a pivotal role in sustainable development. It is the most widely used energy source for electricity generation and an essential input to most steel production. Total global coal resources are estimated at 11,000 billion tons [1], out of which extractable reserves are 909 billion tonnes, less than 10% of the total coal resources. A resource is the occurrence in the earth's crust. A reserve is a mineable part of a resource that is extractable with existing technology.

USA ranks first in coal resources with 237 billion tons. Russia, China, Australia and India come next to USA in coal resources. However, China ranks first in coal production with 3474 million tons in 2014. USA, India, Australia and Indonesia come next to China in coal production.

As estimated by the World Coal Association, coal currently fuels 41% of the world electricity and this proportion is set to remain static over the next 30 years. Poland relies on coal for over 94% of its electricity; South Africa for 92%; China for 77%; and Australia for 76%. Coal has been the world's fastest growing energy source in recent years – faster than gas, oil, nuclear, hydro and other renewable sources. Coal has played this important role for centuries – not only providing electricity, but also an essential fuel for metallurgical and cement production, and other industrial activities. About 70% of the world's steel production is based on coal.

Over the next 30 years, it is estimated that global energy demand will increase by almost 60%. Two thirds of the increase will come from developing countries – by 2030 they will account for almost half of total energy demand.

Average gross energy efficiency of power generation from coal-based power plants employing pulverized coal firing method is 30.5 per cent [1]. Energy efficiency can be improved during combustion stage as well as pre-combustion stage. Processing of the coal and blending the coals of different quality before the coal is combusted are the low cost solutions to increase the energy efficiency in a pre-combustion stage. Clean coal technology aims to improve the energy efficiency and to reduce the harmful emissions.

Chapter 2

Clean coal technology

The term **Clean Coal Technology** (CCT) describes a new generation of processes for the production of electricity and fuels from coal. Clean coal technology addresses atmospheric problems resulting from burning coal. The clean coal technology is of utmost importance because (i) coal is abundant and will remain a major source of energy for future years, and (ii) emission from coal based generation is a matter of serious concern. Thus, clean coal research has begun to:

- Improve the quality of non-coking coal at the pre-combustion stage for use in power generation by value addition
- Adopt new coal combustion and conversion technology for improving efficiency of coal utilization
- Reduce carbon dioxide and other pollutant emissions in the environment through Renovation and Modernization

Adoption of new and efficient technologies for improvement of coal quality at pre-combustion stage, and for combustion and conversion processes not only aims to increase in amount of energy obtained from each ton of coal used but also to reduce emission of greenhouse gases and other pollutants.

A **Greenhouse Gas** (GHG) is a gas in an atmosphere that absorbs and emits radiation within the thermal infra-red range. This process is the fundamental cause of the greenhouse effect. The **greenhouse effect** is a natural process by which thermal radiation from a planetary surface is absorbed by atmospheric **greenhouse** gases, and is re-radiated in all directions. Greenhouse gases normally trap some of the sun's heat keeping the planet warm enough for life. Burning of fossil fuels increases the greenhouse gas levels, leading to an enhanced greenhouse effect. The result is global warming and unprecedented rates of climate change.

Global warming is a significant increase in the Earth's climatic temperature over a relatively short period of time as a result of the activities of humans. In specific terms, an increase of 1 or more degrees Celsius in a period of one hundred to two hundred years would be considered global warming. Over the course of a single century, an increase of even 0.4 degrees Celsius would be significant.

The most abundant greenhouse gases in Earth's atmosphere are water vapor (H_2O), Carbon dioxide (CO_2), Methane (CH_4), Nitrous oxide (N_2O), Ozone (O_3), and Chlorofluorocarbons (CFCs). Other greenhouse gases include sulfur hexafluoride, hydrofluorocarbons and perfluorocarbons. The atmospheric lifetime of green house gases measures the time required to restore equilibrium following a sudden increase or decrease in its concentration in the atmosphere. Major greenhouse gases are well mixed and take many years to leave the atmosphere. The atmospheric lifetime of CO_2 is estimated of the order of 30–95 years. Methane has an atmospheric lifetime of 12 ± 3 years. However, the residence time of water vapor is about nine days. The Global Warming Potential (GWP) depends on both the efficiency of the molecule as a greenhouse gas and its atmospheric lifetime.

The World-watch Institute reports that carbon emissions worldwide have increased from about 1 billion tons in 1900 to about 7 billion tons in 1995. Atmospheric CO_2 levels have increased by more than 40 percent since the beginning of the Industrial Revolution, from about 280 parts per million (ppm) in the 1800s to 400 ppm today [2]. Hence emission to the environment on utilizing the coal is of major concern. Therefore **Clean Coal Technology** (CCT) refers all the technologies applied to coal in order to reduce air emissions, waste product and pollutants on utilizing the coal for its process of energy conversion.

Clean coal technologies are categorized into

1 Coal beneficiation
2 Coal combustion
3 Coal conversion
4 Post-combustion

Coal Beneficiation Technology

Beneficiation of coal produces higher quality coals by increasing percent carbon that can be burned more cleanly and with greater efficiency, reduces the amounts of emitted fly ash and associated hazardous air pollutants, increases calorific Value, produces required sizes of particles, minimize capital, operating and maintenance costs, reduces the need to import higher-quality coals, improves health and safety and mitigates environmental degradation.

Coal Combustion Technology

Coal combustion technology aims in increasing the energy efficiency and reducing the harmful emissions while combusting the coal.

Coal Conversion Technology

It comprises the technology of converting coal into gas through gasification and into oil through liquefaction. Coal conversion processes reduce pollution and increase efficiency, but adds to infrastructure needs for coal suppliers/users.

Post-combustion Technology

In post-combustion technology, pollutants such as SO_x, NO_x, and CO_2 are captured and removed from the atmosphere.

Chapter 3

Coal – its origin and formation

Coal is a natural fuel, occurring in layers in the earth's crust composed mainly of plant material that has suffered partial decay and has been further altered by the agencies of heat and pressure to the varying degrees of completeness. This initial sediment formed by this process is, moist, spongy material, called peat, but this becomes compressed, dried and modified in both texture and composition due to diagenesis associated with burial and tectonic activity. The different kinds of plant material vary in their proportions in different coals, and the decay and subsequent alteration of the material proceeded to different degrees. As a result, coals show great variety in their chemical and physical properties and because of this, in their behaviour in practical use.

Coal is a stratified rock which was formed many millions of years ago from the remains of decaying trees and vegetation. Coal is unique amongst rocks because it is organic in composition. It contains the elements carbon, hydrogen and oxygen with small amounts of nitrogen and sulphur and only traces of inorganic material which are not chemically combined with the organic material forming most of coal.

Coal is a stratified rock, since geologists regards as rocks all natural, solid substances, organic or inorganic, that compose the earth's crust. From petrological point of view, coal may be considered as a mildly metamorphosed sedimentary rock, with properties depending on both the nature of the original parent material or maceral assemblage and the degree of diagenesis or metamorphism to which it has been subjected. Being an unusual rock type, coal is also a highly significant part of the stratigraphic succession in many sedimentary accumulations. Coal beds are widely used as markers for stratigraphic correlation, and as indicators of specific depositional environments in basin analysis. From a more pragmatic viewpoint, coal may be regarded simply as a special kind of economic mineral deposit. All of the above considerations are important in someway to the economic coal geologist, along with aspects such as the most appropriate means of evaluating and developing individual deposits for use. The economical value of coal deposit, and physical, legal and sociological constraints on their extraction and use are likewise of great concern to mining and processing engineers, mineral economists, environmental scientists and host of other technical specialists involved in the various operations of the coal Industry.

In trade, industry, and legal affairs coal is considered as a mineral and it is sometimes spoken of as mineral coal. In restricted technical sense, it is not a mineral, because a mineral according to Dana [3] is an inorganic homogeneous substance with a definite chemical composition and internal atomic structure, all of which requirements coal lacks. A block of coal of appreciable size is not homogeneous and though the composition of certain constituents comprising it may be expressed by a chemical formula, the composition of coal as a whole varies markedly from point to point.

Coal is a primary source of heat and power. It has long been the backbone of industrial life. The popular definition of coal is that of Miss. Stopes and Wheeler [4] according to whom, "Ordinary coal is a compact stratified mass of mummified plants (which have in part suffered arrested decay to varying degrees of completeness)." But the scientific definition of coal is given by E.A.N. Arber [5] who defines, "Coal is a solid stratified rock, composed mainly of hydrocarbons and capable of being used as a fuel to supply heat or light or both."

3.1   ORIGIN OF COAL

Chemical and geological studies have conclusively shown that coal is formed from vegetable material such as trees, vesicular plants, spores etc. The longer remains like tree trunks, bark, leaves and some plant residues can be seen with naked eye. Small structures such as wood cells, spores and algae are identified with the help of a microscope. The various ranks of coal represent different degrees in the conversion of the original plant material. The method of accumulation of the vegetable matter has also influenced the nature and properties of coal.

It is considered that coal was formed from decaying vegetation and mineral matter, compressed beneath many layers of fallen trees, leaves and soils. About 250 million years ago, much of the area now occupied by Great Britain was covered by large shallow lake or swamp surrounded by low lying land, which, here and there, extended into the lake and subdivided it into several parts. The climate at that time is considered to have been warm and humid, with a heavy rainfall, so that conditions were favourable to the growth of luxuriant vegetation. Large trees, many resembling giant ferns, grew in dense forests on the low lying land or in the shallow waters of the lake and succeeding generations of trees as they died and accumulated on the floor of the lake, forming a vegetable sludge.

Two theories, **in situ** and **drift**, have been put forward as to the modes of origin of coal seams. The first, in situ (the growth-in-place) theory says that coal seams occupy more or less the site on which the original plants grew and where their remains accumulated. The coal formed under this theory is not polluted much with the extraneous dirts, and the seams thus formed are not very thick.

In the case of drift theory, the formation is of a quite different in nature. Plants formed to coal seams were drifted from one place, where it actually grew and die, by flood or river transportation and accumulated in a lake or estuary. Under some earth quake or other geological sequence, everything had gone under ground and covered up with earth strata.

From time to time sinking of the floor of the lake or swamp drowned the forests, and sediments (sand and mud) carried by rivers were deposited in layers above the vegetable sludge. Eventually, with a halt in the sinking, the water became shallow again, trees re-established themselves, and the whole cycle was repeated. This occurred many times over, so that there accumulated twenty or thirty or even more layers of vegetable sludge separated by layers of sand and mud. The last two materials, with little more change than hardening, eventually formed sandstone and shale, but the conversion of the plant material into coal involved a considerable change in composition.

Each layer of vegetable sludge which forms further as coal bed is called **Coal Seam**. Coal generally occurs as layered sedimentary rock/bed as part of earth crust and this layer is called the coal seam. In a sequence, wherever a coal seam occurs, irrespective of its geological age, the seam is usually a minor constituent of the rock to which it belongs. Sandstone, shale or carbonaceous shales generally overly the coal seams. Formations of series of coal seams separated by layers of sand and mud (sedimentary rock) are known as **Coal Measure.**

The coal formed under drift theory is naturally contaminated by extraneous dirts with the formation of shale and sandstone bands. Collected evidences indicate that the majority of coal seams in the world are of in situ origin whereas Indian coals are of drift origin. That is why percentage of ash is much higher than the coals under in situ formation. One advantage in this coal is that, the seams are thick due to prolonged accumulation of drifted vegetation in lakes. China has got a seam of over 600 ft, the thickest one in the world. In India, the Jheengurdah seam of Singrauli coalfield in Sidhi district in U.P border is about 152 meters (500 ft) thick, stands in the second position in the world. One may visualize how much drifted plant was accumulated to form such a thick seam which can be worked out simply by open cast system by removing over burden.

3.2 FORMATION OF COAL

Coal is formed from vegetation by coalification. Coalification is the process of the chemical transformation from vegetation into coal. There were two important stages in the formation of coal from vegetable matter. The first one is **Peat stage** or **Biochemical stage** and the second one is **Metamorphic** or **Geochemical** or **Dynamochemical stage.**

3.2.1 Peat stage or biochemical stage

On dry ground, fallen trees and plants are attacked by oxygen from the surrounding air. Cellulose, which is their principal constituent, is slowly converted to carbon dioxide and water and the tree and tree rots, leaving little trace of the trees and vegetation are water logged, however, air cannot penetrate to the cellulose and decay takes place anaerobically (i.e. in absence of air) by the action of bacteria. In this case, decay takes place slowly and is gradually halted as the products of decomposition accumulate and bacteria can no longer survive. During the period of bacterial decay, the trees and vegetation are covered by fresh debris by vegetation, soil and rocks deposited by movements of the earth's crust. Because the bacterial degradation of cellulose is a slow process, the products of decomposition have been buried to a considerable depth by the time the bacterial action ceases. The resulting product thus formed is called as **PEAT**. In a peat, the bacterial processes are only partially completed, because some of the products which accumulate in the deposit are aseptic and prevent the complete break down of the plant tissues. Resins and waxy plant skins resist bacterial decay more strongly than wood, so these compounds tend to accumulate in the deposit.

The principal chemical components of wood from which peat formed are:

Cellulose $n(C_6H_{10}O_5)$	45–65%
Lignin	25–35%
Water and proteins in solution	10–15%
Waxes and resins	0.5–15%

The following is the analysis of wood:

Dry, ash-free material	percent
Carbon	50.0
Hydrogen	6.2
Oxygen	43.8

When wood is subjected to bacterial processes, the cellulose, lignin and protein are partially decomposed and their residuals combine to form products of varying composition that resemble humus, called humic acid. Humic acid occasionally occurs as a thick jelly, also called dopplerite, after its discoverer, Doppler [6].

A typical analysis shows that peat contains 70–90% humic acid and 5–30% resins and waxes. The following is the analysis of peat:

Dry, ash-free material	percent
Carbon	55-65
Hydrogen	5.5
Oxygen	32

The amount of water present in peat varies greatly and may be as high as 90%. Near the surface, peat is light in colour, but at lower depths it becomes darker and finally black.

3.2.2   Metamorphic or geochemical or dynamochemical stage

Soon after burial under an impervious cover, all bacterial action ceases and subsequent chemical changes are taking place in the deposit during metamorphic stage. During this stage, the progressive changes that occur within coals are an increase in the carbon content and a decrease in the hydrogen and oxygen content, resulting in a loss of volatiles. This together with continued water loss and compaction results in the reduction of the coal volume. Products of such coalification are methane, carbon dioxide and water, and are caused by temperature, pressure and time.

a   **Temperature:** Temperature changes can be achieved in the two following ways.

   1   The direct contact of the coal with igneous material, either as minor intrusions or as deep-seated major intrusions. The coals exhibit loss of volatiles, oxygen, methane and water, and the surrounding sediments will show evidence of contact metamorphism, for example, the local development of high rank coal in

the Gondwana coals of South Africa and India, and in the Paleogene–Neogene coals of Sumatra, Indonesia.

2   The rise in temperature associated with the depth of burial. Increasing depth of burial results in a decrease in the oxygen content of the coals, and the increase in the ratio of fixed carbon to volatile matter. In normal coals, exceeding 300°C, temperature increases with increasing depth. For the temperature effect on coal seams, **Carl Hilt** (1873) shows that the rate of chemical change doubles for a rise of 5°C to 10°C so that coals in the lower seams of coal measures are generally more mature (i.e., of higher rank) than those of higher seams, because of the temperature gradient of the earth's crust. This variation of rank with depth is known as Hilt' law [7].

b   **Pressure:** The influence of pressure is at its greatest during compaction and is most evident from the peat to sub-bituminous coal stages. With increasing chemical coalification, pressure has less influence. Pressure changes from a few pounds to many hundred pounds per square inch. Pressure is important mainly in its effect on temperature, particularly dynamic pressure due to resistance to earth movements.

c   **Time:** Temperature and pressure operates for enormous lengths of time. The effect of the time factor is that in various parts of the world, the coal seams in younger geological formations find on the whole to be less mature or less coalified than those in older formations.

Degree of coalification is less where sediments have subsided rapidly and time only has a real effect when the temperature is sufficiently high to allow chemical reaction to occur. Where very low temperatures occur over a very long period, little coalification takes place, for example, the Lower Carboniferous lignites in the Moscow Basin. The influence of time therefore is all the greater when the temperature is higher.

While the main course of coalification was probably decided by the heat and pressure resulting from burial of the coal swamps, in the regions of intense earth movements, pressure accompanied by heat increase the degree of coalification.

Variations in the conditions of temperature and pressure to which the seam was exposed have led to variations in the transformation of the decaying wood as follows:

1   Conditions which were not truly anaerobic led to the formation of peat.
2   Low alkalinity (absorbing carbon dioxide) in the surrounding clay led to the formation of lignites.
3   High alkalinity in the surrounding clay led to the formation of bituminous coals.

The precise nature of the changes that took place in the gradual conversion of plant material into coal is not known. Some scientists suggested the following overall reactions for formation of coal from wood:

1   According to **Regnault** (1900) [8]

$(C_6H_{10}O_5)_4 \rightarrow C_6H_6O + 7\ CH_4 + 3\ H_2O + 8\ CO_2$

    Cellulose   Bituminous

2   According to **Parr** (1910) [9]

$(C_6H_{10}O_5)_5 \rightarrow C_{20}H_{22}O_4 + 3\ CH_4 + 8\ H_2O + 6\ CO_2 + CO$

    Cellulose   Lignite

$(C_6H_{10}O_5)_6 \rightarrow C_{22}H_{20}O_3 + 5\ CH_4 + 10\ H_2O + 8\ CO_2 + CO$

    Cellulose   Bituminous

3   According to **Mott** (1942) [10] the following changes occur in the series wood to anthracite

Stage	Products evolved
Wood to low rank lignite	$64\ H_2O + 8\ CH_4 + CO_2$
Low rank lignite to low rank bituminous coal	CO_2
Low rank bituminous coal to semi-anthracite	1st stage $1.42\ H_2O + 0.43\ CH_4 + CO_2$ 2nd stage $5\ H_2O + 3\ CH_4 + CO_2$ 3rd stage $1.45\ H_2O + 5.8\ CH_4 + CO_2$
Semi-anthracite to anthracite	$36\ CH_4 + H_2O$

From the reactions suggested by Mott, it can be observed that the rate of methane evolved increases rapidly from bituminous coal to semi-anthracite, and from semi-anthracite to anthracite. This results in a fall of the hydrogen content of coal. These reactions account for large quantities of methane associated with coal mines containing carbonaceous coals and anthracites.

Chapter 4

Constituents of coal

Since coal is derived chiefly from vegetal matter, it consists mainly of the elements that go to compose plants, but it differs from plants in composition in as much as certain proportions changed during the fermentation and metamorphic processes that have caused the formation of coal. As the plants accumulated under water, some silt also settled along with them. Thus at a later stage, some mineral matter got mixed with the coal as it formed. In addition to the plant and mineral matter, an appreciable amount of animal matter may have been imprisoned in the coal and this may have caused a variation from normal composition, especially in nitrogen and phosphorous content.

Hence the coal as obtained from the earth's crust is not strictly a coal but consist of **coal** (or coal substance), **mineral matter** and **moisture**.

4.1   COAL SUBSTANCE

Coal substance (or simply coal) is that part of the plant's organic material (or cellulose) which has been later converted during the coalification reactions to form coal beds.

The principal elements from which coals are composed are some ones which make up wood and other vegetal matter: carbon, hydrogen and other elements characteristic of the inorganic matter. Carbon, hydrogen, oxygen, nitrogen and a portion of the sulphur are combined in very complex molecules with high molecular weights, which were produced from the original vegetal substances by the coalification reactions. The exact course of these reactions is not known, but all the evidence points to a gradual loss of carbon, hydrogen and oxygen, most probably by the elimination of water, carbon dioxide and methane. Thus the whole substance suffered wastage but as the hydrogen and oxygen were lost at proportionately higher rates than the carbon, the net result was that the percent carbon of the maturing coal increased with the degree of coalification.

The extent of these changes is shown by the following analysis of wood, representing the starting material, and anthracite which is the most mature form of coal:

	Wood	Anthracite
Carbon %	50.0	96.0
Hydrogen %	6.2	3.0
Oxygen %	43.8	1.0

As a result of the changes in the relative proportions of carbon, hydrogen and oxygen, other characteristics also change. Two elements nitrogen and sulphur amount to about 1 or 1.5% and show no marked variation with the degree of coalification. The part they play in the chemistry of coal is not fully understood, but compared with carbon, hydrogen and oxygen, they are relatively unimportant.

4.2 MOISTURE

The moisture in coal can be considered to occur in two parts, though the dividing line between them is not absolutely definite. One part, called the **free moisture**, occurs on the surface of the coal and in its cracks and joints. It is easily lost by evaporation, and except during unusually wet and cold weather, the amount of free moisture in sized grades of coal is generally small when it reaches the consumer, but washed smalls, which sometimes drain badly, may retain considerable quantities. Large amounts of free moisture are clearly undesirable in the coal as purchased, since they have to be paid for the same price as coal. On the other hand, a limited amount of free moisture is always present in the coal as eventually used, and water is often added to dry smalls to assist combustion.

The other part, called **inherent moisture**, is the amount of moisture in the following forms:

1 **Hygroscopic moisture:** This is the water held inside the capillaries of the coal substance.
2 **Decomposition moisture:** This is the water incorporated in some of the coal's organic compounds.
3 **Mineral moisture:** This is the water which forms part of the crystal structure of clays and other minerals present in the coal.

This inherent moisture is more or less constant for coals of a given rank. Much of it, especially the moisture in the pores of the coal, is driven off by heating to 100°C but some of the mineral and decomposition moisture may not be liberated until temperatures exceed 500°C.

The inherent moisture is also called air-dried moisture because, under normal atmospheric conditions, it is not removed by evaporation. The percent of air-dried moisture can be used as a broad indication of the rank of the coal. It is some extent affected by the atmospheric conditions existing at the time of air drying. For this reason, the conditions under which coal is air-dried in preparation for laboratory examination are carefully specified.

The moisture in the coal reduces the calorific value of coal, increases the consumption of coal for heating purposes and lengthens the time of heating. If coal is exposed to an atmosphere of increasing humidity at a fixed temperature, it absorbs more and more moisture. The quantity of moisture the coal has at saturated atmosphere (96–99% relative humidity) is called **near saturation moisture** or **bed moisture** and is a better measure than the air dried moisture for determination of rank of high volatile bituminous, sub-bituminous and lignitic coals and serves as parameter in some coal classification systems.

4.3 MINERAL MATTER

No coal consists entirely of organic compounds. Inorganic material is also present in the coal as impurities. Mineral matter refers to such impurities as they exist in the coal. The mineral matter is non-combustible. The residue from this mineral matter after coal has been burned is called ash. The average ash content of the entire thickness of a coal seam is at least 2 or 3%, even for very pure bituminous coals, and 10% or more for most commercial mines. Material that is too high in ash for ordinary use is called bone coal, carbonaceous shale, or black slate.

Mineral matter present in coal may be classified broadly into those that form ash and those that contribute sulphur. Ash forming mineral matter is of two types namely **inherent mineral matter** and **extraneous** or **adventitious mineral matter**. The inherent mineral matter represents inorganic elements present in plants giving raise to coal beds. It is very small in amount, about 2% or less of the total ash, different in composition and not possible to separate by usual beneficiation methods. A new process developed at Central Institute of Mining and Fuel Research (CIMFR) Dhanbad (formerly Central Fuel Research Institute CFRI), called oil agglomeration technique which consists mainly of leaching of coal impurities by petroleum oil, can to some extent remove inherent mineral matter. The inherent mineral matter is a useful classification when applied to the practical problems of coal cleaning. Generally speaking, it defines the lower limit to which coal can be separated physically from its mineral impurities. This is true because theoretically all extraneous mineral matter can be removed.

The extraneous mineral matter is due to the substances which got associated with the decaying vegetable material during its conversion into coal, and also due to the rocks and dirt getting mixed up during mining and handling of coal. The former of extraneous mineral matter is in a fine state and intimately associated with the organic mass of coal. Hence difficulties are experienced in removing this from coal by mechanical methods. The second type of extraneous mineral matter is more amenable to coal cleaning methods. The major portion of mineral matter of commercial coal is extraneous. In Indian coals, the mineral matter content is not only high but is of intimately associated due to the drift origin.

The bulk of the mineral matter of coal is due to clay or shale consisting of alumino-silicates of different composition. Other constituents identified are carbonates, sulphides, oxides, chlorides and sulphates. Table 4.3 shows coal minerals and their frequency of occurrence.

When coal burns, shale and other hydrated minerals lose water of hydration while sulphides, sulphates and carbonates usually decompose, resulting in loss of weight, hence the ash of coal is always less than the mineral matter content.

Sulphur occurs in coal in three forms. It is present in organic combination as part of the coal substance, as pyrites or marcasite, and as sulfates. The amount of organic sulphur normally is not over 3%, but in exceptional cases may be as much as 11%. The sulphates, mainly calcium and iron, rarely exceed a few hundredths percent except in highly weathered or oxidized samples. Pyrites and marcasite constitute the principal form of sulphur found in coals. Because of the difficulty in distinguishing one from the other, they usually are designated simply as pyrite. Pyrite occurs in coal in veins, lenses, nodules or balls and pyritized plant tissue. Microscopic pyrite also

Table 4.3 Minerals identified in coal (compiled from various sources).

Group	Minerals	Occurrence*
Clay	Illite	dominant – abundant
	Kaolinite	common – very common
	Montmorillonite	rare – common
	Chlorite	rare
	Biotite	very rare
Carbonates	Siderite	common – very common
	Ankerite	common – very common
	Calcite	common – very common
	Dolomite	rare – common
Sulphides	Pyrite	rare – common
	Marcasite	rare
	Sphalerite	rare
Oxides	Quartz	rare – common
	Hematite	rare
	Magnetite	very rare
	Rutile	very rare
Chlorides	Sylvine	very rare – common
	Halite	very rare – common
Sulphates	Gypsum	rare
	Baryte	rare

*Occurance – Dominant: > 60%
Abundant: 30 – 60%
Very common: 10 – 30%
Common: 5 – 10%   of the total mineral matter content in the coal
Rare: 5 – 1%
Very rare: < 1%

occurs as small globules, fine veinlets, euhedral crystals finely disseminated throughout the coal, cell fillings, and replacement of plant material. Elemental sulphur has been reported to occur in amounts of as much as 0.15% in some coals.

Depending on the nature of the coal, the mineral matter present may be derived from a number of different sources. Nature of mineral matter or impurities present in coal are of the following types:

- residual inorganic matter of coal forming plants
- mineral matter washed or blown into the coal forming mass during the period of its formation
- pyrites formed by the reaction of iron sulphate with coal forming matter
- sedimentary deposits during the coal forming periods
- deposits formed through deposition of bedding planes
- saline deposits
- slate, shale, clay etc. from the underlying and overlying strata

The minerals present in coal are of great significance in aspects of coal classification, testing and use, as well as in problems such as seam correlation and the development of depositional models. The mineral matter can have an effect on the coal's behaviour at low temperature, at medium temperature such as in carbonization, and at the high temperatures of the combustion process.

4.4   PETROGRAPHIC CONSTITUENTS OF COAL

Close examination of coal in hand specimen generally shows it to be composed of different layers. Under the microscope, these layers in turn are seen to be composed of mixtures of discrete entities. Coal petrology is the study of the origin, composition and technological behaviour of these different materials, while the systematic quantification of their proportions and characteristics under the microscope is sometimes known as coal petrography.

The petrology of coal may be studied at either a megascopic or a microscopic scale. From a megascopic point of view, coal may be classified into two broad groups, the banded or humic coals and the non-banded (massive) or sapropelic coals. The humic coals are visibly stratified, consisting of layers or bands of organic material of varying appearance. Such coals are derived from a heterogeneous mixture of a wide range of plant debris. The sapropelic coals are homogeneous, tough materials and made up of spores or algae material.

4.4.1   Lithotypes in banded coals

After careful examination of the different layers in a number of coal seams, Dr. M.C. Stopes [11], a palaeobotanist, in 1910 concluded that there were four distinct types of coal layers or **Banded constituents**, which she defined according to their appearance as seen by the unaided eye, and named as **Vitrain, Clarain, Durain** and **Fusain**. In current usage, these constituents are regarded as **Lithotypes**.

Vitrain is the black, glossy, vitreous material that is probably the most striking component of bituminous coals. Vitrain tends to be more brittle and often breaking with a conchoidal fracture. It is assumed that Vitrain was originated from barks of special type of plants which had first undergone into the chemical and physical changes for coalification than other parts of debris. This will not make hand dirty, if touched. It is coking in nature and is responsible for lustrous black band of bituminous coal. In humic coals, vitrain is widely distributed.

Clarain resembles nearly the same like Vitrain but it is less glossy and can be identified with experience. It has a silky luster and on a vertical face it is seen to be finely laminated. It breaks usually with a splintery fracture. It makes the hand slightly dirty. It includes relatively large plant fragments, particularly in the vitrain bands, and it seems reasonable to assume that the bright coal or clarain was formed from material that was not transported into the swamp but come directly from the trees growing there. Clarain is the most common macroscopic constituent of humic coals.

Durain occurs as grey to black bands with a dull to slightly greasy luster. The material is relatively hard and tends to break into large, blocky fragments. Fracture surfaces of durain are rough. Durain may sometimes be confused with impure coal or carbonaceous shale, which are also often dull and hard, but it can be distinguished by its lower density. Durain was formed possible from trunks and main woody matters.

Fusain is a soft friable material that closely resembles wood charcoal. It is of silky luster, black and frequently somewhat fibrous. Fusain usually occurs as thin lenses between the bands of other types and is only a very minor constituent of most bituminous coal seams on a volumetric basis. It is only 3 to 5% in coal. Fusain is non-coking in nature and soils the hand when touched.

The terms duroclarain and clarodurain have been added to this list to extend the number of terms available for megascopic coal description. They represent material that is intermediate in character between clarain and durain.

Microscopic studies of the four different bands of ordinary coal revealed that two of them, namely the vitrain and fusain, are homogeneous, showing the same kind of material throughout. The clarain and durain bands, on the other hand, are heterogeneous, consisting of different kinds of easily determinable microscopic features.

The distinction between bright components (Vitrain and Clarain) and dull components (Durain and Fusain) is most apparent in bituminous coals, in some lignites, to a less extent in anthracite coals.

4.4.2   Lithotypes in sapropelic coals

Sapropelic coals represent accumulations of algae or spore remains. Sapropelic coals are characteristically fine grained, faintly bedded to homogeneous, massive materials. They are generally dark in colour with a dull to greasy luster and typically display a marked conchoidal fracture. Sapropelic coals may occur as layers or plies within seams of banded or humic coal, often at the roof.

The two major types of sapropelic coal are **cannel coal** composed largely of spores or fine organoclastic detritus, and **boghead coal** composed largely of algae. Cannel coals are black and dull, sometimes with a rather greasy luster. They are homogeneous and compact fine grained coals and breaks with a conchoidal fracture. The most characteristic feature of all cannel coals is the almost uniform size of the constituent particles. The ash content of cannel coal is usually high. Cannel coals occur in most coalfields all over the world. Cannel coals contain little (about 5%) or no algae, whereas boghead coals contain more than 5% algae. Boghead coals, also known as torbanites, are similar to cannels in appearance, except that they tend to be browner in colour.

4.4.3   Coal maceral groups

The constituents of coal were classified microscopically by Thiessen [12] in 1920 as **anthroxylon, attritus** (translucent and opaque) and **fusain** (which corresponds to macroscopic classification of Stopes: vitrain, clarain, durain, and fusain). This classification was based on visual characteristics of the coal constituents in thin sections under transmitted light. The use of thin section was later replaced by measuring the reflectance on a polished surface because of the experimental convenience of the latter technique.

The transmitted-light technique is advantageous for morphological investigations, whereas reflected light is suitable for quantitative measurements. For example, reflectance measurements frequently can be used effectively to:

1   Determine yields of coal carbonization products, such as coke, tar, gas, and light oils.
2   Obtain heating values and specific gravity properties of gases produced in coal carbonization processes.
3   Determine the free-swelling index and heating values of coals.
4   Categorize coals for certain combustion uses.
5   Predict the oxidation tendencies of coals.

The differences between the two techniques led to two different nomenclatures in coal petrology. All of Thiessen's coal constituents – anthraxylon, attritus, and fusain – are present in ordinary coals, regardless of rank. According to the presence or absence of anthraxylon, coals are classified into two major groups:

1   Banded coals – composed of both anthraxylon and attritus.
2   Non-banded coals – composed entirely or almost entirely of attritus.

The banded coals were subdivided into (1) Bright coals contain predominately vitrain and clarain, (2) Semisplint coals contain predominately clarain with some vitrain and durain, (3) splint coals contain predominately durain with some vitrain and clarain. The non-banded coals were divided into cannel and boghead coals contains predominately durain with lesser amounts of vitrain than splint coal.

European workers usually define the micro-constituents of coal as macerals, deriving from maceration of plant matter. These macerals are grouped into **vitrinite, exinite** (liptinite), and **inertinite.** In U.S. nomenclature, vitrinite and exinite are equivalent to anthraxylon and translucent attritus; Inertinite is frequently divided into **micrinite** and **fusinite** and are equivalent to opaque attritus and fusain. Of the four lithotypes, vitrain and fusain are each composed primarily of a single maceral or maceral group. Vitrain is essentially all vitrinite and fusain is essentially all inertinite. Clarain contains predominantly vitrinite while durain contains predominantly micrinite. The macerals and maceral groups of lithotypes are given in Table 4.4.1.

The maceral groups serve as a basis of coal petrography. They are not only physically distinct but also have very different chemical characteristics.

The petrographic composition of the coal influences the ease of winning the coal, since the macerals making up the lithotypes have a definite relationship to the power required to mine the coal. McCabe L.C [14] has stated that fusain require the least power for breakage, vitrain require twice, clarain three times and durain 7.5 times as much. A study found that the amount of power required to mine the tough durain coal was as much as 40% greater than that required for the friable clarain coal. The difference in power consumption in a seam depends upon the physical character of the coal, including petrographic composition, cleat, and fracture, and can be influenced by such other factors as type of miner used and type of mining operation.

Mining method adopted in coal mine influences the distribution of macerals. In the various size fractions of coal from the continuous miner operation, the proportions

Table 4.4.1 Macerals and Maceral groups of Lithotypes [13].

Macroscopic lithotypes	Microscopic	
	Maceral groups	Macerals
VITRAIN	Vitrinite	Collinite and telinite
CLARAIN	Vitrinite dominant	Collinite and telinite
	Exinite and	Sporinite, cutinite, alginite, resinites, and waxes
	Inertinite less prominent	Fusinite, micrinite, sclerotinite, and semifusinite
DURAIN	Inertinite dominant	Fusinite, micrinite, sclerotinite, and semifusinite
	Vitrinite and	Collinite and telinite
	Exinite less prominent	Sporinite, cutinite, alginite, resinites, and waxes
FUSAIN	Inertinite	Fusinite

of group macerals are more consistent than in the coal mined in the ordinary manner. The breaking action of the miner no doubt minimized the influence of the natural breakage characteristics of the coal.

Another problem in coal mining is the size consist. The size consist of the run-of-mine coal is influenced by (1) the macropetrographic structure of the seam and the cleat system, (2) the types of mining machines used, and (3) the location of the mine. The most reliable way to evaluate the overall effect of these parameters is the size analysis of a sample representing a working face, normally a fixed number of mine cars.

The effect of petrographic composition on coal breakage is evident in the preparation plant as well as in the mine. Two methods of breaking coal are used in plants – impact and compression. Natural characteristics of coal components are important factors in impact breakage, and screening the coal results in selective concentration of certain macerals, group macerals, and lithotypes.

In a finely stratified coal seam that does not include any thick layers of dull or bright coal the size consist of micro-lithotypes of macerals of lumps, nuts, and fines is practically the same. By contrast, if a seam includes one or more layers of durain thicker than about 3/8 inch, the hard durain, especially in low rank coals, tend to concentrate in the nuts or, if the durain layers are extremely thick, in the lumps. When a seam contains thick layers of bright coal, the soft and mostly brittle vitrain concentrates in the – 3/8 inch coal; a high content of soft fusain, in the form of layers or lenses, will lead to concentration of this friable lithotype in the fines.

4.4.4   Vitrinite reflectance as a measure of rank

The rank of a coal is characteristic of the stage reached by it in the course of transformation process which began with decayed vegetal debris and the final stage of which is represented by graphite. Hoffman & Jenkner (1932) [15] were first to observe the fact that the reflectance of vitrinite increases progressively with increasing rank. Following on their fundamental findings, the quantitative determination of the rank of coal by making reflectance measurements has become more and more an acceptable parameter of coalification, because it is independent of further genetic peculiarities in the coal mass.

4.4.5 Micropetrographic characteristics of gondwana coals

The petrographic properties of Gondwana coals reveal regional and stratigraphic variations amongst the seams of different coalfields and within the same coalfield respectively. Several authors extensively studied the petrographic compositions of Gondwana coals of different parts of the world. Their work firmly established that the flora and climate resulted in major petrographic differences between these coals and those from Carboniferous periods. In the later case vitrinite is predominant maceral while in the Gondwana coals the inertinite content may reach as high as 70%.

The main petrographic differences are caused by the bio-chemical processes during the first stage of coalification. Petrographic composition explains significant differences in coal chemistry and has a direct effect on utilisation. On account of their low vitrinite content, Gondwana coals are comparatively low in hydrogen and high in nitrogen (1.6–2.6% d.a.f). The substantial proportions of fusinite and semifusinite, with their relatively greater porosity, allow higher in-situ moisture retention and result in lower heating values than those of Carboniferous coals of the same maturity. Volatile matter is also affected. According to Kroger (1968) [16], the increase in volatile matter yield corresponds to a rise in the wax-resin component of vitrinite.

The mineral matter in the Gondwana coals occur mainly in two forms e.g. finely divided state dispersed throughout the coal as well as micro-banding, which is very common and is very difficult to be removed by conventional beneficiation methods, and second one as macroscopically visible bands and lenses. The Gondwana coals have been affected by igneous intrusions in the form of dykes and sills and as a result the mineral matter content of the affected coal seam is further increased, especially with respect to carbonate.

Petrography is a very eminent tool, which enables very quick and reliable information regarding (1) Coal genesis, seam correlation and stratigraphic studies (2) Constitution (both organic and inorganic components), Determination of Rank and reactives (3) Association of maceral-maceral and maceral-mineral matter (i.e. microlithotype study) (4) Coal beneficiation/washability studies for steel & power industries and establishing different blend proportions based on rank and reactive components (5) The char morphology has gained paramount status in deciphering the burnout behaviour of coal in different thermal power plants.

Chapter 5

Sampling of coal

The method or operation of taking the small amount of material from the bulk is called **Sampling**. It is the art of cutting a small portion of material from a large lot. The small amount of material is called **Sample** and it should be representative of the bulk in all respects (in its physical and chemical properties). Sampling was well defined by Taggart [17] as "the operation of removing a part, convenient in size for analysis, from a whole which is of much greater in bulk, in such a way that the proportion and distribution of the quality to be tested are the same in both the whole and the part removed (SAMPLE)". The conditions of the more stringent definition, that the sample shall be completely representative of the whole bulk, are practically never fulfilled when heterogeneous materials are sampled.

Coal is a highly heterogeneous substance in terms of the inorganic and organic constituents and exhibits wide variability with respect to size of the particles. The basic purpose of taking and preparing a **sample** of coal is to provide a test sample which when analyzed will provide the test results representative of the **bulk** or **lot** sampled. In order that the sample represents the coal from which it is taken, it is collected by taking a definite number of **increments** distributed throughout the whole of coal.

The degree which a sample may be representative of a total shipment or lot depend not only on the sampling method used, but also even more on the care exercised by the sampler. The sampler's knowledge, experience, judgment and ability are of greater value because instructions cannot cover every point or combination of circumstances encountered on each inspection.

The procedure for sampling will, however, differ with the purpose and method of sampling. Samples may be required for technical evaluation, process control, and quality control or for commercial transactions. For quality assessment of coals from new sources, samples are to be drawn from in-situ coal seams, either as rectangular blocks or pillars cut from full seam height, or from seam channels or from borehole cores. To check the quality of coal consignments it is desirable to sample from conveyer belt. The reference method of stopped belt sampling is often implemented to standardize the mechanical automatic sampling systems.

5.1 IMPORTANT TERMINOLOGY IN SAMPLING PRACTICE

Lot	is the total amount of material from which a sample is to be taken.
Consignment	is the quantity defined as a shipload, carload, or a day's production or other specified quantity which corresponds to a sample period or billing period for delivery purposes.
Homogeneity	is the condition of the material such that all portions or cuts taken from it are equivalent to the extent that can be determined by methods of analysis applied.
Top size	is the maximum particle size of the material being sampled, determined by the screen size on which less than 5% of the material is retained.
Consist (size consist)	is the particle size distribution of the material.
Cut	is one portion of the material taken by a systematic method.
Increment	is the quantity of sample taken in one cut.
Gross sample	is the accumulation of samples taken from the material before additional reduction is performed
Spot sample	is one cut taken from one place.
Random sample	is composite of cuts taken at several places chosen at random in the material being sampled.
Stratified Sampling	is cuts taken at regular intervals throughout the material being sampled.
Systematic sampling	is the samples collected on a specified time interval or weight delivery interval.

5.2 SAMPLING

A sample can be taken from any type of material dry, wet or pulp. But, in each case, the method of sampling and the apparatus necessary for them are different.

A sample is collected from huge lot of dry material in stages. At first, sample in large quantity is collected from a lot, known as **primary sample** or **gross sample** or **composite sample**, by means of various types of sampling equipment such as mechanical or hand-tool samplers using appropriate sampling methods and techniques.

The gross sample is reduced to a quantity that can be handled with ease by **alternate shoveling** or **fractional shoveling** in stages depending upon the quantity of gross sample. It is essential that the gross sample be thoroughly mixed before reduction in order to obtain a representative sub-sample or laboratory sample. Such reduced samples are called **secondary sample** and **ternary sample** depending upon the number of stages used. Reduction of thus reduced sample to a quantity necessary for analysis, known as **final sample** or **test sample**, is called **sample preparation**. It is the process of reducing the quantity by splitting.

5.3   GENERAL PRINCIPLES OF SAMPLING

The fundamental requirements of sampling are:

- That all particles of coal in the lot to be sampled are accessible to the sampling equipment and each individual particle shall have an equal probability of being selected and included in the sample.
- The dimension of the sampling device used should be sufficient to allow the largest particle to pass freely into it.
- The first stage of sampling is the taking from positions distributed over the entire lot of an adequate number of coal portions known as primary **increments,** to account for the variability of the coal. The primary increments are then combined into a sample as taken or after reducing the mass of the sample to a manageable size. From this sample, the required number and types of test samples are prepared by a series of processes jointly known as **sample preparation.**
- The minimum mass of the gross sample should be sufficient to enable the particles to be present in the same proportions as in the lot of coal from which it is taken.
- To ensure that the result obtained has the required precision, the following issues are to be considered.

  - Variability of the coal
  - Number of samples from a lot
  - Number of increments comprising each sample
  - Mass of the sample relative to the **nominal top size**

The ideal method of sampling is the **stopped belt** method. As implementation of such method will affect the continuity of plant operation, it is not practicable for routine sampling.

Sampling scheme has to be designed based on the purpose of sampling and after ascertaining at what stage of coal handling operation the sample is required.

- **Division of lots:** A lot may be sampled as a whole or a series of sub-lots. Each sub-lot will constitute one sample.
- **Basis of sampling:** It can be either time basis or mass basis. In time basis the sampling interval is defined in minutes/seconds and mass is proportional to the flow rate whereas in mass basis the interval is defined in tones and the mass of increments is uniform.
- **Precision:** In all the methods of sampling, sample preparation and analysis, errors are introduced at every stage and the measured value differ from the true value of the parameter. As the true value is not known exactly it is not possible to assess the accuracy of the results but an estimate of precision of results can be made.

The required precision for a lot for each parameter has to be decided and then the number of sub-lots, number of increments and mass of increment are to be estimated.

The minimum mass of the sample is dependent on the nominal top size of the coal and the precision required for the concerned parameter and relationship of the parameter with particle size. The minimum weight of the sample required for typical analysis are given in the table 5.3.

Table 5.3 Minimum weight of the sample after division.

Nominal top size of coal (mm)	Weight of common sample for general analysis (kg)	Weight of sample for moisture analysis (kg)	Weight of sample (kg) for size analysis to achieve precision of	
			±1%	±2%
300	15000	3000	54000	13500
200	5400	1100	16000	4000
150	2600	500	6750	1700
125	1700	350	4000	1000
90	750	125	1500	400
63	300	60	500	125
45	125	25	200	50
31.5	55	10	65	15
22.4	32	7	25	6
16	20	4	8	2
11.2	13	2.5	3	0.7
8	6	1.5	1	0.25
5.6	3	1.2	0.5	0.25
4	1.5	1	0.25	0.25
2.8	0.65	0.65	0.25	0.25
2	0.25	–	–	–
1	0.1	–	–	–
<0.5	0.06	–	–	–

Source: NTPC Coal Book-2008.

- Satisfaction of the criteria of the minimum mass does not ensure good precision. Precision can be improved by increasing the increments.

Sampling methods are broadly categorized as **Hand sampling** and **Machine sampling**. Hand sampling is usually expensive. It is slow in batch sampling and labor-wasting in stream sampling. The personal element enters so largely that accurate results are difficult to obtain. Machine sampling should be used where possible and hand sampling applied only where material is not suitable for treatment by machine, as with sticky ore, or where machinery is not available, or the expense of its installation not justified, or where the bulk material from which sample is to be collected is huge in quantity and there is no possibility of mixing either by hand or by machine.

5.4   SAMPLING METHODS TO COLLECT PRIMARY SAMPLE

The two methods used to obtain gross sample are **Random sampling** and **Systematic** or **stratified sampling**. The various hand-tool samplers used are Drill, Shovel, Scoop, Auger, Pipe and Slot samplers.

Grab sampling method is used to collect samples from stationary bulk material in heap such as stockpile. Grab sampling consists in taking small, equal portions of material from several places by scoop or shovel (or pipe sampler to take sample from inside the heap) selected at random (random sampling) or at regular intervals (systematic or stratified sampling) from the bulk of material to be sampled. The material thus collected is mixed together to form a primary or gross sample which is a base for the final sample.

While taking the sample, the sampler must avoid **biased** sampling procedures such as preference for easily accessible units or following routine selection patterns that are easily recognized and involve frequent choice of units in the same sequence. Examples of these are: taking items from the same position in containers, stacks, or piles in every inspection; taking items from the top of a container; not taking items from the top of a container; or taking items from the output of certain identical production elements and not from others.

When it is required to collect samples from streams of solids and/or pulps, **manual** or **mechanical sample cutters** are employed to cut and withdraw small quantities from a stream of traveling material at a predetermined frequencies and speed to form a gross sample. In case of pulps, thus collected gross sample is to be dewatered and dried for sample preparation.

5.5   SAMPLE PREPARATION

The gross samples, being huge in quantity, have to be properly "reduced", so that the reduced sample is representative of the collected gross sample. Shovel sampling is one of the methods used to reduce the gross sample to a convenient size.

Shovel sampling, also called **Alternate Shoveling** or **Fractional Shoveling**, can be applied when coal is being loaded or unloaded, or moved from one place to another by shoveling, or to reduce the gross sample.

In shovel sampling, every alternate, or every third, fourth, fifth, or tenth shovelful is taken for the sample, depending upon the size of sample permissible or desired. Common practice is to take the fifth or tenth shovels in unloading a car and to finish sampling by alternate shovels.

The other method in shovel sampling consists of taking a shovelful quantity of the material each time and putting them separately say into five heaps (Fig. 5.5).

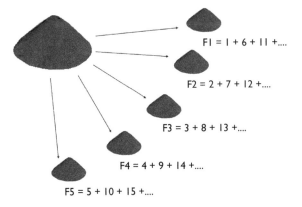

Figure 5.5 Sample reduction by using the Shovel.

The next sixth to tenth shovelful of material is put on the same five heaps. The following eleventh to fifteenth shovelful material is put on the same five heaps and continued till the gross sample is taken completely. Any heap among the five heaps can be taken as a reduced sample. This method can be adopted when the gross sample collected is not very huge and convenient for this method.

The gross sample, after reducing to convenient size, needs to be "prepared" before analysis. Indeed, one could think of this as sampling within sampling. The two major steps in sample preparation by reduction are:

1 **Homogenization:** This is done so that the next step, splitting, is more accurate. This typically involves crushing and/or grinding. At the very least, the sample should be thoroughly mixed before proceeding to the next step.
2 **Splitting:** Reducing the large sample to required smaller amounts. This is done by various techniques such as coning and quartering, riffling and table sampling, to split the sample into two "identical" halves. Splitting is repeated as many times as necessary to obtain the right quantity of material.

Further splitting of the sample can be done by **Coning and quartering** or by using **paper cone splitter, riffle splitter** with smaller slot width, **rotary cone splitter, rotary table splitter** or **micro splitter.**

When the sample is taken and subject to analysis, chances of error in single sample will exist. One must take the number of samples to reduce the error and to keep the overall error within the tolerable working limits.

When a sample is to be taken for analysis, the sample should be re-crushed sufficiently between each cutting down of the sample so that the ratio of the diameter of the largest particles to the weight of the sample to be taken shall not exceed a certain safe proportion. It is to be noted that no amount of mixing and careful division can make the sample and reject alike in value when the lot before division contains an uneven number of particles of different carbon content.

Chapter 6

Size analysis of coal

Size of the particle is most important consideration in Beneficiation because of the two following main reasons:

- Energy consumed for reducing the size of the particles depends on size
- Size of the particles determines the type of Size reduction equipment, Beneficiation equipment and other equipment to be employed

The size of the particle of standard configuration like sphere and cube can easily be specified. For example, the size of a spherical particle is its diameter (d) and that of a cubical particle is the length of its side (l) as shown in the Fig. 6.0.1.

As the real particles are of irregular in shape, it is difficult to define and determine their size. A number of authors have proposed several empirical definitions to particle size. Martin [18] in 1924 defined as the length of the line bisecting the maximum cross-sectional area of the particle. Feret [19] in 1931 defined the size of an irregular particle as the distance between two most extreme points on the surface of a particle. During later years, the size of a particle is defined by comparison with a standard configuration, normally spherical particle.

Equivalent size or **equivalent diameter** of an irregular particle is defined as the diameter of a spherical particle which behaves similar to an irregular particle under specified conditions.

Surface diameter is defined as a diameter of a spherical particle having the same surface area as the irregular particle.

Volume diameter is defined as the diameter of a spherical particle having the same volume as the irregular particle.

It is obvious that each definition has its own limitations.

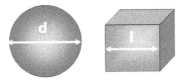

Figure 6.0.1 Representing size of the sphere and cube.

Figure 6.0.2 Test Sieve.

In mineral and coal industry, the side of a square aperture through which a particle just passes is taken as the size of the particle even though little or no importance is given to its shape. Standard Test Sieves are used in mineral and coal industry to measure the size of the small and the fine particles usually down to 74 microns.

The following are the nomenclature used in testing the particles for its size.

Test Sieve	is a circular shell of brass having 8 inch diameter and about 2 inch high as shown in the Fig. 6.0.2.
Sieve cloth	is made of wire, woven to produce nominally uniform cloth apertures (openings). The sieve cloth is placed in the bottom of the shell so that material can be held on the sieve.
Aperture (or **Opening**)	is a distance between two parallel wires.
Mesh number	is the number of apertures per linear inch. Sieves are designated by Mesh number.
Mesh size	is the size of an aperture i.e. the distance between two parallel wires. As mesh number increases, mesh size decreases.
Sieve Scale	is the list of successive sieve sizes used in any laboratory, taken in order from coarsest to finest.
Standard Sieve Scale	is the sieve scale adopted for size analyses and general testing work to facilitate the interchangeability of results and data. In this standard sieve scale, the sizes of successive sieves in series form a geometric progression.

For a standard sieve scale, the reference point is 74 microns, which is the aperture of a 200 mesh woven wire sieve. The ratio of the successive sizes of the sieves in the standard sieve scale is $\sqrt{2}$, which means that the area of the opening of any sieve in the series is twice that of the sieve just below it and one half of the area of the sieve next above it in the series.

In general, mesh number × mesh size in microns ≈ 15,000.
For closer sizing work the sieve ratio of $\sqrt[4]{2}$ is common.

The different standards in use are:

American Tyler Series
American Standards for Testing and Materials, ASTM E-11-01

Table 6.1 Comparison of Test Sieves of different Standards (compiled from various sources).

Tyler Sieve designation mesh no.	Width of aperture mm	Mesh double tyler series	U.S.A ASTM E-11-01 Sieve designation mesh no.	Width of aperture mm	BRITISH B.S 410-2000 Sieve designation mesh no.	Width of aperture mm	INDIAN I.S. 460-1962 Sieve designation mesh no.	Width of aperture mm	FRENCH AFNOR NFX-11-501 Sieve designation mesh no.	Width of aperture mm	GERMAN DIN 3310-1: 2000 Sieve designation mesh no.	Width of aperture mm
–	–	–	–	–	–	–	–	–	38	5.00		5.00
4	4.75	–	4	4.75	3 ½	4.75	480	4.75	–	–		4.50
–	4.00	5	5	4.00	4	4.00	400	4.00	37	4.00	2E	4.00
6	3.35	–	6	3.35	5	3.35	340	3.35	–	–		–
–	–	–	–	–	–	3.15	320	3.18	36	3.15		3.15
–	2.80	7	7	2.80	6	2.80	280	2.80	–	–		2.80
8	2.36	–	8	2.36	7	2.36	240	2.39	35	2.50		2.50
–	2.00	9	10	2.00	8	2.00	200	2.00	34	2.00	3E	2.00
10	1.70	–	12	1.70	10	1.70	170	1.70	33	1.60		1.60
–	1.40	12	14	1.40	12	1.40	140	1.40	–	1.40		1.40
–	–	–	–	–	–	1.25	–	–	32	1.25		1.25
14	1.18	–	16	1.18	14	1.18	120	1.20	–	–	5	1.20
–	1.00	16	18	1.00	16	1.00	100	1.00	31	1.00	6	1.00
20	0.85	–	20	0.850	18	0.850	85	0.850	–	–		–
–	–	–	–	–	–	0.800	80	0.79	30	0.800		0.800
–	0.710	24	25	0.710	22	0.710	70	0.710	–	0.710		0.710
–	–	–	–	–	–	0.630	–	–	29	0.630		0.630
28	0.600	–	30	0.600	25	0.600	60	0.600	–	–	10	0.600
–	0.500	32	35	0.500	30	0.500	50	0.500	28	0.500	12	0.500
35	0.425	–	40	0.425	36	0.425	40	0.425	–	–		–
–	–	–	–	–	–	0.400	–	–	27	0.400	16	0.400
–	0.355	42	45	0.355	44	0.355	35	0.355	–	0.355		0.355
–	–	–	–	–	–	0.315	–	–	26	0.315		0.315
48	0.300	–	50	0.300	52	0.300	30	0.300	–	–	20	0.300
–	0.250	60	60	0.250	60	0.250	25	0.250	25	0.250	24	0.250
65	0.212	–	70	0.212	72	0.212	20	0..212	–	–		–
–	–	–	–	–	–	0.200	–	–	24	0.200	30	0.200
–	0.180	80	80	0.180	85	0.180	18	0.180	–	0.180		0.180
–	–	–	–	–	–	0.160	–	–	23	0.160		0.160
100	0.150	–	100	0.150	100	0.150	15	0.150	–	–	40	0.150
–	0.125	115	120	0.125	120	0.125	12	0.125	22	0.125	50	0.125
150	0.106	–	140	0.106	150	0.106	10	0.106	–	–		–
–	–	–	–	–	–	0.100	–	–	21	0.100	60	0.100
–	0.90	170	170	0.090	170	0.090	9	0.090	–	0.090	70	0.090
–	–	–	–	–	–	0.800	–	–	20	0.80		0.080
200	0.075	–	200	0.075	200	0.075	8	0.075	–	–	80	0.075
–	–	–	–	–	–	0.710	–	–	–	0.071		0.071
–	0.063	250	230	0.063	240	0.063	6	0.063	19	0.063		0.063
–	–	–	–	–	–	0.056	–	–	–	0.056	110	0.056
270	0.053	–	270	0.053	300	0.053	5	0.053	–	–		–
–	–	–	–	–	–	0.050	–	–	18	0.050	120	0.050
–	0.045	325	325	0.045	350	0.045	4	0.045	–	0.045		0.045
–	–	–	–	–	–	0.040	–	–	17	0.40		0.040
400	0.038	–	400	0.038	400	0.038	3	0.038	–	–	130	–

British Standard Sieves, BSS 410-2000

French Series, AFNOR (Association Française de Normalisation) NFX 11-501

German Standard, DIN (Deutsches Institut für Normung) 3310-1: 2000

The Indian Standard (IS) sieves, however, follow a different type of designation. For an IS sieve, the mesh number is equal to its aperture size expressed to the nearest deca-micron (0.01 mm). Thus an IS sieve of mesh number 50 will have an aperture width of approximately 500 microns. Such a method of designation has the simplicity that the aperture width is readily indicated from the mesh number.

Table 6.1 shows the comparison of test sieves of different standards.

For most size analyses it is usually impracticable and unnecessary to use all the sieves in a particular series. For most purposes, alternative sieves are quite adequate. For accurate work over certain size ranges of particular interest, consecutive sieves may be used. Intermediate sieves should never be chosen at random, as the data obtained will be difficult to interpret. In general, the sieve range should be chosen such that no more than about 5% of the sample material is retained on the coarsest sieve, or passes the finest sieve. These limits may be lowered for more accurate work.

6.1 SIEVE ANALYSIS

Sieve analysis is a method of size analysis. It is performed to determine the percentage weight of closely sized fraction by allowing the sample of material to pass through a series of test sieves.

Closely sized material is the material in which the difference between maximum and minimum sizes is less. Also called **closed size material.**

Sieving can be done by hand or by machine. Hand sieving method is considered more effective as it allows the particles to present in all possible orientations on to the sieve surface. However, machine sieving is preferred for routine analysis as hand sieving is long and tedious. Vibrating sieve shaker and Ro-tap sieve shaker are the two principal machines used in laboratory for sieve analysis. These sieve shakers are shown in Fig. 6.1.1 and Fig. 6.1.2

Because of irregular shapes, particles cannot pass through the sieve unless they are presented in favourable orientation particularly with the fine particles. Hence there is no end point for sieving. For all practical purposes, end point is considered to have been reached when there is little amount of material passing through after a certain length of sieving. The most satisfactory results in making a sieve analysis are obtained when the amount of material on each sieve, at the end of the sieving operation, does not exceed that required to form a layer one particle deep. However, a bed of two particles deep can be handled with reasonable accuracy.

Sieving is generally done dry. One of the great hindrances to perfect sieving is the adherence of extremely fine particles to coarser particles, or to each other, through electrostatic action or because of the presence of minute amounts of moisture. The best way to take care of the dust and slime problems is to conduct a wet-and-dry sieving operation. Wet sieving is used when the material is in the form of slurry.

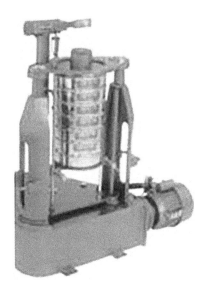

Figure 6.1.1 Vibrating Sieve shaker.
(Courtesy Jayant Scientific Industries, Mumbai).

Figure 6.1.2 Ro-tap Sieve Shaker.
(Courtesy Jayant Scientific Industries, Mumbai).

6.2   TESTING METHOD

The sieves chosen for the test are arranged in a **stack,** or **nest,** starting from the coarsest sieve at the top and the finest at the bottom. A pan or receiver is placed below the bottom sieve to receive final undersize, and a lid is placed on top of the coarsest sieve to prevent escape of the sample.

The material to be tested is placed on uppermost coarsest sieve and close with lid. The nest is then placed in a Sieve Shaker and sieved for certain time. Fig. 6.2.1 shows the sieve analysis at the end of the sieving

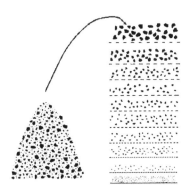

Figure 6.2.1 Sieve Analysis at the end of sieving.

Table 6.2.1 Particle Size Distribution data from sieve analysis test.

Mesh number	Retained mesh size in microns	Weight of material gm
+14	1200	02.5
−14+22	710	18.0
−22+30	500	18.5
−30+44	355	21.0
−44+60	250	27.5
−60+72	210	36.0
−72+100	150	31.5
−100+150	105	26.0
−150+200	74	18.5
−200		50.5
		250.0

+ sign designates particles retained on that sieve.
− sign designates particles passed through that sieve.

The material collected on each sieve is removed and weighed. The complete set of values is known as **Particle Size Distribution** data. Particle size distribution refers to the manner in which particles are quantitatively distributed among various sizes; in other words a statistical relation between quantity and size. Particle size distribution data is presented in a tabular form as shown in the Table 6.2.1.

Another way of representing the material with mesh numbers is 14/22 which means the material passed through 14 mesh and retained on 22 mesh.

The weight percentages of the material retained on such sieve are to be calculated to form differential analysis. Cumulative weight percentage retained is obtained from differential analysis by adding, cumulatively, the individual differential weight percentages from the top of the table. Cumulative weight percentage passing is obtained by adding, cumulatively, the individual weight percentages from the bottom of the table.

All the fractions are fairly closely sized (except first fraction). Hence the size of the particles in each fraction may be calculated as arithmetic mean of the limiting sizes.

For example, the size of −14 + 22 mesh fraction is $\frac{1200+710}{2} = 955$ microns.

It means, the material pass through 14 mesh and retain on 22 mesh are having the mean size of 955 microns. Similarly the mean sizes of each fraction are to be calculated. The Table 6.2.2 shows all values.

Average size of the material is determined by using the following simple arithmetic formula

$$\therefore \text{Average size} = \frac{100}{\sum \frac{w_i}{d_i}}. \tag{6.2.1}$$

where

w is the weight percent of the material retained by the sieve
d is the mean size of the material retained by the same sieve

Table 6.2.2 Calculated values for Particle Size Distribution.

Mesh number	Retained mesh size microns	Mean size d_i microns	Weight gm	wt% retained w_i	Cum wt% retained	Cum wt% passing W
						100.0
+14	1200	1200	02.5	1.0	1.0	99.0
−14+22	710	955	18.0	7.2	8.2	91.8
−22+30	500	605	18.5	7.4	15.6	84.4
−30+44	355	427.5	21.0	8.4	24.0	76.0
−44+60	250	302.5	27.5	11.0	35.0	65.0
−60+72	210	230	36.0	14.4	49.4	50.6
−72+100	150	180	31.5	12.6	62.0	38.0
−100+150	105	127.5	26.0	10.4	72.4	27.6
−150+200	74	89.5	18.5	7.4	79.8	20.2
−200		37	50.5	20.2	100.0	
			250.0	100.0		

6.3   PARTICLE SIZE ANALYZER

Particle size analyzer is an instrument which uses the technique of laser diffraction to measure the size of the particles in a sample of material. It determines the size of the particles by measuring the intensity of light scattered as a laser beam passes through a dispersed particulate sample. This data is then analyzed to calculate the size of the particles that created the scattering pattern. Particle size analyzers can measure the sizes of many particles in a sample very quickly and can provided data on particle size distributions.

A typical system is made up of three main elements:

• **Optical bench:** A dispersed sample passes through the measurement area of the optical bench, where a laser beam illuminates the particles. A series of detectors then accurately measure the intensity of light scattered by the particles within the sample over a wide range of angles.
• **Sample dispersion units (accessories):** Sample dispersion is controlled by a range of wet and dry dispersion units. These ensure the particles are delivered to the measurement area of the optical bench at the correct concentration and in a suitable, stable state of dispersion.
• **Instrument software:** The software controls the system during the measurement process and analyzes the scattering data to calculate a particle size distribution.

There are number of firms available in the market manufacturing the particle size analyzers for measuring the size of solid particles up to 6 mm.

6.4   PRESENTATION OF PARTICLE SIZE DISTRIBUTION DATA

Particle size distribution refers to the manner in which particles are quantitatively distributed among various sizes in a sample of material; in other words a statistical relation

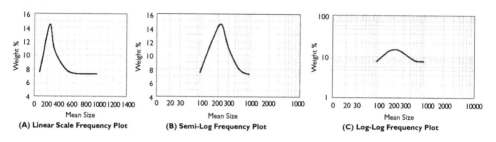

Figure 6.4.1 Graphical presentation of data tabulated in table 6.2.2.

between quantity and size. This data is best presented for use in the form of graphs. The simplest method is to plot a histogram of the weight percent of the material in the size interval against the size interval. When the size intervals are small enough, the histogram can be presented as a continuous curve taking the middle points of histogram. In other words, a graph is plotted between the weight percent of the material as ordinate and the arithmetic mean size as abscissa. It is called as **linear scale frequency plot**. It gives the quantitative picture of the relative distribution of the material over the entire size range. In this plot, the size scale at the fine end is compressed and the data points are congested because the size intervals are in geometric series. Hence a logarithmic scale is used for abscissa of mean sizes. As the distances separating the points corresponding to consecutive mean sizes are equal, the data points at the finer end will spread. This plot is called as **semi-log frequency plot**. In this plot, the area under the curve is in all cases equal to unity or 100 percent. This is often useful. In studies of size distribution in crushed products, often a graph known as **log-log frequency plot** is obtained by plotting logarithm of the weight percent of the material against the logarithm of the mean size. All the three graphs for the tabulated data are shown in Fig. 6.4.1.

In many cases, the data is more commonly plotted as cumulative wt% passing versus actual size of opening. It is called **linear scale cumulative plot**. d_{80}, the size of the sieve at which 80% of the material pass through (simply called 80% passing size) may be found from this plot. Crowding of data points at finer end is not a drawback in this plot since plotting of all points is not necessary. However, logarithmic scale of abscissa for actual size of opening is recommended in which case it is called **semi-log cumulative plot**. Although this plot appears to be a satisfactory presentation of the data, it is not widely used because the S shape of the curve is difficult to express mathematically. These two plots are shown in Fig. 6.4.2. where determination of 80% passing size is also shown.

Size distribution analyses of crushed and ground products are commonly plotted on log-log paper with **W** the cumulative wt% passing as ordinate and the particle diameter **d** in microns as abscissa. This plot is convenient and most commonly used in the mineral and coal industry to describe the size distributions.

Such plots usually show a fairly straight line for the finer particle size range which begins to curve in the coarser size range. Interpolation is much easier from a straight line. Extrapolation of straight line, gives the size distribution data at finer sizes down

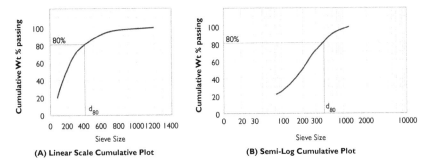

Figure 6.4.2 Linear Scale and Semi-log Cumulative Plots.

to 5 microns. The burden of routine analysis can be greatly reduced as relatively few sieves will be needed to check essential features of the size distribution.

The **Rosin-Rammler** method [20] (developed in 1933) is often used for representing the size distribution of broken coal and relatively fine crushed coal. Such products are found to obey the following relationship

$$W = 100 - 100 \, e^{-\left(\frac{d}{d*}\right)^n}$$

If $d = d*$, $W = 100 - \dfrac{100}{e} = 100 - \dfrac{100}{2.71828} = 100 - 36.788 = 63.212$

Therefore $d*$ is the size at which 63.212% of material pass through. Rosin-Rammler equation can be rewritten as

$$e^{-\left(\frac{d}{d*}\right)^n} = \frac{100 - W}{100}$$

$$\Rightarrow e^{\left(\frac{d}{d*}\right)^n} = \frac{100}{100 - W}$$

$$\Rightarrow \ln\frac{100}{100 - W} = \left(\frac{d}{d*}\right)^n$$

Taking log on both sides

$$\log\left[\ln\frac{100}{100 - W}\right] = n\log\left(\frac{d}{d*}\right)$$

A plot of $\ln\dfrac{100}{100 - W}$ versus 'd' on log-log axes is to be drawn.

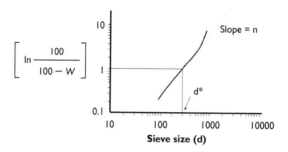

Figure 6.4.3 Rosin-Rammler Plot.

The graph is a fairly straight line for the finer particle size range and begins to curve upwards at the coarser end as shown in Fig. 6.4.3. The value of the 'n' is the slope of the straight line.

As the d* is the size at which 63.212% of material passes,

$$\ln\frac{100}{100-W} = \ln\frac{100}{100-63.212} = 1.0$$

The value of 'd' corresponding to $\ln\dfrac{100}{100-W} = 1.0$ is to be read from the straight line which is the value of d*.

80% passing size (D80) is the size of the sieve at which 80% of the material pass through that sieve. 80% passing size can be determined from the plot of cumulative weight percent passing versus sieve size.

F80   is the 80% passing size of the feed material.

P80   is the 80% passing size of the product material.

80% passing size is used in all calculations to determine energy requirements for reducing the size of the particles by comminution equipment.

Size distribution analyses of crushed and ground products are also plotted on log-log paper with **W** the cumulative wt% passing as ordinate and the particle diameter **d** in microns as abscissa. This plot, frequently referred as **Schuhmann, Gaudin-Schuhmann,** or **Gates-Gaudin-Schuhmann plot** [21], is convenient and most commonly used in the mineral industry to describe the size distributions and is represented in mathematical form as follows:

$$W = 100\left(\frac{d}{d_{100}}\right)^m$$

where

      W = the cumulative weight percent passing
      d = particle size in microns
      d_{100} = Gaudin-Schuhmann modulus or Size modulus
             Maximum theoretical size or 100% passing size
      m = distribution modulus (slope of the line)

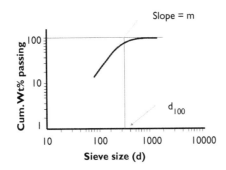

Figure 6.4.4 Gates-Gaudin-Schuhmann plot.

Such plots as in Fig. 6.4.4 usually show a fairly straight line for the finer particle size range which begins to curve in the coarser sizes and often approaches tangency with the 100 percent passing line at the top of the plot. The slope of the straight line is the value of m.

When the straight lower portion of the plotted line is extended at its slope m, it intercepts the 100 percent passing line at d_{100} microns.

This Gates-Gaudin-Schuhmann distribution relationship is applicable for homogeneous brittle materials which have no natural weaknesses, particularly cleavage planes, cracks, and weak grain boundaries. It can be applied to as much as 80% of many materials with useful accuracy.

6.5   SUB-SIEVE SIZING

Sizing of the particles having size less than 40 microns is known as Sub-sieve sizing. The particles at fine sizes are termed as slimes and colloids. The following are the approximate size ranges:

Sands	between 2 mm and 74 microns
Slimes	between 74 and 0.1 microns
Colloids	between 0.1 and 0.001 microns

Size analysis methods used for the particles less than 40 microns are shown in Table 6.5.

Sedimentation and elutriation techniques are based on the settling behaviour of the particles of various sizes and the analysis is made by separating the particles into various size fractions. Microscopic sizing is similar to measurement with a yardstick. The particles are sprinkled on a glass slide or mounted in some way on a slide and the size of individual particles is measured under the microscope. Laser beam particle size analysis is of the recent origin. The PSM system has been installed in several Beneficiation plants for continuous measurement of particle size.

Fine particles are more difficult to handle and beneficiate. Greater stress is to be given to process the fine particles not only to recover the values but also to control the pollution.

Table 6.5 Sub-sieve sizing methods.

Method	Approximate range, μm
Sedimentation (gravity)	40–1
(a) Beaker decantation (b) Andresen pipette	
Elutriation	40–5
Sedimentation (centrifugal) Cyclosizer	5–0.05
Microscope (optical)	150–1
Electron microscope	1–0.005
Electrical Resistance method Coulter counter	400–0.5

6.6   ILLUSTRATIVE EXAMPLES

Illustrative example 6.6.1: *From the sieve analysis data of a sample shown in Table: 6.6.1, determine 80% passing size.*

Table 6.6.1 Sieve analysis data for illustrative example 6.6.1.

Mesh number	Mesh size microns	Direct wt% retained
+18	853	7.0
−18+25	599	10.4
−25+36	422	14.2
−36+52	295	13.6
−52+72	211	9.2
−72+100	152	8.1
−100+150	104	8.2
−150+200	74	5.1
−200		24.2

Solution:

For determination of 80% passing size, cumulative weight percentages are to be calculated from the bottom. All the values are shown in Table 6.6.1.1.

Table 6.6.1.1 Calculated values for illustrative example 6.6.1.

Mesh number	Mesh size microns	wt% retained	Cumulative wt% passing
+18	853	7.0	100.0
−18	853	10.4	93.0
−25	599	14.2	82.6
−36	422	13.6	68.4
−52	295	9.2	54.8
−72	211	8.1	45.6
−100	152	8.2	37.5
−150	104	5.1	29.3
−200	74	24.2	24.2

To determine 80% passing size, a graph between cumulative wt% and mesh size is drawn as shown Fig. 6.6.1.1.

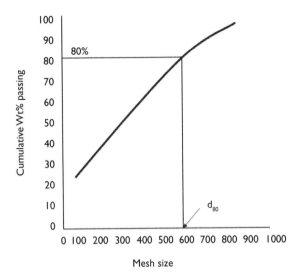

Figure 6.6.1.1 Graph between cumulative wt% and mesh size for illustrative example 6.6.1.

Size corresponding to 80% of cumulative wt% passing is the 80% passing size. It is 580 microns from the graph.

Illustrative example 6.6.2: *For the size analysis of a screen underflow shown in Table 6.6.2, determine Rosin-Rammler equation and Gates-Gaudin-Schuhmann equation.*

Table 6.6.2 Size analysis of a screen underflow for illustrative example 6.6.2.

Mesh number	Mesh size microns	Weight % retained
20	840	3.6
28	595	6.0
35	420	8.3
48	297	8.7
65	210	8.1
100	149	8.4
150	105	7.6
200	74	8.1
−200		41.2

Solution:
Necessary calculations are done and the Table 6.6.2.1 shows different values.

Table 6.6.2.1 Calculated values for illustrative example 6.6.2.

Mesh number	Mesh size microns	Weight% retained	Cum. wt% passing W	100 – W	$\dfrac{100}{100-W}$	$\ln\dfrac{100}{100-W}$
20	840	3.6	96.4	3.6	27.778	3.324
28	595	6.0	90.4	9.6	10.417	2.343
35	420	8.3	82.1	17.9	5.587	1.720
48	297	8.7	73.4	26.6	3.759	1.324
65	210	8.1	65.3	34.7	2.882	1.058
100	149	8.4	56.9	43.1	2.320	0.842
150	105	7.6	49.3	50.7	1.972	0.679
200	74	8.1	41.2	58.8	1.701	0.531
−200		41.2				
		100.0				

A graph is drawn between $\ln\dfrac{100}{100-W}$ and sieve size 'd' on log-log graph sheet as shown in Fig. 6.6.2.1.

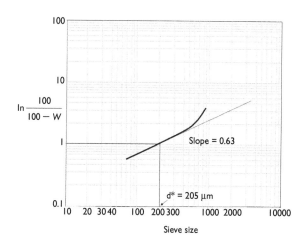

Figure 6.6.2.1 Rosin-Rammler plot for illustrative example 6.6.2.

From the graph Slope = n = 0.63

$$\ln\frac{100}{100-w} = \ln\frac{100}{100-63.212} = 1.0$$

From the graph d* = 205 μm corresponding to 1.0 on ordinate
On substituting these values, Rosin-Rammler Equation becomes

$$W = 100 - 100e^{-\left(\frac{d}{205}\right)^{0.63}}$$

A graph is drawn between Cumulative weight% passing and sieve size 'd' on log-log graph sheet as shown in Fig. 6.6.2.2.

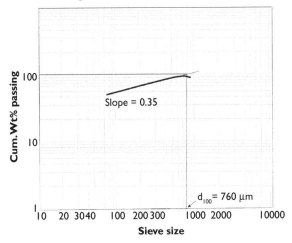

Figure 6.6.2.2 Gates-Gaudin-Schumann plot for illustrative example 6.6.2.

From the graph, slope = 0.35
Corresponding to cumulative wt% passing of 100%, sieve size is d_{100}.
d_{100} = 760 microns from the graph.
Gates-Gaudin-Schumann equation is

$$W = 100 \left(\frac{d}{760} \right)^{0.35}$$

6.7   PROBLEMS FOR PRACTICE

6.7.1: *From the sieve analysis of the rod mill product shown in Table 6.7.1, estimate 80% passing size.*

Table 6.7.1 Sieve analysis of rod mill product for problem 6.7.1.

Aperture size of the sieve, microns	Weight fraction retained
1680	0.005
1190	0.075
840	0.075
595	0.085
420	0.110
297	0.144
210	0.125
149	0.103
105	0.078
105 pass	0.200

[680 microns]

6.7.2: *For the size analysis data of ball mill feed shown in Table 6.7.2, draw frequency plots on linear, semi-log and log-log scales. Also draw cumulative plots on linear and semi-log scales. Obtain Rosin-Rammler and Gates-Gaudin-Schuhmann equations.*

Table 6.7.2 Size analysis data of ball mill feed for problem 6.7.2.

Mesh Number	Mesh Size microns	Weight% retained
12	1410	2.61
14	1190	9.30
20	840	11.80
28	595	12.89
35	420	9.81
48	297	8.19
65	210	7.74
100	149	5.60
150	105	6.09
200	74	3.88
−200		22.09

$$\left[W = 100 - 100e^{-\left(\frac{d}{593}\right)^{0.68}} , W = 100\left(\frac{d}{1450}\right)^{0.55} \right]$$

Chapter 7

Proximate analysis of coal

Analysis of coal is very important from a point of view for the selection of coal for definite purpose like combustion, carbonization, gasification and liquefaction. Proximate analysis is the most often used type of analysis for characterizing coals in connection with their utilization. The proximate analysis determines the percentage of moisture, volatile matter, ash and fixed carbon. Proximate analysis is much more readily made and gives a preliminary indication of quality and suitability for various uses. It also affords a means of providing commercial classification.

Proximate analysis is not an analysis in the true sense since the results do not have any absolute significance. However, if the determinations are carried out under specified conditions, the results are reproducible and enable the coal to be classified into groups and opinion formed about its probable use. Studies have shown that proximate analysis can be used to estimate certain physical, chemical and thermal properties of coal.

The first step in the analysis of coal is the provision of sample of suitable bulk, particle size, and conditions. As coal is a solid substance and varies in nature from seam to seam even from the same mine, a representative sample should be prepared before the actual analysis is done. As the analysis is based on a very small quantity, unless the sample is representative of the main bulk, the results of the analysis, however accurate, are valueless and misleading.

The difficulty in obtaining a representative sample lies in the fact that the coal is heterogeneous in a double sense; firstly, impurities are always present and secondly, the distribution of the impurities is not uniform.

The heterogeneity of coal is measured in terms of average error which is calculated by analyzing the coal from a large number of wagons from the same seam. For example, if 100 wagons of coal are sampled, the ash will vary from wagon to wagon about a mean value which is called the true ash content. If the sum of the deviations from the true ash value (regardless of sign) is divided by the total number of samples, the quotient will give the average deviation from the mean. This is known as the average error of the coal in 100 wagons.

The weight of the gross sample is based on the size of the coal, its variability and the accuracy required. The minimum weight of each increment depends on the size of the coal, while the number of increments required for a given accuracy is function of the average error. The degree of accuracy required in sampling depends on the purpose for which the sample is taken, i.e. whether for commercial purposes, for routine testing in a factory, or in connection with special performance and efficiency trials.

The gross sample is collected from the bulk of coal in heaps or wagons by making holes at different level at equal spacing and keeping the whole amount drawn through the whole. This amount is crushed to –6 mm size and reduced by coning and quartering to 1.2 kg which is ground to pass 72 mesh B.S. Sieve and stored in a stoppered bottle.

7.1   MOISTURE

Coal that has been exposed to contact with water in the seam or in washery, or coal wetted by rain, may carry free or visible water. This water plus the moisture within the coal is called total moisture. The amount of moisture retained by a coal may vary between fairly wide limits. By exposing coal in a thin layer in a dry, well-ventilated place, the coal looses free or surface moisture content in equilibrium with the moisture in the atmosphere.

7.1.1   Determination of moisture

Weigh 2 to 10 gm of –72 mesh B.S. Sieve coal sample in a Petri dish of 10 mm deep and provided with a cover. Spread the sample in such a way that the weight of coal does not exceed 0.3 gm per square centimeter in the dish. Heat the uncovered dish in an electrically heated vacuum oven for an hour between 105° and 110°C. After this, the dish is covered and transferred to the desiccator and cooled. The loss in weight is the amount of moisture.

By using a vacuum oven, the risk of oxidation is minimized and the rate of drying is increased. To prevent oxidation of the coal, drying is also carried out in an atmosphere of nitrogen. The atmosphere within the oven should be changed four to five times in an hour.

For routine purposes, about 1 gm of –72 mesh coal sample is kept in a silica crucible and heated in a muffle furnace at 105°–110°C for one hour. Thereafter, the crucible is taken out, cooled in a desiccator and weighed. The process of heating, cooling and weighing is repeated number of times till the constant weight of coal is achieved. The loss in weight is the weight of moisture.

$$\% \text{ Moisture} = \frac{\text{Weight of moisture}}{\text{Weight of original sample}} \times 100 \qquad (7.1.1)$$

7.2   VOLATILE MATTER

The volatile matter is not a constituent of coal, but consists of a complex mixture of gaseous and liquid products resulting from the thermal decomposition of the coal substance. The amount of decomposition and, therefore, the yield of volatile matter depend mainly on the temperature used during the assay. Hence, in determining volatiles, standard conditions should be maintained, otherwise the results will vary from experiment to experiment and they will not be comparable with each other.

Certain gases like CO, CO_2, CH_4, H_2, N_2, O_2, hydrocarbons etc. are present in the coal which comes out during its heating. These are called volatile matter of coal.

Volatile matter does not include the moisture of coal but it contains water that is formed from the hydrogen and oxygen of coal during decomposition. It also includes the part of mineral matter which escapes into the gaseous and vapour state. When volatile matter is expressed on dmmf basis, it represents only the volatile products from the pure coal or organic mss. This percentage is used to classify the coal.

The coal with higher volatile matter ignites easily, burns with long smoky yellow flame, has lower calorific value, has higher tendency of catching fire when stored in open space and it requires larger furnace volume for its combustion. Volatile matter decreases with increase in the maturity or rank of coal. It is estimated that the volatile matter that comes out from mineral matter is approximately 10% of ash present in the coal.

A standard method for the determination of volatile matter has been recommended by the Fuel Research Board and the British Standards Institution (U.K) in which 1 gm of air-dried coal is heated for exactly 7 minutes in a translucent silica crucible at a constant temperature of 925°C in a muffle furnace. The crucible should be of a specified dimension (38 mm high, and 25 mm external and 22 mm internal diameters) with capsule type lid having internal overall diameter of 27 mm, diameter of well 21 mm, and depth of well 4 mm. The combined weight of the crucible and the lid should be between 12 and 14 gm. The clearance between the crucible and the lid at the top edge should not be more than 0.5 mm.

The furnace may be heated by gas or electricity, but it should give a steady temperature of 925°C. It should also have a well-fitting door at the front and a short flue at the back. The thermocouple used to measure the furnace temperature should be sheathed and calibrated from time to time against a standard thermocouple and indicator.

7.2.1   Determination of volatile matter

1 gm of air-dried coal of −72 mesh B.S. Sieve is weighed in a standard cylindrical silica crucible with lid. The crucible is placed in a muffle furnace of specified dimensions at 925°C for a period of exactly seven minutes. Remove the crucible from the furnace and place on a cold iron plate to cool it rapidly. This prevents any oxidation of the contents in the crucible. Transfer the crucible to a desiccator while still warm. Allow it to cool and weigh. The loss of weight is taken as weight of volatile matter and air-dried moisture.

$$\% \text{ volatile matter and air- dried moisture}$$
$$= \frac{\text{Weight of volatile matter and air- dried moisture}}{\text{Weight of original sample}} \times 100 \qquad (7.2.1)$$

$$\% \text{ Volatile matter } = \% \text{ Volatile matter and air- dried moisture}$$
$$- \% \text{ air- dried moisture} \qquad (7.2.2)$$

7.3   ASH

The ash of a coal is the non-combustible inorganic residue that remains when coal is burned. It does not occur as such in coal, but it formed as a result of chemical changes that take place in the mineral matter during the ashing process. It is an inert material and excess of it may detract the value of coal. It represents the bulk of the mineral matter in the coal, after volatile components such as Carbon dioxide (from carbonates) Sulphur dioxide (from sulphides) and Water (from clays) have been dried off. The amount of ash varies considerably in different coals and in the coals of the same rank.

The terms mineral matter and ash as applied to coal are not synonymous. Mineral matter refers to the various impurities as they exist in the coal, whereas the ash is the solid residue remaining after the coal has been completely burned. The ash produced by the inherent mineral matter is **fixed ash**. The ash produced by the extraneous mineral matter is **free ash**. Although the ash is obviously driven from the mineral matter, it has not the same composition or amount as the mineral matter. Roughly, mineral matter in coal is 10% more than the actual ash formed on combustion of coal.

$$MM = 1.1 \ A \tag{7.3.1}$$

where

MM = percent mineral matter in coal

A = percent ash in coal

The ash from industrial coals is determined by the complete combustion of the weighed sample. It includes inherent ash intimately associated with the coal and partly or mainly derived from the original coal plants and adventitious ash derived from shale, clay, pyrites or directly have become included in mining of coal. The adventitious ash forming constituents can be removed by physical means but the inherent ash forming constituents cannot be removed. Coals having drift origin i.e. Indian coals, contain a large proportion of adventitious ash forming constituents.

7.3.1   Determination of ash

Ash prepared from a given weight of coal would be heavier if prepared at 500°C than if prepared at 800°C, as carbonates and some sulphates stable at 500°C are decomposed at 800°C. Further the composition of coal ash is influenced by the availability of air during the combustion, so that with a restricted supply of air, sulphides may be formed instead of sulphates.

1 gm of air-dried coal of −72 mesh B.S. Sieve is taken in a clean dry silica crucible. The coal is distributed so that the thickness of the layer does not exceed 0.14 gm per square centimeter. The crucible is put into a muffle furnace at 500°C for 30 minutes and raised the temperature to 815±10°C in another 30 to 60 minutes. The crucible is kept for one hour or more at this temperature until there is no loss in weight. The crucible is then taken out, cooled in a desiccator and weighed. The weight of the material left in the crucible is the weight of the ash.

$$\% \ Ash = \frac{Weight \ of \ the \ ash}{Weight \ of \ original \ sample} \times 100 \tag{7.3.2}$$

The percent ash is reported to one decimal place.

The colour of the ash is also to be noted.

It is also in practice to heat the coal sample directly at 750°C till a constant weight is obtained.

7.4 FIXED CARBON

The residue left after heating the coal in absence of air in a closed vessel to drive off the volatile matter is the Coke. This residue contains all the inorganic constituents present in the original coal that go to form the ash. This solid residue also contains hydrogen, sulphur, oxygen and nitrogen in addition to carbon. It may vary from a black powder (non-coking coals) to a highly porous button and its appearance, strength and cellular structure are significant characteristics. The percentage of solid residue minus the percent ash gives the percent fixed carbon.

In other words, the fixed carbon content of a coal is the carbon found in the material that remains after the volatile matter has been expelled. It represents the decomposition residue of the coal's organic components, and carries with it small amounts of nitrogen, sulphur, hydrogen, and possibly oxygen as absorbed or chemically combined material.

The fixed carbon content is used as an index of the yield of coke expected from a coal on carbonization, or as a measure of the solid combustible material that remains in coal burning equipment after the volatile fraction has been liberated. If corrections are applied for ash or mineral matter, it may be used as an index of coal rank and a parameter in coal classification.

Fixed carbon is the pure carbon present in the coal. It is the carbon available in the coal for combustion. Higher the fixed carbon content, higher will be its calorific value.

Total carbon is the fixed carbon plus the carbon present in the volatile matters e.g. carbon monoxide, carbon dioxide, methane, hydrocarbons etc. Total carbon is always more than fixed carbon in any coal. High total carbon containing coal will have higher calorific value.

In anthracites, the volatile matter is very small and the values of fixed carbon and total carbon are almost equal. In other coals, fixed carbon is less than total carbon. The carbon content of coal increases with increase in the rank.

7.4.1 Determination of fixed carbon

Fixed carbon is not determined directly. It is simply the difference between the sum of the other components and 100.

% Fixed carbon = 100 – (% Moisture +% Volatile matter +% Ash)   (7.4.1)

7.5 PRE-WETTING OF COAL SAMPLE

A procedure has been adopted to pre-wet the coal sample when hygroscopic salts are present in coal. In such case, a pre-wash with warm distilled water is desirable.

Take about 20 gm of laboratory sample of coal, wet it thoroughly for 15 minutes and then dry by pressing between the folds of filter paper. When no more water appears to be absorbed, place 10 gm of coal sample in light metal dish of 10 cm diameter. Spread the coal thinly and evenly. Put the dish into uncovered desiccator and keep inside humidity chamber for 48 hrs. Then proceed as usual.

7.6   REPORTING PROXIMATE ANALYSIS

Most analyses of coals are carried out on air dried samples, and the percentages of the various constituents are calculated in proportion to the mass of that material. For many purposes, however, this value is of little significance. In commercial operations, a certain amount of **adventitious** moisture forms part of the coal that is mined, shipped, and delivered to the consumer. The percentage of ash in relation to the total mass of coal supplied in such cases is more meaningful than the percentage in relation to a state that is never attained in practice.

On the other hand, comparison and classification of coals is based essentially on the nature of the organic fraction. It is necessary to allow for the effects on chemical composition and other properties brought about by mineral impurities in order to make use of such classifications, and thus the percentages may need to be re-expressed as part of a **pure coal** rather than of a moist, mineral bearing material.

In both these situations, the analytical results can be modified by appropriate corrections to allow expressions on a different bases. The most commonly used bases for reporting of analytical results are as received, air-dried, dry, daf and dmmf.

7.6.1   As received or as sampled

When the coal is received by a consumer from the mine, then its analysis is reported on **As received basis**. Lot of physical and chemical changes occur during the transportation of coal from mine to the consumer and also during the processing such as size reduction, washing etc. Hence analysis of coal at consumers end is reported on **As received basis**.

7.6.2   Air-dried

Freshly mined coal looses its moisture due to exposure to atmospheric air, during transportation and storage. The data obtained by analyzing the coal at this stage is on **air dried basis**.

In fact the data on **As received** basis and **Air dried** basis may be the same because in both cases coal looses its moisture similarly depending on humidity and temperature of atmospheric air. However, for getting accurate and comparable results, the coal is exposed to an artificial and standard atmosphere at 40°C and 60% relative humidity to get air dried data. Even after air drying, the coal contains some amount of moisture.

7.6.3   Dry or moisture free

When it is required to completely eliminate the effect of moisture on analytical data, the coal analysis is reported on **Dry** or **moisture free basis**. It is the data expressed as the percentages of the coal after all the moisture has been removed.

7.6.4   Dry, ash free (d.a.f.)

If the effect of moisture and ash is to be eliminated, then the data is reported on **dry ash free basis**. The coal is considered to consist of volatile matter and fixed carbon on the basis of recalculation with moisture and ash removed. This does not allow for the volatile matter derived from minerals present in the air-dried coal. This is the simplest way to compare the organic fractions of coals without diluting the effects of inorganic components. This data is suitable for comparing low ash coals (ash <10%).

7.6.5 Dry, mineral matter free (d.m.m.f.)

Here it is necessary that the total amount of mineral matter rather than ash is determined, so that the volatile matter content in the mineral matter can be removed. In case of high ash coals, the mineral matter content is around 10% more than its ash whereas mineral matter is almost equal to its ash in case of low ash coals. Hence the data expressed on **dry mineral matter free basis** is most suitable for comparing high ash coals (ash >10%).

7.7 CALCULATIONS

The details of calculations to express the proximate analysis on different bases are given in the following articles.

7.7.1 As received or as sampled basis

The results of proximate analysis are expressed as percentages of the coal including the total moisture content.

$$\% \text{ Moisture} = \frac{\text{Weight of moisture}}{\text{Weight of coal sample as received}} \times 100 \qquad (7.7.1.1)$$

$$\% \text{ Volatile matter} = \frac{\text{Weight of volatile matter}}{\text{Weight of coal sample as received}} \times 100 \qquad (7.7.1.2)$$

$$\% \text{ Ash} = \frac{\text{Weight of ash}}{\text{Weight of coal sample as received}} \times 100 \qquad (7.7.1.3)$$

$$\% \text{ Fixed carbon} = 100 - (\% \text{ Moisture} + \% \text{ Volatile matter} + \% \text{ Ash}) \qquad (7.7.1.4)$$

7.7.2 Air-dried basis

The results are expressed as percentages of the air-dried coal, including inherent but not surface or free moisture.

$$\% \text{ Moisture} = M = \frac{\text{Weight of moisture}}{\text{Weight of air- dried coal sample}} \times 100 \qquad (7.7.2.1)$$

$$\% \text{ Volatile matter} = V = \frac{\text{Weight of volatile matter}}{\text{Weight of air- dried coal sample}} \times 100 \qquad (7.7.2.2)$$

$$\% \text{ Ash} = A = \frac{\text{Weight of ash}}{\text{Weight of air- dried coal sample}} \times 100 \qquad (7.7.2.3)$$

$$\% \text{ Fixed carbon} = FC = 100 - (M + V + A) \qquad (7.7.2.4)$$

7.7.3   Dry or moisture free basis

The results are expressed as percentages of the coal after the inherent moisture has been removed. By using the percentages on air-dried basis, the results of proximate analysis on dry basis can be calculated as follows:

On Dry basis

$$\% \text{ Ash} = \frac{A}{100 - M} \times 100 \qquad (7.7.3.1)$$

$$\% \text{ Volatile matter} = \frac{V}{100 - M} \times 100 \qquad (7.7.3.2)$$

$$\% \text{ Fixed carbon} = \frac{FC}{100 - M} \times 100 \qquad (7.7.3.3)$$

7.7.4   Dry, ash free (d.a.f.) basis

The coal is considered, in proximate analysis, to consist of only volatile matter and fixed carbon, on the basis of recalculation with ash and moisture removed. The calculations are as follows:

On daf basis

$$\% \text{ Volatile matter} = \frac{V}{100 - M - A} \times 100 \qquad (7.7.4.1)$$

$$\% \text{ Fixed carbon} = \frac{FC}{100 - M - A} \times 100 \qquad (7.7.4.2)$$

7.7.5   Dry, mineral matter free (d.m.m.f.) basis

The coal is also considered to consist of solely volatile matter and fixed carbon, but it is necessary that the total amount of mineral matter rather than ash be determined.

Allowance is also made in dry, mineral matter free data, for the contribution to the air-dried volatile matter that comes from the mineral components. This may be done directly or indirectly. As it is difficult to determine volatile matter that comes from the mineral matter, it is suggested and agreed that the mineral matter of coal contributes to the volatile matter by an amount approximately equal to 10% of the ash.

Accordingly

$$\% \text{ Mineral Matter} = MM = A + 0.1 A = 1.1 A \qquad (7.7.5.1)$$

The calculations are as follows:

On dmmf basis

$$\% \text{ Volatile matter} = \frac{V - 0.1A}{100 - M - 1.1A} \times 100 \qquad (7.7.5.2)$$

$$\% \text{ Fixed carbon} = \frac{FC}{100 - M - 1.1A} \times 100 \qquad (7.7.5.3)$$

All the above bases are indicated pictorially in Fig.7.7.

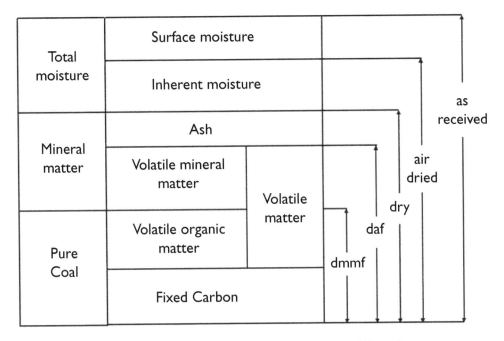

Figure 7.7 Pictorial presentation of proximate analysis on different bases.

7.8   INSTRUMENTAL METHODS FOR PROXIMATE ANALYSIS

Traditionally, the various proximate analysis determinations involve heating the sample to constant weight. These determinations are time consuming and require a significant amount of laboratory equipment. An alternative method for proximate analysis is Thermo Gravimetric Analysis (TGA). It measures weight changes in a material with temperature and provides a convenient method for performing a proximate analysis usually in less than 20 minutes. Because of smaller sample sizes and rapid temperature and atmosphere control in TGA, it substantially reduces the analysis time as well as the equipment necessary for proximate analysis.

In TGA, the sample contained in the pan of a sensitive analytical balance is heated under a flowing atmosphere (inert or reactive) and the weight change is recorded. To obtain a complete proximate analysis in a single TGA experiment, the system is programmed to hold initially at 200°C in nitrogen, then jump to 900°C and hold for a specified period of time in nitrogen before switching to oxygen. Recent advances in TGA instrumentation have made proximate analysis even easier to perform. These include:

- Automated gas switching: With a Gas Switching Accessory, the purge gas change at 900°C can be built into the multi-segment experiment method so that the Thermal Analysis Controller automatically makes the switch.
- Hi-Res™ TGA and the "abort" segment: Historically the time that the TGA remained at a specific set of conditions to ensure that the associated weight loss was completely operator–selected based on experience. In fact, the time was usually set to allow a

"safety" margin which ensured that the weight loss was complete. With the new TGA "abort" segment, the Thermal Analysis Controller can be programmed to automatically proceed to the next experimental step when a weight loss is complete.

7.9   ILLUSTRATIVE EXAMPLES

Illustrative example 7.9.1: *Three samples from medium coking coal were collected for the determination of proximate analysis. The following is the data obtained:*

Sample 1:

Weight of the empty crucible	*= 16.3256 gm*
Weight of the crucible with coal sample	*= 17.1348 gm*
Weight of the crucible with coal sample after heating at 105°C till constant weight	*= 17.1239 gm*

Sample 2:

Weight of the empty crucible	*= 18.5364 gm*
Weight of the crucible with coal sample	*= 19.3579 gm*
Weight of the crucible with coal sample after heating at 925±10°C for 7 minutes	*= 19.1603 gm*

Sample 3:

Weight of the empty crucible	*= 17.0826 gm*
Weight of the crucible with coal sample	*= 17.9301 gm*
Weight of the crucible with coal sample after heating at 750°C till constant weight	*= 17.3846 gm*

Calculate the proximate analysis of the coal.

Solution:

Moisture determination (Sample 1)

Weight of the coal sample	$= 17.1348 - 16.3256 = 0.8092$ gm
Weight of the moisture	$= 17.1348 - 17.1239 = 0.0109$ gm

$$\% \text{ Moisture} = \frac{0.0109}{0.8092} \times 100 = 1.35\%$$

Volatile matter determination (Sample 2)

Weight of the coal sample	$= 19.3579 - 18.5364 = 0.8215$ gm
Weight of volatile matter and moisture (since fresh sample is used)	$= 19.3579 - 19.1603 = 0.1976$ gm

$$\% \text{ Volatile matter} + \text{Moisture} = \frac{0.1976}{0.8215} \times 100 = 24.05\%$$

$$\% \text{ Volatile matter} = 24.05 - 01.35 = 22.70\%$$

Ash determination (Sample 3)

Weight of the coal sample	$= 17.9301 - 17.0826 = 0.8475$ gm
Weight of the ash	$= 17.3846 - 17.0826 = 0.3020$ gm

$$\% \text{ Ash} = \frac{0.3020}{0.8475} \times 100 = 35.63\%$$

% Fixed carbon = 100 − (% Moisture +% Volatile matter +% Ash)
= 100 − (01.35 + 22.70 + 35.63) = 40.32%

∴ Proximate Analysis of Coal is M = 01.35%

VM = 22.70%

A = 35.63%

FC = 40.32%

Illustrative example 7.9.2: *Proximate analysis of a coal was carried out by taking three samples as follows:*

a   *First sample is taken in 25 ml silica crucible of 17.395 gm and weighed as 18.313 gm. It is heated at 105°C in a hot air oven till constant weight is obtained. Its weight is 18.221 gm.*

b   *Second sample is taken in another 25 ml silica crucible of 18.305 gm and weighed as 19.217 gm. It is heated at 800°C in a muffle furnace till all the coal in it completely burns. Its weight is 18.534 gm.*

c   *Third sample is taken in a 18.232 gm silica volatile matter crucible and weighed as 19.055 gm. This is kept in a muffle furnace at 925°C for 7 minutes and then weighed as 18.726 gm.*

> *Calculate*   *i*   *Percent moisture*
>
> *ii*   *Percent mineral matter*
>
> *iii*   *Percent coal substance*

Solution:

a   Weight of the coal   = 18.313 − 17.395 = 0.918 gm

Weight of moisture   = 18.313 − 18.221 = 0.092 gm

$$\% \text{ moisture} = \frac{0.092}{0.918} \times 100 = 10.02\%$$

b   Weight of the coal   = 19.217 − 18.305 = 0.912 gm

Weight of ash   = 18.534 − 18.305 = 0.229 gm

$$\% \text{ ash} = \frac{0.229}{0.912} \times 100 = 25.11\%$$

c   Weight of the coal   = 19.055 − 18.232 = 0.823 gm

Weight of volatile matter + moisture = 19.055 − 18.726 = 0.329 gm

$$\% \text{ volatile matter} + \text{moisture} = \frac{0.329}{0.823} \times 100 = 39.98\%$$

% volatile matter = 39.98 − 10.02 = 29.96%

% fixed carbon = 100 − 10.02−29.96 − 25.11 = 34.91%

% mineral matter = 1.1Ash = 1.1 × 25.11 = 27.62%

% volatile matter from coal substance = volatile matter − 0.1 Ash

= 29.96 − 0.1 × 25.11 = 27.45

% coal substance = % fixed carbon + % volatile matter from coal substance

= 34.91 + 27.45 = 62.36%

Illustrative example 7.9.3: *A coal has 2.46% moisture, 25.73% volatile matter and 42.89% ash. Calculate ash% on dry basis, volatile matter on daf basis and fixed carbon on dmmf basis.*

Solution:

% fixed carbon = 100–2.46–25.73–42.89 = 28.92%

Proximate Analysis of Coal is
$$M = 02.46\%$$
$$VM = 25.73\%$$
$$A = 42.89\%$$
$$FC = 28.92\%$$

$$\% \text{ Ash on dry basis} = \frac{A}{100-M} \times 100 = \frac{42.89}{100-02.46} \times 100 = 43.97$$

$$\% \text{ Volatile matter on daf basis} = \frac{V}{100-M-A} \times 100$$

$$= \frac{25.73}{100-02.46-42.89} \times 100 = 47.08$$

$$\% \text{ Fixed carbon on dmmf basis} = \frac{FC}{100-M-1.1A} \times 100$$

$$= \frac{28.92}{100-02.46-1.1\times42.89} \times 100 = 57.43$$

Alternatively, fixed carbon can also be calculated through volatile matter

$$\% \text{ Volatile matter on dmmf basis} = \frac{V-0.1A}{100-M-1.1A} \times 100$$

$$= \frac{25.73-0.1\times42.89}{100-02.46-1.1\times42.89} \times 100 = 42.57$$

% Fixed carbon on dmmf basis = 100–42.57 = 57.43

7.10 PROBLEMS FOR PRACTICE

7.10.1: *Three samples are taken to determine the proximate analysis of a coal. The following are the observations in a laboratory.*

  a *First sample is taken in a 25 ml silica crucible of 18.395 gm and weighed as 19.313 gm and used for the determination of moisture present in the coal. The weight of the crucible after heating at 105°C in a hot air oven till constant weight is 19.221 gm.*

  b *Second sample is taken in a 19.234 gm silica volatile matter crucible and weighed as 20.055 gm. This is kept in a muffle furnace at 925°C for 7 minutes and then weighed as 19.726 gm.*

  c *Third sample is taken in another 25 ml silica crucible weighing 18.313 gm and kept in a muffle furnace at 750°C till the coal completely burns. The weights of crucible before and after heating are 19.225 gm and 18.542 gm respectively. What is proximate analysis?*

  [08.94, 29.60, 40.95, 20.51]

7.10.2: *A high volatile bituminous coal has 8% moisture, 34% volatile matter and 46% ash. Calculate volatile matter percent on dry, daf and dmmf bases.*

  [13.04; 26.09; 28.99]

Chapter 8

Ultimate analysis of coal

Ultimate analysis refers to the determination of those elements which are the main constituents of coal. These are carbon, hydrogen, nitrogen, sulphur, and oxygen. The first four elements are determined directly, but as there is no satisfactory method for the direct determination of oxygen in coal, the amount of oxygen is found by difference, subtracting the total percentage of the other four elements, expressed on a dry, mineral matter free basis, from 100. By contrast with proximate analysis, the determinations of carbon, hydrogen, nitrogen, and sulphur, are all of an absolute and finite nature. Analytical accuracy only is to be attained to ensure the reproducibility of results.

8.1 DETERMINATION OF CARBON AND HYDROGEN

A known amount of coal is burnt in a current of dry oxygen thereby converting C and H of coal into CO_2 ($C + O_2 \rightarrow CO_2$) and H_2O ($2H_2 + O_2 \rightarrow 2H_2O$) respectively. The products of combustion (CO_2 and H_2O) are passed over weighed tubes of anhydrous calcium chloride and potassium hydroxide which absorb H_2O and CO_2 respectively. The increase in the weight of $CaCl_2$ tube represents the weight of water (H_2O) formed while increase in the weight of KOH tube represents the weight of CO_2 formed.

% of H and C in coal can be calculated as below:

Let, x = weight of coal sample taken

   y = increase in the weight of $CaCl_2$ tube

   z = increase in the weight of KOH tube

$$\therefore \text{ Amount of carbon in the coal sample} = \frac{12}{44}z$$

Since, 44 gm of CO_2 is produced from 12 gm of carbon and 32 gm of oxygen $\Rightarrow \underset{12}{C} + \underset{32}{O_2} = \underset{44}{CO_2}$

$$\therefore \text{ \% Carbon in coal} = \frac{12\,z}{44\,x} \times 100 \tag{8.1.1}$$

Similarly, amount of hydrogen in coal sample $= \frac{2}{18}y$

Since, 18 gm of water is formed by 2 gm of hydrogen and

$$16 \text{gm of oxygen} \Rightarrow \underset{4}{2H_2} + \underset{32}{O_2} = \underset{36}{H_2O}$$

$$\therefore \% \text{ of hydrogen in coal} = \frac{2y}{18x} \times 100 \qquad\qquad (8.1.2)$$

8.2   DETERMINATION OF NITROGEN

Nitrogen estimation in coal is done by Kjeldahl's method (ASTM D-3179; ISO 333). A known weight of powdered coal is heated with concentrated sulphuric acid in presence of potassium sulphate and copper sulphate in a long necked flask (called Kjeldahl's flask) thereby converting nitrogen of coal to ammonium sulphate. When clear solution is obtained (i.e., when whole nitrogen is converted into ammonium sulphate) it is treated with 50% NaOH solution. The ammonia thus formed is distilled over and absorbed in a known quantity of standard sulphuric acid solution. The volume of unused sulphuric acid is then determined by titrating against standard NaOH solution. Thus, the amount of acid neutralized by liberated ammonia (from coal) is determined.

$$\% \text{ nitrogen in coal} = \frac{\text{Volume of acid used} \times \text{Normality}}{\text{Weight of coal taken}} \times 1.4 \qquad (8.2.1)$$

Since, $(NH_4)_2SO_4 + 2NaOH \rightarrow Na_2SO_4 + 2NH_4OH$

One litre of N/10 H_2SO_4 consumed is equivalent to 0.1 gm mole of ammonia or 1.4 gm of nitrogen.

Volume of acid used $= V_1 - V_2$

where
V_1 = Volume of H_2SO_4 neutralised in blank
V_2 = Volume of H_2SO_4 neutralised in determination

8.3   DETERMINATION OF SULPHUR

A known amount of coal is burnt completely in bomb calorimeter in a current of oxygen. Ash, thus obtained contains sulphur of the coal as sulphate which is extracted with dilute hydrochloric acid and the acid extract is treated with barium chloride solution to precipitate the sulphate as barium sulphate

$$\underset{32gm}{S} \xrightarrow{O_2} SO_4 \xrightarrow{BaCl_2} \underset{233gm}{BaSO_4} \qquad\qquad (8.3.1)$$

The precipitate of $BaSO_4$ is filtered, washed, dried and weighed from which the sulphur in coal can be computed as follows:

32 gm of sulphur in the coal will give 233 gm $BaSO_4$

If, x = weight of coal sample taken
   y = weight of $BaSO_4$ precipitate formed

then, % sulphur in coal sample $= \dfrac{32\,y}{233\,x} \times 100$ \hfill (8.3.2)

8.4   DETERMINATION OF OXYGEN

% oxygen in coal = 100 − (% of C + H + N + S + Ash) \hfill (8.4.1)

An additional analysis is also carried out to determine Phosphorus, Arsenic, Chlorine and Carbon dioxide whenever required.

8.5   CHNS-O ELEMENTAL ANALYSER

CHNS-O Analyzer is an elemental analyzer dedicated to the simultaneous determination of the amount (%) of Carbon, Hydrogen, Nitrogen, Sulphur and Oxygen contained in coal. Technique used is DYNAMIC FLASH COMBUSTION.

The sample weighed in milligrams housed in a tin capsule is dropped into a quartz tube at 1020°C with constant helium flow (carrier gas). A few seconds before the sample drops into the combustion tube, the stream is enriched with a measured amount of high purity oxygen to achieve a strong oxidizing environment which guarantees almost complete combustion/oxidation even of thermally resistant substances. The combustion gas mixture is driven through an oxidation catalyst (WO_3) zone, then through a subsequent copper zone which reduces nitrogen oxides and sulphuric anhydride (SO_3) eventually formed during combustion on catalyst reduction to elemental nitrogen and sulphurous anhydride (SO_2) and retains the oxygen excess. The resulting four components of the combustion mixture are detected by a Thermal Conductivity detector in the sequence N_2, CO_2, H_2O and SO_2. In case of oxygen which is analyzed separately, the sample undergoes immediate pyrolysis in a Helium stream which ensures quantitative conversion of organic oxygen into carbon monoxide separated on a GC column packed with molecular sieves.

Many companies are manufacturing CHNS-O Elemental Analysers. They are fully automatic instruments for the most exacting determination of CHNS and O.

8.6   USEFULNESS OF PROXIMATE AND ULTIMATE ANALYSES

The proximate analysis involves the use of inexpensive apparatus and can be done accurately with some practice work. It does not require costly equipment and rare skill and so is very popular. The commercial grading of coal, until recently, was based on proximate analysis. Recently the determination of calorific value (in addition to proximate analysis) has become necessary in fixing the grades of non-coking coals, while for trading of coking coals, proximate analysis alone is enough.

The selection of coals for industrial purposes is largely dependent on the results of proximate analysis. It is a cheap and convenient method for assessing some of the industrial properties of coals.

While the proximate analysis offers an easy means of differentiating between different types of coals, knowledge of the elementary constituents is required for differentiating within types. For scientific study and research on coals, ultimate analysis is therefore very important. It is also required for classifying the coals in respect to their carbon and hydrogen contents along with certain properties. However, it involves the use of costly scientific equipment which again require to be handled by very skilled persons. This provides a limitation on the use of ultimate analysis. In accurate scientific work and in research, results have to be interpreted on the basis of ultimate analysis and so it becomes unavoidable.

The ultimate analysis of coal is used for the checking of combustion conditions during boiler trials, to give indications of the nature of products of coal carbonization, and to help in the classification of different kinds of coal. Sulphur is an undesirable constituent of coal, being concerned with corrosion troubles, atmospheric pollution, and the weakening of metals made with high-sulphur cokes. For these reasons, total sulphur determination is nearly always carried out along with proximate analysis on a coal being evaluated for commercial purposes. Hydrogen in coal increases the calorific value of the coal. It is associated with the volatile matter of the coal. Hydrogen content in coal from the peat to the bituminous stage varies between 4.5 to 6.5% and beyond the bituminous stage, the hydrogen content sharply decreases to a value of 1–2% in anthracites. Nitrogen in coal is present up to 2.5% and comes from the proteinous matter present in vegetable matter. Presence of inert nitrogen decreases the calorific value of the coal. Nitrogen in coal is useful in carbonization industries which recover part of it as valuable by-products like ammonia, ammonium sulphate and pyridine bases. The amounts of carbon and oxygen in coal are characteristic of the rank of the coal, ranging from about 90% of carbon and about 3% of oxygen with anthracites, to about 65% of carbon and about 30% of oxygen with brown coals. Oxygen in coal reduces its calorific value. As the oxygen content of the coal increases, its moisture holding capacity increases and the caking power decreases.

8.7 STANDARD METHODS OF ANALYSIS

Extensive and expanding use of coal brought about a need to develop a standard method of coal analysis. International Standards Organization (ISO), National standardization bodies, such as the American Society for Testing Materials (ASTM), State Standards of Russia (GOST), National Standards of Peoples Republic of China, Standard Association of Australia (AS), Bureau of Indian Standard (BIS) have contributed much to the development of reliable standard testing methods.

All major coal producing countries have developed standardization methods and everyone interested in the analysis of coal properties must be familiar with the standardization methods adopted in that country. New standards of procedures are being developed continually for increased accuracy and precision in the results.

The list of International and National Standards used in Coal and Coke Analysis and Evaluation are given in Annexure – II.

Chapter 9

Calorific value of coal

Calorific value of coal is the quantity of heat generated by complete combustion of unit weight of coal.

Units for the calorific value are:

        Calories/gm   (In C.G.S system)
        Kilo Calories/kg   (In M.K.S system)
        Btu/lb   (In F.P.S system)

Calorie is the amount of heat required to raise the temperature of one gram of water by 1°C at the point of its greatest density (4°C). It is, however, often stated more conveniently as the heat required to raise one gram of water from 15°C to 16°C.

British Thermal Unit is the amount of heat required to raise the temperature of one pound of water from 39.1°F to 40.1°F, which corresponds to the point of greatest density of water. In recent years the unit is often described as the heat required to raise one pound of water from 60°F to 61°F., or from 62°F to 63°F.

        Relationship   1 Kcal/kg = 1.8 Btu/lb

Two types of calorific values in use are Gross or Higher calorific value (GCV) and Net or Lower calorific value (NCV). When the calorific value of coal is determined, the hydrogen present in coal is converted into steam. If the products of combustion are condensed to room temperature, the latent heat of condensation of steam also gets included in the measured heat. The calorific value so calculated is known as **gross calorific value**. Thus the gross calorific value can be defined as the total quantity of heat generated by complete combustion of unit weight of coal and the combustion products are cooled to room temperature. In actual practice, the water vapours escape along with hot combustion gases and thus are not condensed. Hence lesser amount of heat is available and this amount of heat is known as **net calorific value**. Thus the net calorific value can be defined as the quantity of heat generated by complete combustion of unit weight of coal and the combustion products are allowed to escape.

Thus,   NCV = GCV – Latent heat of water vapours formed   (9.1)

Now, since 1 part by weight of hydrogen gives 9 parts by weight of water, the equation 9.1 becomes

$$\text{NCV} = \text{GCV} - \text{Weight of Hydrogen} \times 9 \times \text{Latent heat of steam.} \qquad (9.2)$$

As the latent heat of steam is 587 Kcal/kg, equation 9.2 becomes

$$\text{NCV} = \text{GCV} - \% \text{ Hydrogen} \times \frac{9 \times 587}{100}$$
$$\Rightarrow \quad \text{NCV} = \text{GCV} - 52.83 \times \% \text{ Hydrogen} \qquad (9.3)$$

There is only one really satisfactory method for the determination of the calorific value of coal and that is the use of a high pressure oxygen bomb calorimeter.

When the weighed quantity of coal is burnt in the calorimeter, the heat generated is used up in heating the calorimeter and the water in the calorimeter. By equating the heat given out by the coal with heat taken up by the calorimeter and water, the calorific value is determined.

Bomb calorimeter consists of a strong stainless steel vessel, called bomb, capable of withstanding high pressure. The bomb is provided with a lid which can be screwed firmly on bomb. The lid in turn is provided with two electrodes and one oxygen inlet valve. One of the electrodes is provided with a ring to accommodate the silica crucible.

The bomb is placed in a copper calorimeter having a known weight of water. The copper calorimeter, in turn, is surrounded by an air-jacket and water jacket to prevent loss of heat due to radiation. The calorimeter is provided with an electrical stirrer for stirring water and a Beckmann thermometer.

A weighed amount of the coal is placed in the silica crucible. The crucible is supported over the ring. A fine magnesium wire touching the coal sample is stretched across the electrodes. Oxygen supply is forced into the bomb till a pressure of 25–30 atmospheres is reached. Initial temperature of the water in the calorimeter is noted after thorough stirring. The current is switched on and the coal in the crucible burns with the evolution of heat. The heat produced by burning of the coal is transferred to water which is stirred throughout the experiment by the electric stirrer. Maximum temperature shown by thermometer is recorded. The calorific value of the coal can now be calculated as below:

Weight of the coal taken in crucible $= x$ kg
Weight of water in calorimeter $= y$ kg
Water equivalent of the calorimeter, stirrer, thermometer and bomb $= z$ kg
Initial temperature of water in calorimeter $= t_1 {}°\text{C}$
Final temperature of water in calorimeter $= t_2 {}°\text{C}$

Let the gross calorific value of coal be C Kcal/kg

Heat gained by water $= y(t_2 - t_1)$ Kcal
Heat gained by calorimeter $= z(t_2 - t_1)$ Kcal
Total heat gained $= y(t_2 - t_1) + z(t_2 - t_1)$ Kcal
$= (y + z)(t_2 - t_1)$ Kcal
Heat generated by coal $= x$ C Kcal

Now, heat liberated by coal = heat gained by water and calorimeter
$$x\,C = (y + z)\,(t_2 - t_1)$$

∴ Gross calorific value $\dfrac{(y+z)(t_2 - t_1)}{x}$ Kcal/kg   (9.4)

There are many formulae for the calculation of the calorific value of coal without actually determining the same in the laboratory. GOUTAL (1902) [22] suggested the following formula based on proximate analysis:

$$GCV = 82\,F + a\,V \qquad\qquad\qquad (9.5)$$

where
   GCV = Gross calorific value, Kcal/kg
   F = percent fixed carbon
   V = percent volatile matter
   a = constant depending upon the value of volatile matter expressed as percent
       daf (v′) as shown below:

v′	5	10	15	20	25	30	35	38	40
a	145	130	117	109	103	98	94	85	80

This formula looks upon coal consisting of volatile matter and fixed carbon, each contributing to the calorific value of the coal. The fixed carbon of different coals is assumed of a fixed composition and hence of fixed calorific value. The composition and calorific value of the volatile matter differ from coal to coal and are assumed to depend upon the nature of coal as indicated by the volatile matter on daf basis. These assumptions limit the utility of the GOUTAL formula.

The following formulae have been developed by the **Central Institute of Mining and Fuel Research (CIMFR)**, formerly CFRI, Dhanbad, for the calculation of calorific value of Indian coals from their proximate analysis:
   For low moisture coals (M ≤ 2%)

$$GCV = 91.7\,F + 75.6\,(V - 0.1\,A) - 60\,M \text{ Kcal/kg} \qquad (9.6)$$

   For high moisture coals (M > 2%)

$$GCV = 85.6\,[100 - (1.1\,A + M)] - 60\,M \text{ Kcal/kg} \qquad (9.7)$$

where M, A, V and F are moisture, ash, volatile matter and fixed carbon (all in percent air dried), respectively.

There are also several formulae based on Ultimate analysis of coal. The original DULONG [23] formula is

$$GCV = 80.8\,C + 344\left(H - \frac{O}{8}\right) \text{Kcal/kg} \qquad (9.8)$$

where C, H and O are percent carbon, hydrogen and oxygen respectively.

This formula assumes that heat of formation of coal is zero and the only heat giving elements are carbon and surplus hydrogen. (Surplus hydrogen is the hydrogen in excess of that required to combine with the oxygen of coal to form water). On including the sulphur as a heat giving element the DULONG formula is amended as

$$GCV = 80.8\ C + 344 \left(H - \frac{O}{8} \right) + 22.2\ S\ Kcal/kg \qquad (9.9)$$

where S is percent sulphur.

All these formulae are of limited use because the heat of formation of coal is neither zero nor constant. The modified DULONG formula is, however, fairly useful for all practical purposes.

The calorific value of coal bears a good relationship with the rank. The higher the calorific value the higher is the rank. However, anthracites form an exception to this regularity and have lower calorific values than many bituminous coals. This is due to the sharp fall of hydrogen content in anthracites, the hydrogen having more than four times the calorific value of carbon. The hydrogen content is also responsible for relatively high calorific values of cannel coal, boghead coal and exinites of humic coals.

Useful Heat Value (UHV) means the heat value determined on Equilibrated Basis by the following formula.

$$UHV\ (Kcal/kg) = 8900 - 138(A+M) \qquad (9.10)$$

where A & M represent the equilibrated ash and moisture % of coal.

This formula (9.10) was applicable to high moisture coal only. However a modified formula (9.11) was given by CIMFR for low moisture and low volatile coal

$$UHV\ (Kcal/Kg) = 8900 - 138(A+M) - 150(19 - VM) \qquad (9.11)$$

where A, M, VM are % of ash, moisture and volatile matter respectively.

Net calorific value is more realistic figure as Useful Heat Value. GCV is determined in the laboratory from the heat released by the combustibles in coal whereas UHV is computed by applying ash penalty on the heat value of the combustible matter by applying an empirical formula 9.10. The concept of Useful Heat Value is unique in India and was accordingly conceived by CIMFR. On the basis of various UHV ranges, non-coking coal was graded. As regards coal pricing, the coal companies have switched over from Useful Heat Value (UHV) to Gross Calorific Value (GCV) with effect from 01.01.2012. Now the grading of non-coking coal is being done on the basis of GCV. All the power houses today are analysing the GCV to calculate their thermal efficiency.

9.1   ILLUSTRATIVE EXAMPLES

Illustrative example 9.1: *The proximate analysis (% air dried basis), the ultimate analysis (% dmmf basis) and experimental gross calorific value (Kcal/kg on air dried basis) is shown in Table 9.1.*

Table 9.1 Analysis of coal for illustrative example 9.1.

Proximate Analysis %				Ultimate Analysis %					C.V Kcal/kg
Moisture	Volatile matter	Ash	Fixed carbon	C	H	O	N	S	Experimental value
2	30	16	52	86	6	5	2	1	6900

Calculate its gross calorific value using (a) Modified Dulong formula (b) Goutal formula (c) CFRI formula (d) Difference of gross and net calorific value of coal on (i) air dried basis (ii) complete dry basis.

Solution:

a   GCV by modified Dulong formula

$$GCV = 80.8\,C + 344\left(H - \frac{O}{8}\right) + 22.2\,S$$
$$= 80.8 \times 86 + 344\left[6 - \frac{5}{8}\right] + 22.2 \times 1$$
$$= 8820\ \text{Kcal/kg}$$

This GCV is on dmmf basis

$$GCV \text{ on air dried basis is} = 8820\,(100 - M - 1.1\,A) \times \frac{1}{100}$$
$$= 8820\,(100 - 2 - 1.1 \times 16 \times \frac{1}{100}$$
$$= 7091.3\ \text{Kcal/kg}$$

This GCV is higher than the experimental value by

7091.3 – 6900 = 191.3 Kcal/kg

b   GCV by Goutal formula GCV = 82 F + a V

$$V' = \text{Volatile matter on daf basis} = \frac{30}{100 - 2 - 16} \times 100 = 36.6\%$$

The value of *a* from the table

V'	a
35	94
38	85

$$a = 94 - \frac{94 - 85}{38 - 35} \times (36.6 - 35) = 89.2$$

GCV on air dried basis is GCV = 82 × 52 + 89.2 × 30 = 6940 Kcal/kg
This GCV is higher than experimental value by 6940 – 6900 = 40 Kcal/kg

c   GCV by CFRI formula (for moisture ≤2%) on air dried basis is

$$GCV = 91.7\ F + 75.6\ (V - 0.1\ A) - 60\ M$$
$$= 91.7 \times 52 + 75.6\ (30 - 0.1 \times 16) - 60 \times 2$$
$$= 6795\ Kcal/kg$$

This GCV is higher than experimental value by 6900–6795 = 105 Kcal/kg

d   Difference of gross and net calorific value of coal

$$GCV - NCV = 52.83 \times \%Hydrogen$$

i   on air dried basis

Moisture in coal = 2%
Ash in coal = 16%
Hydrogen in coal = 6% from ultimate analysis

$$\% \text{ hydrogen in coal in organic form on air dried basis} = \frac{6(100 - 2 - 1.1 \times 16)}{100}$$
$$= 4.82\%$$

$$\% \text{ hydrogen in moisture} = \frac{2}{9}\%$$

$$\% \text{ hydrogen in mineral matter} = \frac{0.1 Ash}{9} = \frac{0.1 \times 16}{9} = \frac{1.6}{9}\%$$

$$\% \text{ total hydrogen in coal on air dried basis} = 4.82 + \frac{2}{9} + \frac{1.6}{9} = 5.22\%$$

$$GCV - NCV = 52.83 \times \%Hydrogen = 52.83 \times 5.22 = 275.8\ Kcal/kg$$

ii   on dry basis

$$\% \text{ ash on dry basis} = 16 \times \frac{100}{100 - 2} = 16.3\%$$

$$\% \text{ hydrogen in coal in organic form on dry basis} = \frac{6(100 - 2 - 1.1 \times 16)}{100 - 2} = 4.92\%$$

$$\% \text{ total hydrogen in coal on dry basis} = 4.92 + \frac{0.1 \times 16.3}{9} = 5.1\%$$

$$GCV - NCV = 52.83 \times \%Hydrogen = 52.83 \times 5.1 = 269.4\ Kcal/kg$$

9.2 PROBLEMS FOR PRACTICE

9.2.1: *Calculate the gross and net calorific value of a coal which analyses: C 74%, H 6%, N 1%, O 9%, S 0.8%, moisture 2.2% and ash 8%.*   [7674, 7357 Kcal/kg]

9.2.2: *The proximate analysis of coal is: Moisture 2.4%, Volatile Matter 29.4%, Fixed Carbon 58%, Ash 9.7% and Sulphur 0.5%. Its gross calorific value is 7650 Kcal/Kg. Calculate proximate analysis and calorific value on (a) Moisture free basis (b) Dry ash free basis*
[30.1%, 59.4%, 9.9%, 0.51%, 7838 Kcal/kg; 33.5%, 66%, 0.57%, 8703 Kcal/kg]

9.2.3: *The ultimate analysis of bituminous coal (dry basis%) is: C 77, H 5.8, N 1.7, O 4.8, S 2.5 and ash 9. The moisture content is 5%. The gross calorific power is 7650 Kcal/Kg on dry basis. Calculate*

    a   *Gross calorific value, moist basis*
    b   *Net calorific value, moist basis*
    c   *Net calorific value, dry basis*
    d   *Gross calorific value, dry basis*

[7658.7, 7367.6, 7755.4, 8061.8 Kcal/kg]

Chapter 10

Rank of a coal

The maturity or stage of coalification reached by a coal is referred to as its rank. Rank is not measured in percentages or other units, though it is judged by composition particularly the carbon or the oxygen content of the coal. The term is used only in a comparative sense, in such expressions as high rank, medium rank and low rank. It does not imply any superiority or inferiority of quality; low rank, for example, does not mean poor quality.

As a result of the changes in the relative proportions of Carbon, Hydrogen and Oxygen, other characteristics also change. With increasing coalification i.e., increase of rank, the volatile content of the coal decreases mainly because of decrease in the proportion as the oxygen falls, though in the highest rank coals it becomes slightly lower owing to the sharper decline in Hydrogen. The caking properties, which confer on a coal, the ability to yield coke on carbonization are nil in the lowest rank coals, rise to maximum in the medium rank coals, and fall to nil again in the high rank coals. Two elements nitrogen and sulphur amount to about 1 or 1.5% and show no marked variation with changes in rank.

In Petrography, the rank of coal is measured by the reflectance of vitrinite since vitrinite is the most abundant maceral group. The rank of coal increases as the reflectance of vitrinite increases. The mean reflectance of vitrinite increases from 0.26% to 6.09%.

Rank of a coal is also indicated by the FUEL RATIO.

$$\text{Fuel ratio} = \frac{\text{Fixed Carbon}}{\text{Volatile matter}} \qquad (10.1)$$

The fuel ratio increases from low rank to high rank coals.

Coal is classified by its rank as Peat, Lignite or Brown coal, Sub-bituminous coal or Black lignite, Bituminous coal, Semi-anthracite and Anthracite.

In these varieties of coal, the rank is increased from peat to anthracite. This increase in rank is accompanied by the following factors:

1 Increase in carbon percentage
2 Decrease in hydrogen content, particularly at the high rank end of the series
3 Decrease in oxygen content

4   Decrease in volatile matter
5   Decrease in inherent moisture content
6   Increase in caking power from nil to a maximum in the middle of the range and
    a decrease with further increase in rank
7   Increase in calorific value to a maximum about the middle of the range, and then
    a slight decrease with further increase in rank

Chapter 11

Important properties of coal

11.1   DENSITY

Density of the particle is defined as the mass of the particle per unit volume. The ratio of the density of the particle to the density of water is defined as specific gravity. A bulk solid (bulk material) is combination of particles and space. For a bulk material, the average particle density can be determined by dividing the mass of the material (solids) by the true volume occupied by the particles (not including the voids). The density of the coal can be determined by using density bottle.

The stepwise procedure is:

1   Wash, dry and weigh the density bottle with stopper. Let this weight be w_1.
2   Thoroughly dry the coal sample.
3   Add 5–10 grams of coal sample to the bottle and reweigh. Let this weight be w_2.
4   Now fill the bottle with a liquid of known density. The liquid used should not react with the coal.
5   Insert the stopper, allow the liquid to fall out of the bottle, wipe of excess liquid and weigh the bottle. Let this weight be w_3.
6   Remove the coal and liquid from the bottle and fill the bottle with liquid alone and repeat step. 5. Let this weight be w_4.

$w_2 - w_1$	is the weight of the coal sample
$w_4 - w_1$	is the weight of the liquid occupying whole volume of the bottle
$w_3 - w_2$	is the weight of the liquid having the volume equal to the volume of density bottle less volume of coal sample taken
$(w_4 - w_1) - (w_3 - w_2)$	is the weight of the liquid of volume equal to that of the coal sample

If ρ_l is the density of the liquid

$$\text{Density of the coal sample} = \frac{w_2 - w_1}{(w_4 - w_1) - (w_3 - w_2)} \times \rho_l \qquad (11.1)$$

11.2 SPECIFIC GRAVITY

Specific gravity is the ratio of the density of a material to that of water at a specified temperature, usually 4°C. Apparent specific gravity is the specific gravity of a lump of coal including its inherent moisture, mineral matter and the air in the pore spaces, but not the surface moisture. True specific gravity is the specific gravity of the coal free of air and uncombined water, but including mineral matter. The true specific gravity is most commonly used.

Of the various petrographic constituents, exinite is the lightest maceral group, while fusinite is the most dense group with vitrinite and micrinite intermideate. The specific gravities of exinite and micrinite in coals of sub-bituminous and bituminous ranks range from 1.0 to 1.28 and 1.35 to 1.45, respectively, while that of fusinite exceeds 1.5. The specific gravity of vitrinite first decreases from 1.43 to 1.27 and then increases to 1.35 as moisture-ash-free carbon content increases from 70% to 87% and then to 91%.

The proportion and nature of both the organic mass and mineral matter influence the specific gravity of coal. Coals which contain more ash-bearing minerals have higher specific gravities because the average specific gravities of the minerals are greater than that of the coal substance. For the same type of coal, the higher ash coals have higher specific gravity. The true specific gravity of bituminous coals varies between 1.27 and 1.45.

Among the coals of different types, the specific gravity increases with maturity e.g., peat 1.15 to 1.25, lignite 1.25 to 1.3, bituminous coal 1.27 to 1.45 and anthracite 1.4 to 1.7. Coal of a given rank has a higher apparent specific gravity when wet than when dry. The apparent specific gravity of air-dried coal is lower than that of the same coal fresh or saturated with moisture, but air-dried coal usually regains its original apparent specific gravity if immersed in water at room temperature for 24 hours.

11.3 BULK DENSITY

The bulk material is really a combination of particles and space, the percentage of the total volume not occupied by the particles is referred as the 'voidage' or 'void fraction'. Sometimes the term 'porosity' is applied to bulk material to mean the same as 'voidage'. Thus we can define the particle porosity as the ratio of the volume of pores within a particle to the volume of the particle (inclusive of pores).

The **bulk density** is the overall density of a material kept in large quantities, which can be defined as the mass of the material divided by its total volume (particles and voids) and depends upon the true density of the material and the pore space between the particles. It is a measure of the storage capacity. Three kinds of bulk density that apply to materials handling calculations are (1) Aerated density (2) Packed density (3) Dynamic or Working density.

When the sample of the bulk material is carefully poured into a measuring cylinder to measure its volume, then the computed density is called as 'Aerated', 'loose', or 'poured' bulk density (ρ_a). If the sample is packed by dropping the cylinder vertically a number of times from a height of one or two centimeters on to a table, then the computed density is called 'packed' or 'tapped' bulk density (ρ_c). The dynamic or working density (ρ_w) is a function of Aerated and Packed densities.

The bulk density of packed coal depends on the size analysis of the coal, shape of particles, method of packing and moisture content of the coal. For example, the bulk densities of loosely packed dry coal for a true density of 1300 kg/m³ is as follows:

Lumpy coal (sized or free from fines) = 600–670 kg/m³
Lumpy coal (with fines)   = 690–830 kg/m³
Coal dust   = 480–580 kg/m³
Pulverized coal   = 400–500 kg/m³

The variation of bulk density with free moisture content is very important when coal is charged into coke ovens.

11.4 POROSITY

Coal is porous substance and when brought in contact with an organic liquid (e.g., methanol), it enters the very fine pores and the surface of coal is wetted. The diameters of the smallest pores in coal are about 0.5–1 nm. The true density of coal refers the coal mass per unit volume excluding pores in the coal. The apparent density of coal refers the coal mass per unit volume including pores in the coal. The coal porosity can be calculated as

$$\text{Porosity} = \frac{\text{True density of coal} - \text{Apparent density of coal}}{\text{True density of coal}} \times 100\%$$

The true density of coal can be determined by an ordinary density bottle as described in article 11.1. For determination of Apparent density, about 5 lb sample of coal is dried to constant weight on an electric hot plate and weighed. Later it is kept immersed in boiling water for about half an hour in order to saturate the pores with water. It is taken out and adhering water wiped off and the volume of the coal is measured by displacement of water in a special trough made for the purpose. The apparent density is calculated by dividing the initial weight of the coal by the volume of the coal as determined.

For the same coal sample, the value of the true density of the coal is highest, followed by that of the apparent density, and the value of bulk density is lowest. The densities of minerals are significantly higher than that of organic matter, so the content and composition of the minerals in coal has a significant influence on the coal density. In the study of coal structure, it is usually necessary to eliminate the impact of minerals. The density must be corrected roughly as follows: for every 1% increase in coal ash, the coal density will increase by 0.01%.

The general relationship between the density and the degree of coalification for various macerals is as follows: the true density of inertinite is the highest, followed by those of vitrinite and exinite; when the carbon content on a dry ash-free basis is greater than 90%, the three become similar and increase sharply, indicating that their structures have undergone profound changes. The general relationship between vitrinite density and the degree of coalification is as follows: the vitrinite density begins to decrease slowly with increasing coalification, mainly because the reduction in the oxygen content is greater than the increase in the carbon content, and the atomic weight of oxygen is greater than that of carbon. The density of coal containing 85–87% carbon is at least 1.3 gm/cm³. For coal with a carbon content greater than 90%, the density increases sharply with increasing coalification, mainly because of the increasing amount of more compact aromatic structures.

Porosity decreases with the rank to minimum, at about 89%–90% carbon and then rises in anthracitic region. The following are some values:

Carbon % d.m.m.f	80	89	93
Porosity % d.m.m.f	18–20	2–3	6–8

11.5 REFLECTANCE

The capacity of a polished coal surface to reflect vertically incident light is referred to as the reflective capacity of the coal. The visual performance under a microscope is the brightness of the polished surface. The reflective capacities of different coal types are different. The reflectivity or reflectance, R, of coal is defined as:

$$R_0 = \frac{I_r}{I_i} \times 100\%$$
(11.5.1)

where
  I_r is intensity of the reflected light
  I_i is the intensity of the incident light

Reflectance is an important property of opaque minerals, and is also an important indicator of the degree of coalification. The reflectance is usually determined using a relative method: the reflected light intensity of a standard sheet with a known reflectance is measured under a certain intensity of incident light (typically monochromatic polarized light) and compared with the intensity of reflected light of the material under investigation. Materials such as optical glasses, quartz, and diamond are commonly used as standards. The equation for calculating the reflectance is

$$R = \frac{I}{I_0} R_0 \times 100\%$$
(11.5.2)

where I is the intensity of the reflected light from the material being examined, I_0 is the intensity of reflected light of the standard material, and R_0 is the reflectance of the standard material.

As the resolution of coal in an oil medium is far better than that in air, the reflectance is generally measured under an oil-immersion objective (R_0). At least 20 points for each optical coal sample are used to measure the maximum reflectance. Usually, the average value of the maximum reflectance measured under an oil-immersion objective is used as the analytical indicator.

Reflectance is measured by microscopic examination using a special reflectance microscope. For this purpose, fine coal is made into a small sample using an adhesive, and the top face of sample is polished before it is placed under the reflectance microscope. Oil having a refractive index of 1.585 is spread on the polished surface, and then the objective of the microscope is allowed to come in contact with the oil layer. When light impinges on the polished surface, the extent by which the incident light gets reflected from the surface of the coal sample is a measure of the rank of the coal. An average of 100 such reflectance readings is usually reported as the average reflectance of coal in oil − R_0 (average) (the subscript 0 denotes oil). For a bireflective material, the reflectance varies as the microscope stage is rotated. Following complete rotation of 360°, the two maximas of reflectance that are observed give the maximum reflectance of that particular coal particle. This procedure is repeated for 100 particles (to yield 200 maximas) and the mean of all these measurements of reflectance of separate particles gives the mean maximum reflectance.

For most purposes it is the reflectance of the vitrinite component that is determined for the following reasons:

1   Vitrinite is the preponderant maceral in most coals
2   Vitrinite often appears homogeneous under the microscope
3   Particles of vitrinite are usually large enough to permit measurements to be made easily.
4   In the application of petrographic techniques to the industrial uses of coal, particularly in carbonization, interest is focused on the behavior of virinite which is the maceral principally responsible for the plastic and agglutinating properties of coal.

Vitrinite reflectance increases with the rank of the coal and is perhaps the most significant parameter influencing the coke making potential of any coking coal. Among the micro-components of the same coal, fusinite and micrinite have very high reflectance and exinite has very low reflectance, the vitrinite having intermediate values. Reflectance is a good parameter for the determination of coal rank. Generally the coking property develops in coal if its reflectance is between 0.9–1.3. The ideal value of reflectance will be within 1.3–1.5.

11.6   REFRACTIVE INDEX

The definition of the refractive index is the ratio of the sine of the incident angle to that of the refraction angle when light passes through a material interface, is refracted at the interface, and enters the interior of the substance. The molecular refraction can be obtained from the additive refractive index, an important property in analytical studies of coal structure. The refractive index of coal cannot be directly measured, but the reflectance and the refractive index of vertical incident light are related as follows:

$$R_0 = \frac{(n-n_0)^2 + n^2 K^2}{(n+n_0)^2 + n^2 K^2}$$

(11.6)

where

R_0 is the reflectance of coal (%)
n_0 is the standard medium refractive index, $n_0 = 1.514$ for cedar oil
n is the refractive index of the coal
K is the absorption index of the coal

Based on the reflectance of incident light measured in air and cedar oil, two equations can be obtained using the equation 11.6. On solving the two equations, n and K values are obtained. The refractive index increases with increasing coalification. When the carbon content is higher than 85%, the increase is large.

Refractive Index and Reflectance increases with increase in rank of coal. Following are certain values for vitrain-rich samples:

Carbon % d.m.m.f	75	80	84	91	95
Refractive Index	–	1.6	–	1.9	–
Reflectance % Incident Light	0.51	0.67	0.92	2.23	4.17

11.7 HARDNESS

Coal hardness reflects the coal's ability to withstand external mechanical actions. Hardness increases with the rank, reaches a maximum at 84% carbon and decreases to a minimum at 90% carbon, then increases again. Hardness rapidly decreases from 5% volatile matter to a minimum at about 15% and, thereafter, steadily increases to 40% volatile matter.

The representation and determination of coal hardness differ depending on the applied mechanical force. The scratch hardness (Mohs hardness) is the relative hardness determined by scratching the coal surface with 10 types of standard mineral. The scratch hardness of coal is usually between 1 and 4. Coal hardness is related to coalification. Lignite, which has a low degree of coalification, and coking coal, with medium coalification, have the lowest scratch hardnesses of 2–2.5, whereas anthracite has the highest scratch hardness that is close to 4.

The micro Vickers hardness is referred to as the microhardness. It is determined by pressing a diamond indenter with a static load into the maceral under a microscope. The greater the indentation is, the lower the microhardness of the coal. The value of the microhardness is expressed by the load capacity per contact area between the indenter and the coal (in kilograms per square millimeter). The microhardness determined by the indentation method is widely used in the study of coal chemistry.

11.8 ABRASIVENESS

The abrasiveness of coal is a factor of considerable economic importance in mining, preparation, and utilization. Coal is an extremely abrasive material. Some coals are much more abrasive than others. Abrasiveness of coal may be associated more with the character of the impurities it contains than with the nature of the coal substance itself. The wear on grinding elements due to the abrasive action of coal results in maintenance charges that constitute a major item in the cost of grinding coal for use as pulverized fuel. Under high contact pressures developed between coal and metal in pulverizers, abrasive wear increases many times.

Coarse particles of hard mineral matter, such as quartz, can cause significant abrasion of grinding surfaces in the pulverizing equipment associated with many coal-burning furnaces. The likely extent of the abrasion can be tested by allowing a sample of coal, with a specified size distribution, to be agitated for 12,000 revolutions at 1,500 rev/min. in a special mill equipped with four metal blades. The **Abrasion Index** is determined from the loss in mass of these blades, and is expressed in milligrams of metal per kilogram of coal involved.

11.9 GRINDABILITY

Grindability of a coal is a measure of the ease with which it may be ground to fine size. The grindability of coal is a composite property embracing other specific properties, such as hardness, strength, tenacity and fracture.

There are two methods of determining the ease of grinding coal to fine sizes, viz., Hardgove method and Ball mill method. The former measures the increase of surface produced by the application of a standard amount of work and later method measures the amount of work done in grinding a pre-sized material to a given fineness.

A standard test called **Hardgrove** method is employed to determine the **Hardgrove Grindability Index**. The Hardgrove apparatus has eight 1-inch balls that roll on a stationary ring and are driven by an upper grinding ring which is rotated at 20 ± 1 rpm. 50 gm of air dried coal of size −16 + 30 mesh is subjected to 60 revolutions in Hardgrove apparatus. After grinding, the coal is screened through a 200 mesh sieve. Hardgrove Grindability Index is then calculated as

$$G = \textit{Hardgrove Grindability Index} = 6.93 \, W + 13 \qquad (11.9)$$

where W = weight of sample passing through 200 mesh sieve, gm

Coals which are easy to grind have Grindability Index near to 100.

A high value of Hardgrove Grindability Index indicates a soft and easily grindable coal. Hardgrove Grindability Index of coal initially increases with the rank, reaches a maximum of about 105 for bright coals of 89–90% carbon, and then falls to about 35 for anthracites. Coals that are easiest to grind are found in the medium and low volatile groups. They are easier to grind than coal of the high volatile bituminous, sub-bituminous, and anthracite ranks.

In Ball mill method, 700 ml of −6 mesh coal is grounded in a 12″ × 12″ steel ball mill with 285 balls of specified sizes rotated at 70 rpm. The grindability is the ratio of the net weight of −200 mesh coal formed to the number of revolutions.

The principal advantage of Hardgrove method is its rapidity of the tests; the disadvantage is that it requires an expensive grinding machine. Only softer components of the coal are crushed leaving harder particles unground. The Ball mill method eliminates this error by grinding the entire coal to finished size. The Ball mill method is still used by mill manufacturers when mixtures of coal of varying grindability values are being fired, for high ash content coals, or for coals with large quantities of hard impurities.

11.10　FRIABILITY

Friability of coal is a measure of its ability to resist degradation in size during handling. Friability depends to some extent on toughness, elasticity, fracture characteristics and strength. An important aspect of friability is the increased amount of surface produced incident to the handling of friable coals. This surface allows more rapid oxidation and hence makes conditions more favouable for spontaneous ignition, loss in coking quality in coking coals, and other changes that accompany oxidation.

In general, coals of same rank vary widely in friability. Friability increases with rank through bituminous coals to a maximum of nearly 75% fixed carbon and then decreases for anthracites. Lignites are found to be the least friable of all coals. Anthracites are comparable in friability to sub-bituminous coals; both are stronger than bituminous coals and more resistant to breakage than the very friable low volatile coals. Friability decreases sharply as the inherent moisture increases to about 5% and thereafter decreases steadily but more slowly.

The two widely used methods for measuring friability are the **Tumbler test** and **Shatter test**. In tumbler test, a 1000 gm sample of coal sized between 1.5 and 1.05 inch square-hole screens is tumbled at 40 rpm in the mill without a grinding medium for one hour. The coal is then removed, screened on square-hole sieves of 1.05, 0.74, 0.53, 0.37, 0.047, 0.0117 inch and weighted average particle size is calculated. The friability is reported as the percentage reduction in weighted average particle size (1-P/F)% where P and F are the weighted average particle size of product and feed coal.

In shatter test, a 50 lb sample of coal sized between 3- and 2-inch round-hole screens is dropped twice from a drop-bottom box onto a steel plate 6 feet below the box. The material shattered by the two drops is then screened over round-hole screens of 3, 2, 1.5, 1.0, 0.75, 0.50 inch and weighted average particle size is calculated. The friability is reported as reported in tumbler test.

A comparison of tumbler and shatter methods for measuring friability of coal showed that a coal susceptible to degradation in size by shattering on impact is not necessarily equally susceptible to breakage by abrasion or attrition. A coal may have these two properties in different degrees. The shatter test appears best suited for measuring the breakage that occurs in handling the larger sizes of coal in thin layers, but does not measure as well the breakage that occurs when coal is handled in mass.

The tumbler test utilizes both shatter and attrition forces and therefore is probably better suited to ordinary use. The tumbler test was considered more suitable for estimating the behavior of coals under severe conditions of handling and the shatter test for estimating how coals will withstand gentler treatment.

The relative friability of different coals is of great importance in preparation because the greater the proportion of finer sizes in the feed to the washing plant, the greater the total preparation cost as preparation cost per ton of feed is a function of the number of particles per ton of feed.

11.11 WEATHERING

During storage, coal undergoes a series of changes by exposure to the atmosphere. This is known as the weathering of coal. Weathering is the tendency of coals to break apart when they dry out. Weathering is more pronounced with lower rank coals and greater exposure to air. Weathering reduces the coal size and increases its friability.

Low rank coals show a pronounced tendency to disintegrate or slack on exposure to the weather, particularly when alternately wetted and dried or subjected to hot sunshine. Lignite slacks very readily, sub-bituminous coals slack to some extent but less readily than lignite, and bituminous coals are affected only slightly by weathering.

Coals that slack readily contain relatively large amounts of moisture. When exposed to the weather, such coals lose moisture rapidly. As the coal loses moisture at the surface, the moisture from the interior of the piece gradually drifts outward to the surface. If the loss of moisture at the surface proceeds at a faster rate than that at which it is replaced by moisture from the interior of the piece, undoubtedly the shrinkage of the coal at the surface is greater than that in the interior; consequently, stresses are generated in the surface coal. These stresses cause the coal to crack and disintegrate. Likewise, when the air-dried coal is wetted by rain water, the surface exposed gains moisture more rapidly than the interior, causing greater expansion in the surface coal leading to further breakage.

Slacking, like the handling of a friable coal, causes the formation of an excessive amount of fine material at the expense of the coarser sizes, thus decreasing the value of the coal for most uses. Moreover, storage of coals that slack readily is unsatisfactory, not only because of the loss of the more valuable coarse sizes, but also because slacking increases the tendency of coal to ignite spontaneously because of the increased surface area exposed to oxidation. These coals can be stored with comparatively little trouble from slacking only when the loss of moisture is retarded. For example, in the region of high relative humidity in the winter, the sub-bituminous coals of that region can be stored reasonably well.

The **weathering** or **slacking index** of a coal is an indication of its size stability when stored and exposed to the weather. It denotes the tendency of coal to break on exposure to weather or alternate wet and dry periods.

To determine this property, a known quantity of coal lump (1–1.5 inches size) is air dried and then immersed in water for one hour. Water is then drained and coal lump is air dried for 24 hours. Then the coal lump is screened with 0.263 inch sieve. The weathering index is the percentage passing through the sieve. Weathering indices of 5% or less characterize bituminous coals, whereas values for lignite approach 100%.

11.12 OXIDATION OF COAL

Organic mass of coal is quite susceptible to oxidation. Even atmospheric oxygen brings about oxidation of coal with evolution of heat. The rate of oxidation varies inversely with the rank and it increases with increase in surface area (or decrease in particle size).

If the temperature rise due to oxidation exceeds the critical value (varying from about 50°C for lignite to about 80°C for bituminous coals), spontaneous combustion takes place and the coal is destroyed by fire. Spontaneous combustion is due to heat produced by a slow oxidation process. At the initial stages of oxidation, the coal acts as insulator and prevents the dissipation of heat generated. The temperature, therefore, rises, and the rate of oxidation is accelerated till to a point where combustion or firing occurs. Hence provisions are to be made for dissipation of the heat generated while coal is stored to prevent spontaneous combustion.

For a given weight of coal, the more the surface exposed, the greater the rate of oxidation. For this reason, spontaneous combustion is more likely to occur in coal piles with an excessive amount of fines.

Spontaneous combustion usually occurs within 4 to 5 weeks of mining but may occur up to about 4 months. Coals already stored for more than 6 months are not usually liable to spontaneous combustion. High moisture coal in slack size is especially susceptible to spontaneous combustion.

If the temperature rise due to oxidation does not exceed critical value, combustion does not take place but the quality of coal is effected depending on the degree of oxidation. Low temperature oxidation of coal causes:

- decrease in its caking power and calorific value
- decrease in carbon and hydrogen content
- increase in its oxygen content
- decrease in gas and tar yields on its carbonization
- disintegration of coal

Chapter 12

Classification of coal

The various classifications of coal have been given by different geologists. Most classifications are based upon some property of coal which varies with increasing maturity or rank of coal. The systems of classification fall into two categories:

Scientific
Commercial

For scientific classification, the property used is the ultimate analysis which gives the elementary composition of coal in terms of percentages by weight of the elements present, viz., carbon, hydrogen, oxygen, nitrogen and sulphur. **Regnault** was the first to give a satisfactory classification in 1837. Later, **Gruner** in 1874, **Gruner-Bousquet** [24] in 1911, **Grout** [25] in 1907 and **Ralston** [26] in 1915 have modified the classifications. In 1900, **C.A.Seyler** [27] proposed another classification.

For the classification to be used and developed for commercial purposes, the property used is the proximate analysis which gives percentages of moisture content, volatile matter, ash, fixed carbon and sulphur in coal plus calorific value in cal/gm. There are three major classifications, viz., the **American Standards for Testing and Materials (ASTM)** classification developed in USA, the **National Coal Board (NCB)** classification developed in England and **International classification** or ECE classification developed by the **Economic Commission of Europe**. NCB and ECE classifications also include the coking properties of coal.

Various classifications proposed as above are less familiar. Certain varieties are recognized almost universally in science and commerce. These varieties are classified by ranks i.e., according to the degree of metamorphism in the series from lignite to anthracite. These varieties are not sharply separated and they grade into one another, so that in describing them the proportions of their constituents must be stated as varying within wide limits. Two coals with a certain percentage of fixed carbon may have very different calorific properties owing to the fact that the moisture or the ash may vary considerably and consequently if one constituent is chosen as a standard the others do not necessarily agree.

Since it is so generally admitted that all coals have been derived from peat in some form and that it has arrived at its present state as the result of various geological processes, peat is briefly described with the varieties of coal. It is not regarded as a type of coal, but rather as an incipient stage in the formation of that substance.

The varieties of coal are **Peat, Lignite** or **Brown coal, Sub-bituminous coal** or **Black lignite, Bituminous coal, Semi-anthracite** and **Anthracite**.

12.1 PEAT

Peat is a naturally occurring solid fuel consisting of partly decomposed plant material that has accumulated in-situ under temperate marshy conditions. Peat bogs grow at measurable rates. In general, peat accumulates in an active swamp at the rate of about 3 metres in 2,500 years. It is associated with large content of water. In fact the amount of solid matter in peat bogs is 10% or less. Near the surface of the deposit, peat is light brown in colour and highly fibrous in nature. With the increase in depth, the colour becomes darker and finally black, when vegetable structure is not so obvious. A part of the water content of freshly won peat can be drained off while a much larger part is removed by drying in air. Air drying operation may require 40–50 days.

Peat is not regarded as coal, but it represents the first stage in the conversion of vegetable matter into coal. Most of the world's peatland is in North America and the northern parts of Asia with large areas in northern and central Europe and in Southeast Asia, whilst some are in tropical Africa, Latin America and the Caribbean. 85% of the global peatland area is in only four countries, Russia, Canada, USA and Indonesia.

The composition and properties of peat vary widely from place to place, depending on the nature of the original plant material and the agencies and extent of decay. Raw peat consists of decayed plant material and peat humus. The average properties of peat are as follows:

Proximate analysis % air dried basis		Ultimate analysis (% dmmf)	
Moisture	15–25	C	55–60
Volatile matter	50–55	H_2	6–6.5
Ash	3–10	O_2	30–35
Fixed carbon	25–30	N_2	1.5–2.0
Calorific value (dmmf) = 4,500–5,000 Kcal/kg		S	0.6–1.0

The lower layers of peat have usually higher ash than the upper layers.

Uses: Peat is an important fuel in those countries having large deposits of peat. Its main use is as domestic fuel. It is easy to ignite and burns freely to give a long pleasant flame. Peat is also largely used in steam boilers, power stations and gas producers. The low temperature carbonization of peat is also practiced for getting peat coke and by-products. Peat coke is valuable fuel for some metallurgical processes. Peat is also used as a fertilizer or for making fertilizer. However about 75% of the world production of peat is used in heat generation.

12.2 LIGNITE (OR) BROWN COAL

Lignite occurs in a number of forms distinguished by their physical characteristics

1   woody or fibrous brown coal with the clear structure of plant tissues
2   earthy brown lignite, compact but friable
3   brown coal showing cleavage and slight woody structure

A distinction is sometimes made in the terms lignites and brown coals on the basis of the woody structure which is predominant in the former and not obvious in the latter. Lignite is characterized by high moisture content viz., 30–50%. On exposure to the atmosphere, the brown colour darkens and the moisture content reduces to an equilibrium value of 12–20%. On drying, lignite shrinks and breaks up readily in an irregular manner. Hence it cannot be moved far from the mine. It is also likely to ignite spontaneously as it adsorb oxygen readily and must therefore not be stored in the open without care.

Europe has the largest lignite reserves in the world. Of the global lignite reserves of 283 Gt in 2012, 90.7 Gt (including sub-bituminous) are found in Russia (32% global share), followed by Australia (15.6%), Germany (14.3%), the USA (10.8%), and China (3.9%). Germany is the largest producer of lignite followed by China and Russia.

As in the case of peat, the composition and properties of lignite also vary widely. The immature varieties of woody brown coals cannot be easily distinguished from the mature peat. Likewise, the more mature brown coals are similar to sub-bituminous coal. The following is the typical analysis of lignite:

Proximate analysis % air dried basis		Ultimate analysis (% dmmf)	
Moisture	10–30	C	70–73
Volatile matter	40–45	H_2	4.6–5.5
Ash	3.5–7.5	O_2	22–26
Fixed carbon	30–35	N_2	0.6–1.0
Calorific value (dmmf) = 6,500–6,600 Kcal/kg		S	0.6–1.5

Uses: Compared to bituminous coal, raw lignite is an inferior fuel owing to high moisture, low calorific value, small size, bad weathering properties etc. Lignite is of economic importance in those places where it is available and other fuels do not occur in abundance. Lignite is used in the generation of electricity in thermal power stations and carbonized briquettes are used as smokeless fuel. The tar obtained by the low temperature carbonization of lignite is a valuable raw material for the production of synthetic petrol and other liquid fuels. Lignite is extensively used in the manufacture of producer gas. It is also gasified into synthesis gas for ammonia production.

12.3 SUB-BITUMINOUS COAL (OR) BLACK LIGNITE

In many countries, this fuel is regarded as a variety of mature lignite resembling true coal in colour and appearance. In India and U.S.A, it is regarded as a separate class and term sub-bituminous coal is preferred. It is black in colour with a dull, waxy luster. It is denser and harder than lignite and has lower moisture content (12–25%). Most sub-bituminous coals appear banded like bituminous coal. The bands are parallel to the bedding plane but they are poorly jointed and easily split into slabs instead of breaking into rectangular lumps. Like lignite, sub-bituminous coal disintegrates on exposure to atmosphere and is therefore difficult to transport.

The following is the analysis of sub-bituminous coal:

Proximate analysis		Ultimate analysis (% dmmf)	
Air dried Moisture	10–20%	C	70–78
Volatile matter (dmmf)	40%	H_2	4.5–5.5
Fixed carbon (dmmf)	60%	O_2	20
Calorific value (dmmf) = 6,800–7,600 Kcal/kg			

Uses: It ignites easily and may be used in raising steam for various purposes. If low in sulphur, it may also be used for manufacturing gaseous fuels.

12.4   BITUMINOUS COAL

Bituminous coal is black and is usually banded. The bands are parallel to the bedding plane. The coal breaks along vertical joints (cleats) into rectangular, columnar or cubical pieces. Sometimes the fracture is conchoidal. The luster varies from bright to dull. Bituminous coal is denser and harder than lignite and sub-bituminous coal and does not disintegrate into slacks on exposure to the atmosphere. Owing to the good heating qualities and ease of handling, bituminous coal is the major fuel in most countries.

Bituminous coal is the most common and widely used variety of solid fossil fuel. The raw coal ordinarily sold in the market belongs to this class. The term coal alone ordinarily refers to bituminous coal. In the wider sense, coal covers all the solid fossil fuels.

The following is the analysis of Bituminous coal:

Proximate analysis		Ultimate analysis (% dmmf)	
Air dried Moisture	0.5–14%	C	80–90
Volatile matter (dmmf)	20–45%	H_2	4–6
Calorific value (dmmf) = 7,500–8,900 Kcal/kg		O_2	0.5–15

The limiting figures given above are for the bituminous coals of India and may differ slightly in coals of other countries. Indian coals have high percentage of ash which ranges between 12 and over 40%, the usual range being 15–30%. In the tertiary coals of Assam, the ash is often low (3–8%) and only in particular areas it is rather high (24–26%).

Uses: The chief use of bituminous coal is for combustion in domestic ovens, industrial furnaces and boilers, railway locomotives and thermal power stations. Two other uses are carbonization and gasification, whereby coal is converted into solid fuels (coke and semi coke), liquid fuels (coal tar fuels) and gaseous fuels (producer gas, water gas, coal gas). It is used for the production of activated carbon which is used for decoloration of glycerine and petroleum products. Coal is also source of wide range of coal chemicals, fertilizers and synthetic liquid fuels. Powdered coal is used in dynamite. Treatment of coal with strong sulphuric acid forms a basic exchange agent used in water treatment process.

12.5   SEMI-ANTHRACITE

Semi-anthracite is intermediate between bituminous coals and anthracites. It is harder than most mature bituminous coal. The conchoidal fracture is not so well developed as in anthracite and the cleats are more numerous, making it very friable coal. It crumbles more readily in the fire, and owing to a greater percentage of volatile matter it kindles more readily than anthracite and emits a small amount of yellow flame when ignited. Because of this more rapid consumption, its efficiency is greater than that of anthracite for certain purposes.

The following is the typical composition of Semi-anthracite

Proximate analysis		Ultimate analysis (% dmmf)	
Moisture	3.0%	C	80.2
Volatile matter	8.4%	H_2	3.6
Ash	9.7%	O_2	4.7
Fixed carbon	78.9%	N_2	1.1
Calorific value (dmmf) = 7,700 Kcal/kg		S	0.7

12.6   ANTHRACITE

Anthracite is commonly called Hard coal, Stone coal on account of its characteristic hardness and strength. It is characterized by an iron black colour and dull to brilliant and even sub-metallic luster. It does not soil the hand. It is non-coking and shows absolutely no tendency to soften under load. It commonly breaks with conchoidal fracture. Although there is banded structure, this is not always obvious. The following is the typical composition of anthracite.

Proximate analysis		Ultimate analysis	
Moisture	2.3%	C	86.7%
Volatile matter	3.1%	H_2	2.2%
Ash	6.9%	O_2	2.9%
Fixed carbon	87.7%	N_2	0.8%
Calorific value (dmmf) = 7,700 Kcal/kg		S	0.5%

Uses: The chief uses of anthracites are in boilers, domestic ovens and metallurgical furnaces. It is also used in small quantities as a component of coke oven charges. On calcining, it gives thermo-anthracite which is a raw material for the production of carbon electrodes. It is used for making brushes, battery parts, resistors, carbon refractory, corrosion resisting structural materials. It is used as a filter and as a pigment for paints. It is used for blending with coking coal to check its swelling and improving the coke quality.

Chapter 13

Coking and non-coking coals

From commercial point of view coal may be broadly classified into two categories

1   Coking coal
2   Non-coking coal

    Coking coals are the coals when heated out of contact with air, volatile matter gets removed and carbon particles join each other to form a porous cellular mass with sufficient strength, called **coke**. These coals are also called as **metallurgical coals**. Coking coals form a part of the bituminous group. Peat, Lignite, Sub-bituminous, Semi-anthracite and Anthracite are all non-coking coals. So also are some of the bituminous coals. Non-coking coals are mainly used for power generation.
    There is a difference of opinion as to the meaning of the words **Caking** and **Coking** when applied to coal. The one thing that is agreed is that both apply to those qualities which are important in the production of coke for special purposes, such as for metallurgical use. Several qualities or properties are involved, such as the amount of liquefaction which takes place during carbonization, the strength of the coke, and the extent of swelling when the coke forms. It is clear that no single test could give sufficient information on all these properties, at the same time, and in consequence, the various tests which are all limited in usefulness.

13.1 CAKING AND COKING COAL

When powdered coal is carbonized (i.e. heated in absence of air) it forms an expanded lumpy mass in some cases. Such coals are called caking coal and the phenomenon is called caking of coal. When the residue is vary hard and strong it is called coke and the process is called coking of coal. The coal is called coking coal. All the caking coals do not form strong, hard and coherent residue called coke. Hence all the caking coals are not necessarily coking coals but all the coking coals are necessarily caking in nature.
    When coal is carbonized, the caking coal will first expand and then contract slightly leaving a larger, weak and porous residue. When coking coal is carbonized, it will expand first and then it will contract to a greater extent (than merely a caking coal) to form a very compact, relatively less porous and stronger residue. Strong caking coals are called coking coals.

Why some coals are caking and others are non-caking is an interesting problem for investigation. Caking properties are perhaps due to a chemical process in which the macro-molecular structure of the coal mass is broken down and some products of relatively low molecular weight remain in a softened state for a sufficiently long time in the reaction zone. As a result, the entire mass takes the form of a plastic matter which is converted into a solid lump (re-solidified) on further heating. In this way the powdered caking coals are capable of producing lumpy semi coke and coke. The non-caking coals cannot produce the plastic state and yield on carbonization only a sintered mass.

13.2   COKING COAL

This coal has the property of softening and running together into a pasty mass at the point of incipient decomposition and then at higher temperature giving off its volatile constituents as bubble of gas. There remains a hard, grey, cellular mass called **COKE**.

According to White [28], practically all coals with H:O ratios of 59% or above seen to posses the quality of fusion and swelling necessary to good coking. Most with ratios down to 55% will make coke of some kind and a few with ratios as low as 50%, coke in the beehive oven, though very rarely yielding a good product. Coals changing to anthracite, the weathered coals and the coals of the boghead and cannel group show considerable variation from this rule. It has been shown that the solubility of coal in aniline may serve as an indication of coking properties. Vignon [29] says that the coke given by coal insoluble in aniline is powdery and that of the coal soluble in aniline is agglomerated and swollen.

A simple and satisfactory preliminary test is an agate mortar test. Coals which coke, when rubbed with a pestle in an agate mortar, cling to the sides of the mortar, whereas non-coking coals do not [30].

Experience has shown that vitrain and clarain are best coking constituents in coal. Much of the durain does not posses coking qualities unless mixed with vitrain. Fusain does not posses coking properties.

A measure of the coking properties is necessary for coal classification and for selection of coal for different industries. Coking properties influence not only the production of coke but also the performance of the coal in combustion and gasification. As it is noted earlier, although no chemical or simple physical test is known which will invariably distinguish coking coals, certain tests will usually indicate their coking properties. The standard tests in vogue in different countries are:

1   Crucible swelling number or Free swelling index
2   Agglutinating value or caking index
3   Gray-King low temperature carbonization assay
4   Roga index

The appearance of the residue (coke-button) of the volatile matter test may give an idea of the coking capacity of the coal. The coke-button may indicate five types – Pulverulent, Sintered, Weakly caked, Caked and Strongly caked.

13.2.1   Crucible swelling number (CSN) or free swelling index (FSI) (IS 1353:2010)

The most simple test to evaluate whether a coal is of potential value for coke manufacture is to determine the crucible swelling number or free swelling index. This test is intended solely to give some comparative measure of the swelling properties of coal. From the consideration of the average error, it has been ascertained that the mean result of four tests on the same coal is taken.

1.00 to 1.01 gm of freshly ground coal of −72 mesh B.S.Sieve is weighed into a crucible which is lightly tapped 12 times on the bench to level the surface of the coal. The crucible is covered with the lid. When the temperature of the tubular furnace reaches 820°C after inserting the empty crucible within 2.5 minutes, then the furnace is ready for firing the coal packed crucible. The crucible with the sample is inserted into the tubular furnace with the help of hanger and heated for such time as is required for the flame of the burning Volatile Matter to die out and in any case for not less than 2.5 minutes. The crucible is allowed to cool and the coke button is carefully removed from the crucible. The test is repeated until four buttons have been obtained.

The coke button is viewed through a tube to compare the shape with a set of shapes given in the specification (Fig. 13.2.1).

The crucible swelling number of a button is the number inscribed in the outline that its largest profile most nearly matches, and the mean swelling number of the series of four tests, expressed to the nearest half unit, is reported. For non-swelling buttons, the number '0' is used to describe coals which give a powder residue. The number '½' describes coals which give a coherent residue that will not bear a 500 gm weight without crumbling. Such coal is described as **non-agglomerating**. The number '1' describes coals which give a coherent residue that cracks into a few firm pieces when 500 gm weight is applied. Such coal is distinguished as **agglomerating**. The higher the number, the better the caking and swelling properties. The limitation is imposed by the maximum possible number 9 and the very highly swelling coals cannot be differentiated from one another.

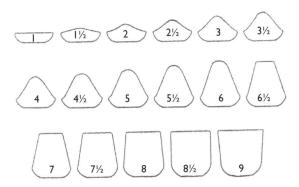

Figure 13.2.1 Standard profiles of coke buttons and corresponding crucible swelling numbers.

13.2.2 Agglutinating value or caking index (IS 1353:2010)

The agglutinating value or caking index is the maximum whole number ratio of sand to coal in a 25 gm mixture of the two. Sand used in this test should be of uniform quality; with regard to size, purity, sharpness etc.

The standard silica sand is not soluble in hot dilute HCl to a greater extent than 0.5%. It consists mainly of angular particles of pure silica, and is free from impurities such as clay, chalk or iron carbonate. It is regarded to pass IS Sieve 30 (296 microns or 52 B.S. mesh) and to be retained on IS sieve 20 (211 microns or 72 B.S mesh) containing not more than 5% of oversize and not more than 10% of undersize. The sand shall not break down on heating for 3 hours at 920°C to such an extent that the percentage of undersize material is increased by 2.5%.

The requisite quantities of sand and finely ground coal of −72 mesh B.S. Sieve to give exactly 25 gm of the mixture is taken in a crucible covered with lid. Then the crucible is put in a furnace at a temperature of 900°±15°C for exactly 7 minutes. Then the crucible is taken out and cooled to room temperature, and remove the lid. The rubber bung is gently inserted in a crucible on the carbonized mixture.

The crucible and bung are inverted on a sheet of white glazed paper on which any loose particles should be collected. The crucible is slowly and vertically removed from the carbonized mixture. The coherent residue is removed from the bung and placed on a level surface.

A 500 gm weight is gently lowered on to the carbonized residue. If the residue withstands the load, the loose powder from the top of the bung is added to the powder on the paper and weighed on a watch glass.

The test is repeated with mixtures of different ratios of sand and coal (25 gm mixture always being used), and find the critical ratio of sand to coal where a residue of coke is capable of supporting a weight of 500 gm without producing more than 5% of loose grains of coke. This critical ratio is agglutinating value or caking index.

Caking index is a measure of the binding or agglutinating property of the coal undergoing carbonization. The higher the agglutinating propensity, the higher the amount of sand that may be bound by coal and hence higher the caking index. If the coal has higher than 17% ash, then the sample has to be washed before testing. A demerit of the test lies in its trial-and-error approach.

Coals having caking index ≥24 are called Prime coking coals. If the caking index lies between 12 and 23 they are termed as Medium coking coals. The coals of caking index <12 are called Semi/Weakly coking coals.

13.2.3 Gray-king low temperature carbonization assay (IS 1353:2010)

The type of coke obtained from Gray-king Assay test characterises coals in regard to their coking properties. Two techniques for Gray-King Assay test are followed depending upon the types of coal under investigation.

Technique I – Applicable to non-swelling and moderately swelling coals giving coke pencils up to G_2.

20 gm of coal of −72 mesh B.S. Sieve is weighed and transferred in the retort without fouling the side arm, which is held almost vertically. By careful shaking, the

coal is spread into an even layer over the 15 cm length and then the retort is lightly tapped on the bench. The soft rubber bung is fitted into the open end of the retort, side arm into the tar receiver and then connected with the ammonia scrubber and gas holder. The whole assembly is then kept in position on the frame carrying the furnace.

The furnace previously raised to a steady temperature of 325°C is drawn smoothly and quickly over the retort; the temperature drops to about 300°C. Then the temperature is raised at the required rate of 5°C/min. At the end of the fifth minute it may come to 325°C. Thereafter the regular increase in temperature at the rate of 5°C/minute is maintained by small increase of current at regular time intervals. When the temperature reaches about 590°C, the current is reduced to maintain the furnace at 600°C by thermal inertia within two minutes. The furnace is held at this temperature for a further 15 minutes. After that the furnace is switched off and when cooled, the tar receiver and bung is removed. The traces of tar fouling the mouth and side arm of the retort are cleaned. The carbonized residue i.e. coke pencil is then taken out of the retort for examination.

Technique II – Applicable to swelling coals, giving coke pencils above G_2.

Here the classification is based on the minimum proportion of electrode carbon or H.T. coke breeze of –100 B.S mesh to be added to the coal to control the swelling. The subscript given to the letter G gives the number of parts of electrode carbon or coke breeze in 20 parts of that coal-electrode carbon or coke breeze mixture which gives a coke of type G. In all the trials carried out by this technique 20 gm of the mixture are carbonized, consisting of a quantity of electrode carbon or coke breeze, say, x gm and (20-x) gm of coal. The quantities are weighed separately and thoroughly mixed. The whole of the 20 gm mixture is then transferred to the retort and carbonized as described for Technique I.

The carbonized residue i.e. coke pencil taken out of the retort is to be visually compared with standard profiles and a letter A to G and G_1 to G_9 is assigned (Fig. 13.2.3).

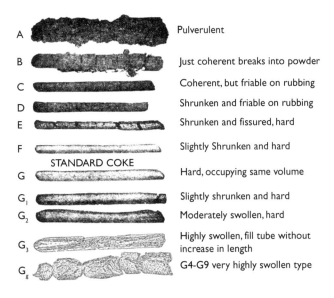

A	Pulverulent
B	Just coherent breaks into powder
C	Coherent, but friable on rubbing
D	Shrunken and friable on rubbing
E	Shrunken and fissured, hard
F	Slightly Shrunken and hard
	STANDARD COKE
G	Hard, occupying same volume
G_1	Slightly shrunken and hard
G_2	Moderately swollen, hard
G_3	Highly swollen, fill tube without increase in length
G_8	G4-G9 very highly swollen type

Figure 13.2.3 Cokes produced from different classes of coal in the Gray-King Assay Apparatus.

The letters represent the Gray-King (Low Temperature) coke type. A means non caking. Letters from B to G_9 indicates the increasing order of caking and swelling capacity. If the coal has higher than 17% ash, then the sample has to be washed before testing.

13.2.4　Roga index

Caking index test, due to difficulty in the procurement of graded silica sand and high processing cost involved to obtain standard sand conforming strictly to specifications as required, has been replaced by Roga test in many countries. The Roga test has been adopted by the International Organization for Standardization as a standard for determining the caking properties of coal and it finds place in the International Coal Classification system also. Roga index is a variation of the agglutinating index or caking index. The Roga test is based on determination, by means of a revolving drum, of the abrasion resistance of coke obtained by carbonizing a mixture of test coal and standard anthracite or H.T. coke dust in proportion of 1:5.

A mixture of coal and specified anthracite in a fixed proportion is carbonized under standard conditions. The strength of the residue is expressed as a numerical figure called Roga Index.

1 gm of the air-dried coal of size 0.212 mm (−72 B.S mesh) is blended in a special Silica crucible with upper diameter of 40 mm, bottom diameter of 20 mm and height of 40 mm with 5 gm of anthracite or H.T. coke dust of 0.3 to 0.4 mm (−36+52 B.S mesh) size and then leveled and weighted down with an iron weight of about 110 gm. Iron weight is of diameter 31 mm, height 21 mm and 15 mm depth. The hole is threaded so that the weight can be removed. The mixture is pressed by means of a special drop-press under a load of 6 kg/cm² for 30 seconds. The crucible is covered by a steel lid with a 2 mm hole in the center and the mixture is carbonized in an electric furnace for 15 minutes at 850°C. When cold, the weight is carefully withdrawn from the crucible and the resultant coke residue is weighed as 'Q' gm. It is then sieved through 1 mm sieve. The weight of the +1 mm fraction is 'a' gm. This material is placed in a rotating drum of diameter 20 cm and is rotated at 50 rpm for three periods of 5 minutes each. At the end of each period the −1 mm fraction is removed by screening. If 'b' gm, 'c' gm and 'd' gm are the weights of the +1 mm residues at the end of first, second and third periods respectively, the Roga Index is given by

$$\text{Roga Index} = \frac{\frac{a+d}{2}+b+c}{3}\times\frac{100}{Q} \qquad (13.2.4)$$

This should range from 0 to 70 in practice.

A general correspondence between Crucible Swelling Number, Gray-King Coke type and Roga Index is shown in Table 13.2.

Whatever test is used, the parameter for the caking properties is significant in defining the nature of coal. The very young (i.e., peat, lignite and sub-bituminous) and the very mature (i.e., semi-anthracite and anthracite) coals are completely devoid of cakability. In the case of bituminous coals, the caking capacity first increases with the rank, attains a maximum and then decreases with the further rise in the maturity or rank. The coals of the highest caking capacity are often called fat coals.

Table 13.2 Comparison of different Indices.

Crucible Swelling Number	Gray-King Coke type	Crucible Swelling number	Roga index
$0-\frac{1}{2}$	A–B		
1–4	C–G_2	$0-\frac{1}{2}$	0–5
$4\frac{1}{2}-6$	F–G_4	1–2	5–20
$6\frac{1}{2}-8$	G_3–G_9	$2\frac{1}{2}-4$	20–45
$8\frac{1}{2}-9$	G_7 and above	>4	>45

13.2.5 Plastic properties of coal

When bituminous coals are heated up, they undergo a series of changes of phase:

1 the coal particles soften (around 400°C) and become fluid-like
2 swelling takes place as soon as the particles are sufficiently fused together to offer appreciable resistance to the flow of the volatile matter which has resulted from decomposition
3 swelling ceases at a temperature around 500°C when the coal has lost its plasticity and begins to re-solidify into a coherent body with a porous structure, called coke

These behaviors of coal, between the softening and re-solidification temperatures are generally referred to as plastic properties of coal. Softening is a pure physical phenomenon of melting, independent of pyrolytic reactions. However, high plasticity can only be observed when decomposition has taken place. The decomposition initially de-polymerizes the coal. Subsequently, it gives rise to fluid products, which plasticize the other components of the coal, and gases, which form bubbles. When the bubbles flow through the macro-pores and fissures of the coal particles, they encounter resistance from the plastic coal. As a result, the entire coal mass swells. The swelling ceases as soon as the coal re-solidifies because the fluid products have further decomposed into volatile matter and re-polymerized to insoluble residue.

The **fluid products** which plasticize the inert components of the coal to form plastic (or fluid) coal during coking are chloroform soluble, stable up to 400°C and volatile only under high vacuum. They are formed as a result of primary decomposition of coal. This chloroform soluble material has been found in the coking coal only. At temperatures higher than 400°C, the yield of fluid products rises rapidly for a short time and then decreases rapidly, indicating that this material re-polymerizes to form insoluble product.

Plastic properties initially increase with increased volatile content and reach a maximum for coals with 25% to 30% volatile content. Subsequently, the plastic properties decrease with increased volatile content and disappear as the volatile content exceeds 35% to 40%. Specifically, when the volatile content increases from 15% to 40%, the softening point initially decreases very rapidly and then very slowly from a range of 430°C to 450°C to a range of 330°C to 350°C. Above a volatile content of 30%, the softening temperature remains rather constant. The re-solidification temperature decreases almost linearly from about 510°C to 450°C as the volatile content increases from 15% to 40%. Thus, the plastic range increases initially with volatile content, passes a maximum at 25% to 30% volatile and then decreases with further increase in the volatile content.

Swelling as measured by a dilatometer also reaches a maximum at a volatile content of 25% to 28% and contraction has been observed in the dilation test for coals with 15% to 18% and 35% to 40% volatile.

The plastic properties of coal are markedly modified by oxidation. In general, oxidation causes an increase in the softening temperature and decrease in the re-solidification temperature, the latter change being much smaller. As a result, the plastic range is reduced. So is the fluidity and swelling. Extensively oxidized coking coals may neither soften nor swell, and the coherent structure of coke can no longer be achieved.

Coal petrography describes the coal quantitatively in terms of optically distinct entities which can be divided into two classes, reactives and inerts, according to their thermal characteristics. The reactives consists of vitrinites, exinites, and reactive semi-fusinites. The inerts consist of micrinites, fusinites, inert semi-fusinites. The reactives soften, flow, fuse, and resolidify, to form coke exhibiting plastic properties during carbonization, whereas the inerts remain relatively unchanged. As the reactives flow around, they envelope and bond the inerts together. Since small particles of the inerts are well assimilated in the plastic matrix, coke strength increases. However, large particles of the inerts are sources of fissures and cracks. The particle size of the inerts is proportional to pulverization of coal.

The melting and fusion phase of the coal particles during carbonization is the most important part of the coking of coal. The degree of melting of the reactives and the degree of assimilation of the inerts into the molten mass determine the characteristics of the coke produced. A coal rich in vitrinite but deficient in fine size inerts produces a weak spongy coke. Conversely, a coal deficient in vitrinite but rich in inerts has insufficient plastic properties necessary for good coke formation. Therefore, there is an optimum ratio of reactives to inerts to produce strong coke. This ratio varies with the vitrinite type. Vitrinite ranges from type 3 to type 22 as the reflectance increases from 0.3 to 2.2. For coals with vitrinite type 3 through type 7 the coke strength increases uniformly as the reflectance of the vitrinites increases but remains relatively low. Coals containing vitrinite type 9 through type 13 are the better coking coals, and their coke strength increases rapidly as the reflectance of the vitrinites increases. Coals containing vitrinite type 14 through type 19 are low-volatile coking coals and their coking strength increases slowly as the reflectance increases. Vitrinites of type 20 and 21 undergo transient fusion and decrease in strength as reflectance increases. Above a reflectance of 2.2 (vitrinite type 22) as in semi-anthracite and anthracite, the vitrinites are virtually non-coking and behave like the inert coal entities.

The dilatometric test is done for the knowledge of the swelling and contraction of a coal during heating under load without the excess air. In this test, the temperature range of plasticity of a coal can also be determined. Coals shrink during carbonization, such volume changes that accompany the heating of a coking coal are measured with a dilatometer. There are a number of dilatometers used in different countries. The most widely used are the Audibert-Arnu and Gieseler plastometer. The basic principles of all dilatometers is to record the expansion or contraction or the fluidity of the coal sample which is heated in absence of air at a constant rate, say 1–3°C/min to a temperature until the plastic mass is re-solidified.

In Audibert-Arnu dilatometer, dimensional changes in a coal can be measured as functions of time. While the temperature of the coal is being raised at a constant rate, curves record the length of a coal sample to define the extent of contraction and dilatation, and the temperatures at which these changes begin or end. These properties are significant in determining the volume of coal that can be fed into a coke oven, and also in blending different coals for coke production. The resultant coke is itself subjected to rigorous testing to confirm its strength and quality for use in commercial operations.

In Gieseler plastometer, a coal sample is pressed around a spindle under torque, as the coal reaches its fluid state, the spindle begins to revolve, the rate at which it turns is measured in 'dial divisions per minute' (d.d.p.m.), which are then plotted against temperature. Until recently, Gieseler plastometer motors were capable of measuring to only 30,000 d.d.p.m., but newer instruments can now measure up to 180,000 d.d.p.m. (Pearson, 2011) [31]. Coals with high and low fluidity may be blended to obtain improved coking properties.

In Russian practice, the caking and plastic properties of coals are determined by the thickness of plastic layer. The apparatus used is known as **Sapozhnikov Plastometer** developed by Sapozhnikov and Bazilevich in 1938 [32]. The apparatus consists of a metallic cup with perforated bottom where 100 gm of coal sample (–2 mm) is charged and a pressure of 1 kg/cm² is exerted on the coal by a weight suspended on a horizontal layer. The temperature is measured by a thermocouple placed at the bottom of the sample. Heating is done by an electrical heating element from the bottom. The sample is quickly heated to 250°C in 30 minutes and then the rate is controlled at 3°C/min up to 730°C.

The volumetric curve of the coal is plotted on the graph paper fixed on a rotating drum as the drum rotates at the rate of 1 mm/minute by a clock work mechanism. During the heating period, the formation of the plastic layer is measured in two levels with the help of a needle, fixed on a metallic scale. The readings of the upper level and the lower level of the plastic layer are plotted on the same graph paper and the maximum distance between these two curves give the thickness of the plastic layer, which is the index for caking property. The nature of volumetric curve gives an idea of the coking nature of the coal. This test is widely used in China, Russia and other Eastern European countries. The test was known as the Sapozhnikov Plastometric Test.

13.3 NON-COKING COAL

This non-coking coal may resemble coking coal in all outward appearance, but in composition it differs in H:O ratio. It does not cling to the sides of an agate mortar when rubbed with pestle. It burns freely without softening, leaving a powdery mass instead of a strong cellular mass. The cherry coal is a variety of non-coking coal. It is usually velvet black in colour, brittle, and crumbles rather readily. Splint coal, slate coal and hard coal are also some varieties of non-coking coal. They are of black to brilliant luster. They fracture in two directions, the longitudinal breaking being curved and slaty and the transverse is uneven and splintery.

Chapter 14

Classification of Indian coals

Coals are classified into various categories to assess the useful value of a coal for a given purpose based on a few tests.

Coals are classified based on various parameters like proximate analysis, calorific value, maturity (rank), ultimate analysis, caking properties etc.

There is no universal classification system of coal because

- Coal is composed of diverse elements i.e., it is a heterogeneous mixture of organic mass, mineral matters and moisture in uncertain proportions
- The organic mass itself being heterogeneous comprises of many microcomponents which means that the coals of same ultimate analysis do not necessarily have the same properties while coals of different compositions may in some respect behave alike
- Both the amount and composition of mineral matters in coal varies widely which greatly influence the properties of the whole coal
- The quality and quantity of the microcomponents vary from coal to coal. The quality of microcomponents is determined by the initial plant material and the coalification processes both of which vary from place to place and time to time

Because of the above reasons, large number of coal classification systems exist. Indian coal is classified into two main categories, namely, coking and non-coking. Although for commercial gradation, ash percentage is the sole criterion, for semi-weakly-coking coal, along with ash percentage, moisture percentage too is considered as an added criterion. For non-coking coal, an empirical formula is used to determine Useful Heat Value (UHV) of coal in kcal/kg. The classification of coal as per the Ministry of Coal is given in Table 4.1.

In order to adopt the best international practices, India decided to switch over from the grading based on Useful Heat Value (UHV) to the grading based on Gross Calorific Value (GCV); and, therefore, on 16.01.2011 the Ministry of Coal notified the switch over. As per the new system, nomenclature as shown in Table 14.2 has been introduced for gradation of non- coking coal. Based on the GCV ranges of proposed gradation and erstwhile (UHV) gradation, a concordance table is generated for better understanding and also shown in the Table 14.2 separately. However, it may be noted that this concordance does not depict exact one-to-one relation between the two systems.

Table 14.1 Classification of coal.

Sl No	Class	Grade	Specification
I	Non-coking coal produced in all states other than Assam, Arunachal Pradesh, Meghalaya and Nagaland	A	Useful Heat Value exceeding 6200 kcal per kg.
		B	Useful Heat Value exceeding 5600 kcal per kg but not exceeding 6200 kcal per kg.
		C	Useful Heat Value exceeding 4940 kcal per kg but not exceeding 5600 kcal per kg.
		D	Useful Heat Value exceeding 4200 kcal per kg but not exceeding 4940 kcal per kg.
		E	Useful Heat Value exceeding 3360 kcal per kg but not exceeding 4200 kcal per kg.
		F	Useful Heat Value exceeding 2400 kcal per kg but not exceeding 3360 kcal per kg.
		G	Useful Heat Value exceeding 1300 kcal per kg but not exceeding 2400 kcal per kg.
2	Non-coking Coal produced in Assam, Arunachal Pradesh, Meghalaya and Nagaland	A	Useful Heat Value between 6200 and 6299 kcal per kg and corresponding ash plus moisture content between 18.85 and 19.57%.
		B	Useful Heat Value between 5600 and 6199 kcal per kg and corresponding ash plus moisture content between 19.58 and 23.91%.
3	Coking Coal	Steel Grade I	Ash content not exceeding 15%.
		Steel Grade II	Ash content exceeding 15% but not exceeding 18%.
		Washery Grade I	Ash content exceeding 18% but not exceeding 21% .
		Washery Grade II	Ash content exceeding 21% but not exceeding 24%.
		Washery Grade III	Ash content exceeding 24% but not exceeding 28%
		Washery Grade IV	Ash content exceeding 28% but not exceeding 35%.
4	Semi-coking and weakly–coking coal	Semi-coking Grade I	Ash plus moisture content not exceeding 19%.
		Semi-coking Grade II	Ash plus moisture content exceeding 19% but not exceeding 24%.
5	Hard coke	By-product Premium	Ash content not exceeding 25%.
		By-product Ordinary	Ash content exceeding 25% but not exceeding 30%.
		Beehive Premium	Ash content not exceeding 27%.
		Beehive Superior	Ash content exceeding 27% but not exceeding 31%.
		Beehive Ordinary	Ash content exceeding 31% but not exceeding 36%.

Source: Indian Minerals Yearbook 2013 Published by IBM.

Table 14.2 Gradation of Non-coking coal based on GCV.

Gradation of non-coking coal		Concordance table	
Grades	GCV Range (kcal/kg)	Old grading based on UHV	New grading based on GCV
G1	GCV exceeding 7000	A	G1, G2, G3
G2	GCV exceeding 6701 and 7000	B	G4, G5
G3	GCV exceeding 6401 and 6700	C	G6
G4	GCV exceeding 6101 and 6400	D	G7, G8
G5	GCV exceeding 5801 and 6100	E	G9, G10
G6	GCV exceeding 5501 and 5800	F	G11, G12
G7	GCV exceeding 5201 and 5500	G	G13, G14
G8	GCV exceeding 4901 and 5200	Non-coking coal Un-graded	G15, G16, G17
G9	GCV exceeding 4601 and 4900		
G10	GCV exceeding 4301 and 4600		
G11	GCV exceeding 4001 and 4300		
G12	GCV exceeding 3701 and 4000		
G13	GCV exceeding 3401 and 3700		
G14	GCV exceeding 3101 and 3400		
G15	GCV exceeding 2801 and 3100		
G16	GCV exceeding 2501 and 2800		
G17	GCV exceeding 2201 and 2500		

Source: Indian Minerals Yearbook 2013 Published by IBM.

Chapter 15

Indian coals

India is endowed with abundant coal resources of the order of 301.6 Billion tones. The proved reserves are 126 Billion tones. India ranks fifth in the world, with 2.7% of the global coal resources. India has a share of about 13.5 per cent of the global coal reserves. India is one way fortunate to have substantial quantity of coal reserves and on the other way equally unfortunate to have coals contaminated with extraneous dirt and shale bands in coal seams due to its drift origin. India is the world's third largest country producing coal and third largest coal importer. The coal occurs in Gondwana and Tertiary formations. In the former, many of the coal fields, especially the developed ones, are from the lower Gondwanas. The Gondwana coals are largely confined to the river valleys – like the Damodar (West Bengal and Jharkhand), Mahanandi (Odisha), and Godavari (Maharashtra and Andhra Pradesh). Coal seams are found within the rocks of two formations viz., the Lower or Barakar Coal Measures and the Upper or Raniganj Coal Measures. Geographically the rocks of the Barakar formation are more extensive and the coal is superior in quality and more in quantity than the coals of the Raniganj formation. Generally the Gondwana coals are represented by bituminous and sub-bituminous coals. Coal fields of North Eastern Region belong to the Tertiary age. The lignite deposits of Jammu and Kashmir, Kerala, Tamil Nadu and Gujarat are also of the same age.

Occurrence of metallurgical grade coal is confined to Barakar formations. Metallurgical coal is found in Jharia, Giridih, Karanpura and Bokaro coal fields of Jharkhand and Raniganj coal fields of West Bengal only. Raniganj formation yields semi-coking coal. Jharkhand has the largest number of coal mines.

There is no consistency in the ash percentage in the coal seams with variation from piece to piece which is the result of the formation of Indian coals under drift theory. Practically all the best coal seams of Raniganj and Jharia fields are nearly exhausted. All good seams every where in India were explored first leaving only enormous quantity of high ash coals. Major coal fields of India are briefly described [33] below.

15.1 GONDWANA COALS

In India 99% of coal production comes from the Gondwana coals.

15.1.1 Coal fields of Jharkhand and Bihar

About one-third of the estimated coal reserves are distributed in the coalfields of Jharkhand and Bihar. Important coalfields of this state are Jharia, Bokaro, Giridih,

Karanpura, Ramgarh, Daltonganj, Auranga and Hutar. Part of the Raniganj coalfield of West Bengal falls in this state. Coalfields of the Damodar valley are the chief source of metallurgical coal in the country and most of the iron and steel plants get coking coal from these fields.

15.1.1.1   Jharia coal field

The Jharia coal field is a large coal field located in the east of India in Jharkhand and it is the principal coking coal resource of the country. This coalfield is situated about 260 km northwest of Kolkata in the heart of Damodar Valley mainly along the north of this river. The coal field lies within the district of Dhanbad and covers an area of 456 sq.km. The Barakar measure and Raniganj measure represent the coal measures of the field deposited in different periods.

The deposits were formed layer after layer with parting of sandstone forming Barakar coal measure with 25 seams. 18 seams of them are workable and are low volatile coking quality. The moisture is low and volatiles vary from 13% to 30% with fixed carbon 50%–70%. Other 7 seams are above these 18 seams and are termed as local seams. Besides these, there are 9 seams under Raniganj measure deposited in latter age. The Raniganj measure coals are of inferior quality in general and there are 3 to 4 major seams of low volatile and semi-coking quality.

The estimated reserves of coal in Jharia coal field is 19.4 billion tones. Most of the metallurgical coal requirement of the country is supplied from the Jharia coal field, which supplies about 30% of India's total coal production.

15.1.1.2   Bokaro coal field

Bokaro coal field is in the form of a long narrow strip extending for about 65 km in an east-west direction with a maximum width of about 11 km in the north-south direction. The Barakar formation is the chief coal bearing horizon. East Bokaro and West Bokaro are two subdivisions of the field separated almost in the middle by Lugu Hill. In the East Bokaro field, out of 15 seams within Barakars, 3 seams namely Kargali, Karo, and Bermo are the principal ones. Kargali seam ranks very important in its thickness and coking properties. The coal is of medium coking variety. The coal of Karo seam is non-coking coal and the coal of Bermo seams overlying the Karo seam is of coking variety. In West Bokaro, there are 13 major seams within the Barakars. The coal is of coking variety with an ash content of 24%–35%. The seventh seam has an ash less than 24%. Most of the coals are medium coking coals.

15.1.1.3   Giridih coal field

Giridih has only 16 sq.km of coal measure. The workable seams are under two groups – the Karharbari (lower and upper) and the Hill seams. The coal of Karharbari seam is one of the excellent coking coal. The coal from the seams are low in moisture (1.40–1.80%), low in ash (9–12.6%), low in volatile, low in sulphur (0.5%) and phosphorous (0.01%).

15.1.1.4   Ramgarh coal field

Ramgarh coal field covers an area of 98 sq.km. mostly within the Barakar measures. The coal from main Ramgarh basin have low moisture content (less than 2%) and fairly high coking characteristics. The coals in the western sub-basin (in Kaitha area) have high moisture (greater than 2%) and weakly coking properties.

15.1.1.5   Karanpura coal field

Karanpura coalfield lies to the west of Bokaro coalfield. This coal field is divided in to two parts – North Karanpura covers 1190 sq.km area and South Karanpura occupies 180 sq.km. In Karanpura coalfield there is full development of Lower Gondwana and the younger rocks. In the North Karanpura, a number of coal seams occur. The ash content of these coal seams is high. In South Karanpura there is good development of Talchir and Barakar Formation. Most of the coals of this area are non-coking. Argada and Sirka seams of South Karanpura are of weakly coking type.

15.1.1.6   North Koel valley coal fields

There are three coalfields – Auranga, Hutar and Daltonganj. The Auranga and Hutar coalfields are in the same alignment with those of Damodar Valley while Daltonganj coalfield is somewhat north of axial line. Hutar and Daltonganj coalfields are of economic importance. In Hutar coalfield, coal seams occur in Lower Barakar. The coals are low in volatile matter (12.6%) and ash content (17.67%).

15.1.1.7   Deogarh coal fields

The Deogarh group of coalfields comprise three isolated Lower Gondwana sedimentary basins and are located in the Santhal Pargana districts of Bihar. The coal seams are reported to occur in the Karharbari as well as Barakar Formation. The coals are high in ash and range in rank from Sub-bituminous to high volatile bituminous.

15.1.1.8   Rajmahal coal fields

The coalfields of this area are assuming importance lately. Based on the coal of this region, a Super Thermal Power Station has been built at Farakka. There are five coalfields in this area. Coals of this region are sub-bituminous to high volatile bituminous in rank.

15.1.2   Coal fields of West Bengal

Raniganj coal field is the important coal field in West Bengal and is the easternmost of the Damodar Valley coalfields. This coal field lie mostly in the West Bengal and partly (Western portion) in Jharkhand. It extends over an area of 1550 sq.km. with Barakar measure and Raniganj measure separated by a barren measure of Iron, stone, shale devoid of any coal. Coals of the Barakar Measures are low in moisture (1–3%), low in volatile matter (20–30%) whereas coals of Raniganj Measures are high in moisture (3–10%) and high in volatile matter (30–36%).

The eastern part of the Raniganj field is totally non-coking with high moisture (9%). This area is meeting up the 25% coal requirement of the country. As regard the utilization efficiency, high volatile non-coking coal of Raniganj series is the best coal in India with immense export market potentiality. Laikdih and Begunia seams of Barakar measure are of medium coking type and Dishergarh, Sanchria and Paniati seams of Raniganj measure are of semi-coking type.

Low ash coals having reasonable coking property have been earmarked as blend-able coal for the steel plants to blend with prime coking coals to manufacture hard coke, and hence its name. Dishergarh seam is the principal blendable coal.

Other coalfields found in West Bengal are Barjora coalfield, Birbhum coalfield and Darjeeling coalfield.

15.1.3   Coal fields of Chhattisgarh and Madhya Pradesh

About one-fifth of the estimated reserves of the country are located in coalfields of these states. Coalfields of these states are traditionally put into four groups:

a   Central Indian coalfields (Singrauli, Sohagpur, Umaria, and Johilla)
b   Satpura coalfields (Pench, Kanhan and Pathakhera)
c   North Chhattisgarh coalfields (Chirimiri, Kurasia, Bisrampur, Jhilimili, Sonhat, Sendurgarh, Tatapani-Ramkola), and
d   South Chhattisgarh coalfields (Hasdo-Arand, Korba, Mand-Raigarh)

Madhya Pradesh and Chhattisgarh produced 29.2% of total production in India.

15.1.3.1   Central Indian coal fields

a   **Singrauli coal field:** This field is situated mostly on the border of Uttar Pradesh and Madhya Pradesh. While most of the field is in Madhya Pradesh a part of it is situated in the Mirzapur district of Uttar Pradesh. In this coalfield coals have been found in Barakar and Raniganj Formation. There are four coal seams. These coals are useful for thermal power generation.
b   **Sohagpur coal field:** Sohagpur is another important coalfield in the Son Valley. Barmni-Chilpa fault trending east-west has divided this field in two parts. In the southern part of the fault there are 5 coal seams within the Barakar Formation. The coal contains 4–7% moisture and 20–27% ash. The coals on the north of this fault are characteristically different from the coals occurring south of the fault. Coking coals have been found in the north of the fault.
c   **Umaria coal field:** This coalfield is situated on the Umrer river a tributary of the Son river. The Lower Gondwana rocks are well developed in this coalfield. Six coal seams have been found in this field. The coals are relatively high in moisture (7–10%) and high in ash (18.6–29.4%).
d   **Johilla coal field:** This coalfield is situated in the Valley of Johilla River. In this field, Talchirs, Barakars and beds of Raniganj age are developed. Johilla seam is the most important seam in the northern area. The seam has a high moisture (10.8%), ash (17.9%) and volatile matter content (31.7%).

15.1.3.2   Satpura coal fields

Satpura coalfields lie within the Pench-Kanhan-Tawa valley, south of Narmada river, known as Satpura Gondwana Basin. The following are the important coalfields in this region.

a   **Mohpani coal field:** This coalfield is one of the country's oldest coal-bearing areas. It is situated in the west of Mohpani. In this coalfield, Talchir and Barakar Formations are overlain by the Upper Gondwana rocks of Bagra Formation (Mahadeva Group) and Jabalpur Formation. The coal seams in this area are weakly coking with moisture content ranging from 4 to 6%.

b   **Pathakhera coal field:** This is an important coalfield in the Tawa valley. In the vicinity of Pathakhera three coal seams have been encountered by boring. The top seam is of poor quality and the other seams are comparatively better in quality.

c   **Kanhan valley coal field:** These are the most important coalfields of Satpura region and covers around 15 sq.km. The area is covered by Barakars. The coal in this region is of high volatile coking type with ash content up to 22%.

d   **Pench valley coal field:** This area is situated in the north-west of Chindwara and lies in the east of Kanhan valley coalfields. The rocks of Barakar Formation are exposed in the area. Important coal seams are exposed in Gajandoh area, Barkuhi area, Chandamata – Dongar Chikhli area etc.

15.1.3.3   North Chhattisgarh coal fields

a   **Tatapani-Ramkola coal field:** This coalfield is located in the Surguja District of Chhattisgarh and covers an area of about 260 sq. km. It consists of two separate areas – the eastern and western. The eastern portion is called Tatapani area where 5 coal seams occur in the Barakar Formation. The coals in the area are non-coking with low ash content. The western part or Ramkola area is separated from eastern part by a patch of Upper Gondwana rocks called the Rajkhatra tract. There are 5 coal seams in the Barakar Formation. The ash content varies between 17 and 34%.

b   **Jhilimili coal field:** This covers 170 sq. km. in the Rewa-Chhattisgarh basin. The coalfield may be divided in to three areas: (i) Northern area; (ii) Central area; (iii) Southern area. Of the five important coal seams, three have weak to moderate coking type of coal with ash less than 16%.

c   **Sonhat coal field:** This coalfield lies west of the Jhilimili coalfield forming the eastern extension of Sohagpur coalfield. The Barakar rocks which occupy the Sonhat plateau have been broadly divided in to three divisions. The lower division consists of more than 15 coal seams. The middle division is devoid of coal seams. In the Upper division although Barakar strata is of considerable thickness in the field, the number of coal seams and their thickness is poor.

d   **Chirimiri area:** Three seams of the Karakot horizon are the most important seams in this area. The composite seam is being worked in the collieries of Chirimiri, New Pouri (New Chirimiri) and Kurasia.

e   **Kurasia area:** In the eastern sector drilling has proved the existence of workable coal horizon in this area. These are: Duman seam; Kaperti seam; Shorgela seam; and Kotmi seam.

f   **Bisrampur coal field:** This coalfield covers an area of about 1036 sq.km. Coal bearing Barakar rocks are developed to a thickness of about 150 metres. Several coal seams have been reported from different localities. In the south-western part of the field, detailed prospecting conducted by Indian Bureau of Mines has indicated more than one horizon of coal. Pasang seam is the thickest seam in the horizon. The coal is of non-coking type in this seam.

15.1.3.4   South Chhattisgarh coal fields

a   **Hasdo-Rampur or Arand (Surguja) coal field:** This coalfield extends from Rampur and Paharbula Lappas in Arand valley to Hasdo river in Bilaspur district. This coalfield is divided in to four parts (i) The eastern or Rampur section in Rer (Arand) valley (ii) North central (Paharbula) area (iii) South Central (Uprora) area (iv) Western (or Mation) area beyond the Gej and Hasdo rivers. The quality of coal in this field varies widely. The contents of moisture varies from 1.56 to 7.40% and ash from 11.26 to 25%.

b   **Korba coal field:** Korba coalfield is located in Korba district of Chhattisgarh and covers an area of about 530 Sq.Km. The coalfield is named after the village Korba on the eastern bank of the Hasdo river which is tributary of the Mahanadi river. The Barakar Formation is the coal bearing measures. As per GSI, a total of 10075 Mt coal reserves available in Korba coalfield. The deposits are restricted into two distinct zones (i) Thick seam/quarry power grade zone comprising of grade E, F, & G having reserves of approx. 9068 Mt. (ii) Thin seam/underground superior grade zone comprising of grade B to D having reserves of approx.1007 Mt.

c   **Mand-Raigarh coal field:** These coalfields are situated in Raigarh district of Chhattisgarh and covers an area of about 520 sq. km. This coalfield comprising of grades A to G and may be exploited through open-cast mining.

15.1.4   Coal fields of Maharashtra

15.1.4.1   Kamptee coal field

This coalfield is situated about 19 km NNE of Nagpur. Detailed exploration has proved a large deposit of coal in the following three blocks:

1   Ghatrohan area to the east of the Kanhan river
2   Silewara area to the west of the Kanhan river
3   Bina area to the south of the Kanhan river

Five workable seams have been proved over the three blocks. The moisture content of the coals varies from 8 to 11% and the volatile matter from 33 to 43%. The coals are non-coking.

15.1.4.2   Bokhara coal field

This coal field is situated 9 km north-west of Nagpur railway station. Seven coal seams have been proved. The moisture content of the coal seams varies from 8 to 11% and the volatile matter from 24 to 29%. The coals are non-coking.

15.1.4.3 Umrer coal field

Umrer is a small town about 44 km south-east of Nagpur. The coal bearing strata is nowhere exposed at the surface. There are four workable seams in the area.

15.1.4.4 Wardha valley coal field

Wardha valley coalfields are situated in the valley of Wardha river, lying mainly in the Chandrapur district. The coalfields extend in a NW-SE direction extending over a distance of 115 km and cover an area of about 4130 sq. km. The coal bearing Barakar rocks are only 76 m thick and occur in patches. Rarely coals are found in the outcrops.

15.1.5 Coal fields of Andhra Pradesh

In Andhra Pradesh important Còalfields lie in the Pranhita – Godavari Valley. In continuation of the Wardha valley there are coalfields in the Pranhita-Godavari valleys covering an enormous area of over 9000 sq. km. Based on geographical and geological considerations, the Godavari valley coalfield is divided in to twelve coal belts. Ramagundam Coal belt is one of such coal belts located along the western margin of the Godavari valley coalfield. Important coalfields of the area Tandur Coalfield; North Godavari and South Godavari Coalfield; Karlapalli or Kamaram Coalfield; Ramagundam Coalfield etc.

15.1.6 Coal fields of Odisha

Out of 57 Gondwana and 14 Tertiary coalfields considered for the national inventory of the coal, Odisha has Talcher and Ib-valley coalfields. Its share in the reserve so far established in the country amounts to 23.6%. A substantial qurriable reserve has been located in northern part of Ib-River coalfield (Gopalpur area) and towards its southeastern extremity in Khinda-Talabira area. Occurrence of coal seems has also been reported from Raniganj Formation of Ib-River coalfield very recently. The importance of Odisha coalfields is further enhanced due to their proximity to the east coast.

Coalfields of Odisha constitute the southern part of the Son-Mahanadi Valley basin. Except the Ib-River coalfield and Talcher coalfield, there are Four more Gondwana basins in Odisha (a) Athagarh (b) Gaisilat (c) Athamalik (d) Katranjia basins.

15.1.7 Upper Gondwana coals

It includes coalfields of Gujarat. Sub-bituminous type of coal is found in association with Upper Gondwana sediments (Cretaceous) in the district of Kutch, Surendranagar and Mehsana district.

15.2 TERTIARY COALS

Tertiary coal fields are found in North Eastern Region (Assam, Meghalaya, Nagaland, Arunachal Pradesh) and some deposits in Jammu & Kashmir, Gujarat and Himachal Pradesh. Tertiary coals account for about 2% of India's total coal production and are high in sulphur content. But even then, these coals are very useful in those areas where they are produced, since those areas are devoid of Gondawana coals.

a   **Assam:** Makum coalfield of upper Assam in Dibrugarh district is the most impor-
    tant coal producing region of the state. It has 6 coal seams. Other coal fields of the
    state include Dilli-jeypore and Mikir hills. Assam coals, although of low rank, have
    high coking properties, have highest calorific value in Indian coals but are of high
    sulphur (3–8% sulphur) coals. High sulphur content makes them unsuitable for
    metallurgical purpose. They are well suited to hydrogenation process to produce
    liquid fuels.
b   **Meghalaya:** The coal deposits of Meghalaya occur in Garo, Khasi and Jaintia
    Hills. Pendenguru coal field with eight seams has good quality coal. Other coal
    fields are Siju, Mawlong, Shella, Bapung, Darangiri and Langrin. Based on vitrin-
    ite reflectance, the rank of these coals has been described to be Sub-bituminous to
    high volatile bituminous.
c   **Nagaland:** Borjan coalfield is the important coalfield of Nagaland. The coal of
    this coalfield was widely known as Nazira coal. These coals are weakly coking.
    Jhanzi, Disai, Tuen sang and Tiru valley are other coal fields of Nagaland.
d   **Jammu and Kashmir:** Important coalfields are Kalakot, Mohogala, Metka
    (western Chenab region), Ladda and Saugar Marg (eastern Chenab region).
    Recently anthracite coal has been discovered in the Riasi area of Jammu but its
    mining is economically not viable.
e   **Gujarat:** O.N.G.C. while drilling for oil has come across a large reserve of
    coal (about 63 billion tones) at a depths ranging from 700 to 1700 m in Kalol-
    Mehsana district in Gujarat. The coal associated with shales, claystone and sand
    occurs in Kalol Formation. Coal associated with shale and sand also occurs in
    Kadi Formation. Both the formations are of Eocene age.

Main coal-fields of Arunachal Pradesh are Namchick- Namphuk, Abor hills,
Miri, Daphla, Aka hills and Miao Bum. Coal has been located in Chauri, Laharu,
Gadhsan and Samet areas of Chamba district in Himachal Pradesh.

15.3   LIGNITE DEPOSITS

Lignite is a low grade inferior coal containing too much of moisture and low percentage of carbon (35–40%). When exposed, it disintegrates easily. Drying and
briquetting are, therefore, necessary before it is put to use. It is mainly used in thermal
power plants and as industrial and domestic fuel. It is also used for carbonisation and
fertilizer production. Lignite deposits are located away from traditional coal mining
areas and, hence, play vital role in substituting coal, saving coal transport cost and
promoting economic development in these areas.

In India, the utilization of lignites in various industries and power generation are
gaining importance. In comparison to coal it is low in ash and sulphur content and
also creates less environmental hazards. Presently, the contribution of lignites is about
4% of the energy needs of our country. The occurrence of Lignites in India is known
in Tamilnadu, Pondichery, Karnataka, Andhra Pradesh, Maharashtra, Gujarat,
Rajasthan, Jammu and Kashmir, Kerala and West Bengal.

Table 15.3 Major sources of Indian coals and lignites.

Type of coal	Major sources
Prime coking	X to XVIII seams of Jharia coal field Karharbari seam of giridih coal field
Medium coking	I to IX seams of Jharia coal field Mohuda series of Jharia coal field Laikdih seam of Raniganj coal field Kargali seam of East Bokaro coal field Ramgarh coal field
Semi-coking	Kanhan coal field Sanchria & Deshergarh seams of Raniganj coal field
Weakly coking	Argada & Sikra seams of Karanpura coal field Jhilmilli coal field
Non-coking	All coal fields excluding Jharia, East Bokaro and Giridih coal fields
Semi-anthracite	Kalakot coal field Jammu & Darjeeling
Assam coals	Upper Assam coal field Khasia & Jaintia coal field
Lignites	South Arcot (Tamil Nadu) Palana & Khari (Rajasthan) Umarsar (Gujarat) Nichahom (Kashmir)

The lignite deposits in the Neyveli field in South Arcot district, Tamil Nadu was first discovered in 1930 and are the sole contributors to the Indian lignite production. The field covers an area of about 250 sq.km. The lignite horizon is of 15 meters thick and is confined to Cuddalore series of Miocene age. Neyveli Lignite opencast mine is the largest mechanical mine producing 24 million tonnes of lignite annually and generating power with installed capacity of 2490 MW.

Table 15.3 shows the major sources of different types of Indian coals and lignites based on the physical and chemical survey data collected by Coal Survey Laboratories of CIMFR (previously CFRI).

15.4 INDIAN COAL RESOURCES

India's geological resources of coal, as on 1st April 2014, are estimated at 301.6 billion tons up to the maximum depth of 1200 metre. including 34.1 billion tones of coking coal. Of this 126.0 billion tones belong to the proved category, 142.5 billion tones are in the indicated and 33.1 billion tones in the inferred segments. It is to be noted that only 11.3% of the total coal resources are of coking coals which are useful for metallurgical purpose. Among these coking coal resources, 79.4% is of medium coking coal, 15.6% is of prime coking coal and the rest 5% is of semi-coking coal. The share of Prime coking coal resources is only 1.76% of total coal resources and these coals are available only from Jharia coal field. The country's lignite reserves are estimated at about 43.22 billion tones as on 1st April 2013, bulk of this (34.35 billion tones) is located in Tamil Nadu.

As per Indian Standards Procedure (ISP) the coal resources are classified into (1) Proved: The coal resources of an area falling within 200 m radius from a borehole point (or observation point) (2) Indicated: Those resources occurring in the area falling between radii of 200 m and 1 km from a borehole point (3) Inferred: Those resources occurring in the area falling between radii of 1 km and 2 km from a borehole point.

If the estimate is based on sufficient data such that it will not vary much from the actual tonnage and grade when mined, such estimate comes under proved category. A 'Proved Resource' is the economically mineable part of a Measured Resource demonstrated by at least a Preliminary Feasibility Study. This Study must include adequate information on mining, processing, metallurgical, economic, and other relevant factors that demonstrate, at the time of reporting, that economic extraction is justified.

Under indicated category, estimate is computed partly from sample analysis and measurements and partly from reasonable geological projections. It carries lesser degree of assurance. An 'Indicated Resource' is that part of a Resource for which quantity, grade or quality, densities, shape and physical characteristics, can be estimated with a level of confidence sufficient to allow the appropriate application of technical and economic parameters, to support mine planning and evaluation of the economic viability of the deposit. The estimate is based on detailed and reliable exploration and testing information gathered through appropriate techniques.

The estimate under inferred category is made by extrapolation of sampling data to areas where there is no data of sampling available. It is based on geological evidence and projection. An 'Inferred Resource' is that part of a Resource for which quantity and grade or quality can be estimated on the basis of geological evidence and limited sampling and reasonably assumed, but not verified, geological and grade continuity. The estimate is based on limited information and sampling gathered through appropriate techniques from locations such as outcrops, trenches, pits, workings and drill holes. Due to the uncertainty that may be attached to Inferred Resources, it cannot be assumed that all or any part of an Inferred Resource will be upgraded to an Indicated or Measured Resource as a result of continued exploration. Confidence in the estimate is insufficient to allow the meaningful application of technical and economic parameters or to enable an evaluation of economic viability worthy of public disclosure. Inferred Resources must be excluded from estimates forming the basis of feasibility or other economic studies.

Detailed state-wise/coalfield-wise/type-wise geological resources of Indian coals as on 01–04–2014 are given in Table 15.4.1. Approximate state-wise resources of coal are shown in Table 15.4.2. World coal reserves are shown in Table 15.4.3.

There are in all 559 operating mines in India. They produced 556 mtpy during 2012–13. Out of these, 215 were opencast while 320 were underground mines. The remaining 24 were mixed collieries. There were 530 public sector mines and 29 mines in private sector. Thrust is now given to further increase production from opencast mines where the gestation period is comparatively shorter. Of 559 mines, 176 mines were located in Jharkhand, West Bengal had 101 mines, Madhya Pradesh (71), Chhattisgarh (60), Maharashtra (58), Andhra Pradesh (50) and Odisha (28). The remaining 15 mines were located in the states of Arunachal Pradesh, Assam, Jammu & Kashmir and Uttar Pradesh.

Coal mining in India is carried out by both opencast and underground methods. Opencast mining contributes over 90% of total production whereas rest of the

Table 15.4.1 Geological resource of Indian coal as of 01.04.2014.

(Resource in million tonne)

State/Coalfield/Type of coal	Proved	Indicated	Inferred (Exploration)	Inferred (Mapping)	Total
GONDWANA COALFIELDS					
West Bengal					
1. Raniganj					
Medium coking	550.42	0.00	0.00	0.00	550.42
Semi-coking	188.05	432.49	168.23	0.00	788.77
Non-coking	12549.84	6868.22	3845.18	0.00	23263.24
2. Barjora					
Non-coking	114.27	0.00	0.00	0.00	114.27
3. Birbhum					
Non-coking	0.00	5721.44	864.57	0.00	6586.01
4. Darjeeling					
Non-coking	0.00	0.00	15.00	0.00	15.00
JHARKHAND					
5. Raniganj					
Medium coking	269.23	17.17	0.00	0.00	286.40
Semi-coking	51.40	40.00	0.00	0.00	91.40
Non-coking	1217.56	409.39	31.55	0.00	2036.30
6. Jharia					
Prime coking	4614.35	698.71	0.00	0.00	5313.06
Medium coking	4360.48	1803.52	0.00	0.00	6164.00
Non-coking	6153.14	1799.86	0.00	0.00	7953.00
7. East Bokaro					
Medium coking	3281.70	3841.21	863.32	0.00	7986.23
Non-coking	104.07	62.50	0.00	0.00	166.57
8. West Bokaro					
Medium coking	3446.51	1294.68	33.66	0.00	4774.85
Non-coking	274.38	14.03	0.00	0.00	288.41
9. Ramgarh					
Medium coking	531.52	37.55	0.00	0.00	569.07
Semi-coking	171.94	431.55	53.45	0.00	656.94
Non-coking	7.13	26.20	4.60	0.00	37.93
10. North Karanpura					
Medium coking	508.67	2799.14	413.43	0.00	3721.24
Non-coking	8990.75	4115.47	1451.53	0.00	14557.75
11. South Karanpura					
Medium coking	0.00	513.40	296.23	0.00	809.63
Non-coking	3230.09	1354.26	1183.99	0.00	5768.34
12. Auranga					
Non-coking	352.05	2141.65	503.41	0.00	2997.11
13. Hutar					
Non-coking	190.79	26.55	32.48	0.00	249.82
14. Daltonganj					
Non-coking	83.86	60.10	0.00	0.00	143.96
15. Deogarh					
Non-coking	326.24	73.60	0.00	0.00	399.84

(Continued)

Table 15.4.1 (Continued)

State/Coalfield/Type of coal	Proved	Indicated	Inferred (Exploration)	Inferred (Mapping)	Total
16. Rajmahal					
Non-coking	3211.18	11219.06	1691.82	0.00	16122.06
BIHAR					
17. Rajmahal	0.00	0.00	160.00	0.00	160.00
Non-coking					
MADHYA PRADESH					
18. Johilla	185.08	104.09	32.83	0.00	322.00
Non-coking					
19. Umaria					
Non-coking	177.70	3.59	0.00	0.00	181.29
20. Pench-Kanhan					
Medium coking	107.83	400.01	158.58	0.00	666.42
Non-coking	1357.95	478.65	533.55	0.00	2370.15
21. Pathakhera					
Non-coking	290.80	88.13	68.00	0.00	446.93
22. Gurgunda					
Non-coking	0.00	47.39	0.00	0.00	47.39
23. Mohpani					
Non-coking	7.83	0.00	0.00	0.00	7.83
24. Sohagpur					
Medium coking	246.66	1160.10	114.25	0.00	1521.01
Non-coking	1504.90	4304.77	78.87	0.00	5888.54
25. Singrauli					
Non-coking	6532.68	5795.61	1893.25	0.00	14221.54
CHHATTISGARH					
26. Sohagpur					
Non-coking	94.30	10.08	0.00	0.00	104.38
27. Sonhat					
Semi-coking	70.77	99.25	0.00	0.00	170.02
Non-coking	128.72	2364.61	1.89	0.00	2495.22
28. Jhilimili					
Non-coking	228.20	38.90	0.00	0.00	267.10
29. Chirimiri					
Non-coking	320.33	10.83	31.00	0.00	362.16
30. Bisrampur					
Non-coking	1010.90	603.80	0.00	0.00	1614.70
31. East of Bisrampur					
Non-coking	0.00	164.82	0.00	0.00	164.82
32. Lakhanpur					
Non-coking	455.88	3.35	0.00	0.00	459.23
33. Panchbahini					
Non-coking	0.00	11.00	0.00	0.00	11.00
34. Hasdo-Arand					
Non-coking	1599.72	3665.40	263.70	0.00	5528.82

(Continued)

Table 15.4.1 (Continued)

State/Coalfield/Type of coal	Proved	Indicated	Inferred (Exploration)	Inferred (Mapping)	Total
35. Sendurgarh					
Non-coking	152.89	126.32	0.00	0.00	279.21
36. Korba					
Non-coking	5651.14	5936.50	168.02	0.00	11755.66
37. Mand-Raigarh					
Non-coking	6219.76	17699.13	2553.92	0.00	26472.81
38. Tatapani-Ramkola					
Non-coking	50.43	2587.68	209.68	0.00	2847.79
UTTAR PRADESH					
39. Singrauli					
Non-coking	884.04	177.76	0.00	0.00	1061.80
MAHARASHTRA					
40. Wardha valley					
Non-coking	3604.85	1497.52	1424.07	0.00	6526.44
41. Kamptee					
Non-coking	1276.14	1204.88	505.44	0.00	2986.46
42. Umrer-Makardhrokra					
Non-coking	308.41	0.00	160.70	0.00	469.11
43. Nand-Bander					
Non-coking	468.08	483.95	0.00	0.00	952.03
44. Bokhara					
Non-coking	10.00	0.00	20.00	0.00	30.00
ORISSA					
45. IB-River					
Non-coking	9134.52	9923.55	5139.92	0.00	24197.99
46. Talcher					
Non-coking	18656.78	27949.69	4268.16	0.00	50874.63
ANDHRA PRADESH					
47. Godavari					
Non-coking	9729.25	9670.43	3068.47	0.00	22468.15
ASSAM					
48. Singrimari					
Semi-coking	0.00	0.39	0.00	0.00	0.39
Non-coking	0.00	3.74	0.00	0.00	3.74
SIKKIM					
49. Ranjit valley					
Non-coking	0.00	58.25	42.98	0.00	101.23
Total	125315.13	142406.95	32349.73	0.00	300071.81
TERTIARY COALFIELDS					
ASSAM					
50. Makum	432.09	20.70	0.00	0.00	452.79
High Sulphur					
51. Dilli-Jeypore					
High Sulphur	32.00	22.02	0.00	0.00	54.02

(Continued)

Table 15.4.1 (Continued)

State/Coalfield/Type of coal	Proved	Indicated	Inferred (Exploration)	Inferred (Mapping)	Total
52. Mikir Hills					
High Sulphur	0.69	0.00	0.50	2.52	3.71
ARUNACHALA PRADESH					
53. Namchik-Namphuk					
High Sulphur	31.23	40.11	12.89	0.00	84.23
54. Miao Bum					
High Sulphur	0.00	0.00	0.00	6.00	6.00
MEGHALAYA					
55. Balphakram-Pendenguru					
High Sulphur	0.00	0.00	0.00	107.03	107.03
56. Siju					
High Sulphur	0.00	0.00	0.00	125.00	125.00
57. Mawlong-shella					
High Sulphur	2.17	0.00	3.83	0.00	6.00
58. Bapung					
High Sulphur	11.01	0.00	22.65	0.00	33.66
59. Jayanti hills					
High Sulphur	0.00	0.00	1.10	1.24	2.34
60. West Daranggiri					
High Sulphur	65.40	0.00	0.00	59.60	125.00
61. East Daranggiri					
High Sulphur	0.00	0.00	0.00	34.19	34.19
62. Langrin					
High Sulphur	10.46	16.51	0.00	106.19	133.16
63. Khasi Hills					
High Sulphur	0.00	0.00	0.00	10.10	10.10
NAGALAND					
64. Borjan	5.50	0.00	0.00	4.50	10.00
High Sulphur					
65. Jhanzi-Disai					
High Sulphur	2.00	0.00	0.00	0.08	2.08
66. Tuen Sang					
High Sulphur	1.26	0.00	2.00	0.00	3.26
67. Tiru Valley					
High Sulphur	0.00	0.00	6.60	0.00	6.60
NAGALAND DGM REPORT					
High Sulphur	0.00	0.00	0.00	293.47	293.47
Total	593.81	99.34	49.57	749.92	1492.64
Total Gondawana	125315.13	142406.95	32349.73	0.00	300071.81
Total Tertiary	593.81	99.34	49.57	749.92	1492.64
Grand Total	125908.94	142506.29	32399.30	749.92	301564.45

Source: Coal Inventory by CMPDI, Ranchi.

Table 15.4.2 Statewise coal resources of India.

State	Billion tonnes
Jharkhand	80.7
Orissa	75.1
Chhattisgarh	52.5
West Bengal	31.3
Madhya Pradesh	25.7
Andhra Pradesh	22.5
Maharastra	11.0
Uttar Pradesh	1.1
Meghalaya	0.6
Assam	0.5
Nagaland, Bihar, Sikkim, Arunachal Pradesh	0.6
Total	301.6

Table 15.4.3 World Proved Coal Reserves at the end of 2013 (By Principal Countries).

(In million tonnes)

Country	Anthracite & Bituminous Coal	Sub-bituminous coal & Lignite	Total
Australia	37100	39300	76400
Brazil	–	6630	6630
Canada	3474	3108	6582
China	62200	52300	114500
Colombia	6746	–	6746
Germany	48	40500	40548
India	56100	4500	60600
Indonesia	–	28017	28017
Kazakhstan	21500	12100	33600
Poland	4178	1287	5465
Russian Federation	49088	107922	157010
South Africa	30156	–	30156
Turkey	322	8380	8702
Ukraine	15351	18522	33873
USA	108501	128794	237295
Other countries	8435	36972	45407
World: Total	403199	488332	891531

Source: Indian Minerals Yearbook 2013 Published by IBM.

production (about 10%) comes from underground mining. Most mines are either semi-mechanised or mechanised. The machinery commonly deployed is drill machines, load-haul-dumper (LHD), ventilation fans, pumps for dewatering, haulage for transport, etc. In order to arrest the decline in production from a few underground mines, "mass production technology" by introducing 'continuous miner' is being practiced. Modern roof-bolting technology with "flexi-bolts" up to 5 m length; 'smart bolting'

Table 15.4.4 Production of Coal, 2012–13 (By Technology).

Technology adopted	Production in million tonnes	Percentage of total
Opencast (Total)	504.195	90.62
Mechanised	503.784	99.92
Manual	0.411	0.08
Underground (Total)	52.207	9.38
Conventional B&P	4.023	7.70
Mechanised B&P	42.119	88.68
Conventional LW	0.097	0.18
Mechanised LW	0.603	1.16
Other methods	5.365	10.28
All India: Total	556.402	

Source: Indian Minerals Yearbook 2013 Published by IBM.

Table 15.4.5 Production of Coal, 2012–13 (By Grade and Sector).

(In '000 tonnes)

Grade	Total	Pub. Sec.	Pvt. Sec.
All Grades	556402	509240	47162
Coking	51582	44274	7308
ST-I	72	72	
ST-II	1370	1370	–
W-I	260	260	–
W-II	1711	1608	103
W-III	12346	10400	1946
W-IV	35656	30397	5259
SC-I	167	167	–
Non-coking	504820	464966	39854
G1, G2, G3	12001	6361	5640
G4, G5	32781	32774	7
G6	22708	16671	6037
G7, G8	59031	55002	4029
G9, G10	125935	120640	5295
G11, G12	157301	150406	6895
G13, G14	84258	79505	4753
G15, G16, G17	10805	3607	7198

Source: Indian Minerals Yearbook 2013 Published by IBM.

for cost reduction of roof support; introduction of mechanised roof bolting using hydraulic bolts for difficult roof are new technology absorptions in Indian Underground Coal Mining. Mechanised Long wall mining (long wall powered support) has also been introduced in a limited scale which yields higher output with high percentage recovery (70–80%). In opencast mines, machinery like draglines, dozers, shovels, dumpers and graders are deployed for various operations.

Production of coal by different mining technologies employed is furnished in Table 15.4.4.

Chhattisgarh was the largest coal producing state with a share of about 21.2% followed closely by Jharkhand and Odisha with contributions of 20.0% and 19.8%, respectively, to the national output. Next in order of share in the total production were Madhya Pradesh (13.6%), Andhra Pradesh (9.6%), Maharashtra (7.0%), West Bengal (4.8%) and Uttar Pradesh (2.9%). The remaining 1.1% of coal production was accounted for by Arunachal Pradesh, Assam, Jammu & Kashmir and Meghalaya. Table 15.4.5 shows the production of all types of coal during 2012–13 by grades and sectors.

Of the total production of coal, 9.3% was coking coal and the rest 90.7% was non-coking coal. Bulk of the coking coal production i.e. about 85.8% was from the public sector. Out of the total production of coking coal in India, bulk quantity i.e. 99% was produced in Jharkhand followed by Madhya Pradesh with 0.6%. The remaining 0.4% was contributed by Chhattisgarh and West Bengal. Production of coking coal during 2012–13 by states and grades are given in Table 15.4.6.

91.5% of non-coking coal came from the public sector. Out of the total non-coking coal production, Chhattisgarh produced 23.3%. Next in order were Odisha (21.8%), Madhya Pradesh (15%), Jharkhand (11.9%), Andhra Pradesh (10.5%), Maharashtra (7.8%), West Bengal (5.2%) and Uttar Pradesh (3.2%). The remaining 1.3% production came from the states of Assam, Arunachal Pradesh, Jammu & Kashmir and Meghalaya. Details of Production of non-coking coal are shown in Table 15.4.7.

Thermal power plants, Iron & Steel, sponge iron and Cement are the major consuming industries for coal in India. Sizeable quantities are also consumed by the railways, collieries and as a domestic fuel. Due to electrification and dieselization programmes, the coal requirement of the Railways is declining. Data regarding consumption in these sectors are not available. However, industry-wise despatches of coal are given in Table 15.4.8.

China is the largest producer of coal and lignite in 2012 with about 46% share in total world production followed by USA (12%), India (8%), Australia (6%), Indonesia (5%), Russia (4%) and South Africa (3%). The remaining 16% of the total world coal production was from other producing countries. Australia is the world's fourth largest producer and world's leading exporter of coal.

Table 15.4.6 Production of Coking Coal, 2012–13 (By State and Grade).

(In '000 tonnes)

State	All-Grades	ST-I	ST-II	W-I	W-II	W-III	W-IV	SC-I
India	51582	72	1370	260	1711	12346	35656	167
Chhattisgarh	157	–	–	–	–	–	–	157
Jharkhand	51065	52	1370	260	1381	12346	35656	–
Madhya Pradesh	330	–	–	–	330	–	–	–
West Bengal	30	20	–	–	–	–	–	10

Source: Indian Minerals Yearbook 2013 Published by IBM.

Table 15.4.7 Production of Non-coking Coal, 2012–13 (By State and Grade).

(In '000 tonnes)

State	All-Grades	G1	G2	G3	G4	G5	G6	G7	G8	G9	G10	G11	G12	G13	G14	G15	G16	G17
India	504820	5899	480	5622	17619	15162	22708	34842	24189	66817	59118	120369	36932	81090	3168	3968	1630	5207
Andhra Pradesh	53190	0	34	0	0	686	0	7270	0	13102	172	15958	0	12522	0	2144	0	1302
Arunachal Pradesh	73	0	0	0	0	0	0	0	0	0	0	0	0	0	0	0	0	73
Assam	605	259	279	1742	67	0	0	0	0	0	0	0	0	0	0	0	0	0
Chhattisgarh	117673	0	0	0	2865	4537	2623	1100	1141	1365	9403	72079	11593	0	2454	1414	1630	3727
Jammu & Kashmir	19	0	0	1291	0	0	0	0	0	0	0	0	0	0	0	0	0	19
Jharkhand	60209	0	77	0	676	3836	6970	1601	4810	20431	3080	17282	0	0	0	69	0	86
Madya Pradesh	75618	0	0	1601	1711	2494	7218	21716	2870	1436	36295	277	0	0	0	0	0	0
Maharastra	39134	0	0	0	0	284	890	1325	7168	29064	0	0	0	62	0	341	0	0
Meghalaya	5640	5640	0	0	0	0	0	0	0	0	0	0	0	0	0	0	0	0
Odisha	110132	0	0	0	0	118	0	35	229	1307	2240	11644	25339	68506	714	0	0	0
Uttar Pradesh	16090	0	0	0	0	158	122	0	7882	0	7928	0	0	0	0	0	0	0
West Bengal	26437	0	90	988	12300	3049	4885	1795	89	112	0	3129	0	0	0	0	0	0

Source: Indian Minerals Yearbook 2013 Published by IBM.

Table 15.4.8 Despatches of Coal, 2012–13 (By Industry).

Industry	Million tonnes
Electricity	433.62
Iron & Steel	15.99
Sponge Iron	14.97
Cement	12.81
Fertilizer	2.51
Others (Chemical, base metals, paper & pulp, textile & rayon, bricks, etc.)	87.24
Total	567.14

Source: Indian Minerals Yearbook 2013 Published by IBM.

In 2012–13, exports of coal and coke from India were 2.95 and 1.12 million tones. Coal was mainly exported to Bangladesh (50%), Nepal (39%) and Bhutan & UAE (6%). Coke was exported predominantly to Bhutan (56%), Nepal (17%), Brazil (12%), and Malaysia (7%). Imports of coal and coke were 138 and 3.08 million tonnes. Coal was mainly imported from Indonesia (58%), Australia (20%) and South Africa (13%), whereas coke was imported mainly from Ukraine (29%), Japan (22%), Poland (13%), Russia (12%), Colombia (10%) and China (3%).

15.5   COAL PRODUCING ORGANIZATIONS IN INDIA

Coal India Limited (CIL) under the Ministry of Energy (Government of India) is the chief producer of coal in India. It accounts for 90% of India's coal production and has emerged as the world's largest producer. The following eight coal companies are its subsidiary companies.

1   Bharat Coking Coal Limited (BCCL)
2   Eastern Coalfields Limited (ECL)
3   Central Coalfields Limited (CCL)
4   Western Coalfields Limited (WCL)
5   South-Eastern Coalfields Limited (SECL)
6   Mahanadi Coalfields Limited (MCL)
7   Northern Coalfields Limited (NCL)
8   North-Eastern Coalfields Limited (NEC)

The Central Mine Planning and Designs Institute (CMPDI) at Ranchi is also under CIL. It is engaged in surveying, planning and designing work with a view to optimise coal production.

In addition to the Coal India Limited, The Singareni Collieries Company Limited (SCCL) is a joint venture of the Government of India and the Government of Andhra Pradesh.

Jharkhand State Mineral Development Corporation Ltd (JSMDC), Damodar Valley Corporation (DVC) and Jammu & Kashmir Minerals Ltd (JKML) are the State Government undertakings engaged in coal mining. Indian Iron and Steel Company Ltd (IISCO) steel plant of SAIL is the only public sector steel unit operating captive mines for coal. Tata Steel, Jindal Steel & Power Ltd (JSPL), Adani, Bhushan Steel, Monnet Ispat, HINDALCO and Bengal EMTA Coal Mines Ltd (BECML) are some of the major companies, operating captive mines in the private sector.

15.6   R & D INSTITUTES WORKING IN THE AREA OF COAL PREPARATION

- CSIR-Central Institute of Mining & Fuel Research, Dhanbad
- CSIR-Institute of Minerals & Materials Technology, Bhubaneswar
- CSIR-National Metallurgical Laboratory, Jamshedpur
- Central Mine Planning and Design Institute, Ranchi
- Research & Development Centre for Iron & Steel, Ranchi
- TATA R & D centre, Jamshedpur
- CSIR-North Eastern Institute of Science & Technology, Jorhat

Part B

Coal processing

Chapter 16

Coal processing

Coal Beneficiation means the separation of coal particles of low ash from the run-of-mine coal by physical and/or physico-chemical treatments. As it comes from the mine, coal is known as **Run-of-mine coal** (**ROM coal**) and consists of a range of sizes from chunks to small particles mixed with some dirt and rocks. In most cases, this ROM coal is subjected to various operations principally size reduction and screening, beneficiation (separation), and dewatering (if wet beneficiation operations are used) to meet certain market requirements as to sizes, ash, sulfur, moisture, and heating values. Coal Processing is a term that is used to designate the various operations performed on the ROM coal to prepare it for specific end uses such as feed to a coke oven or a coal-fired boiler or to a coal conversion process without destroying the physical identity of the coal. Coal Processing is recognized as a combination of science, art and engineering, recognized in its own right as a vital link between the production and marketing of coal.

The mineral matter, which gives ash after burning the coal, present in the coal is intimately associated with the coal substance in ROM coal. When ROM coal is reduced in size, all the coal particles produced will never contain the same quantity of mineral matter. Every coal particle may differ from other coal particles in its mineral matter (or ash) content. These coal particles are separated or beneficiated to obtain low ash coal particles and high ash coal particles as two products. The product of low ash coal particles is called as **clean coal**. Another term **combustibles** is also used for clean coal. The other product of high ash coal particles is called as **refuse** or **rejects**. Some times another product, medium ash coal particles called as **middling**, is also separated depending on the requirement.

The terms coal preparation, coal dressing, coal cleaning, coal washing, coal upgradation and coal concentration are also applied to the same field. All of them are synonymous terms; different terms are used in different countries and different locations. In many plants, wet gravity methods are mostly used for beneficiation of coal. Hence these plants are called as **Coal Washeries** and the low ash coal product is called as **washed coal**.

Coal Processing forms a link between coal mining and coal utilization. Coal Processing literally means increasing the commercial value of coal by suitable preparation. Originally, coal preparation was confined to the hand picking of coarse refuse from conveyor belts and the crushing and screening of coal to give the particular sizes (mainly coarse sizes) required by the market at that time. Mechanical cleaning of coal to remove much of the mineral impurity began in the second quarter of the 19th century, but it took more than 100 years for the practice to become widespread and develop into the multiple process preparation plants that are now an essential part of most mining operations. Depending on the circumstances of production and consumption in each individual case, coal preparation may involve any combination of crushing, screening and removal of a wide range of mineralogical contaminants from different coal products.

The principal coal beneficiation processes used today are oriented toward product standardization and ash reduction, with increased attention being put on sulfur reduction in some of the countries. Coal processing in commercial practice is currently limited to physical processes. In a modern coal processing plant, the coal is typically subjected to (1) size reduction and screening, (2) separation of coal from its impurities, and (3) dewatering and drying. A modern installation is carefully designed assembly of component machines for handling, screening, washing, dewatering and blending of coal and for water clarification. The function of the modern plant is to produce the maximum yield of clean coal of suitable quality for the consumer at an economic cost. Up to the present, commercial practice has largely relied on physical coal washing processes to beneficiate coals. Chemical, microbiological, and other novel coal beneficiation processes are of recent origin and still at various levels of process development.

16.1   NEED FOR COAL PROCESSING

The need for coal processing is more related to consumer demands than to the requirements of the producer, but it is also due to the development of greater environmental constraints than in the past. Coal, by its very nature, is a heterogeneous material, and coal produced from operating mines is even more variable due to the incorporation of non-coal bands, mineral aggregates and possibly a certain amount of roof and floor rock in the mined material. The introduction of mechanized, high productivity extraction methods has resulted in ROM coals that are finer, wetter and dirtier than in the past, and given rise to an increasing need to beneficiate the coal in some way before use.

Inert material associated with the coal often referred as dirt, and varies in amounts. Coal, when put on fire, does not completely burn due to the presence of dirt which will not take part in combustion. The nature and quality of dirt including its mode of association are primarily depends on

1   The sedimentation conditions prevalent during the formation of coal seam
2   The method of mining and loading adopted during the process of its extraction

The presence of dirt (mineral matter) in the coal causes so many disadvantages. Some of the ill effects of dirt in coal can be summarized as follows:

1   As a general rule, dirt in excess of specified limits effect the efficiency of utilization and the load factor and it is more so when there are wide fluctuations in the quality and quantity of dirt.
2   The useless transport of dirt along with coal and its subsequent disposal as cinder or slag also cost money and results in some loss of sensible heat.

3 In thermal power stations, excess amount of ash in feed coal not only calls for additional capital investment but also causes frequent hazards in operation and maintenance.

4 In conventional Iron and Steel metallurgy, an increase in ash content of coke by one percent over a critical limit results in decrease in production by 3% to 6% and involves an increase in coke consumption by 4% to 5%.

5 For combustion of coal in steam locomotives, the ash penalty of each percentage of ash beyond a specified or tolerable limit also becomes quite excessive and leads to uneconomic operation.

Due to the ill effects of dirt, the coal processing is now widely practiced to counteract the affect of deteriorating quality of coal or to remove excess dirt in ROM coal introduced through intensive mechanization in mines.

Apart from the fundamental need to the wide spread use of mechanized mining methods, other factors that have contributed to the increasing use of coal beneficiation and the growing sophistication of beneficiation techniques include the following:

1 The placement of more constraints on coal quality by consumers in an effort to improve the efficiency of their operations and subsequently reduce their costs.

2 The requirement by consumers for a product of consistent quality, with consistency sometimes being more important than absolute quality levels.

3 The attention focused by the community on potential pollutants from coal.

4 The ruling of governments that all coals are to be washed to yield clean coal of particular ash% depending on the environmental constraints prevailing in different countries.

5 The need for the coal producer to maximize the percentage of salable coal from the mine, and thus to obtain the maximum degree of utilization from the available coal reserves while at the same time minimizing the overall cost per ton to the consumer.

Most of the coal charged to steel plants is processed through washeries to reduce the ash content of ROM coals by about ten to fifteen percent. As regards the quality of clean coal, the steel plants desire it to be maintained at the level of 16% to 18% depending on the volatile matter content of the coal so that the ash content of the resulting coke does not normally exceed the limit of 24%. However it is not merely the ash level of the clean coal or of the blended charge to coke-ovens that matters in producing good metallurgical coke but the more vital role in coke making is exercised by the petrographic constituents of the blended charge.

In processing of non-coking coals, the bulk of which are earmarked for power stations, sophisticated beneficiation techniques applied to coking coals are not necessary but there is a need to employ simple deshaling units for removing at least a major portion of the free dirt from the run-of-mine production before the same is offered to the consumers for use. With the application of simple beneficiation techniques, the level and quality of ash in non-coking coals can not only be controlled to great extent but also a reasonable consistency in the supplies to the prospective consumers can be expected. It is equally important on the part of the bulk consumers specially power stations receiving coals from two or more sources, to provide reasonable blending facilities at their end so as to ensure consistent quality of feed to their plants in the interest of efficient operation and higher availability.

16.2 OBJECTIVES OF COAL PROCESSING

The objectives of coal processing are to reduce its ash content, reduce its sulphur and phosphorous contents which are detrimental particularly to metallurgical coals, increase its heating value, improve its coking properties, increase the fusion point of its ash by removing alkali chlorides (which is responsible for lowering the fusion point), reduce the clinkering tendency and to increase its efficiency in use.

Beneficiated coal (also called washed coal or clean coal) being low in incombustible content has following advantages:

1   more efficient combustion and higher heat evolution per unit weight of coal burned
2   maximum useful application of heat
3   lower freight and handling charges per unit of heat value for delivery from coal plant to point of consumption and for the disposal of incombustible refuse or ashes
4   greater cleanliness and less ashes to be handled, this being of particular value in domestic fuels

The following are the benefits of using beneficiated coal for power generation

• Increases generation efficiency and plant availability
• Increases equipment system capacity
• Decreases auxiliary power equipment requirements
• Reduces investment costs
• Reduces operation and maintenance (O&M) costs due to less wear and reduced costs for fuel and ash handling
• Energy conservation in the transportation sector and lower transportation costs
• Less impurities and improved coal quality
• Reduces load on the air pollution control system
• Reduces the amount of solid waste that has to be disposed off
• Reduces CO_2, NO_x, SO_x, and particulate emissions

16.3 COAL BENEFICIATION METHODS

The methods used in the beneficiation of coal are analogous in many ways to those used in the beneficiation of ores. The principles involved in coal beneficiation are similar to that of ore beneficiation. In some instances, the same machines could be used in both fields perhaps with slight modifications. An essential feature of coal beneficiation processes is that the treatment must be rapid and inexpensive, because coal is a cheap product. Accordingly, simple plants consisting of a few units, each capable of handling a large tonnage, are required.

Another factor important in coal processing is that the coal, during all stages of its handling, from mining, through beneficiation, transportation, and finally to its delivery to the consumer, must undergo a minimum of degradation because the value of coal depends on its particle size, and in general, the larger the particle size is, the better price the coal commands on the market.

Gravity separation principles form the basis of most of the coal beneficiation processes. In case of Coal Beneficiation, the valuable part, the coal, is light and the impurities to be removed by washing or cleaning are heavier whereas in beneficiation of ores, the valuable mineral is heavy and impurities (gangue) is light.

16.4 ESSENTIAL OPERATIONS IN COAL PROCESSING PLANTS

The essential operations in coal processing plants are classified as follows:

1   Screening
2   Size Reduction
3   Mechanical washing or cleaning including testing and control
4   Dewatering and Drying
5   Recovery and treatment of fines; Water clarification and circulation
6   Moving coal in the plant
7   Miscellaneous operations

The above classification should not be considered either as a sequence of operations or as a list of operations, all of which will be found in any plant, but rather as a classification convenient for the purpose of discussion.

In a beneficiation operation, the feed coal particles are separated into two products called as **clean coal** (also called **concentrate**) and **refuse** or **rejects** (also called **tailing**). The concentrate is the product contains mostly particles having low ash whereas tailing contains particles with more mineral matter i.e. having high ash. When feed coal particles contains widely varied ash content, a third product called **middling**, having ash content intermediate to that of the concentrate and tailing, is also separated.

Simple mass balance expressions are being in use for performance evaluation of beneficiation operations and controlling those operations in coal washeries.

For a two product beneficiation operation

Total mass balance of the material	$F = C + T$	(16.4.1)
Mass balance of ash	$Ff = Cc + Tt$	(16.4.2)

where
   F = Quantity of feed coal
   C = Quantity of Clean coal (or concentrate) obtained from a beneficiation operation
   T = Quantity of refuse (or tailing) obtained from a beneficiation operation
   f = fraction (or percent) of ash in the feed

p = fraction (or percent) of ash in clean coal (or concentrate)

u = fraction (or percent) of ash in refuse (or tailing)

For a three product beneficiation operation

Total mass balance of the material $F = C + M + T$ (16.4.3)

Mass balance of ash $Ff = Cc + Mm + Tt$ (16.4.4)

where

M = Quantity of middling obtained from a beneficiation operation

m = fraction (or percent) of ash in the middling

All others are as used in two product beneficiation operation

Chapter 17

Screening of coal

Screening is an operation used for separation of particles according to their sizes. Sieving and screening are distinguished by the fact that sieving is a batch process used almost exclusively for test purposes, whereas screening is a continuous process and is used mainly on an industrial scale. Sieves are manufactured with definite dimension and standard aperture sizes. Screens can be manufactured with any dimension and any aperture sizes as per the requirement. In Industrial screening, the particles of various sizes are fed to the screen surface. The material passing through the screen aperture is called **underflow** (undersize or fines) while the material retained on the screen surface is called **overflow** (oversize or coarse).

Screening operations form a very important part of modern coal processing plants of all types. The ROM coal from the mines having assorted sizes with top size of about 1 metre and bottom size 0, cannot be fed to any machine for size reduction or any washer for upgradation. It is, therefore, necessary to screen the coal before size reduction. The crushed coals need to be passed through a number of screens to obtain coals of various size fractions for further treatment by the washing systems. Grading the coal by screening may be the chief market preparation in many localities. Screening in beneficiation plants may be necessary in various parts of the flowsheet as follows:

1   Screening preliminary to beneficiation
2   Grading coal preparatory to marketing
3   Rescreening graded sizes to remove degradation and to ensure uniformity in grading

Screening is generally used for dry treatment of coarse material. Dry screening can be done down to 10 mesh with reasonable efficiency. Wet screening is usually applied to materials from 10 mesh down to 30 mesh (0.5 mm) but the developments in the Sieve Bend Screen have made the wet screening possible at the 50 micron size.

17.1   PRELIMINARY SIZING

Generally screening is the first operation in the plant flowsheet. In the coal preparation plant, screening may be used for the following purposes:

1   Separation of coarse coal for hand picking and for breaking to smaller sizes
2   Removal of fine coal before a size reduction step.

3   Separation of raw coal into two or more sizes for beneficiation in separate machines
4   By-passing fines or other sizes around the beneficiation operations or discarding them entirely
5   Recovering solids from a slurry
6   Recovering the separating medium used in coal beneficiation processes
7   Dewatering
8   Grading the coal into various trade sizes, each size to be beneficiated separately

17.2   GRADING

Separation of the various trade sizes may be carried out by screening before beneficiation in some cases, particularly if it is of advantage to have a closely sized feed to the beneficiation machines used, but it has now become more common to grade the coal finally after beneficiation. The latter method usually yields more uniform sizes with less undersize, as there is a minimum of handling the coal and hence a minimum of size degradation after the grading. The value of the coal also depends on the size of the coal. Each size range has a trade name. The trade names and respective size ranges for coal are shown in Table 17.2. As the size ranges shown are not standardized, they vary from country to country. Size ranges are also not same for all types of coals in a country.

17.2.1   Size specifications in coal preparation practice

The following are the terms and definitions of coals of different sizes used in coal preparation practice: (Size specifications vary from country to country).

1   **Large coal (600–150 mm):** Fraction of run-of-mine coal or crushed raw coal passing through 600 mm screen but retained on 150 mm screen.
2   **Coarse coal (150–25 mm):** Fraction of run-of-mine coal or crushed raw coal passing through 150 mm screen but retained on 25 mm screen.

Table 17.2 Trade names of different sizes of coal.

Trade names	Nominal size range inch	Trade names	Nominal size range inch
Run-of-mine	20 to 0	Pea	$\frac{13}{16}$ to $\frac{9}{16}$
Steam	10 to 1		
Broken	$4\frac{3}{8}$ to $3\frac{1}{4}$	Buckwheat	$\frac{9}{16}$ to $\frac{5}{16}$
Egg	$3\frac{1}{4}$ to $2\frac{7}{16}$	Rice	$\frac{5}{16}$ to $\frac{3}{16}$
Stove	$2\frac{7}{16}$ to $1\frac{5}{8}$	Barley	$\frac{3}{16}$ to $\frac{3}{32}$
Rubble	2 to 1	Slack	$\frac{3}{4}$ to 0
Chestnut or Nut	$1\frac{5}{8}$ to $\frac{13}{16}$	Dust	$\frac{1}{2}$ to 0

3 **Small coal (25–0.5 mm)**: Fraction of run-of-mine coal or crushed raw coal passing through 25 mm screen but retained on 0.5 mm screen.
4 **Fine coal**: Fraction of run-of-mine coal or crushed raw coal passing through 0.5 mm square mesh sieve.
5 **Ultra-fine coal**: Fraction of fine coal passing through 53 micron sieve.
6 **Slime**: Extremely fine or ultra-fine particles forming stable suspension with a portion of circulating water or adhering as thin film to the washed products.
7 **Slurry**: Fine coal remaining mixed in various proportions in the circulating water of a plant.

17.3 SCREENING OF COAL

Consider a simplified screen as in Fig. 17.3.1.

The material is fed at one end of the screen. Screening is affected by continuously presenting the material to be sized (the feed) to the screen surface which provides a relative motion with respect to the feed. The screen surface can be fixed or movable. Agitation of the bed of material must be sufficient to expose all the particles to the screen apertures several times during the travel of the material from feed end to the discharge end of the screen. At the same time the screen must act as a transporter for moving retained particles from the feed end to the discharge end. Particles of size more than the aperture size of the screen are retained and particles of size less than the aperture size of the screen are passed through the apertures. Both the oversize and undersize particles are collected as overflow and underflow separately.

In coal screening, it is desirable to keep breakage and production of fines during screening at a minimum. And also, particularly for grading purposes, accuracy of sizing may be of somewhat greater importance than in ore screening, as the coal consumer may insist on getting a coal with the percentages of oversize and undersize held within rather narrow limits.

The types of screens used for coal are fixed bar grizzlies and moving screens i.e. revolving Trommel, shaking or jigging screens and vibrating screens. Another stationary screen used for fines is sieve bend also known as Dutch State Mines (DSM) screen.

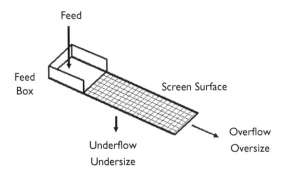

Figure 17.3.1 Simplified screen.

17.3.1   Fixed Bar Grizzly

It consists of parallel bars set at an angle to the horizontal so that the coal delivered to their higher ends slides down over them by gravity. The spacing of the bars fixes the sizes of the products. The smaller coal passes between them and is collected in a hopper. The larger sizes slide off at the lower end. The cross section of the bars is usually wedge-shaped, with the thicker edge at the top. They are simple and cheap to install and operate, have large capacities, require no power and little attention, and withstand rough service. But the sizing is not accurate and breaking of the coal in passing down the screen is sometimes excessive. The disadvantage of fixed bar grizzly is that long, flat pieces, pass through the bars, and with wet coal manual raking may be required to screen the coal and keep it moving. Fixed bar grizzlies are used for sizing coarse coal.

17.3.2   Revolving Trommel

Revolving trammel screens consist of punched plates or wire mesh, bend to form a cylinder, which is rotated about its axis. The speed of rotation is 8–30 rpm. The axis is set at a slight inclination to the horizontal so that when coal is fed at the upper end, oversize material will traverse the screen longitudinally whilst undersize passes through the holes. Trommels can be made to deliver several sized products by having smaller apertures at the feed end and coarser apertures at the discharge end. The main problem is that the fine screen wears quickly, as the whole of the feed must be fed on to it.

   The problem of undue wear on the fine screen trammel is overcome in the compound trammel which has a series of concentric cylinders, with the coarsest screen at the centre, such that the coarsest fraction is removed first. In this compound trammel, it is difficult to observe failure of the inner screens and also difficult to replace when worn. Although trommels are cheap, vibration free and robust, they have poor capacities since part of the screen surface only is in use at any one time and they blind very easily.

17.3.3   Shaking or Jigging screens

Shaking screens have a reciprocating movement mechanically induced in the horizontal direction and are mounted either horizontally or with a gentle slope. Shaking screens consist of rectangular plate, perforated with holes of the required size and shape, fixed in a suitable frame. The screen is mounted on flexible supports and is connected to an eccentric, or other driving mechanism which moves the screen backwards and forwards a distance of between 2 and 6 inches about 100 times per a minute. Usually, the supports are arranged so that during the forward stroke the motion carries the screening surface and the particles on it slightly upwards; on the return stroke, the screen moves backwards and slightly downwards, thus withdrawing itself from under the particles. This motion together with the slope of the screen, causes the particles to slide jerkily in contact with the screen. Screens may be superimposed or may be arranged end to end so as to prepare a number of different grades. Screens of this type are efficient for sizes down to about ¼ inch. They are accessible, cheap to operate, and have a high capacity; in consequence, they are widely used dry in modern colliery practice. They are used when headroom and a conveying action are required.

17.3.4 Vibrating screens

Vibrating screens are flat screens made of wire mesh and mounted at a slope which vary from 16° to 26°. The range of screen aperture sizes is 10 inch to 100 mesh. Vibration is induced vertically either by the rotation of a mechanical reciprocating device applied to the casing or by electric devices operating directly on the screen.

In mechanically vibrated screens, vibrations are produced by Cam and spring, Eccentric or Unbalanced flywheels. Mechanically vibrated screens are most widely used for coarse sizing.

Vibration in the finer screening ranges is often produced by unbalanced weights or flywheels attached to the drive shaft. The vibrator generates an elliptical motion, slanting forward at the feed end; a circular motion at the centre; and an elliptical motion, slanting backwards at the discharge end. Forward motion at the feed end serves to move oversize material rapidly out of the feed zone to keep the bed as thin as possible. This action facilitates passage of fines which should be completely removed in the first one-third of the screen length. As the oversize bed thins down, near the centre of the screen, the motion gradually changes to the circular pattern to slow down the rate of travel of the solid. At the discharge end, the oversize and remaining near-size materials are subjected to the increasingly retarded effect of the backward elliptical motion. This allows the near size material more time to find openings in the screen surface.

Electrically vibrated screens, such as Hummer screen, operate with a high-frequency motion of very small throw, created by a moving magnet activated by alternating current. The electromagnetic vibrator is mounted above and connected directly to the screening surface. The high speed vibrating screen finds favour for separating fine sizes on account of its high throughput of difficult material.

Vibrating screens are used principally in making separations of 3/8 inch coal or less. By the use of screen with two or three decks, each with a different mesh, several sizes of coal can be produced. Table 17.3.4 shows typical applications of vibrating screens in coal processing plants.

17.3.5 DSM Sieve Bend

The sieve bend (Fig. 17.3.5), developed by the Dutch States Mines in the early 1950s, is a stationary curved screen composed of horizontal wedge bars oriented at right angles to the line of flow. The screen surface is curved in a 60° arc at a radius between 20–60 inch. The feed end of the sieve is tangent to the vertical so that discharge end is elevated 30° from the horizontal for a 60° sieve bend. Oversize product tends to slow down at this end, contributing to dewatering.

In operation, the feed slurry is introduced through a feed chamber mounted at the top of the screen and is distributed over the top end of the screen surface. Feed slurry enters tangentially to the upper surface in a direction perpendicular to the openings between wedge bars. This feed slurry action on the concave screen surface imparts centrifugal action in addition to the gravitational force.

Liquid and undersize particles pass through the openings while dewatered over-size particles flows on down the screen. Each wedge bar appears to act as a knife

Table 17.3.4 Vibrating-Screen Applications in Coal Processing Plants [34].

Type	No. of decks	Installation angle	Aperture	Screen deck type	Accessories
Run-of-mine scalper	Single	17°–25°	6 in.	Manganese skid bars, AR perforated plate with skid bars	Feed box with liners, extra high side plates, drive guard enclosures
Raw-coal sizing screen	Double	17°–25°	1 in. / 5/16 in.	AR perforated plate, polyurethane, rubber / Polyurethane, wire 304 stainless steel profile deck rubber	Dust enclosures, drive guard enclosures / Feed box with liners drive guard enclosures
Pre-wet screen	Double	Horizontal	1 in. / 1 mm	Wire, polyurethane, rubber / Stainless steel profile deck, polyurethane	Water spray bar, side plate drip angles, drive guard enclosures, feed box liners
Dense-medium drain and rinse screen (coarse coal)	Double	Horizontal	1 in. / 1 mm	Wire, polyurethane, rubber / 304 stainless steel profile deck, polyurethane	Side plate drip angles, spray bars, shower box cross flow screen or sieve bend, drip lip angles, drive guard enclosures
Dewatering screen (coarse coal)	Single	Horizontal	1 mm	304 stainless steel profile deck, polyurethane	Sieve bend or cross flow screen, dam, discharge drip lip angles, drive guard enclosures
Desliming screen	Single	Horizontal	0.5 mm	304 stainless steel profile deck, polyurethane	Sieve bend or cross flow screen, spray bars, shower box, drive guard enclosures
Classifying screen (fine coal)	Single	28°	100 mesh	Stainless steel woven wire sandwich screens	Three-way slurry distributor and feed system
Dense-medium drain and rinse screen (fine coal)	Single	Horizontal	0.5 mm	304 stainless steel profile deck, polyurethane	Sieve bend or cross flow screen, spray bars, shower box, drip lip angles, drive guard enclosures
Dewatering screen (fine coal)	Single	Horizontal or 27°–29°	0.5 mm	304 stainless steel profile deck or woven wire, rubber, polyurethane	Sieve bend or cross flow screen, spray bars, dam, drip lip angles, drive guard enclosures

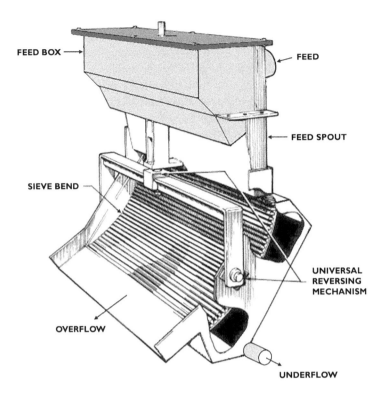

FEED BOX

FEED

FEED SPOUT

SIEVE BEND

UNIVERSAL
REVERSING
MECHANISM

OVERFLOW

UNDERFLOW

Figure 17.3.5 Sieve Bend.

on the underside of the passing slurry. A layer of liquid and undersize particles is sliced off and directed downward through the slot. This slicing action produces an undersize particle which is approximately one half the dimension of the space between the bars.

Sieve bends make a relatively sharp separation at ½ and 2/3 the slot width. This feature is particularly advantageous because it practically eliminates blinding of the screen surface. Sieve bend is gaining wide popularity and it is used in fine coal circuits, especially when processing dilute suspensions of particles up to 2 mm.

17.4   SCREEN SURFACES

Perforated screen plate is used for coarse screening where long service life is a requirement. The openings may be square, rectangular, hexagonal, or round. Round-hole punched plate is commonly used on coal shakers for most purposes. The screens can be made of steel, stainless steel, or rubber coated steel.

Lip screens are used considerably for removing degradation and also to some extent for primary screening. Lip screens have long slotted openings which diverge or widen in the direction of flow of material across the plate. The plate is bent downward at the end of each row of slots to form a step, so that particles which tend to become wedged in the slots are freed on reaching the lower ends of the slots. Where applicable, lip screens have the advantages of high percentage opening and high capacity in small area, reduced tendency to blind, and low coal degradation. However, sizing is not so accurate as with round hole surfaces.

Woven wire cloth has a wide selection of apertures from 5 inch to 500 mesh. The screens can be manufactured from a wide variety of metals and alloys. For coarse screen sizes, steel and high-carbon steel are the preferred choices. For finer sizes, stainless steels are often used because of their resistance to corrosion. Square or rectangular weaving are the two most common screen types. The square mesh gives the best control of size but can be prone to blinding. The rectangular opening screen has less tendency to blind with coal that is difficult to screen. Woven wire and wedge wire find considerable application in the screening and dewatering of fines.

Plastic screens have been developed using rubber and urethane materials. The screens have an extended life over standard screens, although the cost is higher. Advantages claimed are fewer tendencies to blind and uniformity of screen openings throughout the life of the screen.

Screening may be assisted by water sprays or by running water, particularly when applied to products from heavy media separation operations. Here, the process is basically a rinsing operation, intended to wash the medium off the coal and through the screen so that it can ultimately be recovered for re-use.

Screens have gradually become larger and have been designed to have a higher capacity, with an emphasis also on improved screening efficiencies and greater ease of maintenance and replacement. In recent years, polyurethane and rubber decked screens, supported on a steel frame have been introduced. Several of the screens contain replaceable panels and segments to reduce replacement costs, especially when wear is concentrated in particular parts of the screen.

Screening is performed either dry or wet. Wet screening is superior, adhering fines are easily washed off, and it avoids the dust problem. But the cost of dewatering and drying of the products becomes more.

The following are some terms used for screens in coal washing practice according to the purpose:

1   **Raw coal screen:** used to divide run-of-mine coal into two or more sizes for further treatment or disposal; usually employed to remove the largest pieces for crushing.
2   **Dewatering screen:** used to separate water from solids
3   **Desliming screen:** used to remove slimes from coarse coal.
4   **De-mediuming screen, De-pulping screen, medium-draining screen, Medium recovery screen:** used to drain the separating medium.
5   **Sizing screen:** used to divide the product i.e. washed coal into a range of sizes.
6   **Check screen, Oversize control screen:** used to prevent oversize coal to feed into next operation.
7   **Undersize control screen:** used to remove undersize coal from a product.

17.5 FACTORS AFFECTING THE RATE OF SCREENING

A number of factors determine the rate at which particles pass through a screen surface and they can be divided into two groups: those related to particle properties and those dependent on the machine and its operation. Some important factors are:

A Material factors
    1 Bulk density of the material
    2 Size and size distribution of the particles
    3 Size of the particle relative to the aperture
    4 Shape of the particle
    5 Moisture content of the material
B Machine factors
    1 Size of the aperture
    2 Shape of the aperture
    3 Size of the screen surface
    4 Percent opening area
    5 Angle of incidence of the particle on the screen surface
    6 Speed at which the particle strikes the screen surface
    7 Thickness of the material on the screen surface
    8 Blinding of the screen surface
    9 Type of screening, i.e., wet or dry screening
   10 Type of motion given to the screen surface
   11 Slope of the screen deck
   12 Mechanical design for supporting and tightening the screen deck

17.6 THE CHOICE OF A SCREEN

Some of the factors that affect the choice of a screen are listed below:

- Size distribution of the coal to be screened.
- Density of the coal
- Size at which the coal must be screened
- Moisture content of the feed if dry screening must be done
- The reasonable screening efficiency required (this should typically not exceeding 95%).
- Nature of the coal, i.e. it is flaky or wedge-shaped, etc.
- The screening duty i.e. sizing, dewatering, drain & rinse, desliming, etc.

17.7 SCREEN EFFICIENCY

A screen is said to behave perfectly if, in a mixture of different sizes of materials, all material of a particular size less than the screen aperture is separated from the mix. In general, absolute separation of different sized particles using a screen is difficult as it involves probabilities of movement of particles at different stages that may be difficult to determine. Hence it is necessary to express the efficiency of the process.

Screen efficiency (often called the effectiveness of a screen) is a measure of the success of a screen in closely separating oversize and undersize materials. There is no standard method for defining the screen efficiency. Depending on whether one is interested in removing oversize or undersize material, screening efficiencies may be defined in a number of ways.

Screen efficiency can be calculated based on the amount of material recovered at a given size. In an industrial screening operation, it is to be specified whether the required material is oversize or undersize or both.

For the oversize material,

$$\text{Screen efficiency} = \eta = \frac{\text{Weight of actual oversize material present in the feed}}{\text{Weight of overflow material obtained from the screen}}$$

For the undersize material,

$$\text{Screen efficiency} = \eta = \frac{\text{Weight of underflow material obtained from the screen}}{\text{Weight of actual undersize material present in the feed}}$$

In an industrial screen, if there are no broken or deformed apertures and screen is perfectly made, no single coarse particle coarser than the size of aperture pass through. Therefore above definitions are applicable under such assumed conditions. In reality, some coarse particles, may be less in quantity, will report to underflow fraction. Under such cases equations for efficiency can be derived by writing mass balance equations on the screen as follows:

Total mass balance of the material	$F = P + U$	(17.7.1)
Mass balance of oversize material	$Ff = Pp + Uu$	(17.7.2)
Mass balance of undersize material	$F(1-f) = P(1-p) + U(1-u)$	(17.7.3)

where

  F = Amount of material in the feed
  P = Amount of overflow material obtained from the screen
  U = Amount of underflow material obtained from the screen
  f = fraction of oversize material in the feed
  p = fraction of oversize material in the overflow obtained from the screen
  u = fraction of oversize material in the underflow obtained from the screen

On computation of above, we get $\dfrac{P}{F} = \dfrac{f-u}{p-u}$ and $\dfrac{U}{F} = \dfrac{p-f}{p-u}$

The recovery of oversize material into the screen overflow is referred as Screen Efficiency (or Screen Effectiveness), η_p, based on the oversize material

$$\eta_p = \frac{Pp}{Ff} = \frac{p(f-u)}{f(p-u)} \tag{17.7.4}$$

The recovery of undersize material into the screen underflow is referred as Screen Efficiency (or Screen Effectiveness), η_u, based on the undersize material

$$\eta_u = \frac{U(1-u)}{F(1-f)} = \frac{(1-u)(p-f)}{(1-f)(p-u)} \tag{17.7.5}$$

A combined overall efficiency, or overall effectiveness, η, is then obtained by multiplying the above two equations together

$$\eta = \eta_p \times \eta_u = \frac{p(f-u)(1-u)(p-f)}{f(p-u)^2(1-f)} \tag{17.7.6}$$

If there are no broken or deformed apertures and screen is perfectly made, no single coarse particle will pass through the screen, i.e., u = 0. Then the formula for fines recovery, η_u, and the formula for overall efficiency, η, both reduce to

$$\eta_u = \eta = \frac{p-f}{p(1-f)} \tag{17.7.7}$$

This formula is widely used and implies that recovery of the coarse material in the overflow is 100%.

If f, p, and u are expressed in terms of the fractions of undersize material in feed, overflow and underflow respectively, the following are the formulae:

Total mass balance of the material $\qquad\qquad F = P + U \qquad\qquad$ (17.7.8)

Mass balance of undersize material $\qquad\qquad Ff = Pp + Uu \qquad\qquad$ (17.7.9)

Mass balance of oversize material $\qquad F(1-f) = P(1-p) + U(1-u) \qquad$ (17.7.10)

On computation of above, we get

$$\frac{P}{F} = \frac{f-u}{p-u} \quad \text{and} \quad \frac{U}{F} = \frac{p-f}{p-u}$$

The recovery of oversize material into the screen overflow is referred as Screen Efficiency (or Screen Effectiveness), η_p, based on the oversize material

$$\eta_p = \frac{P(1-p)}{F(1-f)} = \frac{(1-p)(f-u)}{(1-f)(p-u)} \tag{17.7.11}$$

The recovery of undersize material into the screen underflow is referred as Screen Efficiency (or Screen Effectiveness), η_u, based on the undersize material

$$\eta_u = \frac{Uu}{Ff} = \frac{u(p-f)}{f(p-u)} \tag{17.7.12}$$

A combined overall efficiency, or overall effectiveness, η, is then obtained by multiplying the above two equations together

$$\eta = \eta_p \times \eta_u = \frac{u(u-f)(1-p)(f-p)}{f(u-p)^2(1-f)} \tag{17.7.13}$$

If there are no broken or deformed apertures and screen is perfectly made, all underflow particles are undersize particles i.e., u = 1. Then the formula for fines recovery, η_u, and the formula for overall efficiency, η, both reduce to

$$\eta_u = \eta = \frac{f-p}{f(1-p)} \tag{17.7.14}$$

These formulae do not give an absolute value of the efficiency, as no allowance is made for the difficulty of the separation. A feed composed mainly of particles of a size near to that of the screen aperture – **near mesh material (near size material)** – presents a more difficult separation than a feed composed mainly of very coarse and very fine particles with a screen aperture intermediate between them. In such cases, it is proposed to define the efficiency as the ratio of the near mesh material taken out by the screen to the near mesh material present in the feed.

17.8   ILLUSTRATIVE EXAMPLES

Illustrative example 17.8.1: *Anthracite coal from a pulverization unit has been found to contain 80% by weight of fine material. In order to remove these fines, it is screened using 1.8 mm screen. If the weight percent of +1.8 mm material in oversize and undersize products are 40% and 10% respectively, estimate the effectiveness of the screen.*

Solution:

Fraction of +1.8 mm material in the feed = f = 1–0.8 = 0.2
Fraction of +1.8 mm material in the overflow product = p = 0.4
Fraction of +1.8 mm material in the underflow product = u = 0.1

Efficiency (effectiveness) of the screen $= \eta = \dfrac{p(f-u)(1-u)(p-f)}{f(p-u)^2(1-f)}$

$$= \frac{0.4(0.2-0.1)(1-0.1)(0.4-0.2)}{0.2(0.4-0.1)^2(1-0.2)}$$

$$= 0.5 \Rightarrow 50\%$$

Alternatively

Fraction of –1.8 mm material in the feed = f = 0.8
Fraction of –1.8 mm material in the overflow product = p = 0.6
Fraction of –1.8 mm material in the underflow product = u = 0.9

Efficiency (effectiveness) of the screen $= \eta = \dfrac{u(u-f)(1-p)(f-p)}{f(u-p)^2(1-f)}$

$$= \frac{0.9(0.9-0.8)(1-0.6)(0.8-0.6)}{0.8(0.9-0.6)^2(1-0.8)}$$

$$= 0.5 \Rightarrow 50\%$$

Illustrative example 17.8.2: *A coal is screened through a 1.5 mm screen to obtain +1.5 mm fraction. The size analysis of feed, overflow and underflow is given in Table 17.8.2.*

Table 17.8.2 Size analysis of feed, overflow and underflow for illustrative example 17.8.2.

Screen size mm	Weight percent retained this size		
	Feed	Overflow	Underflow
3.3	3.5	7.0	—
2.3	13.5	36.0	—
1.5	33.0	37.0	15.0
1.0	22.7	13.0	43.0
0.8	16.0	4.0	25.0
0.6	5.4	3.0	8.0
0.4	2.1	—	3.0
0.2	1.8	—	2.0
−0.2	2.0	—	4.0

Calculate the effectiveness of the screen.

Solution:

Fraction of +1.5 mm material in the feed = f = 3.5 + 13.5 + 33.0 = 50% ⇒ 0.5

Fraction of +1.5 mm material in the overflow product = p = 7.0 + 36.0 + 37.0 = 80% ⇒ 0.8

Fraction of +1.5 mm material in the underflow product = u = 15% ⇒ 0.15

Efficiency (effectiveness) of the screen = $\eta = \dfrac{p(f-u)(1-u)(p-f)}{f(p-u)^2(1-f)}$

$$= \frac{0.8(0.5-0.15)(1-0.15)(0.8-0.5)}{0.5(0.8-0.15)^2(1-0.5)}$$

$$= 0.676 \Rightarrow 67.6\%$$

Illustrative example 17.8.3: *Analysis of vibrating screen's products is given in Table 17.8.3.*

Table 17.8.3 Analysis of vibrating screen's products for illustrative example 17.8.3.

Analysis	Vibrating screen products		
	+ 1/4"	− 1/4" + 1/8"	− 1/8"
	Wt in kg	Wt in kg	Wt in kg
+ 1/4"	6.0	—	—
− 1/4" + 1/8"	0.75	5.5	0.1
− 1/8"	0.25	0.5	6.9

Calculate:

    a   *Recovery of the fraction –1/4"+1/8" material*
    b   *Percentage removal of +1/4" and –1/8" fractions*
    c   *Efficiency of separating the fraction –1/4"+1/8"*

Solution:

a   Since recovery of the fraction –1/4"+1/8" fraction is to be calculated, the other two fractions +1/4" and –1/8" are to be treated as rejects.

Weight of +1/4" fraction   = 7.0 kg;
Weight of –1/8" fraction   = 7.0 kg;
Weight of –1/4"+1/8" fraction = 6.0 kg;
Weight of feed = 7+7+6   = 20.0 kg;

$F = 20$ kg; $P = 6$ kg; $U = 7 + 7 = 14$ kg;

$$f = \frac{0.75 + 5.5 + 0.1}{20} = 0.3175; \quad p = \frac{5.5}{6} = 0.917; \quad u = \frac{0.75 + 0.1}{14} = 0.0607;$$

$$\text{Recovery of} -1/4'' + 1/8'' \text{ fraction} = \frac{Pp}{Ff} = \frac{6 \times 0.917}{20 \times 0.3175} = 0.8665 \Rightarrow 86.65\%$$

b   Percent removal of +1/4" and –1/8" fraction is

$$\frac{U(1-u)}{F(1-f)} \times 100 = \frac{14(1-0.0607)}{20(1-0.3175)} \times 100 = 96.34\%$$

c   Efficiency of separating the fraction –1/4"+1/8" is

$$\frac{Pp}{Ff} \times \frac{U(1-u)}{F(1-f)} \times 100 = 0.8665 \times 96.34 = 83.48\%$$

17.9 PROBLEMS FOR PRACTICE

17.9.1: *A screen of 2 mm opening is used to remove coarser size from a coal consists of 80% of –2 mm. If the weight percent of +2 mm material in overflow and underflow products of a screen are 40% and 10% respectively, estimate the effectiveness of the screen.*   *[50%]*

17.9.2: *A coal is being fed to a double deck vibrating screen for separation. The desired product is –40+60 mesh fraction. A 40 mesh and a 60 mesh screens are therefore used. The feed is introduced on the 40 mesh screen. From the sieve analysis of the feed and the three products shown in Table 17.9.2, calculate the effectiveness of the double deck screen in separating –40+60 mesh fraction.*

Table 17.9.2 Sieve analysis of feed and three products for problem 17.9.2.

Mesh	Feed	Oversize from 40 mesh screen	Oversize from 60 mesh screen	Undersize from 60 mesh screen
		Mass fraction		
−10 + 20	0.097	0.197	0.026	0.0005
−20 + 30	0.186	0.389	0.039	0.0009
−30 + 40	0.258	0.337	0.322	0.0036
−40 + 60	0.281	0.066	0.526	0.3490
−60 + 85	0.091	0.005	0.061	0.2990
−85 + 100	0.087	0.006	0.026	0.3470

[36.6%]

17.9.3: *Coal containing 45% of −0.5 mm coal is screened on 0.5 mm screen at the rate of 700 tons per day. If 280 tons per day of undersize is obtained and it contains no oversize, determine the efficiency of the screen.* [88.89%]

Chapter 18

Size reduction of coal

The particles of run-of-mine coal may be up to 1 m in diameter when mined in open cast and up to about 30 cm in diameter when mined underground. The coal must be reduced in size before beneficiation. The optimum size is generally determined by float and sink test to assess the size necessary for effective liberation of the coal from any shale particles.

Liberation is the process of releasing the individual components in the composite particles to form separate homogeneous fragments of coal and shale. The fragments in broken coal may include homogeneous particles made up entirely of coal or entirely of shale, and composite particles made up of coal and shale layers firmly bound together. Homogeneous particles are more readily separated from each other than composite particles. Composite particles normally exhibit intermediate characteristics and may be expected in a middling fraction.

The degree of liberation may be defined as the proportion of liberated or free particles in relation to the total material. This value generally increases as the size of the particles present is reduced, partly as a result of preferential breakage along the planes of contact between components and partly because composites are less likely to occur in smaller sized materials.

Large coal is turned into more readily usable sizes by crushing and breaking. In general, the term crushing is applied to an indiscriminate reduction in size whilst breaking implies size reduction in a machine designed to give the maximum possible yield of the desired sizes. The crux of the problem of size reduction of coal is to produce minimum fines.

Further size reduction depends on the proposed use or uses for the coal. For example, for pulverized coal power plants, as a rough general rule, the coal is ground or pulverized to 80% passing 200 mesh (75 microns) before it is blown into the boiler furnace as a coal-air suspension.

When it is required to beneficiate the coal before use, the stages of crushing and pulverization from ROM coal to end use are integrated with the coal beneficiation processes. Since different beneficiation processes work better with different ranges of coal size and the degree of beneficiation possible is intimately connected with the size of the coal, much information is required concerning the size distributions produced by different types of machines and how these can be modified by different ways of operating the machines.

18.1   CRUSHING OF COAL

Coal breaking and crushing may serve one or more of the following purposes:

1   Reduction of coarse portion of run-of-mine coal to smaller sizes prior to beneficiation operations, when production of coarse, raw or hand picked lump sizes is not desired.
2   Reduction of hand picked lump coal to smaller sizes for direct marketing or for further processing.
3   Reduction of larger sizes of cleaned coal to smaller sizes when there is a better market or better price for the latter.
4   Freeing coal from impurities in run-of-mine coal or in middlings of a beneficiation operation preparatory to further beneficiation.

The making of a uniform crushed product, with a minimum of oversize and a minimum of undersize and fines is of much greater importance in crushing coal than it is in crushing ore, for several reasons.

In the first place, the coal after crushing and further treatment by screening and beneficiation will eventually find its way into the various grades of market coal, and certain of these grades will have materially better market prices than some of the others. Hence, in crushing lump coal, maximum yield of the more profitable and more marketable sizes is essential.

A second feature is that fines are difficult to deal with in beneficiation operations. If present in too high proportions, not only are they not efficiently beneficiated, but their presence interferes with the beneficiation and other operations on the other sizes as well. In fact, it is not uncommon practice to remove the fines from the coal before beneficiation and depending upon their purity, either add them to the clean coal, or discard them as waste.

The foregoing requirements are reflected in the design and operation of coal crushers. Standard ore crushers are not suitable for efficient and exact crushing of coal, and special types of crushers have been developed especially for coal. The friable nature of the coal is the main reason for the development of special crushers in order to reduce and minimizes the production of fines.

The following are the three general principles of size reduction:

1   A particular type of machine is most efficient in acting on a certain size range of feed.
2   Size reduction is performed most efficiently in a series of stages; no one machine efficiently reduces large sizes to small sizes by repeated breakage.
3   If it is required to break certain sizes rapidly and efficiently in a machine, the mass fractions of those sizes should be kept as high as possible; or, put another way, finer material should be removed as quickly as possible from the crushing action.

18.2   VARIOUS FORCES IN CRUSHING

18.2.1   Impact force

In crushing terminology, impact refers to the sharp, instantaneous collision of one moving object against another. Both objects may be moving, or one object may be motionless.

There are two variations of impact: gravity impact and dynamic impact. Coal dropped onto a hard surface such as a steel plate is an example of gravity impact. Gravity impact is most often used when it is necessary to separate two materials which have relatively different friability. The more friable material is broken, while the less friable material remains unbroken. Separation can then be done by screening.

Material dropping in front of a moving hammer (both objects in motion), illustrates dynamic impact. When crushed by gravity impact, the free-falling material is momentarily stopped by the stationary object. But when crushed by dynamic impact, the material is unsupported and the force of impact accelerates movement of the reduced particles toward breaker blocks and/or other hammers.

18.2.2 Attrition force

Attrition is a term applied to the reduction of materials by scrubbing it between two hard surfaces. Hammer mills operate with close clearances between the hammers and the screen bars and they reduce by attrition combined with shear and impact reduction. Though attrition consumes more power and exerts heavier wear on hammers and screen bars, it is practical for crushing the less abrasive materials such as pure limestone and coal. Attrition crushing is most useful when material is friable or not too abrasive, when a closed-circuit system is not desirable to control top size.

18.2.3 Shear force

Shear consists of a trimming or cleaving action rather than the rubbing action associated with attrition. Shear is usually combined with other methods. For example, single-roll crushers employ shear together with impact and compression. Shear crushing may be used when material is somewhat friable and has a relatively low silica content or for primary crushing with a reduction ratio of 6 to 1.

18.2.4 Compression force

As the name implies, crushing by compression is done between two surfaces, with the work being done by one or both surfaces. Jaw crushers using this method of compression are suitable for reducing extremely hard and abrasive rock. However, some jaw crushers employ attrition as well as compression and are not as suitable for abrasive rock since the rubbing action accentuates the wear on crushing surfaces. As a mechanical reduction method, compression should be used if the material is hard, abrasive and tough, if the material is not sticky or where the finished product is to be relatively coarse, or larger top size.

18.3 CRUSHING MACHINES

The following are the chief machines used for crushing the coal

1 Rotary Breaker
2 Toothed Roll Crusher

3   Hammer mill
4   Feeder Breaker
5   Sizer

18.3.1   Rotary breaker

The rotary breaker is called as Bradford Breaker, after its inventor, Hezekiah Bradford, 1893. It is in reality a combined breaker and cleaner, although in some instances it is used primarily as a breaker. When large tonnages of coal are treated, the rotary coal breaker is often used.

Rotary Breaker (Fig. 18.3.1) is very similar in operation to the cylindrical trammel screen, consisting of 1.8–3.6 meters in diameter and length of about one-and-half to two-and-half times the diameter, revolving at a speed of about 12–18 revolutions per minute. The machine is massively constructed, with perforated walls, the size of the perforations being the size to which the coal is to be broken. The breaker rotates around its longitudinal axis, located in a horizontal position. The run-of-mine coal is fed at one end of the cylinder, at up to 1500 tons per hour in larger machines. The machine utilizes differential breakage, the coal, being much more friable than the associated stones and shales, will be broken to small sizes. In the admitted run-of-mine coal, the small particles of coal and shale quickly fall through the holes. The larger lumps are retained and, as the breaker rotates, are lifted by side plates, known as the longitudinal lifters, within the cylinder. Near the top of the cylinder, the coal slides off the plates and drops back to the bottom. Repeated drops shatter the pieces until they pass through the perforations in the shell. Large pieces of shale and stone do not break easily, and are usually discharged from the other end of the breaker, which thus cleans the coal to a certain degree. Movement of this refuse is facilitated by fixing the side plates at a slight angle on the shell, or by setting the breaker so that the shaft is not exactly horizontal. In the latter case, the discharge end is little lower than the feed end.

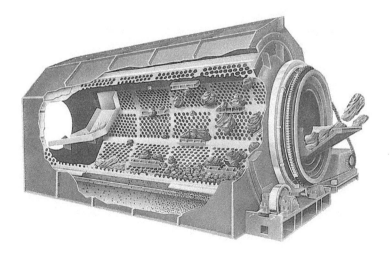

Figure 18.3.1 Rotary Breaker.
(Courtesy Pennsylvania Crusher Corporation)

As the broken coal is quickly removed from the breaker and owing to the relatively slight blows exerted on the coal by drops, the production of fines in a Bradford breaker is at minimum. For hard coal, the length to diameter ratio is increased.

The rotary breaker is relatively trouble free, requiring little upkeep, because the drum rings ride on trunnions, there are no center shaft or shaft bearings, and it is not susceptible to damage by hard rock or tramp iron. Perhaps the greatest objections to its use would occur in situations in which the raw feed contains plastic clayey materials. Such materials often have tendency to roll into balls and plug the perforations, requiring stoppage of breaker and plant until the breaker is cleared. Although this breaker is an expensive piece of equipment, maintenance costs are relatively low, and it produces positive control of top size of the product.

Taggart [17] gives the following empirical formula to determine the approximate power consumption for a rotary breaker

$$P = \frac{d(75 + \pi L)}{44} \tag{18.3.1}$$

where P is horsepower, and d and L are diameter and length of breaker screen, respectively, in feet.

18.3.2   Toothed roll crusher

There are two varieties of Toothed Roll Crusher used for crushing the coal (a) Single Toothed Roll Crusher (b) Double Toothed Roll Crusher.

a   Single toothed roll crusher
Single toothed roll crusher (Fig. 18.3.2.1) is a simplest type of crusher and consists of a heavy cast iron frame on which crushing roll and stationary crushing plate are

Figure 18.3.2.1 Sectional view of Single Toothed Roll Crusher.
(Courtesy aimehq.org)

mounted. The roll shaft is gear driven by the counter shaft, which in turn is driven by the driving pulley. The crushing roll consists of a drum to which toothed segments are bolted. These segments usually have a series of long teeth spaced at intervals and various short teeth covering the entire crushing surface. The coal is squeezed between the revolving roll and the crushing plate. The long teeth act as feeders and also penetrate the lumps of coal, splitting them into smaller pieces, while the smaller teeth make the proper size reduction. The design, spacing and general arrangement of these teeth have considerable influence on the type of product made. The crushing plate is provided with renewable wear plates bolted to the crushing plate. The crushing plate is held in position by a tension rod with a spring relief mechanism for protection against tramp iron.

The capacity of a roll crusher vary with the setting and with the nature of the coal. Usually roll crushers are built with capacities ranging up to about 500 tons of coal per hour. Roll speeds vary from 100 to 150 rpm, the smaller rolls being operated at higher speeds than larger ones.

A single roll crusher can reduce run-of-mine coal to 1.5 inch size in one stage. However, production of fines at the time of crushing is more in a single roll crusher than that of a double toothed roll crusher. Large crushers can crush ROM coal with 48 inch top size to a product size of 80% <6 inch at 1820 tons per hour.

Single roll crushers have the advantages of simplicity, compactness, and ability to operate satisfactorily at high reduction ratios. The crushing action involves a combination of impact, squeezing, and abrasion. The power consumption is very high, owing to frictional forces set up by the abrasive action.

b Double toothed roll crusher

Double toothed roll crusher (Fig. 18.3.2.2) consists of pair of iron or steel cylinders; one roll usually is belt-driven, and second roll is gear driven from the first. Floating gearmatic drive permits crushing roll adjustment over as much as 5 inch and the roll setting can be changed without stopping the crusher when a change in product size is desirable. The most important feature of double toothed roll crusher is rugged construction combined with arrangement of roll design or suitable size crushing.

Tooth design and spacing are important features in the design of the toothed roll crushers. Dull and worn teeth may reduce crushing capacity, increase power consumption, and decrease the yield of the desired coarser sizes. The roll face is usually made up of segments that can be replaced when necessary.

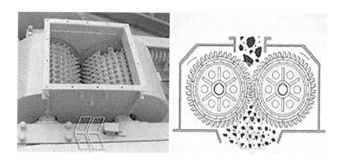

Figure 18.3.2.2 Double Toothed Roll Crusher.
(Courtesy Great Wall Company, Zhengzhou, China)

Double toothed roll crushers are always used in crushing anthracite and are used to a lesser extent in crushing bituminous coal. It can handle run-of-mine coal and make a product to about 1.5 inch size and larger by suitable adjustment of the gap. In order to take care of stone and iron pieces damaging the crusher, one of the roll bearing blocks are provided with suitable relief springs.

Double toothed roll crushers have got certain advantages over single toothed roll crushers. They are

1   materially less power is required for its operation
2   less fines are produced during crushing
3   by way of suitable adjustment of the opening between the rolls, a crushed coal will be obtained which will contain very little oversize coal

The theoretical capacity of a single or double toothed roll crusher can be given by a formula

$$TPH = \frac{D\,L\,S\,\text{rpm}\,60\,W}{1728 \times 2000} \tag{18.3.2}$$

where
      D = Diameter of roll in inches
      L = Length of roll face in inches
      S = Size of the coal in inches
    rpm = Roll revolutions per minute
      W = Weight of coal in lb/ft^3

However, the actual capacity will be 25% to 75% less than the theoretical capacity. It is not always possible to increase capacity by increasing revolutions per minute and horsepower since too high a speed will tend to make the teeth throw material out of the nip region. Larger diameter rolls are used for larger feed sizes, but the ratio depends on the type of teeth used.

18.3.3 Hammer mill

Hammer mill (Fig. 18.3.3) consist of a revolving disk to which heavy blocks or hammers are pivoted. The coal is broken by impact from the hammers. It is thrown against breaker blocks and grate bars and, if necessary, nipped and sheared against the grate bars. The centrifugal force of the hammers is employed to deliver the blow that reduces the material in size. The hammers are pivoted because they can move out of the path of oversize material, or tramp metal, entering the crushing chamber. Pivoted hammers exert less force than they would if rigidly attached. The term hammer mill usually seems to be reserved for equipment with discharge grates, where oversize material is retained and swept up again by the rotor for further impacting until it is reduced to less than the grate opening. The fineness obtained can be varied by adjustments of revolutions per minute or the spacing between the hammer tips and the grate bars. In a reversible hammer mill, the direction of the hammers can be reversed so that both faces of the hammers can be used,

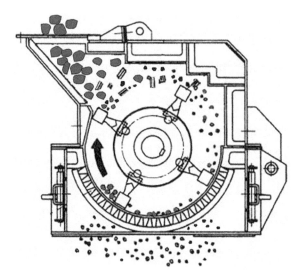

Figure 18.3.3 Hammer mill.

thereby obtaining more uniform grate bar wear, leading to longer time between maintenance outages.

Hammer mills may be used in crushing coal for mechanical stocking, for coking, or for other purposes where the production of fines does not have to be so strictly avoided as in crushing prior to washing. Hammer mills are accordingly used for finer crushing than is usually accomplished in rolls making products with a maximum size of 0.75 inch or under, in some cases as fine as 1/8 inch.

The other two crushers suitable for crushing coal are Needle Crusher and Pick breaker. They operate on the principle of application of force for splitting coal to suitable size without producing much fines. However, compared to the size of the equipment, these crushers are of low capacity and therefore not commonly used in crushing coal.

18.3.4   Feeder breaker

The feeder breaker's function is to accept oversize material from the mine at its maximum rate and break the material into usable size for handling by continuous means or by loading equipment. The feeder breaker is made up of four components, hopper, conveyor, breaker and mounting for transporting to other locations. Hoppers are designed to allow continuous operation from the mine. The conveyor or feeder is designed to receive the material from the hopper and feed the feeder breaker continuously at a rate compatible with mine production. The breaker reduces the mine material to correct size for handling. The mounting components provide for moving the feeder breaker, crawler for frequent moves, powered or non- powered, skids for longer term positioning and permanent locations.

The feeder breaker is a single roll breaker that utilizes the feeder flights and the floor as a second roll. The feeder breaker because of its construction and technology fractures the material so as to keep the amount of fines to the lowest in the industry. The feeder breaker only breaks oversize material and allows undersize to pass and therefore saving energy and wear on the machine. The combination of the feeder and the breaker combined into one machine gives the end-user a very versatile and low cost machine for primary crushing.

The feeder breakers are installed at most of the operating mines where it crushes the ROM coal to 250/200 mm.

18.3.5   Sizer

The basic concept of the Sizer (Fig. 18.3.5) is the use of two rotors with large teeth on small diameter shafts driven at low speed by a direct high torque drive system.

This design produces the three major principles which all interact with each other when breaking materials using SIZER TECHNOLOGY. The Three-Stage Breaking Action, The Rotating Screen Effect. and The Deep Scroll Tooth Pattern are the three unique principles.

1   **Three stage breaking action**
    The first stage of breaking takes place as the large rotor teeth grip the material as it falls on to the shafts. These teeth subject the rock to multiple point loading, which induces stress into the lump causing any natural weakness present in the material to be exploited. The secondary breaking takes place close to the centre line of the rotor, where the three point loading created between the top face of the tooth on one rotor and the top of the two opposing teeth on the other rotor, induces tensile stress in the rock. As the tensile strength of most materials is approximately 10% of the compressive strength, it reduces the amount of power consumed at this stage. Fitting a breaker bar below the centre line of the rotors allows any over size lumps carried by the scroll through the rotors to be broken,

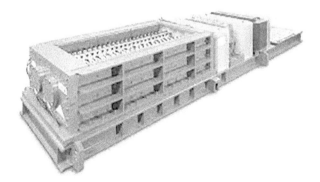

Figure 18.3.5 Sizer.
(Courtesy TerraSource Global, St. Louis, Missouri, USA)

again exploiting the weaker tensile strength of the material. The breaker bar, which forms a comb through which the rotor teeth have to pass, can be adjusted up or down to modify the product size.

2   **The rotating screen effect**
The interlaced toothed rotor design allows free flowing undersize material to pass through the continuously changing gaps generated by the relatively slow moving shafts. Undersize material fed to the Sizer or produced during the first and second stages of breaking flow through the rotors with the assistance of gravity and the constant agitation caused by the rotating shafts. If the machine is fed from one end, this feature gives the added benefit that the smaller material is deposited on the belt first followed by the larger material forming a sealing layer above the dust giving environmental benefits on conveyor systems.

3   **The deep scroll tooth pattern**
The deep scroll conveys the larger material to one end of the machine and helps to spread the feed across the full length of the rotors. This feature can be used to reject oversize material from the machine.

18.4   GRINDING

The ROM coal is crushed to sizes convenient for easy beneficiation in the coal processing plant avoiding the production of excess fines. The fines produced during crushing are separated and either mixed with clean coal or rejected totally depending on their ash percent. Coal is not ground to finer sizes deliberately as fines are difficult to beneficiate and also costly.

The coal is ground to finer sizes at the point of utilization. For example, in a thermal power plant, the coal is ground or pulverized to finer sizes for combustion. Ball mill, Ball and tube mill, Ring and ball mill are the mills used to pulverize the coal to 200 mesh size. The powdered coal from the coal mills is carried to the boiler in coal pipes by high pressure hot air. The pulverized coal air mixture is burnt in the boiler in the combustion zone for the production of steam necessary for turbines to run to produce electric power.

Chapter 19

Pulp/Slurry density

Most of the coal beneficiation operations are wet. Water is added to the particles to aid beneficiation. The mixture of water and solid particles is known as **Pulp**.

Other terms commonly used are:

Suspension: When the solid particles are held up in the water, the pulp is called suspension. In other words, in suspension, the solid particles are well dispersed throughout.

Slurry: A mixture of fine solids (slimes) and water

Sludge: Thick pulp i.e., pulp with less quantity of water

Pulp or slurry density is most easily measured in terms of weight of the slurry per unit volume (gm/cm³ or kg/m³). A sample of slurry taken in container of known volume is weighed to give slurry density directly. Marcy Scale available in the market gives direct reading for the density of the slurry and% solids in the slurry.

The composition of a slurry is often represented as the fraction (or percent) of solids by weight. It is determined by sampling the slurry, weighing, drying and reweighing.

$$C_w = \text{fraction of solids by weight} = \frac{\text{Weight of the particles}}{\text{Weight of the slurry}} \qquad (19.1)$$

$$C_v = \text{fraction of solids by volume} = \frac{\text{Volume of the particles}}{\text{Volume of the slurry}} \qquad (19.2)$$

Knowing the densities of the slurry (ρ_{sl}), water (ρ_w) and dry solids (ρ_p), the fraction of solids (C_w) by weight can be calculated. Since the total volume of the slurry is equal to the volume of the solids plus the volume of the water, then for unit volume of the slurry

$$\frac{C_w}{\rho_p} + \frac{1-C_w}{\rho_w} = \frac{1}{\rho_{sl}} \qquad (19.3)$$

$$\Rightarrow \qquad C_w = \frac{\rho_p\,(\rho_{sl}-1)}{\rho_{sl}(\rho_p-1)} \qquad [\because \rho_w = 1 \text{ gm/cm}^3] \qquad (19.4)$$

Similarly, the total weight of the slurry is equal to the weight of the solids plus the weight of the water, then for unit weight of the slurry

$$C_v\,\rho_p + (1 - C_v)\,\rho_w = \rho_{sl} \tag{19.5}$$

$$\Rightarrow \qquad C_v = \frac{(\rho_{sl} - 1)}{\rho_p - 1} \qquad [\because \rho_w = 1\ \text{gm/cm}^3] \tag{19.6}$$

Where the beneficiation operations are carried out on slurry streams, the slurry is transported through the circuit via pumps and pipelines. The water acts as a transportation medium. The volume of the slurry flowing through the circuit will affect the residence time in unit operations. Volumetric flowrate can be measured by diverting the stream of the slurry into a suitable container for a measured period of time. The ratio of the volume of the slurry collected to the time taken to collect the slurry gives the flowrate of the slurry. This volumetric flowrate is important in calculating retention time of the slurry in any operation. For instance, if 180 m³/hr of the slurry is fed to a flotation conditioning tank of volume of 30 m³, then on an average, the retention time of particles in the tank will be

$$\text{Retention time} = \frac{\text{Tank Volume}}{\text{Flow rate}} = \frac{30}{180} = \frac{1}{6}\text{hr} = 10\ \text{minutes} \tag{19.7}$$

That means, any part of the slurry takes 10 minutes from the time it enters the tank to the time it leaves the tank.

Dilution ratio is the ratio of the weight of the water to the weight of the solids in the slurry.

$$\text{Dilution ratio} = \frac{1 - C_w}{C_w} \tag{19.8}$$

Dilution ratio is particularly important as the product of dilution ratio and weight of the solids in the slurry is equal to the weight of the water in the slurry.

When it is required to prepare a liquid of definite density by mixing two miscible liquids of known densities, the equation can be written as in case of pulp. The total weight of the mixture of two liquids is equal to the weight of one liquid plus the weight of the other liquid; then for unit weight of the mixture

$$C_{v1}\,\rho_1 + (1 - C_{v1})\,\rho_2 = \rho_{12} \tag{19.9}$$

where

ρ_1 = density of liquid 1
ρ_2 = density of liquid 2
ρ_{12} = density of the resultant liquid after mixing two liquids
C_{v1} = fraction of liquid 1 by volume

On computation of equation 19.9, we get $\qquad C_{v1} = \dfrac{\rho_{12} - \rho_2}{\rho_1 - \rho_2} \tag{19.10}$

Similarly, the total volume of the mixture of two liquids is equal to the volume of one liquid plus the volume of the other liquid; then for unit volume of the mixture

$$\frac{C_{w1}}{\rho_1} + \frac{1 - C_{w1}}{\rho_2} = \frac{1}{\rho_{12}} \tag{19.11}$$

where
ρ_1 = density of liquid 1
ρ_2 = density of liquid 2
ρ_{12} = density of the resultant liquid after mixing two liquids
C_{w1} = fraction of liquid 1 by weight

On computation of equation 19.11, we get $C_{w1} = \dfrac{\rho_1(\rho_{12} - \rho_2)}{\rho_{12}(\rho_1 - \rho_2)} \tag{19.12}$

Similar equations can be written for mixture of any number of liquids.

19.1   ILLUSTRATIVE EXAMPLES

Illustrative example 19.1.1: *A filtration experiment on a 2 liter slurry sample of coal (solids specific gravity = 1.4) produced 260 gm of wet filter cake (dry wt. = 196 gm). Calculate*

    a   *% solids by volume in the slurry*
    b   *% solids by weight in the slurry*
    c   *Liquid solid ratio by volume and by weight*
    d   *Density of the slurry*
    e   *% moisture in the filter cake*
    f   *Bulk density of the filter cake*

Solution:

Volume of coal	= 196/1.4 = 140 cm^3
Volume of water in the slurry	= 2000–140 = 1860 cm^3
% coal by volume in the slurry	= 140 × 100/2000 = 7
Weight of water	= 1860 gm
Weight of coal	= 196 gm
% coal by weight in the slurry	= 196 × 100/(196+1860) = **9.53**
Liquid solid ratio by volume	= 1860/140 = **13.29**
Liquid solid ratio by weight	= 1860/196 = **9.49**
Density of the slurry	= (196+1860)/2000 = **1.028**
Weight of moisture in filter cake	= 260–196 = 64 gm
% moisture by weight in filter cake	= 64 × 100/260 = **24.6**
Volume of filter cake	= 140 + 64 = 204 cm^3
Bulk density of the filter cake	= 260/204 = **1.27**

Illustrative example 19.1.2: *It is required to prepare a suspension of specific gravity 1.45 by adding sand of specific gravity 2.6 to the water. How much percent of sand by weight is necessary to prepare the suspension.*

Solution:

$\rho_{sl} = 1.45$ gm/cc; $\rho_p = 2.6$ gm/cc

$$\frac{C_w}{\rho_p} + \frac{1-C_w}{\rho_w} = \frac{1}{\rho_{sl}} \Rightarrow \frac{C_w}{2.6} + \frac{1-C_w}{1.0} = \frac{1}{1.45} \Rightarrow C_w = 0.5043$$

$\Rightarrow$ percent sand by weight necessary to prepare the suspension = C_w = 50.43%

Illustrative example 19.1.3: *Determine % Magnetite by weight in the suspension if the specific gravity of Magnetite 5.0 and the suspension density is 1.8 gm/cm³. Also calculate % water by volume in the suspension.*

Solution:
Let the fraction of magnetite by weight in suspension = C_w;
the fraction of magnetite by volume in suspension = C_v

$$\frac{C_w}{\rho_p} + \frac{1-C_w}{\rho_w} = \frac{1}{\rho_{sl}} \Rightarrow \frac{C_w}{5} + \frac{1-C_w}{1.0} = \frac{1}{1.8} \Rightarrow C_w = 0.5555 \Rightarrow 55.55\%$$

% magnetite by weight = 55.55%

$$C_v\rho_p + (1-C_v)\rho_w = \rho_{sl} \Rightarrow C_v \times 5 + (1-C_v) \times 1.0 = 1.8$$
$$\Rightarrow C_v = 0.2 \Rightarrow 20.0\%$$

% water by volume in suspension = 100.00 − 20.0 = 80%

llustrative example 19.1.4: *A coal slurry has a dilution ratio of 9. If the average specific gravity of the coal particles is 1.5, what is the slurry density?*

Solution:

$$\text{Dilution ratio} = \frac{1-C_w}{C_w} = 9 \Rightarrow C_w = 0.1 \Rightarrow 10\%$$

Density of the coal particles = ρ = 1.5 gm/cc

$$\frac{C_w}{\rho_p} + \frac{1-C_w}{\rho_w} = \frac{1}{\rho_{sl}} \Rightarrow \frac{0.1}{1.5} + \frac{1-0.1}{1.0} = \frac{1}{\rho_{sl}} \Rightarrow \rho_{sl} = 1.034 \text{ gm/cc}$$

∴ Slurry density = 1.034 gm/cc

Illustrative example 19.1.5: *Laboratory flotation test has been conducted for coal slurry with 10% coal by weight. If the specific gravity of the coal particles is 1.7, calculate slurry density and slurry dilution.*

Solution:

$$\frac{C_w}{\rho_p}+\frac{1-C_w}{\rho_w}=\frac{1}{\rho_{sl}} \Rightarrow \frac{0.10}{1.7}+\frac{1-0.1}{1.00}=\frac{1}{\rho_{sl}} \Rightarrow \rho_{sl}=1.043 \text{ gm/cc}$$

Density of the slurry = 1.043 gm/cc

∴ Slurry dilution = Dilution ratio = $\dfrac{1-C_w}{C_w}=\dfrac{1-0.10}{0.10}=9$

Illustrative example 19.1.6: *Two slurry streams, one has a flowrate of 5 m³/hr and the other has a flow rate of 3.4 m³/hr, are discharged to a sump where from it is pumped to a beneficiation plant for treatment. Calculate the tonnage of dry solids pumped per hour if the percent solids by weight in two streams are 15 and 20 respectively and the specific gravity of the solids is 1.6. Also calculate the percent solids by weight of the total slurry pumped from the sump.*

Solution:

For stream 1 $\dfrac{C_w}{\rho_p}+\dfrac{100-C_w}{\rho_w}=\dfrac{100}{\rho_{sl}} \Rightarrow \dfrac{15}{1.6}+\dfrac{100-15}{1.0}=\dfrac{100}{\rho_{sl}}$

$$\Rightarrow \rho_{sl}=1.06 \text{ gm/cc}=1060 \text{ kg/m}^3$$

Mass flowrate of stream 1 = 5 × 1060 = 5300 kg/hr
Mass flowrate of solids in stream 1 = 5300 × 0.15 = 795 kg/hr

For stream 2 $\dfrac{C_w}{\rho_p}+\dfrac{100-C_w}{\rho_w}=\dfrac{100}{\rho_{sl}} \Rightarrow \dfrac{20}{1.6}+\dfrac{100-20}{1.0}=\dfrac{100}{\rho_{sl}}$

$$\Rightarrow \rho_{sl}=1.081 \text{ gm/cc}=1081 \text{ kg/m}^3$$

Mass flowrate of stream 2 = 3.4 × 1081 = 3675.4 kg/hr
Mass flowrate of solids in stream 2 = 3675.4 × 0.20 = 735 kg/hr
Tonnage of dry solids pumped = 795 + 735 = 1530 kg/hr

Mass flowrate of two streams = 5300 + 3675.4 = 8975.4 kg/hr

% solids = $\dfrac{1530}{8975.4}\times100=17.05\%$

Illustrative example 19.1.7: *Calculate the volume of benzene and carbon tetrachloride required to prepare 100 cc of solution of heavy liquid of specific gravity 1.2. Specific gravities of benzene and carbon tetrachloride are 0.8 and 1.6 respectively.*

Solution:

$$C_{vb}\rho_1+(1-C_{vb})\rho_2=\rho_{so} \Rightarrow C_{vb}\times0.8+(1-C_v)\times1.6=1.2$$
$$\Rightarrow C_{vb}=0.50 \Rightarrow 50\%$$

i.e. 50 cc of benzene and 50 cc of carbon tetrachloride is required

Illustrative example 19.1.8: *Two liquids of specific gravities 1.26 and 1.6 are to be mixed to obtain 300 cc solution of specific gravity 1.4. Calculate the quantities of two liquids required by volume and by weight.*

Solution:

$\rho_1 = 1.26$; $\rho_2 = 1.6$; $\rho_{so} = 1.4$

Fraction of liquid 1 by volume $= C_{v1}$

$C_{v1}\rho_1 + (1 - C_{v1})\rho_2 = \rho_{so} \Rightarrow C_{v1} \times 1.26 + (1 - C_{v1}) \times 1.6 = 1.4$

$\Rightarrow C_{v1} = 0.588$

Fraction of liquid 2 by volume $= 1 - 0.588 = 0.412$

Volume of liquid 1 $= 0.588 \times 300 = 176.4$ cc

Volume of liquid 2 $= 0.412 \times 300 = 123.6$ cc

Fraction of liquid 1 by weight $= C_{w1}$

$$\frac{C_{w1}}{\rho_1} + \frac{1 - C_{w1}}{\rho_2} = \frac{1}{\rho_{so}} \quad \Rightarrow \quad \frac{C_{w1}}{1.26} + \frac{1 - C_{w1}}{1.6} = \frac{1}{1.4} \quad \Rightarrow \quad C_{w1} = 0.5294$$

Fraction of liquid 2 by weight $= 1 - 0.5294 = 0.4706$

Total weight of the liquid $= 1.4 \times 300 = 420$ gm

Weight of liquid 1 $= 0.5294 \times 420 = 222.3$ gm

Weight of liquid 2 $= 0.4706 \times 420 = 197.7$ gm

19.2 PROBLEMS FOR PRACTICE

19.2.1: *450 gm of coal is taken and prepared a pulp of 500 cc by adding water to it. If the weight of 500 cc pulp is 600 gm, Calculate the density of coal in kg/m³. Also calculate percent coal in the pulp by weight and by volume.*
[1286, 75%, 70%]

19.2.2: *Calculate the quantity of bromoform and benzene required to prepare 100 cc of solutions of heavy liquids with specific gravities of 1.4, 1.6 and 1.8. The specific gravities of bromoform and benzene are 2.85 and 0.8 respectively.*
[29.3, 70.7, 39, 61, 48.8, 51.2 cc] [83.5, 56.5, 111.2, 48.8, 139.1, 40.9 gm]

19.2.3: *It is required to prepare a pulp of 30% solids by volume with 4.2 litres of water. Determine the weight of solids to be added in kilograms if the specific gravity of solids is 2.65.*
[4.77 kg]

Chapter 20

Washability of coal

Washability of coal means amenability of coal to improvement in quality by benefi-ciation techniques. Washability characteristics of coal vary from locality to locality and from seam to seam in the same locality due to variance in the extent and nature of impurities associated with coal. It is, therefore, necessary to assess the cleaning (beneficiation) potentiality of a coal before sending it to a processing plant.

It will be evident that ordinary mechanical cleaning processes can only separate coal particles of lower ash content from those of higher ash content. They cannot extract ash from coal lumps. The degree of cleaning possible with any particular coal therefore depends upon the distribution of its ash forming constituents.

The ash in the coal can be divided as **Free ash** and **Fixed ash**. Impurities which exist as individual discrete particles when the coal has been broken to the size at which it is cleaned contribute to the free ash content of the coal. The term fixed or inherent ash is used to designate the impurities that are structurally a part of the coal. The former type of impurities can be removed by mechanical means while the latter are difficult to remove. As coal is broken to finer sizes, more and more impurities occur as discrete individual particles and can be separated.

The normal procedure to assess the cleaning potentialities of a coal is to carry out float and sink tests in the laboratory on the representative sample after crushing and screening it to desired sizes. The degree to which the raw coal is crushed prior to tests is closely linked with the nature of its intergrown dirt, often useful to conduct washability tests on a raw coal crushed to different sizes and to ascertain, from the comparative results, the extent of increase in clean coal recovery due to finer crushing. Similarly, studies on the cleaning characteristics of individual size fractions within nar-row limits give greater flexibility in the subsequent combination of results in required size limits that conform to the specifications of commercial washing units. In the case of coking coals containing a large proportion of middlings or sinks, separate wash-ability tests are required to be conducted on middlings/sinks crushed to various sizes to find out the possible recovery of additional clean coal from such treatment. For the evaluation of efficiency of washing baths, float and sink tests are separately carried out on the individual washed products. Thus, the specific objectives for conducting float and sink tests of raw and/or washed products are as follows:

1   To know the cleaning possibilities of a coal including recovery of products, ash content, gravity of cut etc.
2   To study the feasibility of a washery project including selection of washing units and flow scheme for treatment
3   To assess the efficiency of different washing baths in operation
4   To predict the yield of products achievable in practice

20.1   FLOAT AND SINK TEST

Float and sink, commercially called as Heavy Liquid Separation (HLS), is an operation where particles of different specific gravities are separated by using suitable heavy liquid. The principle of float and sink is:

> When two particles of different specific gravities are immersed in a liquid having specific gravity intermediate between that of two particles, lighter particle would float and heavier particle would sink

Float and sink test is based on the difference in specific gravity of coal particles. Specific gravity of clean coal (free from shale, clay, sandstone, etc.) is about 1.20 (1.12 to 1.35) while specific gravity of impure coal varies from 1.60 and 2.60.

The usual organic liquids employed for float and sink test are Benzene (sp.gr. 0.86), Tetra Chloro Ethylene (sp.gr 1.62) and Bromoform (sp.gr. 2.80). By mixing benzene with tetra chloro ethylene in right proportions it is possible to prepare a range of liquid baths with specific gravities lying between 1.25 and 1.62. For testing of samples at specific gravity more than 1.62, mixtures of bromoform and tetra chloro ethylene are used in different proportions. Since tetra chloro ethylene and bromoform are both toxic, all tests using these liquids are necessarily conducted in well ventilated places and where possible, under an open shed out of doors.

Chlorinated salt solutions, employing specially zinc chloride, are often recommended for float and sink testing of coal samples above 6 mm in size. Zinc chloride can be conveniently used to prepare test solutions ranging in specific gravity from 1.25 to 1.70.

In carrying out float and sink tests of coking coals and mature types of non-coking coals, it has also been found advantageous to employ sulphuric acid solutions (specific gravity range 1.25 to 1.80) for size fractions generally above 3 mm but preferably 13 mm, provided carbonate contents in such coals are found to be reasonably low.

20.1.1   Procedure for float and sink test

Laboratory float and sink test is performed on coal to know the washability characteristics of coal thereby to determine the economic separating density. Suitability of heavy medium separation can also be assessed from this test.

Liquids covering a range of specific gravities in incremental steps are prepared and the representative sample of coal is introduced into the liquid of lowest specific gravity. The sink product is removed, washed and placed in a liquid of next higher specific gravity, whose sink product is then transferred to the next higher specific gravity and so on. All the float products are collected, drained, washed, dried and then weighed together with the final sink product, to give the specific gravity distribution of the sample by weight.

A sample of less than 1 gm is prepared separately from each float fraction as well as final sink fraction and ash percentages are determined as detailed in article 7.3.1.

It is desirable to size the coal and make separate float and sink tests on the separate sizes. CIMFR has developed an apparatus, known as Sarkar-Manchanda apparatus, for float and sink tests of fine coal and ores having size below 3 mm. This apparatus has the following advantages:

1   The entire operation including separation and discharge of float and sink products is effected inside a closed system and the evaporation of volatile liquid used for the separation is almost eliminated whereby the worker is exposed very little to toxic vapours.
2   It takes almost half the time required with conventional method using large beakers.
3   It gives very accurate and closely comparable results.
4   Chances of personal error are minimized.
5   The system permits drawing of the separated products readily into a closed filtration system.
6   There is practically no lower size limit of coal to be tested by this apparatus.

Conducting float and sink tests on separate sizes not only assists separation but also gives information regarding the distribution of the impurities according to the size which is essential to select suitable beneficiation process.

The laboratory observations of float and sink analysis on an individual size fraction are to be tabulated. Table 20.1.1 shows such a tabulated values for a hypothetical coal. Hypothetical data is considered for the convenience in discussion.

Table 20.1.1 Laboratory observed values of float and sink analysis.

Specific gravity of liquid used	Weight of watch glass gm	Weight of watch glass with coal floated gm	Weight of empty crucible gm	Weight of crucible with coal gm	Weight of crucible with coal heated at 750°C till constant weight gm
1.30	18.62	31.62	16.843	17.792	16.881
1.35	18.75	38.25	17.346	18.262	17.401
1.40	18.56	44.56	19.982	20.956	20.060
1.45	18.46	50.96	16.827	17.784	16.961
1.50	17.32	30.32	17.924	18.907	18.160
1.55	18.48	24.98	17.465	18.430	17.774
1.60	18.32	24.82	17.638	18.619	18.070
1.75	18.62	25.12	17.239	18.196	17.775
2.00	18.35	21.60	16.347	17.333	16.939
2.00 (sink)	17.52	20.77	16.466	17.439	17.060

From the laboratory observed values of Table 20.1.1, weight of the coal floated at each specific gravity, its weight percentages, cumulative weight percentages and ash percentages in floated coal at each specific gravity are calculated and shown in Table 20.1.2.

In Table 20.1.2, first four columns are the results of float and sink test. Column 5 is the calculated ash% in floated coal at each specific gravity. Column 6 represents the coal floated on percentage basis, also known as differential weight percentage or fractional yield. Column 7 represents cumulative yield percentages of cleans (floats) for each gravity fraction and obtained by simply adding fractional yields of column 6 from topmost value to the value at respective specific gravity.

From the values of Table 20.1.2, it is evident that every coal particle in the sample tested has its own ash and their ash vary from 4% to 61% ash.

From the above results ash percentages corresponding to each cumulative yield percent of floats as well as sinks are calculated. Table 20.1.3 shows values after such calculations:

In Table 20.1.3, the values in column 4 are the product of values in column 2 and 3 and called as Ash product or Ash point. Column 5 and 6 are the simple addition of values in respective columns 2 and 4. The values in column 7 (cumulative ash percentages or ash percentages in total yields at respective specific gravities) is obtained by dividing values of column 6 by values in column 5. The last value 18.4% of column 7 is the ash percent of the coal sample taken for float and sink test. Ash percentages in cumulative sinks is obtained essentially the same manner but the values are cumulated from bottom to top to get cumulative sinks percent, cumulative ash product and cumulative ash percentages.

All the above results are confined to one particular size fraction. Similar tables are to be prepared for all size fractions of coal separately by similar calculations.

Table 20.1.2 Calculated values of float and sink analysis.

Sp.gr. of liquid used	Wt. of coal floated gm	Wt. of coal taken for ash determination gm	Wt. of ash gm	Ash% in floated coal	Wt% of floated coal	Cum wt% of floated coal
1	2	3	4	5	6	7
1.30	13.00	0.949	0.038	4.0	10.0	10.0
1.35	19.50	0.916	0.055	6.0	15.0	25.0
1.40	26.00	0.974	0.078	8.0	20.0	45.0
1.45	32.50	0.957	0.134	14.0	25.0	70.0
1.50	13.00	0.983	0.236	24.0	10.0	80.0
1.55	6.50	0.965	0.309	32.0	5.0	85.0
1.60	6.50	0.981	0.432	44.0	5.0	90.0
1.75	6.50	0.957	0.536	56.0	5.0	95.0
2.00	3.25	0.986	0.592	60.0	2.5	97.5
2.00 (sink)	3.25	0.973	0.594	61.0	2.5	100.0
	130.00				100.0	

Table 20.1.3 Results of cumulative yields of floats and sinks.

				Cumulative floats			Cumulative sinks		
Sp. gr	Wt%	Ash%	Ash product	Wt%	Ash product	Ash%	Wt%	Ash product	Ash%
1	2	3	4	5	6	7	8	9	10
1.30	10.0	4.0	40.0	10.0	40.0	4.0	90.0	1802.5	20.0
1.35	15.0	6.0	90.0	25.0	130.0	5.2	75.0	1712.5	22.8
1.40	20.0	8.0	160.0	45.0	290.0	6.4	55.0	1552.5	28.2
1.45	25.0	14.0	350.0	70.0	640.0	9.1	30.0	1202.5	40.1
1.50	10.0	24.0	240.0	80.0	880.0	11.0	20.0	962.5	48.1
1.55	5.0	32.0	160.0	85.0	1040.0	12.2	15.0	802.5	53.5
1.60	5.0	44.0	220.0	90.0	1260.0	14.0	10.0	582.5	58.3
1.75	5.0	56.0	280.0	95.0	1540.0	16.2	5.0	302.5	60.5
2.00	2.5	60.0	150.0	97.5	1690.0	17.3	2.5	152.5	61.0
2.00 (sink)	2.5	61.0	152.5	100.0	1842.5	18.4	0.0	0.0	0.0

Finally the combined float and sink results of the overall coal can be obtained by adding weights of floated coal in all size fractions at respective specific gravities and computing ash percentages in each floated fraction and then carrying out similar calculations to get cumulative ash percentages.

In addition to expressing the float and sink results of a coal in the form of table as shown in Table 20.1.3, they are represented in the form of curves, familiarly known as **WASHABILITY CURVES** developed in 1902 [35].

The graphical representation of float sink results helps to understand more clearly the washing or cleaning possibilities of coal at any desired ash level of floats or at any desired specific gravity of cut and is therefore more suitable for studying the implications of these results for practical use. The Four different kinds of standard washability curves which are conveniently drawn for this purpose are:

1 The Characteristic curve, also known as elementary ash curve, or fractional yield ash curve
2 Total floats-ash curve or cumulative floats curve
3 Total sinks-ash curve or cumulative sinks curve
4 The yield gravity curve

The characteristic curve is a primary washability curve, also called as Henry–Reinhard plot, and is constructed by plotting the cumulative yield of floats expressed in percentages of the total coal against the ash percentages of the individual fractions. At any yield level of the total floats, it shows directly the ash contents of those particles of the floats which have the highest ash content.

The total floats-ash curve is obtained by plotting the cumulative yield of floats expressed in percentage at each specific gravity against the cumulative ash percentage of floats at that specific gravity. As the total floats ash curve directly tells us the recovery of clean or washed coal obtainable for any desired ash content of the floated coal, this curve finds more frequent use in practice than the characteristic curve.

Total sinks-ash curve is drawn between cumulative yield of sinks expressed in percentage at each specific gravity and the cumulative ash percentage of sinks at that specific gravity. This curve is complementary to the total floats-ash curve and shows directly the ash content of the total sinks at any yield level of sinks or floats.

The yield gravity curve is drawn between cumulative yield of floats expressed in percentage at each specific gravity and the specific gravity. The desired specific gravity of separation corresponding to any yield level of floated coal can be obtained by this curve.

All these four curves are usually drawn on a common diagram as shown in Fig. 20.1.

A   Characteristic Curve
B   Total floats-ash Curve
C   Total sinks-ash Curve
D   Yield gravity Curve
E   Near gravity material Curve

The advantages of drawing all the curves on a common diagram are that all the essential information required for studying the cleaning possibilities of a coal can be readily obtained by cross projections. For example, if one is interested to recover 10% ash clean coal, he has to read first from the total floats ash curve the percent yield of cleans corresponding to 10% ash. Then from this yield point, a horizontal line is drawn to cut the total sinks ash curve and the yield gravity curve. At the cut point of the total sinks ash curve, the ash content of the sinks is read from the ash-axis and at

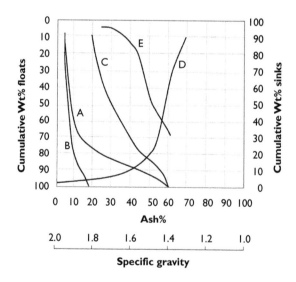

Figure 20.1 Washability curves.

the cut point of the yield-gravity curve, the required specific gravity of separation is read from the gravity axis.

Of these families of curves, the characteristic curve is rightly regarded as the parent curve from which other two curves (total floats-ash curve and total sinks-ash curve) may be derived either by direct calculation or by graphical plotting.

While the basic data obtained from laboratory float and sink analysis is directly used for the construction of the characteristic curve, it is important to realize that the determined ash content of any particular specific gravity fraction represents the weighted average of ash contents of all particles of different specific gravities included in that fraction which leads to an error. This error can be minimized and better accuracy in constructing characteristic curve can be achieved by using more gravity baths in closer intervals (0.025) during float and sink tests.

Both the shape and position of the characteristic curve are of much significance in assessing whether the coal is easy or difficult to wash. If the characteristic curve approaches straight line, the coal becomes more difficult to wash and this is all the more true when the curve approaches vertically i.e., becomes nearly parallel to vertical axis. This nearly vertical shape with steep slope represents relatively small ash and correspondingly small specific gravity differences, hence more difficult to wash.

Flat slope represents the reverse physical condition and correspondingly easy separation. If the characteristic curve lies mostly near the vertical axis and then takes a sudden turn towards horizontality, the coal becomes very easy to wash.

The chief limitation of the standard washability curves is that the yield of middlings of any stipulated ash content cannot be directly read from them.

These standard washability curves do not provide any common and accurate basis for the comparison and correlation of the washability characteristics of different coals. The need for such a basis is felt all the more, when there is wide divergence between the ash contents of raw coals and then the yield levels of clean coal cannot be maintained at any uniform ash or specific gravity level. So more standard criteria have been proposed from time to time to compare and correlate the washibility characteristics of different coals according to the ease or difficulty of washing.

These are:

1 Near Gravity Materials (N.G.M)
2 Yield Reduction Factor (Y.R.F)
3 Washability Index (W.I)
4 Optimum degree of Washability (O.D.W)
5 Washability Number (W.N)

20.2 NEAR GRAVITY MATERIALS

In common usage, the near gravity material is defined as the percent yield of total coal, which is within plus and minus 0.10 specific gravity range of the effective density range of separation. Sometimes an additional curve known as ±0.10 specific gravity distribution curve or **Near Gravity Material Curve** can be constructed along with the standard washability curves to directly measure the ease or difficulty of washing at different densities of cut. The curve can be easily derived from the yield gravity curve.

The near gravity material curves may be of variable nature. For easy washing coals, the near gravity material not only show a tendency to decrease both at lower most and higher most density ranges of cut but becomes maximum in the intermediate density ranges of cut, which generally vary from 1.45 to 1.55. Incidentally, it may be mentioned that the optimum densities of cut for the majority of Indian coals fall in the specific gravity range between 1.45 and 1.55. As a general rule, coal contains more of fixed ash show high percentages of near gravity materials, and those containing more of free dirt show lower percentages of near gravity materials. But precise amount of near gravity materials always depend on the quantum of crowding of the specific gravity fractions around the desired density of separation.

In 1931, B.M.BIRD [36] of America proposed the following classification based on near gravity materials to indicate roughly the degree of difficulty faced in the washing of a coal at any selected density of separation. The basis of BIRD's classification is shown in Table 20.2.1.

As per BIRD's classification, most of the Indian coals can be considered as formidable to washing, whereas most of the American or continental coals fall under simple to moderately difficult washing groups. In Indian coals (except Assam coals), the near gravity materials hardly come down to below 25 to 30% at 15 to 17% ash level. Most of the inferior coal seams of India exhibit much worse cleaning characteristics, as they often contain 60 to 80% near gravity materials at the desired density of separation. Hence major quantity of Indian coals at 75 mm – 13 mm size is treated by Heavy Medium Separation.

Table 20.2.1 BIRD's classification.

±0.10 sp.gr distribution present	Degree of difficulty	Gravity process recommended	Type
0 to 7	Simple	Almost any process High tonnages	Jigs, Tables, Spirals
7 to 10	Moderately difficult	Efficient process High tonnages	Sluices, Cones, HMS
10 to 15	Difficult	Efficient process Medium tonnages Good operation	HMS
15 to 20	Very difficult	Efficient process Low tonnages Expert operation	HMS
20 to 25	Exceedingly difficult	Very efficient process Low tonnages Expert operation	HMS
Above 25	Formidable	Limited to a few exceptionally efficient processes Expert operation	HMS with close control

Table 20.2.2 Values of ±0.10 near gravity material.

Sp. gr	Wt% of ±0.10 near gravity material
1.35	70.0
1.40	70.0
1.45	60.0
1.50	45.0
1.55	22.0
1.60	14.0
1.65	10.0
1.70	6.0
1.75	5.0

Table 20.2.2 shows the values of ±0.10 near gravity material at respective specific gravities deduced from the yield gravity curve for the coal under consideration.

Near Gravity Material curve is also drawn along with standard washability curves in Fig. 20.1.

20.3 YIELD REDUCTION FACTOR

Yield Reduction Factor is expressed as the percent reduction or sacrifice in the yield for each percent reduction or decrease in ash content at any selected ash level of the clean coal. In the present case, the ash content of the raw coal is 18.4%. Let the coal is washed at 1.50 specific gravity. The percent yield and its ash are 80.0% and 11.0% respectively. A reduction of 7.4% ash is effected by sacrificing 20.0% yield and so the Yield Reduction Factor works out to be 20.0 divided by 7.4 i.e., 2.7. It has been observed that the yield reduction factor for any particular coal seam remains reasonably constant so long the size grading of the coal and clean coal ash level do not undergo any appreciable change.

The lower the Yield Reduction Factor, the better is the washability characteristics of the coal. The comparatively easy-washing coals of the Jharia field of India often show 3 to 3.5 yield reduction factor when the raw coal is crushed to below 75 mm and separated at 16.0% ash level. Under similar conditions of treatment, the yield reduction factors of the difficult washing coals are as high as 7 to 10. Except Assam coals, the average yield reduction factor values for Indian coals lie between 4 and 7 as against 1.2 to 2.5 obtained for American and continental coals.

On the basis of yield reduction factors at 15.0% ash level of cleans from raw coals crushed to below 15 mm, coal seams of different washability characteristics may be subdivided as easy coals if yield reduction factor is less than 4, medium coals if the yield reduction factor ranges from 4 to 6, and difficult coals if yield reduction factor is more than 6.

The application of yield reduction factors assumes greater importance in estimating the expected yield of the day to day operation of a washery, receiving supplies of raw coal from varied sources.

20.4   WASHABILITY INDEX

The most important criterion in defining the washability characteristics of coals for the purpose of comparing and correlating the results is the Washability Index proposed for the first time by CIMFR [37] at the Fourth International Coal Preparation Congress held at Harrogate (U.K) in 1962. This Index is expressed by a number ranging between zero and 100 and is independent of the overall ash content of the raw coal or the level of clean coal ash. When this index is low, the coal is difficult to wash and when the index is high the coal becomes easy to wash.

A graph is to be drawn between cumulative weight percent of floats and cumulative ash as percentage of the total ash in the raw coal at different yield levels. For any coal, this yield ash distribution curve originates at zero yield (corresponding to zero ash) and terminates at 100 yield (corresponding to 100 ash). For any hypothetical coal, which is absolutely non-washable, this curve has to take the form of a straight line running from zero yield (with zero ash) to 100 yield (with 100 ash). On the other hand, the greater the concavity of this curve, the better is the cleaning characteristics of the coal. When the area bounded by the curve and the diagonal through zero yield and 100 percent ash is expressed as the percent of the total area bounded by the two axes and the diagonal, **Washability Index** in terms of number is obtained, which has necessarily to lie between zero and 100.

The washability indices of a large number of coals from different coalfields of India, particularly from Jharia coalfield have been evaluated. It has been observed that the Indian coals, except the coals from the Assam coalfield which is of tertiary origin, gave indices between 15 and 43. For Assam coals, these indices varied between 47 and 56. The indices for British, German and American coals range between 45 and 76 indicating that they are comparatively much easier to wash. On the other hand, the indices of Japanese, Australian and South African coals range between 20 and 49 being more or less similar to those obtained for Indian coals.

Since the reserves of Indian coals having washability indices above 40 are limited, it may be convenient to adopt a suitable classification for defining the Washability

Table 20.4 Calculated values to determine W.I.

Sp. gr	Wt%	Ash%	Ash product	Cumulative floats		
				Wt%	Ash product	Ash%
1.30	10.0	4.0	40.0	10.0	40.0	2.2
1.35	15.0	6.0	90.0	25.0	130.0	7.1
1.40	20.0	8.0	160.0	45.0	290.0	15.7
1.45	25.0	14.0	350.0	70.0	640.0	34.7
1.50	10.0	24.0	240.0	80.0	880.0	47.8
1.55	5.0	32.0	160.0	85.0	1040.0	56.4
1.60	5.0	44.0	220.0	90.0	1260.0	68.4
1.75	5.0	56.0	280.0	95.0	1540.0	83.6
2.00	2.5	60.0	150.0	97.5	1690.0	91.7
2.00 (sink)	2.5	61.0	152.5	100.0	1842.5	100.0

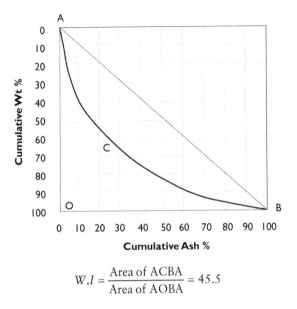

$$W.I = \frac{\text{Area of ACBA}}{\text{Area of AOBA}} = 45.5$$

Figure 20.4 Curve to determine Washability Index.

Index. Thus, coals having washability indices above 40 may be termed as easy coals, those lying between 21 and 40 as medium coals and those below 20 as difficult coals.

Table 20.4 shows the values calculated for drawing the curve to determine washability index for the hypothetical coal under consideration. The last column is the cumulative ash percentages with respect to total ash present in the coal.

Figure 20.4 shows the curve drawn with the above values. The washability index for this coal is 45.5.

20.5 OPTIMUM DEGREE OF WASHABILITY (O.D.W.)

For every coal, there is an optimal cut point, where one can expect the maximum advantage in coal-dirt separation.

While the washability index gives a general impression about the overall washability characteristics of a coal, it fails to locate this optimal cut point. With respect to a coal of some specified top size, the degree of washability at any particular level of cut can be represented by the following expression:

Degree of washability at any particular level of cut

$$= \frac{\text{Recovery percent of clean coal} \times (\text{Ash\% in raw coal} - \text{Ash\% in clean coal})}{\text{Ash\% in raw coal}}$$

$$(20.5)$$

The degree of washability of any coal at zero recovery level has to be zero, as one of the factors in the numerator becomes zero. So also at the recovery level of 100%, where there is no difference between the ash level of raw coal and that of clean coal, the product of the two factors representing the numerator becomes zero, signifying that the degree of washability at that level is again zero. In between these two recovery levels there is a value that represents the optimum degree of washability (ODW).

By plotting the degree of washability against recovery percent of cleans at different specific gravity levels, a peak point is observed for each coal. The degree of washability corresponding to this peak point is designated as the optimum degree of washability. This optimum degree of washability has its values lying between 0 and 100 and generally bears a rectilinear relationship with the washability index. A coal can be considered to have better washability characteristics, when it has higher ODW value and the lower corresponding clean coal ash.

Table 20.5 shows the values calculated for drawing the curve to determine optimum degree of washability for the coal under consideration.

The curve drawn between degree of washability and cumulative weight percent is shown in Fig. 20.5 and the value of optimum degree of washability is obtained as 36.

Table 20.5 Calculated values to determine O.D.W.

Sp. gr.	Wt%	Ash%	Cum Wt%	Cum Ash%	Degree of Washability
1.30	10.0	4.0	10.0	4.0	7.8
1.35	15.0	6.0	25.0	5.2	17.9
1.40	20.0	8.0	45.0	6.4	29.4
1.45	25.0	14.0	70.0	9.1	35.4
1.50	10.0	24.0	80.0	11.0	32.2
1.55	5.0	32.0	85.0	12.2	28.6
1.60	5.0	44.0	90.0	14.0	21.5
1.75	5.0	56.0	95.0	16.2	11.4
2.00	2.5	60.0	97.5	17.3	5.8
2.00 (sink)	2.5	61.0	100.0	18.4	0.0

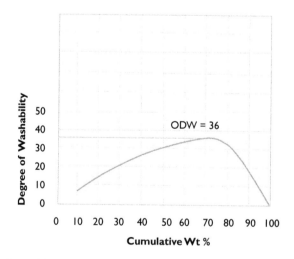

Figure 20.5 Curve to determine optimum degree of washability.

Table 20.6 Washability numbers and Ash% of coals from different countries.

Country	W.N	Optimum cleans ash%	Country	W.N	Optimum cleans ash%
U.K	157	3.5	Yugoslavia	57	7.3
Netherlands	136	4.2	Spain	50	8.9
W. Germany	126	4.4	Czechoslavakia	36	10.9
U.S.A	108	5.0	Rumania	31	12.2
U.S.S.R	98	5.5	Brazil	28	12.6
Canada	96	3.8	Hungary	27	11.9
Nigeria	94	4.0	Phillippines	26	12.5
China	64	6.0	Australia	25	11.4
Japan	60	7.4	South Africa	21	8.4
Turkey	58	8.4	Zaambia	19	15.6
			India	19	13.5

20.6   WASHABILITY NUMBER

To classify coals in accordance with their washablity characteristics, it may be more convenient to express the final value as the ratio of the Optimum Degree of Washability to the clean coal ash at this optimum level.

Since in coals having extremely intractable cleaning characteristics, the value of this ratio is often less than 1, a magnified scale is used by multiplying the resultant value by 10 and rounding up the decimal (if any) to the nearest whole number. This number calculated as

$$\frac{O.D.W}{Clean\ coal\ ash} \times 10 \qquad (20.6)$$

has been designated as Washability Number of a coal.

For the coal under consideration, the clean coal ash corresponding to optimum degree of washability is 8.8%.

Hence the washability number is $\frac{36}{8.8} \times 10 = 41$

Washability numbers and ash percent of optimum cleans for coals from different countries are shown in Table 20.6.

20.7   EFFECT OF SIZING ON WASHABILITY CHARACTERISTICS OF A COAL

It is well known that the size of a coal generally influences its washability characteristics. It is, therefore, expected that the various parameters used to define the washability characteristics of any coal should vary with the size of screening and size of crushing the coal.

Table 20.7.1 Effect of screening on washability characteristics.

Screened fraction mm	Ash%	Optimum sp.gr. of cut	O.D.W	Optimum ash% of cleans	W.N
75–25	27.5	1.54	12.8	21.9	6
25–13	28.7	1.56	16.3	21.5	8
13–3	26.0	1.525	19.3	17.9	11
3–0.5	18.8	1.48	34.1	8.1	42
–0.5	18.9	1.485	38.7	7.3	53
Total coal (75 mm–0)	26.9	1.53	19.9	19.9	8

Table 20.7.2 Effect of crushing on washability characteristics.

Raw coal crushed to mm	Ash%	Optimum sp.gr. of cut	O.D.W	Optimum ash% of cleans	W.N
200	23.6	1.51	11.4	18.8	6
75	23.4	1.52	13.2	18.0	7
13	23.0	1.53	16.9	16.4	10
3	23.6	1.545	21.5	15.3	14
0.5	23.4	1.55	25.0	14.1	18

Table 20.7.1 shows the effect of screening on washability characteristics of a typical coking coal initially crushed to 75 mm and screened at 25, 13, 3 and 0.5 mm.

From Table 20.7.1, it can be readily observed that screening results in yielding coal fractions having widely different washability characteristics caused mainly by the differential segregation of petrographic components in the different size fractions.

Table 20.7.2 shows the effect of crushing on washability characteristics of a very difficult Indian coal.

The values of the Table 20.7.2 evidently show that owing to the intimate association of dirt, little release can be affected by finer crushing.

20.8 MAYER CURVE

The Mayer curve, known as the M-curve, is a method of plotting float-and-sink analysis to predict the results of cleaning properties of coal in a three-component system. The method was first described by F.W.Mayer [38] in 1950 and applications of the method were discussed by him in 1956 and 1957. It is a useful tool to predict cleaning properties of a three-product separation wherein clean coal and middling can be predicted for the required ash percentages of clean coal and refuse. It can also be used in predicting cleaning properties of a product mixture resulting from blending a cleaned coal with un-cleaned coal, or blending two different plant clean coal products.

20.8.1 Construction of M-curve

The M-curve is constructed with the cumulative weight percent on the ordinate and cumulative ash percent on the abscissa. Diagonal lines (known as ash lines) are drawn from the origin to intersect the cumulative ash axis at each cumulative ash percent value from float-and-sink analysis. Each cumulative ash percent value is then plotted on its respective diagonal at the intersection of the corresponding cumulative weight ordinate. The M-curve is drawn through these points. Fig. 20.8.1 shows the construction of M-curve for the float-and-sink analysis data given in Table 20.1.3.

20.8.2 M-curve for a three product system

M-curve can be used to determine yield and ash percentages of clean coal and middling in a three product separation system. The detailed procedure for use of M-curve is explained taking float-and-sink data of Table 20.1.3. as an example.

In predicting the cleaning properties of three product separation system, desired ash contents for the clean coal and refuse are to be selected first. Let these selected values of ash percentages for clean coal and refuse be 10% and 55% respectively. Line OA is drawn (Fig. 20.8.2) from the origin to the selected clean coal ash% value of 10%. The line OA intersects the M-curve at a point C. Weight percent corresponding to this point C is the yield of clean coal and it is 74%. Next, line OB is drawn from the origin to the selected refuse ash% value of 55%. A line parallel to OB is drawn from point R, the ash percent of raw coal. This line intersects the M-curve at a point D. Weight percent corresponding to this point D is the combined yield of clean coal and middling and it is 84%. Subtracting the yield of clean coal percent 74% from the combined yield of clean coal and middling 84%, gives the yield of middling 10%. Finally, line OM is drawn

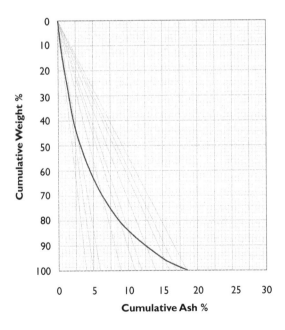

Figure 20.8.1 M-curve for float-and-sink analysis data of table 20.1.3.

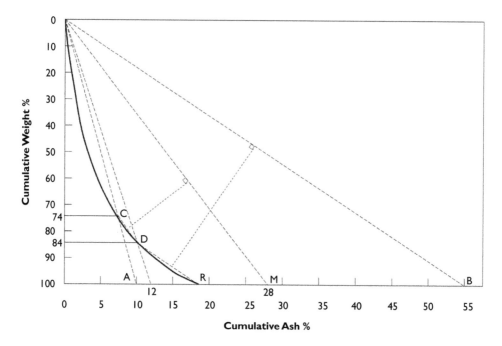

Figure 20.8.2 Example for prediction of cleaning properties in three product system.

from the origin parallel to a line connecting points C and D. The intersection of this line on the ash axis at M gives the ash percent of the middling, 28%. Line OD, drawn from the origin, intersects the ash axis, when extended, at 12% ash. This is the ash% of clean coal and middling together. The specific gravities to be maintained to get three products can be read from yield gravity curve corresponding to respective yields.

This graphical procedure is one of the useful ways to carry out the optimal yield study. The accuracy that is possible depends to a large extent on the degree of curvature exhibited by the curve.

20.8.3   M-curve for blended cleaned and un-cleaned coal

In certain instances, in few of the coal washeries, due to lack of costly fine coal beneficiation facility, un-cleaned fine coal is blended with cleaned coarse coal without affecting the resulted ash percentage much. In such cases M-curve can be used to predict the properties of such blended mixture. Substantial reduction in time and labor may be saved through the use of the M-curve. The practical use of the M-curve in predicting the properties of blended clean coal and un-cleaned coal mixture at optimum conditions is described by taking float-and-sink data of Table 20.1.3. as an example.

Let us consider the blending of an un-cleaned coal of 20% ash with a clean coal product. To prepare the blended clean coal and un-cleaned coal at 12% ash, the M-curve is employed to find the ash percent of clean coal. The ash lines of the blended coal mixture (12%) and un-cleaned coal (20%) are drawn from the origin on the M-curve (Fig. 20.8.3). A tangent parallel line to the 20% ash line is drawn on the M-curve at point C.

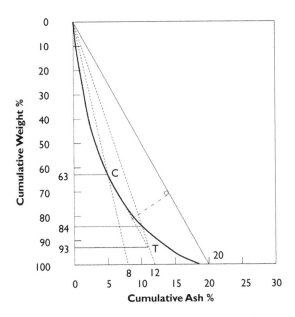

Figure 20.8.3 Predicting clean product by addition of un-cleaned coal to clean coal.

This line intersects the 12% ash line at point T. This corresponds to the ash percent of the clean coal and un-cleaned coal. The ash line is drawn from the origin through point C. On extending this line, it intersects the ash axis at 8% ash. Corresponding to point C, the yield is 63% read on weight axis. This is the yield of clean coal at 8% ash without adding un-cleaned coal. Corresponding to point of intersection of 12% ash line with the M-curve, the yield is 84%. It means that an yield of 84% is achievable if raw coal alone is washed to get 12% ash. From the set of washability curves drawn for the same data in Fig. 20.1, the specific gravity at which the raw coal can be washed to get 84% yield with 12% ash is 1.54. When un-cleaned coal is added to clean coal, the yield is 93% corresponding to point T. It is evident that the weight percent of un-cleaned coal added to the clean coal to obtain resulted 12% ash is 30% (93%-63%). From the set of washability curves drawn for the same data in Fig. 20.1, the specific gravity at which the raw coal can be washed to get 63% yield with 8% ash is 1.42. If 30% of uncleaned coal of 20% ash is added, the ash% of blended coal is 12%.

20.8.4 M-curve for blending clean coal from two plants

Figure 20.8.4 shows the M-curve for two raw coals, A and B, respectively. These two coals are cleaned separately to the required product ash percent of 12% by either an independent cleaning system in the same coal preparation plant or cleaned in two coal preparation plants separately. The 12% ash line of the product mixture is drawn on these two M-curves. This ash line intersects the two M-curves at a_1 and b_1. The intersection points indicate yields of 95% and 65% respectively. The separation specific gravities at ash percent of 12% are 1.80 and 1.48. With an assumed mixture

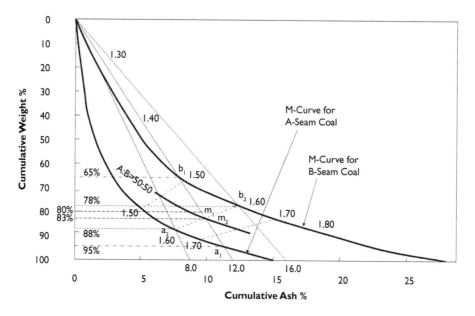

Figure 20.8.4 Mixing of two coals at 50:50 ratio to obtain highest yield for a given ash.

ratio of two raw feed coals A:B = 50:50, a total yield of 80% [(95+65)/2] can be achieved. This is shown in the Fig. 20.8.4 corresponding to point m_1 which is a mid-point of a_1 and b_1. It is to be determined whether 80% is maximum or some other maximum is there by combining two clean coals in the same ratio of 50:50 but washed to yield different ash percentages.

The following are the steps to be followed to determine separation specific gravity at which the yield increases at a mix ratio of 50:50 with 12% ash.

1   Connect equal specific gravity points (1.50, 1.60, and 1.70) on curves A and B.
2   Divide these connected lines according to the ratio 50:50 i.e. midpoint.
3   Connect the midpoints of the connected lines by a curve that represents the curve for a 50:50 mixture of coals A and B.
4   From the 50:50 mixture curve of A and B coals, determine the yield at 12% ash as well as the separation specific gravity at this yield.

As shown in Fig. 20.8.4, an yield of 83% is achievable with the same mix ratio of 50:50, and both the coals are to be washed at 1.60 specific gravity. An yield of 88% at 8% ash for A coal and an yield of 78% at 16% ash for B coal will be obtained.

A comparison between the two methods shows certain essential differences. In the first case, both coals A and B produce a clean coal with an ash percent of 12% and a yield of 95% and 65% are obtained when cleaned at the different separation specific gravities of 1.80 and 1.48 respectively. The combined yield is 80%. In the second case, two raw feed coals with different ash contents are washed at the same separation specific gravity of 1.60 yielding 88% and 78% respectively. The combined yield 83% is achieved at the desired ash percent of 12%. In the second case, the yield has increased by 3% when compared to the first case.

The validity of this method is not limited to the mixing ratio of 50:50 and can be extended to the other ratios. The ratio of 50:50 has been selected to facilitate clarity of the illustration and necessary explanations.

20.9 ILLUSTRATIVE EXAMPLES

Illustrative Example 20.9.1: *When a sample of coal is subjected to float and sink analysis, the values recorded are shown in Table 20.9.1.*

Table 20.9.1 Float and sink analysis data for illustrative example 20.9.1.

Sp.gr of liquid used	Weight of watch glass gm	Weight of watch glass with coal sunk gm	Weight of empty crucible gm	Weight of crucible with coal gm	Weight of crucible with coal heated at 750°C till constant weight gm
1.30	18.48	27.07	16.842	17.707	16.885
1.40	18.25	38.96	17.468	18.405	17.554
1.50	17.87	49.37	17.354	18.199	17.520
1.60	17.54	26.03	17.637	18.457	17.877
1.70	18.36	21.37	16.987	17.767	17.299
1.80	17.65	20.13	17.123	17.918	17.492
1.80 (sink)	18.53	33.75	17.234	18.069	17.865

Calculate the ash percentage of the coal sample taken.

Solution:
Values of wt%, Ash% & Ash product are calculated and tabulated in the Table 20.9.1.1.

Table 20.9.1.1 Calculated values for illustrative example 20.9.1.

Sp. gr	Wt of coal	Wt%	Weight of Coal taken	Weight of Ash	Ash%	Ash product
1.30	8.59	9.55	0.865	0.043	4.97	47.4635
1.40	20.71	23.01	0.937	0.086	9.18	211.2318
1.50	31.50	35.00	0.845	0.166	19.64	687.4000
1.60	8.49	9.43	0.820	0.240	29.27	276.0161
1.70	3.01	3.34	0.780	0.312	40.00	133.6000
1.80	2.48	2.76	0.795	0.369	46.42	128.1192
1.80 (sink)	15.22	16.91	0.835	0.631	75.57	1277.8887

						2761.7193

Ash% of coal sample = 2761.7193/100 = 27.62%

Illustrative Example 20.9.2: *Float and sink test data of a coal of –2+0.5 mm size is shown in Table 20.9.2.*

Table 20.9.2 Float and sink test data for illustrative example 20.9.2.

Sp. gr.	Wt% of floated coal	Ash% of floated coal
1.30	2.10	4.70
1.40	10.00	6.22
1.50	13.67	13.24
1.60	13.52	20.26
1.70	13.21	27.86
1.80	8.62	39.64
1.90	5.54	46.83
2.00	5.13	51.01
2.00 (sink)	28.21	74.23

Determine the washability characteristics.

Solution:
Cumulative wt% of floats and their ash% and cumulative wt% of sinks and their ash% are calculated and tabulated as shown in Table 20.9.2.1.

Table 20.9.2.1   Calculated values for illustrative example 20.9.2.

Sp. gr	Wt%	Ash%	Ash product	Cumulative floats Wt%	Cumulative floats Ash product	Cumulative floats Ash%	Cumulative sinks Wt%	Cumulative sinks Ash product	Cumulative sinks Ash%
1.3	2.10	4.70	9.87	2.10	9.87	4.70	97.90	3841.98	39.24
1.4	10.00	6.22	62.20	12.10	72.07	5.96	87.90	3779.78	43.00
1.5	13.67	13.24	180.99	25.77	253.06	9.82	74.23	3598.79	48.48
1.6	13.52	20.26	273.92	39.29	526.98	13.41	60.71	3324.87	54.77
1.7	13.21	27.86	368.03	52.50	895.01	17.05	47.50	2956.84	62.25
1.8	8.62	39.64	341.69	61.12	1236.70	20.23	38.88	2615.15	67.26
1.9	5.54	46.83	259.44	66.66	1496.14	22.44	33.34	2355.71	70.66
2.0	5.13	51.01	261.68	71.79	1757.82	24.49	28.21	2094.03	74.23
2.0 sink	28.21	74.23	2094.03	100.00	3851.85	38.52	------	---------	------

Percent ±0.1 near gravity material (NGM) at each specific gravity, cumulative ash percentages with respect to total ash present in the coal and degree of washabilty at each specific gravity by using the expression

$$\frac{\text{Recovery percent of clean coal} \times (\text{Ash\% in raw coal} - \text{Ash\% in clean coal})}{\text{Ash\% in raw coal}}$$

are calculated and tabulated as shown in Table 20.9.2.2.

Table 20.9.2.2 Calculated values of NGM & D.W. for illustrated example 20.9.2.

Sp. gr	Wt%	NGM	Ash%	Ash product	Cum Ash%	D.W
1.3	2.10	12.10	4.70	9.87	0.26	1.84
1.4	10.00	23.67	6.22	62.20	1.87	10.23
1.5	13.67	27.19	13.24	180.99	6.57	19.20
1.6	13.52	26.73	20.26	273.92	13.68	25.61
1.7	13.21	21.83	27.86	368.03	23.24	29.26
1.8	8.62	14.16	39.64	341.69	32.11	29.02
1.9	5.54	10.67	46.83	259.44	38.84	27.83
2.0	5.13	—	51.01	261.68	45.64	26.15
2.0 sink	28.21	—	74.23	2094.03	100.00	—

With these values, washability curves are drawn as shown in Fig. 20.9.2.1

1   Characteristic Curve
2   Total floats-ash Curve
3   Total sinks-ash Curve
4   Yield gravity Curve
5   Near gravity material Curve

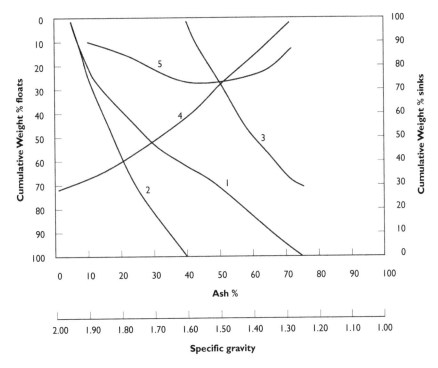

Figure 20.9.2.1   Washability Curves for illustrative example 20.9.2.

Another two graphs, one to determine washability index and another to determine optimum degree of washability, are drawn as shown in Fig. 20.9.2.2 & 20.9.2.3.

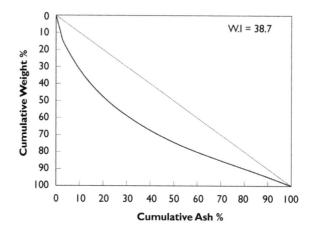

Figure 20.9.2.2   Graph to determine Washability Index for illustrative example 20.9.2.

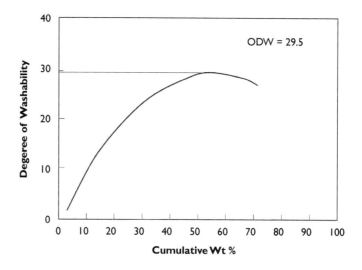

Figure 20.9.2.3   Graph to determine O.D.W for illustrative example 20.9.2.

From the shape of characteristic curve, it is understood that the coal is difficultly washable. The near gravity material at 1.5 and 1.6 specific gravities is more than 25%. Hence the coal is not washable as per the BIRD'S classification. Even at 1.7 specific gravity, the near gravity material is 21.83% and indicates that the coal is exceedingly difficult to wash.

The value of Washability Index (WI) obtained from the graph is 38.7 and the value of Optimum Degree of Washability (ODW) obtained from the graph is 29.5. The yield corresponding to ODW of 29.5 is 56.0% from the graph. From washability curves, ash in clean coal corresponding to this yield is 19.0 from curve.2, corresponding specific gravity of separation is 1.74 from curve.4, this is an Optimum cut point, near gravity material (NGM) at this optimum cut point is 20.0 from curve. 5.

$$\text{Washability Number (WN)} = \frac{29.5}{19.0} \times 10 = 15.5$$

From the values of NGM, WI and WN, it can be concluded that the coal is difficult to wash but not that difficult as indicated at specific gravities 1.5, 1.6 and 1.7. Hence more efficient operation like Heavy Medium Cyclone is to be used for washing the coal at this size range.

Illustrative Example 20.9.3: *By using the float and sink data of a coal sample shown in Table 20.9.3, calculate ash% in coal sample, clean coal and rejects when the coal is washed at 1.5 specific gravity.*

Table 20.9.3 Float and sink data for illustrative example 20.9.3.

Specific gravity	Weight of the coal floated gm	Weight of the ash in floated coal, gm
1.30	11.4	0.5
1.40	24.4	2.0
1.50	5.6	1.1
1.60	2.3	0.7
1.80	2.4	1.0
2.00	3.9	2.5

Solution:
Cumulative Ash for first 3 rows and last 3 rows are calculated separately from the above tabulated data and shown in the Table 20.9.3.1

Table 20.9.3.1 Cumulative ash for illustrative example 20.9.3.

Specific gravity	Weight of the coal floated gm	Weight of the ash in floated coal, gm	Cum. Ash
1.30	11.4	0.5	0.5
1.40	24.4	2.0	2.5
1.50	5.6	1.1	3.6
1.60	2.3	0.7	0.7
1.80	2.4	1.0	1.7
2.00	3.9	2.5	4.2

$$\text{Ash\% in coal sample} = \frac{3.6 + 4.2}{11.4 + 24.4 + 5.6 + 2.3 + 2.4 + 3.9} \times 100 = 15.6\%$$

$$\text{Ash\% in clean coal} = \frac{3.6}{11.4 + 24.4 + 5.6} \times 100 \qquad = 8.7\%$$

$$\text{Ash\% in rejects} = \frac{4.2}{2.3 + 2.4 + 3.9} \times 100 \qquad = 48.8\%$$

Illustrative Example 20.9.4: *The washability test data of a sample of coal is given in Table 20.9.4.*

Table 20.9.4 Washability test data for illustrative example 20.9.4.

Sp. gr	Wt%	Ash%
– 1.30	36.0	2.6
+1.30–1.35	25.7	7.5
+1.35–1.40	11.0	14.1
+1.40–1.45	5.3	19.2
+1.45–1.50	3.5	23.9
+1.50–1.55	2.0	28.1
+1.55–1.60	1.2	31.7
+1.60–1.65	1.1	34.3
+1.65–1.70	0.7	37.5
+1.70	13.5	67.4

When this coal is washed, a clean coal of 8.8% ash is obtained. Find

a   *Recovery of clean coal*
b   *Ash percent in rejects*
c   *Maximum ash in any particle in the clean coal product*
d   *Specific gravity of separation*

Calculate yield reduction factor and assess the washability character.

Solution:
The required values are calculated and tabulated in the Table 20.9.4.1

Table 20.9.4.1 Calculated values for illustrative example 20.9.4.

Sp. gr	Wt%	Ash%	Ash points	Cumulative floats Wt%	Cumulative floats Ash points	Cumulative floats Ash%	Cumulative sinks Wt%	Cumulative sinks Ash points	Cumulative sinks Ash%
1	2	3	4	5	6	7	8	9	10
1.30	36.0	2.6	93.60	36.0	93.60	2.6	64.0	1601.38	25.0
1.35	25.7	7.5	192.75	61.7	286.35	4.6	39.3	1408.63	35.8
1.40	11.0	14.1	155.10	72.7	441.45	6.1	27.3	1253.53	45.9
1.45	5.3	19.2	101.76	78.0	543.21	7.0	22.0	1151.77	52.4
1.50	3.5	23.9	83.65	81.5	626.86	7.7	18.5	1068.12	57.7
1.55	2.0	28.1	56.20	83.5	683.06	8.2	16.3	1011.92	61.5
1.60	1.2	31.7	38.04	84.7	721.10	8.5	15.3	973.88	63.7
1.65	1.1	34.3	37.73	85.8	758.83	8.8	14.2	936.15	65.9
1.70	0.7	37.5	26.25	86.5	785.08	9.1	13.5	909.90	67.4
1.70 sink	13.5	67.4	909.90	100.0	1694.98	16.9	—	—	—

From the 8th row of the table, for floats of 8.8% ash the following are read:

a Recovery of the clean coal = 85.8% (5th column)
b Ash percent in rejects = 65.9% (10th column)
c Maximum ash in a particle of the clean coal product = 34.3% (3rd column)
d Specific gravity of separation = 1.65 (1st column)
Reduction in yield = 100–85.8 = 14.2%
Reduction in ash = 16.9–8.8 = 8.1%

$$\therefore \text{Yield Reduction Factor} = \frac{14.2}{8.1} = 1.75$$

Hence the coal is easy to wash.

Illustrative Example 20.9.5: *The washability test data of a sample of coal is given in Table 20.9.5.*

Table 20.9.5 Washability test data for illustrative example 20.9.5.

Sp. gr	*Wt%*	*Ash%*
1.40	14.32	10.79
1.50	31.32	21.09
1.60	11.06	29.33
1.70	10.98	34.80
1.80	20.33	46.72
1.90	01.23	53.47
1.90 sink	10.76	78.84

By using M-curve, determine yield and ash percentages of clean coal and middlings for the clean coal of 17% ash and refuse of 50% ash.

Solution:
Cumulative weight percentages and ash percentages are calculated necessary for drawing M-curve and shown in Table 20.9.5.1.

Table 20.9.5.1 Cumulative percentages for illustrative example 20.9.5.

				Cumulative floats		
Specific gravity	*Wt% of floats*	*Floats Ash%*	*Ash product*	*Wt%*	*Ash product*	*Ash%*
1.40	14.32	10.79	154.51	14.32	154.51	10.79
1.50	31.32	21.09	660.54	45.64	815.05	17.86
1.60	11.06	29.33	324.39	56.70	1139.44	20.10
1.70	10.98	34.80	382.10	67.68	1521.54	22.48
1.80	20.33	46.72	949.82	88.01	2471.36	28.08
1.90	1.23	53.47	65.77	89.24	2537.13	28.48
1.90 (sink)	10.76	78.84	848.32	100.00	3385.45	33.85

Yield gravity curve is drawn and shown in Figure 20.9.5.1.

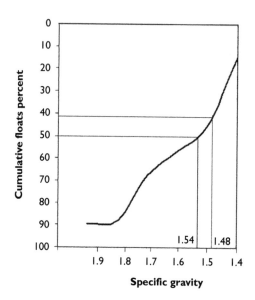

Figure 20.9.5.1 Yield gravity curve for illustrative example 20.9.5.

M-curve is drawn as per the procedure given in article 20.8.1. and yield and ash percentages are determined from M-curve as per the procedure given in article 20.8.2. and shown in Figure 20.9.5.2.

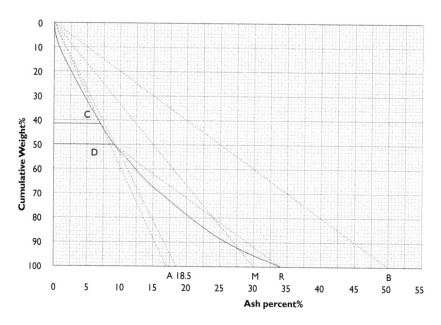

Figure 20.9.5.2 M-curve for illustrative example 20.9.5.

The following results were obtained from the graph:

Yield of clean coal corresponding to point C = 42%
Yield of clean coal and middlings corresponding to point D = 50%
∴ Yield of middlings = 50–42 = 8%

Ash% of middlings at M = 30%
Ash% of clean coal and middlings together = 18.5%
Yield of refuse = 100–50 = 50%

From yield gravity curve,

Specific gravity of separation to get clean coal = 1.48
Specific gravity of separation to get middlings = 1.54

Illustrative Example 20.9.6: *For the problem 20.9.5, determine clean coal product to be obtained in order to blend the uncleaned coal of 35% ash to this clean coal to get blended mixture of 25% ash. Also determine ash% of clean coal.*

Solution:
M-curve is constructed and followed the procedure given in 20.8.3 and shown in Figure 20.9.6.

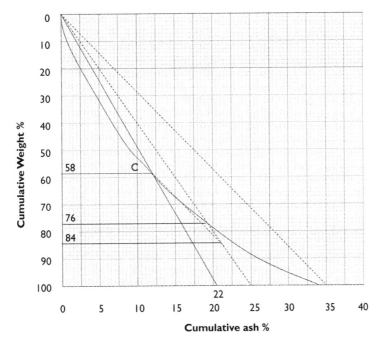

Figure 20.9.6 Prediction of clean coal product required for illustrative example 20.9.6.

From the graph,

Wt% of uncleaned coal to be blended = 84–58 = 26%
Wt% of clean coal = 100–26 = 74%
Ash% of clean coal = 22%

20.10   PROBLEMS FOR PRACTICE

20.10.1: *Float and sink test data of coal of –38+25 mm size is shown in Table 20.10.1. Determine the washability characteristics.*

Table 20.10.1 Float and sink test data for problem 20.10.1.

Specific gravity	Wt% of floats	Floats Ash%
1.40	12.35	15.28
1.50	34.96	22.08
1.60	25.04	33.17
1.70	3.45	42.37
1.80	13.06	48.69
1.90	2.61	53.15
1.90 (sink)	8.53	76.03

[WI = 26, ODW = 21, WN = 9.5]

20.10.2: *Washability test data of a coal sample is shown in Table 20.10.2.*

Table 20.10.2 Washability test data for problem 20.10.2.

Sp. gr.	Differential % of floats	Ash% in differential floats
1.30	7.6	5.9
1.40	21.3	12.7
1.50	36.7	21.8
1.60	13.8	30.5
1.70	11.6	39.6
1.80	4.8	48.3
1.80 (sink)	4.2	63.4

Determine the specific gravity at which the separation should be done for the beneficiation of this coal so that the ash content of the clean coal is not more than 17%. What is the expected yield of clean coal corresponding to this separation? Find out the ash percent in refuse and maximum ash of a particle in the yield. Calculate the yield reduction factor.   [1.50, 65.6%, 40.07%, 21.8%, 4.33]

20.10.3 *Washability test data of a coal sample is shown in Table 20.10.3*

Table 20.10.3 Washability test data for problem 20.10.3.

Sp. gr.	Differential% of floats	Ash% in differential floats
1.40	7.5	14.1
1.50	13.1	26.6
1.60	12.6	36.6
1.70	11.8	42.7
1.80	6.8	47.9
1.90	7.2	53.8
2.00	7.0	61.1
2.00 (sink)	34.0	76.3

Determine yield and ash percentages of clean coal and middlings to get clean coal of 30% ash and refuse of 75% ash.   *[yields-43%, 9%, ash-45%]*

Chapter 21

Coal beneficiation processes

The commercial processes of coal beneficiation are based on the differences in some physical properties of the pure coal and the impure coal (refuse). The difference in specific gravity is the basis for the largest number of coal beneficiation processes in which case they are termed as **Gravity Concentration Processes**. Depending upon the medium used for beneficiation of coal, the various processes are classified as **WET** or **DRY**. Those processes using water as medium are WET processes and are known as **Washing Processes**. The coal beneficiation plants using wet processes are named as **Coal washeries**. For raw coal fines of –0.5 mm, the difference in surface property is utilized since conventional gravity dependent processes are inefficient for this size range.

Among the various wet washing processes, Heavy medium separation (including Heavy medium cyclones & Water only cyclones), Jigging, Spiraling, Froth flotation, Column flotation and Oil agglomeration are the processes used in majority of the coal washeries all over the world. None of these equipments is capable of treating the whole size range of coal. Fig. 21.1 shows the preferred feed size ranges for the major coal beneficiation processes.

The commercial coal processing plants are installed based on the recommendations from the laboratory and pilot plant investigations. The commercial plants may include the beneficiation of coal of desired top size and/or a particular size fraction or to beneficiate the coal at desired quality having specific size range. The beneficiation circuit of the commercial plants depends on the objective of the processing in terms of size, quantity and quality.

There is a wide variation in beneficiation of coal which may be classified in accordance with level or degree of processing. A few levels of coal processing can be summarized as:

Level – I   Crushing and screening only
   II   Coarse Coal Beneficiation only (100–25 mm)
   III   Coarse coal and simple fine coal beneficiation (down to 0.5 mm)
   IV   Coarse coal and fine coal beneficiation including fines of –0.5 mm
   V   Multiple stages of crushing and beneficiation

Those processes using air as medium are dry processes and known as **Cleaning Processes**. Very few coal beneficiation plants are using dry processes. Air dense

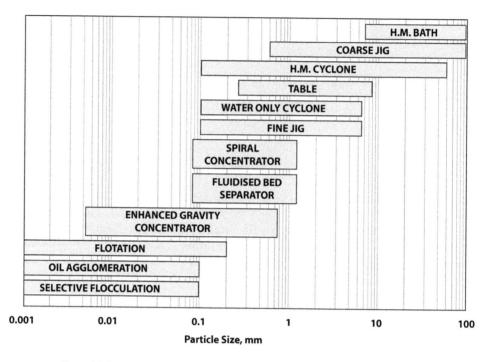

Figure 21.1 Preferred feed size ranges for major coal beneficiation processes.

medium fluidized bed separator, All-air jig, and Air tabling are the dry beneficiation processes employed in few coal beneficiation plants. RAMDARS (RadioMetric Detection And Removal of Stone/Shale) is an indigenously developed Dry coal beneficiation technology for Indian coals. ArdeeSort is the next generation technology to complement RAMDARS. This along with the RAMDARS technology provides complete dry beneficiation solution for coal and lignite. RAMDARS processes material above 50 mm size and ArdeeSort processes material below 50 mm size.

Chapter 22

Principles of gravity concentration processes

Among the several processes, heavy medium separation, jigging, tabling and spiraling are gravity concentration processes and are based on settling characteristics of various particles.

A theoretical analysis on the settling conditions and knowledge of the parameters that influence the motion of particles in a fluid is essential to analyse the gravity concentration processes, to design the suitable equipment and to apply the process for separation of coal.

22.1 MOTION OF PARTICLES IN A FLUID

When a solid particle falls freely in a vacuum, it is subject to constant acceleration and its velocity increases indefinitely, being independent of size and specific gravity. Thus an iron particle and a feather fall at exactly the same rate. But if they are allowed to fall in any medium like air, iron particle lands first due to the resistance offered by the medium.

Consider a single homogeneous spherical particle of diameter d and density ρ_p falling under gravity in a viscous fluid of density ρ_f. Let the particle is falling in a fluid extending in all directions to infinity in a uniform field of force.

There are three forces acts on a particle:

Gravity force, $m_p g$, product of the mass of the particle (m_p) and acceleration due to gravity (g), acts downwards

Buoyant force, $m_f g$, (by Archimedes' principle) product of the mass of the fluid displaced by the particle (m_f) and the acceleration due to gravity (g), which acts parallel and opposite to the gravity force

Drag force, R, (resistance to the motion), which acts on the surface of the particle and is parallel and opposite to the gravity force. This force increases with the velocity of the particle.

According to the Newton's second law of motion, the equation of motion of the particle is

$$m_p g - m_f g - R = m_p \frac{dv}{dt} \tag{22.1.1}$$

where v is the velocity of the particle and $\frac{dv}{dt}$ is the acceleration of the particle

If the drag force or resistance force becomes equal in magnitude and opposite in direction to the resultant of the other two forces (gravity and buoyant) acting on a particle in a fluid, the acceleration of the particle will be nil and the velocity is constant.

This velocity is the maximum velocity attained by the particle. It is known as **maximum velocity** or **terminal velocity**. When once the particle attains this velocity, it will fall with the same velocity thereafter:

When the acceleration is zero, the particle attains the terminal velocity.

Hence when dv/dt = 0, equation 22.1.1 becomes

$$0 = m_p g - m_f g - R$$
$$\Rightarrow \quad R = g(m_p - m_f)$$
$$\Rightarrow \quad R = g\left(\frac{\pi}{6}d^3\rho_p - \frac{\pi}{6}d^3\rho_f\right)$$
$$\Rightarrow \quad R = \frac{\pi}{6}gd^3(\rho_p - \rho_f) \tag{22.1.2}$$

The nature of the resistance (or drag) depends on the velocity of descent. At low velocities, motion is smooth because the layer of fluid in contact with the body moves with it, while the fluid, a short distance away, is motionless. Between these two positions is a zone of intense shear in the fluid all around the descending particle. Hence the resistance to the motion is due to the shear forces or viscosity of the fluid and is called **viscous resistance**.

An eminent English physicist, Stokes (1891) [39], has shown that if the velocity is low enough to cause viscous or laminar flow, the resistance to the motion of a falling sphere, he deduced, is $3\pi d\mu_f v_m$ where μ_f is the viscosity of the fluid and v_m is the terminal velocity of the particle.

Now the equation of motion of the particle, equation 22.1.2, after the particle reaches its terminal velocity, becomes

$$3\pi d\mu_f v_m = \frac{\pi}{6}gd^3(\rho_p - \rho_f) \tag{22.1.3}$$

On computation, this gives

$$v_m = \frac{d^2 g(\rho_p - \rho_f)}{18\mu_f} \tag{22.1.4}$$

This expression is known as Stokes' law and is applicable for fine particles of size less than 50 microns, and is also applicable with small deviations up to 100 microns.

As the size of the particle increases, settling velocity increases. At high velocities, the main resistance is due to the displacement of fluid by the particle and is known as **turbulent resistance**. In this case, the viscous resistance is relatively small.

Sir Isaac Newton [40] assumed that the resistance is entirely due to **turbulent resistance** and deduced as $0.055\pi d^2 v_m^2 \rho_f$.

Now the equation of motion of the particle, equation 22.1.2, after the particle reaches its terminal velocity, becomes

$$0.055\pi d^2 (v_m)^2 \, \rho_f = \frac{\pi}{6} g d^3 (\rho_p - \rho_f) \tag{22.1.5}$$

On computation, this gives

$$v_m = \sqrt{\frac{3gd(\rho_p - \rho_f)}{\rho_f}} \tag{22.1.6}$$

This expression is applicable for the particles of size greater than 2000 microns.

Whether viscous or turbulent resistance predominates, the acceleration of particles in a fluid rapidly decreases and terminal velocity is quickly reached.

From the Stokes' and Newton's laws, it is evident that the terminal velocity of a spherical particle is a function of size and specific gravity of the particle. If two particles have the same specific gravity, then the larger diameter particle has higher terminal velocity and if two particles have the same diameter, then the heavier particle has higher terminal velocity. The velocity of an irregularly shaped particle with which it is settling in a fluid medium also depends on its shape. As almost all natural particles are irregular in shape, it can be stated that

> The coarser, heavier and rounder particles settle faster
> than the finer, lighter and more angular particles

In a large volume of fluid, the particle settles by its own specific gravity, size and shape and uninfluenced by the surrounding particles as particles are not crowded. Such settling process is called **Free settling**. Free settling predominates in well dispersed pulps where the percent solids by weight are less than 10. Fig. 22.1 A shows how the particles of different sizes and two specific gravities settle under free settling conditions.

When the particles settle in relatively small volume of fluid, they are crowded in the pulp and are very close to each other. As a result, the settling of a particle is influenced by surrounding particles. Such settling process is called **Hindered settling**. In this type of settling, particles collide each other during their settling and this collision affects their settling velocities. Thus lower settling velocities are encountered.

Hindered settling predominates when the percent solids by weight is more than 15. Fig. 22.1 B shows how the same particles, as considered in free settling, settle under hindered settling conditions. By comparing Fig. 22.1 A & Fig. 22.1 B, it is evident that more heavier (or lighter) particles can be separated when they settle by hindered settling. This is possible because hindered settling reduces the effect of size and increases the effect of specific gravity. This fact can be obtained mathematically by considering settling ratios.

22.1.1 Equal settling particles

Particles are said to be equal settling if they have the same terminal velocities in the same fluid and in the same field of force.

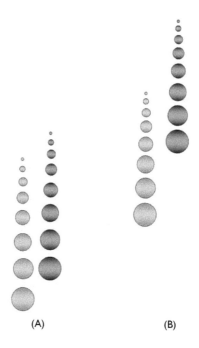

(A)   (B)

Figure 22.1 Settling of particles under (A) Free settling (B) Hindered settling conditions.

22.1.2 Settling ratio

Settling ratio is the ratio of the sizes of two particles of different specific gravities fall at equal rates.

Under free settling conditions, settling ratio is known as **free settling ratio** and can be obtained by equating the terminal velocities of lighter and heavier particles of different sizes:

From Stokes' law (equation 22.1.4)

$$\frac{d_1^2 g(\rho_{p1} - \rho_f)}{18\mu_f} = \frac{d_2^2 g(\rho_{p2} - \rho_f)}{18\mu_f}$$

where

d_1, d_2 are the diameters of lighter and heavier particles
ρ_{p1}, ρ_{p2} are the densities of lighter and heavier particles

$$\Rightarrow \qquad \frac{d_1}{d_2} = \left(\frac{\rho_{p2} - \rho_f}{\rho_{p1} - \rho_f}\right)^{1/2} \qquad (22.1.7)$$

where $\frac{d_1}{d_2}$ is the free settling ratio.

From Newton's law (equation 22.1.6)

$$\sqrt{\frac{3gd_1(\rho_{p1}-\rho_f)}{\rho_f}} = \sqrt{\frac{3gd_2(\rho_{p2}-\rho_f)}{\rho_f}}$$

$$\Rightarrow \qquad \frac{d_1}{d_2} = \left(\frac{\rho_{p2}-\rho_f}{\rho_{p1}-\rho_f}\right) \qquad\qquad (22.1.8)$$

The general expression for free settling ratio can be written as

$$\text{Free settling ratio} = \frac{d_1}{d_2} = \left(\frac{\rho_{p2}-\rho_f}{\rho_{p1}-\rho_f}\right)^n \qquad\qquad (22.1.9)$$

where $n = 0.5$ for small particles obeying Stokes' law and $n = 1$ for large particles obeying Newton's law.

The value of n lies in the range 0.5–1.0 for particles in the intermediate size range of 50 microns –0.2 cm.

Consider a mixture of shale (density 2.4 gm/cm^3) and coal (density 1.35 gm/cm^3) particles settling in water. For small particles, obeying Stoke's law, the free settling ratio is

$$\sqrt{\frac{2.4-1.0}{1.35-1.0}} = 2.0$$

i.e., a small shale particle will settle at the same rate as small coal particle of diameter 2.0 times larger than shale particle. (Fig. 22.2 A shows the settling of small particles).

For coarse particles, obeying Newton's law, the free settling ratio is

$$\frac{2.4-1.0}{1.35-1.0} = 4.0$$

i.e., a coarse shale particle will settle at the same rate as coarse coal particle of diameter 4.0 times larger than coal particle. (Fig. 22.2 B shows the settling of coarser particles).

Therefore the free settling ratio for coarse particles is larger than that of fine particles. This means that density difference between the particles has more effect at coarser size ranges when they settle.

In other words, a particle of shale of density 2.4 gm/cm^3 is equal falling with a particle of density 1.35 gm/cm^3 when the latter is four times its size, so that if this ratio is exceeded, the larger coal falls with the small shale or dirt. Hence to ensure separation of coal from dirt by this principle, the mixture must be sized so that the maximum size is not greater than four times the minimum size, otherwise a large piece of coal would fall faster than the smallest piece of shale or dirt.

As the percent solids in the pulp increases, the effect of particle crowding becomes more and the individual particles tend to interfere with each other and therefore the velocity of motion or rate of settling of each individual particle will be considerably less than that for the free settling conditions. The system begins to behave as a heavy liquid whose density is that of the pulp rather that of carrier liquid. Now the hindered settling conditions prevail. It must be noted that each particle is in fact settling through a suspension of other particles in the liquid rather than through the simple liquid itself.

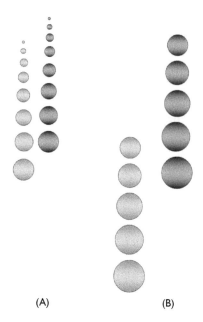

(A)   (B)

Figure 22.2 Free settling of (A) Small particles (B) Coarse particles.

The effective density and viscosity of a concentrated suspension are much larger than those of clear liquid. The settling medium therefore offers high resistance and this resistance to fall is mainly due to turbulence created. Hence the Newton's law can be used to determine the approximate terminal velocity of the particles by replacing ρ_f by ρ_{sl} the density of the pulp or slurry.

$$v_m = \sqrt{\frac{3gd(\rho_p - \rho_{sl})}{\rho_{sl}}} \tag{22.1.10}$$

The lower the density of the particle, the more marked is the effect of reduction of the effective density, $(\rho_p - \rho_{sl})$, and the greater is the reduction in falling velocity. Similarly, the larger the particle, the greater is the reduction in falling rate as the pulp density increases.

Hindered settling ratio can be obtained by equating the terminal velocities of lighter and heavier particles of different sizes

$$v_m = \sqrt{\frac{3gd_1(\rho_{p1} - \rho_{sl})}{\rho_{sl}}} = \sqrt{\frac{3gd_2(\rho_{p2} - \rho_{sl})}{\rho_{sl}}}$$

$$\Rightarrow \qquad \text{Hindered settling ratio} = \frac{d_1}{d_2} = \frac{\rho_{p2} - \rho_{sl}}{\rho_{p1} - \rho_{sl}} \tag{22.1.11}$$

For mixture of shale and coal particles settling in a pulp of density 1.20 gm/cm³, the hindered settling ratio is

$$\frac{2.4 - 1.2}{1.35 - 1.2} = 6.2$$

i.e., a shale particle will settle at the same rate as coal particle of diameter 6.2 times larger than shale particle.

When the hindered settling ratio of 6.2 is compared with the free settling ratio of 4.0, it is evident that hindered settling reduces the effect of size, while increasing the effect of density, which means that more heavier (or lighter) particles can be separated in hindered settling.

Hindered settling ratio is always greater than the free settling ratio. As the pulp density increases, this ratio also increases.

Free settling conditions are used in classifiers, in which case they are called Free settling classifiers (Mechanical classifiers or Horizontal current classifiers), to increase the effect of size on separation. Hindered settling conditions are used in classifiers, in which case they are called Hindered settling classifiers (Hydraulic classifiers or Vertical current classifiers), to increase the effect of density on separation.

The motion of a particle, when it starts settling in the fluid and move through the fluid, can be divided into two stages viz., the acceleration period and the terminal velocity period. Initially the velocity of the particle is zero with respect to the fluid and increases to the terminal velocity during a short period, usually of the order of one tenth of a second or less. During this first stage of short period, there are initial-acceleration effects. When once the particle reaches its terminal velocity, second stage starts and continues as long as the particle continues to settle. Classification, Heavy medium separation and thickening processes make use of the terminal velocity period.

In jigging operation, particles are allowed to settle during the acceleration period.

22.2 HEAVY MEDIUM SEPARATION

In a heavy medium separation process such as Chance Cone process which is outstanding process and widely used for washing the coal, sand in the size range of 30–100 B.S. mesh is used as heavy medium in suspension with water. This suspension is maintained in a conical tank by an upward water current and gentle mechanical agitation. The coal particles are introduced in sand suspension (called as pseudo liquid) which is under hindered settling conditions. The particles lighter than the apparent specific gravity of the suspension will float and heavy particles will sink.

The hindered settling column in the chance cone may be assumed to contain the following:

1   Silica sand, closely sized and averaging about 0.3 mm in size, and specific gravity of 2.65
2   Coal and refuse (shale or slate) particles ranging from 75–13 mm in size and 1.30 to 2.50 in specific gravity

The rising water current in the cone is adjusted to give a suspension density of 1.50, corresponding to the desired point of separation. Assuming that equilibrium is maintained with respect to the sand in the cone, the rising current will be roughly equivalent to the average settling velocity of the sand grains in stable suspension.

The Hindered settling Ratio in this case is

$$\frac{d_c}{d_s} = \frac{\rho_s - \rho_{sl}}{\rho_c - \rho_{sl}} \qquad \qquad 22.2.1$$

where
d_c = Diameter of coal particles, cm
d_s = Diameter of sand particles, cm
ρ_c = Density of the coal particles, gm/cm³
ρ_s = Density of sand particles, gm/cm³
ρ_{sl} = Density of sand suspension, gm/cm³

Substituting the following assumed values in the above equation
d_s = 0.03 cm = Diameter of sand particles, cm
ρ_s = 2.65 gm/cm³ = Density of sand particles, gm/cm³
ρ_{sl} = 1.50 gm/cm³ = Density of sand suspension, gm/cm³

$$\frac{d_c}{0.03} = \frac{2.65 - 1.50}{\rho_c - 1.50} \quad \Rightarrow \quad d_c = \frac{0.03(2.65 - 1.50)}{\rho_c - 1.50}$$

$$\Rightarrow \quad d_c = \frac{0.0345}{\rho_c - 1.50} \qquad \qquad (22.2.2)$$

If the specific gravity of the sand suspension is maintained at 1.50, all particles of specific gravity 1.50 will float, irrespective of hindered settling conditions. On the other hand, it is not true that all particles of specific gravity greater than 1.50 will sink, as occurs in an ideal gravity separation when liquids are used as medium, due to differential settling characteristics of the various particles. For example, specific gravity of coal 1.51 is substituted in the equation 22.2.2, the value of d_c will be 3.45 cm, which means that all particles of specific gravity 1.51 and smaller than 3.45 cm will rise. For particles of specific gravity 1.55, d_c becomes 0.69 cm and all particles smaller than 0.69 cm will rise. For particles of specific gravity 1.60, d_c becomes 0.315 cm and so on.

When the coal particles of size 75–13 mm are treated in Heavy Medium Separation at specific gravity of separation of 1.50, all the particles of specific gravity greater than 1.5265 (the value obtained when diameter of the particle 1.3 cm is substituted in the equation 22.2.2) will definitely sink which means that the particles of size range 3.45 cm–1.3 cm having specific gravity in between 1.5265 and 1.50 will float instead of to sink.

However, among such particles, some particles of specific gravity less than 1.5265 will sink because the sand particles of size less than 0.03 cm are also present in the suspension in which case the size of the equal settling coal particles is less than 3.45 cm. For example, the size of the coal particles of specific gravity 1.51 equally settling with 0.025 cm sand particle is 2.875 cm. Hence the coal particles of size 2.875–3.45 cm will sink if more quantity of 0.025 cm size sand particles is present in suspension.

If the feed coal particles contain less than 1.3 cm size, 0.69 cm particles of specific gravity 1.55 and 0.315 cm particles of specific gravity 1.60 are equally settling with 0.03 cm of sand particles, and these particles are always be in suspension. It means that finer heavy coal particles, equally settling with 0.03 cm sand particles, can not be separated eventhough its specific gravity is much higher than the specific gravity of separation.

If the maximum size of the sand particles is decreased, the minimum size of the coal particles to be treated can also be decreased as coal particle equally settling with less size sand particles is smaller. Therefore, the maximum size of sand particles and minimum size of coal particles are to be calculated and fixed depending upon the required specific gravity of separation. Thus it is very clear that the effect of size of both coal and medium solid particles in Heavy Medium Separation is very important.

In case of heavy medium separation using heavy medium solids like barites of specific gravity 4.00, the size of barite particles must be fine to treat the same size coal particles as in the case of heavy medium separation using sand as medium. The size of barite particles to be used can be obtained from equation 22.2.1 by considering 3.45 cm coal particle of specific gravity 1.51

$$\frac{3.45}{d_b} = \frac{4.00 - 1.50}{1.51 - 1.50} = \frac{2.50}{0.01}$$
$$\Rightarrow \quad d_b = 0.0138 \text{ cm} = 138 \text{ } \mu m$$

From the above discussion it is evident that whenever a particular size range of coal is to be treated in HMS, the gravity of separation for the given size ranges of particles is to be calculated in order to get the required separation. Or minimum size of coal particles is to be calculated for the required gravity of separation. There is no upper size limit of the coal particles to be treated, provided that density difference exists between the particles. The upper size limit is determined by the ability of the equipment to handle the material.

22.3 JIGGING

Jigging is a process of separating the particles of different specific gravity, size and shape by introducing them on a perforated surface (or screen) through which water is made to flow by pulsion and suction strokes alternately.

A jig is a water filled box within which a bed of coal particles is supported on a screen. When the water is pulsed through the screen, the bed dilate, the coal particles are brought into suspension in water and allowed to settle under hindered settling conditions as governed by the initial velocities of the particles rather than the terminal velocities. During the suction period, the bed becomes tight, coarse particles bridge against each other and small particles pass through the interstices between the coarse particles (this phenomenon is known as consolidation trickling). After several such pulsion and suction strokes, the stratified bed of coal particles is obtained in which top layer is of light particles and bottom layer is of heavy particles. This stratified bed is removed from the jig layer by layer by suitable mechanism.

The following three effects contribute to the stratification of jig bed:

1   Hindered settling classification
2   Differential acceleration at the beginning of fall
3   Consolidation trickling at the end of fall

In a jig, the solid fluid mixture is so thick when compared to hindered settling classifier. In a jig, the suspension exists as loosely packed bed of solids with interstitial fluid whereas in classifier, suspension exists as a fluid carrying a large number of suspended solids. The thickest solid fluid mixture in jig can not be maintained for any length of time and solid particles can not rearrange completely. By giving pulsion and suction strokes alternately, the bed is made to more open and compact and a suspension of very high specific gravity is maintained during the bed is opened. When the bed is open, particles settle under hindered settling conditions and rearrange themselves during the short period of pulsion stroke. During this short period, the particle velocity is very small and it is under accelerating period. During this accelerating period, the heavy particles have a greater initial acceleration and speed than the light particles eventhough their terminal velocities are almost the same.

In a jig, the particles are allowed to settle only for short period and particles will never attain their terminal velocities. It means that separation will depend on the initial settling velocities of the particles. This initial settling velocity is extremely low and resisting forces due to frictional effects are not developed.

Now applying equation of motion (equation 22.1.1)

$$m_p \frac{dv}{dt} = (m_p - m_f)g - R$$

where R is practically zero in this case.

The equation becomes

$$\frac{dv}{dt} = \left[\frac{m_p - m_f}{m_p}\right]g = \left[1 - \frac{\rho_f}{\rho_p}\right]g \qquad (22.3.1)$$

where ρ_p and ρ_f are densities of solid particles and fluid.

This clearly shows that the initial acceleration of settling of particle depends on the force of gravity, densities of particle and fluid and does not depend on the size or shape of the particle. This equation also shows that the initial acceleration is maximum in case of most dense particles. This situation indicates that light and heavy particles can be separated by providing extremely short durations of settling. This is possible in jigging.

The Fig. 22.3 shows the settling velocities of six particles of different specific gravities and sizes as a function of time. The area under the curve at any time t, $\int_0^t v \, dt$ represents the distance traveled by the particle in time t.

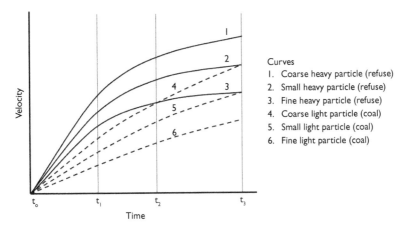

Figure 22.3 Sorting difference on the basis of initial velocity and terminal velocity.

With reference to the curves in Fig. 22.3, the following observations can be made if the settling period is t_3 or more

1   Coarse refuse particles settles faster than coarse coal particles.
2   Coarse coal particles settles equally with small refuse particles as their terminal settling velocities are same
3   Small coal particles settles equally with fine refuse particles as their terminal settling velocities are same
4   Fine coal particles always settle much slower than all refuse particles
5   Terminal velocity controls the separation and it is not possible to make an effective separation between light and heavy particles of varied sizes
6   Only fine coal and coarse refuse particles can be separated

If the time of settling is reduced to t_2, it is not possible to separate coarse coal particles and fine refuse particles as the areas under curve.3 and curve.4 are approximately equal. It means that they fall to an equal distance in a settling period of t_2, in which case they are termed as **equal jigging particles**. The ratio of diameters of these particles is termed as **jigging ratio**. However fine and small coal particles can be separated from all other particles. Similarly, coarse and small refuse particles can be separated from all other particles.

If the time of settling is still reduced to t_1, all refuse particles will fall to a greater distance than all coal particles and the feed particles are completely stratified into all clean coal particles at the top and all refuse particles at the bottom. In this case, no single coal particle is equal jigging with any refuse particles. Hence it is of interest to note that jigging ratio varies with the time of settling.

Moreover, when the particles are lifted during the pulsion stroke, clean coal particles will be lifted to more distance than refuse particles and by the time both particles start settling, a difference in vertical distance exists between coal and refuse particles and this distance increases further as refuse particle settles faster, thus makes the better stratification when settling alone is considered.

From the above discussions, it can be concluded that

1 If the duration of fall is shorter, the particles travel during their initial acceleration period and stratification takes place on the basis of specific gravity alone.
2 A very short settling time must be used if jigging is practiced on unsized or poorly
sized feed.
3 If jigging is practiced on closely sized feed, stratification may result even if a long
settling time is used.

To summarize, in jigging, stratification during the stage that the bed is open is
essentially controlled by hindered settling classification as modified by differential
acceleration and during the stage that the bed is tight, it is controlled by consolidation
trickling. The first process arranges the coarse refuse at the bottom, fine coal at the
top, and coarse coal and fine refuse in the middle.

The second process arranges the particles in reverse order, fine refuse at the bottom, coarse coal at the top and fine coal and coarse refuse in the middle. By varying
the importance of differential acceleration, an almost perfect stratification according
to specific gravity alone can be obtained.

22.4 FLOWING FILM CONCENTRATION

Flowing film concentration has been defined as sorting of particles on flat surfaces in
accordance with the size, shape and specific gravity of the particles moved by a flowing film of water.

When water is made to flow over a bare sloping deck, the velocity of water adjacent to the deck is zero and increases as the distance from the deck increases reaching
maximum at the top surface of water (Fig. 22.4.1). However, velocity at the top surface of water is slightly less than the maximum due to air friction.

If number of spheres, composed of two kinds of materials, one heavy another
light, and are of different sizes, are introduced into a thick layer of water, they will
be separated during their fall through this layer. The biggest heavy sphere falls faster
on to the deck through water and least effected by the current and lies nearest to the
point of entry. The smallest light sphere will be drifted farthest downstream. The others will be drifted to different distances (Fig. 22.4.2).

The flowing water presses the sphere and makes to move downstream. The differential rate at which the water is flowing over the deck causes low pressure on the
bottom of the sphere tending to slide on the deck and causes high pressure at the top
of the sphere tending to roll on the deck (22.4.3).

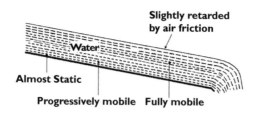

Figure 22.4.1 Flow of water on sloping deck.

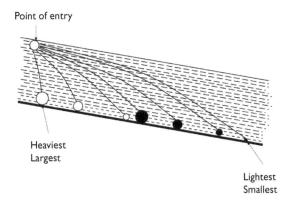

Figure 22.4.2 Particles drift in flowing water.

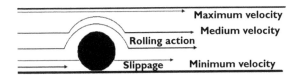

Figure 22.4.3 Forces of flowing water on particle.

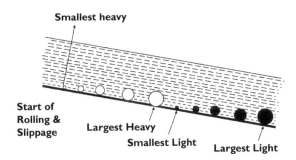

Figure 22.4.4 Arrangement of particles over deck of flowing film.

Since small particles are submerged in the slower-moving portion of the film, they will not move as rapidly as coarse particles. If the combined influence of deck slope and streaming velocity is sufficient to keep all the spheres in rolling movement, they rearrange themselves in the following down slope sequence (Fig. 22.4.4)

1   Small-heavy particles
2   Coarse-heavy and small-light particles
3   Coarse-light particles

It is to be noted that in flowing film concentration coarse-heavy particles are placed with small-light particles which is reverse of the stratification takes place in classification.

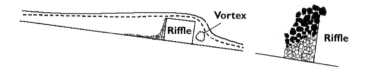

Figure 22.4.5 Effect of Riffle over deck of flowing film.

Spiral concentrator is a unit of stationary flowing film concentration and is used for beneficiation of fine coals ranging in size from 3 mm to 0.1 mm. It consists of a descending spiral launder where the slurry is made to flow down the spiral. The reject particles get thrown towards the inner periphery of the spiral because of their high specific gravity, the middlings stay in the centre and the cleans collect towards the outer periphery of the spiral.

If an obstruction like cross-riffles (bars set across the stream) is placed in flowing film, this obstruction introduce turbulent flow, and vortices; the smallest and heaviest particles occupy the bottom place and are covered by heavy particles of increasing size and then small lighter particles. At the top of the bed are coarsest light particles which may pass over the obstruction (Fig. 22.4.5).

If a reciprocating motion is given to the deck, the heavy particles in between the successive riffles are subject to hindered settling and consolidation trickling and move to one side of the deck whereas lighter particles are washed off across the riffles and along the streaming current. This operation is called as **tabling**.

22.5   CONCENTRATION CRITERION

The possibility of separation by means of gravity is dependent on the range of specific gravities of the particles to be separated and the actual particle sizes. For effective separation by gravity concentration, there must be marked density difference between the particles. Some idea of the type of separation possible can be obtained from the ratio, called **concentration criterion**, and is defined as

$$\frac{\rho_h - \rho_f}{\rho_l - \rho_f}$$

where ρ_h is the density of the heavy particle, ρ_l is the density of the light particle, and ρ_f is the density of the fluid medium. This ratio is a comparison of the buoyancy forces which are at work. If the fluid is water of density 1 gm/cm^3, this expression is the free settling ratio under Newtonian conditions. If the fluid is other than water, this expression is the hindered settling ratio.

In general, when this ratio is greater than 2.5, whether positive or negative, then gravity separation is relatively easy. As the value of this ratio decreases, the efficiency of separation decreases, and if it is below 1.25, gravity concentration is not generally commercially feasible. The following are the values of ratios and particle sizes based on experimental data:

Ratio	Particle Separating Size in Water
>2.50	down to 200 mesh
1.75	down to 65 mesh
1.50	down to 10 mesh
1.25	only material > 13 mm
< 1.25	no separation is possible in water
	Another (heavier) fluid or a psuedo fluid medium heavier than H_2O is needed. An alternative is to alter the effective particle density by causing it to adhere to an air bubble as in flotation.

The motion of a particle in a fluid depends not only on its specific gravity but also on its size; large particles will be affected more than smaller ones. The efficiency of gravity concentration operation, therefore, increases with particle size. Smaller particles respond poorly because their movement is dominated mainly by surface friction. In practice, close size control of feeds to gravity concentration processes is required in order to reduce the size effect and make the particles to move depending on their specific gravities.

22.6   ILLUSTRATIVE EXAMPLES

Illustrative Example 22.6.1: *Calculate the terminal settling velocity of coal particle having 1.4 specific gravity and 20 microns in size settling in water.*

Solution:
    Density of the particle $= \rho_p = 1.4$ gm/cm^3
    Diameter of the particle $= d = 20$ microns $= 0.002$ cm
    Density of water $= \rho_w = 1.0$ gm/cm^3
    Viscosity of water $= \mu_w = 0.01$ poise

As per Stoke's law $v_m = \dfrac{d^2 g(\rho_p - \rho_w)}{18\mu_w}$

$$= \frac{(0.002)^2(980)(1.4-1.0)}{18(0.01)} = 0.00871 \text{ cm/sec}$$

Illustrative Example 22.6.2: *Calculate the size of a spherical silica particle settling in water from rest at 20°C with a terminal settling velocity of 0.5 cm/sec. Specific gravity of silica is 2.65.*

Solution:
    Density of the particle $= \rho_p = 2.65$ gm/cm^3
    Density of water $= \rho_w = 1.0$ gm/cm^3
    Viscosity of water $= \mu_w = 0.01$ poise
    Terminal settling velocity $= v_m = 0.5$ cm/sec

As per Stoke's law $v_m = \dfrac{d^2 g(\rho_p - \rho_w)}{18\mu_w}$

$$d = \sqrt{\frac{v_m 18\mu_w}{(\rho_p - \rho_w)g}} = \sqrt{\frac{0.5 \times 18 \times 0.01}{(2.65-1.0)980}} = 0.074 \; cm$$

Illustrative Example 22.6.3: *Calculate the diameter of the coal particle that settles equally with a shale particle of 45 microns size in water. The densities of coal and shale particles are 1300 kg/m³ and 2500 kg/m³ respectively.*

Solution:

Density of the shale particle = ρ_{sh} = 2.50 gm/cm³
Density of the coal particle = ρ_{co} = 1.30 gm/cm³
Density of water   = ρ_w = 1.0 gm/cm³
Viscosity of water   = μ_w = 0.01 poise

Let the diameters of the shale and coal particles be d_{sh} and d_{co}

By Stokes' law, Free settling ratio $= \dfrac{d_{co}}{d_{sh}} = \left(\dfrac{\rho_{sh} - \rho_w}{\rho_{co} - \rho_w}\right)^{1/2} = \left(\dfrac{2.50 - 1.00}{1.30 - 1.00}\right)^{1/2} = 2.23607$

Diameter of the coal particle = d_{co} = 2.23607 × d_{sh} = 2.23607 × 45 = 100.6 microns

Illustrative Example 22.6.4: *Coal particles of specific gravity 1.40 has been separated from shale of specific gravity 2.60 in a free settling classifier. The size range is from 5.2 to 25 microns. Three fractions are obtained. One is a pure coal, another is a pure shale, and the third is a mixture. Calculate the size range of the coal and shale particles in the mixture.*

Solution:

Density of water   = ρ_w = 1.00 gm/cm³
Density of coal particles   = ρ_{co} = 1.40 gm/cm³
Density of shale particles = ρ_{sh} = 2.60 gm/cm³

Let d_{co} and d_{sh} be the sizes of coal and shale particles

The size of the coal particle that settles equally with the smallest shale particle

$$= d_{co} = \left(\frac{\rho_{sh} - \rho_w}{\rho_{co} - \rho_w}\right)^{1/2} d_{sh} = \left(\frac{2.6 - 1.0}{1.4 - 1.0}\right)^{1/2} \times 5.2 = 10.4\,\mu m$$

The size of the shale particle that settles equally with the largest coal particle

$$= d_{sh} = \left(\frac{\rho_{co} - \rho_w}{\rho_{sh} - \rho_w}\right)^{1/2} d_g = \left(\frac{1.4 - 1.0}{2.6 - 1.0}\right)^{1/2} \times 25 = 12.5\,\mu m$$

Therefore,
All coal particles of size less than 10.4 microns are pure coal fraction.
All shale particles of size more than 12.5 microns are pure shale fraction
The third fraction i.e the mixture contains
Coal particles of size 10.4–25 microns
Shale particles of size 12.5–5.2 microns

22.7 PROBLEMS FOR PRACTICE

22.7.1: *Calculate the terminal settling velocity of shale particle having 2.5 specific gravity and 50 microns in size settling in water.*   [0.204 cm/sec]

22.7.2: R.O.M *Coal contains coal of specific gravity 1.35 and shale of specific gravity 2.40 has size range of 10 microns to 40 microns. When the ROM coal is classified in a free settling classifier, calculate the size range of coal particles separated and those remain with refuse.*   [<20 microns; 20–40 microns]

22.7.3: R.O.M *Coal contains coal of specific gravity 1.35 and shale of specific gravity 2.40 has size range of 10 microns to 40 microns. Will it be possible to separate all the coal particles under hindered settling conditions where the specific gravity of the pulp is maintained at 1.20?*   [yes]

Chapter 23

Heavy medium separation

Present day mining conditions tend to produce coal having more and more complex washability characteristics and therefore lead to an increasing demand for washing processes which will separate coal and refuse with a high degree of efficiency and thus produce the maximum yield of saleable products. Such a separation is accurately accomplished by the simple floating and sinking of the raw coal in a heavy medium, the specific gravity of which may be varied and controlled within very accurate limits to suit the nature of the coal to be treated.

23.1 PRINCIPLE

If a sample of raw coal is introduced into a solution of a predetermined density, a clean coal containing required ash content will be obtained as a float product while the residue of the coal, the refuse, will sink. In practice, solutions of Tetra Chloro Ethylene, toluene and bromoform, which are miscible one in the other, are commonly used in the laboratory to analyse the coals.

In commercial practice, Four types of separating medium have been used. Organic liquids, dissolved salts in water, aerated solids, and suspensions consisting of fine solids suspended in water.

Organic liquids used for coal separations range from 0.86–2.96 specific gravity. They have low viscosities, and therefore serve as ideal separating medium for solid materials. These liquids are stable and virtually immiscible with water. The specific gravity of the liquid can be regulated readily by mixing high and low specific gravity liquids at different proportions.

Solutions of inorganic salts like calcium chloride and zinc chloride are also used as heavy liquid to separate the coal. Lessing [41], Bertrand [42] and Belknap used calcium chloride solution for cleaning the coal. The Du Pont Company in USA, in 1939 used organic liquids of definite specific gravities such as liquid halogen hydrocarbons [43]. These processes did not achieve great commercial success on account of the corrosive and toxic nature of the separating medium, high cost, the difficulty and expense of recovering the solutions from the products of separation and, principally, the development of the heavy medium processes.

23.2 HEAVY MEDIUM

All the processes now in general commercial use employs suspension of finely divided solids in water, termed the **heavy medium**. A suspension may be defined as any liquid in which insoluble solids are dispersed and kept in a state of turbulence. It has been found that such suspensions exhibit many of the properties of true solutions, hence known as **pseudo liquids**, and in particular can support particles with a lower density than the suspension density provided that the mean size of the medium solids are smaller than the coal.

The following equation determines the density of suspension (Heavy medium):

$$\rho_{sl} = \frac{100}{(100 - C_w) + \dfrac{C_w}{\rho_p}} \qquad\qquad (23.2.1)$$

where ρ_{sl} = density of the suspension (or slurry) (gm/cm³)
  ρ_p = density of the solid particles (gm/cm³)
  C_w = percent solids in suspension by weight

From this equation, it will be seen that the density of a suspension can be varied at will by adjusting the proportion of medium solids present in the suspension. There is, however, a natural limit to the proportion of solids imposed by the volume concentration since it is important that the suspension should have a relatively low viscosity to permit the free travel of coal and shale in it. This limiting volume concentration is similar for all suspensions with particles of similar size range, but can be modified to a limited extent by changing the size grading of the medium solids.

The equation 23.2.1 also shows that the density of the suspension is a function of the specific gravity of the medium solids and it naturally follows from this that the medium composed of higher specific gravity solids will have a higher density at the limiting volume concentration than suspensions composed of lower specific gravity solids.

The specific gravities of separation for coals range from about 1.30–1.90. To achieve this range of specific gravity while keeping the volumetric concentration at a reasonable level, it is necessary to select high specific gravity solids or to introduce upward currents in the separating vessel. As the usually accepted volumetric concentration of the suspended solids is between 25% and 40%, their size and specific gravity must be selected to provide the desired medium density while at the same time having the required medium stability. The coarser the solids, the higher the settling rate, the lower the viscosity, and the easier it is to recover the medium. The finer the solids, the lower the settling rate (hence, the greater stability), the higher the viscosity, and the more difficult it is to recover the medium. Additionally, the higher the specific gravity of the suspended solids, the lower is the volumetric concentrations for the given specific gravity, and hence the lower the viscosity.

The term stability is used in heavy medium practice to indicate the rate of settlement of a suspension, and a stable medium is one in which settlement occurs slowly and uniformly throughout the suspension. Unstable medium settle rapidly and there is evidence of differential settlement in the body of the suspension. In practice, there is a further class of medium which is termed as semi-stable medium comprising higher density solids whose settling characteristics are modified by the addition of low density solids at a controlled level to obtain a uniform rate of settlement over a wide range of operating densities.

The most stable medium in commercial use are those in which the solids are very finely divided and are of low specific gravity (2.0–3.0 specific gravity) such as loess and shale. Such a suspension permits separation of the coal under relatively quiescent conditions with a high degree of accuracy of separation, but is limited by the low specific gravity of the solids to a suspension density of 1.60. Above this limit, the volume concentration becomes so high that the suspension exhibits thixotropy. For the same reasons, in the case of such suspension it is extremely important to avoid contamination of the medium with fine coal or shale particles of low specific gravity which are introduced with the raw coal, and considerable care must be taken to ensure the removal of this material in medium recovery process.

High density solids such as magnetite and barites give suspensions which are generally unstable but which permit higher suspension densities up to 2.0 or higher. Fortunately, the stability of such medium can be considerably modified by control of the size grading and by the amount of coal and shale slimes which are present in the suspension. It is found that by fine grinding and in the presence of 30–40% of slimes, semi-stable suspensions can be achieved at densities as low as 1.30–1.35.

The influence of added clay to an unstable medium can be seen from the table 23.2.1 [44] which shows that the settling rate is rather more than halved with each 10% increase in the slimes concentration, and that with the addition of 30% of slimes, the settling rate is so far reduced that such a medium might well be considered to be stable. At higher concentrations of slimes, however, the viscosity rapidly increases and it is not generally possible to operate with more than 50–60% of slimes.

The viscosity is the resistance to flow of a true Newtonian liquid, however, the definition generally is accepted to include suspensions. The viscosity of the suspension in the coal washing process has little effect on the light coal particles or the heavy refuse particles, but becomes critical in the separation of particles having density equal to or nearer to that of the suspension. As the falling velocity of a particle

Table 23.2.1 Settling rate of a semi-stable medium with added slimes (suspension density –1.5).

Proportion of slimes Weight percent	Settling rate min/inch
0	1.78
10	3.98
15	6.31
20	9.55
25	14.13
30	21.38
35	31.62
40	47.86

Table 23.2.2 Medium solids.

Solids	Specific gravity
Sand	2.6
Loess	
Shale	
Barytes	4.0
Magnetite	5.0
Some clays	–

in a fluid is proportional to the density difference between the particle and the fluid, a low viscosity suspension must be maintained to separate near-gravity material at a high rate of feed.

All the heavy medium separation processes employ either unstable or substantially stable suspensions of fine solids in water. Such a medium solids must have the following qualities:

1   The medium solid particles must be sufficiently high in specific gravity to provide the required specific gravity of suspension at moderate non-viscous conditions to allow free travel of the particles to be separated.
2   The medium solid particles must be physically strong and chemically inert.
3   Size and shape of the medium solid particles is important. In general, the coarser the grain size, the more fluid the suspension, but the more agitation is required to maintain the suspension. Angular grains produce stiffer suspensions than rounded grains.
4   The settling rate of the coarsest particles of the medium solids should be less than the settling rate of the smallest particle to be removed by sinking.
5   The medium solid particles should be easily and cheaply recoverable for re-use.
6   The chemical composition of the medium solid particles should be such that the small amount remaining in the product will not be harmful.
7   The medium solid particles must be readily available at a low cost.

The Table 23.2.2 shows some of the medium solids used for making suspensions in Heavy Medium baths for washing coal.

A Heavy Medium coal washing process may be considered to consist of the following four interrelated parts:

•   Separating vessel
•   Raw coal feed and removal of products
•   Medium circulation
•   Medium cleaning and recovery system

23.3   SEPARATING VESSELS

Vessels for washing coal may be shallow or deep baths. Shallow baths (Troughs and drums) contain a relatively small volume of medium and when a stable or semi-stable medium is used, circulation rates can be comparatively low. They cannot be used to carry out a three product separation and they have a limited capacity for overload. Deep baths (cones) have a higher capacity for overload and permit a three product separation, but unless stable medium is used, medium circulation rates are relatively high.

The essential requirements of a separating vessel for continuous operation are as follows:

1   It must have an effective means to maintain the suspension in a reasonably uniform state throughout the vessel with the minimum amount of turbulence.
2   It must have sufficient depth to allow time for the plunging feed particles to loose their initial velocity, thus facilitating the separation of float and sink.
3   It must have sufficient surface area to reduce the particle loading per unit area to a point where float and sink products are actually separated from each other by the medium so that buoyant and settling forces are free to act, and improves the ability to process high tonnages of coal per unit area of floor space.
4   It must be capable of accepting a feed varying in size consist and percentage of impurities without adverse effects on the washing efficiency.
5   It must have a means of introducing the feed into the active separating zone without causing too much turbulence.
6   It must have means for continuous removal of float and sink from the vessel accompanied by a minimum of medium and at the same time allowing a reasonably uniform level of medium to be maintained in the vessel.

The feed is generally introduced at the top of the separating vessel by conveyor belt, shaker or other mechanical means and in some systems, the coal is pre-wetted in a stream of medium before entering the medium bath. In most washers, the clean coal is removed with a portion of the medium overflowing a weir; in a few washers, the floating layer of coal is removed by means of scrapers, paddles and star wheels. In cone washers, the rejects are removed by air lifts, bucket elevator, or through a lock-hopper arrangement. In trough type washers, the sink is removed by a chain conveyor, scraper or rubber belt. In drum washers, sink fraction is removed by lifters mounted on the inside of the revolving drum.

In some vessels, all the medium enters near the top of the separating vessel; in others, a portion enters the bottom of the tank to provide an upward current, in still others, a portion of the medium enters at various levels to form horizontal currents or maintain homogeneity of the medium throughout the vessel.

23.4   MEDIUM RECOVERY SYSTEM

Generally the medium recovery system consists of two screens in series. Washed coal products are sent to these screens. The first screen is a medium drainage screen in which about 85% of the medium is drained and pumped directly to the separating vessel. The remaining 15% of the medium adhering to the coal particles is removed on the second screen by washing with high pressure water sprays. The resulting highly diluted washing are thickened and sent to separating vessel. In case of magnetite medium, diluted medium goes to a magnetizer where magnetite particles get magnetized and flocculated and then further thickened in a thickener. Thickened medium is sent to magnetic separator and the magnetic product is further dewatered in a densifier and returned to separating vessel along with the drain medium. The densifier product must be demagnetized in an alternating current demagnetizing coil to eliminate flocculation and viscosity problems in separating vessel. In case of barites and loess, part of the thickened medium is treated by froth flotation to remove associated coal and clay slimes.

Heavy medium process are widely used for coal washing and offers the following advantages over the other washing processes:

1   Ability to make sharp separations at any specific gravity within the range normally required even in the presence of high percentages of ±0.1 near-gravity material.
2   Ability to maintain constant separating gravity with less fluctuation.
3   Ability to handle a wide range of sizes, up to 14″.
4   Ability to handle fluctuations in feed both in terms of quantity and quality.
5   Ability to change specific gravity of separation to meet varying market requirements.
6   Relatively low capital and operating costs when considered in terms of high capacity and small space requirements.
7   Low medium consumption.
8   A middling product can be separated which is very much needed for Indian coals.

Chance Cone Process, Barvoys Process, Dutch States Mines process, Tromp process, Drewboy process and Wemco Drum separation process are the few of the important commercial heavy medium separation processes. Among these units, Chance cone and Barvoys processes have provision for separation of three products in one operation. Other processes are of shallow bath type and designed to yield two products. For recovery of middlings in washeries incorporating two product units, secondary heavy medium baths have been provided. The size of the coal particles treated in these heavy medium baths are mainly 75 mm–13 mm and the absence of fine coal contributes to the greater efficiency of the separation process. Separations are generally made with the medium at 1.35 to 1.80 specific gravity. The feed capacity depends on both the mean particle size of the coal and the pool area of the equipment used.

23.5   CHANCE CONE PROCESS

Chance cone process is the most popular coal washing process, patented in 1917. The first plant was erected in USA in 1921 for washing anthracite. In 1951, West Bokaro coal washery under the management of TISCO, first Indian coal washery used the chance cone process.

This process employs a suspension of sand in water, the sand having a specific gravity of about 2.60 and a size range of 30–100 B.S.mesh. Such a suspension is unstable as the sand particles at this size settle readily in water. Therefore, the process requires some method of maintaining the sand in suspension. This is accomplished by stirring the sand-water mixture and using rising currents of water of sufficient velocity to hold the sand suspension.

The separating vessel of a Chance cone process (Fig. 23.5.1) consists of an inverted cone with a cylindrical upper section. Three or four water inlets with control valves are arranged in the side of the cone. These water inlets provide the rising currents of water in the vessel and used to control the specific gravity of suspension. Two rotating paddles at the center of the cone driven by bevel gears revolve at a slow speed of 12 rpm and fulfill three functions.

- They scrap away any sand or refuse accumulating on the sides of the cone and break up any banks of sand.
- They impart a rotary motion to the suspension which assists the flow of the coal from the feed chute to the clean coal exit weir.
- They also assist in maintaining an intimate mixture of the sand and water.

The base of the cone is provided with two air operated slide gates. In between them, a refuse chamber is mounted for receiving the sinking refuse. These gates are automatically controlled and operated.

The chamber is first supplied with water from the filling receiver, via the air operated filling valve, closing a pressure switch when full. The closing of this switch automatically opens the top slide gate which allows the refuse that has accumulated in the bottom of the cone to fall into the refuse chamber. After a given time, usually 15–20 seconds, the top gate closes and automatically opens the bottom gate which allows the sand, water and refuse to fall on to the de-sanding screen. The bottom gate closes after the predetermined time and the cycle is recommenced by the opening of the air operated filling valve. The cycle is timed to deal with the maximum rate at which refuse is likely to be delivered and is adjustable. It generally occupies about 1 minute. The whole of the equipment is automatic and is interlocked electrically to prevent both gates being open at any one time.

Raw coal is fed into the top of the separating vessel at one side by means of a chute. The clean coal, being lighter than the suspension, floats at the surface, and

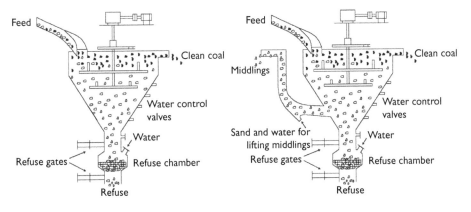

Figure 23.5.1 Two and three product Chance cones.

owing to the rotation induced in the separator by paddles, gradually moves around to the discharge point where it overflows with water and sand. Sand is added to the vessel continuously in the form of thick pulp to keep the level of the suspension up to the level of the overflow lip at the top of the vessel. Thus clean coal floating on the suspension overflows constantly, carrying with it a certain amount of sand suspension. The water required for agitation and maintenance of the suspension is introduced through water inlets at various levels in the cone.

The amount of sand in suspension at any given time and hence the specific gravity of the suspension depends directly on the velocity of the upward water current in the cone. Low water velocities give thick suspensions of high specific gravity; high water velocities give dilute suspensions of low specific gravity. Thus regulation of the water velocity is the means by which the operator is able to adjust the cone to make a separation at any desired specific gravity.

Both the clean coal overflow from the top of the cone and the refuse discharged from the bottom of the cone are de-sanded and de-watered on separate screens (Fig. 23.5.2). Sand and water is carried to main sand sump where, due to the low rising velocity of the water, the sand is retained at the bottom of the sump and the water overflowed into an outer compartment. From this sump, sand and water are pumped back to the top of the cone and the water control valves to the cone water inlets.

Another function of the sand sump is to hold a reserve of sand. If the cone has been operating at a high gravity and is suddenly changed to a low one, the excess of sand automatically leaves the cone and is retained in the sump. This reserve of sand is likewise, available when more sand is required in the cone.

The sand losses in operating the Chance process are around 1.5–2 lb/ton of raw coal treated, and to compensate for this, it is usual to add make-up sand once in a shift. This make-up sand is also stored in the sand sump thus avoiding the inconvenience of adding sand continuously.

23.5.1 Separation of middlings

A Chance cone may be designed for either two product or three product separations. When it is desired to obtain middling product in addition to the clean coal and

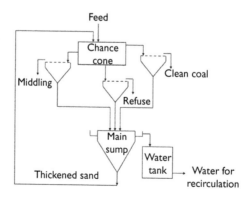

Figure 23.5.2 Chance Cone process flowsheet.

refuse products, a separate middlings column is provided at the side of the cone. This column is in direct communication with the sand suspension in the cone, and is operated by either increasing the gravity at the bottom of the cone or lowering the gravity at the top by adjusting the water control valves. The middlings, floating at the level of higher specific gravity are carried up the tube by introducing additional sand and water at its base. This type of cone can be operated as a single gravity separator or a two gravity separator merely by opening or closing the valves controlling the sand and water for lifting the middlings up the column.

The chief advantages of the Chance Cone process are:

1   As the separation depends solely on difference in specific gravity, the size and shape of the particles does not affect the washing efficiency.
2   Within the maximum capacity of the cone, intermittent or variable feed does not affect the washing efficiency.
3   Coals containing high proportions of near gravity material can be efficiently washed.
4   The operating density can be altered in a few minutes if the products of different seams are to be washed or in accordance with market requirements.
5   Variation in the inherent ash of the raw coal do not affect the efficiency.
6   Breakage in the cone is low.
7   Power consumption is fairly low and is largely a pumping load.
8   A middling product can be separated if required.

23.6   BARVOYS PROCESS

The Barvoys process uses suspensions of higher stability which approach very close to those of a true liquid, and achieves separation under non-turbulent conditions. The Barvoys medium consists of finely divided barites and clay, the size of the barites being of the order of 25 microns while the clay, which is generally obtained from disintegrating shale in the coal treated, is still finer in size. The clay has an effect of stabilizing the barites.

A suspension of this type is virtually stable when the solid concentration is high and settles reasonably quickly when diluted with water. The specific gravity of barites is 4.20 and of shale about 2.20–2.60 and their proportions may be adjusted so that the suspension has the required stability at specific gravity ranging from 1.30–1.60. The concentration of solids in the suspension is usually between 25% and 30% by volume. Above this value, the medium tends to become viscous, and at lower concentrations becomes unstable.

When the products of separation are rinsed with water to remove adhering medium, the resulting dilute suspension of medium can be recovered and densified by settlement in thickeners, but these are of relatively large diameter. Arrangements must be made to remove coal slimes originating from the coal being treated, and for this purpose, a portion of the recovered medium is treated in froth flotation cells to separate the coal slimes and surplus clay from the barites, which is then returned to the washing circuit. Medium consumption is 2–3 lb/ton of coal cleaned.

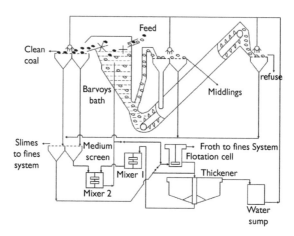

Figure 23.6 Barvoys process flowsheet.

The Barvoys bath (Fig. 23.6) is of the deep pyramid-shaped bath and does not require any agitation. In order to prevent accumulation of middlings, medium is fed at an intermediate level to create a gentle upward current and stronger downward current in the lower zone which separates middlings into floats and sinks. The raw coal is fed to the surface of the bath and the clean coal floated is transported mechanically across the surface of the separator either by a scraper or by rotary paddles while the shale is removed by bucket elevator.

The middlings are removed from the bath by means of middlings tube which rises from the junction of the base of the bath and the refuse elevator. The shale and middlings fall past the entrance to this tube and encounter a brisk ascending current of medium which floats the middlings up the tube and out on to a spraying screen, the medium being returned to elevator casing. The heavier shale sinks past the entrance to the middlings tube and is picked up in the boot of a perforated bucket elevator from which most of the medium on the refuse drains back down the elevator casing, the remainder is removed by sprays and returned to the dilute medium circuit to be reconstituted by thickener. Fine coal is removed by a constant bleed of medium to a froth flotation plant.

23.7 DUTCH STATE MINES PROCESS

The Dutch State Mines process operates like the Barvoys process with a relatively stable medium and employs hydraulic cyclones to recover the medium. In this case, the medium itself was originally natural loess which is a very finely divided siliceous material similar to clay but containing very little colloidal material and not subject to decomposition in water. The specific gravity of loess is about 2.6 and the particles are about 300 mesh in size. Due to these physical characteristics and, in particular, to the absence of colloidal material, the loess medium may contain a high proportions of solids, up to 40% or 50% by volume, without unduly affecting the viscosity of the medium. Despite the low specific gravity of the solids, suitable suspensions of up to 1.6 specific gravity can be employed.

The dilute medium obtained by spraying the products of separation with water was found to be susceptible to thickening in the hydraulic cyclone and, further, that these cyclones provided an effective method of rejecting the finest coal and clay slimes with which the medium became contaminated during use. In plants which include froth flotation equipment, the rejected tailings provide a source of heavy medium and the necessity for using relatively expensive materials like barites is avoided. However, with such low density solids, extreme care must be taken to ensure that the suspension does not become fouled with slimes and, in particular, froth flotation plant has to be included to remove coal slimes. Medium losses are 4–6 lb/ton but this is unimportant where the medium is obtained from the discard and costs no more than its preparation charges.

Dutch State Mines process employs a shallow bath known as Dutch State Mines Leebar bath (Fig. 23.7) of about 4–6 ft. deep through which travels a continuous comb-type scraper. The top flights of the conveyor transports the floating coal across the surface of the separator while the lower strand scrapes the refuse along the bottom of the separator in the opposite direction. The agitation produced by the passage of the conveyor strands and combs through the medium maintains uniform density of the medium in the bath and also prevents the accumulation of middlings. It is, however, generally considered that some circulation must nevertheless be employed in order to ensure that the medium is continuously removed from the bath for cleaning on fine screens in order to remove associated coal.

If a separate middlings product is required, the refuse may be treated in a second bath at higher specific gravity.

Magnetite is used as heavy medium instead of loess in few plants.

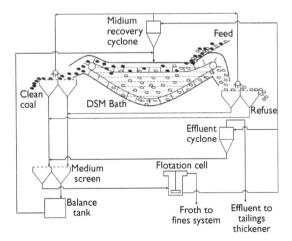

Figure 23.7 DSM process flow sheet.

23.8 TROMP PROCESS

The Tromp process, developed by K. Tromp of Holland, was the first successful commercial process which employs magnetite crushed to −0.1 mm size as heavy medium. The three product McNally Tromp dense medium vessel (Fig. 23.8.1) consists of shallow bath of mild steel plate. A scraper conveyor is provided at its upper section to remove clean coal. A dual purpose scraper conveyor is arranged at its centre and bottom sections for the separate removal of the middlings and refuse products.

The raw coal is introduced at the top of the bath by means of a slow running balanced feeder screen through the chute. The clean coal floating in the top of the bath travels the length of the bath by laminar flow and is removed by the top scraper conveyor, which travels at the same speed as the horizontally flowing medium, and carried up to drain and spraying screens. The middlings are suspended in the bath below the clean coal conveyor at the interface between the low gravity medium and the high gravity medium. The middlings are removed by the combined action of the horizontal currents and the middlings strand of the conveyor. They are then conveyed out of the bath and dropped on to drain and rinse screens. The heavy refuse falls to the bottom of the bath where it is conveyed in the opposite direction of the middlings by the lower strand of the same conveyor. It then passes over a drain and rinse screens for medium removal and subsequent recovery.

Medium enters the bath at two separate points: low gravity medium is fed over the whole width and at varying depths of the top section of the bath by means of four distribution pipes; high gravity medium is fed in a similar manner into the lower section of the bath by a single distribution pipe. In both cases, medium flows horizontally over the whole width and depth of the bath, from the feed end to the middlings discharge, where it overflows. The high gravity medium is confined to the refuse compartment beneath the bottom scraper conveyor, of which a portion flows out through the adjustable bottom drain, another portion through the underflow gate, and the remainder leaves the bath with the refuse at the discharge end.

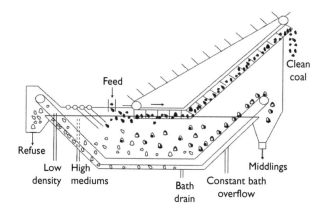

Figure 23.8.1 Tromp shallow bath.

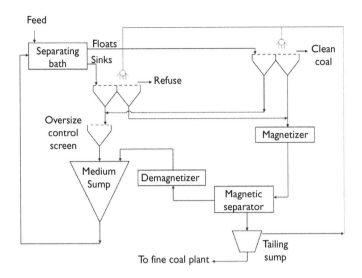

Feed

Figure 23.8.2 Magnetite recovery flowsheet for Tromp process.

The distinctive feature of the Tromp process is that the specific gravity of the magnetite medium gradually increases from the surface downwards. This gradual sedimentation of the solids in suspension is controlled so that the specific gravity at any level in the bath remains constant and by means of slow horizontal currents or laminar flow from end to end of the bath, the bath can simultaneously be kept clear of accumulations of middlings. The absence of vertical currents in the medium and the applicability of a suspension of low viscosity and high fluidity makes for a clear separation at specific gravities ranging from 1.35 to 2.1.

Fig. 23.8.2 shows the magnetite medium cleaning and recovery system in a two product Tromp process plant.

23.9 DREWBOY PROCESS

Drewboy process was developed in France by Preparation Industrielle des Combustibles using the magnetite as heavy medium. The Drewboy separator (Fig. 23.9.1) is a shallow type bath and makes two product separation. The volume of the bath is low and all bearings and working parts are out of contact with the heavy medium.

The raw coal feed with the medium is introduced at one end of the bath. The medium flows with a relatively low speed allowing the feed sufficient time for classification before reaching the discharge point at the opposite end. Clean coal is discharged over the overflow weir by two slowly rotating star wheels with chain scraper flights. The refuse sink to the bottom of the bath and are lifted out and discharged at the outlet by a radial-vaned wheel mounted on an inclined shaft.

The cleans and refuse are sent to separate drain-rinse screens to recover the medium (Fig. 23.9.2). The drained off medium from the first section of these screens

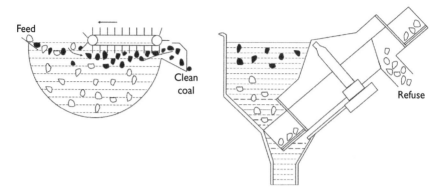

Figure 23.9.1 Drewboy two product separator.

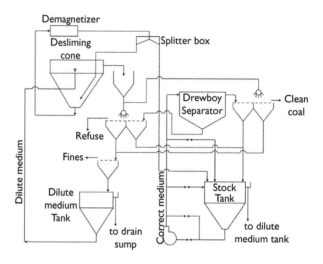

Figure 23.9.2 Drewboy process flowsheet.

is directly sent to stock tank. A circulation system is incorporated to enable the stock tank to be agitated after shut-down periods. This is achieved by bringing into operation a branch line from the pump suction into the stock tank below the surface of the medium in the tank. In this way, water separated as a result of settlement of medium in the tank can be drawn off and pumped into the bottom of the tank through a branch line from the pump delivery. The correct density medium system is arranged so that the medium can be fed into the Drewboy bath directly.

The dilute medium from rinse screens is sent to dilute medium screen to remove fine coal and dirt particles and further sent to dilute medium tank. From this tank, dilute medium is pumped to Simcar desliming cone in which the magnetite medium is cleaned, recovered and densified and the non-magnetic slimes and coal particles are separated from it by taking advantage of the rapid settling rate of the medium when magnetized and flocculated. The densified medium in the foot of the cone is pumped to a splitter box situated above the cone through a demagnetizer. A circulation pipe leads from one side of the splitter and returns the densified medium into the foot of the cone. A second pipe directs the medium from the other side of the splitter to the correct medium stock tank.

The return of the medium from the desliming cone to the correct-medium circuit is controlled manually. The operator is required to use a Simcar density balance to determine the specific gravity of the recirculating, densified and recovered medium at its point of discharge into the splitter box. The flow of medium to the correct medium system is affected by a pneumatically operated motor lever assembly. The motor lever is controlled from a remote panel which also houses the pneumatic instrument indicating the density of the medium in the Drewboy separator. In this way, the plant is controlled from one central position.

23.10   WEMCO DRUM SEPARATION PROCESS

WEMCO drum separators are of two types; the single drum makes a separation at a single gravity while the two compartment drum makes two successive gravity separations in the same vessel by using two separate baths at different specific gravities. Magnetite suspension is used as heavy medium for washing the coal.

In the single drum separator (Fig. 23.10.1), the raw coal feed enters by a chute at one end into the bath of heavy medium. The clean coal rises and overflows a weir at the opposite end of the drum. The refuse fraction sinks and continuously picked up by the lifters fixed to the inside of the drum shell. As the drum rotates on its four rollers, these lifters empty into the discharge conveyor when they pass over the highest position. The rotating drum provides agitation of the suspension. The comparatively shallow pool depth in the drum minimizes settling out of the medium particles giving a uniform gravity throughout the drum.

Whenever a middlings product is required, two compartment drum separator (Fig. 23.10.2) is used where two drum separators are mounted integrally and rotates together. The lighter medium in the first compartment separates clean coal product.

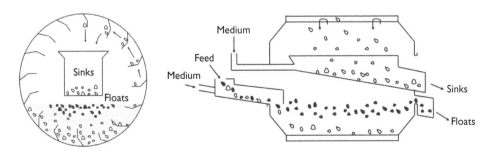

Figure 23.10.1 WEMCO drum separator (single drum).

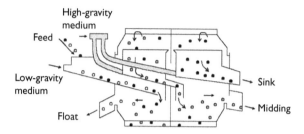

Figure 23.10.2 WEMCO drum separator (two drum).

The sink product is lifted and conveyed into the second compartment where the floats (middlings) and sinks (refuse) are separated by using relatively high gravity medium.

Wemco drum separators are commonly used in the coal industry because of their simplicity, reliability and relatively small maintenance needs.

The medium cleaning and recovery system consists of a thickener to recover the medium following magnetic flocculation to promote its settlement, a magnetic separator to clean the recovered medium, and a densifier and demagnetizer to control its density and to deflocculate it prior to its return to the separator. This type of recovery system is relatively efficient and medium losses can be reduced below 1 lb/ton of coal feed and is particularly valuable where the coal contains high clay content or when a high separating density is required and extreme cleanliness of the medium is essential. The medium cleaning and recovery system is similar to that of Tromp process shown in Fig. 23.8.2.

23.11 BARREL WASHER

Barrel Washer (Fig. 23.11) is a combination of cylindrical and conical construction and works with self generated coal slurry as medium.

In the barrel washer, the beneficiation takes place based on the principles of hindered settling. The coal and water is fed into the top of the cylindrical portion of the barrel which rotates at certain predetermined speed. The water combines with the fine coal and shale particles to form a viscous natural medium. The barrel is angled at 8 degrees and the inside is scrolled. The spiral inside the barrel creates waves in the water in which the pulsation of coal takes place. The combination of the viscosity of the medium and the dynamic effect of the barrel revolution (at 5–20 rpm) causes the lighter coal to float near the top of the flowing stream and discharged at the bottom conical end as low ash coal or clean coal. The shale and high ash coal, which is heavier, sink to the bottom and is carried by the spirals to upper cylindrical portion and discharged at the top conical end as rejects. Thus the rejects and clean coal move in the opposite direction inside the barrel. At the lower end of the barrel a sizing screen is incorporated to drain the water and fine coal. Barrel Washer can wash coal in narrow range (1) 5–12.5 mm (2) 12.5–30 mm (3) 20–50 mm

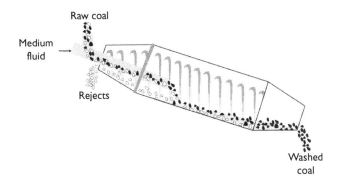

Figure 23.11 Barrel Washer.

The major advantages of this process are:

1   Low capital investment and operating cost.
2   No external medium is required.
3   Simplicity of design with on-line adjustment facility.
4   Easy to operate and control.
5   Low power consumption and low space requirement.
6   Less operating and maintenance staff.
7   Low gestation period.
8   Flexibility due to modular structure.
9   High utilization factor.

Barrel washers are in use in non-coking coal washing plants.

Chapter 24

Jigging

Jigging is the process of separating the particles of different specific gravity, size and shape by introducing them on a perforated surface (or screen) through which a fluid is made to pulsate alternately. Hydraulic jigs use water as the fluid medium whereas pneumatic jigs use air. The device used for this process is called **Jig**. Jigs are one of the oldest and most commonly used methods of coal preparation the world over. Recently, the heavy medium separators have become more popular owing to better performance in the case of difficult coals. In coal plants, Jigs are often called **Jig boxes, Jig washers, Wash boxes**. The extensive use of jigs has been mainly due to low cost of operation, and ability to treat a wide range of size fraction in a single unit. Fines jig can effectively clean from a top size of 13 mm to fines of 100 mesh size. The specific gravity of separation of jigs used in most coal preparation plants varies from 1.30 to 1.90. The optimum capacities range from 200 to 400 tons/hr of feed coal. The basic construction of a Hydraulic jig is shown in Fig. 24.0.1.

It consists of an open tank, filled with a fluid, normally water, with a horizontal or slightly inclined jig screen near the top upon which the particles (the bed) are supported, and through which the fluid flows in alternating directions. The jig includes means to continuously receive raw feed, and means for pulsating the stratified bed into two or more product streams. The jig also includes removal of tailings over the screen or through the screen (called **hutch product**). In operation, the bed is made fluid by a pulsating current of water to provide stratification. These water currents may be all upward (pulsion only), all downward (suction only) or alternating upward

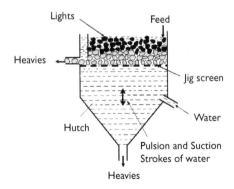

Figure 24.0.1 Basic construction of a Hydraulic jig.

and downward. In most jigs, it is the water which pulsates (fixed sieve jigs), however, in some, the water is stationary and the screen itself pulsates (movable sieve jigs).

On every pulsion stroke, fluid energy of the water acts to lift all the particles in the bed, expanding the contents to the teeter stage. On the reversal of the stroke (suction) the force of gravity supplies the energy to move the particles downward. Stratification (or separation) phenomena can best be explained by considering one heavy particle among many light particles of the same size (Fig. 24.0.2). Under the influence of a rising current of water, light particle will be lifted higher than heavy particle. On the down stroke, the particles fall for a brief instant under free settling conditions.

As initial velocity of heavy particle is greater than light particle, the heavy particle falls faster than light particle and thus increases the distance between the two particles. On next pulsion and suction stroke, the same phenomena continue and increases the distance between two particles further. Such repeated pulsion and suction strokes keeps the heavy particle at the bottom of all light particles. In case of group of many light and heavy particles, repeated pulsion and suction strokes keeps all heavies at the bottom and all lights at the top; thus achieve the separation.

The pulsation of the fluid in a jig can be effected by means of a reciprocating piston. Fig. 24.0.3 shows the displacement of the fluid in a piston type jig as well as its velocity, considering the simple harmonic motion of the jigging cycle.

At the beginning of the cycle, the upward flow of water increases from point A. As the velocity increases, the particles will be loosened and the bed will be forced

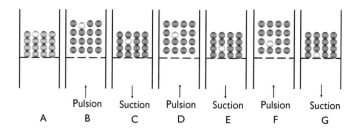

Figure 24.0.2 Stratification phenomena in jig.

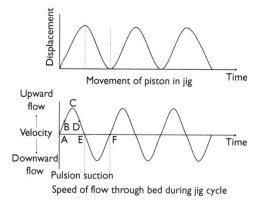

Figure 24.0.3 Harmonic motion cycle of piston jig.

open, or dilated. At point B, the particles are in the form of hindered settling in an upward flow. From B to C, the light fine particles move upward more rapidly than the coarse heavy particles. At point C, the chance of the finest particles, both heavy and light, being carried along with the top flow is the greatest.

Between C and D, the upward force of the rising fluid on the particles will have been spent acting against gravity, and the velocity of the particles will reach zero by about point D, even though the fluid velocity is still upward. At this point, differential acceleration prevails, as each particle reverses its direction and begins to fall. The particles continue to fall during the period D to E by the combination of initial acceleration and hindered settling.

During the suction period, E to F, the fluid flow is downward and the particles are pulled down. The coarse heavy particles arrive first. They are followed by the coarse light particles to form a locked bed, while many slower moving particles continue to settle by the mechanism of consolidation trickling through the interstices of the coarser particles.

One complete jigging cycle is shown in Fig. 24.0.4 depicting how the particles stratify.

Modification to the simple harmonic jig cycle by the addition of a constant flow of hutch water, reduces the compaction of the bed. Suction is reduced in duration by hutch water addition. By adding a large quantity of water, the suction may be entirely eliminated. The coarse heavy particles penetrate the bed more easily and the horizontal transport of the feed over the jig is also improved. However, fines losses will increase partly because the added water increases both the upward flow of water on the pulsion stroke, and the lateral flow across the jig.

The essential requirement in jigging is to produce and maintain a layered bed comprising a top transporting layer, a middle roughing layer and a bottom separating layer.

The functions of the top layer are to spread out the feed entering the jig such that all particles reach the roughing layer and to get slime and other rejected material to the tailboard as quickly as possible. The top layer is thin and fluid. Jigging takes place in the roughing layers and the separating layer. In the roughing layer light particles are immediately rejected back to the top layer whilst indeterminate density particles will be passed down to the separating layer as quickly as possible. The separating layer is the one that accepts and passes heavy particles and rejects middling particles.

Fig. 24.0.5 represents a fully loaded long range jig bed of coal contains different density particles. Slimes remain in the top layer and pass with it rapidly to the

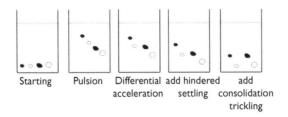

| Starting | Pulsion | Differential acceleration | add hindered settling | add consolidation trickling |

Figure 24.0.4 Particles stratification in one jig cycle.

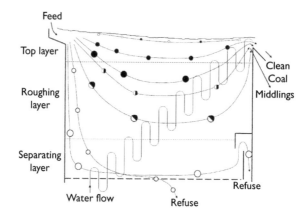

Figure 24.0.5 Flow and solids distribution in jig bed.

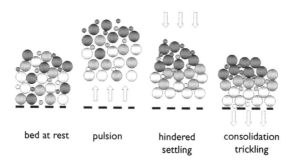

Figure 24.0.6 Particles stratification in a jig bed.

tailboard. Within the roughing layer small light coal particles constitute the top layer with large light coal particles constituting the bottom layer. The total layer moves laterally along the jig to the tailboard and pushed to discharge.

Coarse heavy coal particles (mostly refuse) settle rapidly through the roughing layer to the separating layer. Fine heavies pass to the bottom of the bed by interstitial trickling. Intermediate specific gravity particles, called middlings, arrange into a intermediate layer. Thus all the particles arrange in the increasing order of specific gravity from top to bottom making the light particles float effectively. Fig. 24.0.6 shows how a group of particles stratify in a jig bed. (This figure is only for illustration. Stratification takes place in several jigging cycles but not in one jigging cycle as shown).

24.1 HARZ JIG

The jig, which uses the reciprocating piston or plunger for creating pulsion and suction strokes, is of fixed screen type. Harz jig (Fig. 24.1.1) is a typical example of this type. The piston moves up and down creating the necessary pulsations of water in the

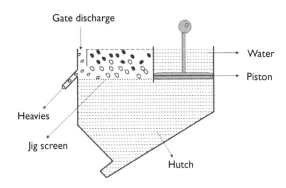

Figure 24.1.1 Harz jig.

jig compartment. A number of compartments are placed in series for successive stages of separation of products of different qualities. The feed is introduced at one end of the first compartment. The light fraction stratifies upward and moves into the second compartment for further separation. The final light fraction overflows from the last compartment. The heavy fractions are removed continuously through a discharge gate at the side of each compartment. Even though the Harz jig is essentially on the screen jig, some fine concentrate will inevitably find its way to the hutch, where it is periodically removed by manual methods. Harz jigs are used in the processing of metallic ores in the size range of 37 mm to 0.5 mm.

24.2   JIGS FOR COAL BENEFICIATION

Four jigs: Baum jig, Batac jig, Feldspar fine coal jig and ROM Jig are commonly used in coal washing plants. All-Air Jig is a pneumatic jig used for dry beneficiation of coal.

24.2.1   Baum jig

The Baum jig is the basis of most of the jigs commonly used in coal washing industry. It is originally designed by Fritz Baum in 1890. The Baum jig (Fig. 24.2.1) consists of a U-shaped steel container divided into two in cross section and longitudinally divided into two or more compartments. On one side of the jig is a perforated screen which supports the particle bed and on which the particle separation is effected. The region below the supporting screen, forming the bottom of the U, is referred as the hutch compartment. Usually a screw conveyor is located at the bottom to remove the fine particles which have passed through the screen with the flowing water.

On the opposite side of the screen plate is a pulsion chamber in which the water pulsations are initiated. A sealed air chamber above the hutch compartment is fitted with an air valve, connected to a compressed air supply. The air valve is actuated mechanically to admit air over the hutch compartment forcing water upward through the perforated screen to produce pulsion stroke. As the valve continues to rotate, the air is released at a controlled rate to atmosphere, and makes the water to move down wards to produce suction stroke. In Baum jig, water pulsation is caused at the rate of 30 to 60 cycles/min.

In its longitudinal phase the U-shaped jig box is divided vertically into compartments. Each compartment, which is essentially a complete jig in itself, is separated by fixed weir and contains the screen and means to remove heavy refuse material either by a gate and dam discharge or a rotary valve mechanism (dirt extractor) at a controlled rate. The heavy refuse drops into the hutch compartment from which a bucket elevator raises the heavy refuse out of the jig. In this jig, primary discharge of heavy dirt is at the feed end and the secondary discharge of lighter dirt, middlings and inferior coal is at the discharge end. It is suited to either steady or fluctuating loads of raw coal, containing at times large proportions of dirt which are quickly disposed at the feed end. An unsized coal is washed with this arrangement. The extraction of dirt must be regulated to correspond exactly with the rate at which it separates, otherwise the dirt will either accumulate in the washer (if the extraction rate is too slow) or coal will pass out with the dirt (if the extraction rate is too fast).

Originally the regulation was by hand, but in modern machines several systems are available for automatic control of refuse material. The most successful system removes the refuse continuously, stabilize the bed and do not impair the stratification. In some systems of automatic control, a float is immersed in the bed in such a way that it takes up a level intermediate between that of dirt and the coal in the stratified bed. If the dirt layer increases in thickness, the float is raised and accelerates the rate of extraction of dirt by increasing the rotation of dirt extractor.

Baum jig has an ability to treat coal of a wide size range and handles large tonnages up to 1000 tons/hr. Because the air chamber in a Baum jig is on the side of the unit, unequal water forces are applied along the width of the jig screen and uneven stratification tends to develop across the bed with a resulting loss in separation

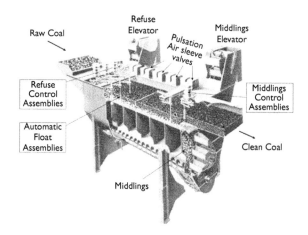

Figure 24.2.1 Baum Jig (Courtesy MBE Coal & Mineral Technology India Pvt Ltd, Kolkata).

efficiency. This tendency is not so important in relatively narrow jigs. As jig size increases, the U-shaped hutch no longer gives an even flow across the whole bed. The efficiency of the jigs is usually good when the NGM is less than 20%.

24.2.2   Batac jig

The **Batac Jig** was developed in Germany in response to a need for jigs of greater capacity. The Batac Jig (Fig. 24.2.2) consists of two compartments and six cells of equal dimensions and is pneumatically operated. In this jig, water pulsations are produced by valve controlled compressed air acting on the water from air chambers arranged underneath the jig bed. This allows the air to be uniformly distributed across the width of the jig. This design promotes more even stratification and gives both improved efficiency and greater processing capacity.

The jig uses electronically controlled air valves which provide a sharp cut-off of the air input and exhaust. Both inlet and outlet valves are infinitely variable with regard to speed and length of the stroke, allowing for the desired variation in pulsion and suction stokes. With this type of sharp control, proper stratification can be achieved for coals of differing characteristics. As a result, the Batac jig can wash well the both coarse and fine sizes of coal.

Because of their high throughput rates and excellent separating performance Batac Jigs have been well accepted in the coal industry worldwide. Batac Jigs in coal

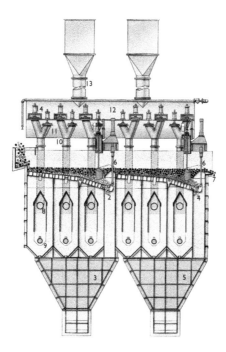

Figure 24.2.2 Batac Jig (Courtesy MBE Coal & Mineral Technology India Pvt Ltd, Kolkata).

are used for de-stoning and for production of final products for the steam coal and metallurgical industry. Units are available to process the full range of coal from coarse size up to 150 mm and down to fine coal in the size range 10–0.5 mm. Common preparation systems based on Batac Jig technology can handle throughput rates between 100 tons/hr and 1,200 tons/hr. The rapid detection of changes in the raw material, the quick reaction of jigs to such changes and easy operation of Batac Jigs make jig plants most reliable for all kinds of applications.

24.2.3　Feldspar jig

The **Feldspar Jig** is an air-pulsated Baum jig utilizing a bed of feldspar (ragging) through which all the refuse materials migrate. It derives its name from the fact that feldspar is used to form an artificial bed.

The feldspar jig works on the same principle as a Baum jig but in view of the small particle size of the feed, an artificial bed with feldspar on the jig screen is provided to prevent the bulk of the feed passing straight through the apertures. Feldspar is used because of its low cost, suitable specific gravity of 2.6 and it has a natural tendency to break into roughly cubical pieces and a high resistance to further breakage or degradation while in use.

The feldspar jig (Fig. 24.2.3) is equipped with three independent cells, each with its own air impulse and water control valves. The cells, not interconnected in any way, provide superior control. The feldspar bed rests on a steel perforated screen plate and transmits the water impulses. The screen perforations are smaller than the feldspar particles but larger than the top size of the feed coal. Under the action of the water pulsations, the raw coal stratifies in the same manner as in the normal Baum jig, i.e.,

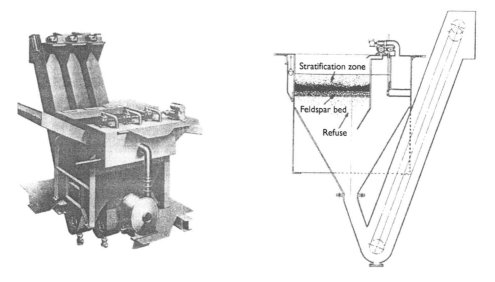

Figure 24.2.3 Feldspar Jig (Courtesy MBE Coal & Mineral Technology India Pvt Ltd, Kolkata).

in to an upper layer of clean coal, an intermediate layer of middlings and a lower layer of shale or dirt. The clean coal is discharged over the sill of the last cell of the jig, while the middlings and the shale comes down through the feldspar until they reach and pass through the jig screen. The density of the feldspar is such that the bed moves under the water pulsations just enough to allow slight relative motion between the pieces of feldspar to permit the downward penetration of the middlings and the shale. The heavier shale and middlings are removed by the bucket elevator.

The pulsation of the water and the 'breathing' of the feldspar bed are separately regulated in each cell of the jig by a float control which gives automatic, sensitive and continuous control of the compressed air supply according to the thickness of the layer of shale or middlings.

A float in the jig bed controls an air valve connected to the air chamber of the jig box. As the quantity of shale decreases, the valve is opened, releasing air from the chamber and thereby reducing the pulsation and the rate of shale removal. Conversely, as the quantity of shale increases, the pulsation is increased. The entire control, apart from the float, is outside the jig box and readily accessible for observation, adjustment and maintenance. The feldspar jigs are available with capacities vary from 30 tons/hr to 100 tons/hr. The feldspar jig is used for the cleaning of – 0.5 inch coal.

The feldspar jig will effect good separations of raw coals containing less than 15% of ±0.10 near gravity material. Where higher percentages of near gravity material are present, efficiency is sacrificed. Although no desliming of the feed coal to a feldspar jig is required, very little reduction in ash is obtained in the –50 mesh (–0.30 mm) material. An attractive feature of the feldspar jig is the small space requirement vs. tonnage treated. The feldspar jig has an automatic control mechanism which compensates for variations in density and rate of feed to provide a more nearly uniform product.

24.2.4 ROM jig

ROM Jig is a movable screen jig and used for deshaling of coal. Separation at relatively high density to remove nearly pure rock is referred as **deshaling**. In ROM Jig, jigging takes place in a water bath. Pulsion and suction strokes required for separation is achieved by lifting and dropping of jig screen to which a hydraulically moved rocker arm is fixed (Fig. 24.2.4). The so induced jigging action causes the separation of rejects from the product, the rejects being on the bottom of the bed, the products on top. The rocker arm movements and the slope pressure result in material transport. The rejects are discharged by a discharge-roll that has the effect of a retaining edge. The hydraulic pressure applied during the upward movement of the rocker arm reflects the reject layer thickness that has accumulated on the screen jig. This value is used as a controlled variable for the discharge-roll velocity. The separated coal is transported over a chute incorporated in the rocker arm. The two products, i.e. rejects and coal are discharged and at the same time de-watered by a twin-type bucket elevator.

The fines dropped through the jig screen in the hutch are directed to fine-grain separation over a gate. The water discharged through the gate and water removed from the coal and rejects are recycled.

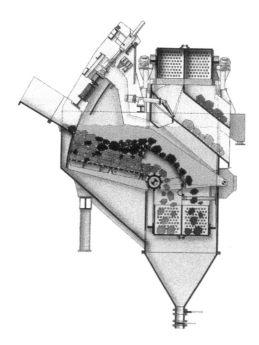

Figure 24.2.4 ROM Jig (Courtesy MBE Coal & Mineral Technology
India Pvt Ltd, Kolkata).

ROM Jig is a single-cut machine developed for primary separation of rejects from the coarse raw coal. The main benefit of the application of the ROM Jig is the reduction of the material to be treated in the next separation steps. Since the material removed is predominantly high mineral content material, the abrasive tendencies of the product will be reduced and the downstream processes will suffer less mechanical wear, thus reducing maintenance costs. The rejects separated in ROM Jigs can be stored in mined-out cavities to alleviate numerous impacts on the environment.

The development of the ROM Jig opened the possibility, to use a very simple process for the beneficiation of the lump size coal –400+30 mm by using only one technologically improved machine and some standard auxiliary equipment.

The removal of a certain portion of the refuse from the uncrushed raw coal offers great advantages for the preparation process, such as for example

- Decrease of power requirements for size reduction
- Increased yield of graded coal in the case of domestic coal production
- Decreased yield of slurry
- Decrease of ash content in the raw slurry
- More favourable homogenizing properties of the raw coal
- Decreased wear in the concentration machines
- More favourable utilization of the preparation capacity, i.e. increased efficiency of the preparation plant

The size of the coal that may be treated in jigs are between 200 mm and 0.5 mm. However, jigs are now often used to wash small coal, say below 25 mm, the larger sizes being treated in heavy medium separators. Heavy medium washers are most suitable for washing the coal that is difficult to wash efficiently because of the presence of near gravity material in large quantity. The recovery efficiency and the sharpness of separation are better for heavy medium vessels than for Baum jigs. However, the capability of the Baum jig to wash particles of wide size range is desirable from the standpoint of capital investment and operating cost.

Jigs cannot wash fines below 0.5 mm and their efficiency drops sharply when the content of sizes below 3 mm grows above 25%. For such fines, cyclone washers are quite suitable. Flotation cells are also used for washing of coal fines. When the feed coal of 200 mm −0.5 mm is jigged, the fines remain unwashed and form slurries which need further treatment for the recovery of combustibles.

Chapter 25

Flowing film concentration

Sorting of different particles on flat inclined surface in accordance with the size, shape and specific gravity of the particles moved by a flowing film of water is called as **Flowing Film Concentration**. The concentration in thin film where the film thickness and size of the particles are of similar magnitude and the rate of shear on the fluid is relatively low is called as **Thin Film Concentration**. Another type of concentration, called as **Thick Film Concentration,** takes place in much thicker films under the conditions of substantial fluid shear.

Spiral concentrator is one of the flowing film concentrators and is used for beneficiation of fine coals ranging in size from 3 – 0.1 mm. Spiral concentrator (Fig. 25.1) consists of a descending spiral launder of a helical conduit with a modified semi-circular cross section wrapped around a central supporting column.

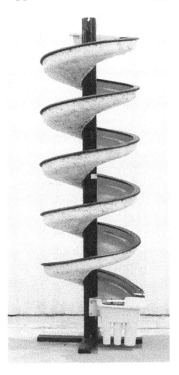

Figure 25.1 Spiral Concentrator.
(Courtesy mine-engineer.com)

The raw coal slurry, having 30 to 40% solids content, is fed through the feed box, which reduces its velocity and establishes the correct pattern of flow. The feed enters the spiral channel as almost homogeneous slurry. As the slurry flows around the helix of the spiral concentrator, stratification occurs in a vertical plane as a result of combination of hindered settling and interstitial trickling and the slurry is subjected to the centrifugal force which places much of the water near the outer rim until the flowing stream reaches an equilibrium between outward centrifugal force and down-ward gravitational force.

In such a curved channel the bottom layer of water, retarded by the friction, has much less centrifugal force and consequently will flow sideways along the bottom towards the inner edge, carrying with it the heavier refuse particles to the lower veloc-ity zone. Simultaneously with this bottom flow of water inward, the upper mass of water flow outward carrying light coal particles to higher velocity zone.

The helical twist of the spiral concentrator causes a flowing film velocity gradient to be set up in a vertical plane and also a radial or centrifugal velocity gradient in a horizontal plane. The difference in centrifugal forces acting upon the varying stream components causes a cross-sectional rotation to develop. The portion of the stream nearest the surface moves outward to the point of maximum stream velocity. From there it moves down into the stream to near the spiral surface. It then follows the spiral surface inward to the inner margin of the stream. This cross-sectional rotation of the stream serves to shift the heavy refuse particles inward and the light, faster flowing, but slower settling coal particles, outward. The heavier and lighter particles of the streams are thus shifted laterally in opposite directions so that one is separated from the other. Cross-sectional rotation in the spiral makes it unique as a gravity concentration device.

The cross section of a spiral concentrator can be divided into various regions (Fig. 25.2), with each region describing the effect it has on the slurry traveling through it. On the outer most region (1) (perimeter), will have mostly water, with fine parti-cles, trapped by the high velocity of the moving water. Moving inward towards the center of the spiral, the next region (2) would consist of a very small area where the maximum water velocity exists, and prevents any separation to occur. This region is defined since it separates the next region (3) from the first region.

Region 3 is a very active region where the velocity begins to slow down and most of the separation occurs, as more heavy particles settle to the bottom and the water velocity keeps the light particles in the stream near the surface, where they eventually wind up in the outer regions (2 and 1). The next region is actually where two regions overlap (region 3 and 4), and is a very narrow region (like region 2). Next to the last region (region 5) is where the heavy refuse particles are collected. The remaining light particles in this region find their way to the top of the slurry surface and are carried off by the fast flowing water to the perimeter of the spiral, with the bulk of the water and the light particles.

Thus the separation of cleans, middlings and refuse takes place because of dif-ferences in their specific gravities. The refuse particles get thrown towards the centre of the spiral because of their high specific gravity. Similarly, the middlings stay in the centre and the cleans collect towards the periphery of the spiral. At the bottom of the spiral, diverters/splitters are provided which guide the three products to get discharged separately.

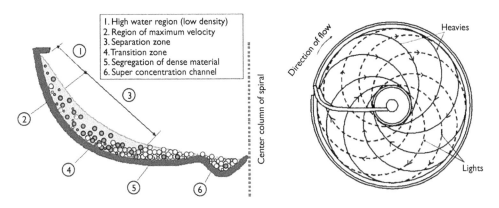

Figure 25.2 Cross section of a Spiral showing particle movement.

Some spirals have a wash water section, where additional water is added to free any trapped light particles in the refuse, and on a wash water spiral, the innermost portion is where this water is added, and it is called region 6. From the innermost region of the spiral, the refuse particles flow to the bottom section of the spiral, where splitter "bars" actually make a cut of the material, channeling the inner most material to the refuse port, a 'middlings' splitter can be used to channel the intermediate to a separate discharge port, and the majority of the water and the coal is cut to a low density clean coal port. These cutter bars are adjustable, and are usually set up during the start up. They can be changed easily, to accommodate differing feed material.

The most important in spiral operation is steady feed rate and density of the slurry. It should be as close as design conditions. Grade of the ROM coal and size range of the particles in feed slurry are important factors that effect the separation.

The available literature shows that spirals are more efficient than water-only cyclones for treating fine coal with appreciable amount of clay. Their separation efficiency is fairly constant over a relatively wide range of solid feed rates. Spirals can be operated at higher feed percent solids and are able to extract rejects of >81% ash at all feed rates.

Spirals concentration was first applied to the washing of coal in 1945, although due to the decline in output of high quality fine coal after the Second World War, their application was limited. Recently, however, there has been renewed interest in the use of spirals for coal cleaning. Reichert has recently developed the spirals specifically for coal cleaning with encouraging performance.

Chapter 26

Cyclone separation

The equipments such as Heavy Medium Separators, Jigs and other gravity concentration devices allow a rather much amount of valuable product to be lost in tailings if the specific gravity of separation chosen is such that the coal to be treated consist large proportion of near gravity material. In all these conventional systems the separation is affected in gravitational field. For materials having small particle size are showing only a slight specific gravity difference, the separating forces in the gravitational fields are too weak to bring about an efficient and sharp separation. Heavy Medium Cyclones provide high centrifugal force and a low viscosity in the medium, enabling much finer separations to be achieved than in gravitational separators.

26.1 CYCLONE

Cyclone is a basic device used for separation of smaller and fine size particles. As the particles are ground smaller they reach a size where the surface drag against the surrounding fluid almost neutralizes the gravitational pull, with the result that the particle may need hours, or even days, to fall a few centimeters through still water. This slowing down of settling rate reduces the tonnage that can be handled and increases the quantity of machinery and plant required. By superimposing the centrifugal force the gravitational pull can be tremendously increased.

The cyclone is one which utilizes centrifugal force to accelerate the settling rate of particles. In a cyclone, the centrifugal force applied is usually 50–500 times greater than that of the gravitational force depending on the pressure at which the pulp is fed to the cyclone and the diameter of the cyclone. Cyclone has found wide acceptance for the washing of fine coal.

Cyclone (Fig. 26.1.1) has no moving parts. It consists of a conically shaped vessel, open at the bottom, variously called the underflow nozzle, discharge orifice, apex or spigot, and connected to a cylindrical section which has a tangential feed inlet. The top of this cylindrical section is closed with a plate through which passes an axially mounted overflow pipe. The pipe is extended into the body of the cyclone by a short, removable section known as vortex finder, which prevents short-circuiting of feed directly into the overflow.

In a cyclone, when the pulp (solids and water), either pumped or flowing by gravity, is fed tangentially under pressure into a cyclone, the pulp is imparted a swirling motion and a vortex is generated about the longitudinal axis (Fig. 26.1.1). At the cen-

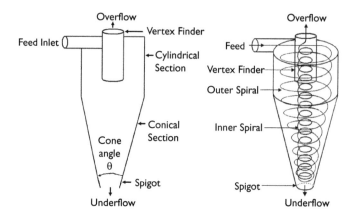

Figure 26.1.1 Cyclone and Flow patterns in cyclone.

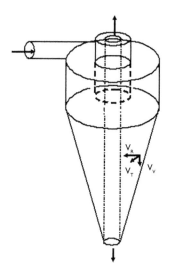

Figure 26.1.2 Velocity components.

tre of the cyclone is a zone of low pressure and low centrifugal force and an air core develops along the axis. The fluid and solid particles fed into the cyclone at a linear velocity 'v' are directed into circular motion. This linear velocity, as a result of the shape of the cyclone and the position of the discharge ports, resolves itself into three components (Fig. 26.1.2):

A radial inward velocity component V_R commencing at the cone periphery, a downward vertical velocity component V_v and a tangential velocity component V_T.

By the law of conservation of energy, the angular or rotational momentum Iω (where I is the moment of inertia, ω is the angular velocity) will be constant for a given moving mass, be it situated at the cone wall or at or near the central part of the cyclone.

$$I = m_p r^2 \qquad (26.1.1)$$

and

$$\omega = \frac{V_T}{r} \qquad (26.1.2)$$

$$\text{Now, rotational momentum} = I\omega = m_p r^2 \left(\frac{V_T}{r}\right) = m_p V_T r = \text{constant} \qquad (26.1.3)$$

where
  m_p = mass of the particle
  r = radius of rotation
  V_T = linear (or) tangential velocity of the particle

$$\text{As } m_p \text{ is constant, } \quad V_T r = \text{constant} \qquad (26.1.4)$$

which means that as the particle or fluid is forced toward the centre i.e., as its radius of rotation becomes less, its linear or tangential velocity must increase. Taking into consideration that some loss of energy occurs due to friction, the equation 26.1.4 becomes

$$V_T r^n = \text{constant} \qquad (26.1.5)$$

where n lies between 0.5 and 1.0.

This equation 26.1.5 holds for all cyclones. As r approaches zero, V_T approaches infinity but this is not so in an operating cyclone since the relationship is valid only until r becomes measurably small and the velocity then decreases rapidly to zero at the air core surface.

For a body moving in straight line F = m_pa
For rotation movement $\qquad\qquad$ F$_c$ = m_pa$_c$

$$F_c = (\text{Apparent mass}) \frac{V_T^2}{r}$$

$$= \text{Volume of particle (density of solid} - \text{density of fluid)} \frac{V_T^2}{r}$$

$$= V_s (\rho_p - \rho_f) \frac{V_T^2}{r}$$

where
  ρ_p = density of solid
  ρ_f = density of fluid
  V_s = volume of solid particle

Therfore, $F_c = V_s(\rho_p - \rho_f)\dfrac{V_T^2}{r} = m_p a_c = V_s \rho_p a_c$

$$\therefore a_c = \frac{V_s(\rho_p - \rho_f)V_T^2}{V_s(\rho_p)r} = \frac{V_T^2}{r}\left(1 - \frac{\rho_f}{\rho_p}\right) \tag{26.1.6}$$

where a_c is the acceleration of the particle at right angles to the direction of rotation due to the tangential velocity V_T.

From this formula, it is seen that the centrifugal acceleration and in consequence the separation force is strongest near the centre of the cyclone. As all solid particles must leave the cyclone near to the centre either by the overflow or the underflow, they must all pass through this region of high centrifugal force.

The tangential fluid velocity increases as fluid and solid particles move from the cone periphery toward the centre line of the cyclone. This tangential velocity increases to a maximum value whose locus is a vertical cylindrical envelope with the axis of cone as its central axis and extending from the apex section to the vortex finder. For any cone, this cylindrical envelope will have a radius of approximately $0.17\ r_c$ where r_c is the radius of cylindrical section of the vessel. From the envelope of maximum velocity toward the face of the air core, tangential velocity drops from a maximum to zero at the air core face.

In a cyclone, there exists a region of downward flow to the apex and an upward flow to the vortex finder. Hence at some point in the cyclone, there must exist an interface between the two flows where there is a zero vertical velocity. At points half way between the air core wall and cone periphery, the vertical velocity is zero. The total envelope of zero vertical velocity is the surface generated by lines joining all these midpoints in the cyclone. This becomes a conical surface.

At all points outside of this conical surface, vertical velocity is downward; at all points inside, vertical velocity is upward. It therefore follows that all particles located outside the envelope of zero vertical velocity move downward while those inside this conical envelope move upward. Fig. 26.1.3 shows different envelopes in a cyclone.

Radial velocity inward toward the cone centre develops as a result of displacement of the fluid mass by incoming feed. The radial velocity is maximum at the cone wall and decreases with the radius until it is zero at the air core interface.

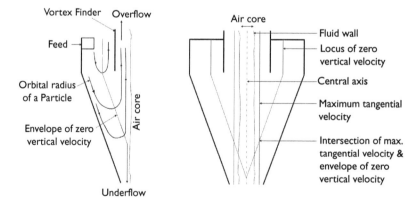

Figure 26.1.3 Different envelopes in a cyclone.

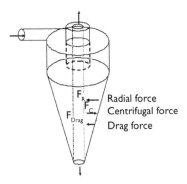

Figure 26.1.4 Forces on particle.

The particles within the pulp flow are subjected to the following three forces (Fig. 26.1.4)

1   The inward drag force resulting from the effect of the inward radial velocity on the particle. i.e., $F_R = f(V_R)$

2   The outward centrifugal force resulting from the acceleration caused by the tangential velocity $F_c = f(\frac{V_T^2}{r})$

3   The inward drag force resulting from the fluid resistance due to the centrifugal acceleration. $F_{Drag} = f(a_c)$

The centrifugal force on a particle at any specified distance from the cone axis is the same regardless of the vertical position of the particle. This centrifugal force is maximum when a particle is positioned on the envelope of maximum tangential velocity. On the other hand, the fluid radial force F_R on the particle increases as the particle moves down the cone between the outside wall and the envelope of zero vertical velocity.

No particle can report to the overflow until it has reached a point on the envelope of maximum tangential velocity where the sum of inward forces $(F_R + F_{Drag})$ is greater than outward force F_c. When the inward force is more, the particle cross the envelope of zero vertical velocity and starts to move upward. Since the fluid force F_R decreases as the particle moves up (V_R decreasing) and F_c remains the same, the particle start to move inward. Below the intersection of the envelopes of zero vertical velocity and maximum tangential velocity, the particles will report to overflow or underflow depending on whether or not they can cross the envelope of zero vertical velocity before they are carried into the underflow. It is clear that particles which do report to overflow will start crossing both the zero vertical velocity line and the maximum tangential velocity line at specific heights.

The water introduced along with the solid particles acts as a vehicle for removing the particles from overflow as well as underflow. The water in the cyclone has four different flow movements: Rotational flow, Inward or radial flow, Downward flow and Upward flow. Particles entering the cyclone with the water are effected both by centrifugal force caused by their own rotation and by the various water flows. As explained above, the balance of two forces i.e. outward centrifugal force and inward drag force, acting on a particle determines whether it leaves with the underflow or the overflow.

The centrifugal force imparts only a low velocity to small light particles and therefore the faster inward flow of the water carries most of these particles towards the vortex. At the vortex, the upward flow carries them through the vortex finder. Some water also leaves via the underflow and therefore carries with it the remainder of the slowly moving fine particles. Heavy and/or large particles have an extremely high velocity and are rapidly thrown to the wall of the cyclone where the downward flow of water carries them to the apex.

Now consider the Stoke's Law for terminal settling velocity of the particle

$$V_m = \frac{d^2 g(\rho_p - \rho_f)}{18\mu}$$

When the driving force is centrifugal, the acceleration due to gravity 'g' is replaced by a_C. Then

$$a_c = \frac{V_T^2}{r}\left(1 - \frac{\rho_f}{\rho_p}\right)$$

Therefore, $$V_m = \frac{V_T^2}{r}\left(1 - \frac{\rho_f}{\rho_p}\right)\frac{d^2(\rho_p - \rho_f)}{18\mu} \qquad (26.1.7)$$

At equilibrium $V_m = V_R$

If this radius, at which equilibrium is reached, is less than the radius of zero vertical velocity envelope, the particle will lie in a rising stream and can overflow. On the other hand, if this radius is greater than the radius of zero vertical velocity envelope, the particle will move downward into the underflow. Thus the particles will get separated and flow through vortex finder and spigot respectively. The vortex finder is so adjusted as to project into the cylindrical section of the cyclone in order to minimize the short circuiting of newly arrived pulp. The particle whose equilibrium radius coincides with the zero vertical velocity line is considered to have a 50:50 chance of going in either direction. This particle size, called the d_{50} size, is the separating size of the cyclone.

The average time of residence of a particle in a cyclone is the cyclone volume divided by the throughput. The residence time in a 10 mm cyclone is of the order of 0.06 seconds and in a low pressure 300 mm cyclone the residence time might go up to 11 seconds.

The main controlling factors in cyclone operation are:

1   Feed inlet diameter
2   Feed pressure
3   Feed rate

4   Solid liquid ratio
5   Position of vortex finder
6   Diameter of vortex finder
7   Diameter of apex
8   Specific gravity of solids in feed

Cyclones are being used in many applications due to the following advantages:

1   Sharper separation
2   Saving of floor space
3   Less power consumption
4   Less maintenance
5   Ability to shut down the mill immediately under load
6   Ability to bring the circuit rapidly into balance
7   Elimination of cyclic surging

The principal applications of cyclones are:

1   Classification (increasingly used in closed circuit grinding)
2   De-sliming
3   De-gritting
4   Thickening (Solids recovery, liquid recovery)
5   Washing of fine coal

As the solid particles are fed with water into the cyclone in the first four applications, it is known as **Hydrocyclone.**

26.2   HEAVY MEDIUM CYCLONE

The Heavy Medium Cyclone or Dense Medium Cyclone also called as DSM Cyclone was developed by M.G.Driessen [45] and his colleagues at Dutch State Mines (DSM) and reported in 1945. It has been developed with an included cone angle of approximately 20°, and is used to treat ores and coal in size range 40–0.5 mm. The principle of operation is very similar to that of the conventional hydrocyclone. The coal particles are fed to DSM cyclone along with the suspension of heavy medium particles.

Instead of water alone, a suspension of heavy particles in water is used in Heavy Medium Cyclone. This suspension, called **Heavy Medium,** is a mixture of −325 mesh particles of magnetite and water in case of beneficiation of coal. The quantity of magnetite added to the water depends on the specific gravity of separation. The fraction of magnetite to be added can be determined by the following formula

$$C_w = \frac{\rho_p(\rho_{hm} - 1)}{\rho_{hm}(\rho_p - 1)}$$

(26.2.1)

where
    C_w = fraction of magnetite by weight
    ρ_p = density of magnetite, gm/cm³
    ρ_{hm} = density of heavy medium, gm/cm³

After preparing the Heavy Medium accordingly, a de-slimed raw coal is added to this Heavy Medium which forms the feed to HM Cyclone. A medium-to-coal ratio of about 5:1 is recommended for coal washing. This feed is forced tangentially into the HM Cyclone through feed inlet orifice.

There are two methods in admitting the feed to inlet orifice. One way is to simply feed the coal directly into the Heavy Medium sump and pump the mixture to the cyclone. Alternatively, the Heavy Medium is pumped to a head tank, which is 5–6 m above the cyclone feed inlet, where the coal is added to prepare the feed. This second method is particularly applicable in case of coal because degradation of coal in the Heavy Medium pump is eliminated. This degradation may occur due to the friable nature of coal.

In a static Heavy Medium bath, the buoyant forces acting on the light coal particles cause them to rise to the surface but the heavy coal particles sink to the bottom. The magnitude of the gravitational and buoyant forces that separate the coal particles is a primary consideration because it governs the velocity with which the particles separate, which in turn determines the capacity of the separating vessel. In a static bath, the net gravitational force minus buoyant force may be written as follows:

$$F_g = (m_p - m_f)\, g$$

where
    F_g = gravitational force
    m_p = mass of solid
    m_f = mass of fluid displaced by the particle

For the coal particles which float, F_g is having a negative value and for sink coal particles, it is positive. In a centrifugal separator, specific gravity separations result from application and utilization of similar forces except that the acceleration of gravity is substituted by a centrifugal acceleration. The equation then becomes:

$$F_c = (m_p - m_f)\frac{v^2}{r} \tag{26.2.2}$$

where
    F_c = centrifugal force
    v = tangential velocity
    r = radius of the centrifugal separator

Cyclones are used to develop this centrifugal force. In a typical cyclone, the centrifugal force acting on a particle in the inlet region is 20 times greater than the gravitational force in a static bath. In the conical section of the cyclone, v is further increased according to the relationship:

$$v\sqrt{r} = constant \qquad\qquad (26.2.3)$$

At the apex of the cyclone where r decreases, the acceleration increases to over 200 times greater than gravity. Thus, the forces tending to separate the light and heavy particles are much greater in a cyclone than in a static bath. This offers two advantages:

1 a relatively high capacity
2 because the forces acting on the small particles are also much larger than static separations, the cyclone is much more applicable to the separation of small particles

The general flow pattern in this HM Cyclone is similar to that of hydrocyclone. As Heavy Medium together with the coal particles are fed through the feed inlet orifice, a vortex with a hollow air core extending from the overflow to the underflow orifice forms in the cyclone. Under the influence of the centrifugal force, high specific gravity coal particles move through the medium to the wall of the cyclone and descend in a spiral flow pattern to the underflow orifice. Those coal particles in the feed stream having the lower specific gravity than the Heavy Medium follow the major portion of the flow to the center of the core where they are caught in the high velocity upward central current and are carried out through the overflow orifice. Some particles arriving in the core leave again under the influence of the centrifugal acceleration imparted to them and move to the apex discharge opening along the wall. At the point, near the apex opening, the non-tangential current is direct upward into the core, the particles can again be selected for discharge through either the apex or the overflow opening.

Particles much below the specific gravity of separation will immediately, after entering the cyclone, move rapidly toward the centre and issue through the overflow opening without being recirculated. Heavy particles, on the other hand, will immediately after getting into cyclone move towards the wall and issue through the apex opening.

Centrifugal force also acts on the very fine magnetite medium and therefore the specific gravity of the medium will increase towards the apex discharge opening. Therefore, the specific gravity of separation is slightly higher than that of the medium.

In this cyclone, floating means moving towards inner air core of the cyclone, while sinking means moving towards the wall of the cyclone. Both movements are rapid as they are under the action of centrifugal force not gravitational force. The specific gravity of separation is related not only to the specific gravity of the Heavy Medium suspension but also to the inward flow towards the centre. The specific gravity of separation is usually slightly higher than that of the medium. Increased overflow diameter increases the difference between the specific gravity of the medium and specific gravity of separation. The cyclone is at its most efficient when the specific gravity of separation is as close as possible to the specific gravity of the medium. To achieve this, the diameter of the vortex finder should be slightly greater than that of the apex.

The capacity of Heavy Medium Cyclone increases with its diameter. Heavy Medium Cyclone diameters normally range from 200 mm up to 1 metre, with the inlet pressure usually being higher for the smaller diameter units. They are operated with inlet pressures as low as 6–8 psig, but pressures of 20 psig and higher are used in practice. At very low pressures, the separation is much less effective than at higher

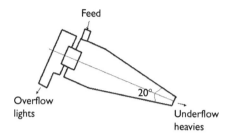

Figure 26.2.1 Typical Heavy Medium Cyclone.

Table 26.2.1 Typical operating data for HM Cyclone.

Cyclone diameter cm	Static head m	Feed capacity t/hr
35	3.20	0–25
40	4.50	25–50
50	5.40	50–75
60	6.75	75–100

pressures, especially for the finer sizes. HM Cyclones with a cone angle of 20° is pretty standard and they are commonly installed with axes inclined at 10–15° to the horizontal (Fig. 26.2.1) in order to enable the unit to be fed at a comparatively low inlet pressure, preferably from a steady head tank and to allow drainage after shut-down. The optimum static head required is approximately 9 times the diameter of the cyclone for washing coal.

Table 26.2.1 shows the typical operating data for HM Cyclone.

The magnetite used to form the heavy medium is required to be about 90% minus 45 microns, but the percentage of ultra-fine magnetite (below 5 microns) should be relatively low, otherwise the fine magnetite particles will be classified in the cyclone, and become incorporated with the clean coal product. This results in heavy losses of the ultra-fine magnetite and, more importantly, a serious reduction in separation efficiency. A medium which is too coarse tends to build up an excessive specific grav-ity differential in the cyclone, preventing near gravity particles from passing through either the zone of high specific gravity into the underflow, or the zone of low specific gravity into the overflow. Excessive recirculation inside the cyclone will result an adverse affect on performance.

Heavy medium have unusual viscosity properties. Agitating the medium has the effect of reducing the viscosity, but in a conventional bath such agitation would ruin the separation of the particles. In a cyclone, the rapid rotation of medium causes lay-ers of medium to move relative to each other. This type of agitation, referred to as "shearing", considerably reduces the viscosity of the medium and is one of the reasons why the cyclone is so effective for small coal.

In spite of the higher settling velocities that occur in a cyclone, there are particles so small that their settling velocity is less than the velocity of the inward current. Such particles will remain with the water and behave as though they were in permanent suspension. Advantage is taken of this to produce stable medium which is not separated by the cyclone. In practice, some small degree of separation of medium particles occurs, i.e., more of the fine particles come out with the overflow than with the underflow, but this separation is not sufficient to be objectionable.

Equipped with considerable operating flexibility, the heavy medium cyclones provide efficient and sharp separations in treating coals of up to 44% near gravity material at separating specific gravities ranging from 1.42 to 1.55. Considering the very short residence time within the cyclone, the sharpness of separation is quite remarkable. The top size of the coal particles to be treated is commonly 13 mm. The bottom size of the coal particle is generally related to the medium recovery system. 0.5 mm is the lowest accepted size for efficient separation and it is due to the difficulty in reclaiming magnetite from very fine size coal.

In HM Cyclone operation, the specific gravity of the Heavy Medium is the main controlling parameter. Other parameters are diameter of the cyclone, feed pressure, cone angle, and sizes of three orifices.

Diameter of the cyclone: The diameter of the HM Cyclone does not have a major effect on its efficiency. Therefore, the larger cyclones are usually used for their higher capacity and ease of operation. The capacity of HM Cyclone increases with its diameter.

Feed pressure: Feed pressure is not a major factor in the efficiency of separation, because even at low feed pressures (less than 8 psig) efficient separations can be obtained with cyclones of various sizes. Above 8 psig feed pressures, the volumetric capacity increases in proportion to the square root of the feed pressure.

Cone angle: It is observed that HM Cyclones of small cone angles provide more efficient separation. Consequently, cone angles for commercial application have been limited to the 14–25° range.

Orifices: An increase in feed orifice diameter increases throughput, decreases retention time, and increases the specific gravity of separation. It may also decrease separation efficiency. An increase in overflow orifice diameter has the same effect as an increase in feed orifice diameter. An increase in underflow orifice decreases the specific gravity of separation and slightly increases overall capacity but markedly increases the capacity of the cyclone for the heavy fraction.

26.2.1   Medium recovery

The basic principles of magnetite recovery is similar to that of magnetite recovery process employed for heavy medium separation; but due to the fine coal feed in heavy medium cyclone, recovery circuit is of large and more complex as the particles of coal are so small and tend to carry large amounts of magnetite with them. Use of sieve bend makes it possible to screen the fine coal at approximately 200 mesh without clogging up the screen deck.

For separation of magnetite medium, concurrent drum magnetic separators are most commonly used in modern circuits. Single stage drum separators are satisfactory for recovery of coarse magnetite, but double drum magnets with the second drum scavenging the coal from the first are generally required for finer magnetite. Furthermore, double drum separators permit higher feed volumes to be treated while obtaining the same recovery that can be achieved at lower rates on single drum separators.

Efficient operation of the magnetic separators is a vital part of the circuit. The magnetite recovery circuit used in heavy medium cyclone process is more sensitive to changes in feed conditions and requires a high standard of operation. Separate recovery circuits for dilute medium from the overflow and underflow can also be used.

Fig. 26.2.2 shows a typical heavy medium cyclone process flow sheet. The deslimed raw coal is mixed with suspension of magnetite and fed to heavy medium cyclone through constant head tank. Both overflow and underflow of heavy medium cyclone are drained separately on sieve bends and on the draining section of drain and rinse vibrating screens. The drained medium of – 28 mesh is fed to constant head tank for reuse. The clean coal and refuse are rinsed on the rinsing screen with water sprays separately and are discharged. The refuse is rejected as it is whereas clean coal is dewatered in centrifuge. The underflow of rinsing screens is processed in two stage magnetic separators for recovery of magnetite. The magnetite recovered from mag-

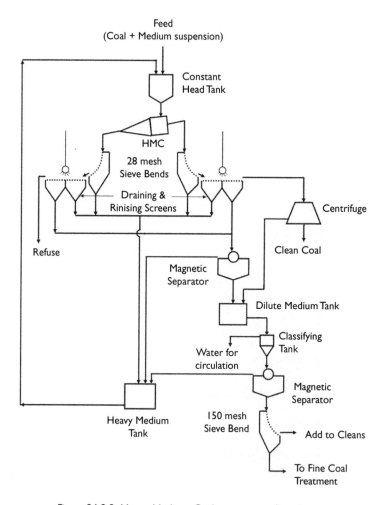

Figure 26.2.2 Heavy Medium Cyclone process flowsheet.

netic separators is reused by adding it to the heavy medium tank. The non-magnetic part of the primary magnetic separator is fed to classifying cyclone to thicken it and then processed it in secondary magnetic separator for further recovery of magnetite. The non-magnetic fraction is screened on 150 mesh sieve bend from which overflow is added to clean coal product and underflow is either sent for fine coal treatment or thickened and filtered to add to clean coal product depending on its ash content.

Several features of this flowsheet are very important to the industry in order to make modifications depending upon the quantity of different fractions obtained at each and every stage.

In order to extend the effective cleaning range of the cyclone down to zero and to improve overall separation efficiency, Pittsburgh Energy Technology Centre of the department of Energy under the auspices of the High Efficiency Coal Preparation Program has been studying the use of heavy liquid cycloning using Freon-13 as the separating liquid in 50 mm cyclone. The study found an exceptional separation of ultrafine coal down to 37 microns in size. Even though Freon-13 is found to be an ideal heavy liquid, for the reason of environmental acceptability, other heavy liquids are to be identified and developed. Possible liquids are brine, sucrose solutions, trichloro-ethane, perchloroethylene and micronized magnetite suspension.

26.3 WATER–ONLY CYCLONE

By giving a special shape to the cone and to the cylindrical part of the cyclone, it is possible to affect separation based on specific gravity utilizing water as a separating medium (i.e., without using Heavy Medium). Such cyclone is known as **water-only cyclone** or **water washing cyclone**.

Water-only cyclones essentially consist of a tangential feed inlet to which a cylindro-conical body is attached. The included cone angle ranges from 80° to 140°. The water-only cyclone has a long-large vortex finder extending down through the length of the cylindrical body and it has a small vortex finder clearance (h) i.e., the vertical gap between the lower tip of the vortex finder and the apex opening.

When feed slurry is injected into the body of the cyclone through a tangential feed inlet, the water adopts a swirling path thus giving a typical flow pattern of spiral within a spiral. When the outer spiral (containing heavy particles) touches the wide-angle conical bottom, the movement of particles is suddenly seized. This results in crowding of the particles in the conical region forming an autogenous Heavy Medium through which the sinks have to penetrate to enter the underflow. The fine light particles which cannot penetrate this Heavy Medium, escape upwards through the vortex finder. Thus the separation takes place on the basis of specific gravity rather than size. As this cyclone create denser bed composed of heavy or intermediate particles of raw coal which further utilized for separation, it is also called as Autogenous cyclone.

As per the acceleration theory proposed by Fontein & Dijksman [46] in 1953, all particles are subjected to the centrifugal forces. The initial movement of a particle outwards towards the wall of the cyclone will be dominated by the particle acceleration and the drag force will be low. Thus acceleration of a particle is given by

$$a_p = \frac{F_c}{m_p} = \frac{(m_p - m_f)}{m_p} \frac{v^2}{r} \qquad (26.3.1)$$

For the particles occupying the same radial position in the cyclone, having r and v the same and since m_f is the mass of an equal volume of fluid, then this simplifies to

$$a_p = \left(1 - \frac{m_f}{m_p}\right)C = \left(1 - \frac{\rho_f V_p}{\rho_p V_p}\right)C = \left(1 - \frac{1}{Sg_p}\right)C \qquad (26.3.2)$$

where

$C = v^2/r$ which is constant and equal for all particles
Sg_p = Specific gravity of the particle

Now for a shale particle of Specific gravity 2.4 and a coal particle of specific gravity 1.3, the initial acceleration of the particles outwards will be given by

$$a_{shale} = \left(1 - \frac{1}{2.4}\right)C = 0.583C \quad \text{and} \quad a_{coal} = \left(1 - \frac{1}{1.3}\right)C = 0.231C$$

That is, the acceleration on the shale particle is about 2.5 times that on the coal particle. The shale particle is therefore more likely to move out of the ascending vortex to the descending vortex and thus report to the cyclone spigot. The coal particle then is more likely to remain in the ascending vortex and report to the overflow independent of its size.

As the particle size decreases, the fluid resistance becomes a significant factor. For large particles, the residence time in the cyclone is not long enough for the fluid resistance to become significant. This is not the case for the finer particles and hence the very fine particles tend to report to the light fraction regardless of their density.

Water-only cyclones may be classified in to three types (1) DSM hydrocyclone (2) Var-a-Wall cyclone (3) Compound water-only cyclone (or) Tricone as in Fig. 26.3.1.

These three types differ in cone angles. The DSM hydrocyclone has uniform tapered constant angle of about 80°. Var-a-Wall cyclone consists of two cone angles

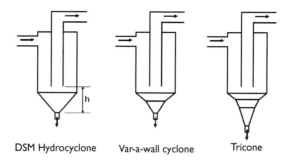

DSM Hydrocyclone   Var-a-wall cyclone   Tricone

Figure 26.3.1 Types of water-only cyclones.

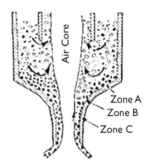

Figure 26.3.2 Compound water only cyclone.

in two stages, the first ranges from 100° to 140° and the second ranges from 80° to 100°. The tricone has cone in three stages. The cone angle of first stage ranges from 80° to 140° and subsequently dropping to 60° and 30° in the second and third stages.

The separation in compound water only cyclone takes place in three stages. In the first stage, as the feed slurry enters the cyclone tangentially into the cylindrical portion, the particles of high density and large size will have higher centrifugal force. These particles will form a thick bed in Zone A as shown in Fig. 26.3.2. In this zone, stratification of coarse heavy particles takes place due to the hindered settling phenomenon. This bed mainly consists of the coarse heavy particles and acts as a carrier for the bed of light particles, so the light particles (having less teetering effect) cannot penetrate the bed of heavy particles and will be swept of Zone B. In zone B, the central currents are much stronger, resulting in the peeling-off of the top of the bed thus exposing the middlings which are swept up. Finally, the small particles that have escaped the central currents enter zone C along with the remainder of the bed. In this zone, the cone angle is very narrow and hence fine particles will be dragged towards the air core leaving coarse heavy particles to be discharged through the apex of the cyclone.

Water-only cyclones have been widely used over the last 35 years for washing coal fines below 0.5 mm. Cyclone diameters may be as small as 50 mm and such units are commonly used as an alternative to froth flotation. They are particularly useful where the coal is prone to oxidation and may therefore be difficult to recover by flotation technique. They are not applicable for difficult coal having large percent near gravity material or at low specific gravity of separation.

The separation efficiency of water-only cyclone is much lower than that of HM Cyclone, and separation is also less sharp. To improve the efficiency, cyclones are often installed as two stage units wherein the underflow of first cyclone is fed to second cyclone for re-treatment.

26.3.1 Design variables

Vortex finder clearance: Vortex finder clearance 'h' is one of the most critical design variables of the water-only cyclone. It should be as small as possible. The relative shortness of this dimension means that the vertical path traveled by the particles in the upward central current of the cyclone is reduced sufficiently so that large low-specific gravity particles caught in the upward current will not reach their terminal settling velocity and settle out to the wall, but will be captured inside the vortex finder and discharged with the light specific gravity fraction. Increasing the clearance 'h' decreases the specific gravity of separation and yield of overflow product. Decreasing the clearance 'h' increases the specific gravity of separation. The optimum length of this dimension depends on the particular feed processed. In most of the water only cyclones, some two-thirds of the total volume of the cylindrical body is occupied by the vortex finder.

Diameter of the Vortex finder: The diameter of the vortex finder is large in relation to the cyclone diameter and it varies from 0.56 to 0.40 times the cyclone diameter. Vortex finder is much longer in relation to the total cyclone length and it varies from 1.25 to 2.00 times the cyclone diameter.

Cone angle: The cone angle of the cyclone is the major factor that determines the specific gravity of separation. For effective separation, the cone angle should not be less than 80°. Low cone angle leads to classification effects and decreases the separation efficiency. Wide angle conical bottom creates intense hindered settling conditions leading to sorting effect. An increase in cone angle from 80° to 140° increases the specific gravity of separation from 1.35 to 1.60–1.95, depending on the amount of fines (−75 mm) present. For optimizing the effect of a particular cyclone cone angle, the operator has available variation in (1) the size of the cyclone orifice (2) the length of the vortex finder (3) feed concentration and (4) feed pressure. Furthermore, modifications of the shape or profile of the conical portion of the cyclone have been developed. For example, in one design modification, the single angle wall of the conical section is replaced by a wall that descends through three angles (Tricone).

Cyclone diameter: Various sizes of water only cyclones in use vary from 5- to 24-inch. Cyclone diameters may be as small as 50 mm and such units are commonly used as an alternative to froth flotation. In general as the diameter of the cyclone increases, capacity of the cyclone increases.

Sizes of feed, overflow and underflow orifices: Increasing the diameter of the feed orifice increases the capacity, decreases the retention time, and increases the specific gravity of separation. The effect of overflow orifice is similar to that of the feed orifice. Increasing the diameter of the underflow orifice increases the capacity of underflow, decreases the specific gravity of separation and decreases the efficiency of the cyclone.

The performance of a water-only cyclone is affected by the relationship of the diameter of the overflow orifice to that of the underflow orifice. This relationship determines the flow ratio of the cyclone, i.e., the ratio of apex flow to feed flow. Generally, the ratio of the diameter of the overflow orifice to that of the underflow orifice for water only cyclones ranges from 1.5:1 to 2:1. The feed orifice is generally slightly smaller in diameter than the overflow orifice.

The two major operating variables affecting the performance of the water-only cyclone are feed pressure and feed solids concentration. Water only cyclones are generally operated at feed pressure of 15 psig or greater to assure high separation efficiencies. An increase in feed pressure increases the separation efficiency and also increases the capacity of the cyclone. High feed pressures are required to improve the separation ability of the cyclone when finest sizes are processed.

Slurry density affects the quality of the product. To create hindered settling conditions and resultant autogenous medium, a bed of heavy solids in the conical region is to be formed. The formation of the bed of heavy particles depends on the solids concentration and also on the size composition of the feed material. Hence water only cyclones are always operated at high slurry densities. An increase in feed solids concentration increases the specific gravity of separation and slightly decreases the efficiency.

The Table 26.3.1 illustrates the effect of feed solids concentration on the specific gravity of separation for processing of coal:

Table 26.3.1 Effect of feed solids in water only cyclone.

% solids in feed	Sp. gr. of separation
8.7	1.59
17.0	1.75
24.6	1.96

The selection of the size of water only cyclone depends on the size of the cyclone diameter required, which in turn is dependent on the size range of the material being treated. The selection of other design parameters may in general be made using the following rule of thumb. If 'D' is the diameter of the cyclone then

Maximum size of the particle to be treated	D/10
Recommended maximum particle size	D/20
Diameter of the vortex finder	D/2
Length of the vortex finder	7D/4
Diameter of the spigot	D/4

Chapter 27

Froth flotation

In a beaker of water, if air is introduced from the bottom, air bubbles are produced and rise to the surface of water (Fig. 27.1 A) as the density of air bubble is much less than that of water. Similarly air bubbles also rise if air is introduced in a pulp containing solid particles. If a solid particle of high density adheres to the air bubble, air bubble along with solid particle rise to the surface because the apparent density of air bubble and the adhered solid particle is less than that of water. If many number of solid particles are adhered to the air bubble, still air bubble rise to the surface (Fig. 27.1B) as the apparent density of air bubble and adhered solid particles is less than that of water due to relatively large volume of air bubble. This concept is the basis for froth flotation operation.

To use this concept or phenomenon, the following two are required:

1 Method to make the solid particles adhered to the air bubble.
2 Method to keep the air bubble alive when it reaches the surface of water. It is known that the air bubble collapses when it reaches the surface of water. When it is collapsed, the adhering solid particles are dropped into the water. So air bubble must be kept alive on the surface of water for sufficient length of time till it is removed from the surface.

The following are the methods adopted in practice:

1 To make the solid particles adhered to the air bubble while it is rising through the pulp, the solid particles are treated with suitable chemical to acquire adhering property for the solid particles.
2 For making the air bubble not to collapse, some other chemical is used to prevent the collapsing of air bubble or in other words to increase the life of the air bubble.

The required solid particles after adhering to the air bubble float to the surface along with the air bubble. The aggregation of several such solid adhered air-bubbles forms the froth on the surface of the pulp (Fig. 27.1C). Hence this operation of solid separation is named as **Froth flotation**.

Froth Flotation is a method of separating the required solid particles in a relatively finely divided state. It utilises the differences in physico-chemical surface properties of particles of various solids. This method can only be applied to relatively fine particles (less than 150 mm). Particles smaller than 400 mesh (37 micron) often will

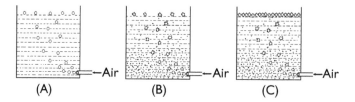

Figure 27.1 Process of rising air bubbles and forming froth.

not attach to the air bubble. If the particles are too large, the adhesion between the particle and the bubble is less than the weight of the particle and the bubble drops the solid particles. The air bubbles can only stick to the solid particles if they can displace water from the solid surface. This can only happen if the solid is water repellent or hydrophobic. Air bubbles, after reaching the surface, can continue to hold the solid particles if they can form a stable froth. If not, air bubbles will burst and drop the solid particles. In order to achieve the favourable conditions for froth flotation, the pulp is treated with various chemical reagents known as flotation reagents. The chemicals used for treating the solid particles so as to make them to adhere to air bubble are called as collectors and the chemicals used to increase the life of air bubbles are called as frothers.

The ordinary simple froth flotation comprises the following steps:

1   The solids are ground in water to at least 48 mesh
2   The pulp thus formed is diluted with water to a consistency between 25% and 45% solids by weight
3   Small quantities of surfactant chemicals called modifiers are added to the pulp to modify the surfaces of specific solid particles
4   Another reagent called collector specifically chosen to affect the solid particles, to be recovered by flotation, is added. It coats the solid particles with an aerophilic surface (i.e., water repellent)
5   Another reagent called frother is then added which imparts persistence to bubbles when they reach the surface and assists in establishing a stable froth at the surface.
6   The chemically treated pulp is aerated either by agitation or by air injection through the porous bottom of the containing tank, or through pipes, during which the coated solid particles become more or less firmly attached to air bubbles.
7   The solid bearing froth which rises to the surface is skimmed off. The pulp passes on through a series of containers or cells in order to provide both time and opportunity for the solid particles to come in contact with air bubbles and to be recovered in the froth.

These steps frequently follow the sequence stated. Dilution is usually affected in the classifier. Modifiers and the collector are added in a separate tank called conditioning tank. Sometimes they may be added to the grinding mill. The frother is normally added in flotation machine where aeration is going on.

The crux of the froth flotation process is the existence of a selective tendency for some particles to adhere to air and for other particles to adhere to water.

The beneficiation of coal by froth flotation is based on the selective attachment of the coal particles to air bubbles in a liquid medium, the bubbles rising and being removed from the surface of the flotation vessel as a froth. Shale or mineral particles, such as pyrite, having different surface properties, stay in the liquid medium and are removed separately as a refuse slurry or tailings.

Froth flotation is the most efficient method of beneficiation of coal having particle size below 0.5 mm. Intensive mechanization and poorer quality of seams now left for exploitation, makes beneficiation of –0.5 mm coal unavoidable. If this fraction is not treated in froth flotation, the losses can be as high as 15–20% of ROM coal. Besides this, the untreated fines, when mixed with washed coal, appreciably increase its ash.

When the seams with friable coal are mined, the production of –0.5 mm size fraction can be as high as 30% of ROM coal. Impurities also get intimately mixed with the fines necessitating their beneficiation through froth flotation.

For washing coals below 0.5 mm size, flotation is one of the main washing units in the fine coal washing circuits. But the ash reduction achieved in all the washeries is very low because of the following reasons:

1   Froth flotation is very sensitive process and involves large number of variables.
2   It is very difficult to control the flotation circuit with the fluctuating conditions that are encountered in the washeries.

The main aim of beneficiating the coal is to produce maximum amount of clean coal at desired level of ash content and at an economic operating level. This can be achieved only if the feed going to the flotation cell is consistent in quality and quantity besides maintaining the operating and design variables at an optimum level.

The froth flotation process is largely used in the beneficiation of mine dust, slack coal, washing rejects, and slurries. It is especially suitable for producing super-clean coal required for making electrodes used in aluminum and magnesium metallurgy. Tailings of the coal flotation are sometimes used as the suspension media in heavy medium plants.

27.1   CONTACT ANGLE

Contact angle (θ) is an angle of contact of an air bubble with the surface of a solid measured across the water. It is a convenient measure of the forces of adhesion between the bubble and the solid surface. The contact angle marks the position of equilibrium between the solid-water and water-air surfaces on a wetted surface i.e., it is the position of equilibrium between three tension forces; the surface tension of water T_{WA}, surface tension of solid coal T_{MA} and interfacial tension T_{MW} between the solid coal and water (Fig. 27.1.1).

If the surface tension of the solid coal T_{MA} is more, the water is pulled over the solid till an acute angle θ is reached, when the component of water tension T_{WA} together with the interfacial tension T_{MW} is sufficient to bring about the equilibrium. Under these conditions, the solid shows a preference for water. If the interfacial tension T_{MW}

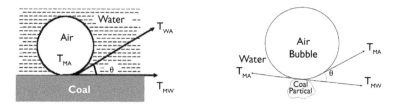

Figure 27.1.1 Contact angle.

is greater, the water will be drawn back and an obtuse angle will form. Under these conditions the solid has a preference for air.

When solid shows affinity for water $\qquad T_{MA} = T_{MW} + T_{WA} \cos \theta$
When solid shows affinity for air $\qquad T_{MW} = T_{MA} + T_{WA} \cos \theta$

Therefore, $T_{WA} \cos \theta$ is a measure of degree of wetting. When the contact angle is nil, $\theta = 0$, $\cos \theta = 1$, the degree of wetting is maximum. When the contact angle is 180°, $\theta = 180°$, $\cos \theta = -1$, the water will contract its extent and the degree of wetting is at a minimum. Since there is always some adhesion between solids and liquids in contact, there is no such thing as complete non-wettability, i.e., a contact angle of 180°. Adherence of the coal particle to the air bubble depends on contact angle. As the contact angle increases, adherence increases and hence floatability increases. Solids with high contact angle are called aerophilic (hydrophobic), i.e. they have higher affinity for air than for water. Most minerals are aerophobic (hydrophilic) in their natural state. To make the valuable mineral particles aerophilic, reagents called collectors are added to the pulp which adsorb on mineral surfaces, increases contact angle and facilitates bubble attachment. Many freshly formed mineral surfaces exhibit a natural contact angle of a few degrees. Graphite and some coals have a high contact angles to float without aid of a collector. They are said to have natural floatability.

27.2 FLOTATION REAGENTS

Flotation reagents (also known as surfactants) are substances added to the pulp prior to or during flotation in order to make possible to float required solid particles and not to float the unwanted or gangue particles. The interfacial tensions normally existing between solid particles and water are generally insufficient in the magnitude and range to be used effectively in flotation, and it is the function of the flotation reagents to intensify the characteristics of the interfaces in each of the required directions in order to separate the required solid particles from the associated constituents. Since flotation surfactants are, in general, supplied to the interfaces through the aqueous solution phase, mainly those reagents which are somewhat soluble in water are used in flotation. In some cases it is necessary to use insoluble hydrocarbons or other oils; these liquids are dispersed in the aqueous phase as emulsions, with the help of soluble surfactants, in order to facilitate their reaching the interfaces in a reasonably short

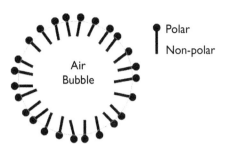

Figure 27.2.1 Action of the frother.

time period. Important flotation reagents for coal are frothers, collectors, depressants, and pH regulators.

27.2.1 Frothers

Frother is a surface active organic reagent and is heteropolar in nature; polar part of it has an affinity for water and non-polar part has an affinity for air or repulsion for water. Frother acts upon the air water interface. When surface-active molecules react with water, the water dipoles combine readily with the polar groups and hydrate them, but there is practically no reaction with the non-polar hydro-carbon group. The result is to force the latter into the air phase.

The frother molecules are adsorbed on the air-water interface and arranged in a way such that the hydrophilic or polar groups are oriented into the water phase, and the hydrophobic or nonpolar hydrocarbon chain in the air phase (Fig. 27.2.1).

The addition of a frother decreases the surface tension of water and increases the life of bubbles produced. The main objective of a frother is to permit the production of a sufficiently stable froth to hold the coal particles that form a network around the bubbles until they are removed from the flotation unit.

In fact, the frother creates conditions for froth formation. The flotation froth is a three-phase system. The frother concentrates at the interface of water and air bubbles, forming an envelope around the bubbles, which prevents them from colliding or touching. The forces created around the air bubble in the presence of a frother prevent the bubbles from collapsing.

As a result of the addition of a frother, the gas bubbles, formed under the surface of water, are more or less completely lined with monomolecular sheath of frother molecules which allows each bubble to come in contact with other bubbles without coalescing. This forms a froth. Thus a froth is simply a collection of coal bearing bubbles. The effect produced by the addition of a frother is proportional to the amount of frother. Past a certain point, the effect of further additions of frother is less than that of preceding additions and addition of further amount results in a decrease of the frothing action and finally in the total absence of frothing. The point at which total absence of frothing is obtained corresponds to the saturation by the dissolved substance of the solution.

The most effective frothers include one of the following polar groups in their composition.

The hydrophobic group consists of a hydrocarbon chain or a cyclic hydrocarbon radical. The most common fothers are those containing the OH group, i.e. cresylic

Hydroxyl	$-OH$
Carboxyl	$-C\overset{\displaystyle O}{\underset{OH}{\parallel}}$
Carbonyl	$=C=O$
Amino	$-NH_2$
Sulfo	$-OSO_2.OH$ or $-SO_2.OH$

acid $CH_3C_6H_4OH$ and pine oil $C_{10}H_{17}OH$. The OH group has strong hydrophilic properties and is only sparingly adsorbed on solid particles, thus producing a minimum collecting effect. Frothers with a hydroxyl polar group (– OH) alcohols have no collector properties and for this reason they are preferred over other frothers.

A wide range of synthetic frothers are now in use in many plants. Methyl Iso-Butyl Carbinol (MIBC) $C_5H_{13}OH$ is most important among the synthetic frothers. The synthetic frothers have a guaranteed composition which makes for ease of control in the plant.

Pine oil, cresylic acid, methyl isobutyl carbinol (MIBC) and kerosene are the more common frothers used in coal flotation. The following are the chemical formulae of most used organic reagents.

Pine oil	Cresylic Acid	Methyl Isobutyl Carbinol (MIBC)

Overfrothing is a condition of a froth which involves an uncontrollable amount of froth. Over-oiling produces an overfrothing condition in which the froth contains small bubbles, the froth is highly fluid and carries a heavy solid load with little or no selectivity. Overfrothing can be corrected by a reduction in quantity of frother.

27.2.2 Collectors

Collector is a chemical reagent, an organic compound, either an acid, base or salt, and is hetero-polar in nature; polar part of it has an affinity towards a specific solid particle and non-polar part has an affinity towards air bubble. The non-polar portion of the collector molecule is a hydrocarbon radical, which does not react with water and is therefore water-repellent. In contrast to the non-polar part of the molecule, the polar part can react with water. Small amount of collector is added to the pulp and agitated long enough so that the polar part is adsorbed on to the coal particles while the non-

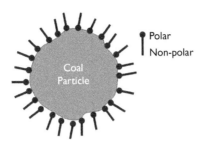

Figure 27.2.2 Collector adsorption on surface of a coal particle.

polar part is oriented outwards and makes the surface of coal particles hydrophobic (Fig. 27.2.2).

The collector must be selective and must not coat the particles that are not to be floated. Collector increases the contact angle of the solid particles on which it is adsorbed. Generally either diesel oil or kerosene is used as collector. Some frothers, such as kerosene and MIBC, have collecting properties also. The reagents having both frothing and collecting properties are known as **frother-collectors**. Kerosene is a frother-collector used in coal flotation. Certain alcohol-type frothers, such as pine oils, cresylic acid, etc. act as froth modifiers. To have an independent control, the frother should not have a collecting property. Though a combination frother-collector may suffice for some coals, oxidized and lower rank coals respond more effectively to froth flotation if a collector is added.

27.2.3   Depressants

Depressants are inorganic chemicals. They react chemically with the particle surfaces to produce insoluble protective coatings of a wettable nature making them non-floatable even in the presence of a proper collector. Thus formed protective coatings prevent the formation of collector film. The depressants generally used in coal flotation are lime and sodium silicate.

27.2.4   pH regulators

pH regulators are used to modify the alkalinity or acidity of a flotation circuit or in other words to control the pH of the pulp. With few exceptions, the effectiveness of all flotation reagents depends greatly on the concentration of hydrogen or hydroxyl ion in the pulp solution. pH determines the driving force for various interactions between the solid particles and the reagents in solution, and therefore it is an important control parameter for regulating flotation. Lime and sodium carbonate (soda ash) are most commonly used pH regulators.

27.3 THEORIES OF FLOTATION OF COAL

The following three theories have been proposed for flotation of coal with an oily collector and a frother or with only a frother for easily floatable coals.

a   **Carbon hydrogen ratio theory:** Coals of different ranks, and sometimes even of
the same rank, have divergent flotation characteristics. Taggart [47] suggested
that the variation in floatability between bituminous and anthracite coals is
caused by the variation of carbon hydrogen ratio. This is not applicable to the
relative floatability of other coals and carbons.

b   **Carbon content theory:** Wilkins [48] proposed that the floatability of coal was
directly proportional to the carbon content or rank. The higher the carbon content,
the greater the floatability. This theory is handicapped by the fact that bituminous
coals that possess moderate carbon contents are actually more floatable than anthracite coals that have high carbon contents. Sun reported that the floatability of coals,
carbons, and hydrocarbon minerals belonging to the same rank could be roughly
correlated with their contents of fixed carbon, volatile matter, and moisture.

c   **Surface component theory:** Surface component theory has been proposed by Sun
[49]. Coals being heterogenous, they are composed of floatable and non-floatable
chemical constituents. Their flotation characteristics are governed by the balance
between these components. Coals with dominant floatable surface components
are more floatable than those with predominating non-floatable components.
The floatable components are oil-avid and water-repellent, whereas the nonfloat-
able components are water-avid and oil-repellent.

27.4   FLOTATION MACHINES

A flotation machine is equipment used to carry out flotation operation. It provides the
hydrodynamic and mechanical conditions which effect the separation. Basically the
flotation machine must include

1   means for receiving and discharging the pulp
2   means for agitation and mixing the pulp
3   means for air introduction and dispersion
4   means for settling the pulp away from the froth
5   means for discharging the froth and conveying it to the next processing step

Regulation of rates of intake and discharge of pulp, of rate of air introduction and
dispersion, and of the pulp level is essential for better control of flotation operation.

The most commonly used flotation machines are of two types namely mechanical
type and pneumatic type. In a mechanical type flotation machine, mechanically driven
impeller agitates the pulp and disperses the incoming air into small bubbles. The air
may be drawn in by suction created by the impeller or may be introduced to the base
of the impeller by an external blower. These flotation machines are often composed
of several identical cells arranged in series in such a way that one cell receives the de-
frothed pulp (tailing of preceding cell) as feed. Such a series of cells called as bank.
The Denver sub-aeration machine (Fig. 27.4.1) is well known cell-to-cell machine.

The pulp from the weir of the preceding cell flows through the feed pipe on to
the rotating impeller. The positive suction created by the impeller draws air through
hallow standpipe, sheared into fine bubbles by impeller and intimately mixed with the
pulp. The diffuser arranged around the impeller prevents the agitation and swirling of

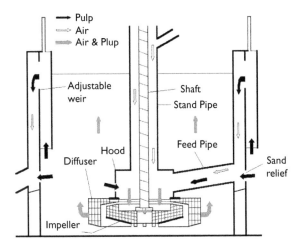

Figure 27.4.1 Denver Sub-A Flotation Machine.

the pulp above the impeller. The stationary hood above the impeller prevents the pulp in the cell to have direct contact with the impeller. The mixture of bubbles and pulp leaves the impeller and bubbles ascend with their solid load to form the froth. As the bubbles move to the pulp level, they are carried to overflow lip by crowding action of succeeding bubbles and removed by froth paddles. Pulp from the cell flows over the adjustable weir on to the impeller of the next cell. Particles which are too heavy to flow over the weir are by-passed through sand relief ports.

In an "open-flow" or "free-flow" type machine, intermediate partitions and weirs between cells are eliminated. The pulp is free to flow through the machine without interference. The pulp level is controlled by a single tailings weir at the end of the trough. Flotation efficiency is high, operation is simple, and the need for operator attention is minimized.

The Wemco Fagergren flotation cell is an open-trough type, self-aerating mechanical flotation cell (Fig. 27.4.2), and is most commonly used in coal washeries. The mechanism consists of a star-like rotor, which rotates inside the shroud or disperser. When operating, the rotor creates a fluid vortex inside the standpipe and in the draft tube, this vortex being at a sufficient vacuum to induce air into the standpipe through the air inlet from above the cell surface. The induced air is mixed inside the rotor-stator zone with the pulp that has been sucked into the rotor from below. The large capacity Wemco flotation cells have a false-bottom draft-tube system that enhances the circulation of the pulp. It permits a low rotor submergence, even for the large-capacity cells. The three-phase mixture leaves the shroud (disperser) through the disperser apertures in radial direction. The new disperser fulfils the shrouding effect perfectly, since the tangential velocity of the three phase mixture imparted on it by the rotor is converted to an entirely radial direction. The particle-loaded air bubbles rising to the froth surface are separated outside the disperser, and the remaining pulp, which flows down the tank walls and returns to the rotors, is separated in the large cells through the false bottom and the draft tube. The conical stator hood is to quieten the cell surface and to keep any turbulence created by the rotor away from the froth layer.

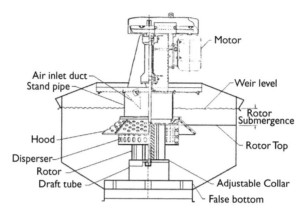

Figure 27.4.2 Wemco Fagergren Flotation Cell.

The function of the mechanism in a Wemco flotation cell is therefore threefold: to circulate pulp, to mix pulp with air, and to draw in air. These functions depend on the shape and geometric dimensions of the rotor and stator, on the speed and submergence of the rotor, on the vertical distance between the rotor and the real tank bottom.

The special features of Fagergren flotation cell are:

a   The power required to suck air into the cell is less (except Denver cell of equal capacity) than any other type cells
b   Dispersion of air bubbles is highly effective
c   Good froth removal systems makes the larger particles to float effectively

In pneumatic machines, air is introduced through the porous bottom of the cell. The air used in these machines not only creates aeration and produce froth but also maintain suspension by circulation. Pneumatic machines are now rarely seen, except in a few old concentrators. Mechanical machines are better suited to difficult separations, particularly where fines are present.

27.5   FLOTATION OPERATION

Industrial flotation is a continuous process and often requires several stages to produce the desired quality of the product. These stages are combined in various ways and referred to as **Flotation Circuits**. Cells are arranged in series forming a **bank**. Pulp enters the first cell of the bank and gives up some of the clean coal as froth. The overflow from the first cell passes to the second cell, where some more coal froth is removed, and so on down the bank to the last cell of the bank. The froth of this bank contains high grade coal and the cells are called **rougher** cells. The overflow from the rougher cells, which may still contains some coal particles, is treated in another bank of cells called **scavenger** cells. The froth from the **scavenger** cells normally contains

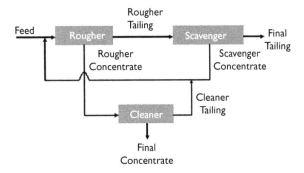

Figure 27.5.1 Flotation Circuit.

middling particles which are often re-circulated to the first cell of the rougher bank. The high grade froth collected from rougher cells is diluted and re-floated in another bank of cells called **cleaner** cells. In this rougher-scavenger-cleaner system (Fig. 27.5.1), the cleaner cells receive comparatively high grade feed which is further upgraded to get the final concentrate. Tailings from the cleaner cells can be re-circulated to the rougher cells along with scavenger froth. The tailing of last scavenger cell is the final tailings.

It is to be noted that the pulp is treated in a conditioner, called **conditioning**, with necessary reagents like depressant and collector prior to flotation in order to convert the coal particles to respond readily in a flotation cell. Conditioning the pulp reduces its residence time in the flotation cell and hence the capacity of the cell increases.

27.6 NUMBER OF FLOTATION CELLS REQUIRED

The number of flotation cells required for coal flotation circuits range from 3 to 6 cells in series in a bank. The usage of number of cells depends on retention time. This is generally ranges from three to four minutes. Using three cells in a bank may lead to the loss of coal to the tailings, while six cells in a bank makes the gangue to report to the clean coal. Hence, using four cells in a series is absolute and five cells are preferable. However, the criteria to determine the number of cells required is given below by using the formula:

$$N = \left[\frac{P}{QR}\right]T \tag{27.6.1}$$

where
    N = Number of cells required
    P = Quantity of pulp entering the cell in m^3/minute
    Q = Chamber capacity in m^3
    R = Ratio of the pulp volume in the chamber to the chamber's geometric volume
    T = Time required for the given flotation in minutes

The value of P can be estimated as follows:

$$P = \frac{W}{1440}\left(X\frac{1}{\rho}\right) \text{ m}^3/\text{minute}$$

(27.6.2)

where
W = the amount of coal to be treated in tons/day
X = the solid liquid ratio
ρ = the density of the coal (kg/m³)

27.7 FACTORS AFFECTING THE FLOTATION OF COAL

The following are some important factors that affect the flotation of coal:

a   Preparation of the pulp
b   Particle size
c   Oxidation and rank of coal
d   Pulp density
e   pH and water characteristics
f   Flotation reagents
g   Conditioning time
h   Retention time and Flow rate
i   Pulp aeration
j   Flotation machine operation

27.7.1   Preparation of the pulp

It is inevitable that there will be always changes in the behaviour of the raw coal being fed to the flotation circuit. Fluctuations in the nature and proportion of minerals in the run-of-mine coal invariably occur when the coals are mined from more than one location besides the variation observed by partial oxidation of raw coal. This may happen due to the environmental changes or due to delayed transportation of broken coal from the place of mining to the washing plant. Oxidation also occurs as a result of overlong storage in stock piles. In order to feed a consistent quality of raw coal to the flotation circuit, provision of blending yards nearby the washeries to blend the coals received from different mines is of paramount importance.

27.7.2   Particle size

The size of the coal particles to be floated by froth flotation is very important, due not only to the mechanics of the process but also to economics.

Standard equipment for coal beneficiation, other than flotation, are based on specific gravity and do not go down below 48 mesh. It is, therefore, more economical to beneficiate by these devices up to the lowest size they can effectively beneficiate. This helps in reducing flotation of particles that can be cheaply beneficiated by other means.

Though particles up to 4.5 mm may be floated by froth flotation, this method is considered uneconomical for particles above 0.5 mm. The optimum sizes for flotation are between 48 to 150 mesh. Particles beyond this range pose problems of recovery and flotation time rate. This is much more for the coarser than the finer particles. Detachment of coal particles of size coarser than 0.5 mm from the air bubble becomes more pronounced and increasing quantity of good coal starts reporting to tailings. The effect of particle size below 150 mesh is not as great as for large particles because this can be counteracted to a considerable extent by pulp dilution.

27.7.3 Oxidation and rank of coal

Oxidation adversely affects the flotation characteristics of coals. Even easily floatable coals become difficult to float if highly oxidized. If the surface of the coal particle is oxidized, it also tends to behave like a shale particle, and will not be recovered with the froth. With correct and judicious use of reagents, effects of oxidation can be overcome. The floatability of oxidized coals improves with the addition of a cationic collector such as a long chain amine.

Rank is also affects the floatability of coals. Low volatile coals are easier to float than most high volatile coals. Amongst the petrographic constituents, vitrain is easier to float than durain. Anthracite is more difficult to float than high volatile bituminous coal. Lignite is the least floatable of all coals. The contact angle increases from 10° to 60° as the rank increases from high volatile bituminous to medium/low volatile bituminous coal. The contact angle decreases as the rank further increases from low volatile bituminous coal to anthracite. Longer retention time in the flotation cell is generally required for oxidized coals. Most highly floatable coals require only one or two minutes retention time, the oxidized and the lower rank coals require three to four minutes or more.

27.7.4 Pulp density

Pulp density of the feed slurry directly effects flotation. To counteract particle sizes, higher pulp densities are used for coarser particles and lower for finer particles. To a certain extent, increase in pulp density reduces the conditioning time, stirring power and the reagent consumption. A thick pulp is preferred to get stabilized froth. The pulp density maintained for coal flotation is about 15% solids by weight. This sometimes drops down to 10% if the coals to be treated are finer in size that is below 100 microns to zero size. For ultrafine coal particles, use of very dilute pulp densities of 3–5% is also employed. It is to be noted that cleaner products are obtained at lower pulp densities while percentage recovery is higher with higher pulp densities. It is also to be noted that at lower pulp densities, greater quantities of frother are required as the volume of water is greater. It is proved that the effect of pulp density variation on the performance of floatation process is of lesser magnitude than that due to the variation caused by reagent dosages.

27.7.5 pH and water characteristics

Flotation is known to be adversely affected within certain pH ranges. This influences both the quality and recovery. The best results are obtained when the pH is between 6 and 7.5. Ash content increased with increase of pH.

Quality of water should be given due consideration in order to achieve efficient flotation. Low pH is normally controlled by additions of lime. High pH helps to inhibit the flotation of pyrite. Colloidal clays or slimes in the water inhibit froth flotation. Use of fresh water in the floatation circuit and the proper use of chemical agents to flocculate them out in the tailings thickener enable them to be removed as tailings. In severe conditions it may be necessary to hydro-classify slimes out ahead of the flotation cells.

27.7.6   Flotation reagents

Selection and dosages of reagents are very important factors as they are the most expensive items in the process. Generally speaking, for most coals it is desirable to use both frother and collector. For flotation of high ash coals, diesel oil is recommended as a collector. It has been claimed that use of kerosene, diesel oil and probably some other mineral oil fractions minimize the dewatering problem thus helping the economy of the process. Collectors used in coal flotation are invariably oils of some type including paraffins, kerosene oil, diesel oil, fuel oil, gas oil etc. The depressants generally used in coal flotation are lime and sodium silicate.

Dosages vary widely depending on prevailing conditions. Normal dosage for frothers is 0.1–0.5 kg/ton of feed. Collectors are added in higher dosages, usually between 0.5–1.0 kg/ton. Higher collector dosage inhibits the functioning of the frother. It has been found that part of the frother is consumed as an emulsifying agent for the collector and this helps the collector to coat the particles effectively. Generally pine oil (0.5 kg/ton) is used as frother and either diesel oil or kerosene (1.0 kg/ton) is used as collector.

Point of addition of reagents plays an important part in the proper functioning of flotation plant. It is essential that the collector and frother are well mixed with the pulp and given sufficient time to act. Addition of collector is done in conditioning tanks placed prior to bank of flotation cells, whereas frother is always added at the feed box of the flotation tank, since it does not react chemically and only require dispersion in the pulp. Adding frother early tends to produce a froth floating on the surface of the pulp during the conditioning stage. This is due to entrained air which can cause uneven distribution of the collector. Stage addition of reagents has been the good practice for improved flotation operation.

The essential requirements for addition of flotation reagents to the circuit are that the addition should be uniform and capable of accurate control. This can be achieved by a variety of different types of feeders. A cup and disk feeder is a typical example of reagent feeders. In this feeder a wide control of feeding is obtained by adding or removing cups, by changing their capacity or point of suspension, and by modifying the speed of the disk.

27.7.7   Conditioning time

Conditioning time is a prerequisite for a good flotation. When the collector is added to the pulp in the conditioning tank, sufficient time should be allowed for the mixing during which coal particles are exposed to contact with the collector. The optimum time required for this operation is known as conditioning time. The conditioning time is an important operating variable. The conditioning time is usually between zero and 5 minutes. It reduces with increase in pulp density. The conditioning efficiency depends on particle size distribution.

27.7.8 Retention time and flow rate

The retention time and flow rate are interlinked in a flotation operation. For good flotation, sufficient long time is given to the particles to enable them to come in contact with air bubbles. This criterion is important in selecting the number of cells and the banks required for flotation. Too large a residence time is also undesirable as this reduces the overall throughput of the flotation plant.

Flow rate in flotation machines differ primarily according to character of raw coal, size of raw coal, and kind of the machine. There is a maximum flow rate for any cell under given conditions, but there is no minimum rate other than that imposed by economic considerations in design. That is to say, recovery in a given cell under given conditions is maximum at the minimum flow rate, but the fall in recovery with increasing flow rate is very slow until the overload point is reached, then recovery falls rapidly with further increase. Constant flow rate is important, for the reason that other variables, particularly reagent addition, are based on a given flow rate. Change in flow rate changes the proportions and usually results in poorer performance.

27.7.9 Pulp aeration

In flotation, the extent of aeration and the size of air bubbles formed are of extreme importance. The extent of aeration depends on size, number and even distribution of the air bubbles in the pulp. Pulp aeration determines the flotation speed, grades of products and reagents consumption. Best flotation conditions are obtained with an optimum degree of pulp aeration. In mechanical type machines, the usual bubble size is 0.8–1.0 cm in diameter, for which an amount of optimum frother is needed. In case of pneumatic type cells, the bubble size varies from 2.5 to 4.0 mm in diameter.

The amount of air-bubbles in the pulp is directly proportional to the volume of air entering the flotation cell and inversely proportional to the speed of air passing through the pulp i.e.

$$V = \frac{100 \times T \times A}{B} \, percent \qquad (27.7.1)$$

where
   V = Total volume of bubbles in a unit of pulp volume as percent of total effective machine capacity
   T = Average time in seconds spent by bubbles in the pulp
   A = Air flow in m^3/sec
   B = effective capacity of the chamber in m^3

Therefore, it is essential to introduce a large volume of air into the pulp for high output of flotation machine.

27.7.10 Flotation Machine Operation

Some of the important factors which affect the operation of flotation machine are listed below:

1 Peripheral speed of the impeller
2 Pulp density
3 Height of the pulp above the impeller
4 Impeller diameter and its angular velocity
5 Clearance between impeller and the stator blades

Amongst the above five, the most important factor is the impeller diameter and its angular velocity, because air consumption and power requirement of a flotation machine depends on the diameter and angular speed of the impeller. Power consumption is approximately proportional to the cube of the impeller diameter and proportional to square of the impeller speed.

The quantity of air consumed can be approximately related by an equation of the form

$$Q_{air} = 135D^3 \left[n^2 - \frac{100}{D} \right] \qquad (27.7.2)$$

where
$\qquad$ Qair = amount of air in litres/minute
$\qquad$ D = diameter of the impeller in metres
$\qquad$ n = impeller speed in rpm

27.8 EVALUATION OF FLOTATION PERFORMANCE

The general parameters that are used for evaluating the performance of any flotation (or any beneficiation process) operation are the grade and recovery. These two parameters are always interrelated with each other in inverse proportion. An increase in recovery will decrease the grade and vice-versa depending upon the selectivity of the process. Under such cases, the performance evaluation of the cleaning unit can be estimated by using the Efficiency Index values presented by Tsiperovich and Evtushenko [50]. This contains mainly three parameters viz., yield, tailing ash and product ash and is defined as

$$E = \frac{\text{Yield} \times \text{Tailings ash}}{\text{Product ash}} \qquad (27.8.1)$$

The value obtained is an index which is nothing but a dimensionless number indicative of performance. For better operation, efficiency index should be as high as possible. The limitation of the above index is that this index can not be used to compare the performance of two or more flotation units operating with coals of different feed ash values. In order to overcome this difficulty, Rao and Vanangamudi have modified the equation for comparing performances of flotation units as

$$E = \frac{\text{Recovery of non – ash material}}{\text{Product ash}} \times \text{Tailing ash} \qquad (27.8.2)$$

In this case also higher values of efficiency index will indicate better performance of flotation unit.

27.9 FLOTATION COLUMN

In flotation of coarse coal, collectivity is the major concern whereas in ultrafine coal flotation, selectivity is of prime importance. Because of the small mass and momentum, fine particles may be transported to the froth by either entrainment in the liquid, or by mechanical entrapment by floating particles. The resulting effect of this entrainment is to increase the ash content of the clean coal product. To overcome this physical limitation, a number of potential solutions have been found out and design of flotation column is one among them.

The column flotation technique uses the principle of counter current wash-water flow for better separation particularly when operating on fine materials. The flotation column is a simplest form of pneumatic type flotation machine. It consists of a tall cylindrical column having the height to diameter ratio of more than 10 (Fig. 27.9).

The reagent conditioned feed pulp is admitted into the upper portion, usually to the depth of 1/3 to 1/5 of the total column height and flotation tailings are discharged in the bottom part of the column. Compressed air is admitted into the sparger (or diffuser or aerator) at the bottom of the column so that air bubbles are generated and move upward in counter direction of downward flow of slurry. Coal particles are attached in the lower enrichment section, also called recovery section, of the column between the feed point and air inlet known as collection zone or flotation zone.

Coal particles attached to the air bubbles are transported to the top part of the column, called washing section, also referred as cleaning zone or frothing zone.

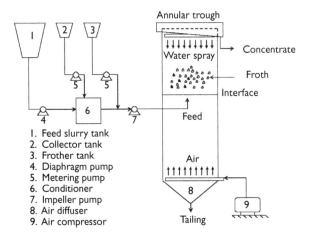

1. Feed slurry tank
2. Collector tank
3. Frother tank
4. Diaphragm pump
5. Metering pump
6. Conditioner
7. Impeller pump
8. Air diffuser
9. Air compressor

Figure 27.9 Flotation column.

This frothing zone is a mobile packed bubble bed that is contacted counter currently with wash water introduced from the top of the column in the form of spray. Refuse particles that are loosely attached to the bubbles are washed down by water sprays in the washing section and sent back to the flotation zone. Only clean froth rises to the top of the column and flows to the annular trough surrounding the column, from where it is removed through a launder by gravity.

Large froth depths (long washing section) ensure that ample opportunity is provided for coal-laden air bubbles to be washed free of trapped refuse particles. The wash water also serves to suppress the flow of feed slurry up the column towards the froth outlet. There is a downward water flow in all parts of the column preventing the bulk flow of material into the concentrate.

The basic advantage of column flotation is the production of high grade concentrate without the loss of recovery. For equal recovery, the volume of a column is larger than the volume of the bank of conventional cells. This is for two reasons.

Firstly, the much deeper froth in a column means that the pulp occupies a relatively smaller proportion of total unit volume and, for any flotation unit, it is the pulp volume which determines average residence time and, hence, total recovery.

The second reason relates to the flow pattern of pulp in the two units. In a column, there is no major impediment to the flow of air upwards through the pulp and hence there is no impediment to pulp flow between the feed entry and the tailings exit. This means that for equal average residence times, flotation column is skewed towards shorter times when compared to a bank of conventional cells.

The capital cost per unit volume capacity for columns is lower than for conventional cells as the former are constructed without impellers, which are the major cost component in the latter. In addition, the fabrication of columns with circular cross-sections is a relatively simple, low cost operation.

A single flotation column can replace five to six stages of operations involving conventional cells and yet achieve better performance. The flotation column has an ability to treat finer feeds. There is considerable savings in reagent requirement. The column occupies less floor space. However, the water requirement per ton of feed processed and consequently the frother requirement will be more.

27.10 JAMESON CELL

The Jameson cell was devised in the period 1985–86, when the inventor was undertaking a collaborative research project at Mt. Isa Mines Limited, Mt. Isa, Queensland. It is an innovative flotation process driven by fluid mechanics. It overcomes the design and operating inadequacies of column and conventional flotation cells. It is a type of flotation column in which the air and the pulp are brought together in a vertical tube. The Jameson cell consistently produces fine bubbles and subjected to intense mixing between air and slurry which results fast and efficient flotation. The way the air bubbles are generated and the bubbles and particles interact make the Jameson Cells unique.

The simplest Jameson cell consists of a riser section which is often referred as cell tank, and a single downcomer (Fig. 27.10). Some of the larger units incorporate up to 30 separate downcomers in combination with a common cell tank.

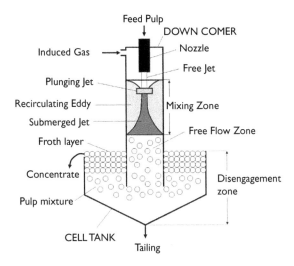

Figure 27.10 Jameson Cell.

The downcomer consists of a vertical tube sealed at the top except for a regulated air inlet and a vertical nozzle through which the slurry feed is introduced. The base of the downcomer is located below the pulp level inside the cell tank. The downcomer is the heart of the Jameson Cell where intense contact between air bubbles and particles occurs. On startup, the air inlet at the top of the downcomer is closed, and the pulp feed is pumped through the nozzle creating a high pressure jet. The air in the down-comer is entrained into the pulp, which forms the seal in the bottom of the cell; conse-quently, the pulp is drawn upward from the cell into the downcomer. The pulp level reaches the tip of the nozzle quite quickly, and as a consequence of the hydrostatic suction developed by the head of this pulp, the pressure in the head of the downcomer is less than atmospheric pressure. When the inlet is opened, air is drawn into the head-space at the top of the downcomer where it is entrained into the downcomer contents by the plunging jet. The entrained air is broken up into fine bubbles that are quickly dispersed into the pulp and carried downward by the bulk fluid motion. The very high interfacial surface area and intense mixing result in rapid particle attachment to the air bubbles, and high cell carrying capacities.

The three-phase mixture passes from the base of the dowcomer into the pulp zone of the cell tank, which has a much greater cross-sectional area than the downcomer. Consequently the downward superficial velocity of the mixture is reduced, allowing the particle-laden bubbles to disengage from the water. The design velocities and operating density in this pulp zone keep particles in suspension without the need for mechanical agitation. Due to rapid kinetics and separate contact zone in the down-comer, the cell tank is not sized for residence time. Therefore, tank volumes are much smaller than equivalent mechanical or column cells. Jameson cells are contact depend-ent, not residence time dependent.

After particle laden bubbles disengage from the water, they rise to the surface and form a layer of froth. This zone is called a froth zone. The froth drains before overflowing into a collection launder, while the water and unrecovered particles leave through a valve at the base of the cell. In the froth zone, the grade of the concentrate is controlled by froth drainage and froth washing. Cells are designed to ensure an efficient, quiescent zone that maximizes the froth recovery. Froth travel distance and concentrate lip loadings are integral to the tank design.

Bubble particle collision, attachment and collection occur in the downcomer. Different hydrodynamic regions of the downcomer are Free jet, Plunging jet, Induction trumpet, Mixing zone and Pipe flow zone.

Free Jet: The free jet is the stream of water (pulp) feed between the tip of the nozzle and the horizontal free surface inside the downcomer. Pulp passing through the nozzle under pressure creates the Free Jet which shears the surrounding air and entrains it into the pulp.

Plunging Jet: The plunging jet is the region where the free jet impacts with the horizontal free surface at the top of the downcomer, resulting in air entrainment.

Induction Trumpet: At the point of impact of free jet, a depression is formed in the horizontal free surface, which is referred as the induction trumpet. The free surface at the top of the downcomer is drawn downward by the momentum of the free jet. The induction trumpet has a wide opening at the top, which tapers down to a thin annular film adjacent to the effective boundary of the free jet.

Mixing Zone: The mixing zone is the volume occupied by the fluid inside the submerged jet immediately below the plunge point that expands to occupy the cross-sectional area of the downcomer and the body of fluid recirculating between the submerged jet boundary and the column wall – often referred to as the recirculating eddy. The high velocity gradients between the submerged jet and the recirculating eddy result in high energy dissipation rates within the mixing zone, which are responsible for the breakup of the air once it is entrained by the plunging jet. The entrained air is broken into fine bubbles before being transported downward into the pipe flow zone by the bulk fluid motion.

Pipe Flow Zone: The pulp flow zone is the region below the mixing zone inside the downcomer. This is the region of uniform multiphase flow. The downward water velocity counteracts the upward flow of particle laden air bubbles. The air bubbles and particles pack together to form a downward moving expanded bubble-particle bed. The dense mixture of bubbles and pulp discharge at the base of the downcomer and enters the tank pulp zone where the particle laden bubbles disengage from the pulp.

Disengagement Zone: When the bubbly mixture reaches the bottom of the downcomer, it passes out into a tank of larger cross-section, and the bubbles then disengage from the main pulp flow. For efficient action, the base of the downcomer is below the liquid level in the cell tank, and a hydraulic seal is maintained. Because of its low effective density, the bubbly flow initially hugs the outer wall of the downcomer, but as it rises it tends to entrain slower-moving fluid and then spreads laterally. The bubbles rise relative to the liquid and pass from the pulp layer into the base of the froth layer. The processes taking place in the froth are very important in the determination of the overall grade and recovery. If the air superficial velocity is too small or the froth depth is too large, the bubbles coalesce and the froth degrades, leading to squeezing of the least hydrophobic particles and loss of recovery. If on the other hand the air rate is too high and the froth depth is too shallow, the recovery may be high but at a low grade due to entrainment of refuse. Consequently, the cell must be operated to give optimum grade and recovery by manipulating the air rate and froth depth. Wash water can be used with the Jameson cell as with other flotation columns, when high-grade products are required.

Froth depth, Superficial gas velocity, Particle size, Bubble size, Air/feed ratio, Wash water ratio, Reagents, Downcomer void fraction and carrying capacity are the chief operating parameters of Jameson cell. Froth depth and wash water ratio are the important control requirements. Froth depth control is essential for concentrate grade stability. It can be readily achieved by some type of direct or indirect level sensor (e.g., bubble pressure probe, diaphragm pressure sensor, ultrasonic sensor, float level indicator) or by a simple gravity overflow. Where wash water is used, some measure of control is desirable in order to maximize recovery while maintaining required concentrate grade.

In the Jameson Cell, particle-bubble contact takes place in the downcomer. The tank's role is froth-pulp separation and may incorporate froth washing to assist in obtaining product grade. With no agitators, blowers or compressors Jameson Cell installation is simple and operation is extremely energy efficient. As the energy for flotation is delivered by a conventional pump, power consumption is significantly lower than the equivalent mechanical or column flotation cell. Optimum Jameson Cell performance is maintained by delivering a constant volumetric flowrate of pulp to each downcomer. While operating plants experience fluctuating process flows, the Jameson Cell is equipped with a tailings recycle system that automatically compensates for feed variations. In addition to maintaining consistent and optimal downcomer operation, the tailings recycle improves metallurgical performance by giving particles multiple 'passes' through to downcomer contacting zone. The Jameson Cell's ability to provide better selectivity and to control entrainment means product grade is not affected.

The advantages of modern Jameson Cells are

1   Consistent fine bubble generation with no external equipment or spargers.
2   Intense mixing with small bubbles achieving rapid flotation without mechanical agitation.
3   High throughput in a small footprint
4   Froth washing maximizes concentrate grade in a single flotation stage.
5   Fast response and easy control.
6   Steady operation and performance irrespective of changes in feed flow.
7   No moving parts, simple to install and maintain, excellent availability.

27.11 OLEO FLOTATION

The process of oleo-flotation has been developed at Central Institute of Mining and Fuel Research for the beneficiation of natural slurry (−0.5 mm) and dewatering of concentrate with cyclone cleans in centrifuge.

The thickened slurry at about 30% pulp density is conditioned with two reagents comprising diesel oil and a fraction of tar oil i.e. wash oil from high temperature carbonisation of coal. The diesel oil and tar oil are mixed in the ratio of 10:1 and well dispersed. This is added to the conditioner at a rate of 1% by weight of dry coal fines.

The conditioned pulp after dilution to 20% pulp density is treated in flotation cells, with controlled aeration to separate concentrate as oiled flocs/aggregates in dense phase with better drainage characteristics. After partial removal of water, the concentrate is mixed with oversize cyclone cleans (+0.5 mm) and the combined clean coals are dewatered in continuous basket centrifuge to a final product having moisture content 6–8%.

An oleo-flotation pilot plant of 20 tph capacity with around 40 tph dewatering arrangements of combined cleans has been setup in the circuit of Sudamdih Coal Washery of BCCL in India.

27.12 OIL AGGLOMERATION

Oil agglomeration is a process in which fine coal particles are bonded together to produce low-ash and compact-coarse-sized agglomerates in liquid suspension by selective wetting (conditioning) with an immiscible liquid (usually diesel oil) and agglomerating the conditioned pulp with a second immiscible liquid (usually furnace oil).

Like flotation, it is based on the surface properties of the coal particles. In this oil agglomeration technique, advantage is taken of the oleo-phillic nature of the coal macerals to separate them under controlled conditions in presence of moderate doses of selected oil from the associated minerals, which are hydrophilic in nature. No aeration is required in this process and the concentrates, which are obtained in the form of agglomerates or micro-pellets can be readily separated from the dirt-laden water by simple screening.

The basic steps involved in oil agglomeration process are:

1 Grinding of coal in a ball or rod mill either in dry or in wet condition. In case of natural slurry, this grinding operation is not necessary
2 Conditioning of the ground coal or natural slurry at 30–40% solids with 1–2% diesel oil under controlled pH (alkaline for coking coals and acidic for non-coking or oxidized coals)
3 Diluting the conditioned slurry to 15–20% solids and subjecting it to a high speed agitation in a specially designed tubular vessel with stirrer-baffle arrangements and simultaneously adding furnace oil/tar oil at a dose of 5–10% by weight depending on the nature of the coal. At this stage, the coal particles agglomerate and the minerals remain in suspended condition.
4 Separation of the agglomerates from suspended minerals on a sieve bend and vibrating screen successively.

Oil agglomeration process is simple in operation and requires less capital investment. Operational and maintenance problems are less and ensure increased availability and higher utilization of plant capacity. Eventhough it has an ability to beneficiate a wider range of particle sizes than froth flotation, it is especially suitable for finer slurry or finely ground coal of below 100 microns. It yields a dense, coarse agglomerates of acceptable strength from the screen at a sufficiently low moisture content. Since the agglomerates have much easier dewatering characteristics, costly provision for thickening of the slurry can be minimized and the use of filtration or thermal drying can be avoided. The product is consistent in quality irrespective of fluctuation in the quality of feed coal.

Oil agglomeration process, when applied to inferior grade coking coals, increases the recovery by 20%–30% when compared to conventional processes like cyclone-cum-floatation and yields only two products viz., clean coal of low ash and refuse of more than 60% ash. The presence of oil in the agglomerates increases the coking propensity of coal and bulk density of coke oven charge.

The tailings of oil agglomeration process are almost free from carbonaceous material (ash content 80%) and can be advantageously used as stowing material for mines. Depending on the mineral matter constitution, valuable trace metals can be recovered from the tailings by hydrometallurgical techniques.

Where the mineral matter in coal is finely disseminated throughout its mass, finer crushing and grinding often becomes imperative for proper release of minerals from coal. In such cases, oil agglomeration technique is the best one. It is best suited for beneficiation of high ash coals with difficult washability characteristics. The only disadvantage of the oil agglomeration process is the requirement of about 10% of oil.

In India, extensive laboratory studies were carried out at CIMFR and Indian School Mines. A 100 kg/hr bench scale unit was installed at CIMFR and all the design and processes parameters were studied for beneficiation of coking coals. Based on the data generated from the bench scale studies a 2-tph pilot plant was designed, fabricated and installed at Lodna washery of BCCL. The plant was operated for more than 500 hrs and the results obtained were found encouraging. Later a 10-tph oil agglomeration unit has been designed by CIMFR and fabricated by McNally Bharat Engineering Company and was installed at Patherdih washery to upgrade a portion of the slurry produced in a 400-tph coking coal washery at Patherdih. The plant was commissioned in 1993, producing clean agglomerates of desired quality and quantity.

Application of oil agglomeration technique for the preparation of (1) super power station fuels (2) colloid fuels or coal oil mixture for blast furnace injection and/or proportionately reducing fuel oil consumption in all oil-fired furnaces and (3) low ash coals for special uses including direct hydrogenation and solvent refining/chemical demineralization can have far-reaching advantages in the present day energy crisis all over the world.

27.13 ILLUSTRATIVE EXAMPLES

Illustrative example 27.13.1: *A pulp consists of 9% coal with an average specific gravity of coal particles of 1.7 is passing through the conditioning tank at the rate of 100 tons/hr of dry solids. It is required to condition the pulp with reagents for 3 minutes before feeding to flotation cells for treatment. What is the volume of the conditioning tank required for this purpose?*

Solution:

$$\text{Volumetric flowrate of solids} = \frac{100 \times 1000}{1700} = 58.8 \text{ m}^3/\text{hr}$$

$$\text{Mass flowrate of water} = \text{Mass flowrate of solids} \times \text{dilution ratio}$$
$$= 100 \times \frac{1-0.09}{0.09} = 1011.1 \text{ tons/hr}$$

Volumetric flowrate of water $\qquad = 1011.1 \text{ m}^3/\text{hr}$

Volumetric flowrate of slurry $= 1011.1 + 58.8 = 1069.9 \text{ m}^3/\text{hr}$

Retention time = 3 minutes

Volume of conditioning tank required $= 1069.9 \times \frac{3}{60} = 53.5 \text{ m}^3$

Illustrative example 27.13.2: *Fine coal having specific gravity of 1.8 is to be floated at the rate of 1000 tons/day with a pulp of 10% solids and flotation time of 10 minutes. Find the number of flotation machines of mechanical type required, if each machine has a capacity of 0.75 m³ with 70% effective capacity.*

Solution:

Weight fraction of coal in the pulp $= C_w = 0.10$

Density of coal = 1.8 gm/cc

Let the density of the pulp $= \rho_{sl}$

Apply $\dfrac{1}{\rho_{sl}} = \dfrac{C_w}{\rho} + \dfrac{1-C_w}{\rho_w}$

$\Rightarrow \quad \dfrac{1}{\rho_{sl}} = \dfrac{0.10}{1.8} + 0.90$

$\Rightarrow \quad \rho_{sl} = 1.0465 \text{ gm/cc}$

Weight of solids = 1000 tons/day

Weight of the pulp = 1000/0.10 = 10,000 tons/day

$$= \frac{10000 \times 1000}{24 \times 60} = 6{,}944.44 \text{ kg/minute}$$

Volume of the pulp = 6944.44/1046.5 = 6.64 m³/minute

Volume of the pulp in 10 minutes = 6.64 × 10 = 66.4 m³

Effective volume of each machine = 0.75 × 0.7 = 0.525 m³

Number of machines required = 66.4/0.525 = 126.5 ≈ 127

Chapter 28

Centrifugal separators

As already mentioned in chapter 26, Heavy Medium Cyclone separation has now become widely used in the treatment of coal. DSM cyclone technology was the single most important development in coal washing in the 20th century. Other similar cylindro-conical type washers includes Mc Nally cycloids, Krebs cyclone and Kilborn cyclone.

28.1 COARSE COAL SEPARATORS

In recent years, work has been carried out in many parts of the World to extend the range of particle size treated by centrifugal separators. The DSM work pioneered the development of cylindrical separators such as Vorsyl separator, LARCODEM, Dyna Whirlpool and Tri-Flo separator. Vorsyl separator was designed and developed by the Mining Research and Development Establishment (MRDE) of British Coal in 1967 for the treatment of coal sized from 50 mm to approximately 0.5 mm. A further refinement of the Vorsyl separator was developed by the MRDE, named the Large Coal Dense Medium Separator or LARCODEMS to treat a wide size range of coal (–100 mm) at high capacity in one vessel and it is similar in concept to the Vorsyl.

Dyna Whirlpool is developed in USA by the Minerals Separation Corporation of Arizona in 1976 and used for treating coal of size range 0.5–30 mm. Tri-Flo separator is an Italian development in 1984 which can be regarded as two Dyna Whirlpool separators joined in series.

28.1.1 Vorsyl separator

The Vorsyl separator (Fig. 28.1.1) consists of vertically mounted completely cylindrical separating chamber with a cylindrical inlet at the top and an annular opening, the throat, at the bottom. The throat is encircled with a shallow shale chamber which is provided with a tangential outlet and is connected by a short duct to a second shallow chamber known as vortextractor. This is also a vertically mounted cylindrical chamber with a tangential inlet for rejects and the medium and an axial outlet. A vortex finder is incorporated in a separating chamber eccentrically passing in a downward direction to the bottom of the chamber.

The feed consisting of de-slimed raw coal, together with the separating medium of magnetite in water, is introduced tangentially, or more recently by an involute

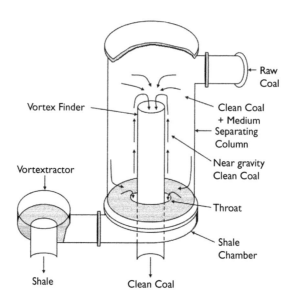

Figure 28.1.1 Vorsyl separator.

entry, at the top of the separating chamber, under pressure. Coal particles of specific gravity less than that of the medium passes into the clean coal outlet via the vortex finder, while the near gravity particles and the heavier shale particles move to the wall of the vessel due to the centrifugal acceleration induced.

The particles move in a spiral path down the chamber towards the base of the vessel where the drag caused by the proximity of the orifice plate reduces the tangential velocity and creates a strong inward flow towards the throat. This carries the shale, and near gravity material, through zones of high centrifugal force, where a final precise separation is made. The shale and a proportion of the medium, discharge through the throat into the shallow shale chamber and enters the vortextractor through the tangential inlet. Here an inward spiral flow to the outlet is induced, which dissipates the inlet pressure energy and permits the use of a large outlet nozzle without passing of an excessive quantity of the medium. The throat opening must be big enough to remove the largest sink particle. The actual volume passing through the throat is determined by an interchangeable orifice in the vortextractor outlet and the volume is therefore made independent of the throat size.

Like any other small coal heavy medium separator, when a three-product separation is required, this has to be achieved by re-treatment of the reject from the primary separator at a higher specific gravity in a secondary unit.

28.1.2 LARCODEMS

The LARCODEMS (Large Coal Dense Medium Separator) is also consists of a cylindrical vessel, but mounted at an angle of approximately 30 degrees to the horizontal. An involute tangential inlet at the lower end and an involute tangential outlet

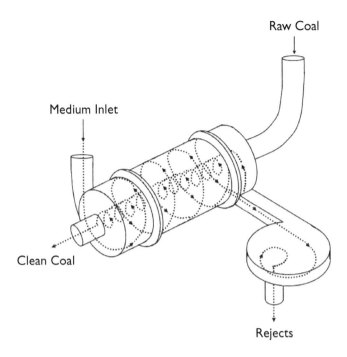

Figure 28.1.2 LARCODEMS.

connected to the vortextractor at the upper end of the cylindrical vessel are provided for medium inlet and rejects outlet respectively. Top and bottom ends of the cylindrical vessel are equipped with suitable piping or chutes to introduce the raw coal at the top end and discharge the clean coal from the bottom end.

Feed medium at the required relative density is introduced under pressure, either by pump or static head, into the involute tangential inlet at the lower end. Raw coal of 0.5–100 mm is fed into the separator by a chute connected to the top end. The medium flow and the raw coal flow are in counter-current direction. The clean coal after separation is discharged through the axial outlet at the bottom. High relative density particles pass rapidly to the separator wall and are discharged through the top involute outlet and the vortextractor.

The vortextractor regulates the medium exit rate. This extractor is different from the one on the Vorsyl separator in that the outlet of the extractor of the LAR-CODEMS is off-centre, which gives improved control. The medium split between discard and product outlet can be varied from 60/40 to 40/60, to suit the yields of product and discard, without detrimental effect on the separation. Furthermore, the separating efficiency is not materially affected when handling a feed with large percentages of discard material, which is an issue with dense medium cyclones. Efficiency characteristics can be maintained from discards yields as high as 100% and low as 20%.

LARCODEMS is much larger in diameter than other heavy media cyclone separators and it is used for coarse coal cleaning. The efficiency of the washer seems to be high as very attractive E_p values are claimed which are given as follows:

Size Range (mm)	Ep (Separation Efficiency)
100.00–50.00	0.008
50.00–12.50	0.010
12.50–6.70	0.017
6.70–3.35	0.029
3.35–2.00	0.035
2.00–1.00	0.044

28.1.3   Dyna Whirlpool

The Dyna Whirlpool (Fig. 28.1.3) is a straight walled cylindrical vessel installed at an angle of approximately 25 degrees to the horizontal. It has two identical tangential sections, one near the lower end of the vessel for the medium inlet and another near the upper end for the rejects discharge. As in LARCODEMS, Top and bottom ends of the cylindrical vessel are equipped with suitable piping axially to introduce the raw coal at the top end and discharge the clean coal from the bottom end.

The majority of the medium (approximately 90%) of required density is pumped under pressure through the tangential medium inlet at the lower end of the vessel. The

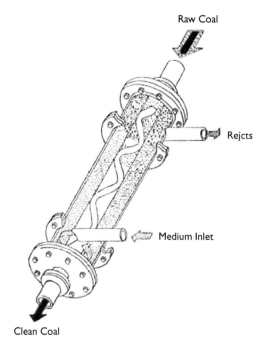

Figure 28.1.3 Dyna Whirlpool.

rotating medium creates an open vortex and spirals upwards towards the rejects outlet. Raw coal is mixed with the remaining medium and enters the separator at a static head of 1 to 2 m through the axial feed pipe, and a rotation movement is quickly imparted to it by the rotation of the medium at the vortex. As the coal moves down, the centrifugal forces move the heavier reject particles towards the wall in the outer spiral, and upwards with the medium and get discharged through the rejects outlet. The lighter coal particles move towards the inner spiral under centripetal forces, and with the rest of the medium out towards the product outlet at the bottom of the separator. The wear is greatly reduced as clean coal particles do not contact the outer walls of the vessel. Since the rejects discharge is close to the feed inlet, the rejects are removed from the vessel almost immediately, again reducing wear considerably. Only near-gravity particles which are separated further along the vessel actually come into contact with the main cylindrical body. The tangential sink discharge outlet is connected to a flexible sink hose and the height of this hose may be used to adjust back pressure to finely control the cut-point.

There is a gravity differential between the float medium coming out at the clean coal discharge outlet and the sink medium leaving the vessel at the rejects discharge outlet. The gravity inside the vessel itself increases upward with the rising medium, reaching its maximum at the rejects discharge pipe. Hence, the feed experiences a higher density at the entrance of the separator, which aids the separation. The gravity also increases in the direction from the inner face of the open vortex towards the outer wall of the vessel.

Less horsepower will be required to supply the energy required to create the vortex, as this energy only needs to be applied to the medium that enters at the bottom. The feed enters at the top non-pressurized. This has an influence on the capital and operating costs of the process.

The material of construction for the separator is crucial since the more abrasive material (the rejects) is moving with significant velocity against the wall of the vessel. Lining with ceramic as well as special nickel based hard metal alloys is used to prevent excessive erosion. An advantage of the Dyna Whirlpool's design is that the length of the vessel exposed to the harshest conditions is shorter as the highest concentration of reject material is closest to the outlet. Apart from the reduced wear, which not only decreases maintenance costs but also maintains performance of the separator, operating costs are lower, since only the medium is pumped. The separator has a much higher sinks capacity and can accept large fluctuations in sink/float ratios. These separators are also capable of handling large size coal particles (up to 100 mm). The cylinder length is of the order of five times its diameter, although longer units are preferred for difficult separations as this increases the residence time of the lights in the separator, thereby giving any near density fine heavies time to report to the correct orifice.

28.1.4 Tri-Flow separator

The Tri-Flo separator (Fig. 28.1.4) combines two stages of dense medium cylindrical cyclones separation in a single unit operation installed with a slope of 20° from horizontal. It consists of two consecutive cylindrical chambers with an axial orifice. Involute medium inlets and sink outlets are used, which produce less turbulence than tangential inlets.

The device can be operated with two media of differing densities in order to produce sink products of individual controllable densities.

The feed is sluiced with a small amount of dense medium and added to the first chamber of the vessel at atmosphere pressure, produced float and sink 1. The float

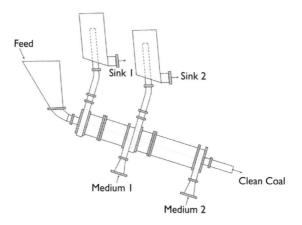

Figure 28.1.4 Tri-flow separator.

from the first stage is the feed to the second chamber, at lower specific gravity, produced a sink 2 (middling) and the final float product. Two-stage treatment using a single medium density produces a float and two sinks products with only slightly different separation densities. Where the separator is used for washing coal, the second stage cleans the float to produce a higher grade product. Two stages of separation also increase the sharpness of separation. Operation of Tri-Flow separator can be fed by gravity flow using head tank. Thus, there is no need of pumping feed coal. Additionally, the low level feed entry makes a lower building and shorter feed conveyors, resulted in saving of space and cost.

28.2 FINE COAL SEPARATORS

Gravity separation process is very efficient for the particles of size larger than 0.5 mm and when there is a large difference in density between the particles. For the finer particles and for the particles having small density difference, the speed with which the particles will move apart may be slower than the retention time in the device. This prevents the particles from separating each other. By applying centrifugal force, settling velocities of the finer particles can greatly be enhanced to aid better separation. The plot of Fig. 28.2 shows the settling velocity of spherical particles of pure coal, shale and pyrite having specific gravities of 1.3, 2.5, and 4.8, respectively. Two sets, one under a normal gravitational field of 1 g (solid lines) and the second under an artificial gravitational field of 200 g's (dashed lines) have been plotted in this figure. As shown, the settling velocity of particles subjected to the normal gravitational field rise very rapidly above 1 mm. Since the gravitational force is proportional to particle mass, particles smaller than 1 mm separate slower, and hence less efficiently, than do particles in the larger size ranges. However, by applying an artificial gravitational field i.e. centrifugal force, particle settling velocities can be increased and the effective size range over which efficient separations are achieved can be extended down to much smaller sizes. As shown in Fig. 28.2 [51], high settling velocities can be main-

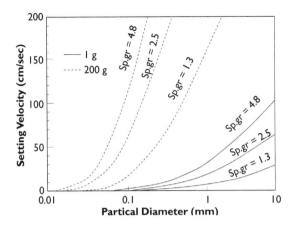

Figure 28.2 Effect of particle diameter on the free-settling velocity of coal (SG = 1.3), shale (SG = 2.5) and pyrite (SG = 4.8) under gravitational fields of 1 and 200 g's.

tained down to 0.1 mm by applying an artificial gravitational field of 200 g's. The additional force will permit efficient separations to be achieved even at these very fine particle sizes.

More coal fines are created when the coal is crushed to smaller sizes for better liberation of dirt. Adoption of mechanized mining increases the quantum of fines generation. For cleaning of these coal fines, number of centrifugal enhanced gravity separators are available. These are water-based devices and the centrifugal force is applied by using a rotating bowl into which the slurry is fed. They are capable of upgrading particles once believed to be too fine for water-based gravity separators. In the case of coal, efficient separations have been achieved down to particle sizes of 325 mesh and finer. These units are particularly well-suited for pyritic sulfur removal because of the large density difference between pyrite and coal. Falcon Concentrator, Kelsey Jig, Knelson Concentrator and Mozley Multi-Gravity Separator are the few enhanced gravity separators.

28.2.1 Falcon concentrator

The Falcon concentrator (Fig. 28.2.1), is a vertical axis spinning fluidised bed semi-continuous enhanced gravity concentrator developed by Falcon Concentrators Inc and Hy-G Manufacturing Company targeting at fine gold recovery. It consists of a smooth-surface truncated cone which rotates at a very high speed.

Feed slurry is injected near the bottom of the cone and is accelerated up the cone wall by the centrifugal field (up to 300 g's). The slurry forms a thin flowing film and stratifies according to particle density before passing over a concentrate bed fluidised from behind by back pressure water. Light particles atop the stratified layer are discharged over the top of the cone lip, while heavy particles located at the bottom of the bed are trapped into the inter-riffle spaces sliding along the inner surface of the cone and are discharged through the cone wall via small reject ports. Periodically the feed is stopped and the refuse rinsed out. Rinsing frequency, which is under

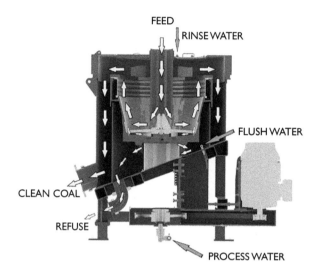

FEED

RINSE WATER

FLUSH WATER

CLEAN COAL

REFUSE

PROCESS WATER

Figure 28.2.1 Falcon concentrator (Courtesy: Sepro Mineral Systems Corp. Canada).

automatic control, is determined from grade and recovery requirements. Cone rotational speed and the fluidisation water velocity are the two major variables of the Falcon concentrator.

Since the discharge rate is fixed under constant operating conditions, the use of this unit in the coal industry may be limited to coal feeds which have a relatively constant amount of reject. To overcome this limitation, a control system which regulates the discharge rate by varying the bowl speed has been suggested.

Falcon concentrator is able to treat particles in size down to 15–20 microns. It is relatively simple mechanically and robust. It has high capacity and requires low operator attention.

28.2.2   Kelsey jig

The Kelsey jig consists of a rotating bowl with a series of individual hutches wrapped around it. The hutches hold the pulse water and discharge concentrate through their spigots. Within this bowl, there is a feeder assembly and a cover to assist an even slurry distribution and a wedge wire screen to retain a ragging bed (Fig. 28.2.2). A diaphragm, whose stroke is controlled by a cam-motor assembly, independent of the main drive, provides the pulsation.

Over the wedge wire screen a specific ragging material, having intermediate density between the heavy and the light minerals likely to be separated, are placed. The feed slurry enters the unit through the central feed pipe and the centrifugal force, maximum 60 g, imparted by the bowl rotation forces the slurry to make contact with the ragging material. The high frequency sequential strokes of the pulse arms create an inward pulse of water through the ragging bed that causes the bed to dilate and contract. This, in turn, results in differential acceleration of the feed and the ragging particles according to their specific gravity.

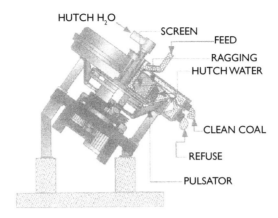

HUTCH H₂O

SCREEN

FEED

RAGGING

HUTCH WATER

CLEAN COAL

REFUSE

PULSATOR

Figure 28.2.2 Kelsey jig (Courtesy: Downer Mineral Technologies, Australia).

Low density particles flow across the ragging material and overflow the top of the unit, while the high density particles pass downward through the ragging/screen and are discharged through the spigots in the concentrate launder. Thus, separation of low density and high density particles occurs in this machine. In most cases, the unit forms its own ragging material from coarser and heavier feed particles.

The need to constantly replenish the bed of ragging appears to be the major short-coming of this particular design. However, narrowly sized clean-coal (1.2–2 mm) cycloned from coarse spiral products have been successfully used for this purpose.

28.2.3   Knelson concentrator

The Knelson concentrator (Fig. 28.2.3) is a compact batch centrifugal separator with an active fluidized bed to capture heavy particles (Knelson, 1992). A centrifugal force up to 200 times the force of gravity acts on the particles.

Knelson concentrator consists of a rotating truncated cone which is stair-stepped by several ring-type partitions. Water is introduced into the rotating cone through series of perforations in the rotating cone. Feed slurry is introduced through the stationary feed tube and into the rotating cone. When the slurry reaches the bottom of the cone it is forced outward and up the cone wall under the influence of centrifugal force. The slurry fills each ring to capacity to create a fluidized bed of particles between each partition. It flows countercurrent fashion from partition to partition until it overflows the top of the rotating cone. The flow of water that is injected into the ring is controlled to achieve optimum bed fluidization. Particles which have a density higher than that of the fluidized bed are captured and retained in the cone, while lighter particles are flushed out over the partitions and get discharged through launder. When the concentrate cycle is complete, the heavies are flushed from the cone into the launder. Under normal operating conditions, this automated procedure is achieved in less than 2 minutes in a secure environment.

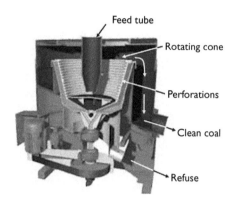

Figure 28.2.3 Knelson concentrator. (Courtesy: FLSmidth).

A continuous flow Knelson concentrator was also designed for industrial application. One of the major disadvantages of this unit is the large fresh water requirement (up to 2–3 times the feed flow) needed to fluidize the particle bed.

28.2.4 Multi Gravity Separator

The Mozley Multi Gravity Separator, known as MGS, was invented and developed by Richard Mozley Limited with backing from the British Technology Group. It is a new device developed for the separation of fine and ultrafine coal. The principle of MGS can be visualized as scrolling the horizontal surface of a conventional shaking table into a drum, then rotating it so that many times the normal gravitational pull can be exerted on the coal/mineral particles as they flow in the water layer across the surface.

The MGS (Fig. 28.2.4) basically consists of a slightly tapered open ended drum that rotates in a clockwise direction generating forces between 5 and 15 g at the drum surface and a sinusoidal shake in an axial direction with an amplitude variable between 4 and 6 cps is superimposed on the motion of the drum. A scraper assembly is mounted inside the drum on a separate concentric shaft, driven slightly faster than the drum but in the same direction.

Feed slurry is introduced continuously midway onto the internal surface of the drum via an accelerator ring launder. Wash water is added via a similar launder positioned near the open end of the drum. The slurry flow a spiraling pattern at the revolving drum surface. Heavy particles are pinned to the surface of the drum as a result of the centrifugal forces to form a semisolid layer. The scraper scrapes the settled solids up the slope of the drum, during which time they are subjected to countercurrent washing before being discharged as rejects at the open, outer, narrow end of the drum. The lighter coal particles along with the majority of the wash water flow down stream to discharge as clean coal via slots at the inner end of the drum.

Separation of the heavy and light particles into layers is greatly accelerated because of the centrifugal acceleration imparted to the particles which is many times greater than the normal gravitational force acting on a conventional shaking table. The shake provides an additional shearing force on the particles in the flowing film,

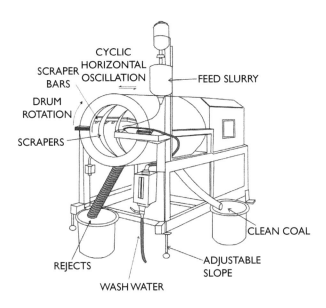

Figure 28.2.4 Multi Gravity Separator.

resulting in improved separation, whilst the specially designed scrapers moving across the drum surface continually re-grade the particles.

High upgrading ratios (typically 20 to 1) can be obtained with MGS. Separation is very selective with fine sized particles (typically −74 + 10 microns). The throughput capacity of the MGS is very low compared to the other enhanced gravity separators as it operates under a low centrifugal field. It is mechanically quite complex and expensive and requires reasonable amount of operator attention.

Enhanced gravity concentrators have tremendous possibilities to overcome the constraints associated with the established process of froth flotation in fine coal beneficiation. Based on the performance evaluation of each laboratory model enhanced gravity concentrators treating coal fines of different characteristics, it is established that considerable ash reduction is possible in fine coals by applying centrifugal force. Amongst the enhanced gravity concentrators, Kelsey jig appears to be the most promising in fine coal beneficiation as the mode of particle separation inside this unit is continuous and the capacity of each unit is much higher than the other units.

Although the mode of operation of a MGS is also continuous, the main disadvantage with this machine is its low capacity. The mine scale unit is only capable of treating up to 5 tons of solids per hour. However, a new twin drum design has been constructed which is claimed to treat up to 25 tons/hr of coal. The excellent performances of the Knelson concentrator and the Falcon concentrator in upgrading coal fines of different characteristics re-establishes the effectiveness of using high centrifugal force while processing coal fines.

The major advantage of the enhanced gravity concentrators appears to be their ability to reject composite particles more efficiently than flotation. In particular, particles containing a high specific gravity component such as pyrite are rejected very efficiently by this new generation of fine particle separators.

Chapter 29

Dry beneficiation of coal

Coal continues to play a major role in the economic development of a country, especially in metallurgical industries and conventional power generation plants. For effective utilization of high ash coals, it is necessary to beneficiate them. The wet beneficiation process for coal cleaning is currently the predominant method of beneficiation of coal in the world. Wet beneficiation techniques are well adopted mainly due to the sharper separation achieved in modern wet processing techniques such as heavy media separation, jigging, spiraling and flotation.

In the present scenario, the dry beneficiation of coal has aroused potential interest not only due to the scarcity of fresh water in coal-producing countries, but also due to process benefits in downstream utilization. The economic consideration of dry beneficiation is obvious as coal is mainly used as a fuel and no energy is expended in drying the coal.

From a theoretical standpoint, gravity separation in water has a considerable advantage over gravity separation by pneumatic means. Assuming that a separation is intended between coal of specific gravity 1.35 and shale of specific gravity 1.50, the ratio of the apparent specific gravities in air separation is practically 1.50/1.35 or 1.11 to 1, the specific gravity of air being negligible. However, in water the ratio of the apparent specific gravities is (1.50–1.00)/(1.35–1.00) or 1.43 to 1. The larger ratio is somewhat more favourable to a good separation with less close sizing. This comparative disadvantage of dry beneficiation may be greatly offset by careful adjustment and operation of the dry process, but nevertheless wet washing is probably more effective and efficient in beneficiating difficult coals.

Dry cleaning machines do not function efficiently on coal carrying an appreciable amount of moisture. Drying of the feed coal may be employed, but in many cases this remedy may be too expensive.

Since air is lighter and flows more readily than water, the velocity and volume of air required to give mobility to particles in a jig bed are greater than with water. This is more pronounced as the material becomes coarser.

When wet washing is used, the clean coal must be dewatered before delivery to the consumer. Coal of above 6 mm size with low percentages of fines are quite satisfactorily and cheaply dewatered by draining, but finer sizes below this limit become increasingly difficult and more expensive to dewater. On the other hand, dry cleaning yields a clean coal requiring no further treatment before marketing.

Fine coal in wet washers also brings up another problem namely that of water clarification and its implications in the washing process. The fines or sludge tend to be carried with the water and if not removed during the water circulation cycle, they increase the density of the water to such an extent that washing becomes more difficult. Fine clay and refuse in the water are just as bad as fine coal and in many respects worse. The recovery of coal fines in a marketable form is also an important part of the problem.

Wet beneficiation plants generate waste slurry containing water, coal fines, silt, clay, and other fine mineral particles that must be discarded into a waste impoundment, which can pose safety and environmental risks if not properly constructed, monitored, and maintained. The use of dry cleaning technology eliminates these problems.

While dry cleaning eliminates the sludge difficulty, it introduces another problem of dust. Precautions must be taken to prevent the escape of dust into the atmosphere. Dust catchers are required on the outlet air from the cleaners and the apparatus is to be tightly enclosed. The majority of the dust is confined within the plant and the particulate emission to the atmosphere away from the plant is virtually nonexistent if cloth filters are used.

Wet washing processes are used for all sizes up to 3 or 4 inches, but frequently used for smaller sizes down to 0.5 inch. However, efficiencies of dry methods on sizes smaller than 14 to 20 mesh tend to be lower than by wet methods. Dry cleaning processes requires closely sized feed for efficient operation and these cannot satisfactorily clean the coals of difficult washability.

Wet process often is not the appropriate method because of inefficiencies due to:

- Chemical breakdown of contained materials.
- Physical degradation leading to excessive fines – this is common with very friable materials and when clays are present.
- Handling problems, environmental hazards, excessive water consumption and losses.
- Insufficient density difference between components.
- Difficult floatability of the coal, and excessive energy consumption and/or high costs for chemicals used in flotation.

Ash content in raw coal is increasing. In many new coal blocks, raw coal having + 45% ash is being mined. If conventional wet technology is to be adopted, to derive one unit of usable energy, water requirement will be far higher than present. In thermal coals, addition of moisture has the same deleterious effect on heat value as ash. Drying of clean coal in most cases is not commercially feasible due to its huge costs as well as further loss of coal fines when moisture is expelled. There is increasing resistance to washery effluents finding their way into drains, streams, rivers and aquifers. Handling these problems requires far higher level of investments for effluent control and recycling than is being envisaged in present washery proposals.

Dry beneficiation processes have the potential to offer significant advantages over wet beneficiation operations. One of the principal advantages of the dry beneficiation is environmental friendliness. As dry beneficiation requires no water it is the only option in locations where water is scarce or expensive. Other advantages are production of dry coal with higher calorific value per ton and lower transportation costs of dry coal. The dry beneficiation requires the lowest initial capital investment and has the lowest maintenance costs of all currently used methods of upgrading fine coal. The processing cost for upgrading coal with dry technology is often low and further enhanced by the elimination of water treatment and fines dewatering and disposal.

Clean coal obtained from dry beneficiation is more amenable to oil treatment for dust control and it flows freely and does not arch in bins and hoppers. In transit, dry cleaned coal will shed rain and arrive with only the surface of the car wetted, whereas wet washed and thermally dried coal may act as a sponge and soak up water. It is more economical to pre-dry the coal for dry processing than to dry the washed coal after it is recovered from the water.

Dry beneficiation may not be suitable since target ash in cleans required for their processes are lower than what is feasible with dry beneficiation. This was true in most of the dry beneficiation methods.

Rotary Breaker explained in article 18.3.1 utilizes differential breakage wherein the coal being more friable than the associated stones and shales will be broken to small sizes and large pieces of stones and shales are discharged unbroken thus achieve certain degree of separation. Rotary breaker is suitable for softer coals and lignite and not for the coals which have no appreciable difference in friability between coal and shale.

Air dense medium fluidized bed separator, All air jig, and FGX separator are currently used dry gravity concentration operations.

29.1 AIR DENSE MEDIUM FLUIDIZED BED SEPARATOR

Air dense medium fluidized bed separator is a dry gravity separator and works on the principle of fluidization. It uses air-solid fluidized bed as separating medium. This fluidized bed is created by suspending solid particles in an upward air flow. The bed behaves like a liquid and can be called as pseudo-fluid. The bed density is more or less same throughout fluidizing region. Particles with density less than the bed density float to the top of the surface of the bed, while particles denser than the bed density sink to the bottom of the container. The dynamic stability of the medium plays an important role in the sharpness of the separation and the system can be made to operate particulate fluidization. The fluidizing medium is of closely sized particles that are appreciably finer than the feed material to be separated. The feed can be a wide size range, the limits being determined by the difficulty of maintaining the air velocity between the minimum needed to fluidize the largest particles and below the terminal settling velocity of the finest particles. Fine particles that are to be separated can themselves combine to form "autogeneous" fluidized medium, and they float or sink according to their size and density.

The separator shown in Fig. 29.1 uses fine magnetite as medium solids fluidized by compressed air introduced from bottom of a vessel through air distributor located under the bed. By varying the volume of the magnetite, the operating specific gravity of the fluidized bed can be maintained at required level. The feed coal particles are admitted at the top of the separator. The coal particles of specific gravity lower than that of the medium floats to the top of the bed where they are conveyed by upper strand of a conveyor and discharged at one end of the vessel. The heavier refuse particles sink to the bottom of the vessel where they are conveyed by the lower strand of the conveyor and discharged at the other end of the vessel.

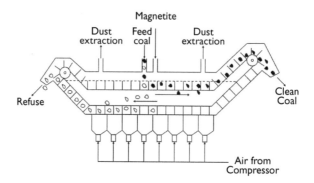

Figure 29.1 Air Dense Medium Fluidized Bed Separator.

It is claimed that the separation efficiency of this fluidized bed separation process is similar to that of the heavy media vessel or cyclones. The following are the additional advantages of Air dense medium fluidized bed separator.

a   It can be utilized in an arid region where water supply is scanty.
b   It produces a dry product requiring no additional dewatering and coal slime treatment process.
c   The air flow removes most of the surface moisture present in the feed.
d   Magnetite medium can be recovered and loss of magnetite medium is less (0.5 kg/ton of feed coal)

The limitations of the process are:

a   Difficulty in maintaining specific gravity of media which can be affected by a whole host of variables – particle size and specific gravity variation in magnetite, nozzle clogging, drop in air pressure and moisture content in raw coal.
b   The bed area increases significantly with the increase in feed rate, and the desired fluidization condition becomes difficult to achieve due to occurrence/initiation of the channeling phenomenon in the bed.
c   There is a restriction on the top size of the feed coal (i.e. below 50 mm).
d   Limiting surface moisture (below 5%) required for the feed coal may restrict its applicability to some high moisture non-coking coals.
e   The exhaust air carrying fines has to be passed through filters/electrostatic precipitator/cyclone to control the air pollution.

29.2 ALL-AIR JIG

The All-air Jig (Fig. 29.2) is a deep-bed separator that exploits the advantages of hindered settling and consolidation trickling. It is a dry separator and the medium is air instead of water. The screen deck is made of stainless steel perforated plate. Feed is introduced to the deck of the jig from a surge hopper using a variable speed star gate.

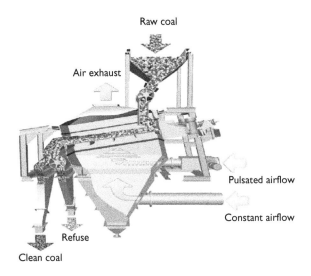

Figure 29.2 All-Air Jig.
(Courtesy Allmineral.asia).

The feed star gate provides an even feed distribution over the jig width. Each revolution of the star gate delivers a controlled volume of feed and the engineered design of the discharge throat eliminates material bridging. Transport of the material across the jig bed is enhanced with external vibrating mechanism.

Air is provided to the jig in a continuous flow and a superimposed pulsated airflow that provides the impetus for stratification and consolidation trickling. The hutch structure uniformly distributes air to all areas of the jig bed, reducing turbulence and dead spots. A superimposed pulsated air on a constant stream of rising air currents allows the All-air Jig to independently control stroke amplitude, frequency and acceleration. Thus, stratification of the feed material is enhanced. The perforated deck and hutch design work together to provide an even distribution of air across the deck, independent of the coal burden on the deck.

Raw coal is fluidized by a constant rising airflow across a perforated deck. Pulsated air provides the jigging action. The raw coal stratifies according to their specific gravities. That means the coal particles stratify on the top layer while the refuse particles stratify in the bottom layer. A clean stratification depends mainly on the best possible stratification and fluidization. This is influenced by the particle size and density distribution of the feed material. As a consequence, different jigging stroke characteristics are required for different feed materials.

At the discharge end of the jig a star gate continuously discharges the refuse material from the stratified layer. The discharge control system maintains the thickness of the refuse layer constant at the end of the jig. This discharge system speeds up or slows down according to the depth of the refuse layer even when the amount of refuse in the feed changes over time. This maintains a consistent refuse layer while discharging the clean stratified coal. Thus the amount of misplaced material is minimized and quality variations in the feed are automatically compensated.

The All-air jig is designed to handle material up to a maximum particle size of 2 inch (50 mm). The maximum feed capacity depends on the particle size distribution of the feed material and reaches up to 100 tons/hr. A throughput of 40 TPH per meter of width for coarse material (50 mm top size), and 30 TPH per meter of width for fine feeds (6 mm top size) will ensure optimum performance. The air jig's limitation is that separation efficiency is low, target ash in clean coal is difficult to obtain and cross-migration is on the higher side apart from high power consumption and dust pollution caused. The latter can be addressed with some change in the design related to enclosure of the equipment, but other limitations persist. On the plus side, air jigs do not need water and cost of beneficiation is a fraction of wet technologies. Given the levels of efficiency, air jigs can at best be at transient phase, till better dry beneficiation technologies replace them. The dedusting of the All-air jig is usually realized with a bag house type filter.

The pneumatic process of beneficiation is the best suited option for coals which has very high percentage of near gravity material. Advantages of All-air jig used for dry processing of coal are reduced costs that are associated with process water, environment and maintenance. Improvement in performance efficiency of All-air jig extends the boundaries of dry processing of coal. It is now possible to upgrade coal into a salable product that was previously discarded. This extends the life of resources.

29.3 FGX DRY CLEANING SYSTEM

The FGX dry cleaning system employs the separation principles of an autogenous medium and a table concentrator. The FGX Separator is shown Fig.29.3.1 and consists of a perforated separating deck, three air chambers, a vibrating mechanism, and a hanging support mechanism (not shown in figure). The separating deck, having riffles on its surface which direct the coal particles toward the back plate, is suspended inclined both in longitudinal and transverse directions. The deck width is reduced from the feed end to the final refuse discharge end.

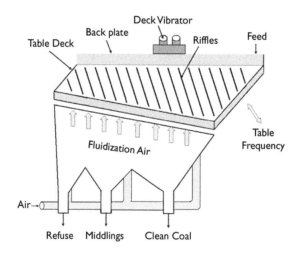

Figure 29.3.1 FGX Separator.

Figure 29.3.2 Simplified process flowsheet for the FGX
air table separator system.

The feed coal, discharged from the surge bin by a controlled electro-magnetic feeder (Fig. 29.3.2), is introduced at the far right corner of the separation deck (Fig. 29.3.1) at a predetermined mass flow rate. On introduction of feed coal onto a deck, a particle bed of certain thickness is formed on the deck. A centrifugal fan provides air that passes through holes on the deck surface at a rate sufficient to fluidize and to transport the light particles. The presence of about 10–20% of feed coal finer than 6 mm is needed to develop a fluidized autogenous medium particle bed.

The particles near the bottom of the bed maintain contact with the table surface where both vibration and the continuous influx of new feed coal move the material along riffles toward the back plate. Upon striking the back plate, the particles move upward and inward toward the discharge side of the table. Light particles are lifted up the back plate at a higher elevation than the heavy refuse particles before turning inward toward the discharge point. As such, light particles create the upper layer of particles that are collected along the length of the table. Particles of sufficient density are able to settle through the autogenous medium formed due to the fluidized bed of particles and report back to the deck surface. These heavy refuse particles are forced by both vibration and the continuous influx of new feed coal to transport toward the narrowing end of the table where the final refuse is collected. The separation process generates three products, i.e., clean coal, middlings, and refuse (Fig. 29.3.3). Two dust collection systems are employed to clean the recycled air and to remove the dust from air before being emitted into the atmosphere. It is very difficult to control the quality of the product from the FGX separator.

The FGX dry cleaning system has been found to operate efficiently and provide high density separation at around 1.8 to 2.2 relative density range and for 50 mm to 6 mm particle size. However, for finer size fractions (6 mm to 1 mm range), the cleaning efficiency is found to be less than desirable. The operating parameters such as air flow rate, table vibration frequency, table amplitude and inclination angles can be adjusted to modify the fluidized air table separator to be applicable for finer fractions.

High separation efficiency along with low cleaning costs has resulted in the widespread application of the FGX Dry Separator in China. The first commercial installation of this technology in the United States took place in the year 2009.

Figure 29.3.3 Stratification on the FGX Deck.

29.4 RADIOMETRIC TECHNIQUES

Emergence of radiometric technologies has a large extent overcome the limitations of dry gravity operations. Radiometric techniques are of two kinds viz. RAMDARS and ArdeeSort. What differentiates radiometric from earlier dry beneficiation techniques is that separation is based not on physical form, colour or friability of the particle but on its inherent properties.

RAMDARS (RAdioMetric Detection and Automatic Removal of Shale/Stone) is the new generation technology where a combination of gamma rays and laser height profile measurement helps detect high ash particles. Screened coal in a size range, for example 50–100 mm, is fed as a monolayer on the belt which enables particle by particle analysis. Ejection is done by nozzle bank at transfer point which in turn is actuated after time delay by the evaluation unit.

ArdeeSort is a multi-energy x-ray differential attenuation technology developed as an answer to the need for beneficiating smaller size fractions using similar principles as RAMDARS. While RAMDARS is for coarser size particles, viz. 50–200 mm, ArdeeSort is for –50+6 mm size fraction. Thus, along with RAMDARS, it provides the comprehensive technology for improving coal quality with required accuracy for obtaining target ash in clean coal.

RAMDARS is a world-first technology developed in India by M/s Ardee Business Services Pvt. Ltd. It has been successfully tested in a pilot plant scale and, thereafter, operated in a quasi-commercial scale at Singareni Collieries Company Ltd, Talcher (MCL) and WCL. The technology has been developed and commercialized by ARDEE through their in-house R&D (recognized by DSIR, Govt. of India). The RAMDARS plant operations are fully automatic and can handle + 50 mm size coal.

The RAMDARS dry Beneficiation technology consists of two components Detection and Removal system. The plant is modular in construction consisting of screens, surge hoppers for different sizes, vibratory feeder for mono-layer feeding, flat conveyor belt on which the detection system is located and removal system at discharge point of belt (Fig. 29.4.1).

The detection system consists of a set of nucleonic gauges and laser sensors located on a flat belt. The output of these sensors is fed to a high-speed processor where the signals are processed based on system design requirements. Presence of stone or shale is detected and control signals are automatically generated by the system.

The detection system uses differential radioactive gamma ray absorption principle for differentiating coal from extraneous material. Radioisotopes of required strength are placed in emitters located between the forward and return belts of the RAMDARS system carrying the raw coal. From the emitter, a collimated beam of gamma rays, are directed vertically upwards such that they penetrate through the conveyor belt and the material on the belt. Gamma rays are absorbed by material on the conveyor belt and a detector, located vertically above the emitter, on top of the belt, measures the attenuated rays. The attenuation depends on loading height and type of material on the belt.

Typically, gamma rays get less attenuated by coal than high ash stone or shale or Shelly coal since attenuation is broadly correlated with the density of the material and most ash materials have higher densities than carbon.

Loading height measurements and the instantaneous height of the material is measured with high-speed laser sensors. Both the attenuation signals and the loading height signals from the two probes are processed in real time processors to calculate the apparent density of the particle on the belt. Once the particle is detected to be high ash material to be removed from the stream, the particles are digitally tracked on the conveyor till the end of the belt and are automatically diverted to a secondary line.

Broadly, density of coal is dependent on the ash content and as per the quality norms, materials having density above 1.8 are undesired materials, which should be eliminated. The system is designed to detect and separate out material with selectable density parameters as per the quality requirements. The density parameters can be set in a user-friendly software menu available to the operator. The system once calibrated

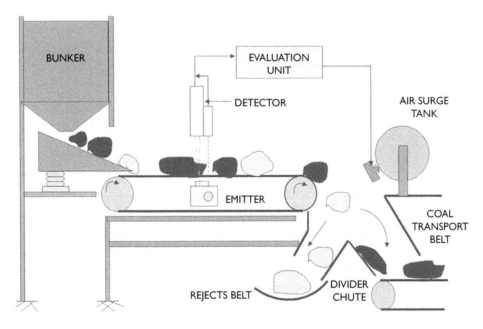

Figure 29.4.1 RAMDARS Plant.
(Courtesy Ardee Hi-Tech Pvt. Ltd., Visakhapatnam, India).

does not require frequent recalibration. The interlinked electrical and electronic controls ensure that operations can be handled from a single point, and staff requirements and man-induced errors are minimal.

The removal system consists of a number of fast response pneumatic solenoid valves in direct alignment with the sensors, which are activated by signals generated from the processor and divert the unwanted materials. The solenoid valves operate air jets. A bank of compressors through large storage tanks meets the requirement of the compressed air. Below the removal system is an inverted v-chute, which diverts the materials on the belt. Unwanted materials are "blasted away" by high-pressure air jets from the normal trajectory into the reject path. The clean coals are then taken by conveyor to storage bunkers and the rejects evacuated by a reject belt. The system is modular and capacity can be increased, by merely adding modules on an as-and-when-required basis, with minimal changes to the existing installations.

RAMDARS system at present is the only cost-effective solution for beneficiating power grade coals. The installation, operation and maintenance costs are much lower as compared to wet methods. Finally, the gestation period for setting up and commissioning these plants are a fraction of that for a conventional washery. Environmental hazards in terms of effluent and waste disposal and rejects are absent.

ArdeeSort uses multi-energy x-ray technology where differential attenuation aided by appropriate high speed image processing software yields a density profile of particles being analysed. A reflex value is, thereby, obtained which has a direct correlation with ash content in coal. Ejection is achieved by tiny high speed air nozzle jets specifically designed for the sizes these modules are supposed to handle. (Fig. 29.4.2).

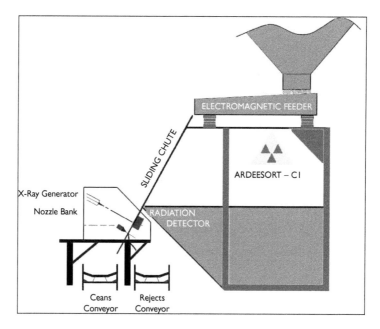

Figure 29.4.2 ArdeeSort Plant.
(Courtesy Ardee Hi-Tech Pvt. Ltd., Visakhapatnam, India).

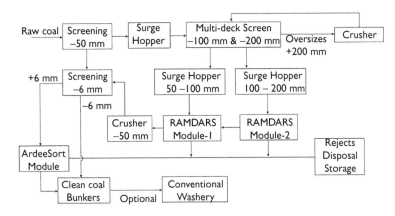

Figure 29.4.3 RAMDARS Process Flowsheet incorporating ArdeeSort.

Sequential beneficiation in RAMDARS and ArdeeSort after appropriate resizing of products will help maximize yield and minimize ash in the cleans. Figure 29.4.3 is a typical process flowsheet incorporating a dry beneficiation technology where the end product can either be directly used (thermal grade coal) or can serve as an input to conventional washing systems (coking coal).

It is possible to plan for target ash in clean coal by fixing threshold reflex value in the control software, very similar to what is done in a conventional dense media beneficiation system. The added advantage is no moisture is added, no magnetite is to be recovered and no tailings generated.

The advantages offered by dry processing, especially the low cost, the low environmental impact as well as the fact that these plants can be constructed and commissioned in a short time, make it a very attractive proposition for a coal producer – especially for a small company with limited funds available.

Chapter 30

Dewatering

Dewatering is the separation of a mixture of solids and water into two parts, one of which is relatively solid-free and the other relatively liquid-free, with respect to the original mixture. Virtually all of the processes used in coal preparation involve the addition of substantial amounts of water at various stages, both as a means of dust suppression and as a medium in washing operations. It is generally necessary that as much of this water as possible be removed from the coal before it leaves the washing plant, mainly because it is undesirable component for most of the coal utilization processes.

Dewatering of coal is required not only prior to loading the clean coal product but may also be required on the feed to some cleaning units. For example, before feeding raw coal to a heavy media bath, the coal should be sized, pre-wetted, and dewatered; fine coal fed to heavy media cyclones should be sized by wet screening methods and dewatered before mixing with heavy media.

Reduction of the moisture content of coal, particularly of the smaller sizes, has the advantages of raising the calorific value, reducing transport costs and reducing coking times in coke oven and gas retorts. In the manufacture of coke, the rate of carbonization reaches a maximum with a moisture content of coal from 5% to 6% and the greatest output is obtained.

The degree of difficulty and the cost of dewatering process increase as the surface area of the particles to be dewatered increases. Thus the fine coal or fine refuse fractions are the most difficult and the most expensive components to dewater and the dewatering costs represent a large part of the total preparation costs for these materials.

A number of machines and processes are available to the coal industry for efficient dewatering of various sizes of coal and refuse. Based on the dewatering methods adopted, coal particles can be divided into the following three groups:

1 coarse coal, particles of +8 mm size
2 small coal, particles of −8 +0.5 mm size
3 fine coal, particles of −0.5 mm size

30.1 DEWATERING OF COARSE COAL

Natural drainage is satisfactory means for reducing the moisture content of coarse sizes of coal down to about 8 mm to nearly the inherent moisture content. The chief equipment used for dewatering by drainage include stationary, shaking and vibrating screens; elevators with perforated buckets; and drainage bins and pits. Drainage during shipment in railroad cars is also a factor. In using screens for dewatering, special types of screening surface such as wedge wire is used in some cases. The water drains away freely from the solid particles giving a total moisture content of around 5% for most bituminous coals.

Washed coal coming from a wet cleaning unit usually is accompanied by large volumes of water that must be removed from the coal when it is graded into market sizes. Vibrating screens usually can dewater coal larger than 8 mm to the extent necessary to meet market requirements. Coarse coal to be dewatered can either be pre-sized or dewatered with all its fines. If it is pre-sized with the fine coal removed, it can be dewatered at openings from 0.5–8 mm. Dewatering screen selections are based on average particle size and a bed depth of coal thin enough to be free-draining. The depth of coal is a function of the size of the coal being dewatered. The smaller the average particle size, the more difficult it is to drain and the thinner bed is to be maintained. The presence of fine coal particles tends to fill the voids and hold the water. Dewatering screens are usually 12 ft or more in length, depending upon the dewatering efficiency required and analysis of the coal being dewatered.

30.2 DEWATERING OF SMALL COAL

Where the particles are between about 8 mm and 0.5 mm, dewatering is mainly accomplished by the use of centrifuges. Centrifuges are the machines which effectively create high gravity forces for purposes of dewatering coal. They find application in virtually every wet washing coal plant. The centrifuges developed for the coal industry are reliable and efficient machines. Their products are consistent, uniform, and easily handled. Properly centrifuged coal can be further dewatered only by evaporation of the moisture remaining on the coal.

When a solid-liquid suspension is rotated in a cylindrical container the suspension is subject to a centrifugal force in the radial direction. Centrifugation is a process by which solid particles are sedimented and separated from a liquid using centrifugal force as a driving force. Depending on the rotational speed and distance from the axis of rotation, the centrifugal force can be many times greater than the force of gravity, allowing even very small particles or particles slightly denser than the fluid to settle.

When a body rotates about an axis, some force is required to keep it in rotational motion. For example, liquid revolving in a cup exerts a force on the side of the cup and the cup in turn exerts a force on the liquid to keep it rotating. In this example the liquid exerts centrifugal force on the wall of the cup. The cup exerts centripetal force on the liquid. These accelerations, equal and opposite, can be expressed by the equation:

$$a = \frac{V^2}{R} \tag{30.1}$$

where

      V = linear peripheral speed in ft/sec

      R = radius of curvature in ft

Usually the acceleration in a centrifuge is expressed in terms of the number of times this force exceeds the accelerating force of gravity, **the number of g's of force**. This number can be found by dividing both sides of the equation by the acceleration of gravity.

$$\text{Number of g's of force} = \frac{a}{g} = \frac{V^2}{gR} = \frac{(2\pi RN/60)^2}{gR} = \frac{4\pi^2 RN^2}{3600g} = \frac{\pi^2 dN^2}{1800g} \qquad (30.2)$$

where

      $V = 2\pi RN/60$

      N = number of revolutions per minute

      $R = \dfrac{d}{2}$

Changing d from feet to inches and multiplying all constants

$$\text{g's of force} = \frac{N^2 d}{70,471} \qquad (30.3)$$

For example, a 48 inch machine rotating at 250 rpm will create

$$\text{g's of force} = \frac{N^2 d}{70,471} = \frac{250^2 \times 48}{70,471} = 42.6$$

In centrifuging any material, moisture content will not be reduced in proportion to the force applied as shown in the equation 30.3. Materials that deform or become plastic or materials that break or degrade obviously will not be dewatered proportionally to the applied forces. Moreover, horse power, wear, maintenance, and degradation will increase with forces applied in the machine.

The Perforated Basket Centrifuge (Fig. 30.2), simplest of all centrifuges, is used to dewater small coal. It consists of a perforated basket rotating round a vertical axis. Inside the basket is a helix or spider carrying scraper blades of similar form but rotating at different speed to give distribution and a conveying action to the coal.

The coal slurry is fed at the top of the centrifuge. When the coal passes through the annular space between the basket and the spider, centrifugal force drives the liquid through the caked solids and the mother liquor is discharged through perforations in the basket circumference. If required, a wash liquid is introduced and is driven through the caked solids. The plug flow action of the wash liquid purifies the solids and removes residual mother liquor. Residual liquors are driven from the caked solids and are discharged through the basket perforations to achieve maximum cake dryness. A scraper knife advances into the rotating basket to discharge the solids to downstream equipment. The coal drops to the bottom of the centrifuge and discharges into a chute or hopper.

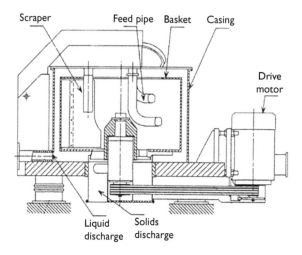

Figure 30.2 Perforated Basket Centrifuge.

After scraping, a 6–10 mm layer remains inside the rotating basket. With the scraper in an advanced position, high pressure nitrogen or air is used to dislodge this residual coal. This step can be performed after several centrifuge cycles, or after each cycle.

The vibrating form of perforated basket centrifuges is one of the most commonly used for dewatering of coal. This machine is distinguished from other basket types in that the rotating basket is vibrated in such a manner as to cause the solids to move through the machine. The slurry is fed into a rotating screen basket which revolves round a vertical axis and is vibrated along the same axis. The centrifugal force and the vibration cause the solids to flow to the larger diameter of the basket from where they are discharged, the liquid passing through the mesh and being collected separately. The vibration motion in this type of centrifuge loosens the bed of particles aiding the drainage. The rotation and vibration are supplied by separate drives and can be varied relative to each other to give optimum results.

The throughput of such machines is relatively high and water content of 25% in the feed is reduced to 5%–7%. Because of the perforations in the basket, these centrifuges are not suitable for feeds having a significant proportion of fines.

30.3 DEWATERING OF FINE COAL

High frequency vibrating screens are probably the most common dewatering screens for fine coal of −2 mm size, as they are generally simple, cheap and robust. Generally, moistures of 30% plus can be expected on −1 mm +0.2 mm material.

30.3.1 High frequency vibrating screen

The high frequency vibrating screen (Fig. 30.3.1) incorporates a 45° sloping back plates screen with 5° uphill flat deck screen, fitted with cross flow slotted apertures. The hi-frequency screens work on the principle of Low strokes and high RPM thus

Figure 30.3.1 High Frequency Vibrating Screen
(Courtesy Metso Minerals).

the screens have twin unbalanced 4 pole vibrating motors. Two contra-rotating unbalanced vibrator motors impart a linear motion. Incoming slurry is fed across the back of the deck. Slurry pools at the lowest point of the screen and solid particles bridge over the apertures and forms a bed. The bed of solids allows the water percolate through the screen apertures and the bed is compacted during vibrations. This in turn squeezes the water out of the fines bed as it is conveyed up the deck. The bed of solids is discharged at the lip as a cake. Adjustable discharge dam provides the ability to vary the bed depth of the feed material to Maximize dewatering efficiency.

Filtration by Vacuum filters and Bowl centrifuges are the currently used dewatering methods for the fine coal particles of size – 0.5 mm. The surface moisture obtained from vacuum filters is about 22% and that from the centrifuges is about 17%.

A combination of methods is employed for dewatering the fine coal slurry. In general, as much water as possible is to be removed from the slurry in order to reduce the volume to be handled by vacuum filter or centrifuge which are more costly operations. Vacuum filter and centrifuge function better with a relatively thick feed. Much water can be removed from the slurry by using **classifying and thickening cyclones** or **thickeners** and can make the slurry denser over 60% solids. The simplicity and cheapness of the hydrocyclone make it very attractive eventhough it yields less thick slurry and overflow contains fine solid particles.

30.3.2 Classifying and thickening cyclones

Hydrocyclones are extremely versatile in thickening the slurry. In principle, hydrocyclone separates solid particles of the dispersed phase from the liquid on the basis of the density difference between the phases and the separation depends heavily on particle size. Thickening means concentrating the solids present in a suspension into a smaller amount of liquid. The aim in using the hydrocyclone as a thickening cyclone is to set the cut size sufficiently low to obtain high concentration of solids in the underflow (i.e. dewatering of solids). The underflow concentration that can be achieved with hydrocyclones may be as high as 50% by volume. Figure 30.3.2(a) shows a hydrocylone used as a thickener to pre-thickening the feed to vacuum filters or dewatering centrifuges.

Series connections of separators are a common way of improving the performance of single units. In case of hydrocyclones, due to their low capital and running costs, multiple series arrangements are quite frequently used. If the required degree of

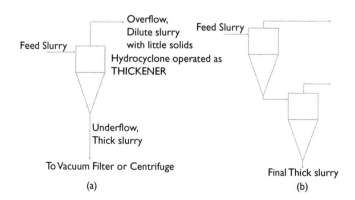

Figure 30.3.2 (a) Pre-thickening with hydrocyclone (b) Two hydrocyclones in series
for thickening.

thickening cannot be achieved with one cyclone, two or more in series may be used
as in Figure 30.3.2(b). The overflow from the second or subsequent stages may be
partially recycled back to the feed of the first stage.

30.3.3 Thickener

Thickener consists of a large cylindrical tank with a very short conical bottom as
shown in Fig. 30.3.3. The feed is introduced continuously through a central semi-
submerged feed well at a rate that allows the solid particles to settle at a safe distance
below the overflow level. Thus clear water overflows into the top peripheral launder.
Thickening is improved by the addition of flocculating agents that cause the particles
to coagulate and accelerates the settling. The settled solids are swept by a slowly
revolving raking mechanism attached to the central rotating shaft and positioned
slightly above the tank bottom. Slow agitation of the slurry helps in reducing the
apparent viscosity of the suspension. The denser slurry with a higher solids content
swept by the rakes is directed towards the center to facilitate easy removal by a suitable pump such as diaphragm pump. The speed of the raking mechanism is normally
about 8 m/minute at the perimeter which corresponds to about 10 rev/hr for a 15 m
diameter thickener.

In a thickener, the surface area must be large enough so that the upward velocity
of liquid is at all times lower than the settling velocity of the slowest-settling particle
which is to be recovered. The degree of thickening produced is controlled by the
residence time of the particles and hence by the thickener depth. Hence the diameter
of the thickener is usually large compared with the depth. In thickening operation,
the feed pulp containing about 15–30% solids is thickened to a pulp of about 60%
solids.

The methods of supporting the drive mechanism depend primarily on the tank
diameter. In relatively small thickeners of less than 45 m diameter, the drive head is
usually supported on a superstructure spanning the tank with the arms being attached
to the drive shaft. Such thickeners are referred to as **bridge** or **beam thickeners**.
For larger thickeners of about 180 m diameter, drive mechanism is supported on a

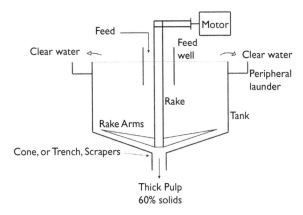

Figure 30.3.3 Thickener.

stationary steel or concrete centre column. In the **traction thickener,** a single long arm is mounted with one end on the central support column while to the other are fixed traction wheels that run on a rail on top of the tank wall. **Cable thickeners** have a hinged rake arm fastened to the bottom of the drive cage or centre shaft. The rake arm is pulled by cables connected to a torque or drive arm structure.

The thickeners often incorporate substantial storage capacity so that if the filtration section is shut down for maintenance, the concentrator can continue to feed material to the dewatering section. During such periods the thickened underflow should be recirculated into the thickener feed well. At no time should the underflow cease to be pumped, as chokage of the discharge cone rapidly occurs.

Conventional thickeners suffer from the disadvantage that large floor areas are required. The availability of new and powerful flocculants made possible thickeners with a very small area per unit weight of solids per day. The high rate thickener is such a thickener which utilizes the flocculant effectively by introducing the feed and flocculant in a flocculation chamber to ensure thorough mixing and dispersion of flocculant and slurry in order to increase the settling rate.

30.3.4 Vacuum filters

Drum and disc filters and horizontal belt filter are the commonly used vacuum filters for dewatering –0.5 mm fines.

The **Rotary Vacuum Drum Filter** (Fig. 30.3.4.1) consists of a cast cylinder mounted horizontally and rotated at a very low rpm (typically from 0.1 to 4 rpm). The cylinder has perforated surface over which the filter medium is wrapped tightly. The periphery of the drum is divided into compartments. Each compartment is provided with a number of drain lines passing through the inside of the drum and connected to a rotary valve head (Fig. 30.3.4.2) on the central drum shaft. The rotary valve is a control valve and is an essential component in all vacuum drum and disc filters. Its purpose is to connect the each of the points on the drum, in sequence, to a vacuum (for filtration, cake washing, and air-drying) then either to vent to atmospheric pressure or to give a small back-flow of pressurized air for cake discharge.

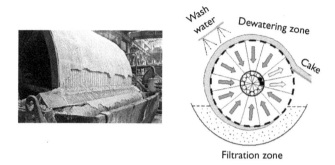

Figure 30.3.4.1 Rotary Vacuum Drum Filter & zones in Filter.

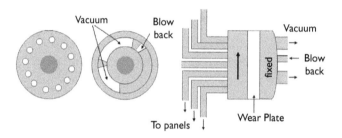

Figure 30.3.4.2 Rotary Valve Head.

The drum is immersed to the required depth in the slurry which is kept agitated to prevent settling of solids. By the action of automatic rotary valve on the drum shaft, vacuum is applied to the immersed compartments and results in cake buildup on the filter medium surface. As the drum rotates, the cake is raised above the slurry level and wash water is sprayed on the surface if required. On further rotation, the cake is dried. The vacuum is continuously applied till the end of drying stage. Air is admitted in to the compartment before it re-enter in to the slurry, thus permitting the cake to be blown away from the filtering surface where it is removed by scraper on to a belt conveyor. The heart of the filter is the valve assembly which at a predetermined position causes a change from vacuum to pressure (or blowback).

The **Rotary Vacuum Disc Filter** (Fig. 30.3.4.3) is similar to the drum filter except that instead of a cylindrical drum it consists of a number of circular discs mounted on a horizontal tubular shaft and spaced by means of hubs. A line of holes is drilled from outside of the shaft into each of the tubes for the insertion of the sector nipple. Each disc consists of ten sectors. Filter medium consists of cloth bags are covered over the sector and fastened to the nipple. The completed sector is joined to the central shaft by screwing the nipple into the holes of the shaft. The cycle of operation is similar to that of drum filter.

Among the drum and disc filters, disc filter is having the following advantages:

1   It has more filtering area when compared to drum filter
2   Head room required per unit filter area is less
3   It is possible to filter several products in single unit
4   Worn out cloth can be replaced without interrupting the process for long time

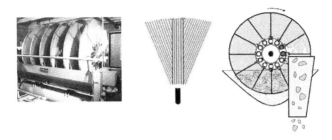

Figure 30.3.4.3 Rotary Vacuum Disc Filter, Sector & Operation
(Courtesy Westech Process Equipment India Pvt.Ltd.).

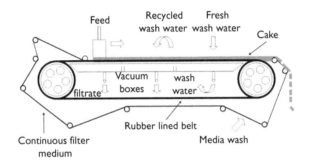

Figure 30.3.4.4 Horizontal Belt Filter.

The **horizontal belt filter** (Fig. 30.3.4.4) consists of an endless perforated rubber drainage deck supporting a separate belt made from a suitable filter cloth.

At the start of the horizontal travel, slurry flows by gravity on to the belt. Filtration immediately commences due to gravity and the vacuum applied to the suction boxes at the underside of the drainage deck. The cake formed is dewatered, dried by drawing air through it, and then discharged as the belt reverses over a small-diameter roller. If required, one or more washes can be incorporated.

Hyperbaric disc filter is a vacuum filter used for dewatering finest grain suspensions with increased pressure differential by using pressure vessel. The dewatering of fine particles is widely considered to be the most difficult operation in coal preparation plants. The difficulty is due to the very high specific surface area of fine coal. Any piece of vacuum equipment can only achieve a maximum differential of one bar (one atmosphere to zero bar) which is not enough to reduce the moisture to the required level due to high specific surface. Pressure differential is increased by using a pressure vessel in a hyperbaric filter. Over the years, Hyperbaric filters have been the subject of sporadic attention by South African companies. Hyperbaric filters are essentially disc filters placed inside a pressure chamber. A hyperbaric chamber can ostensibly increase the atmospheric pressure and thereby increase the pressure differential. A pressure of up to 7 bar may be applied. It is recognized that they can produce moistures between that of other mechanical equipment like vacuum filters and thermal drying. Feed is supplied using a positive displacement pump into the slurry tank, which is kept well agitated. The problem is that of cost and complexity, particularly that of the discharge

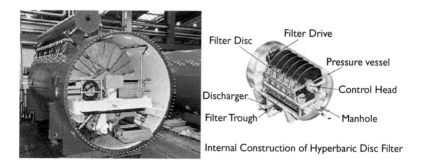

Internal Construction of Hyperbaric Disc Filter

Figure 30.3.4.5 Hyperbaric Disc Filter
(Courtesy Andritz separation).

valves, which operate as high pressure airlocks. A hyperbaric filter can be made using any type of vacuum filter of preference, or availability, such as discs or drum filters. Fig. 30.3.4.5 shows the Hyperbaric Disc Filter and the internal construction.

The following are the Advantages of hyperbaric filtration:

- Continuous system reduces cost for conveyors and other peripheral equipment
- Fully automated continuous cake discharge in combination with pressure filtration
- Variable cake thickness selected by the operator provides highest flexibility.
- Thin filter cakes allow low residual moisture with high throughputs.
- This filter provides maximum filtration area at minimum cost and floor space (footprint) and gives clear filtrate
- Filter sectors are made of stainless steel to reduce wear and can be changed quickly.
- Closed system reduces impact on environment and allows outdoor installation.
- Proven for various applications
- High unit availability even in high abrasion applications

30.3.5 Pressure filters

Because of the virtual incompressibility of solids, filtration under pressure has certain advantages over vacuum. Higher flow rates and better washing and drying may result from the higher pressures that can be used. However, the continuous removal of solids from the pressure-filter chamber can be extremely difficult and consequently, although continuous pressure filters do exist, the vast majority operate as batch units.

Filter presses are the most frequently used type of pressure filter. They are made in two forms: the plate and frame press and the recessed plate or chamber press.

The **plate and frame filter press** is one of the oldest types of batch pressure filter. It consists of vertical plates clamped together alternately by an externally operated screw system or hydraulic ram (Fig. 30.3.5.1). A series of hollow frames which are placed side by side and hung from two parallel rails on either side of the plates. The filtering medium is placed against the sides of the plates and the slurry is pumped between them. The slurry pressure presses the pulp against the medium forcing the

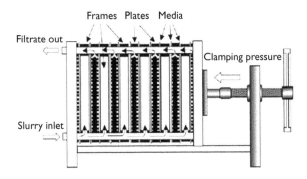

Figure 30.3.5.1 Plate and frame filter press.

liquid through the filter medium and leaving the solids as a cake, on both surfaces of the frame.

In operation, feed in the form of slurry is pumped in through a common channel entering the filters through individual ports. This ensures uniform distribution of feed in each chamber. The feed can be charged either through top or bottom ports in the frame. The filtrate passes through the filter medium and runs down the grooved surfaces of the plates and removed through ports to a common discharge channel. The cake remains in the frame and, when the frame is full, the filter press is opened and each plate and frame is moved manually or with automatic plate shifters so the cake can be discharged through the floor to a conveyor belt or hopper. The filter press is closed again, the feed is admitted and pressure gradually increases as the cake deposits.

Recessed plate filter press or **Chamber filter** is improved plate and frame filter. These filters are used in the coal industry for many years as the principal method of dewatering of fine tailings, usually from the froth flotation process. The tailings solids in the slurry are often of a very fine particle size up to 40% minus 20 microns, and often contain high quantities of clays.

In chamber filters, when recessed plates are clamped together form chambers (Fig. 30.3.5.2). Recessed plates in chamber filters are supported on rails, fastened to two ends. Each plate is covered by backing cloth and filter media on each side. The press is closed, either mechanically or hydraulically, by squeezing the ends together so that each adjacent plate is forced together to form watertight enclosed chambers between the plates.

The slurry to be filtered is pumped under pressure into the chambers via ports. When the chambers are full, filtrate is forced through the filtration media and discharges from the press. Particles too large to pass through the filter medium collect as cake on the surface of the cloth and becomes a filter medium. Eventually the particles become so packed into the chamber that no more solids can be accepted, at which point the filling cycle is considered complete. However, at this point, the interstitial spaces, the ports and the core are still filled with filtrate, a compressed air blow is used to remove the wet core. At this point, options of normal discharging, additional fill pressure, membrane squeeze or air blow can be used to attain different levels of product moisture for different cycle times. The press is opened by releasing the pressure on

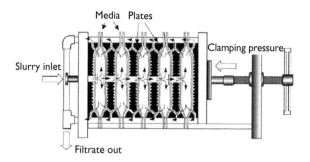

Figure 30.3.5.2 Recessed plate filter press.

each end and opening the chambers, either singly or as multiple plates. When all the cake is discharged from the press the press is closed and the cycle is repeated.

In recent times, filter presses have become larger as it is cheaper to install larger units than smaller for the same tonnage and operating costs tend to be lower. Up to the 1960's most presses were 1.3 m × 1.3 m operating at 7 bar. Presses are now commonly 2 m × 2 m and can work up to 15 bar. Large presses have the additional advantage of producing heavy cakes which discharge more easily, as well as increasing the mass processed per cycle. A 2 m × 2 m press processes nearly seven times more slurry per cycle than a 1.3 m × 1.3 m unit.

30.3.6 Centrifuges

Bowl centrifugation process is widely used for fine coal dewatering and is well accepted by many coal beneficiation plants due to its relative ease of operation and maintenance, low operating and capital cost, and high capacity of producing low-moisture content product. Solid bowl centrifuge and Screen bowl centrifuge are the two most commonly used centrifuges to dewater fine coal. These have achieved some popularity for dewatering the entire −0.5 mm range and can replace the vacuum filter.

Solid Bowl Centrifuge (Fig. 30.3.6.1) consists essentially of a horizontal revolving bowl, cylindro-conical in shape, inside which a screw conveyor of similar section rotates in the same direction at a slightly higher speed.

The slurry is fed through a stationary pipe into the feed zone located in the center of the screw conveyor. The liquid and solid constituents thereby receive an angular momentum and a high centrifugal force is imposed on the suspended solids which causes the solids to settle on the bowl surface at a greatly accelerated rate depending on the rotational speed employed normally 1600 to 8500 revolutions per minute. When the liquid reaches a predetermined level, it overflows through discharge ports at the large end of the bowl. The separated solids are conveyed by the screw conveyor out of the liquid towards the small end of the bowl and are discharged. The solids are continuously dewatered by centrifugal force as they proceed from the liquid zone to the discharge end. After leaving the liquid and before discharge, the solids may be washed by clean water jets. Excess water drains away towards liquid discharge port through the particle bed.

Screen Bowl Centrifuge consists of a rotating cylindro-conical bowl having both solid and perforated sections as shown in Fig. 30.3.6.2. This is a countercurrent flow design, in which feed slurry is introduced at the conical section of the bowl through a feed pipe. The primary solid-liquid separation takes place at the solid section of the bowl. Under the action of high centrifugal force in the range of 500 to 900 g-force, the solid particles tend to settle on the inside wall of the bowl, whereas the separated water flows towards the large diameter end of the bowl and is discharged. The thickened solid is moved counter-current to the water by a screw conveyor towards the screen section of the bowl. This thickened solid form a filtration bed on the screen section, which facilitates the final dewatering of the solid material allowing most of the residual water to drain through the screen openings. Clearly, the centrifugal sedimentation and filtration mechanisms are both utilized in the screen bowl centrifuge to dewater fine coals.

As the products of vacuum filters and bowl centrifuges are relatively high in moisture content, these are mixed with other sizes of low moisture content so that there will not be serious raise in moisture content of the final product. If further reduction in moisture is necessary, heat drying is to be applied.

Screen Scroll Centrifuge is a modification of the standard basket centrifuge used to dewater finer particles. Vertically mounted Screen Scroll Centrifuge manufactured by Centrifugal & Mechanical Industries (CMI), shown in Fig. 30.3.6.3, is built with the main components of screen, scroll, basket, housing, and helical screw. Curved scraper blades are mounted in a helical pattern which run in the same direction as the basket but run at a slightly different speed, developed by a dual speed planetary gearbox, so that the scraper conveys the coal down the basket which enhances the basket loading and the retention time. This type of machine normally runs at a high g between 200 and 400.

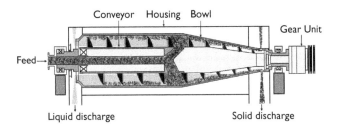

Figure 30.3.6.1 Solid Bowl Centrifuge.

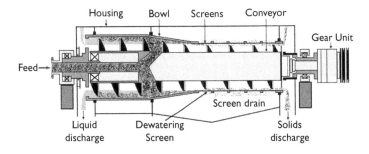

Figure 30.3.6.2 Screen Bowl Centrifuge.

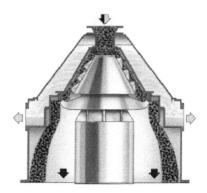

Figure 30.3.6.3 CMI Screen Scroll Centrifuge (Courtesy: Elgin Separation Solutions, St.Louis, Missouri, USA).

Feed containing liquid and solid materials is introduced into vertical screen scroll centrifuge from the top and is deflected into an acceleration chamber. The feed is sped up by centrifugal acceleration produced from the rotating parts contacted. As such, centrifugal force slings liquid through the openings, while solids are held on the screen surface as they cannot pass through because of granular particles larger than the screen pores or due to agglomeration. Movement of solids across the screen surface is controlled by flights, which move relative to the screen. Liquids that have passed through the screen are collected and discharged through effluent outlet from the side of machine. Solids collected from the screen fall by gravity through the bottom discharge opening of the machine. Screen Scroll centrifuge will provide efficient and consistent moisture reduction, even with fluctuating feed rates.

The screen scroll centrifuge has an advantage of having a driven scroll helical conveyor which gives a small differential speed relative to the conical basket. The helical conveyor is installed in the centrifuge to control the transport of the incoming feed, allowing the residence time of the solids in the basket to be increased giving enhanced process performance. Moreover, the helical conveyor and conical basket sections are designed in certain angle of 10°, 15° and 20° being common such that solid particles are dragged on the conveyor along the cone towards the discharge point. As a result, there is no formation of even solids layer but form piles of triangular section in front of the blades of the conveyor. The residence time within screen scroll centrifuge is typically about 4 to 15 seconds which is longer than normal simpler conical basket centrifuge. This permits a sufficient interaction time between wash liquid and cake. However, the presence of the conveyor causes crystals breakage and abrasion problem as well as the formation of uneven solids layer which can lead to poor washing. This can be controlled by conveyor speed.

Scroll centrifuges work on particles from 12 mm to 100 microns, with a feed concentration of 30 to 65% solids. These machines seem to have become the latest standard for treating spiral concentrates.

Chapter 31

Coal washing efficiency

In a laboratory float and sink test, the separation is clean and accurate as sufficient time is given to allow complete separation to take place. The data from such tests indicate what should be obtained under ideal conditions of operation. Such conditions do not exist in plant practice. In a continuously operating process, with constant discharge of float and sink, particles having specific gravity nearer to the medium may not have time to be separated and will be misplaced into the other product. Particles of high or low specific gravity are least effected. The difficulty, or ease, of separation depends on the amount of the material present having specific gravity nearer to the medium. Conversely, the efficiency of a particular separating process depends on its ability to separate material of specific gravity close to that of the medium. Some of the reasons for improper separation are:

1 Degradation of coal during separation process
2 Use of suspensions as the separating media
3 Disturbances created in separating medium due to the introduction of feed and the removal of float and sink fractions
4 Agitation or upward currents used in the vessel to keep the separating medium in suspension
5 Lack of sufficient retention time for the particles especially near gravity particles to separate perfectly due to the use of high throughput

Different expressions for coal washing efficiency have been evolved to accurately reflect the quantitative and/or qualitative aspects of a washing operation. Evaluation of performance of a washer is based on two types of criteria namely dependent and independent.

31.1 DEPENDENT CRITERIA

The criteria that depend both on the washability characteristics of the coal and on the characteristics of the washing equipment are usually called dependent criteria. They include Organic efficiency, Anderson efficiency, Ash error and Yield error. Separation efficiencies or dependent criteria are used to evaluate different equipment for application to different reserves.

31.1.1   Organic efficiency

Organic efficiency, also called as recovery efficiency, is suggested by Fraser and Yancey [52] and is defined as the ratio between the actual yield of a desired product and the theoretically possible yield at the same ash content. Normally it is expressed as a percentage as follows:

$$\text{Organic Efficiency} = \frac{\text{Actual yield of washed coal}}{\text{Theoretical yield of floats of same ash content}} \times 100 \qquad (31.1.1)$$

Organic Efficiency cannot be used to compare the efficiencies of different plants, as it is dependent criteria, and is much influenced by the washability of the coal. It is possible, for example, to obtain a high organic efficiency on a coal containing little near gravity material, even when the separating efficiency, as measured by partition data is quite inefficient.

Another formula evolved by Drakeley [53] is based entirely on float and sink analyses at one specific gravity of the raw coal, the cleaned coal, and the refuse. The specific gravity used for the analyses is that considered most suitable for a separation. The General Efficiency is the product of two separate efficiencies designated as the Qualitative Efficiency and the Quantitative Efficiency.

$$\text{Qualitative Efficiency} = \frac{(\%\ \text{float in washed coal} - \%\ \text{float in feed})}{100 - \%\ \text{float in feed}} \times 100 \quad (31.1.2)$$

$$\text{Quantitative Efficiency} = 100 - \frac{\%\ \text{float in refuse} \times \%\ \text{weight of refuse}}{\%\ \text{float in feed}} \qquad (31.1.3)$$

General Efficiency is the mere multiplication of the above two efficiencies.

The Qualitative Efficiency may be called the efficiency of dirt removal, as it is equal to the percent reduction in sink by washing divided by the percent sink in raw coal, and does not take into account the loss of coal in the refuse. The Quantitative Efficiency represents the percentage recovery of float coal in the washing operation.

31.1.2   Anderson efficiency

Anderson efficiency [54] indicates the correctly placed material and is defined as

$$\begin{aligned}\text{Anderson Efficiency} = 100 - (\text{Float in refuse} + \text{sink in clean coal} \\ \text{at the effective density of cut}).\end{aligned} \qquad (31.1.4)$$

31.1.3   Ash error

Ash error is closely related to recovery efficiency and it is the difference between the ash content of clean coal and the theoretical ash content obtained from the washability data at the same yield. Therefore, the smaller the ash error the larger the yield for a given ash content of the clean product.

31.1.4   Yield error (or) yield loss

Yield error is the difference between the actual yield of the clean coal obtained in the washing unit and the theoretical yield to be obtained from the washability data at the ash content of the actual yield. The smaller the yield error, the more accurate is the separation.

31.2   INDEPENDENT CRITERIA

The criteria that depend on the characteristics of the washing unit and independent of the washability characteristics of the coal are called Independent criteria. Independent criteria are also referred as the sharpness of separation criteria or equipment performance measures. They include **Probabale Error, Error Area** and **Imperfection.** Sharpness of separation criteria may be used to evaluate different equipment for application to a specific coal reserve.

Independent criteria reflects the inherent ability of the cleaning unit to make a sharp separation between coal and impurities, and this criteria must be as free as possible from the influence of the effects of coals of dissimilar character and separations at different densities. It assists in predicting the actual clean coal yields and ash contents of a cleaning operation from standard float and sink washability analysis. Hence, such criteria are useful in formulating performance guarantees for new plants and in calculating the quantity and quality of products obtainable by treating a new coal in an existing unit of known performance characteristics.

In commercial coal cleaning, coal of specific gravity well below the specific gravity of separation and impurities of specific gravity well above the specific gravity of separation report largely (or entirely) to their proper products, clean coal and refuse, respectively. As coal approaches the specific gravity of separation, however, more and more material tends to report to an improper product. Finally, an infinitesimal increment of coal, at the specific gravity of separation, is divided equally between the clean coal and refuse. The specific gravity of this increment is defined as the specific gravity of separation.

A bar chart showing the percentage of each specific gravity fraction of the feed coal that was recovered in clean coal was devised in 1912 by Hancock. In 1938 Tromp [55] and Fraser and Yancey has independently developed a curve which is plotted between percentage recoveries and mean specific gravities of the specific gravity fractions. This curve has several names such as **Tromp Curve, Partition curve, Distribution curve, Recovery curve,** and **Error curve.** The **Tromp Curve** is used to assess the sharpness of separation or to predict the performance of a washing unit. It is the curve drawn between **Partition coefficient** and the mean or nominal specific gravity for each specific gravity range. Partition coefficient is the percentage of feed coal of a certain nominal specific gravity which reports to floats.

To construct the Tromp curve, three sets of coal analytical data are required:

1   recovery of clean coal
2   float and sink washability analysis of the clean coal product
3   float and sink washability analysis of the refuse product

The recovery of clean coal can be determined either by direct weight or it can be predicted by using material balance equations, if the ash percent of feed coal, clean coal and refuse are known.

Let A_f, A_c and A_r are the ash percentages of feed coal, clean coal and refuse respectively. Y_f, Y_c, and Y_r are the recovery or Yield percent of feed coal (100%), clean coal and refuse respectively. Then

Yield balance equation $\quad Y_c + Y_r = Y_f$ $\qquad\qquad$ (31.2.1)

Ash balance equation $\quad\;\; A_c.Y_c + A_r.Y_r = A_f.Y_f$ $\qquad$ (31.2.2)

Solving these two equations

$$\Rightarrow \qquad\qquad Yc\% = \frac{(A_r - A_f)}{(A_r - A_c)} \times 100 \qquad\qquad (31.2.3)$$

Let an example be taken where ash percent of feed coal, clean coal and refuse are 18.65, 12.20 and 49.26 respectively. Then percent clean coal obtained is

$$Y_c\% = \frac{(A_r - A_f)}{(A_r - A_c)} \times 100 = \frac{(49.26 - 18.65)}{(49.26 - 12.20)} \times 100 = 82.6\%$$

i.e., Yield percentage of clean coal $= \dfrac{\text{Ash \% in refuse} - \text{Ash \% in feed}}{\text{Ash \% in refuse} - \text{Ash \% in clean coal}} \times 100$

$Y_r\% = Y_f - Y_c = 100 - 82.6 = 17.4\%$

For obtaining float and sink washability analyses of clean coal and refuse product, representative samples of clean coal and refuse are collected separately from the washing unit after the machine has come to the normal operating state. The individual samples of clean coal and refuse are subjected to complete float and sink analysis in the same way as a sample of raw coal is tested for the evaluation of its washability characteristics. Table 31.2.1 shows the float and sink data of clean coal and refuse products.

The percent weights of the fractions totaling 100 (in case of both clean coal and refuse) as shown in Table 31.2.1 are then expressed as percent weights of the feed coal by multiplying the individual weights by the actual yield percentages of clean coal (82.6%) and refuse (17.4%) and dividing the resultant figures by 100.

Reconstituted feed is then calculated by adding values of percent weights of feed coal for clean coal and refuse at each specific gravity range. Nominal specific gravity is determined by averaging lowest and highest specific gravity at each specific gravity range.

The partition coefficient is calculated as fraction of percent weights of feed coal for clean coal to the reconstituted feed at each nominal specific gravity and multiplied the resultant figures with 100. The partition coefficient can also be calculated as fraction of percent weights of feed coal for refuse to the reconstituted feed at each nominal specific gravity and multiplied the resultant figures with 100. Then the Tromp curve can be constructed by plotting the partition coefficient against the nominal specific gravity.

Table 31.2.2 shows calculated values for drawing Tromp Curve for 82.6% yield of clean coal and 17.4% yield of refuse.

Table 31.2.1 Float and sink washability analyses of clean coal and refuse.

	A	B
	Clean coal analysis	Refuse analysis
Sp. Gr.	Wt%	Wt%
− 1.30	83.34	18.15
1.30–1.40	10.50	10.82
1.40–1.50	03.35	09.64
1.50–1.60	01.79	13.33
1.60–1.70	00.30	08.37
1.70–1.80	00.16	05.85
1.80–1.90	00.09	05.05
1.90–2.00	00.07	40.34
+2.00	00.40	24.45
Total	100.00	100.00

Table 31.2.2 Calculated values for drawing Tromp Curve.

	A	B	C	D	E	F	G	H
Sp. Gr.	Clean coal analysis Wt %	Refuse analysis Wt %	Clean coal % of feed 0.826A	Refuse % of feed 0.174B	Recon-stituted Feed % C + D	Nominal Sp.gr	Partition coefficient for clean $\frac{C}{E} \times 100$	Partition coefficient for refuse $\frac{D}{E} \times 100$
− 1.30	83.34	18.15	68.84	03.16	72.00	-----	95.61	04.39
1.30–1.40	10.50	10.82	08.67	01.88	10.55	1.35	82.18	17.82
1.40–1.50	03.35	09.64	02.77	01.68	04.45	1.45	62.24	37.75
1.50–1.60	01.79	13.33	01.48	02.32	03.80	1.55	38.95	61.05
1.60–1.70	00.30	08.37	00.25	01.45	01.70	1.65	14.62	85.38
1.70–1.80	00.16	05.85	00.13	01.02	01.15	1.75	11.30	88.70
1.80–1.90	00.09	05.05	00.07	00.88	00.95	1.85	07.37	92.63
1.90–2.00	00.07	40.34	00.06	00.76	00.82	1.95	07.32	92.68
+ 2.00	00.40	24.45	00.33	04.25	04.58	-----	07.21	92.79
Total	100.00	100.00	82.60	17.40	100.00			

While drawing Tromp curve, assumptions are required in plotting the lightest and heaviest fractions because they have no exact limiting specific gravities. If 1.30 is the lowest specific gravity used in the analysis, as frequently is the case, the point for the float should be plotted at a specific gravity that is midway between that of the lightest particle present and 1.30. Specific gravity of 1.26–1.28 is generally used. Any error involved in making this assumption generally has very little influence on the shape and position of the curve; it becomes important only when the specific gravity of separation

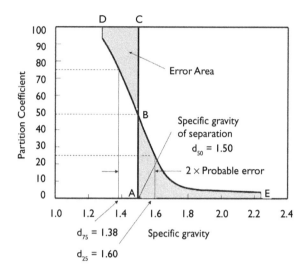

Figure 31.2.1 Tromp Curve relates to Clean coal.

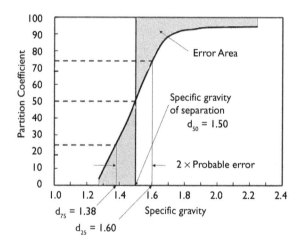

Figure 31.2.2 Tromp Curve relates to Refuse.

is unusually low. If the highest specific gravity is 1.80 in the analysis, the sink is usually plotted at 2.20–2.30, depending on what is known about its composition.

Fig. 31.2.1 shows the Tromp Curve drawn for the partition coefficient relates to clean coal in which case it will decrease with increasing specific gravity. Similarly, Tromp Curve can also be drawn for the partition coefficient relates to refuse (Fig. 31.2.2) in which case it will increase with increasing specific gravity.

The Tromp curve of a particular washer remains unchanged with varying composition of raw coal provided that the feed coal having the same size grading are treated nearly at the same specific gravity of cut under more or less similar load conditions. The shape and gradient of the Tromp curve is a measure of the sharpness of separation of a washer. The steeper the slope, more sharp the separation. For an ideal separation, the misplaced materials in either of the products (clean coal and refuse) being zero, the curve is represented by a straight vertical line. It shows that all the particles lighter than separating specific gravity report to floats while all the heavier particles report to sinks. On the other hand, a Tromp curve tending to be horizontal throughout its length represents an extreme case where practically no separation is achieved. However, most of the Tromp curves remain in between these two extremes.

The Tromp curve for real separation shows that efficiency is highest for particles of specific gravity far from the operating specific gravity and decreases for particles approaching the operating specific gravity. The shape of the tails or loops at the extremities of the Tromp curve indicate the amount of high ash refuse particles and low ash coal particles misplaced in the clean coal and refuse products respectively. The shorter the length of the tails, the better is the efficiency of separation.

The value of the ordinate corresponding to any point on the abscissa gives the probability that a particle will be found in the sinks. 100 minus this value gives the probability that a particle will be found in floats.

The value of the specific gravity corresponding to partition coefficient of 50% is called the **partition specific gravity (partition density)** or **Effective specific gravity of separation** or **Tromp cut point**. At this specific gravity, a particle has an equal chance of going to either clean coal fraction or refuse fraction. Since the partition density is obtained from the curve, it need not coincide with any density in practice or with the operating density. All most all Tromp curves gives a reasonable straight line relationship between partition coefficient values of 25% and 75% and the slope of the line between these two values is used to indicate the accuracy of separation (or efficiency of separation) process.

It is found that partition curve is a function of particle size. Larger particles give closer separation. Hence coals of the same grading should be used when comparing the performance of different washers.

In Fig. 31.2.1, the vertical straight line ABC represents the theoretical separating specific gravity. The actual separation is represented by the curve DBE.

It is common practice to use parameters which is derived from the Tromp curve, instead of using the whole Tromp curve for measuring the technical efficiency of a cleaning unit. The Ecart probable Moyen, Error area and Imperfection are widely used to describe the characteristics of the Tromp curve.

31.2.1 Probable error (or) Ecart Probable Moyen (E$_p$)

The Probable error of separation or the Ecart Probable Moyen (E$_p$) is a guide to the efficiency of separation of a washing unit. It represents the sharpness with which the coal and impurities are separated. It is a measure of the deviation of the Tromp curve from a perfect separation. It is defined as half the difference between the specific gravities corresponding to partition coefficient values of 25% and 75% and is calculated as:

$$E_p = \frac{1}{2}(d_{25} - d_{75})$$

(31.2.4)

Generally, the steeper the Tromp curve, the lower the E_p value. The lower the E_p value, the smaller the difference in specific gravity between the 25% and 75% partition coefficient. The line is nearer to vertical between 25% and 75% partition coefficient, and hence the more efficient is the separation. Conversely a higher E_p value indicates a wider spread of specific gravity and a less efficient separation. In other words, a low E_p denotes a sharp separation, and a high E_p denotes a separation that is not sharp. An ideal separation has a vertical line with an $E_p = 0$. The usual range of E_p is from about 0.020 to 0.30 or more.

For the example considered, $d_{25} = 1.60$ and $d_{75} = 1.38$ from Figure 31.2.1

$$\text{Ecart Probable Moyen} = E_p = \frac{1}{2}(d_{25} - d_{75}) = \frac{1}{2}(1.60 - 1.38) = 0.11$$

The E_p is not commonly used as a method of assessing the efficiency of separation in units such as tables, spirals, cones etc., due to many operating variables like wash water, table slope, speed etc. which can effect the separation efficiency. It is however, ideally suited to the relatively simple and reproducible Heavy Medium Separation process.

31.2.2   Error area or tromp area

Error area is a measure of the sharpness of separation between clean coal and refuse. It is defined as the area between the actual Tromp curve and the theoretically perfect Tromp curve. In Fig. 31.2.1, the area DBC represents the true floats that have reported to the sinks while the area ABE represents the true sinks that have reported to the floats. These two areas are not necessarily equal. These areas are called Error areas. These areas represent deviation from ideality. For a theoretically perfect separation, the error area is zero.

31.2.3   Imperfection

As Probable error depends on relative specific gravities, the imperfection is used as a further method of comparing separation processes. Imperfection involves the influence of the specific gravity of separation on the shape of the Tromp curve. It has been observed that there is a tendency for the curve to steepen as the specific gravity of separation decreases. In other words, separations at low specific gravity tend to be sharper than those at high specific gravity.

This concept contradicts the well-established principle that efficiency increases with increase in the specific gravity of separation. In an effort to develop criteria for sharpness of separation that would be independent of the specific gravity of separation, the term Imperfection (I) was originated and it is calculated as

$$I = \frac{E_p}{d_{50} - 1} \qquad \text{for Jigs} \tag{31.2.5}$$

$$I = \frac{E_p}{d_{50}} \quad \text{for Heavy medium baths} \tag{31.2.6}$$

For the example considered, $E_p = 0.11$ and $d_{50} = 1.50$ from Figure 31.2.1

$$\text{Imperfection} = I = \frac{E_p}{d_{50}} = \frac{0.11}{1.50} = 0.0733$$

Imperfection is a numerical figure that characterizes a particular cleaning device regardless of the separating gravity. It is the coefficient to be preferred in expressing the performance of a washer.

All the three measures of separation, Ecart probable Moyen, Error area and Imperfection, have been developed due to cumbersomeness and inconvenience of using Tromp curve for evaluation of efficiencies. These measures of separation are defined as sharpness of separation criteria.

Table 31.2.3 shows the values of Effective density of separation (d_{50}), Ecart probable Moyen (E_p) and Imperfection (I) for different types of processes.

From the data of Table 31.2.3, it can be seen that Heavy medium processes are more efficient than other coal cleaning methods.

The Tromp curves are specific to any process for which they were established and are not effected by the type of material fed to it, provided

a   The feed size range is the same – efficiency generally decreases with increase in size. Fig. 31.2.3 shows typical efficiencies of bath (drum, cone, etc.) and centrifugal separators (cyclone, Dyna Whirlpool etc.) versus particle size.
It can clearly be seen that, in general, below about 10 mm centrifugal separators are better than baths.

b   The specific gravity of separation is approximately in the same range – the higher the effective specific gravity of separation the greater the probable error, due to the increased medium viscosity. It is shown that the Ep is directly proportional to the specific gravity of separation, all other factors being the same.

c   The feed rate to the unit is same.

d   The vessel parameters and product handling method remain the same.

Table 31.2.3 Values of Independent criteria for different washing units.

Process Unit	D_{50}	E_p	I
Heavy medium bath	1.50	0.02	0.04
Heavy medium cyclone	1.60	0.03	0.05
Jig (25 mm × 10 mm)	1.65	0.06	0.09
(10 mm × 3 mm)	1.70	0.10	0.14
Water washing cyclone	1.65	0.15	0.23

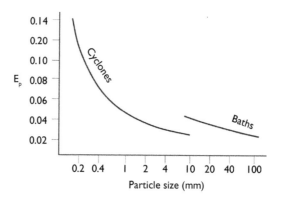

Figure 31.2.3 Effect of particle size on efficiency of Heavy medium separators.

31.3 PLANT EFFICIENCY MEASUREMENT [56]

Processes such as dense medium separations are capable of 'sharp' separations, whereas water-only processes such as jigs are not generally able to effect equally sharp separations. A dense-medium cyclone is therefore said to be more efficient than a jig. In practice, it is often found that even inherently efficient equipment, such as dense-medium vessels and cyclones, does not perform at the expected level of efficiency for a number of reasons. Some of the reasons for this failure to perform at optimum level are:

- Units operating at more than their design capacity
- Intermittent feeding of units
- Unequal feed distribution to a number of units operating in parallel
- Size segregation of the feed coal
- The presence of flat particles, often found in the roof and floor of a coal seam, in the feed coal
- Poor screening of the feed coal, which results in fines being carried over from the screens into the medium and thus increasing the viscosity of the medium
- Unfavourable washability characteristics of the feed coal
- Coal containing a high proportion of fines
- Using the incorrect size grade of magnetite as a dense medium
- Poor state of repair of the equipment
- Insufficient feed pressure at the inlet of a cyclone
- Partial or complete blockage of one of the orifices in a cyclone
- Poor control of the medium density
- Cyclones in a multiple cyclone module not cutting at the same relative density.

Any of the above factors may negatively affect the efficiency of a plant and result in reduction of yield. It is very important that all the equipment in a coal processing plant should operate at the best possible level of efficiency at all times. However, it is not always possible to detect when a unit is operating at reduced levels of efficiency.

If a unit becomes blocked or breaks down, it is usually obvious that there is a problem and corrective action can be taken immediately. There are, however, times when a unit may appear to be functioning normally but in fact there is something wrong, reducing the efficiency of the unit without being noticed. An example of this is the partial blockage of the feed inlet of a cyclone. In such a case, clean coal is being lost without being detected and this situation may continue for extended periods.

It is also possible to lose yield of clean coal even when the equipment is in a good state of working and being operated correctly. This type of situation may arise for a number of reasons, control of medium density and product quality, quality of different size fractions and moisture are some of them.

31.3.1 Control of medium density

Under normal conditions, a fluctuation of the density about the set-point value will occur due to the nature of the control system. In some plants, the variation of density, both below and above the set point, can be relatively large. This may be due to large tank volumes, insufficient amounts of density-control water, poor design of the density-control system or incorrect operation of the system. Although the overall, average density of the medium is the same as the set-point value, yield is lost. The net effect of this is that the product quality is higher than specification for half the time and below it for half of the time. The overall product is still on specification. The larger the variation in quality between the upper and lower limits of the range of qualities produced, the more severe will be the negative effect on the product yield. It is therefore necessary to control the relative density of the medium as accurately as possible and within as narrow a range as possible.

31.3.2 Control of product quality

When coal is produced at a quality that is better than required, yield is lost. On most plants there is a delay of several hours between producing coal and knowing what the quality of the coal produced is. This is due to the process of procuring samples of the coal production, and then drying and analysing these samples.

It is possible to eliminate the delay between the time when the coal is produced and the time when the quality of the coal is known by using on-line analysers. This allows a plant to respond much more quickly to deviations in coal quality and therefore will allow the quality of the coal produced to be controlled within a narrower range and also closer to the target specification.

On-line analysers may be used in conjunction with control software, such as COALTROL and ULTRAMAX to provide accurate control over the quality of the coal produced from a plant.

31.3.3 Quality of different size fractions

Another area where yield may be forfeited is in the control of the quality of coal produced from the differing size fractions in the plant feed. In the case where a coarse coal and a small coal fraction are processed separately, say via a Wemco drum and cyclones respectively, the easiest method of ensuring that the overall combined product is within specification is to produce both the coarse and the small coal products at exactly the same quality. However, this is not the optimal approach in terms of plant yield. In most cases, a higher overall plant yield may be realised by producing the coarse and the small coal at slightly different product qualities. The difference in liberation between the coarse and the small coal very often results in the small coal exhibiting better washability characteristics than the coarse coal. Exploitation of this phenomenon may result in a higher overall yield.

31.3.4   Moisture content

The moisture content of product coal is a very important consideration in the overall efficiency of a coal processing plant. The influence of moisture content on the yield of coal produced can be very large for a higher moisture content in the product coal, the coal must be processed to a higher calorific value to maintain the specified heat value. This has a significant influence on the product yield.

31.4   METHODS TO MEASURE PLANT EFFICIENCY [56]

Ideally, one would like to know the yield that should be obtained from the coal if a product of the correct quality is produced before the coal is processed. Moreover, any deviation from this yield should be signalled and the unit or the reason responsible for this deviation should be identified to allow immediate rectification. Unfortunately, in practice, only limited information is available in this regard. There are, however, some techniques available that may be applied to provide at least some of the information required to control a coal processing plant effectively.

A number of methods, technologies and operating procedures are being used in the coal industry to measure, monitor and control the inputs and outputs of coal processing plants and to attempt to optimise the process. Some of these methods are described below.

31.4.1   Mass meters

In-line conveyor belt mass meters have been used for years to measure the tonnages of coal fed into coal processing plants and the products leaving the plant. Theoretically, mass meters should be able to provide a rapid means of knowing the yield of coal produced since the masses of feed, product and discard coal can be measured. However, a number of factors complicate this measurement, some of which are:

- Inherent inaccuracy of the mass meters, especially at low tonnage rates
- Build-up of coal on the weigh idlers, resulting in faulty readings
- Moisture content of the different products
- Difficulty in calibrating the units.

It may be possible, in conjunction with on-line moisture analysers and personal computers, to use the moisture-corrected masses from mass meters to compute and display the yield of coal produced from a plant.

31.4.2   Measurement of misplaced materials

By taking samples of the coal and discard produced, and performing a single-density float-and-sink analysis, usually at the required set-point density, an indication of the efficiency of the particular unit can be obtained, based on the amount of 'misplaced' material present in the sample. The analysis can be done quite quickly.

A more accurate assessment of plant efficiency is obtained by conducting a float-and-sink analysis on samples of discard coal. However, such an analysis takes longer to complete and in order to assess the results gainfully, the 'acceptable' amount of misplaced material in the sample should be known for comparison. Careful handling of the samples is very important since 'misplaced' material can result from rough handling of the sampling.

31.4.3   Efficiency testing

The most widely used and accepted method for measuring the efficiency of a plant, or a unit within the plant, is to conduct an efficiency test. The test consists of taking samples of the feed, product and refuse from the particular unit to be measured. The product and reject samples are subjected to float-and-sink analysis, using a range of closely spaced density intervals. The ash content of the feed sample, and the float-and-sink fractions of the product and reject samples are determined as detailed in article 20.1. By doing necessary calculations as described in article 31.2, Tromp curve is to be drawn from which a number of parameters, describing the efficiency of the processing unit, can be derived.

Apart from day-to-day control of and troubleshooting at coal processing plants, efficiency testing also serves the following functions:

• To ascertain whether a newly commissioned plant meets the guaranteed specifications given by the contractor who built the plant. The efficiency test conducted for this purpose is known as an 'acceptance test' and is usually a very thorough test carried out in great detail.
• To typify the efficiency of particular processing unit. The results of efficiency tests have been built into computer simulations which are used in forecasting practical plant results from washability data. These results are then used to assist with plant design and with the techno-economic evaluation of alternative plant configurations. The models are also used for day-to-day control by comparing or benchmarking the results obtained on any unit processing a specific raw coal feed with those that would have been obtained on a similar unit (of known performance) processing the same feed coal.

Efficiency tests are labour-intensive and expensive. The results of efficiency tests are often only available after several weeks have elapsed. This obviously reduces the value of the results, especially when the tests are aimed at detecting operational problems.

31.4.4   Tracers

In an effort to overcome the problems associated with conventional efficiency testing, tracers have been used. Tracers are polymer particles to which specific amounts of high relative density filler material have been added to adjust the density of the particles to within the range covered by coal and the impurities found in coal. This range is typically from 1.30 to 2.50. Metal salts and barites are often used for this purpose. By varying the amount of filler material used, particles with a range of densities can be manufactured. Pigments are sometimes added to the tracer particles to render them in bright colours. This makes them easier to detect amongst coal particles.

To determine the efficiency of a processing unit, a number of tracers, covering a range of densities, are introduced into the feed to the unit. The tracer particles are separated within the unit into 'floats' and 'sinks', in the same way that coal would be separated. The tracers are recovered from the float and sink screens and counted. The number of tracers of a certain density recovered from the floats screen, expressed as a percentage of the tracers of that density fed into the unit, provides the partition coefficient for that particular density. Tracers with other densities are evaluated in the same manner. These data are used to construct a partition curve – without the need for any time-consuming laboratory analyses. The number of tracers used for the test is very important as this defines the statistical accuracy of the results. It is customary to use about 10 relative density ranges for efficiency tests. In practice 40 tracers are used per relative density interval. The total number of tracers used per test therefore amounts to between 300 and 400.

The fact that the results obtained from the tracers are available soon after the start of the test makes tracers ideal for troubleshooting and day-to-day control purposes. A disadvantage of tracers is the fact that they have to be found in order to be included in the final count that is used to construct the Tromp curve. In practice, it is very difficult to recover the tracers from the screens, especially if the layer of coal on the screen is relatively thick. The tracers themselves are normally inexpensive enough for their loss not to be a serious problem, but if only a few tracers are recovered then the test results may become statistically meaningless.

When using large tracers, for example larger than 30 mm, the tracers tend to rise to the top of the layer of coal on the vibrating screen due to stratification. This makes the tracers relatively easy to recover by hand. The number of tracers lost is quite low under these conditions and it is possible for tests to be conducted with normal load on the plant. In the case of small tracers, the situation is different and the loss of tracers can be very high. Some tracers can also "hang" in cyclones or may get stuck in chutes or behind weir-bars on screens.

A new type of tracer that utilises radio waves for detection was developed. Each tracer contains a small radio transponder. Each transponder is coded with a unique digital number. The tracer system has been named "Supertracer". The CSIR in South Africa has developed and patented a process that uses radiotracers to measure the efficiency of dense-medium plants on line.

A radio-frequency antenna and reader system is used to detect the tracers when they emerge from the product or reject streams of a dense medium unit. The antenna is mounted over the lip of the screen or may be suspended above the conveyor carrying the product or reject coal from the screen. As each tracer passes underneath the antenna, the electromagnetic radiation from the antenna powers the transponder within the tracer. The transponder then transmits the unique digital code programmed into it to the antenna and reader. The digital code makes it possible to identify each tracer by density and size. This makes it possible to add tracers of different densities and sizes all at the same time. The information from the antenna and reader is fed into a computer running specially developed software to derive a partition curve almost instantaneously.

This greatly enhances the value of the data, as any problems detected within the plant can be rectified immediately. Since the tracers can be detected even when covered by coal or minerals, they can be used under conditions of full plant loading.

The tests can be easily carried out by one person and take only a few minutes to complete. Because the tracers can be detected even when they are covered by coal, they can be used to test the efficiency of a processing unit while the unit is on coal.

Tracers provide a rapid, easy means to determine the efficiency of a processing unit. Tracers are very useful for providing a quick check on the efficiency of any particular processing unit and provide an excellent method for 'troubleshooting'. Tracers are not intended to replace conventional efficiency testing but rather to supplement it.

31.4.5   Strain gauge measurement in chutes

A novel system used for measuring the mass flow rate of coal from individual screens in a coal processing plant consists of an open-ended chute suspended from chains that are connected to a load cell. The chute is fitted with internal baffle plates to ensure that coal passing through it will impact on a surface within the chute. The chute is placed in such a position that all the coal from a screen must pass through it. The coal, by virtue of the internal baffle plates, impacts on the chute and the force is transferred to the load cell. The load cell output is used to indicate the tonnage of coal passing through the chute. The load cell values are calibrated using a series of manual mass rate determinations.

By monitoring the tonnages from individual screens in a plant in this fashion, it is possible to obtain a continuous record of the tonnage produced from individual units. By measuring both the product and reject streams from a unit, the yield from that unit can be continuously monitored. Proper calibration of the system is required on a routine basis. One problem that was reported during testing of the system is that coal will tend to build up in the measuring chute and this could affect the accuracy of the mass determination. Non-stick surfaces, such as high-density plastics, could be used to line the chutes and thus minimise this problem.

31.4.6   On-line ash and moisture monitors

Most plants control the quality of product produced by taking regular samples of the coal, analysing the samples and then adjusting the relative density of the circulating medium according to the results of the analysis. This method works quite well when the raw coal feed into the plant is relatively consistent. Variations in quality are usually not large and therefore only minor adjustments to the medium density are occasionally required.

When variable coals are being processed, however, the situation becomes more problematic. Coal quality often changes rapidly and frequent adjustments to the medium density may be required. The delay between sampling of the coal and receiving the result back from the laboratory may be as long as three to four hours. Changes in the raw coal quality can occur during this period and control of the product quality can become very difficult.

On-line quality monitors can assist greatly in this area of product quality control. Different types of on-line analyser are available. The type of on-line ash monitor with the lowest cost is that utilising dual-gamma technology. The measurement of ash is only independent of the thickness of the coal layer above a certain minimum layer thickness. This thickness is approximately 100 mm but varies for different types and particle sizes of coal. Provided the minimum layer thickness of coal is presented to the ash monitor, these units are capable of sufficient accuracy to be used for quality control in coal processing plants. Ash monitors of the dual-gamma type cannot replace a plant's control laboratory but can supplement it very successfully.

A more sophisticated, and very much more expensive, type of on-line analyser uses prompt gamma neutron activation analysis (PGNAA) technology to determine all the major elements in coal. These types of analyser can be used to measure not only the ash content of the coal but also sulphur, carbon, hydrogen, nitrogen, chlorine and the major elements contained in the ash of the coal. A separate microwave moisture monitor is used to measure the moisture content of the coal. The heat value and other properties of the coal can be computed from the available data.

The latest addition to the range of on-line analysers is X-ray diffraction (XRD) monitors. These units can be positioned directly over a conveyor belt and have the advantage that no radioactive sources are used. Like the PGNAA monitors, they measure a number of coal quality parameters. A Coalscan 9000 has been successfully employed at a coal-loading terminal in Australia to measure the quality of coal during loading operations.

The relative roles of the monitor and the laboratory should, however, be clearly defined. The on-line monitor is used as a control and an early warning device. The quality of coal produced from the plant can be obtained from the monitor continuously, and almost immediately, after the coal leaves the plant. These results can be used to adjust the medium relative densities to ensure that the quality of coal produced remains within the specified limits. The role of the laboratory then becomes one of 'monitoring the monitor'. Samples of the coal production are taken and analysed to ensure that the on-line monitor's calibration remains valid.

31.4.7   Automatic density control

The output from an on-line monitor can be used to adjust the relative density of the washing medium in a plant automatically in order to control the quality of coal produced within narrower limits than is possible with manual control.

COALTROL is a computer program developed jointly by the CSIRO and BHP in Australia. It is used to control the washing medium density in a coal preparation plant in order to maintain the quality of coal produced from the plant within a narrow range. The system uses the data obtained from on-line quality monitors. It is claimed that a 5% increase in plant yield was achieved due to the use of COALTROL.

31.4.8   Control of d50

Heavy medium cyclones with a diameter of 600 mm are used extensively in coal preparation plants in South Africa. Because these cyclones can process only about 80 tons per hour of raw coal each, they are used in modules in which two or more cyclones are operate in parallel. It is often found that the cyclones in a module do not operate at the same cut-point density, or 'd50'. This may be due to uneven wear of the cyclones, uneven feed distribution to the cyclones or any one of a number of reasons. When this happens, yield of clean coal is lost.

BHP in Australia has carried out research into methods that can be used to control the cut-point densities of different cyclones in a module. It was found that there is a correlation between the relative density of the cyclone overflow medium and the cut-point density for a cyclone. Using conventional density-measurement devices and a U-tube arrangement, continuous measurement of the cyclone overflow densities is possible. By measuring the overflow medium density of individual cyclones, and controlling the density of the feed medium to each cyclone, it is possible to control the cut-point density.

By monitoring the cut-point densities of individual cyclones in a single module, it is still possible to correct for deviations, even if such corrections cannot be made by adjusting the medium density. Often, simply changing worn spigots can correct the situation. Unless one is aware that there is a difference in the cut-point densities, however, the situation may not be corrected for some time.

31.4.9 Control of medium viscosity and contamination

Contamination of the washing medium by fine coal or non-magnetic material occurs to some extent in the circuits of all plants. If the contamination is not controlled, the medium will eventually become viscous and this will have a negative effect on the separation efficiency of the plant. Contamination of the medium is due mostly to inefficient de-sliming of the feed coal and to worn screen panels on the drain area of the drain-and-rinse screens.

The amount of contamination in the medium can be controlled by bleeding a portion of the medium to the magnetic separators for cleaning. The degree of contamination of the circulating medium in a plant is difficult to estimate, especially for less-experienced plant operators. However, it is possible, using a combination of density gauges and Ramsey coils, to measure the level of contamination in the circulating medium. Once a measurement is available, corrective action can be taken if required.

It can be concluded that no single method is yet available which will provide a continuous, real-time report on the status of a coal preparation plant. There are, however, a number of separate actions, procedures and methods that can be employed to provide the necessary data for effectively controlling a plant. Some of these methods are already in use at some plants.

31.5 ILLUSTRATIVE EXAMPLES

Illustrative Example 31.5.1: *Float and sink analysis data of a feed coal shown in Table 31.5.1 has been washed in a Heavy Medium Separation Unit at 1.50 specific gravity.*

Table 31.5.1 Float and sink analysis data for illustrative example 31.5.1.

Specific gravity	Wt% of sink coal	Ash%
1.70	19.1	76.1
1.65	3.2	70.4
1.60	2.6	65.0
1.55	3.9	52.0
1.50	4.2	35.5
1.45	4.2	24.7
1.40	4.7	19.4
1.35	8.6	16.2
1.35 (float)	49.5	8.3

Calculate the ash percent of feed coal. What is the yield of clean coal that can be expected from HMS? What would be the ash percent of clean coal and rejects?

Solution:

It is clear that the given data was obtained by doing sink and float analysis starting from 1.70 specific gravity. Hence it is to be converted as float and sink analysis starting from 1.35 specific gravity. The first three columns of the Table 31.5.1.1 is so converted data. Cumulative wt% of floats for whole coal, Cumulative wt% of floats from 1.35 floats to 1.50 floats, from 1.55 floats to 1.70 sinks, Ash product values for whole coal, Cumulative ash product up to 1.50 floats and 1.50 floats to 1.70 sinks are also calculated and shown in the Table 31.5.1.1.

Table 31.5.1.1 Calculated values for illustrative example 31.5.1.

Specific gravity	Wt% of float coal	Ash%	Cum wt%	Cum wt%	Ash product	Cum.ash product
1.35	49.5	8.3	49.5		410.85	
1.40	8.6	16.2	58.1		139.32	
1.45	4.7	19.4	62.8		91.18	
1.50	4.2	24.7	67.0	67.0	103.74	745.09
1.55	4.2	35.5	71.2		149.10	
1.60	3.9	52.0	75.1		202.80	
1.65	2.6	65.0	77.7		169.00	
1.70	3.2	70.4	80.9		225.28	
1.70 (sink)	19.1	76.1	100.0	33.0	1453.51	2199.69
					2944.78	

Ash percent in coal sample = 2944.78/100 = 29.45%
Yield of clean coal   = 67.00%
Ash percent in clean coal = 745.09/67.0 = 11.12%
Ash percent in rejects   = 2199.69/33.0 = 66.66%

Illustrative example 31.5.2: *A coal washery cleans the coal stock by Dense media separation using magnetite-water suspension as the medium. A sample of coal was tested using the float and sink experiment and the data obtained is shown in Table 31.5.2.*

Table 31.5.2 Float and sink experiment data for illustrative example 31.5.2.

Sp.gr.	Wt% of coal floated	Ash% in floated coal
1.287	5.52	0.91
1.314	19.16	3.17
1.341	16.22	8.39
1.377	20.58	12.75
1.423	19.12	14.67
1.461	9.97	21.44
1.461 (sink)	9.43	27.73

If the ultimate ash content of clean coal should not exceed 6%, determine the specific gravity of the medium to be used and the percent recovery.

Solution:

Cumulative wt% and cumulative ash% are calculated and shown in the Table 31.5.2.1.

Table 31.5.2.1 Calculated values for illustrative example 31.5.2.

Sp.gr.	Wt% of coal floated	Ash% in floated coal	Cum.wt% coal floated	Ash product	Cum. Ash product	Cum ash%
1	2	3	4	5 = 2 × 3	6	7 = 6/4
1.287	5.52	0.91	5.52	05.02	5.02	0.91
1.314	19.16	3.17	24.68	60.74	65.76	2.67
1.341	16.22	8.39	40.90	136.09	201.85	4.94
1.377	20.58	12.75	61.48	262.40	464.25	7.55
1.423	19.12	14.67	80.60	280.49	744.74	9.24
1.461	9.97	21.44	90.57	213.76	958.50	10.58
1.461 (sink)	9.43	27.73	100.00	261.49	1219.99	12.19

Total floats ash curve and yield gravity curve are drawn and shown in Figure 31.5.2.

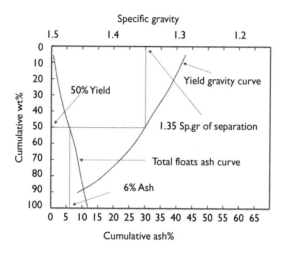

Figure 31.5.2 Total floats ash curve & Yield gravity curve for illustrative example 31.5.2

From the graph, Yield is read corresponding to 6% ash and it is 50%. The specific gravity of separation for this 50% yield is read as 1.35.

∴   Specific gravity of the medium to be used is 1.35
        Percent recovery is 50%

Illustrative Example 31.5.3: *A Jigging plant is intended to treat coal of –1+1/2" size. During the trial work, several parameters have been changed and set the plant to obtain clean coal of 18% ash. For a 250 TPD capacity, 100 tonnes of refuge material is obtained when a coal of 32% ash is treated. What is the percent ash in refuge? Calculate yield reduction factor.*

Solution:
Tonnage of coal fed = F = 250 tons/day
Tonnage of refuge obtained = T = 100 tons/day
Tonnage of clean coal obtained = C = F – T = 250–100 = 150 tons/day

Percent ash in feed = f = 32%
Percent ash in clean coal = c = 18%
Let percent ash in refuge = t

$$Ff = Cc + Tt$$
⇒ $250 \times 32 = 150 \times 18 + 100t$
⇒ $t = 53\%$

∴ Percent ash in refuge = 53%

Yield reduction factor = $\dfrac{F-C}{f-c} = \dfrac{250-150}{32-18} = 7.1$

Illustrative Example 31.5.4: *70 gm of –200 mesh coal of 30% ash is subjected to oil agglomeration process at 10% pulp density. First 2% by weight of diesel oil is added and pulp is conditioned for 10 minutes at 700 rpm. Later 15% by weight of furnace oil is added and agitated for 15 minutes (agglomeration period) at 1200 rpm by adding sufficient amount of water. At the end, whole contents are screened on 30 mesh and agglomerates are removed and analysed. The agglomerates weighs 49 gm and their ash percent is 15%. Calculate the yield reduction factor.*

Solution:

Feed to the oil agglomeration process = F = 70 gm
Agglomerated clean coal obtained = C = 49 gm
Tailing from agglomeration process = F–C = 70–49 = 21 gm

Ash% of feed = f = 30%
Ash% of agglomerates = c = 15%

$$\text{Yield Reduction Factor} = \frac{F - C}{f - c} = \frac{70 - 49}{30 - 185} = 1.4$$

Illustrative Example 31.5.5: *When a coal of 29.2% ash is washed, an yield of 18.5% ash and a refuse of 45.8% ash is obtained. If the theoretical recovery is 63.3% at the same ash level, estimate the performance of the washery.*

Solution:

Percent ash in feed = f = 29.2%
Percent ash in clean coal = c = 18.5%
Percent ash in tailing = t = 45.8%

Let the feed to the washery be 100 tons.

$F = C + T \Rightarrow 100 = C + T$
$Ff = Cc + Tt \Rightarrow 100 \times 29.2 = 18.5C + 45.8T$

Solving these two equations gives C = 60.8 tons
The plant yield of clean coal = 60.8 tons
Theoretical recovery = 63.3%

$$\text{Fraser and Yancey efficiency (Organic efficiency)} = \frac{60.8}{63.3} \times 100 = 96.0\%$$

Illustrative Example 31.5.6: *A Coal with 49.9% ash was treated in a Baum Jig to obtain clean coal and refuse. Samples from clean coal and refuse were collected and analysed for their ash and found as 35.8% and 65.1% respectively. Float and sink analysis of clean coal and refuse are shown in Table 31.5.6.*

Table 31.5.6 Float and sink analysis of clean coal and refuse for illustrative example 31.5.6.

Sp.gr.	Floats of Clean coal	Floats of Refuse
1.40	12.50	0.50
1.45	9.40	0.60
1.50	9.50	0.80
1.55	12.40	1.00
1.60	12.00	1.50
1.65	9.00	2.50
1.70	6.90	4.00
1.80	10.70	11.30
1.90	4.90	8.40
2.00	5.50	12.40
2.10	3.40	11.50
2.20	3.80	45.50
	100.00	100.00

Draw the tromp curve and determine specific gravity of separation, Ecart probable and Imperfection for this Baum jig operation.

Solution:

Ash% in feed   = 49.9
Ash% in cleans = 35.8
Ash% in refuse = 65.1

Yield percentage of cleans

$$= \frac{\text{Ash \% in refuse} - \text{Ash \% in feed}}{\text{Ash \% in refuse} - \text{Ash \% in clean coal}} \times 100 = \frac{65.1 - 49.9}{65.1 - 35.8} \times 100 = 51.90$$

Percentage of refuse = 100–51.90 = 48.10

The necessary calculations for drawing Tromp curve were done and shown in the Table 31.5.6.1.

Table 31.5.6.1 Calculated values for Tromp Curve for illustrative example 31.5.6.

Sp.gr.	Floats of Cleans	Floats of Refuse	Cleans % feed	Refuse % feed	Calculated feed	Mean Sp.gr	Partition Coefficient for cleans
1.40	12.50	0.50	6.49	0.24	6.73	1.400	96.43
1.45	9.40	0.60	4.88	0.29	5.17	1.425	94.39
1.50	9.50	0.80	4.93	0.38	5.31	1.475	92.84
1.55	12.40	1.00	6.44	0.48	6.92	1.525	93.06
1.60	12.00	1.50	6.23	0.72	6.95	1.575	89.64
1.65	9.00	2.50	4.67	1.20	5.87	1.625	79.56
1.70	6.90	4.00	3.58	1.92	5.50	1.675	65.09
1.80	10.70	11.30	5.55	5.44	10.99	1.750	50.50
1.90	4.90	8.40	2.54	4.04	6.58	1.850	38.60
2.00	5.50	12.40	2.85	5.96	8.81	1.950	32.35
2.10	3.40	11.50	1.76	5.53	7.29	2.050	24.14
2.20	3.80	45.50	1.98	21.90	23.88	2.150	08.29
	100.00	100.00	51.90	48.10	100.00		

Figure 31.5.6 shows the Tromp curve drawn with the values of the table 31.5.6.1.

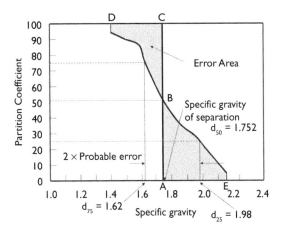

Figure 31.5.6 Tromp curve for illustrative example 31.5.6.

From the tromp curve, specific gravity of separation, $d_{50} = 1.752$
$$d_{75} = 1.62$$
$$d_{25} = 1.98$$

Ecart probable $E_p = \frac{1}{2}(d_{25} - d_{75}) = \frac{1.98 - 1.62}{2} = 0.18$

Imperfection $I = \frac{E_p}{d_{50} - 1} = \frac{0.18}{1.752 - 1.0} = 0.239$

31.6   PROBLEMS FOR PRACTICE

31.6.1: *Float and sink data of a coal is shown in Table 31.6.1. This coal is washed in three product chance cone employing 1.5 and 1.7 specific gravities. Assuming 100% efficiency, calculate the yield of cleans, middlings and rejects. Also calculate their ash percentages.*

Table 31.6.1 Float and sink data for problem 31.6.1.

Specific gravity	Wt% of coal floated	Ash%
1.40	12.35	15.28
1.50	34.96	22.08
1.60	25.04	33.17
1.70	3.45	42.37
1.80	13.06	48.69
1.90	2.61	53.15
1.90 *(sink)*	8.53	76.03

[Yield 47.31%, 28.49%, 24.20%, Ash 20.31%, 34.28%, 58.81%]

31.6.2: *When a coal of 31% ash is treated in a froth flotation cell, a froth of 15% ash and a tailing of 55% ash is obtained. Calculate the percent yield of clean coal.*
[60%]

31.6.3: *Raw coal feed to a coal washery has the following float and sink analysis as shown in Table 31.6.3.*

Table 31.6.3 Float and sink analysis of raw coal for problem 31.6.3.

Sp.gr	Yield%	Ash%
below 1.25	1.5	2.6
+1.25–1.35	25.9	7.3
+1.35–1.45	38.4	20.0
+1.45–1.55	15.2	26.7
+1.55–1.65	7.7	37.1
+1.65–1.75	2.2	43.2
above 1.75	9.1	57.1

On washing in a plant, a clean coal of 18% ash at an yield of 82% is obtained. Evaluate its performance.   *[Efficiency 97.6%]*

Chapter 32

Coal washing practice in India

Indian Gondwana coals of drift origin, formed some 225 to 275 million years ago, are different in their physico-chemical characteristics from the carboniferous coals of Northern Hemisphere deposited 50–100 million years earlier than Gondwana coals due to environment of deposition and post-depositional features. The original plant material, which were later transformed into coal, were transported by rivers to a distance, carrying along other impurities after which coalification process took place. As a result the coal matter is finely disseminated with mineral matter causing deterioration in its quality during its formation stage itself. Hence these coals become difficult-to-wash. The extraneous ash which gets mixed with coal, mostly during mining can be removed more easily. The inherent ash of Indian coals cannot be taken off easily because it is embedded in the coal matrix and thus results into more near gravity materials.

32.1   COKING COAL WASHING

Coking coals are used for making coke for steel industry. The ash percent in coal for making coke for use in blast furnace of steel plants should be within 18%. The higher ash adversely affects the productivity of blast furnace. It has been observed that 1% increase in the ash results in the reduction of the blast furnace productivity by 3–6%. Prior to 1950, the requirement of coal for steel making in India was very small and the required quantity and quality of coal was available directly from the mines. The method of mining was predominantly manual and handpicking which permitted careful selection of good quality coal. Gradual depletion of high quality coal seams and adoption of modern mechanized mining methods led to the production of low quality coals with higher dirt. Coking coal requirements for the Indian steel industry are estimated to be around 67 Mt in the year 2016–17.

In 1938, after carrying out washability studies on Jharia coals, A. Farquhar of M/s Tata Iron and Steel Company (TISCO) found that Jamadoba, Malkera and Bhowra Coals can be washed economically. After further studies during 1938 to 1940, TISCO established West Bokaro Washery in 1951 and Jamadoba Washery in 1952 to meet the requirements of the fast expanding steel making capacity. Thus Coal washing technology was introduced in India by the pioneering efforts of TISCO.

In both West Bokaro and Jamadoba Washeries, upper seam coals of underground mine of Jharia Coal Field were crushed to 75 mm and size fraction +25 mm was washed by Chance Cone process. The Sinks were further crushed for liberation and their recycling facility was also incorporated. Once the efficiency of coal washing was demonstrated by these two coal washeries, attention has been directed to the efficient methods of mining and better preparation of coal in India. In addition, the meager reserves of metallurgical quality coals in India force the beneficiation of low grade coals of higher ash content to yield the coal of 15% to 17% ash. Apart from the ash reduction, a consistent clean coal product is essential for improved efficiency in blast furnace operation. All these factors together prompted the coal washing and a chain of coal washeries came up in India.

In view of the low average production from the individual mines and to meet the increasing requirement of coal for metallurgical use, central washeries have been planned and installed. A washery which receives coal from different number of collieries of varied washability and coking characteristics is known as **Central washery.** A washery which receives coal from one or two collieries of the same nature is known as **Pit-head washery.** The washing scheme adopted in central washery is known as composite washing scheme and is complicated when compared to the washing scheme of pit-head washery which is simple.

Early washeries included Chance Cones constructed by Fraser and Chambers and Baum Jigs constructed by Acco and McNally. These early processes developed into more modern systems based on Dense Media separation and Batac Jigs. Also common are Baum jigs which are used for deshaling prior to cleaning. There are a broad range of the types of processes and configurations adopted in India. Each plant was individually designed taking into consideration the wide variation in raw coal quality and washability characteristics. There is little rationalization of types of equipment either within plants or throughout the industry.

Different schemes have been adopted for different washeries to tackle various problems and to upgrade a wide variety of coking coal feed. The washing schemes which have so far been introduced in the existing coking coal washeries can be classified into three broad groups which are outlined below:

Group I: The washing scheme relating to this group covers mostly coals having comparatively easy washability characteristics. These ROM coals are initially crushed to 75 mm and then classified into −75 mm + 25mm or −75 mm + 13 mm and small size −25 mm + 0.5 mm or −13 mm + 0.5 mm fractions for treatment in H.M. baths and that of small coals in Jigs or H.M. cyclone. In some installations, the coarse sized sinks separated from H.M. baths are crushed and rewashed in H.M. cyclone to recover additional cleans. The washeries at Bhojudih, Durgapur (SAIL) and Kargali as well as the modified washeries at Jamadoba and West Bokaro more or less conform to this group. Kargali washery was later converted to non-coking coal washery. Durgapur washery was closed.

Group II: The treatment under this group is similar to that of the first group except that a pre-washer is incorporated to eliminate the free dirt e.g. Dugda I and Patherdih washeries. Dugda I washery was later converted to non-coking coal washery. The Patherdih washery was closed.

Group III: This scheme is meant for the upgrading of difficult-to-wash coals which are required to be crushed to below 20 mm or 13 mm prior to washing. Whenever so warranted, the whole coal or the fraction above 20 mm

Table 32.1.1 The details of the coking coal washeries in India.

Sl No	Name of the washery	Company	Coalfield/ Location	Commissioning yr	Capacity mtpy	Washing equipment Particle sizes in mm	Slurry treatment	Final products with size in mm
Prime coking coal washeries								
1	Jamadoba	TISCO	Jharia	1952	1.71	HM Cyclone (15–0.5)	Flotation	Cleans (15–0) Middlings (15–0.5) Refuse (15–0.5)
2	Bhelatand	TISCO	Sijua	N.A	0.86	HM Cyclone (20–0.5)	Flotation	Cleans (20–0) Middlings (20–0.5) Refuse (20–0.5)
3	Bhojudih	BCCL	Jharia	1962	2.00	Leebar bath (75–25) Baum Jig (25–0.5)	Flotation	Cleans (75–0) Middlings (75–0.5) Refuse (75–0)
4	Chasnalla	IISCO	Jharia	1968	2.00	Two Stage Leebar bath (75–20) Batac Jig (20–0.5)	Spiral, Flotation	Cleans (75–0) Middlings (75–0.5) Refuse (75–0)
5	Dugda-II	BCCL	Jharia	1968	2.40	HM Cyclone (13–0.5) Rewashing Komag Jig (13–0)	Flotation	Cleans (13–0) Middlings (13–0) Refuse (13–0)
6	Sudamudih	BCCL	Jharia	1981	2.00	Two Stage HM Cyclone (37–0.5)	Flotation	Cleans (37–0) Middlings (37–0.5) Refuse (37–0)
7	Moonidih	BCCL	Jharia	1983	2.00	Two Stage HM Cyclone (37–0.5)	Dewatering	Cleans (37–0) Middlings (37–0) Refuse (37–0)
8	Madhuban	BCCL	Jharia	1998	1.50	Batac Jig (13–0.5)	Flotation	Cleans (13–0) Middlings (13–0.5) Refuse (13–0)

(Continued)

Table 32.1.1 (Continued)

Medium Coking Coal Washeries

Sl No	Name of the washery	Company	Coalfield/ Location	commission ing yr	Capa city mtpy	Washing equipment Particle sizes in mm	Slurry treatment	Final products with size in mm
9	Kathara	CCL	East Bokaro	1969	3.00	Prewashing; Drew Boy (75–13) HM Cyclone (13–0.5)	Flotation	Cleans (13–0) Middlings (13–0) Refuse (75–13)
10	Swang	CCL	East Bokaro	1978	0.75	Prewashing; Baum Jig (80–20) HM Cyclone (20–0.5)	Dewatering	Cleans (20–0) Middlings (20–0) Refuse (80–20)
11	West Bokaro –II	TISCO	West Bokaro	1982	1.80	Two Stage HM Cyclone (15–0.5)	Flotation	Cleans (15–0) Middlings (15–0.5) Refuse (15–0)
12	West Bokaro– III	TISCO	West Bokaro	N.A	2.10	Two Stage HM Cyclone (15–0.5)	Flotation	Cleans (15–0) Middlings (15–0.5) Refuse (15–0)
13	Nandan	WCL	Pench Kanhan	1984	1.20	Komag Jig (75–10) Komag Jig (10–0.5)	Flotation	Cleans (75–0) Middlings (75–0) Refuse (75–0.5)
14	Rajrappa	CCL	Ramgarh	1987	3.00	Batac Jig (80–13) Batac Jig (13–0.5) Rewashing HM Cyclone (10–0.5)	Flotation	Cleans (80–0) Middlings (80–0.5) Refuse (80–0)
15	Mahuda	BCCL	Jharia	1990	0.63	HM Cyclone (25–0.5) Middling Rewashing Jigging (25–0.5)	Flotation	Cleans (25–0) Middlings (25–0.5) Refuse (25–0)
16	Kedla	CCL	West Bokaro	1997	2.60	Batac Jigs for coarse & small coal, HM Cyclone	Flotation	N.A

or 13 mm is first deshaled and the floats crushed and retreated for the recovery of cleans and middlings. In this case, the fraction above 0.5 mm is treated in HM cyclones and the slurry below 0.5mm in water only cyclones or flotation cells. Dugda II, Kathara, Swang, and all the washeries recently commissioned fall under this group.

A total of 23 coking coal washeries were installed in India. Coal India Limited had 19 washeries and the rest four washeries are of TATA Group of companies. Over the years, reserves of good quality coal have been depleted in the neighboring mines resulting in radical deterioration in raw coal feed quality and characteristics. Several modification attempts were made and some are in progress to deal with the problem. But on date few of the washeries are closed and some were converted to non-coking coal washeries. Table 32.1.1 shows the details of the 16 coking coal washeries presently under operation in India.

In majority of the washeries, when they were installed and operated, the coal was washed by Heavy Medium Separation. This was because of the accuracy of separation at any predetermined specific gravity within the range of 1.2–2.50 and continuous maintenance of pre-selected value of specific gravity within ± 0.005 of its value, which are the salient features of heavy medium separation. This accuracy of separation is all the more essential in view of the high percentage (30%) of near gravity materials in Indian coals.

Out of six BCCL washeries, **Bhojudih** washery, an oldest central washery, is most successful coking coal washery because of easy washability characteristics of coal and the design and construction made by the Belgium Company incorporated HM Bath for 75–25 mm coarse coal and Jigs for smalls worked well. Fig. 32.1.1 shows the Simplified flowsheet of Bhojudih Coal Washery.

In **Dugda-II** washery of BCCL, another central washery, raw coal is reduced to −13 mm, deslimed at 0.5 mm and washed in HM cyclones. The feed ash is 24–28% and yield of cleans is about 50% at 17% ash. The dirty slurry coming out of the Cyclone sinks' rinsing screen is fed to a series of Hydrocyclones and the underflow is dried by solid bowl centrifuge. Later Komag jig is used for rewashing. **Moonidih** washery of BCCL, a pit head washery, is based on two stages of HM cyclones for the principal separation. All the coal is crushed to −37 mm, deslimed at 0.5 mm, and gravity fed to two stages of HM cyclones produce clean coal and middlings. **Madhuban** pit head washery was originally designed for washing coking coal of 13–0.5 mm size in Batac Jigs. Due to non-availability of Coking Coal because of stoppage of Block-II OCP, the washery was temporarily converted for washing Non-coking coal which has been reverted back to washing coking coal again from October 2008. In **Mahuda** pit head washery, raw coal is crushed to −25 mm and washed in HM cyclones. Middlings are rewashed by Jigging.

Sudamdih washery was the first indigenously-built pit head coal washery in India. Except magnetic separators used for preparation of magnetite medium for HM Cyclones, centrifuges and few pumps, the entire equipment was from indigenous sources. The following are some of the outstanding features of this washery:

1   Installation of a full sized rotary breaker of 3.6 metre diameter for crushing, screening and de-shaling of coarser fraction of ROM coal.
2   Installation of two stage HM Cyclone washers with top feed size of 37 mm first time in India.

3   The first washery in the Jharia coalfield to include a slurry beneficiation system
    with flotation units.
4   Introduction of an experimental oleo-flotation circuit to study the commercial
    feasibility of this indigenous technology patented by Indian scientists.
5   The washery provides adequate safeguards for pre-concentration of low grade
    magnetite before the ground magnetite is fed to the heavy medium circuit.
6   The streamlined set-up of the individual groups of units in respective floors with
    adequate space is quite attractive from the maintenance point of view.
7   In structural features and excellence, this washery can compare well with any
    other good washery in the world.

Figure 32.1.2 shows the process flowsheet of Sudamdih washery.
    Rajrappa and **Kedla** washeries of CCL use Batac jigs for washing coarse and
small coal. The middlings from the coarse coal Batac jig are crushed, mixed with
middlings of small coal Batac jig and rewashed in a HM Cyclones. Pre-washing is
carried out by **Kathara** and **Swang** pit head washeries of CCL. Kathara washery
uses Drew boy bath for coal of 75–13 mm size whereas Swang washery uses Baum
Jig for coal of 80–20 mm size. Washing of smalls is done by HM Cyclones. **Chas-nalla** washery of IISCO wash the coal by two stage Leebar bath of 75–20 mm size

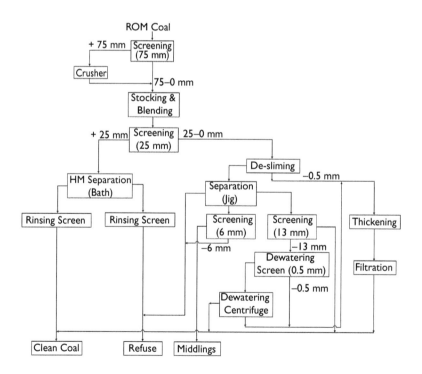

Figure 32.1.1 Simplified Process Flowsheet of Bhojudih Coal Washery.

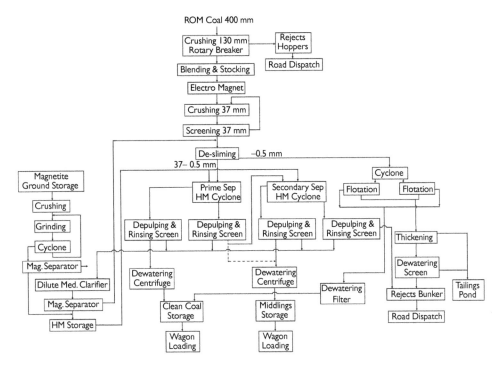

Figure 32.1.2 Simplified Process Flowsheet of Sudamdih Coal Washery.

coal and Batac jig for 20–0.5 mm coal. A secondary HM Bath operating at high gravity rewashes the primary HM Bath's sinks to recover sweetened middlings. Thus, the real rejects have very high ash making it suitable for U/G sand stowing. Subsequently, spirals are also installed to reduce the load on Jigs, by feeding the coarser fines (3 mm–0.4mm) to spirals. **Nandan** washery is the only washery of WCL. ROM coal is crushed to 75 mm and screened at 10 mm. Both the coarse (75–10 mm) and small coals (10–0.5 mm) are washed in Komag jigs with usual desliming at 0.5 mm. What is unique in Nandan Washery is the automatic sampling, sample preparation, even up to bottling in size −3 mm, by a series of crushers, dividers, etc, untouched by human hand.

At present, the prime coking coal of Jharia collieries of Tata Steel is treated in two captive washeries, namely Jamadoba and Bhelatand. **Jamadoba** washery, the second oldest washery in India was treating only −75 + 8 mm fraction, in the chance cone gravity process. The fine coal (−8 mm) were used directly. The HM Cyclone unit was installed at Jamadoba Washery in the early seventies to treat −8 + 0.5 mm coal. Fine coal slurry of −0.5 mm size is dewatered and added to the cleans. Fig. 32.1.3 shows the detailed Process Flowsheet of Jamadoba Coal Washery as adopted on 1979.

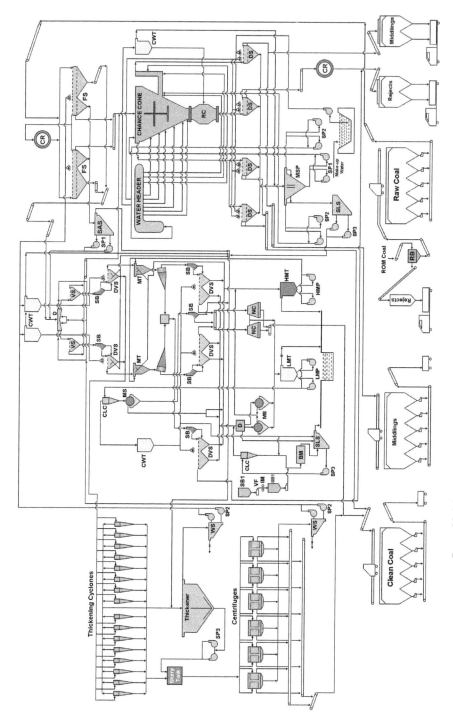

Figure 32.1.3 Detailed Process Flowsheet of Jamadoba Coal Washery as of 1979.

The following are the names of the equipment as labeled in the detailed process flowsheet of Jamadoba Coal Washery:

RB – Rotary Breaker	CR – Toothed Rolls Crusher
FS – Feed Shaker	SAS – Sand Sump
CWT – Circulating Water Tank	RC – Refuse Chamber
DS – De-sanding Screen	MSP – Main Sump
SLS – Slurry Sump	D – Distributor
VS – Vibrating Screen	SB – De-sliming Sieve Bend
DVS – De-sliming Vibrating Screen	MT – Mixing Tank
HMC – Heavy Media Cyclone	NC – Nael Centrifuge
HMT – Heavy Media Tank	LMT – Light Media Tank
HMP – Heavy Media Pump	LMP – Light Media Pump
CLC – Classifying Cyclone	MS – Magnetic Separator
SB1 – Storage Bin	VF – Vibrating Feeder
IM – Impactor	BM – Ball Mill
WS – Water Sump	SP1 – Sand Pump
SP2 – Circulating Water Pump	SP3 – Slurry Pump

Continuous deterioration of the washability characteristics of the mined coal and poor performance of chance cone, chance cones were replaced by HM cyclones in 1986 and coal was washed in two circuits. In the coarse circuit −15 mm + 0.5 mm coal was washed in two stages while the fine coal of −0.5 mm was treated in froth floatation cells. **Bhelatand** washery treats coarse coal (20–0.5 mm), of about 80% of feed coal, in HM Cyclones and fines (−0.5 mm) in flotation circuit.

West Bokaro I washery is not in operation now. The current **West Bokaro** washeries (West Bokaro II and III) are designed to reduce Ash from 36% to 17% at a yield of 38%. Both the washeries crush the ROM coal to about 15 mm and the fraction −15 + 0.5 mm is washed in two stage HM Cyclones, whereas the coal fines are washed in flotation cells. The primary product of West Bokaro is the metallurgical grade coal (also called coking coal), for Coke Ovens, which converts coal into coke for use in the Blast Furnaces.

Coal washeries did not initially include fines treatment circuits. The raw coal fines were simply blended with the washed coarser coals to give steel grade clean coals. With fast depletion of the good quality coals, the quality of coal fines has deteriorated to a great extent and it has become practically impossible to maintain the quality of washed coal at desired level, while mixing the coal fines directly with the clean coal.

The generation of coal fines in the washeries not only increased in quantity but its quality also deteriorated due to the feed from lower horizons and opencast mines. Due to non-availability of the coal fines treatment circuits, the substantial quantities of fines were discharged to nearby ponds and lagoons, there by polluting the surroundings. The problem was taken up by the coal companies and coal fines beneficiation circuits were installed in most of the coking coal washeries in India after 1980.

In Moonidih and Swang washeries, fines treatment circuits are installed with incorporation of Water only cyclones. Flotation circuit is the fines treatment circuits in all other washeries. Flotation plant of chasnalla washery is the first flotation plant where a U-tube type Mass Flow meter was installed to monitor the flow and solid content of the slurry, so as to proportion the reagents dose systematically. Most of the existing coal flotation circuits are unable to run under high efficiency besides being responsible in loosing higher amount of coaly matter through tailings. The ash content of tailings varies from 45 to 50%.

It was observed that the general instability and overall poor performance of the flotation plant was due to:

- Variation in pulp density of feed slurry
- Variation in quantity of slurry (cum/min) from thickener underflow
- Improper conditioning
- Inconsistency and poor quality of frother
- No provision for multiple dosing
- Less solids content and higher proportion of ultra fine particles (−0.053 mm) in concentrate
- Poor recovery of cakes from vacuum filter

The fine coal beneficiation circuits in most of the public sector coal beneficiation plants are not being operated due to various constraints like insufficient poor quality of fines, low recovery of desired quality etc. In short, it may be stated that the coal fines treating circuits in India are not producing desired quantity and quality of clean concentrates for their useful utilization in metallurgical industries.

The real breakthrough in utilizing high ash difficult-to-wash but sufficiently matured (Ro = 1.15 to 1.25 or even 1.3 and low Sulphur) Gondwana coals was the concept of limiting Characteristic ash at the point of cut to about 25%, beyond which the individual coal particles lose their intrinsic coking property. This is a universally proven fact, even in Europe or America, the limiting Characteristic ash content at the point of cut for Steel Plant use is at the same level. That means all the particles having Characteristic Ash <25%, included in cleans, contribute to the coking propensity. If the coal particles of > 25% ash are included in cleans even if the overall ash content is 17% in India or 8 to 9% in Europe or USA, those particles will not have required coking property. Hence such particles are to be eliminated from cleans before use.

32.1.1   Low volatile coking coals

Availability of good quality coking coal (with low ash%) is scarce in India. The practice till now was to take up washing of coal up to 35% ash content (Washery Grade IV) and coal with higher ash% was being linked/supplied to other consumers as the washing of such coal would have given a very low yield resulting into very high cost of clean coal. To conserve the scarce indigenous resource of coking coal, it has become imperative to use such coals also for the steel industry. These coals are termed as Non Linked Washery (NLW) coal or Low Volatile High Rank (LVHR) coking coal and they generally occur in lower seams (combined seam V/ VI/ VII/ VIII and even seam IV, III, II) of Jharia Coalfield and Karo group of seams (IV to XI) in East Bokaro Coalfield.

The lower seam coals presently being mined are mostly low volatile coking coal (LVCC). They constitute about 50% of the total coking coal reserves in India. These coals are characterized by high raw coal ash content and poor washability characteristics. Beneficiation of the lower seam coals in the existing washery circuits (2 or 3 product) does not yield requisite quality demanded by the steel sector of the country and thus almost entire production is being supplied to the thermal power stations.

Low volatile coking (LVC) coal, though inferior in qualities but abundantly available in Eastern part of the country. These coals, being of lower seams are likely to be more matured (Ro ~1.30%) than the upper seams and consequently exhibit lower values of volatile matter.

Of the existing 16 coking coal washeries, only three are less than 20 years old, whereas most are 40–50 years old. These washeries, except for those owned by Tata Steel, operate at a yield level of 30–45%. Most of the existing coal washeries are being operated basically as 2-product washeries producing steel plant cleans (40–45% yield at 19% ash) and remaining middlings at 40–45% ash with little or no rejects. When lower seam coals are directly treated in these washeries, the sink becomes more than 55% ash with no market potentiality. Such coals, though technically very difficult, likely to produce hardly 25–30% of cleans at 18% ash and 70–75% will require disposal as waste, which is not cost effective. Hence, these NLW/LVC coals are being presently sent to thermal power stations.

The LVC coals are difficult-to-wash as these coals have high percentage of near gravity materials, generally over 50% at the primary separation gravity and in most cases yield considerable proportion of co-products like middlings, sinks etc. The liberation characteristics of this type of coal are very poor due to highly intergrown nature of the coal. Generally, there is no commensurate increase in yield of cleans at equivalent ash level by crushing the coal gradually down to below 13 or 6 mm.

Two decades ago, when it became quite obvious that LVC coal would be the mainstay of metallurgical coal production in India, The Central Fuel Research Institute (CFRI) in Dhanbad had proposed a composite scheme for washing the LVC coal. ROM coal is crushed to −75 mm and pre–cleaned in a three product jig followed by multi level washing of the de-shaled coal by Heavy Medium Bath (HMB), Heavy Medium Cyclone (HMC) and flotation. The other major product, middling, was meant for foundry fuels and power plants.

The numerous laboratory tests and pilot scale studies have confirmed that these coals, if it is beneficiated to 17.5 ± 0.5 percent ash level exhibit good caking properties and may be blended to produce blast furnace coke. Realizing the importance, Coal India Ltd. is already in the process to set up six NLW coking coal washeries on private–public cooperation concept (Table 32.1.2). Coal India is providing land, water, electricity and other infrastructure while private sector is providing state of art technology and erecting, commissioning and operating these washeries. These washeries will be three product washeries producing Clean Coal of 18% ash, Middlings of less than 40% ash and Rejects.

The flow sheet of the washery being constructed by Monnet at Patherdih washery is shown in Fig. 32.1.4. The LVC coal may be deshaled first in jigs and then crushed to 13 mm size for beneficiation in HM Cyclones. The fines generated by desliming crushed coal may be subjected to floatation for recovery of 18% ash content cleans which will enhance the total yield of cleans in the circuit. The sinks of HM Cyclones having ash around 40% may be used as Thermal Coal.

Table 32.1.2 Proposed new coking coal washeries.

Sl No	Proposed washery	Company	Capacity
1.	Madhuban Washery	BCCL	5.0
2.	Patherdih Washery-I	BCCL	5.0
3.	Dugda Washery	BCCL	2.5
4.	Dahibadi Washery	BCCL	1.6
5.	Patherdih Washery-II	BCCL	2.5
6.	Dhori Washery	CCL	2.5

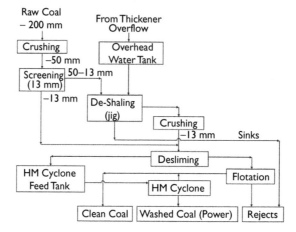

Figure 32.1.4 Simplified Process Flowsheet of Patherdih Coal Washery.

32.1.2 New private coking coal washeries

Electro Steel Coal Washery is a coking coal washery installed at Jharia Coalfield, near Bokaro where captive mine block was allotted to this group. This washery treats the coal of $-13 + 0.5$ mm size by HM Cyclone and -0.5 mm fraction by conventional flotation cells. Another washery, Tata Steel and SAIL's equal joint venture, of 1.8 mtpy capacity at Bhelatand in Jharkhand, through an investment of Rs. 200 crore will be setup. The circuit includes HM Cyclone for washing 13–1 mm fraction, Teeter Bed Separator (TBS) for washing $-1 + 0.25$ mm and flotation for washing -0.25 mm fraction.

32.2 NON-COKING COAL WASHING

It is needless to mention about the importance of non-coking coals used in number of industries. Though the availability of non-coking coals is reported from many locations in India, they cannot be used directly because of their high ash content. Most of the earlier work carried out in the beneficiation studies of high ash non-coking coals indicated that they are difficult to wash mainly due to their drift origin. In 1970s, to boost up the industrial growth, Government decided to increase power generation capacity manifold. After the nationalization of coal industries in mid 1970s, the expansion of coal industry was also taken up on massive scale due to rising demand from thermal power plants. With the heavy investments and coming up of large open-cast mines, mining of low grade non-coking coal has become feasible which was earlier neglected by the private operators prior to nationalization. While power houses are asking for better coal (with ash below 30%), natural resources can offer only raw coal with higher percentage of ash (40% or above) in future years. So the only alternative left is to use beneficiated coal by various end users.

The non-coking coal used in power plants in India is mined by mechanized mining technique which produces small and fine sizes of coal and receives the coal from multiple sources. These are the major constraints in India for achieving efficiency besides high ash and moisture contents of coal. The average quality of non-coking coal has been progressively deteriorating due to inferior grades of coal reserves available from open cast mining and the high degree of mechanization introduced in the large open cast mines. Besides, majority of the coal seams are inter-banded and the bands within the same seam or between the seams are thin and their number is more. Since, such bands cannot be separated during the mining operations, these get mixed with the coal, increasing the ash% of the ROM coal. Weak and soft roof and floor of the coal seams are also a contributory factor to deterioration in the quality of ROM coal. These dirts are disseminated in all the size fractions of coal as well as in the coal matrix. These factors are responsible for inconsistency in the quality of ROM coal, particularly with regard to ash and the moisture content.

Many coal consuming plants including the power plants obtain coal from more than one source and the coal is of varying quality and size. Due to the fluctuations in the grain size distribution, top size, ash and moisture content in the coal fed to the thermal power plants, it is not possible to ensure adequate homogenization of coal quality in the absence of proper and adequate blending facilities at the power plant end. In view of the above situation, beneficiation of power coal appears to be the only solution to reduce ash of the coal and the quantity of coal to be transported, mainly by rail thus reducing demand for railway rakes and resulting in overall savings in expenditure of freight.

The purpose of beneficiation of a non-coking coal is not only to reduce its inert content for transportation or to minimize abrasive materials but mainly to improve its combustion qualities. The combustion properties of coal like heating value, volatile matter content, char characteristics, abrasivity, etc., that govern the performance of the coal have obvious dependence on some inherent properties like ash and maceral composition. Most of the coals presently mined in India are of Lower/Middle Barakar formation. In general, the coals have diversified characteristics, both favorable and adverse, towards power plant utilization. Some of these are

- Thick coal seams, highly inter-banded in lithological make up
- More micro-fragmental in nature; the mineral matters are embedded mostly in the core of the grains and therefore, the fines are difficult to separate by physico-chemical processes

- Inferior in quality with ash content 30–40% (excluding dirt/bands)
- Dominance of inertinite (45–55% or even up to 70%) and less (25–45%) vitrinite content
- Intimate mixing of inertinites with mineral matter leading to higher ash content
- Predominant formation of semi-fusinite and fusinite components that are responsible for sub-hydrous nature (4.2–5.0% Hydrogen, dmmf basis) of the coals in general; because of their relatively higher porosity, the coals possess higher in-situ moisture-retention capacity resulting to lesser heating values

Fortunately, considerable portions of these inertinites have good reactivity. As a result, the coals when prepared by reducing the ash and moisture level to an extent comparable to foreign coals show better combustion characteristics. Other qualities favorable to power plant utilization are

- Low Sulphur content (<0.6%)
- Refractory nature (flow temperature >1400°C)
- Low Chlorine content (<0.1%)
- Low Iron and Phosphorous content
- Low toxic elements
- Volatile matter content 35–40% (dmmf basis)
- Favourable acid/base ratio (0.2–0.3%)

However, with advent of more and more open cast, mechanized mining (accounts for 85–90% of total production of power grade coal), the quality of the coals being supplied is deteriorating. The average calorific value of coal produced from the coal-fields have reduced significantly from an average of 5000 kcal/kg in 1970 to an average of 3000–3400 kcal/kg in 2014. The problem is further aggravated because of the multiplicity of coal sources fed to the power plants. There are very few power plants (except some pit head plants) getting coal from a single, dedicated source. Most of them are supplied mainly with grade E & F coals (i.e. 85–90% by wt.) and partly grade D coals (i.e.10–15% by wt.). Consequently, the Thermal Power Stations (TPS) are getting coals of heterogeneous nature, in both quality and size. The result is lower Plant Load Factor, higher maintenance & operating cost, higher investment in coal handling, ash disposal and specially, more environmental pollution. The major issues and challenges lies in beneficiation of the coals above 34% ash level whose share is more than 77%. The challenge lies in optimal utilization of high ash non-coking coal resources mainly, because of the different nature of the constraints involved in their utilization pattern, prevalent practice, existing infrastructure, etc.

Based on the studies carried out by different organizations and inferences drawn from their studies and several committees constituted by the government between 1978 and 2003 have debated whether 'to wash or not to wash' non coking coal. In 1988, real time tests were carried out at Sarni power plant by burning washed coal from Nandan washery, just to establish the benefits of using coal with lower ash and uniform quality in the power plant boilers. The results of the study, which was carried out by an independent agency were considered positive and clearly in favour of using beneficiated coal in power plant boilers.

Ministry of Environment and Forests (MoEF), Government of India has stipulated that from 1st day of June 2001 raw coals be cleaned to less than 34% ash if the thermal power plant is located beyond 1,000 km or situated in an urban area or an ecologically sensitive area or a critically polluted industrial area, irrespective of its distance from the pit-head. As the amount of coal which is transported beyond 1000 km increases, MoEF has reduced the distance to 500 km with effect from the 5th day of June, 2016.

In the meantime, realizing the importance of Non-Coking Coal (NCC) washing, Coal India Limited (CIL) began setting up NCC washeries and commissioned its first NCC washery integrated with Piparwar opencast mine project in 1997, North Karanpura coalfield with annual throughput capacity of 6.5 million tonnes per year. The second NCC washery, also integrated with mine was commissioned at Bina opencast mine project, Singrauli coalfield in 1999. Due to non-availability of suitable quality of coking coal, CIL also converted three nos. of earlier coking coal washeries i.e. Dugda I (BCCL), Gidi (CCL), Kargali (CCL), to non coking coal washeries during the period 1998–99.

To promote coal washing in private sector, Ministry of Coal issued Guidelines in September 2005 for setting up of coal washeries on Coal Company's land by the coal consumer who has a Fuel Supply Agreement (FSA) or long term linkage with the coal producer or by any operator on his behalf for obtaining desired quality of washed coal and to meet the demand-supply gap of washed coal. In this case, Coal Company has to work as a facilitator. Accordingly, Punjab State Electricity Board (PSEB), Singareni Collieries Company Limited (SCCL) and Andhra Pradesh Generation Corporation (APGENCO) have set up washeries by engaging washery operators. CIL is also implementing a massive program for setting up of washeries on BOM concept.

It was only recently that Coal India finally decided to supply washed coal to all power plants except the pithead ones. This policy decision has virtually rejuvenated the coal preparation industry in India. Hoping that the progress on Coal India's plan of setting up of 19 washeries on 'build-operate-maintain' format will yield positive benefits, it is definitely going to change the old approach of 'take it or leave it'. Going by the growth in production of thermal coal from most of the coalfields, it can be safely anticipated that coal industry encompassing all aspects of coal washing and blending will see a very encouraging growth cycle during the 12th five year plan period.

32.2.1 Technology used for washing Indian non-coking coals

32.2.1.1 Wet beneficiation

The wet processes have been well established and universally accepted for the beneficiation of coal. These are precise, efficient, economical and viable. A wide range of particle size can also be treated by a single process. Hence, the wet processes have become attractive and all the coal producing countries prefer to beneficiate the coals by wet processes. Several technologies based on wet methods have been developed and quite a number of renowned manufacturers are designing, fabricating and marketing the washing equipment (washer) working on the same basic principle with different trade names.

Barrel-cum-cyclone washing process consists of beneficiation of raw coal (−50 mm) in barrel washer (see article 23.11) with self generated slurry as media or separator. The barrel floats are crushed and beneficiated by a set of cyclones. Some of the private coal washeries like Aryan and Global had adopted this technology for washing high ash Indian non coking coals.

Jigging is one of the oldest methods to be adopted for coal beneficiation, about 100 years ago. It is considered as an efficient washer for cleaning coals having NGM (Near Gravity Material) about 20% or below. The development of the ROM Jig (see article 24.2.4) opened the possibility, to use a very simple process for the beneficiation of the lump size coal −400 + 30 mm by using only one technologically improved machine and some standard auxiliary equipment. Such plants have been installed at Bina and Kargali washeries to separate refuse and clean coal. Piparwar washery uses Batac jig for washing −100 + 20 mm coal.

A highly efficient VARI-WAVE Jig, a Japanese coal washing technology by NEDO and JCOAL, was introduced in a new washing plant of Monnet Ispat & Energy Limited at Angul, for treating the coals of Talcher under MCL.

HM Baths are more efficient compared to Jigs and use magnetite as medium. A 100 tph heavy medium bath was installed by McNally Humboldt Wedag India Limited at ACC Limited, Baragarh cement work for treating high ash coals to obtain clean coal for use in their cement factory. Similarly M/s Bhatia International Limited installed a 3.3 mtpa coal washery with heavy medium bath as a main separating unit for treating coals of WCL. Monnet Ispat & Energy Limited installed a 4.2 mtpa plant at Khalari (Ranchi) in N.K.Coalfields in collaboration with M/s Daniels of USA, where a Daniels heavy medium bath is in operation.

HM Cyclones are more efficient compared to Jigs and use magnetite as medium. Non-coking coal washeries under private sector like Jindal Steel and Power Limited, Bhushan Steel Limited, Adani Group etc., use Heavy Medium Cyclone process for beneficiation of the coarser fraction while Bilaspur washery, installed for its own power plants, has introduced large diameter HM cyclone for 50–1 mm size coal.

Coal washeries with HM Cyclone process are in operation in JSPL, BPSL, BSL, Grasim Cement & Gujarat NRE to name a few while ACC, UltraTech are in the process of setting up their captive coal washeries at different locations which includes 3 product washery with either two stage HM Cyclone process or combination of jigging with heavy media process having provision to operate, as and when required, one circuit to produce two products. More are being set up to wash non coking coal in different locations adjacent to WCL, MCL & SECL mines by private entrepreneurs to meet the rising demand of washed coal.

32.2.1.2 Dry beneficiation

Rotary Breaker (see article 18.3.1), a combined breaker and cleaner, generates two products, one is large unbroken high-ash tailings and the other is broken product having better liberation characteristics. Rotary breaker has proven to be a robust machine of very low operating costs, and a high capacity up to 2000 tph. Some private washeries in Maharastra and Chattisgarh have installed rotary breakers for partial beneficiation. Dry Beneficiation Plant at Integrated Baranj OCM near Nagpur, Aryan Coal Beneficiation plant at Korba are the two examples where rotary breakers are installed.

All Air Jig (see article 29.2) is a deep-bed dry separator using air as medium designed by Allmineral Ltd. The Indian coal industry has reacted very positively to the Allair jig, and as a result more than 28 air jigs are in operation in the coal dominated states of Orissa, Chhatisgarh and Jharkhand. These air jigs are upgrading Indian coals from CIL mines of Mahanadi Coal Fields (MCL) to the South Eastern Coal Fields (SECL). A 250 tph demonstration plant is also being set up at Bharatpur under MCL.

FGX Separator (see article 29.3) is a special type of air table that consists of a perforated separating deck, air chambers, a vibrating mechanism, and a hanging support mechanism. It is designed by FGX SepTech. High separation efficiency along with low cleaning costs has resulted in the widespread application of the FGX Dry Separator in China. The first commercial installation of this technology in the United States took place in the year 2009. The National Metallurgical Laboratory, Jamshedpur is procuring a FGX Separator and further R & D studies will be carried out.

Ore Sorting (see article 29.4) through Radiometric technologies have emerged as a viable option and recently few industrial installations were seen in South Africa and China. Radiometric techniques are of two kinds – gamma ray plus laser height profiling technology and multi-energy x-ray differential attenuation technology. In India a deshaling plant based on X-ray sorting is being set up at Madhuband Wahery and one dry deshaling plant based on gamma ray is in operation at Talcher.

32.2.2 Non-coking coal washeries in India

At present 61 non coking coal washeries with a total throughput capacity of 181.61 mtpy are in operation in the country. CIL operates 5 non – coking coal washeries with a total throughput capacity of 18.72 mtpy and other non coking coal washeries with a total throughput capacity of 162.89 mtpy. Table 32.2.1 shows the list of non-coking coal washeries with their annual capacity.

Dudga-I central washery of BCCL, commissioned in 1962, was originally a coking coal washery, later converted to non-coking coal washery. This washery originally comprised a deshaling Baum Jig and Tromp baths for cleaning down to 13 mm. A Komag Jig (a type of Batac Jig), and froth flotation were incorporated in 1985. At present the circuit comprised of Deshaling Baum Jig, screening at 25 and 6 mm, and HM Baths for both the size fractions (75–25 and 25–6 mm) with individual media control measures to maximize the yield of cleans. The smalls (below 6 mm) were dry screened and mixed with the cleans. The average feed ash was 24%, yield was 60 to 70% at 17% ash, and sinks were dispatched by conveyors to nearby Chandrapura Thermal Power Station.

Gidi washery was installed in 1973 to wash non-coking coals for the Railways. ROM coals from under ground mines were crushed to 150 mm, screened at 25 mm and coarse fraction was treated in HM DISA Bath. As a standard circuit, the smalls were washed in Baum Jig, after deslimming at 0.5 mm.

Piparwar washery is a CCL washery having capacity of 6.5 mtpy, highest capacity among the other CIL washeries. It is based on a single process for cleaning coal. ROM coal is crushed to 200/100 mm, screened at 20 mm using banana screen and +20 mm coal is washed in a Batac Jig. All the –20 mm coal is fed untreated into the cleans. The slurry from cleans dewatering screen is thickened in hydrocyclones and its underflow after dewatering in high speed screen is mixed with the cleans. The overflow of the thickening cyclone goes to settling cone and slime ponds to re-circulate the wash water. The Piparwar plant has unusual construction features. It is entirely of a steel construction with concrete used only for foundations. There is no side sheeting on the plant allowing good ventilation and light into the plant. All floors are open grating and, consequently, the plant is considerably cleaner than any other Indian plant. Fig. 32.2.2.1 shows the simplified flowsheet of Piparwar washery.

Kargali washery was originally a coking coal washery and has undergone several changes since its inception. Coal feed size of −80 mm is screened at 12 mm. Two stage

Table 32.2.2 Non-coking coal Washeries in India.

Sl No	Washery & Operator	State of location	Capacity (mtpy)
Non-Coking coal Washeries			
	CIL		
1	Dugda-I, BCCL	Jharkhand	2.50
2	Gidi, CCL	Jharkhand	2.50
3	Piparwar, CCL	Jharkhand	6.50
4	Kargali, CCL	Jharkhand	2.72
5	Bina, NCL	Uttar Pradesh	4.50
	Private		
1	Dipka, Aryan Coal Beneficiation Pvt. Ltd.	Chhattisgarh	12.00
2	Gevra, Aryan Coal Beneficiation Pvt. Ltd.	Chhattisgarh	6.25
3	Pandarpauni, Aryan Coal Beneficiation Pvt. Ltd.	Maharashtra	3.00
4	Gauri, Aryan Energy Pvt. Ltd	Maharashtra	2.00
5	Chakabura, Aryan Energy Pvt. Ltd.	Chhattisgarh	7.50
6	Indaram, Aryan Energy Pvt. Ltd.	Andhra Pradesh	2.00
7	Talcher, Aryan Energy Pvt. Ltd.	Odisha	2.00
8	Balanda, Aryan Energy Pvt. Ltd.	Odisha	2.57
9	Himgir, ACB (India) Ltd.	Odisha	5.00
10	Binjhri, ACB (India) Ltd.	Chhattisgarh	0.96
11	Patharaapali-Faguram, ACB (India) Ltd.	Chhattisgarh	0.96
12	Korba, ST-CLI Coal Washeries Ltd.	Chhattisgarh	5.20
13	Wani, Kartikay Coal Washeries Pvt. Ltd.	Maharashtra	2.50
14	Sasti, Gupta Coalfield & Washeries Ltd.	Maharashtra	2.40
15	Wani, Gupta Coalfield & Washeries Ltd.	Maharashtra	1.92
16	Parasia, Gupta Coalfield & Washeries Ltd.	Maharashtra	1.50
17	Umrer, Gupta Coalfield & Washeries Ltd.	Maharashtra	0.75
18	Bhandara, Gupta Coalfield & Washeries Ltd.	Maharashtra	0.75
19	Pimpalgaon, Gupta Coalfield & Washeries Ltd.	Maharashtra	4.00
20	Gondegaon, Gupta Coalfield & Washeries Ltd.	Maharashtra	2.40
21	Majri, Gupta Coalfield & Washeries Ltd.	Maharashtra	2.40
22	Ghugus, Gupta Coalfield & Washeries Ltd.	Maharashtra	2.40
23	Bilaspur, Gupta Coalfield & Washeries Ltd.	Chhattisgarh	3.50
24	Karanpura, Gupta Coalfield & Washeries Ltd.	Jharkhand	5.00
25	Ramagundam, Gupta Coalfield & Washeries Ltd.	Andhra Pradesh	2.40
26	Talcher, Global Coal Mining (P) Ltd.	Odisha	2.50
27	Ib Valley, Global Coal Mining (P) Ltd.	Odisha	5.00
28	Balanda, Global Coal Mining (P) Ltd.	Odisha	2.91
29	Ramagundam, Global Coal Mining (P) Ltd.	Andhra Pradesh	1.17
30	Manuguru, Global Coal Mining (P) Ltd.	Andhra Pradesh	1.06

(Continued)

Table 32.2.2 (Continued)

Sl No	Washery & Operator	State of location	Capacity (mtpy)
Non-Coking coal Washeries			
31	Wani, Bhatia International Ltd.	Maharashtra	3.73
32	Ghugus, Bhatia International Ltd.	Maharashtra	4.00
33	Jharsuguda, Bhatia International Ltd.	Odisha	2.00
34	Raigarh, Jindal Steel & Power Ltd.	Chhattisgarh	6.00
35	Tamnar, Jindal Steel & Power Ltd.	Chhattisgarh	6.00
36	Wani, Indo Unique Flame Ltd.& Nair Coal Services Ltd.	Maharashtra	2.40
37	Nagpur, -do-	Maharashtra	0.60
38	Punvat (Ghugus) -do-	Maharashtra	2.40
39	Annupur, -do-	Maharashtra	1.20
40	Ratija, Spectrum Coal & Power Ltd.	Chhattisgarh	3.33
41	Ratija, Spectrum Coal & Power Ltd.	Chhattisgarh	10.00
42	Kalinga, Spectrum Coal & Power Ltd.	Odisha	9.52
43	Bilaspur, Chattisgarh Power & Coal Beneficiation Ltd.	Chhattisgarh	1.25
44	Rajnandan, Allied Minerals	Chhattisgarh	0.94
45	Raigarh, MSP Steel & Power Ltd.	Chhattisgarh	0.60
46	Angul, MP Ispat & Power Ltd.	Odisha	2.50
47	Chandrapur, Sidhbali Ispat Ltd.	Maharastra	0.25
38	Chandrapur, Solar Industries Ltd.	Maharastra	0.25
49	Chandrapur, Anshul Impex Pvt. Ltd.	Maharastra	0.25
50	Chandrapur, Fuel Coal Washeries India td.	Maharastra	2.50
51	Chhattisgarh, Trumax Ispat Ltd.	Chhattisgarh	0.88
52	Jharia, Ranchi Casting Pvt. Ltd.	Jharkhand	0.88
53	Khalari, Monnet Group	Jharkhand	4.20
54	Durgapur, Shyam Steel Industries Ltd.	West Bengal	0.88
55	Raniganj, Chariot EXIMP Ltd.	West Bengal	2.00
56	Dharamsthal, BLA Industries	Madhya Pradesh	0.33

Wemco Drum for coarse coal and Jig for the smalls washing are used. Sinks of the first Jig is rewashed in a smaller capacity second Jig for reducing the overall costs. The flowsheet was subsequently modified to utilize two Baum jigs in parallel and increase the plant throughput. HM Cyclone is incorporated to clean the sinks of Wemco Drum after crushing to −16 mm. In the latest flowsheet, a Batac jig has replaced the HM cyclones and small coal Baum jigs and Wemco drums carry out the separation for the coarse coal. The replacement of the HM cyclones was an attempt to overcome the difficulties caused by poor-quality magnetite and the high maintenance requirement of HM systems. A dry deduster was installed, in the early 1980s, along with the Batac jig. Fig. 32.2.2.2 shows the three flowsheets of Kargali washery.

Bina washery was constructed by Humboldt Wedag at Singrauli coalfield. The novelty of the plant is to wash ROM coal of size −200 mm by a rocking pan Jig, which separates cleans and rejects into two streams while the coal is winnowed on an

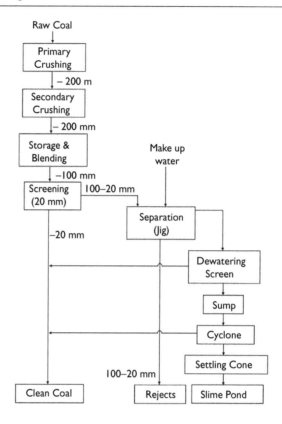

Figure 32.2.2.1 Simplified Process Flowsheet of Piparwar Washery.

inclined screen, dipped in water. The most interesting part is the low water consumption (8 m³/hr) and almost no slurry is thrown out of the plant.

Indaram washery is one of the coal washery setup by Aryan Energy Pvt Ltd at Indaram, near Ramagundam of Andhra Pradesh in the command area of Singareni Collieries Company Limited. In this washery, +200 mm coal is broken by Rotary breaker and rejects are removed. −200 mm coal is crushed to −50 mm and rejects are picked in picking station. −50 + 20 mm and −20 + 10 mm fractions are separated and washed in two separate Barrel washers. Fig. 32.2.2.3 shows the flowsheet of Indaram washery.

32.2.3 Present status of washing

Most of the non coking coal washeries in India concentrated mainly on partial beneficiation, i.e., coarse coal beneficiation, the finer fraction (generally, of lower ash content but prone to higher moisture take up) is allowed to bypass the washing circuit. Since most of the free dirt and banded materials are included in the coarser fraction, beneficiation of this fraction only and mixing of the washed product with the untreated smaller fraction gains first acceptance for maintaining presently desired ash at 34%.

Kargali Coal Washery Flowsheets

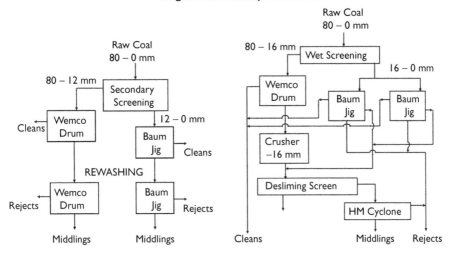

A : Initial flowsheet   B : Modified flowsheet

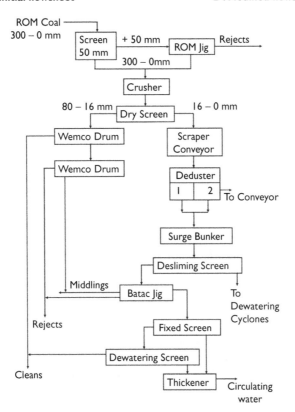

C : Latest flowsheet

Figure 32.2.2.2 Flowsheets of Kargali Non-coking Coal Washery.

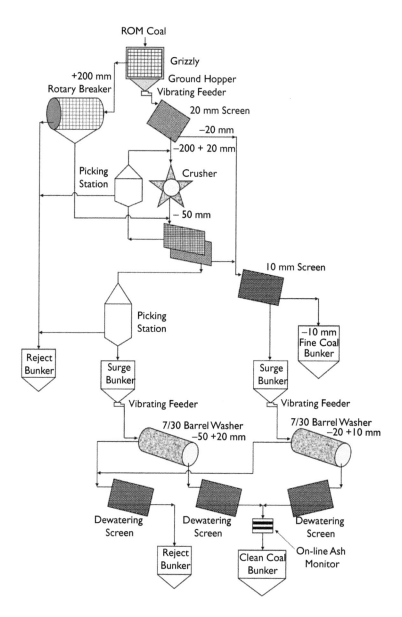

Figure 32.2.2.3 Simplified Process Flowsheet of Indaram Coal Washery.

If the purpose of beneficiation is to meet the Govt. stipulations and the ash content of the raw coal is more than 45%, then a jig washer is sufficient as it will be a much simpler unit to operate, the washability characteristics will be very helpful in this regard, due to the fact that it will provide insights to the cut density to be maintained, the amount of NGM present at the cut density, etc. Even though, HM Washer is efficient in producing low ash cleans with better yield, it is not desirable to use this circuit for producing washed coal of ash 34% as the cost and availability of magnetite plays a vital role and it may be difficult to operate with media having specific gravity more than 1.8, mainly due to viscosity of the media. The HM circuit may produce deep cleaned washed coal having ash as low as 25% or even less suiting for sponge and cement industries.

The choice of washing circuit has to be made depending on the degree of intermixing and the separation criteria. It is essential, therefore, to take utmost care of the constraints, before selection of washers, during planning and designing any circuit such as fluctuating quality of ROM coal, high amount of NGM at cut density, moisture in the raw coal and its effect in washed product and frequent deterioration in the quality of feed from multiple sources. Finally, the washing scheme should depend upon raw coal characteristics and quality demand. A combination of different washing circuits may also be required for higher ash, 'difficult-to-wash' coal. Moreover, the washing circuit should have the optimum flexibility of either by passing or washing the intermediate/ finer fractions.

32.2.4 New non-coking coal washeries

Coal India Limited (CIL) has planned to set up 20 numbers of coal washeries (Coking and Non-Coking) having total capacity of 111.1 Mt of raw coal throughput as shown in Table 32.2.4.

Table 32.2.4 Proposed coal washeries by CIL.

Sl No	Subsidiary	Washery	Capacity (mtpy)	Type	Scheme
1	ECL	Chitra	2.5	Non-coking	BOM
2	ECL	Sonpurbazari	8.0	Non-coking	BOM
3	BCCL	Madhuband	5.0	Coking	BOM
4	BCCL	Patherdih	5.0	Coking	BOM
5	BCCL	Patherdih	2.5	Coking	BOM
6	BCCL	Bhojudih	2.0	Non-coking	BOM
7	BCCL	Dugda	2.5	Coking	BOM
8	BCCL	Dahibari	1.6	Non-coking	BOM
9	CCL	Ashoka	10.0	Non-coking	BOM
10	CCL	New Piparwar	3.5	Non-coking	TURNKEY
11	CCL	Karo	2.5	Non-coking	BOM
12	CCL	Konar	3.5	Non-coking	BOM
13	CCL	Dhori	2.5	Coking	TURNKEY
14	SECL	Kusmunda	10.0	Non-coking	BOM
15	SECL	Baroud	5.0	Non-coking	BOM
16	MCL	Basundhara	10.0	Non-coking	BOM
17	MCL	Jagannath	10.0	Non-coking	BOM
18	MCL	Hingula	10.0	Non-coking	BOM
19	MCL	IB Valley	10.0	Non-coking	BOM
20	WCL	Kolarpimpri	5.0	Non-coking	BOM
TOTAL			111.1		

In addition, more than 30 washeries have been proposed to set up by ACB (India) Ltd., Gupta Coalfields and Washeries, Bhatiya group, Monnet group and few cement plants. Spectacular growth will be witnessed with more than 130 coal washeries in total in India within three years.

Chapter 33

Global coal washing

Many varieties of coal washing plants are presently being used in various parts of the world. They vary from simple screening and crushing operations to very complex flowsheets employing different types of washing equipment. Among the several washing equipments, Jigs are most common. Around 60% of the coal washing is done by Jigs in United Kingdom. Next to Jigs, Heavy medium processes are widely used. India and South Africa washes more than 60% of coal by Heavy medium processes. Among the countries where Heavy medium cyclone installations account for 8% to 40% of total cleaning capacity, Australia tops the list followed by India, Japan, South Africa, Belgium, France and United Kingdom. Froth flotation and water only cyclones are increasingly used to upgrade the slurry of 0.5 mm size. Oil agglomeration technique for slurry treatment is being tried out on pilot/demonstration scale in Japan, India, USA and Australia.

Piston jigs and diaphragm jigs were in use earlier. During 1892, **Fritz Baum** of Germany has developed Baum jig for coal cleaning and was able to treat coal of wider size range. By the late 1950s, Baum wash boxes are treating almost half of the mechanically cleaned coal in the world. Later, Humboldt Wedag Batac Jig was designed with air chambers situated under the grid plates. In early 1980's attention was drawn towards moving screen jigs with the need to deshale run-of-mine coal prior to conventional cleaning. Humboldt Wedag, German company, designed a movable screen jig, called as ROM Jig, as a single-cut jig to separate large stones. Vari-wave Jig was another development in which the wave pattern in the jigging chamber can be changed such as from sinusoidal wave to trapezoidal wave.

Till 1930s Launder washers and Ascending current washers were in use. Chance Cone, Barvoys and Tromp processes replaced them and gained popularity during 1930s to treat coarse coal too difficult for jig washers and remained in prominent use for easy coals. By mid 1950s, dozens of different designs were being used in many parts of the world. Later, equipment like Wemco drum and Mc Nally Tromp vessel were designed for three product separations. A Drewboy bath is two product separator which uses radial vaned wheel to discharge heavies and working parts are out of contact with the dense medium. Barrel washer with coal slurry as a heavy medium was the latest equipment used for non-coking coal washing.

Heavy medium cyclone washer was developed at Dutch State Mines (DSM). Other similar cylindro-conical type washers include Mc Nally cycloids, Krebs cyclone and Kilborn cyclone. Heavy medium cyclones are in very common use today. There is a trend towards increasing the top size and decreasing the bottom size of the feed to

HM cyclone. There are commercial plants treating feed sizes down to zero. The DSM work pioneered the development of cylindrical separators such as Vorsyl separator, Dyna Whirlpool, Tri-Flo separator and LARCODEMs.

Another development is the Water only cyclone treating sizes from 35 mm to zero. Use of variable vortex finders and ceramic liners improved the operation of water only cyclones. These are increasingly used for fines below 0.5 mm particularly for oxidized coal that cannot be treated by froth flotation.

Compared to all the coal cleaning processes, heavy medium cyclones provide the most efficient cleaning for fine coal. Spiral concentrators are currently the most widely used technology worldwide for treating fine coal, due to their low capital cost and operational simplicity. However, fluidized-bed separators, also commonly referred to as teeter-bed or hindered-bed separators, have gained popularity when low separation density values are required to achieve product quality specifications.

Froth flotation continues to be the most widely accepted technology for the treatment of coal slurries of –0.5 mm size. Column flotation technique is the recent one. A flotation reagent metering device is in use in Soviet coal washing plants. This device measures the flow rate of the pulp together with percent solids and delivers necessary quantities of frother.

Dry cleaning methods did find wide acceptance for treating coal between 1930 and 1960. Dry methods were adopted in the United Kingdom and the United States up to 1960. Pneumatic jigs and tables were the major equipment used for dry cleaning of coal. In recent years, the only commercial application of dry methods is the use of rotary breaker. Hezekiah Bradford of Pennsylvania is attributed with the invention of the first breaker in 1893 and his Bradford Breaker design is still in use today. These breakers are being widely used in U.K., U.S.A., Australia, West Germany and India. A modified version of rotary breaker known as Brodpactor has been developed in U.S.A. wherein ROM coals could be crushed to 50 mm without any appreciable loss of good coal.

33.1   WET WASHING PROCESSES

Ascending current washers, Launder washers and Concentrating tables were in use previously for easy to wash coal varieties.

33.1.1   Ascending current washers

Ascending current washers are the classifiers of both free and hindered settling type. These may be used for making separations of coal and its impurities under proper conditions. In these washers, the coal and mineral matter are separated by regulating the speed of an ascending current of water, in which the raw coal is suspended, so that the larger and heavier particles fall downward against the upward current of water while the smaller and lighter particles are carried upward.

Theoretically, the feed to ascending current washers should be well sized, at least within the limits determined by the settling ratio of the raw coal constituents whose separation is desired. The fine particles have the effect of increasing the specific gravity of the separating fluid. In water with a density of 1 gm/cc, the ratio of the sizes of coal particles with a specific gravity of 1.35 that can be separated from ash particles of 2.50 specific gravity is 4.3 : 1. In case the suspended particles serve to increase the effective specific gravity of the water to 1.10, the ratio of sizes becomes 5.6 : 1.

The **Menzies Hydroseparator, Menzies Cone separator** and **Hydrotator** are three of the better known washers of this group. In Menzis hydroseparator, coal is separated on a sloping screen by rising current of water. Menzies cone separator is similar to chance cone wherein the coal is separated by rising current of water only. The refuse is discharged by a conveyor. In hydrotator, there is a floating effect of the pulp bed in the tank which acts similarly to the sand suspension in chance cone process in addition to the rising current of water.

33.1.2 Launder washers

Launder washers or trough washers are one of the oldest devices used for washing coals. When a stream consisting of coal, or other material of non-uniform density, and water is directed down a trough, stratification occurs according to the hindered settling rates of the particles. The heavier particles settle rapidly and reach the bottom quickly. The lighter particles settle more slowly and are carried farther down the stream before they can reach the bottom.

In the launder washer, the efficiency of separation is accentuated because the main body of the stream is flowing rapidly, while the layer of heavier material is retarded by friction with the bottom and moves more slowly. Consequently, the heavy portions of the coal accumulate as a relatively slow-moving layer, above which the coal is carried rapidly.

The earlier launder washer consisted of a long wooden trough arranged at a slope and divided by low cross-sectional dams at intervals along its length. Raw coal was fed in at the upper end of the trough in a stream of water. Refuse was removed from the trough at stated intervals by an attendant with a rake. These early forms of trough washers are simple, cheap, and fairly convenient, but they are characterized by a very high water consumption. Also they possess two further marked disadvantages: (1) in order to produce a clean coal, a high loss of coal is sustained in the waste, and (2) the effect of a flowing stream of water upon the material to be separated is so delicate and the character of the raw coal influences the washing and hence uniform results are obtained only with great difficulty.

Later forms of launder washers have various automatic provisions for periodic or continuous refuse removal. The **Rheolaveur washer** is an important among the launder washers. In this washer, the coal is fed into a short steeply inclined portion so that the particles move under the influence of gravity and the water current tend to acquire relatively high velocities. Under these conditions, the particles stratify quickly and completely. Later the particles and water reach a less steeply inclined portion where the speed of the water current decreases and the lowest layer of the bed is deposited. Further progressive deposition occurs along the length of the trough. Dirt and middlings are removed from the bottom of the trough without disturbing the stratification or flow of coal by means of Rheo boxes attached to the trough below the slotted openings. Among the two types of Rheo boxes, sealed discharge Rheo box is used for washing the coal of coarser sizes whereas free discharge Rheo box is used for relatively fine coal washing. The Rheolaveur washer has a wide range of applicability to all types of coals.

33.1.3 Concentrating tables

The concentrating table consists of a rectangular or rhombohedral deck which is slightly inclined to the horizontal and moves with a longitudinal differential motion. The slurry is fed at the upper corner of the table. The deck may be equipped with riffles to impede the downward movement of coarse and heavy particles to some extent. Wash water is also applied to remove the fine and lighter particles across the table. Coarse and heavy particles move longitudinally on the deck.

The chief disadvantage in using tables for coal washing is their low capacity, commonly is of the order of 10–12 tons per hour per table. However, in spite of their low capacity, concentrating tables are used to a considerable extent for washing finer sizes of coal.

The use of Ascending current washers, Launder washers and Concentrating tables is limited to coals of close size ranges and good washability characteristics. The efficiency of these washers is low in the case of difficult coals. Hence they are not in use now.

33.2 DRY CLEANING PROCESSES

Dry cleaning processes, even though simple and cheap, are limited only to fairly dry coals of closer size ranges containing large amounts of free dirt. They are not generally applicable to the medium washing or difficult washing coals.

33.2.1 Hand picking

Hand picking was the first dry cleaning process extensively used for removing refuse from coal. It was largely used even for coal as small as 1 or 2 inches. Picking is always a dry operation except when the material carries surface moisture from the mine or from preliminary water spraying given to clean the lumps from adhering fines and dirt.

Generally hand picking is done on picking belts. Picking belts consist of slow moving conveyors, down each side of which men stand who lift out the dirt and inferior material from the belt as it passes. In some instances bright and dull coals are separated in this way when these constituents having different properties are required by different consumers.

33.2.2 Mechanical pickers

Mechanical pickers make use of several differences in properties between shale or slate particles and coal particles. Some mechanical pickers make a separation on the basis of differences in properties which affect the relative movements of coal particles and slate particles down an inclined chute or other inclined surface. Slate has a higher coefficient of sliding friction and a higher specific gravity than coal; also it tends to break into flat pieces which have considerably more surface in contact with the chute bottom than coal particles of roughly cubical shape. The combined effect of these differences is that coal particles in passing down a chute will acquire higher velocities than slate particles accompanying them.

Pardee spiral separator is similar to Humphrey spiral. When the raw coal is fed at the top of the spiral, it moves in spiral path. The coal particles move outward due to more centrifugal acceleration and collected near the periphery of the spiral whereas the slate particles move inward and collected near the centre shaft of the spiral.

The property resilience may be utilized to accentuate the differences in velocity by taking advantage of the tendency of the coal particles to roll and to bounce under conditions for which the slate simply slides. The Berrisford process is based upon the difference in the resilience of clean coal and the slate. The raw coal is dropped on to an inclined plane containing a gap of chosen width. The clean coal bounces and falls on a receiver while the slate falls through the gap. One Berrisford plant was working for some years at the Singareni collieries of Andhra Pradesh, India. But that is non existent now.

33.2.3 Pneumatic tables

Several types of dry cleaning tables are being used. In operation, air is blown continuously through a perforated and riffled sloping deck which is rapidly reciprocated. The combined action of the air through the deck and the deck motion gives a mobile bed which rapidly stratifies with the heavier refuse particles at the bottom and the lighter coal particles on top. The coal flows down the slope over the riffles while the refuse is held between the riffles. The various tables in use differ mainly in the shape of the deck and in the provisions for separating and the discharging the various products. Some of the shapes of tables are SJ, Y and V. These shapes are designed for quick separation and discharge of most of the clean coal, and a slower treatment and purification of the remainder spread out over a larger area.

Size and specific gravity relations between particles in different portions of the stratified bed on pneumatic tables differ somewhat from those obtained on wet tables as a result of the difference in action between the vertically rising air current in dry tabling and the transverse, nearly horizontal flow of water in wet tabling. The action on a wet table favors the best cleaning of coarser sizes of coal and tends to give the smaller sizes contaminated with larger refuse sizes, whereas the action on dry table favors the production of coarse refuse free from coal and various sizes of coal will each be associated with smaller sizes of refuse.

33.2.4 Pneumatic jigs

Pneumatic jigs are stationary devices utilizing pulsating air currents for stratification of the coal. They consist of a perforated deck over which a pack of marbles is provided. Both the deck and pack are oscillated with short, rapid strokes. As a result of the pulsating air currents supplied from the bottom of the deck and the movement of the deck, coal is stratified so that cleaned coal rises to form an upper layer and the refuse sinks to the bottom. The Roberts and Schaefer Super-Airflow cleaner is a type of pneumatic jig which is used for cleaning coal smaller in size than 10 mesh.

33.2.5 X-Ray based sorting

Coal sorting with an X-ray transmission (XRT) sensor has experienced a lot of development since 1974. Powerful computers and increasingly sensitive X-ray scintillation counters enabled the development of high-performance sensor-based sorting machines. There are two main machine types of sensor-based sorters viz., belt-type sorters and chute-type sorters. The first industrial installation of a belt-type XRT sorting for coal has been in operation since 2004. It is upgrading high-quality coal from 1% ash to 0.7% ash for cathode production. Since 2010 chute-type sorters are in the South African market and, next to production, have been used for extensive test work. Improvements on both separation efficiency and availability of containerized semi-mobile systems have been achieved.

The machine must be fed with properly screened material. A small ratio between top and bottom size ensure an effective separation through the air blasts. A minimum of undersize material is beneficial for both the operational stability and the separation efficiency. Typical size ranges are 20–30 mm, 30–60 mm, and 60–100 mm. In practice, a screen directly feeding onto the sensor based sorter is advisable. The screened feed then enters the machine and is placed in a monolayer onto the fast-running conveyor belt. The belt passes the detection system and the particles are scanned individually. The computer then makes a decision for each particle based on predefined separation criteria. According to this decision an array of high-speed air valves is controlled. There are usually around 150 valves placed per meter working width. Single particle is ejected, thus deflected from their flight parabola. As the logic can be switched around, both fractions can be set as discard and product fractions. The lower amount fraction is ejected to save compressed air and, therefore, energy and operating costs.

33.3 COAL WASHING IN IMPORTANT COUNTRIES

Annual worldwide production of Hard Coal is approximately 7900 Mt. Currently more than 2700 coal preparation plants are in operation in the world. More than one-third of world's coal production is beneficiated. The following are the brief details of coal washing practices in China, USA, Australia, Russia, South Africa, Germany, and Poland [57].

CHINA ranks first in coal production with 3474 million tons of coal in 2014 and had 961 coal preparation plants in 2005 and the total number has been increased over 2000 by 2012. Largest steam coal processing plant is of 34 mtpy and the largest coking coal processing plant is 30 mtpy. During the same period total annual coal washing capacity has increased from 837 Million tonnes to 2150 million tonnes. Thus total coal processing rate has increased from 32% to 56.3% of country's total coal production.

China has made rapid progress in the development of coal processing technology and equipment manufacturing capacity. A large number of advanced technology, excellent equipment and super large scale coal preparation plants have been built. More than 61% of the plants are based on heavy medium coal washing methods.

The following are the coal washing practices in china:

- ROM coal is crushed to 100/50 mm.
- Coarse coal is washed at sizes 100/50 mm mainly by jigs. Dense medium separators (Drewboy, Vertical lifting wheel separator) are also used in some plants.
- For small coal of size 50/25/13 mm, 2-product HM Cyclones of 660–1300 mm diameter and 3-product HM Cyclones of 1000–1400 mm diameter are in use.
- Fine coal of −0.5 mm is washed mostly by flotation. Column flotation is used in few plants for very fine coal.

- Dry separation using compound dry separators and Air dense medium separators are of limited application.
- Dewatering is performed using mainly high frequency screens. Vertical and Horizontal centrifuges, Pressure filters and Fast diaphragm filters are also used. Plate-and-frame filters are in use for slime recovery.

The coal processing development targets are set to increase processing capacity from 1.65 Bt in 2010 to 2.54 Bt by the end of 2015.

UNITED STATES OF AMERICA produced about 924 million tones of coal in 2014. About 90% of the coal produced is being beneficiated by 286 coal processing plants in 16 states of USA.

Each coal washing plant employs 3 or more independent processing circuits for different size fractions. Coarse coal (100–10 mm) is washed by Heavy Medium Vessel. Heavy Medium Cyclones of different diameters upto1000 mm are in use for washing 10–1 mm size coal. Small coal (1–0.15 mm) washing is performed by Water Only cyclones, Spirals or combination of both. Fine coal of size –0.15 mm is treated by froth flotation after de-sliming at –35/40 microns.

Basket Type Dryers are in use for dewatering Coarse size fraction and Screen bowl centrifuges and combination of vacuum filter and thermal dryers are in use for dewatering fine size fraction. Filter presses have gained popularity to dewater –0.15 mm tailings down to 18–30%.

AUSTRALIAN Coal Industry underwent a major expansion between 2005 and 2012, driven by overseas demand for metallurgical and thermal coal. Coal production in Australia is 480 million tones in 2014. The following are the coal washing practices in Australia:

- Run of mine (ROM) coal is sized to 50–60 mm prior to the wash plant
- Plant feed is usually classified (de-slimed) at between 0.7 and 2 mm on large multi-slope (banana) screens
- For washing coarse coal, dense medium cyclones are almost universal – mostly 1000 mm in diameter or larger, with most new installations using 1150, 1300 or 1450 mm diameter units.
- There are still some plants with heavy medium vessels (drums, baths) and a few with jigs.
- Coking coal plants traditionally process –0.5 mm size coal by froth flotation. Most new or upgraded plants producing a coking coal have employed a "mid" circuit with spirals or hindered bed separators (Teeter Bed Separator or Reflux classifier) treating the –2+0.3 mm fraction and the –0.3 mm processed by flotation (mostly Jameson or Microcel technology)
- For thermal coal plants, the fines are generally de-slimed at about 0.1 mm, and then processed in spirals or a combination of spirals and TBS
- Coarse and mid size coal fractions are invariably dewatered in vibrating or scroll-type basket centrifuges, while the flotation product is dewatered on vacuum filters (mainly horizontal belt and disc) or screen bowl centrifuges

About 70 coal washing plants are existing in Australia. 13 plants of total capacity of 17,000 t/hr are under construction.

RUSSIA ranks second in the world in proven coal resources with 195 billion tons and ranks sixth in coal production of 355 million tons. Russia is having 56 coal preparation plants, 30 sorting plants and 11 preparation units. Russian coal is generally low in sulphur (<1%). All the coking coal is being beneficiated while about 23% of thermal coal is only beneficiated.

More than 50% of the coal is beneficiated by Heavy Medium baths and cyclones. Jigging is the next principal unit used. Flotation, water only cyclones and spirals are the units used for fine coal washing. High frequency screens, centrifuges, belt press filters and disc filters are the units used for dewatering fine coal.

SOUTH AFRICA is a country where Coal plays a vital role in South Africa's economy due to non-availability of oil resources. Coal processing is therefore an important part of the coal industry. Coal production in 2014 is 265 million tons. About 92% of electricity is generated from coal which is highest in the world.

- There are approximately 60 coal preparation plants in operation in South Africa and a number of new plants are under construction or in the planning phase. New generation coal preparation plants utilize the benefits of economies of scale employing single large volume units.
- Coarse coal of 80–8 mm size is mainly washed by large diameter pump fed heavy medium cyclones. Wemco drum, Drewboy bath and Jigs are used for washing in some plants.
- Largest plant is Grootegeluk complex – 7000 tons per hour
- Small coal of 8–0.8 mm size are washed in small diameter cyclones.
- Spirals are in use for fine coal washing. Froth flotation is of limited use.
- Most plants use heavy medium cyclones and spirals.
- Many of the plants have two-stage washing to produce export coal (6000 kcal/kg) as primary product and thermal coal (5000 kcal/kg) as secondary product which is fed to domestic power stations.
- Latest developments includes 3-product cyclone, filter presses for water circulation, FGX and X-Ray sorting for dry separation.

GERMANY has produced 188 million tons of coal in 2014. Hard coal industry in Germany has declined due to gradual exhaustion of mineable resources. It is likely to be completely phased out by 2018. Coal washing is done mainly using jigging and flotation processes. Jigging of coarse coal fractions is by ROM-type jigs to avoid additional generation of fines.

POLAND coal production is 137 million tons in 2014. It is a country where all coking coal is washed. About 60% of steam coal is washed (depending on Customer demand). The washing technology in vogue are:

- Lump coal and middle size coal (200/100/50–20/10 mm) is processed in HM Separators (DISA) and Jigs
- Fine coal (20/10–0.5 mm) is washed in Jigs and HM Cyclone
- Froth Flotation and Spirals are used for treating slimes of –0.5 mm
- Water slurry management is through DORR Thickeners, Settlement Concrete Tank, Centrifugal Drainer, Filtration Press, Belt Filter Press and Disc Vacuum Filter.

Chapter 34

Recent developments in coal processing

The main objective of beneficiation of coal is to recover as much lump coal as possible. The fines generated during the mining, size reduction and beneficiation are discarded as plant refuse. However, during the past few years, more emphasis is on fine coal because of the following factors:

1   Increasing use of coal instead of oil or natural gas to generate electric power
2   Increasingly stringent environmental controls for burning the coal and for the disposal of refuse
3   Increased mechanization in the coal mines, which results in more fines in ROM coal
4   Increasing need to beneficiate every part of coal deposit to conserve the coal

As a result, more and more emphasis is being placed on processing the fine-size coal to recover usable coal and minimize the amount discarded as refuse. Considerable research effort is currently being expended to develop new processes.

34.1   CHEMICAL COMMINUTION FOR COAL CLEANING

Chemical comminution is the recently developed size reduction operation wherein fragmentation is strongly controlled by boundaries between maceral and mineral matter resulting in greater mineral matter liberation and small amount of fines generation. The chemicals (generally concentrated aqueous ammonia solutions or gaseous ammonia) induce a fracture of the coal along already existing boundaries which contain the pyrite and mineral matter, thereby liberating the impurities present in the coal. The chemically comminuted coal is then subjected to conventional beneficiation methods wherein the coal matter is separated from the liberated impurities.

Chemical comminution requires the following four major steps:

1   Treating the raw coal of −37 mm with a chemical reagent e.g., ammonia as a gas, liquid, or aqueous solution
2   Removing the adsorbed ammonia from the coal, e.g., by hot-water washing
3   Recovering ammonia from the wash water for recycling by distillation followed by compression, with or without liquefaction

4   Delivering the comminuted coal to a physical cleaning operation as an aqueous slurry or as a partially dewatered product

Chemical comminution produces larger particle sizes and tends to release greater amounts of impurities when compared to mechanical comminution methods. Coal cleaning plants utilizing chemical comminution will largely eliminate the expensive equipment needed for processing fine coal, thus makes the cleaning system more profitable. Chemically comminuted coal can be readily stored and easily shipped, thus eliminating problems associated with mechanically ground fine coal.

34.2   ULTRASONIC GRINDING

The US Department of Energy along with Energy & Minerals Research Co. has developed a method that uses ultrasonic sound to grind coal to micron sizes. Ultrasonic grinding produces rapid size reduction with a narrow product size distribution and liberates sulphur bearing and ash forming minerals without excessive grinding. Ultrasonic grinding is as much as 500 percent less energy intensive when grinding coal to micron sizes.

34.3   GRAVITY SEPARATION

Otisca process is a waterless heavy liquid separation employing chlorofluoromethanes as parting liquid. All the raw coal particles are placed in a static bath or cyclone separator of parting liquid with a specific gravity between that of coal and free mineral matter which causes the coal to float, making it easily removable from the surface of the bath. At the same time, the more dense mineral matter and sulphur compounds sink to the bottom of the bath and are recovered separately. Both the products of separation, coal and refuse, are transported directly to their respective evaporators where the parting liquid is recovered by evaporation for reuse in the process.

Otisca process is able to recover more fine coal with less misplaced material at a lower processing cost than alternate processes which are currently available. It can tolerate wide fluctuations in raw coal feed rates, size distributions and chemical analyses. The parting liquids used in the process is non-flammable, non-toxic, virtually odour free, and non-corrosive, and allows for inexpensive construction of material handling and electrical equipment. The parting liquid permits complete dispersion of coal particles from the refuse material eventhough surface moisture is present, thus could ensure near theoretical recovery of the coal product. Otisca-cleaned coal has not only been found to result in higher BTU yields, it also produces far less sludge, boiler refuse, noise and dust. At the same time, it extracts more pyritic sulfur and mineral impurities than can be accomplished through water cleaning.

The Otisca Process offers the following promises:

- higher sulfur coal can be cleaned to levels more competitive with coal containing less sulfur
- jobs threatened by the unsuitability of "dirty" coal reserves could be saved

- the cost of abatement devices such as precipitators and scrubbers, presently required to meet clean air standards, would be reduced and
- the environmental penalties associated with less efficient, conventional washing techniques (i.e., energy, noise, dust, black water, boiler refuse, greater sulfur and ash levels and lower BTU yield) would be lessened

Floatex density separator (FDS) is an advanced hindered settling classifier, also referred as counter-current or autogenous teetered bed separator. It uses differential particle settling rates to segregate particles according to size, shape and density. This is also called as Teetered Bed Separator or Fluidized Bed Separator. This equipment is considered to be the most advanced commercial separator for particle classification and is able to treat material whose size in between what would be considered optimal for screen and hydrocyclone.

It works on the principle of hindered settling and fluidization where the settling rate of a particle in a liquid suspension is influenced by the presence of particles. The transition from free to hindered settling occurs as the concentration of solids in suspension increases. This reduces the distance between particles sufficiently such that the drag force created by the settling particles will affect the surrounding particles. If the density of the fluid is higher, the larger/heavier particle will remain suspended in the fluid hence it is a function of particle size, density and fluid viscosity as well as the pulp density. When pulp density increases abundantly with particles crowded, lots of particles will have a thin film of water and surface tension keeps the mixture together in perfect suspension. This condition is called full teeter. The particles heavier than the viscous pulp can fall through and settle against the rising teeter water through a bed of artificial heavy medium and get accumulated at the bottom forming a teeter bed, whereas all other particles simply float above the teeter zone.

Since the size and density of the particles are not uniform, the particles are aggregated according to their mass. In general, the coarser heavier particles form a layer at the bottom of the bed and the coarser lighter forms the top layer. Other particles are distributed throughout the bed depending on their density and size. Both the apparent density and viscosity of the bed of solid particles that is developed are higher than the liquid medium and hence often more resistance to settling in terms of the drag force and the buoyant force to a moving particle develops. Unlike dense medium separation where the medium density is the apparent density, both the effective suspension density and upward liquid velocity have substantial influence on the separation density.

The particles settle with different settling velocities depending on their size and density leading to segregation. Segregated particles are separated by the action of upward force resulting from the raising teeter water. Therefore the separation can be described by the relative velocity of each particle with respect to the velocity of water, which is called slip velocity. Particles having a slip velocity equal to the raising velocity of the water have equal chances of settling on being transported upward by water. However, if the slip velocity of a particle is greater than the raising water velocity, the particle settles downwards and reported to the under flow. Otherwise it is carried away to the over flow.

The floatex density separator consists of an upper square tank and a lower conical section and is divided into six main zones viz., Overflow collection zone (zone A),

Upper intermediate zone (zone B), Feed zone (zone C), Lower intermediate zone (zone D), Thickening zone (zone E) and Underflow collection zone (zone F)

Feed slurry is introduced through a central feed well that extends to one third of the length of the main tank and the teeter water is introduced over the entire cross-sectional area through evenly spaced water distribution pipes at the base of the teeter chamber. The teeter water flow rate is dependent upon feed particle size distribution, density and the desired cut-point for the separation. The separator is equipped with a pressure sensor mounted in upper intermediate zone above the teeter water pipes and an underflow discharge control valve. The pressure, as measured by a level sensor, is transmitted to the underflow discharge control valve using a set-point controller resulting in maintaining a constant height of the teeter bed and a steady discharge of the underflow. It is an effective equipment for discarding the fine impurities like silica and other gangue minerals of the raw coal.

Reflux classifier, a new high throughput device for solid–liquid processing, combines the uniform flow conditions of the liquid fluidized bed and the proven throughput advantage of the inclined lamella separator. Structurally, the elemental unit of the reflux classifier consists of a section of a rectilinear conventional fluidized bed and a set of parallel inclined plates spanning the whole cross section of the fluidized bed section. Particulate solids are suspended by an upward flow of liquid from the bottom of the vessel. Particulate solids are fluidized uniformly within the fluidized section of the reflux classifier. As the fluidized suspension enters an inclined channel between the plates, some particles settle onto the upward facing surface within the channel to form a sediment layer. The sediment slide down rapidly on the wall and return to the zone below. Some particles remain in the suspension, and hence are carried through the channel to the zone above. Clarified liquid is formed below the downward-facing wall, as a result of the particle flux leaving the suspension for the sediment layer. There are three layers formed within the inclined channel: a clear liquid zone below the downward facing wall of the channel, a layer of sediment on the upward facing wall, and a suspension of particles in between. The returned sediment is mixed with the rest of the suspension in the fluidized zone below and returned to the inclined channel as a result of the fluidization. This internal self-recycling effect, referred to as the reflux action, is an interaction between the inclined channels and the suspension of particles. The nature of the fluidized zone, referred to as the mixing zone of the reflux classifier, is very different to that present in a conventional fluidized bed.

The reflux classifier consists of a conventional fluidized bed with a set of parallel inclined plates and providing a stable response to large changes in the solid throughput. At bottom of the inclined section, a pressure transducer senses the high-density suspension, resulting in their discharge when the suspension density exceeds that of the set point. In the absence of high density particles the fluidized water maintains a suspension within the vessel and the excess suspension reports to the overflow. The effective sedimentation area of the vessel is increased by these inclined plates and fluidized suspension passes up through the inclined channels. Faster settling particles segregate onto the inclined plates and slide back down to below the fluidized zone. The reflux classifier was used to separate coal and mineral matter in a number of studies, covering a broad range of vessel geometries and feed conditions.

34.4   THREE PRODUCT CYCLONE

The three-product cyclone was originally developed in Russia and is now extensively used in China. The cyclone has recently entered the South African coal industry, and with the obvious advantages that this item of process equipment offers our ever-evolving industry, it is safe to assume that it will add value to dense medium circuits in South Africa. The three-product cyclone consists of a cylindrical dense medium vessel, similar to a LARCODEMS, with a conventional dense medium cyclone attached to the rejects outlet of the primary unit. The cyclones can be pump fed or gravity fed. The three-product cyclone has proven itself as an effective means to produce multiple products utilizing a single dense medium stream. It is important to understand that determination of the efficiency of the three-product cyclone is complicated by the fact that the sinks from the primary cyclone (which is also the feed to the secondary) cannot be sampled. This means that neither the primary nor the secondary stage partition curve can be computed directly. By following iterative procedure it is possible to obtain the partition data for the two cyclones and the efficiency of the cyclone was found good while operating South African coals.

34.5   FLOTATION

The new flotation machine Heyl and Patterson Cyclo-cell has been developed and installed in about 25 U.S. Preparation plants. This cell has no moving or mechanical parts. Agitation is accomplished by submerged vortex chambers which impart cyclonic motion to the slurry before it discharges in the form of a jet-like spray. The vortex chamber can be placed in an open tank or chamber of any size needed. Low pressure air is introduced into the centre of the discharge spray and is sheared into fine bubbles which are dispersed through the cell.

The flotation of low rank and/or oxidized coals and selective separation of pyrite from coal are two main problems associated with coal flotation. Because of the limited pyrite rejection achieved by coal flotation, a two-stage **reverse flotation** process has been developed. This process involves a first-stage conventional coal flotation step to reject most of the high-ash refuse and some of the coarser or liberated pyrite as tailing. The coal froth concentrate, with some dilution water, then goes to a second-stage froth flotation where a hydrophilic colloid is added to depress the coal, followed by a sulphydryl collector to float the pyrite. The coal depressant and pyrite collector used in most of the pyrite flotation work reported are Aero Depressant 633 and Potassium amyl xanthate.

Spray flotation is the latest technique emerging out for the beneficiation of fine coals where the advantages of turbulence for adhering more fine coals caused by spraying the slurry may be utilized along with that of counter-current pneumatic laminar transport of the fines.

Stack Cell Flotation is a new high-intensity flotation system. Stack Cell flotation makes use of pre-aeration coupled with a high-shear feed canister. This arrangement provides efficient bubble-particle contacting, thereby substantially shortening the residence time required for coal collection and virtually eliminating most of the column height.

Stack Cell is a proprietary flotation system that concentrates the energy used to generate bubbles and provides bubble-particle contact into a relatively small volume. An impeller in the aeration chamber located in the center of the cell shears the air into extremely fine bubbles in the presence of feed slurry, thereby promoting bubble-particle contact. Unlike conventional, mechanically-agitated flotation cells, the energy imparted to the slurry is used solely to generate bubbles rather than to maintain particles in suspension. This leads to reduced mixing in the cell and shorter residence time requirements.

During operation, feed slurry is introduced to the cell through a side (or bottom) feed port. At this point, low pressure air is added to the feed slurry. The aerated feed slurry then travels into the aeration chamber where significant shear is imparted to the system. The shear forces imparted to the system are used to create bubbles for bubble-particle collisions. In fact, all of these bubble-particle collisions occur in the aeration chamber prior to discharge into the outer tank. Once the slurry enters the outer tank, phase separation occurs between the froth and pulp. A pulp level is maintained in the outer tank to provide a deep froth that can be washed to minimize the entrainment of ultrafine high-ash clay material. The froth overflows into a froth collection launder, while the tailings are discharged using either a control valve or mechanical weir system. The system is specifically designed to have both a small footprint and a gravity-driven feed system. This allows multiple units to be "stacked" in series on subsequent levels in the plant or placed ahead of existing column or convention flotation circuits.

During the past few years, the **Air-Sparged Hydrocyclone** (ASH) has been developed for the fast and efficient flotation of fine coal particles in a centrifugal field. The air-sparged hydrocyclone consists of a right-vertical cylinder having a porous wall, a conventional cyclone header, and a froth pedestal located at the bottom of the porous cylinder. The slurry is fed tangentially through the conventional cyclone header into the porous cylinder to develop a swirl flow of a certain thickness in the radial direction (called the swirl-layer thickness) and is discharged through the annular opening between the cylinder wall and the froth pedestal. Air is sparged through the jacketed porous cylinder wall and is sheared into small bubbles by the swirl flow.

Hydrophobic particles in the slurry collide with these bubbles and after attachment, are transported radially into a froth phase which forms on the cylinder axis. The froth phase is stabilized and constrained by a froth pedestal at the underflow and thus moves towards the vortex finder of the cyclone header and is discharged as an overflow product. Hydrophilic particles generally remain in the slurry phase and are discharged as an underflow product through the annulus created by the froth pedestal.

PNEUFLOT pneumatic flotation machines are of latest development and are being developed by MBE Coal & Minerals Technology GmbH since 2009. The flotation pulp is first directed to a single aerating unit arranged in the vertical pipe above the flotation cell. The aerator (self-aerated) is installed in the vertical feed pipe. Following aeration, the pulp flows through the central pipe to the slurry distributor ring located at the bottom of the cell where it is vertically deflected upward through high wear resistant ceramic nozzles. The air bubbles covered with hydrophobic particles ascend to the upper cell area and form a froth layer on the surface which flows off into a froth launder surrounding the cell like a ring.

Particles not clinging to air bubbles are discharged with the pulp from the bottommost point of the cell. The pulp level is kept constant either by a level probe which actuates a valve controlling the discharge or by a device known as a "gooseneck discharge". The kinetic energy required for adhesion at the bubble/particle interface is generated by the turbulent flow of the pulp in the aerator unlike any other technology which takes place in the vessel. The necessary flow rate and pressure are delivered by the appropriate slurry feed pump. The pulp distributor injects the aerated pulp in an upward motion into the flotation vessel. The cell is only responsible for separating the remaining pulp from the froth formed by the loaded bubbles.

Self-aerating units which do not require compressed air have been developed. The slurry is pressed through small wear-proof ceramic nozzles distributed in circles pointing to a large Venturi and thus creating a vacuum when the pulp is pumped through it. This effect pulls air into the pulp. The circular arrangement of the nozzles distributes the pulp flow creating the necessary turbulence for intensive air bubble/coal particle contact. Only one aerator unit per flotation cell is needed to achieve high performance.

PNEUFLOT is applicable for flotation of coal both coking and steam coals. Pneuflot has shown its efficiency in many mines around the world. The energy consumption, the space and manpower requirements are considerably reduced by the application of Pneuflot cells. Better recovery and more yield can be obtained with Pneuflot because of optimal particle and bubble contact. Other advantages are higher selectivity and no re-sliming. Small air bubbles for fine material or bigger air bubbles for coarse feed material can be produced with the same aerator design.

34.6   HIGH GRADIENT MAGNETIC SEPARATION (HGMS)

High Gradient Magnetic Separation can be applied to remove inorganic sulphur and ash-forming minerals from coal. Most of the mineral impurities in coal, which contribute to its pyretic sulphur, sulphate sulphur and ash content, are weakly magnetic (paramagnetic). These can be separated normally from the pulverized diamagnetic or practically non-magnetic coal by magnetic means. Both wet and dry magnetic separation processes can be used.

In the wet magnetic separation process, coal is separated by passing a water slurry of finely pulverized coal (generally 70%–200 mesh) through a container where it is subjected to a high-intensity, high-gradient magnetic field. The container is packed with a "capture" matrix made of stainless steel wool. In the presence of magnetic field, pyrite and mineral matter becomes magnetized and is trapped in the matrix while the unaffected coal particles pass through the container. When the matrix is loaded to its magnetic capacity, the slurry feed is stopped and the electric power is cut off. The matrix is then backwashed to remove pyrite and mineral matter. Afterwards, the feed and the power are resumed and the entire process is repeated.

In the continuous separator, the "capture" matrix is a continuous, segmented metal belt which passes through the magnetic section of the separator where the coal slurry is introduced and beneficiated. The belt then travels into the washing section to wash off pyrite and mineral matter trapped on the belt. The cleaned belt section then returns for the entire process to repeat. Small amounts of flocculant and dispersant solutions are added to the coal slurry to facilitate the beneficiation process.

In the dry process, either an air entrained flow or recirculating air fluidization is used. The recirculating air fluidization can effectively beneficiate 70% to 80% of –200 mesh coal without any external size classification, ultra fines removal and coal drying prior to magnetic separation.

Preliminary studies have shown the HGMS can be used to beneficiate coal dispersed in fuel oil or suspended in methanol.

Physical methods such as thermal treatment, microwave radiation and the selective adsorption of specially prepared dispersions of colloidal magnetic particles can be used to alter the magnetic characteristics of pulverized coal and its impurities for efficient magnetic separation.

34.7   ELECTOSTATIC SEPARATION

The basis of any electrostatic separation for finely divided matter is the interaction between an external electric field and the electric charges acquired by the various particles. Small particles can be charged by tribo-electrification, conductive induction or corona charging. The charges developed depend on the particle characteristics such as composition, crystal structure, and surface state, as well as environmental factors such as temperature and humidity. After charging, particles of different types can be separated according to the charge to mass ratio using forces in an electric field.

Tribo-electric separation of coal from minerals has been successfully demonstrated by laboratory experiments and pilot plant studies. The basic principle of tribo-electrification is that when two types of particles (A & B) placed on surface are made to repeatedly contact one another as well as the surface, the surface will acquire electrons from one type of particles (say particle A) and give electrons to another type of particles (particle B) so that particle A will become positively charged and particle B will become negatively charged.

In tribo-electric separation of coal, the coal is first pulverized into a fine powder of size 5–750 μm. The powder is then charged electrostatically by impaction against a metal surface such as copper. On contact with copper, the organic coal particles become positively charged and the pyrites and inorganic mineral particles become negatively charged. This powder material, after tribo-charging, passes through an electrostatic separator consisting of two conducting plates across which a high voltage is applied. The organic coal particles are attracted toward the negative plate, whereas the pyrites and mineral particles are attracted toward the positive plate.

Tribo-electrification is the dominant charge transfer mechanism and is extremely sensitive to surface state. Any transient surface changes and time of contact will have profound effects on the charge transfer. The tribo-electric separation process is very attractive from both energy usage and economic points of view. However, an understanding of the surface science involved in the electrostatic charging mechanisms of coal and mineral particles is required to make the process successful commercially.

Electrostatic methods applied to coal in a fluidized state are the newest in the field of separation. Fluidization is an ideal means of "individualizing" and charging electrically fine particles while subjecting them to the influence of an electric field. Under certain conditions, the repeated collisions generate contact or tribo-electrification.

Various types of equipment for electrostatic beneficiation of coal have been tried in laboratories around the world. The most promising equipment for application to coal are Free-fall separation tower in combination with fluidized bed tribo-electrification for particles around 50 to 500 μm size and the Dilute-phase loop for particles of – 50 μm.

34.8   CHEMICAL BENEFICIATION

The chemical cleaning of coals shows that the methods used include acid leaching, alkali leaching under high pressure and at elevated temperatures, and leaching by molten caustic baths. Demineralization and desulfurization of coal by aqueous or fused sodium hydroxide alone or followed by treatment with mineral acids has been reported by many investigators. They achieved different levels of success in removing mineral matter and sulfur from coal of different sources by treatment with sodium hydroxide alone or in combination with other substances.

Meyers, Battelle hydrothermal, Ledgmont, KVB, and PERC processes are some of the chemical beneficiation processes. Among them, Meyers process is the most developed one. In this process, raw coal grounded to –14 mesh is reacted with an aqueous ferric sulphate solution at temperatures ranging between 90°C and 130°C and at pressures up to 120 psig. The coal matter goes through the process virtually unchanged, but the pyretic sulphur present in the coal is leached out by the ferric sulphate solution and the majority of the pyrites are converted to ferrous sulphate, sulphuric acid, and elemental sulphur. High-purity oxygen is also added to the reaction mixture to simultaneously regenerate the ferric sulphate from the spent ferrous sulphate solution.

The coal is filtered from the spent solution, washed with recycle water and dried using centrifuges. The moist coal is then flash-dried by high temperature steam and cooled to yield the cleaned coal. Excess ferrous sulphate generated in the process is separated and recovered as a by-product. The elemental sulphur that vaporizes during flash-drying is also recovered by either steam distillation or solvent extraction as a by-product.

The Meyers process is especially suited to process coals of high percentage pyritic sulphur. The process is capable of removing up to 95% of the pyritic sulphur and reducing the ash content of the feed coal by 10% to 30%. As a result, the process can yield a product coal that has up to 5% higher heating value than the feed coal.

In the context of growing industrial importance of clean coal and coal derivatives, and with the implementation of stringent environmental regulations, ultraclean coal technology development programs have gained significant importance world wide. No significant effort has been made in chemical beneficiation for Indian coals, which are of drift origin and have high-ash content with finely distributed mineral matter. Besides, all the studies have been carried out at diversified operating conditions and an elaborate research report is nonexistent. Most of the research works have been carried out for thermal coals and hence the effect of this chemical treatment method on coking properties has not been investigated thoroughly.

TATA Steel, studied the effect of aqueous alkali leaching along and in combination with acid leaching and washing on the removal of mineral matter from five different Indian coals containing high ash at temperatures from 45°C to 85°C under atmospheric pressure. Effect of the process and operating conditions on various properties of coal has been studied in detail for West Bokaro clean coal. It is possible to reduce the ash content of physically beneficiated Indian coals by treatment with caustic solution followed by acid washing. The degree of demineralization improved by increasing the reaction time, alkali concentrations, and temperature, and by reducing the coal particle size. A reduction is noticed in the Alumina (Al_2O_3) to Silica (SiO_2) ratio. A marginal reduction in sulfur content and significant reduction in phosphorous content was observed after the acid treatment. Improvements in the Crucible Swelling Number of the coals were observed after the acid treatment.

Part C

Coal utilization

Chapter 35

Coal utilization

Coal is used mainly for

1   Carbonization
2   Combustion
3   Gasification
4   Liquefaction

Coal is one of the cheapest and most important sources of energy, responsible for 41% of electricity production worldwide and for more than 60% of Steel Making. Access to modern energy services not only contributes to economic growth and household incomes but also to the improved quality of life that comes with better education and health services. All sources of energy will be needed to meet future energy demand, including coal.

Coal has many important uses worldwide. The most significant uses of coal are in electricity generation, steel production, cement manufacturing and as a liquid fuel. Global coal consumption has grown faster than any other fuel. The five largest coal users – China, USA, India, Russia and Japan – account for 76% of total global coal use. Different types of coal have different uses. The following are few of them.

35.1   COKING COAL

These coals, when heated in the absence of air, form coherent, strong and porous mass, free from volatiles, called coke. These coals have coking properties. They are mainly used in steel making and metallurgical industries and also used for hard coke manufacturing. Hence they are also known as metallurgical coals. Steel Industry is the second largest user of coal after the Electricity Industry. Metallurgical coke, produced from coking coal, is used as a fuel to smelt Iron in Blast Furnace. This Pig Iron which is produced is further refined to make Steel. Around 0.63 tonnes of coke is required to produce 1 tonne of Steel.

35.2   SEMI COKING COAL

These coals, when heated in the absence of air, form coherent mass not strong enough to be directly fed into the blast furnace. Such coals are blended with coking coal in adequate proportion to make coke. These coals have comparatively less coking properties than coking coal. They are used mainly as blendable coal in steel making, merchant coke manufacturing and other metallurgical industries.

35.3 NON LINKED WASHERY (NLW) COAL

Some of the coking coals of Jharia coalfields in India contain very high ash and they are characterized as difficult-to-wash. These coals when fed to the existing coking coal washeries results in low yield at the required ash level. These coals have been termed as NLW coals and are used for power utilities and non-core sector consumers.

35.4 NON COKING COAL

These coals are not having coking properties. The chief use of non coking coals is for power generation. These non coking coals are also called as thermal coals, power coals, steam coals. The second largest users of non coking coals are sponge iron and the cement industry. These coals are also used by fertilizer, glass, ceramic, paper, aluminium, chemical and brick industries, and also used for other heating purposes.

35.5 BENEFICIATED COAL

These coals have undergone the process of coal washing or coal beneficiation, resulting in value addition of coal due to reduction in ash percentage. Beneficiated coking coals are used in manufacturing of hard coke for steel making. Beneficiated non-coking coal is used mainly for power generation and also used by sponge iron, cement, fertilizer, glass, ceramic, paper, chemical and brick industries.

35.6 MIDDLINGS

Middlings are by-products of the three stage coal washing / beneficiation process, as a fraction of feed raw coal. They are used for power generation, cement plants, domestic fuel plants, brick manufacturing units, etc.

35.7 REJECTS

Rejects are the products of coal beneficiation process after separation of cleans and / or middlings, as a fraction of feed raw coal. They are used for Fluidized Bed Combustion (FBC) Boilers for power generation, road repairs, briquette (domestic fuel) making, land filling, mine back filling, etc.

35.8   COAL FINES

These are the screened fractions of raw coal. These are used in boilers, industrial furnaces as well as for domestic purposes.

Other important users of coal include alumina refineries, paper manufacturers, chemical and pharmaceutical industries, users of stone, clay and glass. Several chemical products can be produced from the by-products of coal. Refined coal tar is used in the manufacture of chemicals, such as creosote oil, naphthalene, phenol, and benzene. Ammonia gas recovered from coke ovens is used to manufacture ammonia salts, nitric acid and agricultural fertilizers. Thousands of different products have coal or coal by-products as components: soaps, aspirins, solvents, dyes, insecticides, explosives, plastics, synthetic rubber, synthetic fibres such as rayon and nylon, food preservatives, ammonia, fingernail polish and medicines. Coal is also an essential ingredient in the production of specialist products such as **Activated carbon** which is used in filters for water and air purification and in kidney dialysis machines, **Carbon fibre** which is an extremely strong but light weight reinforcement material used in construction, mountain bikes and tennis rackets, **Silicon metal** which is used to produce silicones and silanes, which are in turn used to make lubricants, water repellents, resins, cosmetics, hair shampoos and toothpastes.

By-products generated from burning coal in coal-fired power plants such as fly ash, bottom ash, boiler slag and flue gas desulphurisation gypsum are also used in Concrete Production. Fly ash can be used to replace or supplement cement in concrete. Fly ash produces a concrete that is strong and durable, with resistance to corrosion, alkali-aggregate expansion, sulphate and other forms of chemical attack. Coal combustion products are expected to continue to play a major role in the concrete market. Their use in other building products is also expected to grow as sustainable construction becomes more prominent, and more architects and building owners understand the benefits of using coal combustion products. Among the most significant environmental benefits of using fly ash over conventional cement is that greenhouse gas (GHG) emissions can be significantly reduced. For every tonne of fly ash used for a tonne of portland cement (the most common type of cement in general use around the world) approximately one tonne of carbon dioxide is prevented from entering the earth's atmosphere. Fly ash does not require the energy-intensive kilning process required by portland cement.

A process of converting coal to a liquid fuel, called as coal liquefaction, allows coal to be utilised as an alternative to oil. Current Transportation Industry does not make much use of coal as Fuel. However the increasing cost of Oil has made it economical to consider converting Coal into Gas and Liquid which can be used to power vehicles, ships etc. Fuels produced from coal also have potential outside the transportation sector. Coal-derived dimethyl ether (DME) is receiving particular attention today as it is a product that holds out great promise as a domestic fuel. DME is non-carcinogenic and non-toxic to handle and generates less carbon monoxide and hydrocarbon air pollution than LPG. DME can also be used as an alternative to diesel for transport, as well as for on and off-grid power applications.

The biggest market for coal is Asia, which accounts for over 67% of global coal consumption; although China is responsible for a significant proportion of this. Many countries do not have natural energy resources sufficient to cover their energy needs, and therefore need to import energy to help meet their requirements.

Chapter 36

Carbonization

Carbonization is the process of heating coal at a temperature of several hundred degrees centigrade in the absence of air to produce the following types of material

1   A carbon enriched solid, called **coke** if vesicular and fused or **Char** if less porous and not fused
2   liquid products, made up of a mixture of hydrocarbons called tar and aqueous solutions containing a variety of dissolved materials called ammonical liquor
3   Hydrocarbon and other compounds that remain in the form of gas on cooling to normal temperatures

Carbonization is the basis for manufacture of coke and also of many gasification and liquefaction techniques. The relative amounts of each type of product that can be derived from a given coal depend on its petrographic features and on the details of the carbonization process employed.

The most significant use of carbonization processes is in the manufacture of coke for metallurgical operations. Coke is the solid residue that remains when coal is heated out of contact with air until a substantial part of the volatile constituents have been driven off. Its principal use is in iron and steel manufacture, where it provides heat energy and acts as a reducing agent for the iron ore and support for other raw materials in iron making blast furnace.

Coke for this purpose is usually dense and relatively strong material, produced in a coke oven from a single coal or blend of selected coals. However, where the residue from the carbonization process is non-porous powder or granular mass, it is known as char. Char may also be used, in the form of specially moulded briquettes, in much the same way as coke (a product known as formed coke) or as a raw material for industrial products such as electrode carbon.

Depending upon the operation, temperature of the process, coal carbonization may be of three categories

1   Low Temperature Carbonization (L.T.C) at 500–600°C
2   Medium Temperature Carbonization (M.T.C) at 600–900°C
3   High Temperature Carbonization (H.T.C) at 900–1000°C

L.T.C. is commercially practiced for the production of semi-coke, also called as soft coke or char. The various products of low temperature carbonization of coal are: Semi-coke, low temperature tar, liquor, crude low temperature spirit and gas. Semi-coke is highly reactive and can be easily ignited into a smokeless flame. Semi-coke is an ideal domestic solid fuel. Semi-coke is also used for the production of iron in low shaft furnaces, for gasification into fuel gas or synthesis gas for fertilizers and chemicals, and for the preparation of coke oven blends etc.

H.T.C is carried out for the production of hard coke and coal gas. M.T.C does not have commercial application. However, many H.T.C.s approach the conditions of M.T.C. Because of the important use of hard coke in blast furnace and cupola, the H.T.C is practiced on a much bigger scale than L.T.C.

H.T.C. is commercially practiced in coke ovens and to much lesser extent in gas retorts. The coke oven may be **Beehive** type or **By-product** type. The by-products are recovered only in the latter type of coke ovens while they are burnt off in the former. Coke, tar, crude benzol, ammonia (as concentrated aqueous solution or ammonium sulphate crystals) and coke oven gas are usually produced in by-product ovens. Beehive ovens, even though by-products are not recovered, are still in use in India because of good quality coke production and also the coke production is not connected with the availability of the market for by-products. Different types of coke are produced from coking coals.

- **Metallurgical coke** is produced in coke ovens and is mainly used in the reduction of iron ore to pig iron in blast furnace. The iron and steel industries consume 90 percent of the metallurgical coke produced every year. It is also consumed in blast and electric furnaces for ferro-alloy production, reduction of metal oxides to metals and chlorides, reduction of phosphates and sulphates, and in the reduction of carbonates to carbides. Metallurgical coke is also used in those products which require high performance carbon and high resilience factor. For instance, the metallurgical coke is used in drilling applications, conductive flooring, electrolytic process, frictional materials, corrosion materials, ceramic packing, foundry carbon raiser, and heat treatment and foundry coatings. One of the primary reasons why metallurgical coke is so useful is because of its stable burning temperature which makes the production of metal products and other metal applications easier.
- **Foundry coke** is produced in beehive or non-recovery coke ovens and is used at foundries to melt iron and various copper, lead, tin and zinc alloys in cupolas. The basic coke requirements are the same as for metallurgical coke but the size specification varies, depending on the size of the cupola. Foundry coke is almost always of larger size than metallurgical coke.
- **Domestic coke**, or more often semi-coke, is used as a fuel. A low ash, easily ignited coke of high specific energy with very low sulphur content is required.
- **Gas coke** is the coke obtained from the gas retorts. Owing to its poorer strength it is not suitable in blast furnace operation. It is used as a fuel in miscellaneous industries and domestic ovens. The gas produced in gas retorts is known as coal gas or Town gas.

36.1   COKING MECHANISM [58]

There are several necessary conditions for coal to be transformed into coke. The more important are

- Heat supply
- Enclosure to prevent oxygen contact with the coal
- Close contact between the coal particles during the carbonization process

In conventional vertical coke ovens, the heat is supplied from gas-burning flues located within the walls of each oven. Charging of the coal into the oven and pushing of the product coke from the oven are accomplished via openings in the oven that can be sealed to prevent incursion of air. The coal particles are charged into the oven by being dropped from a height so that the particles are packed together between the opposite walls of the oven, causing contact between particles. In this configuration, even for cubic particles and excluding contact with gas pockets, each particle, on average, comes into contact with six other particles.

Upon heating, coal molecules undergo many reactions. The primary reactions involve pyrolysis and formation of radicals having lower molecular weight than in the original coal. Some of the radicals, enriched with hydrogen, form liquid and gaseous products. In other reactions some radicals form more stable substances of higher molecular weight and less hydrogen content. Surface tension on the liquid components promotes additional contact between these components to further facilitate fusing the coal particles as they are heated.

When coal is charged into the hot coke oven, the heat is transferred from the heated brick walls into the coal charge. From about 375°C to 475°C, the coal particles adjacent to the coke oven walls and doors begin to de-volatilize and soften immediately. The softened, or fluidized, particles sinter into each other and are further de-volatilized to form a layer of fully sintered coal particles, i.e. coke against the oven walls and doors. Away from these hot surfaces are successive layers of coal in various stages of softening, melting, fusing, and re-solidifying. This arrangement results in the existence of an envelope of "plastic" coal that continues to move inward, away from the heated surfaces, until the plastic envelope converges at the center of the coal charge. What results are three separate regimes of coal/coke transformation that occur simultaneously in a given coke oven until the plastic envelope is consumed. Formation and movement of the plastic envelope is shown in Fig. 36.1.1.

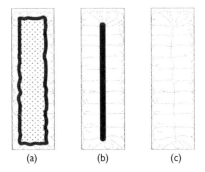

(a)   (b)   (c)

Figure 36.1.1 Development of plastic layer movement during coking: (a) about midway in coking cycle; (b) convergence of plastic envelope; and (c) end of coking cycle. The thick, dark, solid line represents the plastic envelope, defining the boundary between coal and semicoke; and represents the plasticized coal.

The plastic envelope represents a barrier to gas movement. Although gases generated in the envelope move out in both directions, gases generated on either side of the envelope do not generally cross this barrier. At about 475°C to 600°C, there is a marked evolution of tar, and aromatic hydrocarbon compounds, followed by re-solidification of the plastic mass into semi-coke. The semi-coke adjacent to the envelope still contains much volatile gas which continues to be driven off as it reaches higher temperatures from the oven walls and doors. The remaining volatiles in the semi-coke decrease to nearly zero as proximity to the hot surfaces increases. During this heating, carbon crystal structure grows and become increasingly oriented. The porosity of the carbon decreases as the pore wall thickens and densify. After semi-coke is formed and continues to degas, it tends to physically shrink. The volume of this material is lowered as the carbon atoms align into more compact forms. This effect tends to cause the coke mass to contract away from the oven walls and doors. However, buildup of gas pressure within the plastic layer and thermal expansion of the coal particles produce forces that tend to continue pressing the coke in contact with the oven walls and doors. The force keeping the coke in contact with the walls and doors acts to maintain good heat transfer from the oven surfaces into the coke mass.

At 600°C to 1100°C, the coke stabilization phase begins. This is characterized by contraction of coke mass, structural development of coke and final hydrogen evolution. The coking cycle starts when coal is charged into the hot oven and ends when the last of the volatiles are degassed from the coke at the center of the charge, which is the coolest part of the charge. The incandescent coke mass thus formed is pushed from the oven and is wet or dry quenched prior to its shipment to the blast furnace. A complete coke making cycle requires 18 hours or more.

36.2   COKE OVENS

Coke ovens are primarily of two types. (a) Beehive or non-recovery coke oven (b) By-product coke oven

36.2.1   Beehive coke oven

Beehive Coke Ovens are called that because they are built in a beehive-like hemispherical shape and then covered with earth. The Beehive Ovens are built in banks of ovens, called a battery, connected by common walls and operated as a unit, where coal undergoes destructive distillation under negative pressure to produce coke. A strong retaining wall is built in front, and then covered with earth. The earth cover helped to insulate the ovens so that they will retain the heat after firing to help fire the next batch or charge of coal. It is designed for the combustion of coke oven gas from which byproducts are not recovered.

To heat a coke oven, a wood fire is first started and then gradually increased in intensity. Lump coal is added within 2 to 4 days to gradually heat a cold oven. Once the ovens are heated, they will burn continuously until the fire brick in them burned out. Then they will have to be rebuilt with new brick, and the heating process would begin again.

A small charge of coal is dumped in through the "tunnel head" (the hole at the top of the oven), and the front door is partially bricked up, leaving a gap for draft. The product of this first small charge, used to finish heating the oven, is called "black jack;" and it will be used to start other ovens. The oven is heated sufficiently in 4 or 5 days. The "black jack" is removed, about two-thirds of the front door is closed off with firebrick, and the oven is ready for a full charge of coal. The "Charger," running a "Larry," will charge the oven. About 1½ tons of coal will yield about 1 ton of coke.

The "Leveler" level the charge with a tool which resembled a large, toothless rake. A typical leveler consisted of a 3" × 16" iron bar welded at right angles to a 15 foot long pipe with a loop handle at the end. The "Leveler" pull the charge from side to side in the oven and level the charge. Once the first oven is leveled, the "Leveler" will move on to the next oven and so on. Once the charge is leveled, the door is bricked up by the "Mason" up to within 1½ inches of the top and the brick is daubed with clay to make it airtight. Fig. 36.2.1 shows the Beehive coke oven battery.

An oven attendant regulates the small opening. The burning time varied from 44 to 72 hours, depending upon the size of the charge and the oven temperature. The gases generated by the intense heat of the ovens ignited and burned slowly downward. When sufficient burning had taken place, the door is closed tightly, and the tunnel head is closed either partially or completely. Once the controlled burning is completed, the "Puller" will open the door and insert a spray pipe connected to a water hose for quenching. After quenching, coke will be discharged.

36.2.2 By-product coke oven

By-product Coke oven (Fig. 36.2.2.1) [58] is of slot type and consists of a narrow, rectangular refractory coking chamber equipped with removable doors at both ends and charging hole lids so that it can be sealed and the coal is heated in the absence of air. The removable doors at both ends enable the hot coke to be pushed out with a ram. The width of the coke discharge side is slightly more, 3–4 cm more than the pusher side. The side of the coke oven where the pusher machine works is known as **ram side** or **pusher side** and the other side is known as **coke side**. The chamber is also equipped with a gas collecting system for the removal of the volatile matter distilled from the coal. The coking chamber and its coal charge are heated by heating walls located on each side of the coking chamber. The heating walls contain a series of vertical heating flues in which a fuel gas is burned. A large number of ovens with heating flues in between are arranged in a battery.

Figure 36.2.1 Beehive coke oven battery.

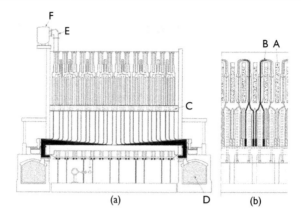

Figure 36.2.2.1 (a) By-product coke oven and (b) a section therein.
A – coke oven chamber containing coal; B – oven wall heating flue; C – sole heating flue;
D – air preheating; E – standpipe; F – collecting main.

Coal is usually received on railroad cars or barges. Conveyor belts transfer the coal as needed to blending bins. The blended coal is transported to the coal storage bunkers on the coke oven battery (Fig. 36.2.2.2).

A weighed amount or specific volume of coal is discharged from the bunker into a larry car, which is the charging vehicle driven by electric motors that can travel the length of the battery on a wide gauge rail. The larry car is positioned over the empty hot oven, the lids on the charging ports are removed, and the coal is discharged from the hoppers of the larry car into the oven.

After completion of charging and reseating of the charging hole doors, a small sub-door at the top of one of the oven doors is opened and a steel leveling bar is inserted along the length of the oven at the top of the coal charge. The leveling bar is moved back and forth over the coal charge to produce a level coal charge having sufficient free space above the charge. This free space is important in ensuring balanced heating of the coal and is needed for conveying the carbonization volatiles out of the oven. Most coke batteries charge wet coal into the ovens, however, a few facilities are equipped with coal pre-heaters that not only remove all moisture from the coal, but preheat it to 150–200°C in order to quicken the carbonization process.

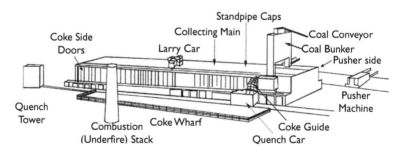

Figure 36.2.2.2 By-product Coke Oven Battery.

The oven walls are made of silica bricks. Each pair of ovens is separated by a system of vertical flues. Air for combustion is preheated in regenerators. Gaseous fuels (usually coke oven gas or blast furnace gas) and pre-heated air are supplied to the heating flues and hot combustion gases are passed through the regenarator or waste heat boiler and finally let off to atmosphere through the chimney. Modern coke ovens are always provided with regenerators, built underneath the ovens. The heat recovered in the regenerators are utilized for pre heating of air and blast furnace gas used for heating of the oven. Coke oven gas could not be preheated as it get cracked in the brickwork of the regenerators resulting in deposition of carbon soot on regenerator walls thereby reducing its heat transfer capacity. Carbon soot may also choke the smaller diameter burners in the heating chambers. Regenerators work on the principle of alternative heating and cooling cycle usually at bout 30 minutes interval.

The volatile gases, generated from the coal during carbonization, flow to the top of the oven, into the free space, and out the standpipes. The standpipes are all connected to huge collecting mains that run the length of the battery. These mains transport the gases to the by-product plant in which the gases are processed into various materials. Cooling water is sprayed into the mains in order to cool the gases and to condense some of the tar out of the gas. During charging, standpipe valves are positioned so that all gases pass directly into the collecting main.

Flue temperature in the heating chamber is maintained at about 1200–1300°C. The carbonization proceeds for the average coking period of 15–18 hours. At the end of each oven's coking cycle, the doors on both sides of coke ovens are opened and the pushing ram pushes the red hot coke into the quenching car. Swelling and shrinking of coal during carbonization as the temperature rises puts some pressure on the walls. Hence the oven should not be pushed until the coke has shrunk clear of walls.

The red hot coke is then quenched with large amount of water. An alternative dry quenching uses inert circulating gases (N_2) which transfers the heat to waste heat boilers. After quenching, the hot car again moves to dump the coke onto a refractory covered coke wharf sloped away from the hot car. The coke flows to the bottom of the wharf at which point it drops onto a conveyor system for transportation to blast furnace, storage pile, or for further transportation out of the plant.

Heating chamber (located on both the sides of an oven) is divided into several sections by partition walls. Burners are located at the bottom and are (called under firing burners) in pairs. In the first cycle the gas burns in one and the flue gas passes through other set of burners. After 20 or 30 minutes the gas flow is reversed i.e. the gas burns in other set of burners and the flue gas is taken out through the burners which were initially fired. This reversal of flow of gas/air and waste gas (flue gas) is done continuously at fixed interval (generally 20 or 30 minutes). Regenerators which are normally made of fireclay bricks are used for waste heat recovery from the flue gas and in the next cycle air or gas are preheated in the hot regenerator before entering the burners. Each heating chamber is provided with two regenerators. While the waste gas (flue gas) passes through the one set (thereby heating its bricks) the fuel gas (Blast furnace gas, Coke oven gas, Producer gas etc.) and air is heated in the other set before firing in the burner.

In yet another heating system of coke oven called cross over flue system, the flue gas passes from one heating chamber to another through the cross over flue at the top of the oven.

The coke oven battery may be suported either diectly on the foundation or on a set of tall columns created on foundation, called underjet ovens. In some coke ovens, coke oven gas (rich gas) is only used as fuel, these are called simple ovens and in other coke ovens, mixture of coke oven gas and blast furnace gas (lean gas) are used as the fuel, these ovens are called compound ovens. The design of these coke ovens vary from each other depending upon the arrangement of flue. Semet-Solvey design deals with the horizontal flues. Due to the horizontal flue pass, the stability of the ovens are lower than the ovens with vertical flue. Kopper cross regenerative, Simon Carves, Wilputte, Otto, soviet PVR, Dider, Koppers-Becker, Soviet PK are the examples of coke ovens with vertical flue pass.

The coke oven gas is subjected to the following treatment to recover the by-products (chemicals) present in it, before it is used as a fuel gas:

- Cooling of the gas for condensation of tar and ammoniacal liquors
- Electrostatic separation of remaining tar
- Recovery of ammonia as ammonium sulphate by reaction with H_2SO_4
- Gas is oil washed to recover naphthalene and benzol
- Desulphurisation of gas with moist ferric hydroxide (bog iron)
- Distribution of fuel gas to consumer furnaces

Typical yields in high temperature carbonization of coking coals in a by product coke oven is given in Table 36.2.2.

36.2.3 Non-recovery coke oven

Coke making started with the beehive ovens, which were later enhanced to non-recovery type of coke ovens. The by-product ovens because of the value addition due to the recovery of coal chemicals were preferred over non-recovery ovens as a more viable and profitable investment. The stringent pollution laws and the high cost involved in the installation of pollution control equipment led to many by-product coke oven plants to face closure in the 80's and 90's. This led to the revival of interest in the non-recovery coke oven technology as it was realized that it could be used with minimum investment and complied with the pollution control regulations. Non-recovery coke ovens are used for production of coke, whereby products are not recovered. All of the coke oven gas is burned, and instead

Table 36.2.2 Typical yields in H.T.C. in By-product coke oven.

Products	Yield, wt%
Coke	75
Gas	15
Tar	3
Benzol	1
Ammonia	1
Water vapour	5
Total	100

of recovery of chemicals, this process recovers the heat. Power can be generated by means of waste gas heat recovery. In this way waste can be converted to wealth. Hence non-recovery type of coke oven is energy efficient and environment friendly.

Non-recovery ovens are of a horizontal design with a typical range of 30 to 60 ovens per battery. Each oven is equipped with two doors. The oven is charged through the oven doorway with a coal conveyor. After an oven is charged, carbonization begins as a result of the hot oven brick work from the previous charge. Combustion products and volatiles that evolve from the coal mass are burned in the chamber above the coal, in the gas pathway through the walls, and beneath the oven in sole flues. Each oven chamber has two to six down-comers in each oven wall, and the sole flue may be subdivided into separate flues that are supplied by the down-comers.

Primary combustion air is introduced into the oven chamber above the coal through one of several dampered ports in the door. The dampers are adjusted to maintain the proper temperature in the oven crown. Outside air may also be introduced into the sole flues; however, additional air usually is required in the sole flue only for the first hour or two after charging. Gas flow is a result of natural or induced draft, and the oven is maintained under a negative pressure. Consequently, the ovens typically do not leak as do the byproduct ovens maintained under a positive pressure. However, door leaks can occur if the pressure in the oven becomes positive because of a plugged uptake damper, fouling of the heat exchanger used for heat recovery, and other operating problems.

The non-recovery ovens are provided with sufficient free space between the oven top and the coal bed where the volatile matters coming out from the coal charged during carbonization get combusted. The adequate free space as well as controlled supply of air ensures efficient combustion of the hydrocarbons present in the volatile matter. The un-burnt volatiles along with the hot flue goes to the sole via volatile chamber provided at the side walls of the oven where secondary air is injected to facilitate the complete combustion of the remaining hydrocarbons. The burning of the volatile matter in the sole increases the temperature of the coke oven bed that increases the efficiency of the coke oven. Also an additional combustion chamber has been provided for complete combustion of volatiles and settling down of particulate matters. All the above mentioned pollution control devices are inbuilt in the oven system. The clean flue gas can also be utilized in heat recovery units.

The combustion gases are removed from the ovens and directed to the stack through a waste heat tunnel that is located atop the battery centerline and extends the length of the battery. At the end of the coking cycle, a worker inspect each oven by opening one of the damper ports to assure the completion of coking. This inspection procedure cannot be performed on byproduct coke batteries because they are operated under positive pressure. Pushing and quenching operations are similar to those at byproduct coke oven batteries. One slight difference in pushing is that the height of fall of the hot coke is less for the non-recovery oven because of its horizontal design.

36.2.4 Coke production

Most of the coke oven plants were an integral part of iron and steel industry. Due to increasing demand of iron and steel, there has been a considerable increase in the coke oven capacity. As per IEA clean coal centre, annual production of coke in the world has increased from 343.75 million tones in 2000 to 592.74 million tones in 2010. Over 80% of coke oven batteries around the world are by-product coke ovens. In India, coke oven batteries had been built since beginning of this century but the major thrust came when batteries were built in fifties based on USSR, UK and German designs as part of steel plants.

36.3   ROLE OF COKE IN BLAST FURNACE

The coke plays the following three major roles in a blast furnace

1   It is a fuel providing heat for meeting the endothermic requirements of chemical reactions and melting of slag and metal.
2   It produces and regenerates reducing gases for the reduction of iron oxides.
3   It provides an open permeable bed through which slag and metal pass down into the hearth and hot reducing gases pass upwards.

Simple understanding of the Blast furnace process for production of pig iron makes clear of the role of coke in blast furnace.

36.3.1   Blast furnace process

Blast furnace consists of the foundation, the hearth, the bosh, and the stack as shown in Fig. 36.3.1. A Bell and hopper arrangement made at the top of the furnace is used for charging the solid material. Four exhaust pipes are connected to the furnace top which are further joined to a bigger pipe called down-comer through which the gas is delivered to the gas cleaning system. Air from hot blast stove is supplied through a bustle pipe to the tuyeres arranged at the bosh level.

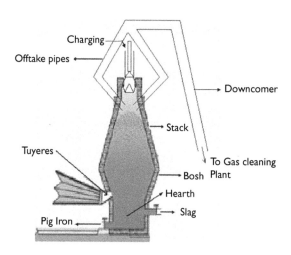

Figure 36.3.1 Blast Furnace.

The raw materials called **charge** (Iron ore, Coke, Limestone, Dolomite) are fed separately in the desired sequence at the top of the stack through a charge distribution system. The hot air blast heated to 800–1300°C is blown through tuyeres at a velocity of around 200–300 m/sec and at a pressure of 2–4 atm.

The oxygen from the preheated blast combines with the carbon of coke which get heated to nearly 1500°C during its descent from top to bottom of the stack and burns as $2C + O_2 = 2CO$ generating temperatures of the order of 1900–2000°C. This represents the main source of heat and reducing gas. The gases containing mainly nitrogen and carbon monoxide ascend upwards through the charge. As the charge descent from the upper part of the stack, it attains a temperature of 400°C and looses almost all its moisture. As the charge further descends, it meets higher temperatures at which the reducing intensity of C and CO increases and the ore is reduced through the stages to metallic Iron as follows at temperatures below 570°C

$$3Fe_2O_3 + CO = 2Fe_3O_4 + CO_2 \qquad (36.3.1)$$
$$Fe_3O_4 + 4CO = 3Fe + 4CO_2 \qquad (36.3.2)$$

At temperatures above 570°C, ore is reduced as follows since wustite (FeO) is stable only above 570°C

$$3Fe_2O_3 + CO = 2Fe_3O_4 + CO_2 \qquad (36.3.3)$$
$$Fe_3O_4 + CO = 3FeO + CO_2 \qquad (36.3.4)$$
$$FeO + CO = Fe + CO_2 \qquad (36.3.5)$$

Main reactions occur in the range of 700° to 1200°C. Besides the reduction of iron oxide, higher oxides of manganese are also reduced to lower oxides.

The reduction of Fe_2O_3 and Fe_3O_4 to FeO is completed before the reduction to metallic iron starts as Fe_2O_3 and Fe_3O_4 are more stable at upper portion than FeO and Fe. Even if some Fe_2O_3 happens to be reduced to metallic iron in the upper portion, it would have a strong tendency to re-oxidize atleast to FeO until the charge has descended to the lower portion where FeO and Fe are more stable.

$$3Fe_2O_3 + 6CO = 4Fe + 6CO_2 \qquad (36.3.6)$$
$$Fe + CO_2 = FeO + CO \qquad (36.3.7)$$
$$Fe + CO = FeO + C \qquad (36.3.8)$$

The reaction between CO and iron ore in the upper part of the stack, where the temperature is too low for the coke to react, is called **indirect reduction**. The reduction of Fe_2O_3 to metallic iron also takes place by reacting directly with coke at the lower part of the stack where high temperature of about 1200°C exists.

$$3Fe_2O_3 + C = 2Fe_3O_4 + CO \qquad (36.3.9)$$
$$Fe_3O_4 + C = 3FeO + CO \qquad (36.3.10)$$
$$FeO + C = Fe + CO \qquad (36.3.11)$$

These reactions are sometimes called **direct reduction**. Major part of the reduction of oxides takes place indirectly by CO generated at the tuyere level and small amount of oxide is reduced directly by solid carbon. While the gases are ascending, part of CO_2 formed during reduction also react with coke and regenerates the CO.

$$CO_2 + C = 2CO \qquad (36.3.12)$$

This regeneration reaction, known as **Boudourd reaction,** is sometimes called **solution loss reaction,** the meaning being that some carbon reacts (dissolves) before it reaches the tuyeres. Thus, in the ascending gases, the percentage of CO in the total $CO + CO_2$ decreases from 100% at lower level to 70% at the throat.

Limestone and dolomite, added as a flux in the charge, get calcined as

$$CaCO_3 = CaO + CO_2 \qquad (36.2.13)$$
$$MgCO_3 = MgO + CO_2 \qquad (36.3.14)$$

in the temperature zone of 800°-1000°C. The resulting basic oxides combine with the gangue oxides and coke ash to form the slag. $CaO + Al_2O_3 + SiO_2 =$ silicates

The flux makes the gangue and coke ash fusible at a relatively low temperature, reduces the viscosity of the slag and decreases the activity of some of its components to make them stable or unstable in the slag phase.

Reduction of oxides of iron is practically over while it is in the solid state. This reduced iron is impure because of associated gangue constituents of the ore. The charge materials begin to soften and fuse as they come down into the bottom of the stack. In the bosh, melting of the charge, except coke, takes place. Melting and direct reduction of wustite by carbon of the coke ($FeO + C = Fe + CO$) are the main processes occurring in the bosh region. The charge permeability in this region is maintained because of the presence of solid coke. Liquid iron and slag percolate through the solid coke and collect in the hearth.

The slag, while percolating through the moving active zone of coke, absorbs the ash released from the coke on burning. Any iron oxide contained in the slag is reduced fully during percolation through the stagnant coke percolator. Partial reduction of other oxides like those of manganese, silicon, phosphorus, chromium also occurs along with and that makes the metal impure.

The specific gravity of the slag is much lower than that of the metal and therefore they stratify into two distinct layers of molten immiscible liquids. Both these go on accumulating in the hearth up to a certain level and then these are tapped out separately. The slag is tapped every 2–3 hours and the metal is tapped every 5–6 hours in a normal practice. The gas comes out from the top of the furnace, called Blast Furnace Gas, is cleaned thoroughly through dust catcher, scrubber and electrostatic precipitator for preheating the air and for other uses.

Approximate quantities of ore, fuel and flux required for the production of one tonne of pig iron under Indian conditions are:

Iron Ore (60%Fe)	1.7–1.8 tonnes
Coke	0.8–0.9 tonne
Fluxes	0.4–0.5 tonne
Air	4.0–4.5 tonne

The coke to be a good fuel, the carbon content of coke should be maximum and it should contain minimum of ash and other deleterious impurities. As a regenerator of reducing gasses and as a heat producer it should have a high reactivity with oxygen, carbon dioxide and water vapour. Permeability of the charge, particularly in the bosh region, where everything else except coke is either plastic or molten, is maintained by the coke alone. It cannot be replaced by anything else. This function of coke is of relatively greater importance than its heat generation and ore reducing functions. In other words a modern blast furnace cannot be run without a certain amount of coke as a charge material.

Natural coal is too dense for the blast to penetrate it quickly. It is not strong enough to stand nearly 25 m of burden lying over it inside the furnace. Hence, the coke is the right type of fuel needed to run blast furnaces. It should be of a narrow size range and suffer minimal breakdown in its passage to and through the furnace until it burns at the tuyere level.

The size of the coke has to be sufficiently lumpy. The proportion of +40 mm size in the charge coke should be at least 80% to ensure a sufficiently high permeability of the charge. It was found that for a mean size of burden of 13 mm the mean size of coke should not be less than 53 mm and this corresponds to an average coke burden size ratio of about 4:1. In general, it has been suggested that the optimum size of coke should be 3–5 times that of the iron bearing material. However, coke of +80 mm size is to be eliminated in the charge since it has lower stability than −80 mm. Major portion of the coke burns at the tuyere level to provide major portion of the heat necessary for the process. A certain proportion of the coke is consumed in the stack in solution loss reaction. Coke costs nearly 20% of the overall cost of iron and steel production together.

Too large an ore size would result in unreduced material coming down the stack into the tuyere area and increase the total demand of heat. Maximum top size of the ore to be charged into the Blast Furnace should be 50 mm–55 mm. Major portion is expected to be in the range of 25 mm–50 mm. Particles of size −10 mm are considered as fines and should not be present in the charge.

The productivity of a blast furnace mainly depends upon the rate of blast that can be pushed through the furnace. The more is the blast the more is the oxygen pushed in for combustion of coke and more is the rate of coke burning and consequently more heat generation. This results in more rate of melting of the charge as well as higher rate of stack reduction. This is possible only if the charge is permeable inside the furnace.

36.4 SELECTION OF COAL FOR METALLURGICAL COKE

While selecting the coal for metallurgical coke, due attention should be paid to the presence of objectionable constituents such as ash, sulphur and phosphorous.

The nature of ash from coal has some influence on its actual performance in the blast furnace. Silica in the coke requires the addition of lime as a flux when the coke is used in the furnace, which results in an increase of slag formed and the heat loss. Therefore, a ferruginous ash is advantageous than siliceous ash.

Table 36.4.1 Quality parameters of Indian Coking Coals (Charged to coke oven).

Parameters	Desirable	Tolerance limit
Size in %		
Fraction below 0.5 mm	<25	<30
Inherent Moisture %	<1.5	2
Ash %	<17	20
Max.Ash % of Particle at cut point	25–27	27–30
Volatile Matter (Air dried) %	22–32	>20
Coke Type	G–G$_3$	F/G
Swelling Index	5	3
Max. Fluidity (ddpm)	500	100
Fluidity Range (deg C)	60	50
Mean Reflectance %	1.10–1.30	1.05
Total Reactive %	60	55
Vitrinite Distribution % $(V_9 - V_{14})$	80	70

Sulphur is objectionable and should be as low as possible. Sulphur may be present in coal in the form of pyretic sulphur, sulphate sulphur and organic sulphur. Of these, only pyretic sulphur can be reduced by mechanical processes of beneficiation. Thus the distribution of the forms of sulphur in coal should be known in addition to the total sulphur present in order to be sure whether the coal can be cleaned to the required extent or not. Phosphorus is another objectionable constituent and may be present in the form of calcium phosphate in the mineral matter of the coal. Both sulphur and phosphorus retard the quality of coke and influence the quality of steel.

The quality parameters of Indian Coking coals which can be used for the production of metallurgical coke are shown in Table 36.4.1.

While selecting proper coal for the manufacture of metallurgical coke, it is necessary to satisfy oneself that the coke obtained fulfils certain specifications. Coke Reactivity Index (CRI), coke strength after reaction (CSR) and certain special physical tests for the properties of coke such as Shatter, Micum and Heaven tests are of great significance in its use for metallurgical purposes, gasification and for boilers. Porosity is important for the coke to be used for metallurgical purposes.

36.4.1   Reactivity to CO$_2$

Reactivity to CO$_2$ (RCO$_2$) is determined by the Fuel Research Station`s Apparatus. The reaction tube is made of 48 cm long transparent silica tube including 20 cm long capillary end of 7–8 mm of out side diameter and of 1.5 mm of bore. Coke of −14+25 mesh is charged in the tube to a length of 7 cm. The temperature of the coke bed is read by a pyrometer connected to a 34 gauge platinum, Pt-Rh thermocouple in a suitable sheath placed at the centre of the coke bed. The temperature of the tubular furnace is first raised to 950°C in 1 hour in a current of pure dry nitrogen gas and maintained at this temperature for another hour. Pure CO$_2$ stored in a gas holder graduated in a two portion of 100 cc capacity each, is passed through the coke bed at the rate of 5 cc/minute by displacement with conc. MgCl$_2$ solution. The first 100 cc is utilized to flush the system. The gases resulting from the passage of the second 100 cc of CO_2 are collected in a nitro-meter over KOH solution to absorb the reacted CO_2 gas. The volume of gases collected mainly consisting of CO is directly taken as an index of reactivity of the coke towards CO_2 and termed RCO_2.

36.4.2   Coke reactivity index (CRI) & coke strength after reaction (CSR) (IS 4023:2013)

200 gm sampled and sized $(-21 + 19$ mm) coke pieces are dried thoroughly to constant weight at 105°C and charged into a reaction tube. The reaction tube is placed in the furnace and heated to 1100°C in a stream of nitrogen. A soaking time of 15 minutes is allowed after the specific reaction temperature of 1100°C is reached. Nitrogen flow is stopped and CO_2 is then passed at the rate of 5 litre/minute for 120 minutes maintaining the temperature at 1100 ± 5°C. Then CO_2 is stopped, furnace is switched off and cooled to room temperature in a stream of nitrogen. Coke pieces are carefully withdrawn and weighed (W_1). The coke is transferred to a I-Type drum of 130 mm diameter $\times$ 70 mm length and rotate at 20 rpm for 30 minutes. The coke pieces are then taken out and screened on a 10 mm round hole screen. Weigh +10 mm fraction of coke pieces (W_2).

$$\text{Coke Reactivity Index (CRI)} = \frac{200 - W_1}{200} \times 100$$

$$\text{Coke strength after reaction (CSR)} = \frac{W_2}{W_1} \times 100$$

36.4.3   Shatter test (IS 1354:2010)

The test is designed to simulate the effect of dropping coke on loading, dropping into bunkers and to the charge level of blast furnace. It measures, therefore, the resistance to shattering or the impact hardness. It is desirable for a blast furnace coke to be of high impact hardness so that little small coke or breeze is formed in the handling between the screens of the coke oven plant and the charge level of the blast furnace.

The box required for the shatter test is 71 cm long, 46 cm wide and 38 cm deep, supported by pulleys and wire ropes so that the inside of the bottom of the box is 183 cm above the base plate when the coke is dropped. The bottom of the box consists of two doors, hinged length wise and provided with a latch for rapid opening. The doors are of 6 mm plate so that they swing open rapidly and not impede the fall of coke. Base plate is rigid and of not less than 12.5 mm thick, 122 cm long and 97 cm wide. The base plate has side plates 20 cm high and 6 mm thick on all sides to prevent loss of coke during the test.

Take 25 kg air dried coke of +51 mm and place by hand in the box. Raise the box to the standard height of 183 cm, close and latch the front plate of the base and displace the latch of the shatter test box to allow the coke to fall on the base plate. Close the bottom door of the box and replace the latch. Lower the box until the lower stop halts it. Drop the front base plate and shovel the coke from the base plate into the box. Care being taken to lower the coke into the box without dropping. Return the coke of +13 mm in size from the base plate to the box using shovel and without sweeping at this stage. Repeat this process until 4 drops in all have been given. The percentage of the coke retained on 51 mm, 38 mm and 13 mm screens are recorded and are called shatter index.

It is usually satisfactory to record only the 51, 38, 13 mm shatter indices. For the standard shatter test, the records noted are cumulative percentages on sieves of 102, 76, 51, 38, 25, and 13 mm in kg. The loss during the test which should not amount to more than 50 gm should be distributed more or less uniformly on the different fractions. The average of 3 results obtained shall be reported for each shatter index.

36.4.4   Micum test (IS 1354:2010)

This test is a relative measure of the resistance of coke to degradation mostly by abrasion. In this test, 50 kg of +5 cm size air dried coke is put in Micum drum of 100 cm × 100 cm size and rotated for 4 minutes at 25 rpm or a total of 100 revolutions. The coke is removed, and screened through 40 mm and 10 mm screens.

The percentage of coke retained on 40 mm screen is called M_{40} index whereas the percentage of coke that passes through 10 mm screen is called M_{10} index. M_{40} gives the resistance of the coke to breakage by impact i.e., it is a measure of the strength of the coke. M_{10} gives the resistance of the coke to breakage by abrasion i.e., it is a measure of hardness of the coke. High M_{40} values and low M_{10} values are desirable for metallurgical coke.

36.4.5   Heaven test

This test is also used to find the abrasion index of coke. In this test, 10 kg of +5 cm coke is taken in a drum of 9.15 cm diameter and 45.7 cm length. The drum is rotated at 24 rpm for a total of 1400 revolutions. The percentage of coke retained on 25 mm screen is known as Heaven index.

36.4.6   Porosity of coke

Percentage porosity is given by

$$\frac{\text{True density} - \text{Apparent density}}{\text{True density}} \times 100\%$$

The true density can be determined by an ordinary density bottle as described in article 11.1. For determination of Apparent density, about 5 lb sample of coke is dried to constant weight on an electric hot plate and weighed. Later it is kept immersed in boiling water for about half an hour in order to saturate the pores with water. It is taken out and adhering water wiped off and the volume of the coke is measured by displacement of water in a special trough made for the purpose. The apparent density is calculated by dividing the initial weight of the coke by the volume of the coke as determined.

Table 36.4.2 Coke quality parameters.

Parameters	Desirable	Tolerance limit
Moisture %	<4	4
Ash %	22	25
Volatile Matter %	<1.5	1.5
Sulphur %	<0.7	0.7
Phosphorous %	<0.25	0.25
Micum		
M40	80	75
M10	10	12
Porosity %	38–45	38–45
CRI	<25	25
CSR	>55	50

The coke produced from the coal should possess the required strength, size and reactivity. The coke quality parameters for Indian Blast Furnaces are shown in Table 36.4.2.

Requirements of hard coke used for gasification, in water gas generators, gas producer, boilers etc., are much less stringent than that of metallurgical coke. However, at present, there is no separate standard for hard coke used for different purposes.

36.5 CLASSIFICATION OF COKING COALS

Coking coals used for coke manufacture are broadly classified into four groups as Prime, Medium, Semi-coking, and weakly-coking coals.

36.5.1 Prime coking coals

The strongly caking coals which with or without beneficiation produce coke of metallurgical specification on carbonization at high temperature by conventional practice are classed as Prime Coking Coals.

It has to be borne in mind that strong coking property is not the only criterion for a metallurgical coal. The other criteria which determine the suitability of coals for coking are high fluidity combined with a not too low and too high volatile matter. For all practical purposes, this range in volatile matter is between 24% and 32% on dmmf basis.

36.5.2 Medium coking coals

These are caking coals which with or without beneficiation produce coke just inferior to the standard metallurgical coke and when used in blends with suitable matching coals produce coke of metallurgical specification. These coals may be sub-divided into two groups: (a) Low volatile medium coking coals and (b) Medium volatile medium coking coals.

36.5.3   Semi-coking coals

These are caking coals which with or without beneficiation are not capable of yield-ing even border-line metallurgical coke on their own except in blends with suitable matching coals.

These coals may also be sub-divided into (a) Low volatile semi-coking coals (b) High volatile semi-coking coals

36.5.4   Weakly coking coals

These coals show weakly caking properties and can be used in blends only in small proportions. Semi-coking and Weakly coking coals supplied to steel plants are com-monly termed as blendable coals.

The reserve of Prime Coking Coal in India is about 4% and blendable coal is about 17% of the total reserve. The reserves of Prime Coking Coals are local-ized in the coalfields of Jharia and Giridih only. Dishegarh seam is the principal blendable coal. Partly because of limited availability and high cost of Prime Cok-ing Coal, most present day plants make use of coal blends for their carbonization process.

To achieve best results, blending must aim to mix intimately two or more compo-nents in such a manner that each particle of any one component lies as close as pos-sible to a particle of each of the other components so that resulting mixture delivered to the carbonization plant is uniform in every respect.

Blending of Prime Coking coals with other sub-standard coals in order to con-serve better type of coking coals is an accepted practice in all the major coke oven plants of India and use of binary or ternary blends for the production of metallurgical coke is the rule rather than the exception.

Investigations at CIMFR have shown that coking blends containing Medium cok-ing coal (30% to 40%), Semi- to Weakly coking coal (10% to 20%) and matching proportion of Prime coking coal (40% to 50%) yield hard coke of stipulated proper-ties suitable for steel plants. Each of the constituents of such a ternary blend should be crushed to the requisite fineness and properly mixed prior to coking. Large capacity blast furnaces require coke of much greater hardness and purity than those specified by ISI. To produce coke of such superior quality, greater proportions of Prime coking coal should be used if carbonized in conventional way.

For manufacture of metallurgical coke medium coking coals from Ramgarh and Bokaro field and weakly coking coals from Karanpura and Raniganj field are blended with prime coking coal of Jharia and Giridih. Thus in India, coke is manufactured by blending all classes of coal in suitable proportion.

Requirements of coal quality may be changed to conserve the coking coals by improvement in technology of coke making and blast furnace operation. The follow-ing are some developments made in coke making technology with the aim to reduce the cost of blast furnace coke and to extend the range of ranks and types of coals used for blending:

a   **Addition of Semi-coke in coal blend:** Semi-coke can be mixed to the coal blend for coke making. Semi-coke is produced by low temperature carbonization process.

This process normally uses low rank coals and lignite. The coke produced being lower in ash content will give added economy in coke rate in blast furnace.

b **Preheating of coal charge:** Coal charge of the coke oven can be preheated by the hot flue gases coming out of coke oven regenerators. Thus heat in the flue gases is recovered. Preheating of coal increases its bulk density resulting in increased productivity of the oven besides lowering the time of carbonization and heat required for carbonization. Preheating results in the production of coke of improved quality, uniformity and stability.

c **Use of coal briquettes:** Use of 30%–50% of coal briquettes made with the help of binder increases the charge density by 7%–9% and improves the coking properties of the charge by expansion of briquettes during carbonization. This allows the use of non-coking coals upto 10%–20% in the coke oven.

d **Addition of coking agents:** Low coking property of some weakly coking coal can be improved by the addition of coking agent like asphalt, tar, pitch etc., but the presence of sulphur in the coking agent is detrimental. It permits the use of non-coking coals upto 5% and is suitable for existing ovens.

e **Stamped charging of coal:** In gravity charging of coal in the coke ovens the coal particles are loosely packed. In stamped charging, the coal is first pressed mechanically and then charged in the coke ovens, thus significantly increases the bulk density of coal charge. Stamping enables the utilization of larger proportion of substandard coking coal. 20%–30% non-coking coal can be used by stamping process whereas in top charging process, even 15% non-coking coal fail to produce satisfactory coke.

f **Formed coke process:** A technology for production of formed coke has been developed by CIMFR for use in Indian furnaces. Formed coke is made from low rank, high volatile non-coking coal with low swelling umber. It is carbonized at a low temperature of 500°C to produce char. The hot char produced is blended with either about 20% of coking coal or with tar or with a mixture of these and formed by pressing into briquettes of suitable shape and size. These briquettes are then heated to carbonize the binder and to consolidate the char to a suitable strength and reactivity. The final product is called Formed coke.

Since it has go standard shape and size, better control over its behaviour in the blast furnace can be achieved as the size and size distribution determines the burning characteristics of coke and influences the flow of materials through blast furnace and hence the productivity and efficiency of iron making process.

Table 36.5.1 Formed coal specification.

Average size	45 mm
3.8 cm Shatter	90% (max)
M40	70%
M10	12–14%
Ash	22%
VM	3%
Moisture	<3%
Sulphur	0.7%

Formed coke made from low rank non-coking coal can be used as a metallurgical coke with suitable control of quality, thus conserving the reserve of coking coal. Keeping in view the available raw materials, the acceptable limit of formed coke specification for normal blast furnace used in India is shown in the table 36.5.1. (as recommended by CIMFR).

g   **Form coal process:** In form coal process, part of the normal crushed coke oven blend is briquetted with a binder. The briquettes are then blended back into the normal coke oven blend before the mixture is fed into the coke ovens. This process permits the use of about 20% of non-coking coal in coke oven feed.

Coke rate in the Indian steel plants is very high compared to other developed countries. The following are some of the technological measures responsible for reduced coke consumption and improved blast furnace performance:

1   Increased usage of agglomerates and self fluxing sinter
2   High hot blast temperature
3   Humidification of hot blast by injection of steam in the hot blast
4   Oxygen enrichment of hot blast
5   Use of high blast rates with high top pressure
6   Use of large volume blast furnace
7   Proper burden distribution in the furnace
8   Increased auxiliary fuel injection

36.6   PULVERIZED COAL INJECTION

Pulverized Coal Injection (PCI) is a process that involves blowing large volumes of fine coal into the Blast Furnace. This provides a supplemental carbon source to speed up the production of metallic iron, reducing the need for coke production. The necessity to adopt fuel injection in a blast furnace arises from the fact that coke is not only costly but it is becoming more and more scarce and hence it should be replaced by other cheaper and readily available fuels to run blast furnace without impairing their efficiency. Either solid, liquid or gaseous fuels can be injected in the tuyeres.

Prior to the 1980's the preferred injection fuel was oil, but sharply increasing oil prices led to other fuels being used, such as natural gas and coal. PCI has now been implemented in most steelworks around the world.

Increased injection of coal was initially driven by high oil prices but now increased use of PCI is driven by the need to reduce raw material costs, pollution and also by the need to extend the life of ageing coke ovens. The injection of coal into the blast furnace has been shown to increase the productivity of the blast furnace, reduce the consumption of the more expensive coking coals, improve the consistency of the quality of the hot metal, and reduce greenhouse gas emissions. In addition, coal injection has proved to be a powerful tool in the hands of the furnace operator to adjust the thermal condition of the furnace much faster than would be possible by adjusting the burden charge from the top.

PCI is a recognized method of controlling costs in iron making. The PCI amounts have been increasing in the majority of furnaces worldwide, approaching values between 150 kg/thm to 220 kg/thm. These values differ from shop-to-shop because of various factors not only on the equipment side (mill capacity), but also from coke quality, which limits the amount of pulverized coal. Efficient PCI is obtained by convenient pretreatment of coal as far as moisture and grain size are concerned, appropriate mixing of coal and hot blast, uniform distribution across all tuyeres, low nitrogen input into the blast furnace, and by maximizing the retention time of the coal in the tuyeres.

A considerably wider range of coals can be injected than those suitable for coking. These range in rank from sub-bituminous to anthracite. The ash content of the coal should be low and that no deposition takes place in the tuyere region. The melting point of the ash should be as high as possible but not that much so as to influence the melting characteristics of the slag inside the furnace. At high PCI rates, the preference is for coals with both the ash and moisture contents below about 10%, sulphur content below 0.8%, and low phosphorus and alkali contents. These are good quality, and hence more expensive, coals. Blending coals will extend the range of acceptable coals and increase the number of supply options. The importance of blending is likely to increase as injection rates approach the theoretical maximum and will provide furnace operators with the flexibility in coal selection to meet their particular needs. With better prediction and improved understanding of the effect of coal properties and how operating conditions can be optimised, there is the potential to identify suitable, as well as cheaper, coals. This could provide significant cost savings whilst maintaining a high productivity. The development of modern PCI methods has greatly improved the combustion of coal within the tuyere. For coals with a volatile matter greater than 10% there are only small differences between the combustibility of coals and it is likely that these differences can be accommodated by adjustment of blast furnace operating conditions.

Low volatile coals, compared to high volatile coals, are generally softer and thus require less energy to grind, but they require a higher energy to dry the coal down to a moisture level required to eliminate the risk of handling problems. Free moisture in the pulverized coal can lead to handling problems in bins and transport lines. Clays in the coal may also increase the risk of the handling problems when there is excess free moisture.

Chapter 37

Combustion

Combustion represents a series of exothermic reactions between the coal (fuel) and oxygen or air at elevated temperatures.

The reactions are:

$$2C + O_2 \rightarrow 2CO + 52.8 \text{ Kcal} \tag{37.1.1}$$
$$2CO + O_2 \rightarrow 2CO_2 + 135.3 \text{ Kcal} \tag{37.1.2}$$
$$C + O_2 \rightarrow CO_2 + 94.1 \text{ Kcal} \tag{37.1.3}$$

Conditions for firing coal to the best advantage consist in distributing the air required for combustion in such a manner as to avoid the escape of unburned gases while using the minimum excess of air.

Coal may be burned in the form of a bed of granular or solid coal or as a stream of finely ground pulverized fuel.

In solid coal combustion, air is passed through a permeable bed of crushed and graded coal. The thickness of the fuel bed and the particle size distribution of the coal are among the most important factors that influence combustion efficiency, as these control the rate of flow of air for the combustion process. If the bed of coal is too thin, the air may pass through too readily and provide little opportunity for contact between the oxygen and the fuel. If the bed is too thick, the rate of air flow may be reduced to a level where the fuel becomes starved of oxygen and incomplete combustion occurs. A small sized coal, with particles crushed to less than 50 mm, or even less than 30 mm, is generally used for coal combustion. A minimum proportion of fine particles (−3 mm) is also generally required, to maintain permeability in the fuel bed.

In a fixed bed of solid coals, the air used to effect combustion within the coal bed itself is called primary air. Secondary air is injected above the fuel bed to assist in combustion of the volatile constituents released from the coal in the primary combustion process.

In a fluidized bed combustion, a mass of fine coal particles are kept in a state of suspension or fluidized by means of an upward current of air.

In the combustion of pulverized fuel, an intimate mixture of air and finely ground coal is injected into the furnace through special burners that produce turbulent flow. Turbulent flow is necessary to ensure efficient and rapid combustion. Thermal power plants and cement rotary kilns fire coal in the powdered form. For use in most power station boilers, coal must be pulverized so that 70–80% have −75 micron size. Normally, ball mills are used for pulverizing the coal. However, the use of air-swept mills such as Raymond mill reduces the necessity for drying before grinding except in case of very wet coals. Otherwise hot gas dryers should be used for drying the coal. Wide varieties of coals can be used as pulverized fuel.

Smoke is formed from the tarry distillation products which escape from the fuel bed before they can be completely burned. Brown smoke is tarry matter given off at low temperatures, while black smoke consists mainly of particles of carbon derived from the cracking of hydrocarbons at high temperatures. Smoke is visible sign of incomplete combustion of the gases over the bed and therefore of poor distribution of air.

Clinker is the name given to an agglomerated mass that forms in fuel beds as a result of fusion of the coal ash. Clinker clogs the furnace grate and reduces the flow of air because spaces in between coal particles on grates get blocked resulting in uneven combustion of coal on grates thereby producing less heat and uneven distribution of heat. Clinker removal from the grate is very difficult. Clinker sometimes contains parts of the refractory walls of the furnace and can damage metal grates by dissolving the metal in the molten slag.

80–95% of residue from complete combustion of coal in a pulverized fuel boiler occurs in the form of extremely fine particles of mineral matter and is known as fly ash. This is entrained in the flue gases and must be collected before these gases are discharged to atmosphere. Fly ash is generally collected from the flue gases by electrostatic precipitation. Alternative methods are the use of fabric filters and cyclones.

37.1   USE OF COAL FOR POWER GENERATION

The first main use of coal was for power generation and to provide heat for factories and houses. About 41% of the total electricity, generated all over the world from all sources, is produced from the coal. The conversion from coal to electricity takes place in three stages [59].

Stage 1: The first conversion of energy takes place in the boiler. Coal is burnt in the boiler furnace to produce heat. Carbon in the coal and Oxygen in the air combine to produce Carbon Dioxide and heat.

Stage 2: The second stage is the thermodynamic process.

1   The heat from combustion of the coal boils water in the boiler to produce steam. In modern power plant, boilers produce steam at a high pressure and temperature.
2   The steam is then piped to a turbine.
3   The high pressure steam impinges and expands across a number of sets of blades in the turbine.
4   The impulse and the thrust created rotates the turbine.
5   The steam is then condensed and pumped back into the boiler to repeat the cycle.

Stage 3: In the third stage, rotation of the turbine rotates the generator rotor to produce electricity based on Faraday's Principle of electromagnetic induction.

Pulverized Coal (PC) firing is the oldest method of power generation in thermal power plants (Fig. 37.1). Coal is first milled to a fine powder, which increases the surface area and allows it to burn more quickly. In this pulverised coal (PC) firing method, the powdered coal is blown into the combustion chamber of a boiler where it is burnt at high temperature. The hot gases and heat energy produced converts water into steam.

The high pressure steam is passed into a turbine containing thousands of propeller-like blades. The steam pushes these blades causing the turbine shaft to rotate at high speed. A rotor of generator is coupled to end of the turbine shaft and consists of a large cylindrical magnet so that when turbine rotates, the rotor turns with it. The stator has heavy coils of copper bar in slots. Electricity is produced by rotating the rotating magnetic field created by rotation of exciter motor. After passing through the turbine, the steam is condensed and returned to the boiler to be heated once again.

The electricity produced by stator winding is transmitted to transformer into the higher voltages (up to 400,000 volts) used for economic, efficient transmission to long distance with low losses via power line grids. When it nears the point of consumption, such as our homes, the electricity is transformed down to the safer 100–250 voltage systems used in the domestic market.

In practice to effect the three stages of conversion, many systems and sub systems have to be in service. Also different technologies, like combustion, aerodynamics, heat transfer, thermodynamics, pollution control, and logistics are involved.

As an example for typical coal fired power plant of capacity 500 MW:

- Around 2 million tons of coal will be required each year to produce the continuous power.
- Coal combustion in the boiler requires air. Around 1.6 million cubic meter of air in an hour is delivered by air fans into the furnace.
- The ash produced from this combustion is around 2,00,000 tons per year.
- Electrostatic precipitators capture almost all of this ash without dispersing this to the atmosphere.
- The boiler produces around 1600 tons per hour of steam at a temperature of 540°C to 600°C. The steam pressures are in the range of 200 bar. The boiler materials are designed to withstand these conditions with special consideration for operational safety.
- Heat transfer from the hot combustion gases to the water in the boiler takes place due to Radiation and convection.

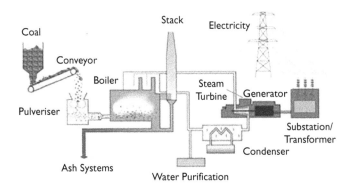

Figure 37.1 Thermal Power Plant.

- The Electrical generators carry very large electric currents that produce heat and are be cooled by Hydrogen and water.
- The steam leaving the turbine is condensed and the water is pumped back for reuse in the boiler. To condense all the steam it will require around 50,000 cubic meter per hour of cooling water to be circulated from lakes, rivers or the sea. The water is returned to the source with only an increase of 3°C to 4°C to prevent any effect to the environment.
- Apart from the cooling water the power plant also requires around 400 cubic meter per day of fresh water for making up the losses in the water steam cycle.
- Pollutants from coal power plants like carbon dioxide, sulphur dioxide, and nitrogen oxide can also affect the environment. Thermal power plants are the biggest producers of Carbon Dioxide.

All thermal power plants have the following four main circuits, though each plant is unique in itself in terms of specific features and functionalities.

1   **Coal and Ash Circuit:** This circuit deals mainly with feeding the boiler with coal for combustion purposes and taking care of the ash that is generated during the combustion process and includes equipment and paraphernalia that is used to handle the transfer and storage of coal and ash.
2   **Air and Gas Circuit:** For the coal to burn inside the boiler it needs a sufficient quantity of air which is supplied using either forced draught or induced draught fans. The exhaust gases from the combustion are in turn used to heat the ingoing air through a heat exchanger before being let off in the atmosphere. The equipment which handles all these processes fall under this circuit.
3   **Feed Water and Steam Circuit:** This circuit deals with supply of steam generated from the boiler to the turbines and to handle the outgoing steam from the turbine by cooling it to form water in the condenser so that it can be reused in the boiler plus making good any losses due to evaporation etc.
4   **Cooling Water Circuit:** This circuit deals with handling of the cooling water required in the system. Since the amount of water required to cool the outgoing steam from the boiler is substantial, it is either taken from a nearby water source such as a river, or it is done through evaporation if the quantity of cooling water available is limited.

37.1.1   Pulverized coal firing thermal power plant

Coal received from the mines is stored in the coal yard adjacent to the power plant. It is then conveyed on a daily basis and stored in a **Coal Silo. Coal feeder** continuously feed the required amount of coal to the **Coal Pulveriser** to grind the coal to a very fine powder. Hot air from the Primary Air Fans dry the coal in the pulveriser and carries the dry coal powder to the burners in the boiler furnace. In the burners the coal powder is mixed with the required amount of Combustion air. Correct amount of air is the most essential ingredient for Combustion. More air or less air both makes the combustion process inefficient.

   Forced Draft Fan supplies most of the Combustion air. This fan takes air from the atmosphere and blows it into the furnace through air ducts. The **Air Heater**, utilizing the heat of the hot flue gases that leave the boiler heats the air before it enters the Furnace. Coal burns in the furnace giving out heat and forming flue gases. The hot flue gases are drawn out by the Induced draft fan and the gases pass through the various heating surfaces of the boiler and the Electrostatic Precipitator for capturing fly ash and discharges to the atmosphere at the top of the stack or chimney. The residue after combustion called Bottom Ash collects at the bottom of the furnace.

Volume of one unit mass of steam is thousand times that of water. When water is converted to steam in a closed vessel the pressure will increase. Boiler uses this principle to produce high pressure steam. **Boiler feed water** is pumped at high pressure into the boiler from the **feed water tank. Feed water heaters,** using extracted steam from the turbine, heat the water before the water enters the boiler. Conversion of Water to Steam in the boiler evolves in three stages viz., heating the water from cold condition to boiling point or saturation temperature (sensible heat addition), boiling of water at saturation temperature to produce steam (latent heat addition), heating steam to higher temperature called Superheating.

The **Economiser** which has a set of coils made from steel tubes located in the tail end of a boiler heats the feed water by utilizing the heat in the exhaust flue gases before leaving through the chimney. From the economizer, the water is fed to the **drum,** a large cylindrical vessel that functions as the storage and feeding point for water and the collection point for water and steam mixture. This is the largest and most important pressure part in the boiler. Boiling takes place in the **Water Walls** which are water filled tubes typically welded into the sides of the boiler that form the walls of the furnace. Water walls get the water from the large pipes connected to the drum called **down-comers.** As the water heats up, a part of the water in the water wall tubes becomes steam. This water steam mixture has a lower density than the water in the down-comers. This density difference creates a circulation of water from the drum, through the down-comers, water walls and back to the drum. Steam collects at the upper half of the drum. Steam from the drum passes to the **Super Heater** coils placed in the Flue gas path. The super heater increases the temperature of saturated steam without raising its pressure till the maximum required for operation. The superheated steam then finally goes to the turbine. Final Super heater temperatures are in the Range of 540°C to 570°C for large power plants and Super Heated steam pressures are around 175 bar.

Steam from the exhaust of the first stage turbine goes back to the boiler for reheating and is returned to the second stage. Reheater coils in the flue gas path does the reheating of the returned steam. The reheat steam is at a much lower pressure than the super heated steam but the final reheater temperature is the same as the super-heated steam temperature. Reheating to high temperatures improves the output and efficiency of the Power Plant. Final reheater temperatures are normally in the range of 560°C to 600°C. Reheat steam pressures are normally around 45 bar.

The most important requirement to burn coal is the correct quantity of air. More Air or less Air is an energy loss. The coal is ground to fine powder to ensure that each coal particle comes in contact with air so that the chemical reaction can take place. If the furnace is only provided with the theoretical air there may be a possibility that some coal particles do not get sufficient air. If this happens, that part of the coal will not burn and will be an energy loss. To avoid this, air is provided in excess of the theoretically calculated value. In large coal fired power plants, the excess air is around 20%.

If the air is less than required, part of the coal will not burn and goes out through the ash as un-burnt coal particles. This is equivalent to losing a part of the potential energy of the coal. This is known as Unburnt Carbon Loss. In the normal combustion reaction, carbon and oxygen combine to form carbon dioxide giving out heat. Actually this takes place in two stages, first is the formation of carbon monoxide and then the carbon monoxide reacts to form carbon dioxide. If the air is less, the second stage does not take place, and carbon monoxide is formed. This means a part of the potential energy of the coal is not released. This is an energy loss. Also carbon monoxide is a toxic pollutant.

If the air supplied for combustion is more than required, the air that is in excess of the combustion requirement does not contribute to the combustion process, but takes away a part of the combustion heat then goes up the stack as waste heat. This is an energy loss. This is called the Dry Gas loss. Modern combustion control systems in power plants optimise the air requirements to minimize the effects of both these conditions.

It can use any type of coal and is relatively insensitive to the quality of coal burnt. Until the twentieth century most thermal power generation around the world was from direct combustion of coal in boilers. In India too, most coal-based power generation with installed capacity up to 500 MW is based on pulverized coal-fired units, while some use gas turbines. Average gross efficiency of generation from coal-based power plants is 30.5 per cent.

Efforts have been made to render coal combustion more efficient and less polluting. Improving the efficiency of conventional pulverised coal fired power plants has been the focus of considerable efforts by the coal industry. In a **Fluidized Bed Combustion** (FBC) process, it was found that chemical reactions were accelerated due to the turbulent mixing and close contacts of materials within a fluidized bed.

Fluidized Bed Combustion (FBC) uses a fluidized bed of fine coal particles suspended in air. At high pressures, solid coal behaves like a fluid and allows rapid transfer of heat. The efficiency of the burning process gets enhanced because the motion of coal brings a constant supply of hot particles to the surface. The heat is extracted and utilized in a conventional power generation cycle. It works at lower temperatures than the pulverized coal firing process, and hence, reduces NOx emissions in the atmosphere.

FBC is also being widely adopted and in some cases getting performance over the conventional burning systems due to its inherent advantages, viz.,

- Reduced sensitivity to fuel quality, thus permitting use of carbonaceous matter of even low calorific value containing ash of about 75% (max) and volatile matter as low as 1% in fluidized bed. This is a major advantage of the system from coal utilization point of view.
- Reduced crushing cost of coal compared to PC system, since larger size coal particles can be used.
- High heat transfer rate resulting in reduced heat transfer surfaces.
- Reduced environmental pollution since emission of SOx and NOx is restricted.
- High sulphur coals can be used by mixing with limestone to capture more than 90% of the sulphur released from the coal when it burns.

The two types of fluidized bed combustion are Atmospheric Fluidized Bed Combustion (AFBC) and Pressurized Fluidized Bed Combustion (PFBC). An atmospheric fluidized bed combustor performs roughly the same functions as a conventional boiler in driving a steam turbine, except with far fewer emissions. Two types are being developed: bubbling bed and the circulating bed. In a Bubbling Fluidized Bed Combustion

(BFBC), the gas velocity is increased until the whole bed becomes a turbulent mass of solids and bubbles, but there is no carry-over of bed material with the combustion gases. In Circulating Fluidized Bed Combustion (CFBC) coal particle size is reduced to 0.07–0.3 mm and the fluidization velocity is kept at 5–10 m/sec, so that the particles are ablated in the steam gas. Since the gasifier is compact, higher heat release rate per unit area can be achieved. In India, CFBC has been developed for high ash coals having high heat value of less than 3000 kcal/kg. The first CFBC boiler of 175 tons/hr capacity was commissioned by BHEL at Sinarmas Pulp and Paper (India) Ltd. in Pune. It has proved to be a promising technique for increasing efficiency of power generation, and its use in commercial systems is growing rapidly.

Pressurized Fluidized Bed Combustion (PFBC) uses crushed coal with a limestone suspension as a sorbent (to absorb the sulphur content in the coal). As air pressure inside the boiler is increased to 16 to 20 bars at a temperature around 850°C, the limestone sorbent captures the sulphur in the coal and forms a dry paste, which gets collected at the bottom of the boiler and can be removed. This technique is particularly suitable for high sulphur coals. A pressurized fluidized bed combustor, because of the increased energy in its high pressure gases exiting the boiler, can drive both gas turbine and steam turbine, an arrangement known as a combined cycle. These systems can boost power generation efficiencies to well above 40%; much greater than the 30% to 35% efficiencies of conventional coal fired technology.

Over the years continuous developments are taking place in pulverized coal power generation technology to increase thermal efficiency and improve environmental performance. One of the significant developments has been the adoption of supercritical combustion. The term supercritical refer to the critical point of water 221.2 bar and 374.15°C. The critical pressure of water is the maximum pressure that liquid and vapor can coexist in equilibrium. At this critical point, the density of steam and the density of water are equal and there is no distinction between the two states.

Super-Critical (SC) combustion and Ultra-Super-Critical (USC) combustion are thermodynamic cycles that improve thermal efficiency of coal combustion. At supercritical pressures, water is heated to produce superheated steam without boiling. Main steam conditions in super-critical power plants are 246 Bar pressure and 538–565°C temperature. Ultra-super critical combustion technology, operates at the steam conditions of 270 Bar pressure and 565–625°C temperature. In Advanced Ultra Super Critical (AUSC) combustion, the steam conditions are 270 Bar pressure and temperature of above 625°C. Increase in efficiency of supercritical plant has brought benefits of reduced coal consumption, reduced GHG emissions of CO_2, NO_x and SO_2. The most significant aspect of supercritical plants is the development of materials that are resistant to high temperature and pressure conditions associated with the assurance of the reliability of the high temperature and high pressure materials. Change over from Ferrite to Austenitic steels has opened host of opportunities of increasing parameters.

37.1.2   Power generation

For about 100 years, coal is used for generating electrical energy at coal-fired thermal power plants worldwide. The world's power generating capacity has grown 15 times since 1950. As per IEA clean coal centre, there were over 1600 pulverised coal fired power plants in the world, comprising more than 4000 units by the end of 1999. As per the World Bank data, 9,129.3 TWh (terawatt hour) of electricity is produced in the world in 2011 by coal fired thermal power plants. This accounted for almost 41.2% of total electricity production of 22,158.5 TWh. The total installed capacity of coal fired thermal power plants in India as on 31 March 2015 is 164,635.88 MW. Coal's share in the fuel market, especially for power generation, is expected to continue at the same level over the next two decades. In spite of advances in coal-fired power-plants design and operation worldwide they are still considered as not environmental friendly due to producing a lot of carbon-dioxide emissions as a result of combustion process plus ash, slag and even acid rains.

37.1.3 Selection of coal for boiler firing

The coal to be used for boiler firing should be high in calorific value and low in moisture and ash contents. Uniform size of coal is desirable and fine dust layer lumps are objectionable. The ash should be refractory and infusible. Coals of easily fusible ash will form clinker and spreads over the grates if the temperature is high enough.

Fieldner and Selrig have classified coals on the basis of their fusion/softening point temperature as follows:

Class I – Coals whose ash does not fuse at 1427°C (2600°F)
Class II – Coals whose ash fusion temperature is between 1427°C to 1204°C (2600°F to 2200°F)
Class III – Coals whose ash fusion temperature is below 1204°C (2200°F)

Class I coals are the best from the point of view of clinker formation and can be used for boiler firing without any trouble whereas class III coals are worst. The clinkering properties of class II coals depend upon the nature of mineral matter in the coal and the kind of stocker used.

A coal which gives a hard and non-porous coke should be avoided as it is not sufficiently free burning to permit sudden increase in the load on the boiler to be rapidly taken up. Moreover, a large excess of air is necessary to avoid excessive carbon loss in the solid refuse. Hence strongly caking coals should be avoided.

While low ash is desirable, if the coal is to be used on a traveling grate stoker, the ash should not be below 7%. If the ash content falls appreciably below this minimum, the links of the grate burnout rapidly, unprotected from the full heat of the fire by a sufficient layer of ash.

The sulphur in the coal should be low. The mixture of sulphurous and sulphuric acids formed by the combustion of sulphur may cause serious corrosion in economizers and air heaters. Sulphur dioxide released causes atmospheric pollution.

Hand fired boilers are likely to give smoke with heavy loss of combustible gases and vapours when high volatile coals are used. Hence for these boilers, low volatile coals are most suitable. The coal should be free from large lumps (+75 mm) and should contain little dust (–4 mesh). Mechanically fired water tube boilers can handle coals of more widely varying characteristics with high efficiency.

For steam raising, almost all other types of coal which are not suitable for carbonization and gasification can be used. Even coal middlings of ash upto 45% can be pulverized and used in the boilers. Use of washed coal is expected to reduce CO_2 emissions from 0.326 to 0.266 kg/kWh of electricity generation, besides other benefits. Normal quality requirement of coal for power plants is given in Table 37.1.

37.2   USE OF COAL FOR SPONGE IRON PRODUCTION

Blast Furnace process for extraction of pig iron needs coking coal in order to meet its energy requirements, acts as a reducing agent and provides an open permeable bed through which slag and metal pass down into the hearth and hot reducing gases pass upwards. As coking coal deposits are depleting fast through out the world, attention has been paid in searching other processes which uses more abundantly available sources of energy like non-coking coal, Natural gas, etc. Direct Reduction process is one which uses non-coking coal to reduce iron oxides of iron ore in solid state to metallic iron. This is also a measure for conserving coking coals.

Direct reduction of iron ore results a solid porous metallic mass, called a **sponge** because of its appearance like a honey comb structure with minute holes all over the surface. It acquires this peculiar appearance because of escape of gaseous products through the mass of ore which itself looses weight as a result of reduction. This is an approach to steel making without recourse to the blast furnace.

As many as 100 DR processes have been invented and operated at least on an experimental basis since 1920. These are catagorised as Gas-based processes, Fluidised-bed processes, and Coal-based processes. Of these, Stelco-Lurgi-Republic Steel-National Lead process, called in short as SL/RN process with solid coal as fuel and reductant, which is developed in 1964, is the most popular and acceptable Coal-based DR process in the world. Rotary kiln is used as a reactor in this SL/RN process. India entered the sponge iron industry in 1980.

The reduction processes have essentially been designed to carry out in a long, slightly inclined to the horizontal, slowly rotating **Rotary Kiln** (Fig. 37.2) using non-metallurgical coal. The coal not only acts as a reducing agent but also supplies the heat required for maintaining the temperature profile of the charge within the kiln. Some additional liquid or gaseous fuel may be burnt to generate the working temperature. The charge (sized ore and a coarse fraction of non coking coal) is fed from the end which is at higher level. Some time a flux such as limestone or dolomite must be

Table 37.1 Coal quality requirement for power plants.

Sl. No.	Characteristics	Requirement
1	Total Moisture content %	8 to 12 max
2	Volatile Matter (air dry basis) %	19 min
3	Ash % (annual average)	34 max
4	Sulfur %	0.8 max
5	Chloride %	0.01 max
6	Size, mm	250 max

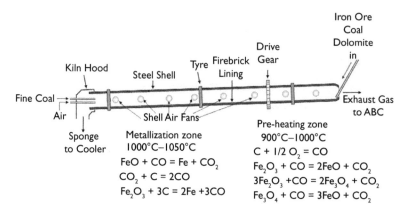

Figure 37.2 Rotary kiln for Sponge Iron production.

added to the coal charged into the kiln to control the sulphur absorption in sponge iron, since non-coking coal contains Sulphur.

The charge travels under gravity aided by the rotating motion, through several heating zones of a rotary kiln. In the preheating zone, moisture is driven off first, and then hydrocarbons and hydrogen are formed by the thermal decomposition of the coal. As the combustible gases from the coal rise from the bed of solid material, portions of these gases are burned in the freeboard above the bed by the controlled quantities of air that are introduced through the tuyeres connected to shell air fans placed evenly along the kiln. The combustion of these gases in the freeboard radiates heat to the surface of the bed of material and also to the exposed surface of the kiln lining. As the kiln rotates (about 0.45 rpm), the lining carries this heat down into the bed and transfers it to the solid materials.

In the preheating zone, the coal present in the charge burns and produces CO.

$$C + \tfrac{1}{2} O_2 = CO \tag{37.2.1}$$

Reduction of iron oxide proceeds to the ferrous oxide (FeO) according to the following reactions

$$Fe_2O_3 + CO = 2FeO + CO_2 \tag{37.2.2}$$

(or)

$$3Fe_2O_3 + CO = 2Fe_3O_4 + CO_2 \tag{37.2.3}$$
$$Fe_3O_4 + CO = 3FeO + CO_2 \tag{37.2.4}$$

The final reduction to metallic iron takes place in the metallization zone. Primary air through the central burner and coal through the injector are fed from the discharge side of the kiln to maintain proper temperature in the metallization zone of the kiln. It is believed that this final reduction is accomplished by the reaction of carbon monoxide with FeO to form carbon dioxide and metallic iron according to reaction

$$FeO + CO = Fe + CO_2 \tag{37.2.5}$$

Most of the carbon dioxide from this reaction is converted back to carbon monoxide by reacting with the excess solid fuel in the kiln according to the Boudouard reaction

$$CO_2 + C = 2CO \tag{37.2.6}$$

Because of the importance of Boudouard reaction, it is important for the solid fuel to have a relatively high reactivity for the successful operation of the process. The more reactive the fuel is, the more rapidly the CO_2 is converted to CO and consequently, the greater the reducing power of the gases in the kiln.

Iron oxide may also be reduced by directly reacting with Carbon to metallic iron according to the following reactions

$$Fe_2O_3 + 3C = 2Fe + 3CO \tag{37.2.7}$$
$$Fe_2O_3 + 3/2C = 2Fe + 3/2CO_2 \tag{37.2.8}$$

The cycle of reactions continues, maintaining the reduction conditions prevailing in the kiln. The reduced charge, **Sponge**, with a high degree of metallization exhibits a honey comb structure under microscope, discharged from the other end of the kiln.

The sponge is indirectly cooled in a rotary cooler to room temperature so that no water comes in the direct contact with the reduced product which being a non equilibrium material is prone to re-oxidation. Reduced and cooled product is screened and the oversize is subjected to magnetic separation to obtain clean sized sponge while the non magnetic oversized portion as well as the under size are re-circulated.

The rotary kiln based DR processes operates on the countercurrent principle in which gases moves in a direction opposite that of the flow of solids. Various unit operations occur both in parallel and in series e.g., transport, mixing, grain separation, heating, gas generation and reduction. Segregation of charge material (ore, coal, flux) because of size and density differences, as well as because of the slope and rotation of the kiln, must be prevented by adopting an appropriate design and practicing correct operating measures. Another area of critical importance is the prevention of localized areas of high temperature which can result in the formation of accretions on the kiln lining and ball shaped clusters within the bed. Temperatures maintained within the kiln at various zones vary from plant to plant depending on the quality of raw materials used. Typical temperatures maintained are about 900°C to 1000°C in the preheating zone and about 1000°C to 1050°C in the metallization zone.

As the Boudouard reaction is endothermic, it holds down the temperature of the bed in the reducing zone so that bed can absorb heat rapidly without reaching such a high temperature that melting or sticking would become a problem. As the reactivity of the fuel increases, the bed temperature in the reduction zone decreases and the relative throughput rates increases. With high reactivity fuels, the temperature of the bed of material and the temperature of the gases in the freeboard remain in a satisfactory range even at very high throughput rates.

Most of the established rotary kiln based DR processes operates on the principle that the reduction is carried out exclusively by CO obtained by the gasification of the fixed carbon content in the coal. In case the CO generation falls short, fine coal can be injected to make up for the lack of CO. In this situation about 25 to 50% of the total coal requirement is injected in to a zone where the fresh coal is immediately subjected to temperature above 800°C at which reduction reaction takes place. The balance coal is introduced at the charging end of the kiln together with the ore desulphurizing agent and sometime an amount of recycled char.

The volatile content of the concurrent coal is released at temperature up to approximately 600°C i.e. before reduction reaction starts. Some of these volatiles are utilized to preheat the kiln with the waste gases without contributing to the actual process of reduction. In order to lower the overall energy consumption, it is therefore essential to optimize the utilization of the hydrocarbons in the volatiles.

Non-coking coal is a vital raw material for the production of direct reduced iron (DRI) being the reductant for the reduction of Iron Ore. Non-coking coals should have the following desirable characteristics:

1   High reactivity
2   Adequate volatile matter
3   High ash softening temperature
4   Low ash and low sulphur

Reactivity is a measure of the ability of carbon in coal to react with CO_2 to form CO by gasification of carbon according to the Boudouard reaction. Reactivity is often measured by reacting coke with carbon dioxide at high temperature. The term reactivity as applied to coke may relate either to its behaviour towards carbon dioxide or to its reaction with oxygen. Due to the presence of volatile matter, the reactivity of raw non-coking coals cannot be directly determined. Hence, char or coke is generated from known amount of coal and reactivity of char or coke determined and is related to the non-coking coal used.

In the SL/RN process, as much carbon monoxide as possible is required in the bottom part of the rotating kiln, but the upper temperature limit of operation is, to a certain extent, limited by the ash fusion point of the coal. Above this temperature, unacceptable clinkers may occur. Therefore, to maintain satisfactory reduction of iron ore by carbon monoxide maximum gasification of the reductant is to be ensured and this is controlled by the reactivity of coke expressed in terms of amount of CO generated per gram per second.

With increase in reactivity of the fuel, the throughput rate of the rotary kiln can be increased within certain limits and permits rotary kiln operation with low reduction temperature. Generally the reactivity of the coal increases with increase in volatile matter of parent coal. Volatile matter primarily contributed to heat generation for raising the temperature of the kiln from normal temperature of around 30°C to 1000°C. Part of the volatile matter also re-helps in the reduction of charge. Charge with low volatile matter will not produce adequate heat and reducing conditions. In those cases, a supplementary fuel such as natural gas or fuel oil is fed through the central burner or through the shell air fans to maintain the proper temperature along the kiln. Coal with very high volatile matter can lead to waste of heat from kiln exhaust gases. They may also result in abnormally high temperature at the kiln inlet. The residence time in the reactor decreases with increase in reactivity of the fuel. Coals of high reactivity such as lignite and sub-bituminous coals are preferable since they would permit operation at lower working temperature in the rotary kiln and hence a shorter preheating time. Due to this shortening of preheating zone, the capacity of given kiln can be raised. Thus reactivity has a significant bearing on the reduction process. Lower kiln operating temperatures also decreases the tendency for formation of accretion rings inside the kiln.

Since reduction is effected by the contact of coal with the charge in the solid state, any coking property in the coal would lead to agglomeration adversely affecting the surface area available for reduction. It will also impede the material flow characteristics. The caking and swelling index should be as low as possible to avoid problems of formation of rings.

Ash in coal required to be as low as possible. Greater the ash content, greater will be the heat wasted in the process of heating ash which is an inert matter of coal. Higher ash in coal also reduces the productivity of the kiln by reducing the active kiln volume available for iron bearing materials. This effect is more in respect of coals having a rigid ash structure preventing degradation of coal in the kiln during the process.

The temperature at which the ash of coal fuses is important because of the effect of clinkar formation and efficiency of combustion. Clinker is the fusion or melting together of the inorganic ash constituents of the coal into masses that interfere with air passage. A shortage in the amount of air means a shortage in the amount of oxygen supplied for combustion. This increases the amount of carbon monoxide produced and also the amount of unburnt material passing out with the ash. Coals having percentage of pyrite iron have a low ash fusion temperature and often the ash will flow through like molasses. A low ash-fusion temperature is undesirable because it promotes the formation of accretions. Generally, ash fusion temperature should be 150°C above the reactor operating temperature.

The composition of the ash is also important because if it is too siliceous, it may react with ferrous oxide to form the low-melting compound, ferrous silicate, and this would interfere with the reduction to metallic iron. Sulphur in the Sponge Iron is mainly picked up from the fuels. Sulphur in coal is of three forms such as sulphate-sulphur, pyrite sulphur and organic sulphur. Most of the sulphur from inorganic constituents volatilizes as H_2S at 600°C, but organic sulphur remains unaffected upto 1000°C. This sulphur is responsible for sulphur pick up in the sponge iron. Sulphur content of the coal should be normally below 1% to avoid sulphur pick-up by DRI.

Further, factors of importance are bulk density and the properties of the char discharged as surplus fuel from rotary kiln. As the bed of the material in a rotary kiln is thin and being in permanent movement, the permeability of the bed for reducing gas is of lesser importance. The optimum mean size of the coal from the stand point of heat and mass transfer is about one half of the mean size of the ore. Normal quality requirement of coal for sponge iron production is given in Table 37.2.

37.2.1 Sponge Iron production

Sponge Iron has now succeeded in becoming a preferred raw material in secondary steel making. A coal based sponge iron plant was first built in 1980 at a place called Paloncha in Andhra Pradesh, India, which had a capacity of just 0.03 million tones per annum. In a span of 35 years, the sponge iron industry has become well developed in India and is presently operating in eight different States of India. As per the world

Table 37.2 Coal quality requirement for sponge iron industry.

Sl. No.	Characteristics	Requirement
I	Total Moisture Content (at 60% RH and 40°C), %	6 max
2	Grade & UHV, Kcal/Kg	B/C, 4940–6200
3	Fixed Carbon %	42 min
4	Volatile Matter (air dry), %	30 min
5	Ash %	22–25
6	Initial deformation Temp.	>1280°C
7	Size, mm	−25+3

steel association, India is the world's largest producer of sponge iron with a production of 19.42 million tones of sponge iron in 2014. Iran stood second with a production of 14.55 million tones.

Coal based sponge iron technology has gained higher economic viability by its ability to generate a considerable quantity of electricity through use of hot waste gases and kiln waste (char) materials. The power generation capabilities are high and economical such that a company which was primarily producing sponge iron, can now also become a producer of power and add 'POWER' to its name.

37.3   USE OF COAL FOR COREX PROCESS

COREX process is the reliable alternative route of Iron making and emerged as one of the most lucrative hot metal producing process. It eliminates the coke making step and uses directly non-coking coal as fuel as well as the reducing agent. Corex process is the first commercially established, industrially proven, flexible, cost affective and environment friendly process for production of the hot metal. Corex process is the only direct smelting process that is in commercial operation operating in South Africa, Korea, India and the USA. Corex process (Fig. 37.3) consists of two reactors viz., the Reduction Shaft and the Melter Gasifier. Reduction shaft is placed above the melter gasifier for easy decent of the material.

Iron ore (lump ore, pellets, or a mixture thereof), limestone and dolomite are continuously charged into the reduction shaft via lock hopper system located on top of the shaft. With a downstream distribution system, the burden descends in the shaft. The gas generated in the melter gasifier enters the reduction shaft at 800 to 850°C and over 3 bar gauge pressure. The gas moves in the counter current direction to the top of the shaft and exits from the shaft. It is termed as top gas. The top gas temperature is around 280°C. The top gas is subsequently cooled and cleaned in a scrubber. This gas is a highly valuable export gas with a net calorific value of about 1,700–1,900 Kcal/m^3 and is suitable for wide range of applications like power generation, DRI production, natural gas substitution etc. Some amount of coke is also added to the shaft to avoid clustering of the burden inside the shaft due to sticking of pellets and to maintain adequate bed permeability. After the residence time of about 6–7 hours inside the shaft, the iron bearing material gets reduced to over 80–85%

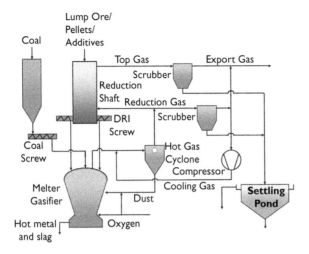

Figure 37.3 COREX Process flowsheet.

metallization and is termed as DRI (Directly Reduced Iron). Subsequently, DRI from the reduction shaft is discharged by screw conveyor and falls into the melter gasifier by gravity through the downpipes. Oxygen is blown into the melter gasifier through tuyeres and dust burners.

Coal is directly charged into the melter gasifier. It is gasified by the oxygen blown resulting the generation of highly efficient reduction gas. This gas leaves the melter gasifier at the dome via refractory lined gas ducts. Cooling gas is added directly to cool the gas from 1050°C to 850°C down to the required reduction gas temperature for the reduction shaft. The gas passes to the hot gas cyclones for dust separation. The dust, separated by the hot gas cyclone, is recycled back into the melter gasifier via Dust Recycling System where the dust is burned by passing Oxygen to Dust Burner. The cleaned and cooled reduction gas is blown into the reduction shaft. DRI charged from the reduction shaft to the melter gasifier undergoes the rest of the reduction and melts to liquid hot metal and slag at about 1480–1500°C. Hot metal and slag are tapped from melter gasifier as in blast furnace. Melter gasifier also operates at an elevated pressure in excess of 3-bar gauge.

The coal used in the corex process must supply heat for the devolatilisation of the coal, the gasification of the char and the melting of the reduced iron. It must also provide sufficient gas to the reduction shaft to reduce the iron ore feed. The gases generated from a low volatile coal, say below 27% volatile content are insufficient for carrying out the reduction of iron bearing materials inside the shaft. On the other hand, very high volatile content say above 30% increases the heat demand inside the melter gasifier dome and causes various consequential problems, such as, high oxygen and fuel rate, high carbon dioxide in the reduction gas, more tarry material in the gas cleaning system due to low dome temperature in the melter gasifier, scum formation in the process water systems etc. Similarly, the ash content in the corex coals is limited to 12% (max). Coals most suited for use with the corex process must contain atleast 60% fixed carbon. This is to ensure good gas flow within the melter gasifier and to reduce the carry over of coal and/or char. The moisture of the coal is maintained below 4.5% by passing it through coal dryers.

Besides chemical analysis of the coal, one of the prime requirements of corex coal is that the char (contains fixed carbon and ash) formed after coal devolatalisation should be physically stable to maintain the bed permeability. The characteristic of coal char is compared to that of the coke to evaluate its stability for corex. Various coal tests, such as thermal decrepitation test, CSR (strength after reaction), CRI (coal reactivity index), free- swelling index, tumbler test, shatter test etc, are typical for selection of corex coals. Thermal decrepitation test indicates the extent of size degradation of coal once exposed to high temperature in order of 1000°C. Similarly CRI and CSR indicate the stability of the coal chars after devolatalisation. A CSR value above 40% and a CRI value below 30% assure better size retention of the coal char till the tuyeres level and thus maintaining adequate bed permeability.

The mean particle size (MPS) of the coal has a major role to play in corex process. Decrease in coal MPS decrease the permeability of the char bed, which results in gas channelling. Thus the sensible heat of the gases is not transferred to the char bed which causes sudden drop in hot metal temperature and quality. For this reason maintaining a steady MPS of coal is very important for corex operation. The coal MPS should be > 20 mm. The amount of fine coal (minus 5 mm material) that is fed to the corex process must be minimised. Therefore all coals must be sized or agglomerated before use.

37.4   USE OF COAL FOR CEMENT PRODUCTION

India is the second largest producer of cement in the world. The cement industry is the third largest consumer of coal in the country. The cement industry is an energy intensive industry with energy typically accounting for 30–40% of production costs (i.e. excluding capital costs). Traditionally, the primary fuel used is coal. During cement manufacturing process, coal is usually burnt in the form of powder.

Cement is a mixture of artificial mineral-like oxide-type compounds, similar in composition and probably in structure to the natural silicates. It is a hydraulic binder, a finely ground material, when mixed with water, forms a paste which sets and hardens by means of hydration reactions and processes and after hardening retains it's strength and stability even under water. The principal cement compounds are given in Table 37.4.1.

Of these compounds, C_3S and C_3A are mainly responsible for the strength of the cement. High percentages of C_3S (low C_2S) results in high early strength but also high heat generation as the concrete sets. The reverse combination of low C_3S and high C_2S develops strengths more slowly (over 52 rather than 28 days) and generates less heat. C_3A causes undesirable heat and rapid reacting properties, which can be prevented by adding gypsum ($CaSO_4.2H_2O$) to the final product. C_3A can be converted to the more desirable C_4AF by the addition of Fe_2O_3 before heating, but this also inhibits the formation of C_3S. C_4AF makes the cement more resistant to seawater and results in a somewhat slower reaction which evolves less heat.

Most cements contain small quantities of MgO, Na_2O and K_2O, which are almost invariably present in the raw materials and minute amounts of one or more of the oxides TiO_2, P_2O_5, Mn_2O_3 etc.

Table 37.4.1 Principal cement compounds.

Cement compounds	Symbol	Chemical formula	Typical concentration
Tricalcium silicate (Alite)	C_3S	$3CaO.SiO_2$	50–65%
Dicalcium silicate (Belite)	C_2S	$2CaO.SiO_2$	10–30%
Tricalcium aluminate	C_3A	$3CaO.Al_2O_3$	4–10%
Tetracalcium aluminoferrite	C_4AF	$4CaO.Al_2O_3.Fe_2O_3$	2–10%

There are around 11 different types of cement. Some of the various types of cement are:

- Portland Cement
- Portland Pozzolana Cement
- Portland Blast Furnace Slag Cement
- Rapid Hardening Portland Cement
- Oil Well Cement
- White Cement
- Sulphate Resisting Portland Cement
- Clinker Cement

Portland cement is the most common type of cement in general use around the world, because it is a basic ingredient of concrete and mortar. It is a fine powder produced by grinding portland cement clinker (more than 90%), a limited amount of calcium sulphate which controls the set time, and up to 5% minor constituents (as allowed by various standards).

Portland cement clinker is a coarse agglomerate of synthetic minerals that is produced by burning a raw meal, consisting of a homogeneous mixture of raw materials to a sintering temperature of about 1450°C in a specialized kiln system. It consist of at least two-thirds by weight of calcium silicates ($3CaO.SiO_2$ and $2CaO.SiO_2$), the remainder consisting of aluminium- and iron-containing clinker phases and other compounds. The ratio of CaO to SiO_2 shall not be less than 2.0. The magnesium content (MgO) shall not exceed 5.0% by weight.

Cement is prepared by grinding the clinker with some gypsum into a fine powder.

There are four fundamental distinct stages in the production of Portland cement: (1) Quarrying (2) Raw Material Preparation (3) Clinkering and (4) Cement milling.

1 **Quarrying:** The raw material for cement manufacture, a rock mixture containing about 80% limestone and 20% clay or shale having silica (SiO_2), alumina (Al_2O_3) and ferrous oxide (Fe_2O_3) are quarried and stored separately. The lime and silica provide the main strength to the cement, while the iron reduces the reaction temperature and gives the cement its characteristic grey colour.

2 **Raw material preparation:** The steps involved here depend on the process used. There are two main cement manufacturing processes currently used: the dry process and the wet process. The dry process uses more energy in grinding but less in the kiln. The individual raw materials are first crushed to below 50 mm. In

many plants, some or all of the raw materials are then roughly blended in a pre-homogenization pile. Silos of individual raw materials are arranged over the feed conveyor belt. The proportions of each material mixed together is determined by calculations which take into account the analyses of the raw materials, the combining ratios in the kiln, and the chemical specifications for the finished cement. The raw mix is fed into a mill where the rock is ground until more than 85% of the material is less than 90 μm in diameter. It is important that the raw mix contains no large particles in order to complete the chemical reactions in the kiln, and to ensure the mix is chemically homogenous. In the case of a dry process, the raw mill also dries the raw materials, usually by passing hot exhaust gases from the kiln through the mill, so that the raw mix emerges as a fine powder. This is conveyed to the blending system by conveyor belt or by a powder pump. In the case of wet process, water is added to the raw mill feed, and the mill product is a slurry with moisture content usually in the range 25–45% by weight. This slurry is conveyed to the blending system by conventional liquid pumps.

3   **Clinkering:** This is the stage which is characteristic of Portland cement. The finely ground material is dried, heated (to enable the sintering reactions to take place) and then cooled down again. While it is being heated various chemical reactions take place to form the major mineral constituents of Portland cement.

The powder from the dry process doesn't contain much moisture, so can be dried in a pre- heater tower. As it falls through the tower (which takes 30 seconds) it is heated from 70 to 800°C. The moisture evaporates, up to 20% of the decarbonation (loss of CO_2) occurs and some intermediate phases such as CaO and Al_2O_3 begin to appear. The mixture is then fed into the kiln.

The slurry from the wet process contains too much moisture is fed directly into the kiln where it is formed into dry balls by the heat and rotation of the kiln. Because of this extra role of the kiln, wet process kilns are generally longer than dry process kilns.

The rotary cement kiln (Fig 37.4) [60] consists of a tube made from steel plate, and lined with heat-resistant bricks. The kiln is inclined on a shallow angle (1–4°) and slowly rotates on its axis at between 30 and 250 revolutions per hour. Raw mix is fed in at the upper end, and the rotation of the kiln causes it gradually to move downhill to the other end of the kiln. At the other end, pulverized coal is blown in through the burner pipe, where it spontaneously ignites due to the very high temperatures, producing a large concentric flame in the lower part of the kiln tube. As material moves under the flame, it reaches its peak temperature of 1400–1450°C, before dropping out of the kiln tube into the cooler. Air is drawn first through the cooler and then through the kiln for combustion of the fuel. In the cooler the air is heated by the clinker, so that it may be 400 to 800°C before it enters the kiln, thus causing intense and rapid combustion of coal.

A complex succession of chemical reactions take place as the temperature rises. The peak temperature is regulated so that the product contains sintered but not fused lumps. Sintering consists of the melting of 25–30% of the mass of the material. The resulting liquid draws the remaining solid particles together by surface tension, and acts as a solvent for the final chemical reaction. Too low a temperature causes insufficient sintering and incomplete reaction, but too high a temperature results in a molten mass, destruction of the kiln lining, and waste of fuel. When all goes correctly, the resulting material is clinker.

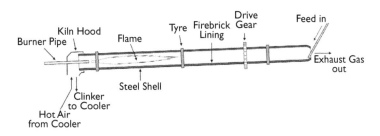

Figure 37.4 Rotary Cement Kiln.

The kiln reactions, in order of occurrence, are (1) evaporation of free water, (2) dehydration of clay or shale and calcination of $MgCO_3$, (3) calcination of $CaCO_3$, and (4) formation of cement compounds. Each of these reactions requires a higher temperature than the one preceding it; therefore, the kiln is fired at the discharge end so that the stream of material flow through successively hotter zones. The successive zones traversed by the material from the feed end are usually designated as **drying, heating, calcining, burning** (clinkering), and **precombustion** (or cooling).

Drying: The length of the drying section of a wet process kiln usually ranges from 20–30% of the total kiln length, whereas a dry process kiln requires little or no length for drying. Gas temperature at the feed end of a wet kiln is maintained in the range of 200°C–260°C.

Heating: Approximately 30% of the kiln length is occupied by the heating section which heats the material from 100°C–900°C. Heat is absorbed by the endothermic reactions of calcination of $MgCO_3$ at about 330°C and of dehydration of clay at about 500°C.

Calcination: Dissociation of the calcareous component of the mix ($CaCO_3$) into lime (CaO) and CO_2 occurs at about 900°C. Since the calcination reaction is endothermic and involves a large percentage of the solids in the kiln, substantially all of the heat input is consumed in driving this reaction and the temperature of the solids remain virtually constant for 15% of the kiln length. During this period the gas temperature drops sharply. The lime (CaO) appears in appreciable quantities when the rate of calcination exceeds the rate of reaction of CaO with the remaining uncombined acidic oxides. Calcination is accelerated by the additional heat generated by the exothermic cement reactions and the approach of the material to the burning zone. The free lime content then passes through a maximum and decreases rapidly as $CaCO_3$ is exhausted.

Burning: Due to exothermic cement compound forming reactions, temperature rises rapidly from 1000°C. The beginning of fusion of the cement compounds and clinker formation starts approximately at 1250°C. This is the hottest zone of the kiln. Material temperature in this area rises to about 1450°C with subsequent temperature drop resulting from completion of the exothermic reactions, passage into the precombustion zone, and absorption of heat from the hot solids by continuing clinker fusion.

Precombustion: This zone is the last zone in the kiln next to burning zone and occupies nearly 10% length of the kiln.

The reaction processes occurring within the kiln are not easily understood due to the wide variations in raw-mix chemistry, raw-mix physical properties and kiln operating conditions, and the physical difficulties of extracting hot materials from the process for investigation before they cool. The Table 37.4.2. shows chemical transformations take place during cement formation process.

By using the dry process, the kiln is shorter by a length corresponding to the drying zone and further more the heat required for drying is saved. The dry kiln is more or less replica of the wet kiln with the drying zone omitted.

The calcining process of the raw mix is the most energy consuming process in the kiln system requiring about half of the total energy input and half of the kiln volume. By moving the calcining process outside the kiln in a preheater, it is possible to reduce the kiln length and in some cases also the diameter, thus greatly reducing the size of the kiln tube for a given production.

Two types of preheaters are grate preheater and gas-suspension preheater. The grate preheater consists of a chamber containing a chain-like high-temperature steel moving grate, attached to the cold end of the rotary kiln. A dry-powder rawmix is turned into a hard pellets of 10–20 mm diameter in a nodulizing pan, with the addition of 10–15% water. The pellets are loaded onto the moving grate, and the hot combustion gases from the rear of the kiln are passed through the bed of pellets from beneath. This dries and partially calcines the raw mix very efficiently. The pellets then drop into the kiln.

The cyclone is key component of the gas-suspension preheater. When a dust-bearing gas-stream is passed tangentially in to a cyclone, it produces a vortex within the vessel. The gas leaves the vessel through a vortex-finder. The solids are thrown to the outside edge of the vessel by centrifugal action, and leave through a spigot. It is found that in a cyclone, the gas is efficiently cooled, hence producing less waste of heat to the atmosphere, and the raw mix is efficiently heated. This efficiency is further increased if a number of cyclones are connected in series.

The precalciner is a development of the suspension preheater. If part of the coal necessary to burn the raw mix is burned outside the kiln, the output of the system can be increased for a given kiln size. Users of suspension preheaters found that output could be increased by injecting extra fuel into the base of the preheater.

A specially designed combustion chamber at the base of the preheater is installed and pulverized coal is injected. This is referred to as an Air-through precalciner,

Table 37.4.2 Course of Reaction in a Cement Kiln.

Temperature (°C)	Chemical Transformations
Below 800	Formation of $CaO.Al_2O_3$, $2CaO.Fe_2O_3$, and $2CaO.SiO_2$ begins.
800–900	Formation of $12CaO.7Al_2O_3$ begins.
900–1,100	$2CaO.Al_2O_3.SiO_2$ forms and decomposes again. Formation of $3CaO.Al_2O_3$ and $4CaO.Al_2O_3.Fe_2O_3$ starts. All $CaCO_3$ decomposes and free CaO reaches a maximum.
1,100–1,200	Formation of major part of $3CaO.Al_2O_3$ and $4CaO.Al_2O_3.Fe_2O_3$. Content of $2Cao.SiO_2$ reaches a maximum.
1,260	First liquid formation starts
1,200–1,450	Formation of $3CaO.SiO_2$ with progressive disappearance of free lime.

because the combustion air for both the kiln fuel and the calciner fuel all passes through the kiln. This kind of precalciner can burn up to 30% (typically 20%) of coal in the calciner. If more coal is injected in the calciner, the extra amount of air drawn through the kiln would cool the kiln flame excessively. The feed is 40–60% calcined before it enters the rotary kiln. The ultimate development is the Air-separate precalciner, in which the hot combustion air for the calciner arrives in a duct directly from the cooler, bypassing the kiln. Typically, 60–75% of the fuel is burned in the precalciner. In these systems, the feed entering the rotary kiln is 100% calcined. The kiln has only to raise the feed to sintering temperature.

Immediately following the kiln is a large cooler designed to drop the temperature of the clinker from 1000°C to 150°C. This is achieved by forcing air through a bed of clinker via perforated plates in the base of the cooler. The plate within the cooler slide back and forth, shuffling the clinker down the cooler to the discharge point and transport to a storage area. If the clinker is cooled very slowly, some of the reactions would be reversed resulting the loss of tricalcium silicate, which is important to the strength development of the cement, by dissolving in the liquid. During rapid cooling, the liquid solidifies quickly and there is no appreciable loss of tricalcium silicate.

4   **Cement milling:** To produce the final product cement, the clinker is mixed with 2–8% (but typically 5%) of gypsum ($CaSO_4.2H_2O$) and ground for approximately 30 minutes in large tube mills. The cement, flowing from the inlet to the outlet of the mill, first ground with 60 mm then 30 mm diameter steel balls. The first grinding breaks up the material and the second grinds it to a fine powder. The grinding process is controlled to obtain a powder with a broad particle size range, in which typically 15% by weight consists of particles below 5 μm diameter, and 5% of particles above 45 μm. The cement is conveyed by belt or powder pump to a silo for storage.

37.4.1   Cement production

The cement industry is the building block of the nation's construction industry. As per the CEMBUREAU, The European Cement Association, global cement production is 4,300 million tones in 2014, with an increase of 6.9% compared to the 4,000 million tones recorded in 2013. China is the largest producer of cement in the World with a production of 2,500 million tones. India is the second largest producer of cement with 280 million tones. USA is next to India in cement production with 83.3 million tones of cement production.

37.4.2   Selection of coal for cement manufacture

Coal plays an important role in the manufacturing process of cement. The selection of coal for cement industry should be judiciously done. Table 37.4.1.1 shows coal quality requirement for cement industry.

In a cement plant two systems of coal firing are used, namely, (a) Direct firing and (b) Indirect firing. In direct firing system, coal is milled on line and is directly fed to the kiln. The primary air is used to dry the coal. High moisture coals are not suitable

Table 37.4.1.1 Coal quality requirement for cement industry (IS 12770:2010).

Sl. No.	Characteristics	Requirement
1	Total Moisture Content (at 60% RH and 40°C), %	8 max
2	Volatile Matter (air dried), %	24 min
3	Ash %	
	(a) Dry process	27 max
	(b) Wet process	24 max
4	Sulfur, %	0.8 max
5	Chloride, %	0.01 max
6	Size, mm	250 max

for direct firing, as this has the effect of lowering the flame temperature and therefore the process efficiency. Excess of primary air should not be allowed, as this has also a similar effect like high moisture. In indirect firing system, coal is milled off line and stored in a bunker from where it is fed to the kiln as per the requirement. During storage of coal the propensity for spontaneous heating should be kept in mind.

Coal fineness has a direct relationship with its reactivity. Hence in the cement plant, a special significance has been given to the milling behavior of coal. It has been observed that low volatile matter in coal can be compensated by finer grinding. It is also desirable that coal must have a high Hardgrove Grindability Index (HGI).

To get the temperature of clinker around 1500°C in a kiln, the flame temperature should be maintained at 1700°C. This is achieved by providing preheat to the secondary air. If high moisture coal is used in direct firing system, there may be an excess of moist primary air and required temperature may not be obtained. However, in indirect firing system using dry primary air, a satisfactory flame temperature can be achieved even with low energy coal.

In the clinkering zone of the kiln, excessive build up of deposits can hinder the movement of solids through the kiln. The deposit formation is commonly associated with the presence of chlorine, sodium, potassium and sulphur. Hence coal with high chlorine or sulphur is not favoured in the cement plant.

The temperature vis-à-vis heat required in the rotary kiln depends on the composition of raw feed. Hence the coal should be selected in such a way that it should be able to generate requisite gross calorific value. In direct firing system, high moisture coals are not suitable. One advantage of using coal as a fuel is that the ash left after burning coal may be utilized in cement production. When cement clinkers are finally milled, the ash may be mixed in requisite proportion.

Chapter 38

Gasification

Gassification is the process of partial combustion of the entire solid fuel in the presence of a limited amount of air or oxygen. This partial combustion of carbon yields carbon monoxide which is a combustible gas.

Solid fuels may be gasified through reactions with air, oxygen, steam, carbon dioxide or mixtures of these into a product that is suitable for use either as a fuel or as a raw material for making chemicals, liquid fuels or other gaseous fuels. Carbonization may be considered as a partial gasification process yielding solid, liquid and gaseous products from the initial solid fuel.

One reason for coal gasification is to make up the shortage of liquid and gaseous fuels. Now the world economy depends on energy provided principally by oil and natural gas. As the world petroleum and natural gas production declines because of increasing world population and aspirations for improvement in quality of life, the coal gasification will be a primary way to produce liquid fuels for transportation and gaseous fuels for heating and chemicals production.

The major difference between combustion and gasification from the point of view of the chemistry involved is that combustion takes place under oxidizing conditions, while gasification occurs under reducing conditions. In the gasification process, carbon of the coal reacts with water in the form of steam and oxygen at relatively high pressure typically greater than 30 Bar and at temperatures typically reaching 1,225°C in a reaction vessel called a gasifier to produce raw synthesis gas or **syngas**, a mixture primarily of carbon monoxide and hydrogen and some minor byproducts. The byproducts are removed to produce a clean syngas that can be used as a fuel to generate electricity or steam, as a basic chemical building block for a large number of uses in the petrochemical and refining industries, and for the production of hydrogen.

38.1 GASIFICATION OF COAL

Gasification of coal is a process that converts coal from a solid to a gaseous fuel through partial oxidation. Coal is converted into synthesis gas by reaction with steam and oxygen (or air). When coal is gasified under practical conditions of coal gasification, coal is first heated in a closed reaction chamber called gasifier where it undergoes a pyrolysis process (reaction 38.1.1) at temperatures above 400°C. Pyrolysis or devolatilization accounts for loss of a large percentage coal and occurs rapidly during the initial stages of coal heat up. At any given temperature only a certain fraction of the volatiles is released. Significant devolatilization begins when the coal temperature is about 500°C. As the temperature is increased more volatiles are released. The maximum volatile yield occurs when the temperature is > 900°C.

$$\text{Coal} \xrightarrow{\text{Pyrolysis}} \text{Char (C)} + \text{Coal Volatiles} \qquad (38.1.1)$$

The chemistry of gasification is quite complex and involves many chemical reactions, some of the more important gasification reactions are:

- Reactions in the solid phase:

Partial oxidation	$C + \frac{1}{2} O_2 \rightarrow CO$	$-\Delta H$	(38.1.2)
Combustion	$C + O_2 \rightarrow CO_2$	$-\Delta H$	(38.1.3)
Gasification with steam	$C + H_2O \rightarrow CO + H_2$	$+\Delta H$	(38.1.4)
	$C + 2 H_2O \rightarrow CO_2 + 2H_2$	$+\Delta H$	(38.1.5)
Boudouard	$C + CO_2 \rightarrow 2CO$	$+\Delta H$	(38.1.6)
Hydrogenation	$C + 2 H_2 \rightarrow CH_4$	$-\Delta H$	(38.1.7)

- Reactions in the gas phase:

Partial oxidation	$CO + \frac{1}{2} O_2 \rightarrow CO_2$	$-\Delta H$	(38.1.8)
Water shift	$CO + H_2O \rightarrow CO_2 + H_2$	$-\Delta H$	(38.1.9)
Methanation	$CO + 3H_2 \rightarrow CH_4 + H_2O$	$-\Delta H$	(38.1.10)
Hydrogen oxidation	$\frac{1}{2} O_2 + H_2 \rightarrow H_2O$	$-\Delta H$	(38.1.11)
	$CO + 2H_2 \rightarrow CH_4 + CO_2$	$-\Delta H$	(38.1.12)
Tar hydrocracking	$VM + H_2 \rightarrow CH_4$	$-\Delta H$	(38.1.13)

Main gasification reactions are the gasification reactions (38.1.4 & 38.1.5) in the solid phase where the reaction of carbon with steam at temperatures and low pressures results in hydrogen and carbon dioxide. These are highly endothermic reactions. Reactions 38.1.2 and 38.1.3 are exothermic oxidation reactions and provide most of the energy required by the endothermic gasification reactions. The oxidation reactions occur very rapidly, completely consuming all of the oxygen present in the gasifier, so that most of the gasifier operates under reducing conditions. The Boudouard reaction 38.1.6 is endothermic and, in absence of catalyst, occurs very slowly at temperatures under 700°C. The reaction is inhibited by the CO produced in the partial oxidation and carbon gasification with steam. Methane formation, hydrogenation reaction 38.1.7, is favored by high pressures and low temperatures and is, thus, mainly important in lower temperature gasification systems. Reaction 38.1.9 is the water-gas shift reaction, which in essence converts CO into H_2. The water-gas shift reaction is used to adjust the H_2/CO ratio in the final gas mixture. As it is an exothermic reaction it occurs at low temperatures in presence of a catalyst and pressure has no effect on increasing hydrogen yield. Mineral matter in the coal catalyzes this gas-phase reaction. Other gas-phase reactions are the combustion of CO, H_2, and tar cracking (reactions 38.1.8, 38.1.11, 38.1.12, 38.1.13).

The fraction of the devolatilization gas that condenses at room temperature and pressure is called tar. It is a mixture of hydrocarbons. The yield of tar depends on the

coal rank; higher rank coals produce lesser amounts of tar. Higher gasifier temperature also reduces the amount of tar in the gasifier products because of increased cracking of tar into lighter gases. The amount of tar also decreases with increasing pressure
and decreasing heating rates. The devolatilization gas that does not condense at room
temperature and pressure consists mainly of CO, CO_2, CH_4, H_2, and H_2O. Steam or
water (coal-water slurry feeding) can be added in order to increase the amount of
Hydrogen produced in the gas.

The solid product left over from devolatilization is char. Char in an oxygen
atmosphere undergoes combustion. In gasifiers, partial combustion occurs in an
oxygen-deficient, or reducing, atmosphere. The heat released by the partial combustion provides the bulk of the energy necessary to drive the endothermic gasification
reactions. The oxygen is rapidly consumed in the combustion zone, which occupies
a small volume of the reactor. Further conversion of char occurs through the much
slower, reversible gasification reactions with CO_2, H_2O, and H_2.

Methane formation reactions in solid (reaction 38.1.7) and gaseous phases (reaction 38.1.10) are exothermic reactions that does not consume oxygen and, therefore,
increases the efficiency of gasification and the final heating value of the synthesis gas.
Overall, about 70% of the fuel's heating value is associated with the CO and H_2 in
the gas, but this can be higher depending upon the gasifier type. Depending on the
gasifier technology employed and the operating conditions, significant quantities of
H_2O, CO_2, and CH_4 can be present in the synthesis gas, as well as a number of minor
and trace components. Fig. 38.1 shows the reactions in coal gasification.

Many other reactions, besides those listed, occur. Under the reducing conditions
in the gasifier, most of the fuel's sulfur converts to hydrogen sulfide (H_2S), but 3–10%
converts to carbonyl sulfide (COS). Fuel-bound nitrogen generally converts to gaseous nitrogen (N_2), but some ammonia (NH_3) and a small amount of hydrogen cyanide
(HCN) are also formed. Most of the chlorine in the fuel is converted to HCl with
some chlorine present in the particulate phase. Trace elements, such as mercury and
arsenic, are released during gasification and partition among the different phases,
such as fly ash, bottom ash, slag, and product gas.

The raw syngas produced is cleaned of most pollutants (almost 99% of its sulphur and 90% of nitrogen pollutants). Modern gasification systems produce a syngas
at par with natural gas called Synthetic Natural Gas (SNG). The syngas produced

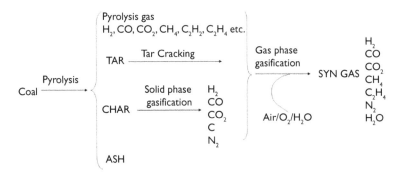

Figure 38.1 Reactions in coal gasification.

from coal gasification is shifted to produce a H_2/CO ratio of approximately 3:1. The carbon dioxide produced during shifting is removed, and CO and H_2 react to produce methane (CH_4), or SNG, and water in a methanation reactor.

38.2 TYPES OF GASIFIERS

Gasifiers are usually classified by the flow regime inside the reactor. There are three main categories:

1   Fixed or Moving bed gasifiers
2   Fluidized bed gasifiers
3   Entrained flow gasifiers

   Each type of gasifier depending on the operation characteristics can be classified as

• Pressurized and non-pressurized
• Autothermal or allothermal
   In Autothermal gasification, the heat required for gasification reactions is supplied by partial oxidation of the syngas. Air or a steam/oxygen mixture are used as oxidant agents.
   In Allothermal gasification, the heat required for gasification reactions is afforded by an external source. Steam is used as the gasification agent.
• Using air or oxygen as gasificant agent
• Slagging, agglomerate or dry ash

Gasification slag: It is vitrified ash containing some unconverted carbon.

Agglomerate: If operating temperature is over the Initial Deformation Temperature of Ash, it starts to melt and get sticky creating agglomerates.

Dry ash: If the operating temperature is under the Initial Deformation Termperature of Ash, the ash will not melt.

38.2.1   Fixed or moving bed gasifiers

Fixed-bed or Moving-bed gasifier is the oldest gasification device in use. Most of these gasifiers are used with oxygen and steam which are injected into the bottom of the reactor while the coal is fed at the top. In this gasifier, large particles of coal move slowly down through the bed while reacting with gases moving counter-currently. Reaction "zones" are often used to describe the reactions occurring along the length of the gasifier. In the drying zone at the top of the gasifier, the entering coal is heated and dried by the countercurrent flow of syngas, while simultaneously cooling the syngas before it leaves the gasifier. The moisture content of the coal mainly controls the temperature of the discharge gas from the gasifier. As the coal continues down the bed, it enters the carbonization zone where the coal is further heated and devolatilized by higher temperature gas. In the gasification zone, the devolatilized coal is converted to syngas by reactions with steam and CO_2. In the combustion zone near the bottom of the reactor, oxygen reacts with the remaining char to consume the remaining carbon and to generate the necessary heat for the gasification zone.

Depending upon the operation of the combustion zone, the moving bed gasifier can be made to operate in one of two distinct modes, i.e., dry ash or slagging. In the dry-ash version, the temperature is maintained below the ash slagging temperature by the endothermic reaction of the char with steam in the presence of excess steam. In addition, the ash below the combustion zone is cooled by the entering steam and oxidant. In the slagging version, much less steam is used so that the temperature of the ash in the combustion zone exceeds the ash fusion temperature of the coal and molten slag is formed. Temperature varies from 400°C at the top to 800°C–1400°C at the bottom for slagging gasifiers and 1000°C for dry ash gasifiers.

This type of gasifier accepts coal of size from 5 to 80 mm. Minor fragments have to be briquetted before entering into the gasifier. The requirement of a sized coal is one of the main disadvantages of this technology. The residence time is long (15 to 60 min) for high pressure steam/oxygen gasifiers and several hours for atmospheric pressure steam/air gasifiers. The syngas outlet temperature is low (400°C to 600°C) depending on the coal moisture content. The produced syngas has a high heating value due to the high methane content and the consumption of oxygen in the reactor is very low. As a result, the thermal efficiency of the process is very high.

38.2.2 Fluidized bed gasifiers

Fluidized-bed gasifiers operate in a highly back-mixed mode, thoroughly mixing the coal feed particles with those particles already undergoing gasification. Coal enters at the side of the reactor, while steam and oxidant enter near the bottom, thereby suspending or fluidizing the reacting bed. Char particles entrained in the raw gas leaving the top of the gasifier are recovered by a cyclone and recycled back to the gasifier. Ash particles removed below the bed give up heat to the incoming steam and oxidant. Because of the highly back-mixed operation, the gasifier operates under isothermal conditions at constant temperatures (900°C–1100°C) below the ash fusion temperature of the coal, thus avoiding clinker formation and possible collapse of the bed. The low temperature operation of this gasifier means that fluidized-bed gasifiers are best suited to relatively reactive feeds, such as low-rank coals, or high ash coals. Gasifying agent is usually air. It has to be fed with a minimum fluidizing velocity to ensure the bubbling of the bed. For velocity values higher than the MFV the particles of the bed will flow up causing a circulating bed.

This type of gasifier has great fuel and load flexibility and can only operate with coal sizes of 0.5–5 mm. The syngas outlet temperature is usually within 700°C–900°C. It is free of tars and with low fly ash content. Suitable coals for this gasifier are lignites and brown coals because of their higher ash content. Higher rank coals can operate in agglomerated ash gasifiers. Part of the H_2S and COS can be retained by the bed (up to 90%) with sorbents as limestone. This reduces as well the corrosion.

Fluidized bed gasifier offers the advantage of promoting excellent mass and heat transfer due to the intensive mixing. On the other hand, individual particles have widely varying residence time in the bed volume. Therefore, unreacted carbon particles are inevitably removed from the bed along with fully reacted particles. The best existing fluidized bed devices offer a carbon conversion of 97%. In comparison, both moving-beds and entrained-flow processes offer carbon conversions of 99%.

38.2.3   Entrained flow gasifiers

Entrained flow gasifiers are characterized by higher velocities and higher temperatures than the fixed or fluidized bed gasifiers. Coal particles are having the size 200–300 μm. These fine coal particles react with steam and oxidant at temperatures well above the ash fusion temperature. The residence time is very short (0.5–5 sec) and high temperatures are required to achieve high carbon conversion. Oxygen consumption is higher because of the need to combust more coal to generate the required heat. Oxygen consumption can be minimized by using high quality coals. The produced gas is free of tars and phenols and contains small amounts of methane.

Two types of entrained flow gasifiers are down-flow and up-flow gasifiers. In down-flow gasifier coal is fed dry or with water at the top of the reactor. Gasification occurs at high temperatures and moderate pressures. The gas flows downwards and it is cooled or quenched with water at the bottom of the reactor. The slag drops into a water pool. In a up-flow gasifier, coal is fed at the bottom of the gasifier. Gas flows upwards and leaves the gasifier at the top part while the slag flows down and is quenched with water. This type of gasification can be in one or two stages. When a two stage gasifier is used, 75% of the coal is fed by the bottom part and the rest is directly injected into the hot gas in order to take advantage of its high temperature. Some char and hydrocarbons are produced in this second stage.

The advantage of the entrained flow gasifiers is the ability to handle any coal and produce a clean, tar-free gas. Additionally, the ash is produced in the form of inert slag. The majority of the coal gasification processes that have been developed after 1950 are based on entrained-flow, slagging gasifiers operating at pressures of 20 to 70 bar and at high temperature ($\geq 1400°C$). Entrained-flow gasifiers have become the technology of choice for hard coals, and have been selected for the majority of commercial-sized IGCC plants.

38.3   OTHER FUEL GASES

Producer gas is a mixture of Carbon monoxide and hydrogen with little carbon dioxide. It is the gas which is formed by partial combustion of coal with air. The solid fuel is completely consumed by means of partial oxidation and gives a combustible gas and leaves no combustible residue. The oxygen for combustion is obtained from air and water. The producer gas may be produced from coal or coke.

Water gas or **blue water gas** is produced by passing steam on red hot coke. The resulting gas contains large quantities of carbon monoxide and hydrogen. The reaction is highly endothermic. Therefore, to heat the coke, air is blasted. The purpose of passing air and steam at different intervals is to ensure that the large quantity of nitrogen does not reach the gas. The gas is called blue water gas because the combustion of carbon monoxide gives a blue flame.

Carbureted water gas is the water gas enriched by hydrocarbon gases to increase the calorific value of the gas. Enrichment is usually done in a carburetter sprayed with suitable fuel oil.

Table 38.3 Typical Analysis of Fuel gases.

	Components % by volume							
	CO_2	O_2	N_2	CO	H_2	CH_4	others	c.v
Producer gas	4.5	0.6	50.9	27.0	14.0	3.0	–	1360
Water gas	5.5	0.9	27.6	28.2	32.5	4.6	0.7	2125
Carburetted water gas	6.0	0.9	12.4	26.8	32.2	13.5	8.2	4000
Coal gas	1.7	0.8	8.1	7.3	49.5	29.2	3.4	4150
Coke oven gas	2.2	0.8	8.1	6.3	46.5	32.1	4.0	4520
Blast Furnace gas	11.5	–	60.0	27.5	1.0	–	–	820

c.v = Net calorific value Kcal/m³ at 15.5°C 1 atm. Pressure.

Coal gas or **town gas** is the gas manufactured by high temperature carbonization of coal in gas retorts. It is used for town supply. The main product of high temperature carbonization is the gas while coke is a secondary by-product.

Coke oven gas is the by-product of coke oven. The composition of coke oven gas is similar to coal gas but the carbonization temperature in coke oven gas is lower and more closely controlled.

Blast furnace gas is a low grade producer gas. In the blast furnace, coke reacts with air to give carbon dioxide which rises upwards and reacts with coke to give carbon monoxide. It has low calorific value; hence it cannot produce high temperature. It is used for operating gas engines, to heat by-product coke ovens, and in various other heating processes. The analysis of some of the fuel gases is shown in Table 38.3.

38.4 SELECTION OF COAL FOR GASIFICATION

A high volatile coal is advantageous as the products of decomposition enrich the gas. The coals having volatile contents of 33%–37% are preferable for gas production. The lower the rank of coal higher the volatile matter content and easier to react with oxygen and steam for gasification reactions to take place. As the carbon content of coal increases, the reactive functional groups present in coal decreases and reactivity reduces.

The coal should have low moisture. The ash should be low and as infusible as possible. Fusible ash gives rise to serious clinkering troubles and may slag with the lining of the gasifier. The extra force necessary to dislodge clinker causes undue loss of carbon in the refuse, and much stirring up of the fuel bed leads to rising of the ash into the hottest part of the fire with increased clinker formation.

Strongly coking coals are unsuitable, since by the formation of large lumps of coke, uneven resistance is setup in the fuel bed and the gasification rate and quality of gas fails off. A slightly coking coal is advantageous, particularly if the coal is dusty or tends to break down into dust when heated.

A closely screened coal is of advantage, a more even distribution of the blast through the fuel bed will result and this will lead to more even working and a gas of more constant composition will be obtained.

38.5   INTEGRATED GASIFICATION COMBINED CYCLE (IGCC)

If the syngas is to be used to produce electricity, it is typically used as a fuel in an **Integrated Gasification Combined Cycle** (IGCC) power generation system, which is the cleanest, most efficient means of producing electricity from coal. IGCC plants use a two-step process to produce electricity. In the first step, coal is converted into synthetic gas or syngas. Gasifiers convert the coal into a syngas composed mainly of hydrogen and carbon monoxide, both are combustible. Gasification normally takes place by heating the coal with a mixture of steam and oxygen. This can be carried out in a fixed bed, a fluidized bed or an entrained flow gasifier. The syngas is used as fuel in a gas turbine which produces electrical power. In the second step, the hot combustion gas from the gas turbine is sent to a heat recovery steam generator, where it produces steam, which in turn, drives a steam turbine/generator to produce additional electrical power (hence the term **combined cycle**). Such plants are considered **integrated** because the two steps occur at the same facility in tandem. Electric power is produced from both the gas and steam turbine-generators. Thermal efficiencies of over 55% can be achieved in such plants. By removing the emission-forming constituents from the syngas under pressure before combustion, an IGCC power plant produces lower levels of air pollutants viz., nitrous oxide, sulfur dioxide, and particulate matter and volatile mercury. Figure 38.5 shows the IGCC Plant.

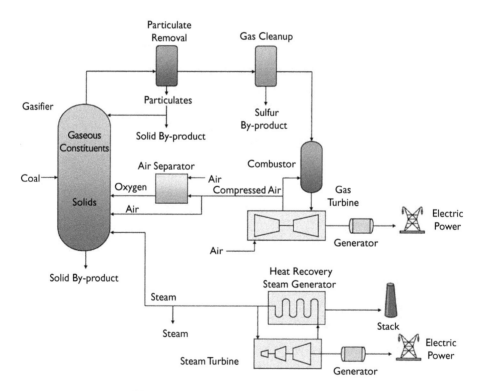

Figure 38.5 Integrated Gasification Combined Cycle Plant.

38.6   UNDERGROUND COAL GASIFICATION

Underground Coal Gasification (UCG) is the process of gasifying coal in-situ, that is, within an underground coal seam. It is similar to surface gasification, with syngas produced through the same chemical reactions. The main difference is that surface gasification occurs in a manufactured reactor whereas the reactor for a UCG system is a natural geological formation containing unmined coal.

Vertical wells, called injection well and production well, are drilled into the coal seam and linked together horizontally within the seam (Fig. 38.6). Coal ignition is initiated through the use of an electric coil or gas firing near the face of the coal seam. Compressed gasification agent (air or oxygen) is pumped into the injection well to allow for combustion of coal. Combustion produces heat, carbon dioxide and some syngas through partial combustion. Through a series of chemical reactions involving pressure, heat and carbon dioxide from combustion, steam (generated from water in the coal) and carbon from the coal, syngas is produced.

The gasification channel is normally divided into three zones: oxidization, reduction, and dry distillation and pyrolysis. In the oxidization zone, multiphase chemical reactions occur involving the oxygen in the gasification agents and the carbon in the coal. The highest temperatures occur in the oxidation zone, due to the large release of energy during the initial reactions. In the reduction zone, the main reactions involve the reduction of $H_2O(g)$ and CO_2 into H_2 and CO at high temperatures within the oxidation zone. Under the catalytic action of coal ash and metallic oxides, a methanation reaction takes place. Within the distillation (pyrolysis) zone, the coal seam is decomposed into multiple volatiles including H_2O, CO_2, CO, C_2H_6, CH_4, H_2, tar, and char. At the exit of the gasification channel, the volatile composition of the syngas consists mostly of CO, H_2, and CH_4.

The UCG process can also have other products, including H_2S, As, Hg, Pb, and ash. The composition of syngas is highly dependent on the gasification agent, air

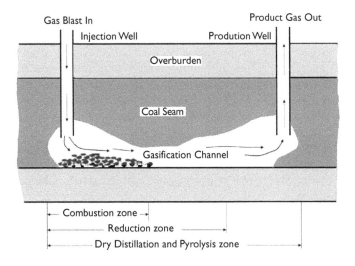

Figure 38.6 Underground Gasification System.

injection method, and coal composition. During operation, the three gasification zones move along the direction of the air flow, ensuring continuous gasification reactions. A distinguishing feature of UCG, compared to surface gasification, is that drying, pyrolysis, and char gasification occur simultaneously within the coal. The syngas flows from the gasification chamber through the horizontal connection in the coal seam and flows to the surface through the production well. When the syngas reaches the surface, it is cleaned and undesired by-products are removed from the product stream.

UCG offers the potential to use the energy stored in coal deposits that are uneconomic to mine by conventional methods. As there is no need to mine the coal, safety hazards associated with underground coal mining are eliminated. The syngas product can be used in a variety of industrial processes including power generation, liquid fuel production and chemical manufacture. Significant environmental benefits are reduced surface disturbance and land use conflicts, and avoidance of greenhouse gas production associated with coal mining. UCG technology could also be regarded as an enabling technology for carbon capture since it has the ability to deliver an enriched CO_2 stream suitable for carbon capture and storage. With an approximate 21 per cent reduction in greenhouse gas emissions, UCG is a lower carbon emitting technology for power generation when compared to coal-fired power stations.

38.7   GASIFICATION INDUSTRY

There are more than 272 operating gasification plants worldwide with 686 gasifiers. There are currently 74 plants under construction worldwide that will have a total of 238 gasifiers and produce 83 MWth (Megawatt thermal power). Gasification plants had been fairly evenly distributed between Asia/Australia, Africa/Middle East and North America. The gasification capacity (both operational and under construction) in the Asia/Australia region now exceeds the rest of the world put together. Currently, China has the largest number of gasification plants.

Gasification for chemicals has been, and will remain, the most important gasification application for the foreseeable future. A recent study conducted by Higman and Tam determined that about 25% of the world's ammonia and over 30% of the world's methanol are now being produced via gasification. Gasification for liquid and gaseous fuels is becoming increasingly important. Gasification for substitute natural gas has also shifted to Asia. The high cost of importing Liquefied Natural Gas or LNG and the concerns about energy security have prompted a number of new plants under construction in Asia. Coal is now the dominant feedstock and will continue in future.

Gasification projects are becoming both larger and smaller. The large industrial coal and petroleum coke gasification projects (for chemicals, hydrogen, power) are getting bigger. Worldwide gasification capacity is expected to grow significantly by 2018, with the primary growth occurring in Asia (primarily China, India, South Korea, and Mongolia).

Chapter 39

Liquefaction

Coal liquefaction, also called Coal To Liquid (CTL) Technology, is an industrial process in which coal as raw material is converted into liquid hydrocarbon mixture through chemical reaction, which, under further processing, becomes the desired liquid fuels or chemical feedstock. The liquid fuels produced through this process are suitable for transportation application by the removal of carbon or addition of hydrogen, either directly or indirectly. In this way coal can act as a substitute for crude oil. However, the cost effectiveness of coal liquefaction depends to a large extant on the world oil price with which in an open market economy, it needs to compete.

In analogy to gasification the term liquefaction is used to cover all the processes for converting solid fuels into liquid products which may be either used directly as fuel or converted into chemicals or other liquid fuels. Owing to the recovery of crude benzol and coal tar, the carbonization process may be described as partial liquefaction of coal. Coal liquefaction is possible by raising the hydrogen-to-carbon ratio. It can be achieved either by direct conversion or by indirect conversion of coal through the gasification route. The most important property of coal in order to predict liquid yield from coal is the percentage of volatile material in it. The liquid yield from coal varies between 35 and 45 per cent. One tonne of coal can produce about one to three barrels of oil and 200 to1,000 cu.m. of gas. Wide ranges of by-products are obtained in different liquefaction processes. Fig. 39.1 shows some of the products that can be obtained from the coal through gasification and liquefaction.

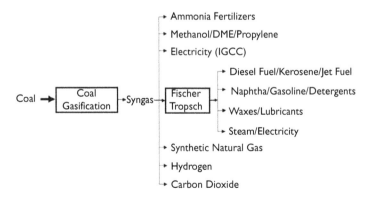

Figure 39.1 Products from the coal gasification and liquefaction.

39.1 PRODUCTION OF LIQUID FUELS

Hydrocarbon type liquid fuels are produced from coal by the following routes:

1　Hydrogenation of coal e.g. Bergius process
2　Solvent extraction of coal and hydrogenation of coal extracts
3　Refining of tar and oil obtained by carbonization of coal
4　Gasification of coal into synthesis gas and conversion of latter into liquid fuels. e.g. Fischer-Tropsch process

39.1.1　Bergius process

The **Bergius process** is a method of production of liquid hydrocarbons for use as synthetic fuel by hydrogenation of high-volatile bituminous coal at high temperature and pressure. The process is also called as **Direct Coal Liquefaction (DCL)**. It was first developed by Friedrich Bergius in 1913, who was later awarded the Nobel Prize in chemistry for his development of high pressure chemistry.

In the Bergius process, coal is splitted, in presence of catalyst, into shorter hydrocarbons resembling ordinary crude oil by adding hydrogen under high pressure and temperature as per the reaction 39.1.1.

$$nC + (n+1)H_2 \rightarrow C_nH_{2n+2} \tag{39.1.1}$$

The hydrocarbons thus formed again react with hydrogen to produce saturated hydrocarbons. These saturated hydrocarbons at high temperature and pressure decompose to give high yield of liquid hydrocarbons and also some gas and coke.

The coal is ground and mixed with coal derived heavy oil recycled from the process to form coal-oil slurry. The slurry containing 30–50% coal is then fed to the reactor and heated to about 450°C in hydrogen atmosphere of 170 bar pressure. A second reactor completes the liquefaction, operating at higher temperatures. The reaction catalyst for both the stages may be iron based one, dispersed in the slurry. Liquid yields may be in excess of 70% of the dry weight coal feed, with thermal efficiencies of around 60–70%. The resulting liquids are of much higher quality and can be used unblended in power generation or other chemical processes as a synthetic crude oil (syncrude). However, further treatment is needed before they are usable as a transport fuel and refining stages are needed in the full process chain. A mix of many gasoline-like and diesel-like products, as well as propane, butane and other products can be recovered from the refined syncrude mainly by distillation. These products are only partially refined. They must be further refined into finished liquid fuel products at conventional refineries, where additional H_2 is added to bring the H/C ratio up to ~2 for the final products.

Processes have been developed to use coals from low rank lignites to high volatile bituminous coals. Higher rank coals are less reactive and anthracites are essentially non-reactive.

39.1.2　Solvent extraction

In solvent extraction process, much of the organic matter in some types of coal is dissolved in solvents, such as coal-tar oils generated within the process, at temperatures above 400°C, leaving the mineral matter and some inert constituents as a residue.

This process is combined with the addition of hydrogen where hydrogen is transferred to the coal molecules for liquid fuel production.

39.1.3   Refining carbonization products

High temperature carbonisation is the oldest process for producing liquids from coal. When the coal is heated to around 950°C in a closed container in absence of air, decomposition takes place, and the volatile matter is driven off. This is typical of the coke making process, and the hydrocarbon liquid products, made up of a mixture of hydrocarbons called tar and aqueous solutions containing a variety of dissolved materials called ammonical liquor are the byproducts. The tar and oil thus obtained by carbonization of coal is refined to yield liquid fuels.

39.1.4   Coal gasification and fischer-tropsch process

This is an indirect liquefaction process to produce liquid fuels. The first step in indirect liquefaction is the production of synthesis gas. The synthesis gas of carbon monoxide and hydrogen is produced using fixed bed gasification process at 800°C–900°C by coal gasification. The composition of this synthetic gas is adjusted to give the required balance of hydrogen and carbon monoxide. Sulphur compounds are removed at this stage to prevent poisoning of the reaction catalyst as well as to provide low-sulphur transport fuels.

The synthesis gas is converted into liquid hydrocarbons by a catalytic process known as **Fischer-Tropsch process.** It was first developed by Franz Fischer and Hans Tropsch in Germany, in 1923. The Fischer-Tropsch process for making synthetic hydrocarbons can be summarized, in a simplified manner, by the following two catalytic reactions that build up large hydrocarbon molecules from the small CO and H_2 molecules produced by gasification:

$$n\ CO + 2n\ H_2 \rightarrow n\ H_2O + C_nH_{2n}\ \text{(olefins)} \tag{39.1.2}$$
$$n\ CO + (2n + 1)\ H_2 \rightarrow n\ H_2O + C_nH_{2n+2}\ \text{(paraffins)} \tag{39.1.3}$$

The Fischer-Tropsch process involves a series of catalyzed chemical reactions in which carbon monoxide and hydrogen are converted into liquid hydrocarbons of various forms. The catalyst used is a chemical compound that increases the rate of a chemical reaction without altering the final equilibrium. In this process, synthesis gas is passed over iron or cobalt catalyst at a temperature between 200°C–300°C forms mixture of saturated and unsaturated hydrocarbons. These are latter fractionated to give various products.

39.2   PRACTICE OF LIQUEFACTION OF COAL

History of coal liquefaction dates back to early 20th century. Germany had successfully used both direct and indirect routes for production of oil during Second World War on commercial scale. South Africa under geopolitical compulsion produced most of its oil requirement at Sasol through indirect process from mid 1950's to 1980's.

The only operating process for the 'indirect' liquefaction of coal is South Africa's Sasol process, with three operating plants. The first plant, Sasol 1, was built at Sasolburg in the mid 1950s with a capacity of ~6000 bbl/day (1 bbl = 158.987 litres) of gasoline. The much larger Sasol 2 and 3 plants were completed at Secunda in 1980 and 1982 respectively. These plants were each designed to produce 50,000 bbl/day of gasoline, together with substantial quantities of other products for use as chemical feedstocks, from the processing of 30,000 tons/day of coal. It is reported that up to 60% of the fuel requirements for transportation are met from the coal through indirect hydrogenation route.

Significant coal liquefaction research and development (R&D) was started up in the early 1970s, particularly in USA, UK and Japan, in response to various oil price shocks. Japan has been pursuing activities in large-scale process development, with a 150 tonnes/day plant in operation. China is currently co-operating with USA, Japan and Germany on feasibility studies with the plan of installing the first commercial coal liquefaction (direct) of the world. Direct liquefaction is the most efficient route currently available. The single stage direct processes were developed in the mid-to-late 1960s. Some developers added a second stage during the 1970s, following the oil crisis, to increase the production of light oils.

Activities pertaining to coal to oil is being pursued in India since 1960's primarily at CIMFR, Dhanbad. Based on these studies CIMFR has developed two low severity processes. One of which is for conversion of coal to oil with high distillate yield (~90%) while the other one deals with development of coal-water emulsion. One 0.5 tpd high pressure plant was set up at CIMFR to study the hydrogenation of coal. The single stage process yielded 25% oil and operation problems were too many e.g., valve erosion, choking of the reactors, etc. Amenability studies of Indian coals for hydrogenation had been carried out in detail and based on the information generated, a new generation indigenous and innovative process named as "Multi Stage Hydrogenation of Coal (MSHC)" was developed. The concept of MSHC envisages conversion of oil to syncrude at a much less severity condition compared to the other processes.

Although there are no CTL plants currently operating, a number of projects are proposed. The most recent involves Jindal Steel & Power Ltd (JSPL), India and Sasol. This will produce SNG that will be used in a JSPL steel plant and to feed an 80,000 bbl/day facility for motor fuels. There is also a pre-feasibility study under way for a plant involving Tata and Sasol. Fischer-Tropsch technology will be used to convert ~30 Mt/y of high-ash opencast coal into 80,000 bbl/day of liquid products (diesel, naphtha, jet fuel, and LPG). The project will also generate 1500 MW of electricity. Reliance Industries, allied with Coal India, has also proposed an US$8 billion indirect coal liquefaction project based on US technology. This would use up to 30 Mt/y of Mahanadi coal to produce 80,000 bbl/day of synthetic oil products.

Chapter 40

Carbon capture and storage

The term **Clean Coal Technology** (CCT) refers all the technologies applied to coal in order to reduce air emissions, waste product and pollutants on utilizing the coal for its process of energy conversion. As already indicated in chapter 2, clean coal technologies are categorized into beneficiation technologies, combustion and conversion technologies and post-combustion technologies. Coal beneficiation technologies have been discussed in Part-B for which this book is mainly intended for. Coal combustion and conversion technologies have been briefly described in Part-C to give an idea to the reader about these technologies.

Post-combustion technologies are the ultimate technologies where carbon dioxide (CO_2) is captured and removed from the atmosphere. CO_2 Sequestration – **Carbon Capture and Storage** (CCS) technology is one of the emerging clean coal technologies to meet the global emission stabilization targets while meeting the national energy needs.

Carbon Capture and Storage is a set of technologies that can capture up to 90% of the carbon dioxide emissions produced from the use of fossil fuels in electricity generation and industrial processes such as making cement, steel or in the chemical industry, preventing the carbon dioxide from entering the atmosphere. The Carbon dioxide Capture and Storage technologies involve capture of CO_2 in the atmosphere and its permanent fixation away from the atmosphere. If the power plant and the storage sites are not near each other, it will involve transport of CO_2 in liquid form over longer distances. Essentially, the CCS is a three step process as follows:

- Capture of CO_2 from power plants or industrial processes
- Transport of the captured and compressed CO_2 (usually in pipelines)
- Underground injection and geologic sequestration (also referred as storage) of the CO_2 into deep underground rock formations.

40.1 CARBON DIOXIDE CAPTURE

The first stage in the CCS process is the capture of CO_2 released during the burning of fossil fuels, or as a result of industrial processes. Capture technologies allow the separation of carbon dioxide from gases produced in electricity generation and industrial processes by one of three methods viz., pre-combustion capture, post-combustion capture and oxyfuel combustion.

Pre-combustion capture involves first converting solid, liquid or gaseous fuel into a mixture of hydrogen and carbon dioxide using one of a number of processes such as 'gasification' or 'reforming'. Reforming of gas is well-established and used at refineries and chemical plants around the world. In gasification process, the coal is gasified to produce a synthetic gas, contains mainly carbon monoxide and hydrogen. The former is reacted with water to produce CO_2 and hydrogen. CO_2 is then separated, by using physical or chemical solvents. CO_2 can also be separated by solid sorbents or membrane removal. The hydrogen-rich fuel can be used in many applications, such as boilers, furnaces, gas turbines, engines and fuel cells. Pre-combustion capture is suitable for use in integrated gasification combined cycle (IGCC) plants.

One disadvantage of the pre-combustion method is that it cannot be retro-fitted to the older pulverised coal power plants that make up much of the world's installed base of fossil fuel power. It could perhaps be used in natural gas stations, where a synthetic gas is first produced by reacting the methane with steam to produce carbon dioxide and hydrogen. But the economic advantage of this method over post-combustion is yet to be proven.

Post-combustion capture process involves scrubbing the power plant's exhaust gas using chemicals. CO_2 is separated from the exhaust gas of the power station by bubbling the gas through an absorber column packed with liquid solvents (such as ammonia) that preferentially take out the CO_2. In the most commonly-used techniques, once the chemicals in the absorber column become saturated, a stream of superheated steam at around 120°C is passed through it. This releases the trapped CO_2. Carbon dioxide can be captured from the exhaust gas by dissolving it in a specially formulated liquid. The concentrated carbon dioxide is then removed from the liquid. Other methods for separating CO_2 include high pressure membrane filtration, adsorption/desorption processes and cryogenic separation.

Oxyfuel combustion consists of burning the coal in an atmosphere with a higher concentration of pure oxygen. In this environment, virtually all the waste gas will be composed CO_2 and water vapour. The latter can be condensed out while the former can be piped or transported directly to a storage facility.

40.2 CARBON DIOXIDE TRANSPORT

After capture, carbon dioxide is compressed and then transported to a site where it is injected underground for permanent storage, also known as **sequestration**. Carbon dioxide is commonly transported by pipeline, but it can also be transported by train, truck, or ship. The technologies involved in pipeline transportation are the same as those used extensively for transporting natural gas, oil and many other fluids. In some cases it may be possible to re-use existing but redundant pipelines. Each CCS project would choose the most appropriate method for transporting carbon dioxide and be subject to planning and health and safety regulation. The pipelines are usually buried.

Up to 40% of a power station's energy is consumed to run the CCS scrubbing and transport systems and hence retro-fitting to old power stations will be costly.

40.3   CARBONDIOXIDE STORAGE

Carbon dioxide storage or sequestration is burying the carbon dioxide so that it does not escape into the atmosphere and contribute to climate change. Carbon dioxide is stored in porous geological formations that are typically located several kilometres under the earth's surface. At the storage site the carbon dioxide is injected under pressure into the geological formation. After injection, the carbon dioxide moves up through the storage site until it reaches an impermeable layer of rock (which can not be penetrated by carbon dioxide) overlaying the storage site; this layer is known as the **cap rock** and traps the carbon dioxide in the storage formation. This storage mechanism is called "structural storage".

Structural storage is the primary storage mechanism in CCS and is the same process that has kept oil and natural gas securely trapped under the ground for millions of years providing confidence that carbon dioxide can be safely stored indefinitely. As the injected carbon dioxide moves up through the geological storage site towards the cap rock some of it is left behind in the microscopic pore spaces of the rock. This carbon dioxide is tightly trapped in the pore spaces by a mechanism known as "residual storage".

Over time the carbon dioxide stored in a geological formation will begin to dissolve into the surrounding salty water. This makes the salty water denser and it begins to sink down to the bottom of the storage site. This is known as "dissolution storage". Finally "mineral storage" occurs when the carbon dioxide held within the storage site binds chemically and irreversibly to the surrounding rock. As the storage mechanisms change over time from structural to residual, dissolution and then mineral storage the carbon dioxide becomes less and less mobile. Therefore the longer carbon dioxide is stored the lower the risk of any leakage.

Geological formations, deep underground saline aquifers or disused oil fields are few of the suitable sites for sequestration. The last method is often used in a process called "enhanced oil recovery", where CO_2 is pumped into an oil field to force out the remaining pockets of oil that would otherwise prove difficult to extract. Deep saline aquifers represent the largest potential carbon dioxide storage capacity in the long term. Unmineable coal seams are also potential reservoirs for CO_2 storage. By injecting CO_2 in coal seams, coal bed methane recovery can be enhanced. Potential sequestration sites must undergo appropriate site characterization to ensure that the site can safely and securely store CO_2.

Applications of computers

Computer application in coal processing had an increasingly important role in recent years. Broadly the applications can be classified in the following groups [61]:

1   Data bank of the coals fed to the washery.
2   Mathematical analysis of the washability data.
3   Plant Simulation.
4   Plant Optimization.
5   Control strategy and data acquisition system.
6   Plant accounting.

1   DATA BANK

The area of data handling covers the storage, systematic retrieval and simple mathematical analysis of the large volume of screening and washability data generated from different collieries/seams. This allows data from drill cores, adits, channel samples and run-off-mine coal to be combined so that the characteristics of a raw coal from a given mining scenario may be calculated. Furthermore, the washery personnel can use data of individual coals to generate the washability characteristics of the blended coal that goes as feed to the washery. In recent years microcomputers has found wide application for data handling, display of operating and accounting data in a coal processing plant.

2   MATHEMATICAL ANALYSIS

A. Raw washability data of plant feed: The set of data generated through washability studies are often subjected to error arising due to sampling and analytical methods. Before utilizing the data for generating the washability curves and subsequent prediction of practical yield, considering the performance efficiency of relevant washers, it is essential to identify the errors in the data and apply the suitable numerical techniques to correct the data. For the generation of the fractional yield and ash at any density interval other than the intervals for which the float & sink data are available, several mathematical methods such as cubic spline interpolation, mathematical programming based on the classical optimization principles etc. are being used. The smoothen data sets are extremely useful for plant simulation studies and can easily be done with the help of a computer.

B. Plant data: Data generated in a coal processing plant/washery include the size/density data of the feed and product streams from individual process units along with the measured values of different assays such as ash%, %solids, etc. To obtain the performance efficiency of the individual units, it is necessary to calculate the mass flow in the input and output streams from the units. This is being normally done with the help of balancing the suitable assays, such as ash, size, % solid, etc. in the respective streams. In the case of washers working on the principle of gravity separation, the mass flow values of the products are used in conjunction with the float & sink data of the product streams to determine the reconstituted feed.

The use of reconstituted feed for generating the partition data are based on the assumption that the mass yields and mass distribution in the individual density fractions of the products are accurate which in most cases may not be strictly true. Hence, a separate method for generating the partition data using the mass distributions of the feed and the products should be preferred. This can be achieved with the help of a computer; utilizing a suitable data adjustment algorithm based on the principle of weighted least squares to obtain the best estimates of the mass yields that satisfy the mass balance constraints.

Another important area where computerised soft wares are of extreme importance is the material balance of the washery circuit. In order to obtain a material balance measurements of assays on each stream can be obtained. However, due to errors present in the measurements, it is usually not possible to find a set of mass flow rates which satisfy all the mass balance constraints at the individual process units. Two distinct approaches are being used to get the total mass flows and the component mass flows in all the streams in the plant. The first approach use all the available plant data to produce the best estimate of the material balance and in the second one only that assay is chosen to obtain the material balance which has minimal sensitivity to experimental error. For routine plant auditing purpose where minimum sampling and sample preparation is required, the second approach is preferred. The choice of the suitable assay should be made by considering that the chosen assay is well separated in the product streams and has the minimum relative error. In case where there are more than one assay which can be used to find the material balance, it is more appropriate to use all the relevant assays, subject them to minimum adjustment so as to produce a consistent set of mass and component flow rates. The method that is being used to handle such redundant data is based on the principle of weighted least square minimization technique. The weighting/confidence factor is being used on the principle of assigning high weightage factor to the assay data which has minimum error and vice versa. Several robust material balance soft wares are available which utilize either the method of Lagrange Multipliers, direct search method or the method of 'independent path'.

3 PLANT SIMULATION

Computer simulation technique is a powerful tool in the hands of plant engineers and designers to achieve a wide range of objectives. Besides providing a tool for quality control, this helps in the (a) development of flowsheets, (b) retrofitting of existing washery circuits, (c) choice of alternate circuit configurations to produce the desired products, (d) plant optimization. In the Indian context, the application of this tool has become extremely necessary, due to the wide variation of the raw coal characteristics that are being fed to the washeries, arising due to gradual depletion of easy to wash coals and also due to mechanized mining which consequently has led to complications in the operations of the existing washeries to the optimum level. It is imperative to use such techniques to identify the suitable operational parameters of individual process units, their interconnections, to produce the products of desired quality. This will also help to suggest the suitable modifications for retrofitting the existing washeries to accommodate the abundant resource of 'difficult-to-wash' coals of the lower seams of Jharia coalfield.

For simulation studies, the following procedures are to be followed:

a   Identify all the process units and their interconnections.
b   Identify the feed streams and the final products and refuse streams.
c   Generate the washability data of individual size fractions of the feed and obtain a balanced raw density and size data using suitable error minimization techniques.
d   Develop suitable models for individual process units such as crushers, grinding mills, screens, jigs, gravity separators etc. Several mathematical models have been developed for the respective units which can be used after proper validation of the models with the existing plant data. Empirical models utilizing plant data can also be used for simulation and predictive purposes of the existing plants.
e   In case of gravity separators, the model can be represented by a set of partition curves or generalized curves for individual size fractions. The methodology involved in the generation of partition data from the feed and product streams of individual washers and subsequent plotting of the partition curves are outlined in the ISO standard. The partition data represents the fraction of the feed in a density interval which goes to the cleans and d_{50} is the density at which the 50% of the feed in that density that goes to the cleans. The parameters derived from the partition/Tromp curves are the (a) Relative density at the cut point d_{50}; (b) Ecart Probability **Ep**; (c) Imperfection **I**; (d) Error area. In general, the partition curves are specific to the separation units for which they are established and are independent of the density distributions of the feed and depend on size composition, feed rate and other operating conditions. Strictly speaking this is not true. The Ep value derived from the linear mid-portion region is independent of feed characteristics but the error area which embraces the 'tails' is influenced by the nature of the feed. The Ep value also increases with the density of cut and also increases with the decreasing size of the feed .

As relative density is a controlling variable in a density separation process, variation in the relative density of cuts will yield different set of curves. The product distribution at any other density can be obtained by suitably shifting the curve at the desired density. However, a more accurate method of obtaining the same is to generate a generalized distribution curve for a washer using the data obtained from the set of partition curves, which is independent of density. This is obtained by plotting the partition data against the reduced density, a dimensionless variable defined as d/d_{50}. From this generalized curve the partition data at any density of cut can be obtained and used with washability data to predict the product yield and quality.

In simulation studies of a gravity washer treating a particular size range of the feed, the input data of the separating density can predict the product distribution. But this itself is not sufficient since the d_{50} of the entire size range will not give the density of cut of the different size fractions within the size range which is necessary to know the distributions of different size fractions in the products. To obtain this, beside the generalized curve of the composite feed, generalized curves for individual size fractions need to be generated from the same plant data. Furthermore, the following parameters would also be required.

a z_{50} is the ratio of d_{50} of a size interval to the d_{50} of the entire size.
b Z_{Ep} is the ratio of probable error of a size interval to that of the entire size.
c   S is the ratio of the mean size interval to that of the entire size.

A functional relationship between these parameters can be derived from the existing data which subsequently will be used to get the separation data of individual sizes from those given for the entire feed.

The data generated from the simulation studies are

1   The flow rate, size distribution and ash contents of the individual streams.
2   The float and sink analysis and ash contents of the final and intermediate products, on a size by size basis.
3   For gravity washers, the performance criteria, the organic efficiency and the percentage of misplaced materials on a size by size basis.

The data generated from the simulation can be linked with a suitable optimization criteria to optimize the separation densities for gravity separation systems so as to maximize the yield of cleans at the desired quality.

4   PLANT OPTIMIZATION

The ultimate objective of any simulation studies is to select the process variables of individual process units to satisfy some optimum criteria set by the plant manager. The optimum criteria may be of achieving maximum yield of the products of desired quality or producing a product mix of different grade/quality to fetch the maximum returns. In a coal preparation plant which consists of different units ranging from crushers, screens, jigs, dense medium washers, secondary crushers for precleans, middlings etc., flotation, optimal setting of the process variables can be achieved to produce the desired products from individual units. However, as practiced in most of the existing washeries, gravity separation plays the dominant role and produces the maximum amount of the desired products along with some flotation cleans. It is thus necessary to evolve a suitable strategy to optimise the gravity separation processes, in particular. As the density is the most important controlling variable in a dense medium washer, beside the other operational variables such as feed rate, medium/coal ratio and vortex diameter in case of cyclones, it is judicious to select the optimum cut points of different gravity separators so that the combined cleans from the different washers produce the desired products

5   CONTROL STRATEGY AND DATA ACQUISITION SYSTEM

A considerable amount of advancement has recently occurred in overall automatic control of coal processing plants. Programmable controllers are now widely used for plant start-up and shut down, and the computer is used to monitor the states of individual circuits, which can be displayed on visual display units and if necessary, retained in hard copy. The British and German plants have given the lead in this area, but Australian, South African, American and Canadian plants are being built incorporating a considerable amount of process control equipment.

In general terms, the application of computers in plant operational control is taken only as far as reliable and well proven hardware, especially in-plant transducers, will permit. That is to say that the objective from the outset is to utilize computer control to the fullest extent for controlling all plant functions amenable to this form of control providing that they can be shown to be reliable.

There is still the role of computer usage in the control of individual units. For example, some common pieces of coal processing equipment that embody computer control are:

1   Batac Jig – where a microcomputer controls pulsion and water injection.
2   Baum Jig – where a micro computer is used to control raw-coal feed and shale extraction.
3   Dense medium cyclone washing – where a microcomputer can be used in conjunction with a nuclear density gauge and flowmeters for controlling relative density of the medium.
4   Coal on-line analysers – where computers are employed to provide rapid analytical processing and results reporting.

6   PLANT ACCOUNTING

Many plants now incorporate some form of computerized accounting system, whereby all important operating parameters are collected by the various measuring devices and systematically stored for computer processing. Each piece of information can be immediately tabulated if required or retained to facilitate on-going calculation of shift-by-shift, daily, weekly, monthly or annual values of any measured or related parameter.

Typical input data include: operating hours, delay, throughput raw coal and production of cleaned coal and rejects, quality figures, stores consumed, etc.

Typical reported information includes:

1   Full production statistics and stockpile inventory
2   Analysis of plant operations, including plant availability, utilization and analysis of breakdowns, magnetite and reagent consumption etc.
3   Maintenance status of screen surfaces, pump parts, conveyor belts, including logged running hours and maintenance time.

Monthly management reports, which for many years have required tedious analysis and much professional interpretation, may now be simply generated in any desired format from within the computer controlled system that is also running the plant. A report format can be evolved which meets the needs of all concerned from plant operator to mine manager.

List of international and national standards used in coal and coke analysis and evaluation

The following are the standards for coal and coke as used in different standards. The list is selective and includes standards necessary for coal processing and does not cover all coal standards. Figures given after the Standard number indicate the year of most recent approval.

I INTERNATIONAL ORGANIZATION FOR STANDARDIZATION (ISO) CASA POSTALE 56, CH 1211, GENEVE 20, SWITZERLAND

Standard No.	Title
ISO 157-1996	Hard coal – determination of forms of sulfur.
ISO 331-1993	Coal – determination of moisture in the analysis sample, direct gravimetric method
ISO 334-1975	Coal and coke – determination of total sulfur, Eschka method.
ISO 335-1974	Hard coal – determination of caking power, Roga Test.
ISO 348-1981	Hard coal – determination of moisture in the analysis sample, direct volumetric method.
ISO 349-1975	Hard coal – Audibert–Arnu dilatometer test.
ISO 501-1981	Coal – determination of the crucible swelling number.
ISO 502-1982	Coal – determination of caking power, Gray–King coke test.
ISO 561-1989	Coal preparation plant – graphical symbols.
ISO 562-1998	Hard coal and coke – determination of volatile matter content.
ISO 589-1981	Hard coal – determination of total moisture.
ISO 602-1983	Coal – determination of mineral matter.
ISO 609-1996	Coal and coke – determination of carbon and hydrogen (high temperature combustion method).
ISO 616-1995	Determination of coke shatter indices.
ISO 923-2000	Coal cleaning test, expression and presentation of results.
ISO 924-1989	Coal preparation plant – principles and conventions for flowsheets.
ISO 1013-1995	Determination of bulk density of coke (large container).
ISO 1170-1977	Coal and coke – calculation of analyses to different bases.
ISO 1213-1993	Part 1, vocabulary of terms relating to solid mineral fuels. Part 2, terms relating to coal sampling and analysis.
ISO 1928-1976	Solid mineral fuels – determination of gross calorific value by the calorimeter bomb method and calculation of net calorific value.
ISO 1953-1994	Hard coals – size analysis.

ISO 1988-1975	Hard coal – sampling.
ISO 1994-1976	Hard coal – determination of oxygen content.
ISO 2325-1986	Size analysis of coke, nominal top size 20 mm or less.
ISO 5074-1994	Hard coal – determination of Hardgrove grindability index.
ISO 7404.2-2009	Method of preparation of coal samples.
ISO 7936-1992	Hard coal: determination and presentation of float and sink characteristics – apparatus and procedures.
ISO 8264-1989	Hard coal – determination of the swelling properties using a dilatometer.
ISO 10329-2009	Coal – determination of plastic properties – constant-torque Gieseler plastometer method.
ISO 10752-1994	Coal sizing equipment – performance evaluation.
ISO 11760-2005	Classification of coals.
ISO 12900-1997	Hard coal: determination of abrasiveness.
ISO 13909.1-200	Hard coal and coke – mechanical sampling – Introduction.
ISO 13909.2-200	Hard coal and coke – mechanical sampling – Coal: sampling from moving streams.
ISO 13909.3-200	Hard coal and coke – mechanical sampling – Coal: sampling from stationary lots.
ISO 13909.4-200	Hard coal and coke – mechanical sampling – Coal: preparation of test samples.
ISO 13909.5-200	Hard coal and coke – mechanical sampling – Coke: sampling from moving streams.
ISO 13909.6-200	Hard coal and coke – mechanical sampling – Coke: sampling from stationary lots.
ISO13909.7-200	Hard coal and coke – mechanical sampling – Methods for determining the precision of sampling, sample preparation and testing.
ISO 15585-2006	Hard coal – determination of caking index.

2 BRITISH STANDARDS INSTITUTION (BS) BRECKLAND, LINFORD WOOD, MILTON KEYNES MK14 6LE

British Standards are referred as BS. A number of the latest Standards are now designated BS ISO where identical parameters are used.

Standard No.	Title
BS ISO 562-2010	Hard coal and coke. Determination of volatile matter.
BS ISO 687-2010	Solid mineral fuels. Coke, Determination of moisture in the general analysis test sample.
BS ISO 923-2000	Coal cleaning equipment. Performance evaluation.
BS ISO 1170-2008	Coal and coke. Calculation of analyses to different bases.
BS ISO 1171-2010	Solid mineral fuels. Determination of ash.
BS ISO 1928-2009	Solid mineral fuels. Determination of Gross calorific value by the Bomb calorimetric method and calculation of Net calorific value.
BS ISO 11760-2005	Classification of coals.
BS ISO 13909.1-2001	Hard coal and coke. Mechanical sampling. General introduction.
BS ISO 13909.2-2001	Hard coal and coke. Mechanical sampling. Coal sampling from moving streams.
BS ISO 13909.3-2001	Hard coal and coke. Mechanical sampling. Sampling from stationary lots.
BS ISO 13909.4-2001	Hard coal and coke. Preparation of coal test samples.

BS ISO 13909.5-2001	Hard coal and coke. Mechanical sampling. Sampling coke from moving streams.
BS ISO 13909.6-2001	Hard coal and coke. Mechanical sampling. Preparation of coke test samples.
BS ISO 13909.7-2001	Hard coal and coke. Mechanical sampling. Methods for determining the precision of sampling, sample preparation and testing.
BS ISO 15239-2005	Solid mineral fuels. Evaluation of the measurement performance of on-line analysers.
BS ISO 17246-2010	Coal proximate analysis.
BS ISO 17427-2005	Ultimate analysis of coal.
BS ISO 18283-2006	Hard coal and coke. Manual sampling.
BS ISO 20904-2006	Hard coal. Sampling of slurries.
BS ISO 21398-2007	Hard coal and coke. Guidance to the inspection of mechanical sampling systems.
BS ISO 23499-2008	Coal. Determination of bulk density.
BS 1016.1-1989	Total moisture of coal.
BS 1016.7-1977	Ultimate analysis of coke.
BS 1016.100-1994	Methods for analysis and testing of coal and coke, introduction and methods for reporting results.
BS 1016.102-2000	Determination of total moisture of coke.
BS 1016.104.1-1999	Proximate analysis: determination of moisture of general analysis test sample.
BS 1016.104.2-1991	Proximate analysis: determination of moisture content of general analysis sample of coke.
BS 1016.104.3-1998	Proximate analysis: determination of volatile matter content.
BS 1016.104.4-1998	Proximate analysis: determination of ash content.
BS 1016.105-1992	Determination of gross calorific value.
BS 1016.107.1-1991	Caking and swelling properties of coal: determination of crucible swelling number.
BS 1016.107.2-1991	Caking and swelling properties of coal: assessment of caking power by Gray–King coke test.
BS 10160.107.3-1990	Caking and swelling properties of coal: determination of swelling properties using a dilatometer.
BS 1016.108.1-1996	Coke tests: determination of shatter indices.
BS 1016.108.2-1992	Coke tests: determination of Micum and Irsid indices.
BS 1016.108.3-1995	Coke tests: determination of bulk density (small container).
BS 1016.108.4-1995	Coke tests: determination of bulk density (large container).
BS 1016.108.5-1992	Coke tests: determination of density and porosity.
BS 1016.109-1995	Size analysis of coal.
BS 1016.111-1998	Determination of abrasion index of coal.
BS 1016.112-1995	Determination of Hardgrove grindability index of hard coal.
BS 1017.1-1989	Methods for sampling of coal.
BS 1017.2-1994	Methods for sampling of coke.
BS 3323-1992	Glossary of terms relating to sampling, testing and analysis of solid mineral fuels.
BS 3552-1994	Glossary of terms used in coal preparation.
BS 7763-1994	Method of evaluation of the performance of coal sizing equipment.

3   ASTM INTERNATIONAL (FORMERLY KNOWN AS AMERICAN SOCIETY FOR TESTING AND MATERIALS; ASTM) 100 BARR HARBOR DRIVE, CONSHOHOCKEN, PENNSYLVANIA, UNITED STATES

Standard No.	Title
D 121-2007	Definitions of terms relating to coal and coke.
D 197-2002	Sampling and fineness test of pulverised coal.
D 293-2004	Sieve analysis of coke.
D 346-2004	Collection and preparation of coke samples for laboratory analysis.
D 388-1999	Classification of coals by rank.
D 409/D409M-2009	Grindability of coal by the Hardgrove-machine method.
D 440-2002	Drop shatter test for coal.
D 441-2002	Tumbler test for coal.
D 720-2004	Free swelling index of coal.
D2013-2007	Samples, coal, preparing for analysis.
D2234/D2234M-2009	Collection of a gross sample of coal.
D2492-2002	Forms of sulfur in coal.
D2639-2007	Plastic properties of coal by the constant-torque Gieseler plastometer.
D2797-2007	Preparing coal samples for microscopical analysis by reflected light.
D2798-2009	Microscopical determination of the reflectance of the organic components in a polished specimen of coal.
D2799-2009	Microscopical determination of the maceral composition of coal.
D3038-2004	Drop shatter test for coke.
D3172-2007	Proximate analysis of coal and coke.
D3173-2002	Moisture in the analysis sample of coal and coke.
D3174-2002	Ash in the analysis sample of coal and coke from coal.
D3175-2002	Volatile matter in the analysis sample of coal and coke.
D3176-2002	Ultimate analysis of coal and coke.
D3177-2002	Total sulfur in the analysis sample of coal and coke.
D3180-2002	Calculating coal and coke analyses from As-determined to different bases.
D3302/D3302M-2009	Total moisture in coal.
D3402-1993	Tumbler test for coke.
D4182-1997	Evaluation of laboratories using ASTM procedures in the sampling and analysis of coal and coke.
D4371-1998	Washability characteristics of coal.
D4749-2002	Sieve analysis for coal, performing and designating coal size.
D4916-1997	Practice for mechanical auger sampling.
D5114-1998	Method for laboratory froth flotation of coal in a mechanical cell.
D5341-1999 Method	for measuring coke reactivity index (CRI) and coke strength after reaction (CSR).
D5515-1997	Method for determination of the swelling properties of bituminous coal using a dilatometer.
D5865-2004	Standard test method for gross calorific value of coal and coke.
D6610-2001	Standard practice for manual sampling coal from surfaces of stockpiles.
D7430-2010	Standard practice for mechanical sampling of coal.

4 BUREAU OF INDIAN STANDARDS
MANAK BHAVAN, 9 BAHADUR SHAH ZAFAR MARG,
NEW DELHI 110002, INDIA

Standard No.	Title
IS 436 (Pt I/Sec 1): 2013	Methods for sampling of coal and coke: Part I Sampling of coal Section 1: Manual sampling
IS 436 (Pt I/Sec 2): 2013	Methods for sampling of coal and coke: Part I Sampling of coal Section 2: Mechanical sampling
IS 437-2013	Size analysis of coal and coke for marketing
IS 770:2013	Classification and codification of Indian coals, lignites, and semi-anthracites
IS 1350 (Pt 1):2013	Methods of test for coal and coke: Part I Proximate analysis
IS 1350 (Pt 2):2010	Methods of test for coal and coke: Part II Determination calorific value
IS 1350 (Pt 3):2010	Methods of test for coal and coke: Part III Determination of sulphur
IS 1350 (Pt 4/Sec 1): 2010	Methods of test for coal and coke: Part IV Ultimate analysis, Section I Determination of cabon and hydrogen
IS 1350 (Pt 4/Sec 2): 2010	Methods of test for coal and coke: Part IV Ultimate analysis, Section 2 Determination of nitorgen
IS 1353-2010	Methods of test for coal carbonization-caking index, swelling number and Gray–King assay
IS 1354:2010	Methods of Test For Coke Special Test
IS 3746-2010	Graphical symbols for coal preparation plant
IS 3810(Part 1)-2010	Solid mineral fuels-vocabulary: Part 1 Terms relating to coal preparation
IS 3810(Part 2)-2010	Solid mineral fuels- vocabulary: Part 2 Terms relating to Sample Testing and analysis
IS 4023:2013	Methods For The Determination Of Reactivity Of Coke
IS 4311:2010	Method for the determination of mineral matter in coal
IS 4433:2010	Method for determination of hardgrove grindability index of coal
IS 5209-2010	Coal preparation plant- principles and conventions for flow sheets
IS 6345-2013	Methods of sampling of coal for float and sink analysis
IS 7190:2010	Methods Of Determination Of Bulk Density Of Coke
IS 12770:2010	Coal For Cement Manufacture – Product specification
IS 13810-2010	Code of practice for float and sink analysis of coal.
IS 15438:2010	Coal – Determination of forms of sulphur
IS 15439:2010	Hard coal –Determination of oxygen content
IS 16143: Part 1: 2014	Hard Coal And Coke – Mechanical Sampling Part 1 General Introduction
IS 16143: Part 2: 2014	Hard Coal And Coke – Mechanical Sampling Part 2 Coal – Sampling From Moving Streams
IS 16143: Part 3: 2014	Hard Coal And Coke – Mechanical Sampling Part 3 Coal – Sampling From Stationary Lots
IS 16143: Part 4: 2014	Hard Coal And Coke – Mechanical Sampling Part 4 Coal – Preparation Of Test Samples
IS 16143: Part 5: 2014	Hard Coal And Coke – Mechanical Sampling Part 5 Coal – Sampling From Moving Streams

5 STANDARDS ASSOCIATION OF AUSTRALIA (AS) 80–86 ARTHUR STREET, NORTH SYDNEY, NSW, 2060, AUSTRALIA

Standard No.	Title
AS 2418.4-1982	Terms relating to sampling, sample preparation, analysis, testing and statistics.
AS 1038.1-2001	Total moisture in hard coal.
AS 1038.2-2006	Total moisture in coke.
AS 1038.3-2000	Proximate analysis of higher rank coal.
AS 1038.4-2006	Proximate analysis of coke.
AS 1038.6.3.1-1997	Determination of total sulfur (Eschka method).
AS 1038.6.4-2005	High rank coal and coke. Ultimate analysis. Determination of carbon, nitrogen and hydrogen by instrumental methods.
AS 1038.11-2002	Forms of sulfur in coal.
AS 1038.12.1-2002	Determination of crucible swelling number of coal.
AS 1038.12.2-1999	Carbonization properties of higher rank coal, determination of Gray–King coke type.
AS 1038.12.3-2002	Determination of the dilatometer characteristics of higher rank coal.
AS 1038.12.4.1-1996	Plastic properties of higher rank coal by the Gieseler plastometer.
AS 1038.18-2006	Coke – size analysis.
AS 1038.19-2000	Determination of the abrasion index of higher rank coal.
AS 1038.20-2002	Hardgrove grindability index of higher rank coal.
AS 1038.21.1.1-2008	Determination of the relative density of hard coal and coke, analysis sample – density bottle method.
AS 1038.21.1.2-2002	Determination of the relative density of hard coal and coke, analysis sample – volumetric method.
AS 1038.24-1998	Guide to the evaluation of measurements made by on-line coal analyzers.
AS 2434.1-2002	Determination of the total moisture content of lower rank coal.
AS 2434.2-2002	Determination of the volatile matter in low rank coal.
AS 2434.6.1-2002	Ultimate analysis of lower rank coal.
AS 2434.7-2002	Determination of moisture in the analysis sample of lower rank coal.
AS 2434.8-2002	Determination of ash in the analysis sample of lower rank coal.
AS 2856.2-1998	Maceral analysis.
AS 3880-1991	Bin flow properties of coal.
AS 3881-2002	Higher rank coal-size analysis.
AS 3899-2002	Higher rank coal and coke-bulk density
AS 2096-1987	Classification and coding systems for Australian coals.
AS 4156.1-1994	Coal preparation of higher rank coal, float and sink testing.
AS 4156.4-1999	Coal preparation – flowsheets and symbols.
AS 4156.8-2007	Coal preparation – drop shatter test.
AS 4264.1-2009	Coal and coke – sampling of higher rank coal – sampling procedures.
AS 4264.2-1996	Coal and coke – sampling of coke – sampling procedures.
AS 4264.3-1996	Coal and coke – sampling of lower rank coal – sampling procedures.
AS 4264.5-1999	Coal and coke – sampling – guide to the inspection of mechanical sampling systems.

6 NATIONAL STANDARDS OF PEOPLES REPUBLIC OF CHINA

Standard No.	Title
GB/T 189-1997	Classification standards for size fractions of coal.
GB/T 211-1996	Determination of total moisture in coal.
GB/T 212-1996	Proximate analysis of coal.
GB/T 212-1996	Determination of total moisture in coal.
GB/T 212-2001	Determination of inherent moisture in coal.
GB/T 212-2001	Determination of ash content in coal.
GB/T 212-2001	Determination of volatile matter in coal.
GB/T 213-2003	Determination of calorific value in coal.
GB/T 214-1996	Determination of total sulfur in coal.
GB/T 217-1996	Determination of true relative density of coal.
GB/T 397-1998	Technical condition of coal for metallurgical coke.
GB/T 474-1996	Preparation of coal samples.
GB/T 475-1996	Sampling for commercial coal.
GB/T 479-2000	Determination of plastometric indices of bituminous coals.
GB/T 481-1993	Sampling method of coal sample for production.
GB/T 483-1998	General rules for analytical and testing methods of coal.
GB/T 1341-2001	Gray–King assay for coal.
GB/T 2001-1991	Determination of moisture in coke.
GB/T 2001-1991	Determination of ash in coke.
GB/T 2001-1991.	Determination of volatile matter in coke
GB/T 5447-1997	Determination of caking index of bituminous coals.
GB/T 2565-1998	Determination of Hardgrove grindability index in coal.
GB/T 3715-1996	Terms relating to properties and analysis of coal.
GB/T 4634-1996	Determination of ash content in coal.
GB/T 5448-1997	Caking index of coal.
GB/T 5448-1997	Determination of Roga index of bituminous coal.
GB/T 5448-1997	Determination of free swelling index(FSI)/crucible swelling number (CSN) in coal.
GB/T 5450-1997	Audibert–Arnu dilatometer test of bituminous coal.
GB/T 5751-1986	China coal classification.
GB/T 6949-1998	Determination of apparent relative density of coal.
GB/T 7186-1998	Terms relating to coal preparation of coal.
GB/T 7560-2001	Determination of mineral matter in coal.
GB/T 15458-1995	Determination of abrasion index of coal.
GB/T 15459-1995	Determination of shatter strength of coal.
GB/T 15591-1995	Method of reflectance of commercial coal.
GB/T 16417-1996	Method of evaluating the washability of coal.
GB/T 16772-1997	Codification systems for Chinese coals.
GB/T 19092-2003	Methods of fine coal float and sink analysis.
GB/T 19494.1-2004	Mechanical sampling of coal – Part 1 Method for sampling.
GB/T 19494.2-2004	Mechanical sampling of coal – Part 2 Method of sample preparation.

References

1 **Malti Goel:** Implementing Clean Coal Technology in India, Barriers and Prospects, *India Infrastructure Report 2010.*

2 **WMO Greenhouse Gas Bulletin:** *No. 10 | 9 September 2014.*

3 **Read, H.H.:** Rutley's Elements of Mineralogy, *First Indian Edition, CBS Publishers & Distributors, Delhi, 1984.*

4 **Stopes, Marie, C., and R.V.Wheeler.** Monograph on the Constitution of Coal, *H.M.Stationery Office., London. 1918.*

5 **Arber, E.A.N.:** Natural History of Coal, Cambridge University Press, *1911.*

6 **Tideswell, F.V., Wheeler, R.V:** CCLXXXII – On dopplerite. Studies in the composition of coal, *J. Chem. Soc., Trans., 1922.*

7 **Larry Thomas:** Coal Geology, *Second edition, Wiley-Blackwell, A John Wiley & Sons Ltd., 2013.*

8 **Regnault, B:** Bull. Soc. Indust. Miner., *Series 3, 13–14, 1899–1900.*

9 **Parr, S.W:** Illinois Geol. Survey, *Bull. 3, 1906.*

10 **Mott, R.A.** The Origin and Composition of Coals. *Fuel, Vol. 21, No. 6, 1942, Vol. 22, No. 1, 1942.*

11 **Stopes, M.C:** On the Petrology of Banded Bituminous Coal, *Fuel, Vol. 14, No. 1, 1935.*

12 **Thiessen, R:** Compilation and composition of bituminous coals, *Journal of Geology, Volume 28, No. 3, 1920.*

13 **Joseph W. Leonard:** Coal Preparation, Fourth Edition, *The American Institute of Mining, Metallurgical and Petroleum Engineers, Inc., Newyork, 1979.*

14 **McCabe, L.C:** Practical significance of the physical constitution of coal in coal preparation, *Journal of Geology, Volume. 50, 1942.*

15 **Hoffman. E. and Jenkner, A:** Die Inkohlung und ihre Erkennung im Mikrobildung, *Gluckauf, 68, 1932.*

16 **Kröger, C:** Der Wachs/Harz-Komplex und das Kohlebitumen, Brennst. *Chemie, 40, 1968.*

17 **Taggart, Arthur F:** Handbook of Mineral Dressing, *A Wiley-Interscience publication, John Wiley & Sons, New York, 1945.*

18 **Martin, G., Blyth, C.E. and Tongue, H:** *Trans. Brit. Ceramic Soc., 23 (1923–24).*

19 **Feret, L.R:** Assoc. Internat. pour l'Essai des Mat., *Zurich, 1931, 2, Group D.*

20 **Rosin, P. and Rammler, E:** The Laws Governing the Fineness of Powdered Coal, *J. Inst. Fuel, 7, 1933.*

21 **Schuhmann, R., Jr.:** Principles of comminution, I – Size distribution and surface calculation, *Tech. Publs. AIME No.1189, 1940.*

22 **Goutal, M:** Sur le pouvoir calorifique de la houille, *Compt. Rend., Vol. 135, 1902.*

23 **Samir Sarkar:** Fuels and Combustion, *Orient Longman Ltd, 1974.*

24 **Gruner, E. and Bousquet, G:** Atlas general des houilleres, *Deuxieme partie, Texte, 1911.*

25 **Grout, F.F:** The composition of coals, *Econ. Geology, Vol. 2, 1907.*

26 Ralston, O.C: Graphic studies in the ultimate analysis of coal, *U.S. Bur. Mines, Tech. Paper 93, 1915.*

27 Seyler, C.A: Chemical classification of coal, *Proc. S. Wales Inst. Eng., Vol. 21, and Vol. 22, 1900.*

28 White, David: The effect of oxygen in coal, *U. S. Geol. Survey, Bull. 382, 1909.*

29 Vignon, Leo: Sur les dissolvants de la houille, *Compt. Rend., Tome 158, 1914.*

30 Pishel, M.A: A practical test for coking coals, *Econ. Geology, Vol. 3, 1908.*

31 Pearson, D.E: Coal Quality from Automated Fluorescence Imaging Microscopy, *Brochure, Pearson Coal Petrography Company, South Holland, IL, 2011.*

32 Sapozhnikov, L.M. and Bazilevich, L.P: Investigations of the Coking Process, *State Publishing House, Karkov, Ukraine, 1938.*

33 www.geologydata.info.

34 Groseclose, G.E: The Role of Vibrating Screens in Modern Coal Preparation Plants, *Coal Age, Jan. 1976.*

35 Coe, G.D. (Glendale D.): An explanation of washability curves for the interpretation of float-and-sink data on coal, *Information circular No.7045, US Bureau of Mines, 1938.*

36 Bird, B.M: Interpretation of Float-and-sink Data, *Proceedings of the Third International Conference on Bituminous Coal, Pittsburgh. Vol. 2. 1931.*

37 Sarkar, G.G., Bose, R.N., Mitra, S.K. and Lahiri, A: An Index for the comparison and correlation of washability characteristics of coal, *Presented to Fourth International Coal Preparation Congress, Harrogate (U.K), May–June 1962.*

38 Mayer, F.W.: A new curve showing middling composition, *Gluckauf, 86, 1950.*

39 Stokes, G.G: Mathematical and Physical Paper III, *Cambridge University Press, 1891.*

40 Sir Isaac Newton: The Mathematical Principles of Natural Philosophy, Book II, *Translated into English by Andrew Motte, 1729.*

41 Berthelot, Ch: Epuration, sechage, agglomeration et broyage du charbon, *Dunod, Paris, 1938.*

42 Bertrand, Maurice F: Pure coal and Its Applications, *J. Inst. Fuel, 1935.*

43 Foulke, W.B: The Use of Halogenated Hydrocarbon "Parting Liquid" in a Sink-and-float Process, *Am. Inst. Mining Met. Engrs., February, 1939.*

44 Cremer, H.W. and Davies, T: Solid systems, Chemical Engineering Practice, *Volume 3, Butterworths, London, 1956.*

45 Driessen, M.G: The use of centrifugal force for cleaning fine coal and heavy liquids and suspensions with special reference to the cyclone washer, *Journal, Institute of Fuel, 1945.*

46 Fontein, F.J. and Dijksman, C: Recent Developments in Mineral Dressing, *Institution of Mining and Metallurgy, London 1953.*

47 Taggart, A.F. et al: Oil-Air Separation of Non-Sulfide and Non-Metal Minerals, *Trans. AIME, Vol. 134, 1939.*

48 Wilkins, E.T: Coal Preparation: Some Development to Pulverized Practice, *Conference on Pulverized Fuel, Harrogate, England, 1947.*

49 Sun, S.C: Hypothesis for Different Floatabilities of Coals, Carbons, and Hydrocarbon Minerals, *Trans. AIME, Vol. 199, 1954.*

50 Tsiperovich, M.V. and Evtushenko, V: Preparation and carbonization of coals, *Vol. 1, Sverdlovsk, Metallurgizdat, 72, 1959.*

51 Luttrell, G.H., Honaker, R.Q. and Phillips, D.I: Enhanced Gravity Separators: New Alternatives for Fine Coal Cleaning, *12th International coal preparation conference, Lexington, Kentucky, 1995.*

52 Fraser, T. and Yancey, H.F: Interpretation of Results of Coal Washing Tests, *Trans AIME, Vol. 69, 1923.*

53 Drakeley, T.J: Coal Washing: A Scientific Study, *Transactions, Institution of Mining Engineers, Vol. 54, 1917.*

54 Anderson, W.W: Quantitative efficiency of separation of coal cleaning equipment, *Trans AIME, 187, 1950.*

55 Tromp, K.F.: New method for the evaluation of coal preparation, (German) *Gluckauf, 73, 1937.*

56 de Korte, G.J: Real-time Plant Efficiency Measurement, *Division of Mining Technology, CSIR, Coaltech 2020, October 2002.*

57 Sachdev, R.K: Global Overview of Coal Preparation Industry, *CPSI Journal, Volume V, Number 13, December 2013.*

58 Dennis Kaegi, Valery Addes, Hardarshan Valia and Michael Grant: Coal Conversion Processes, Carbonization, *Kirk-Othmer Encyclopedia of Chemical Technology, 2000.*

59 Johnzactruba: Coal Fired Thermal Power Plant: The Basic Steps and Facts, *Bright Hub Engineering, 2011.*

60 en.wikipedia.org/wiki/Cement_kiln.

61 Atma Manthan: Past achievements and future prospects of coal R&D, *Diamond Jubilee Celebrations, Central Fuel Research Institute, Dhanbad, 2006.*

Further readings

1 **Elwood S. Moore:** Coal, Its Properties, Analysis, Classification, Geology, Extraction, Uses and Distribution, *Johan Wiley & Sons, Inc. London, Chapman & Hall Ltd., 1922.*

2 **OM Prakash Gupta:** Elements of Fuels, Furnaces and Refractories, *Khanna Publishers, New Delhi, Fifth Edition, 5th Reprint: 2011.*

3 **Godfrey W.Himus:** Fuel testing: Laboratory methods in Fuel Technology, *Leonard Hill Ltd., London, 1953.*

4 **Pope, P.C.:** Coal, Production, Distribution, Utilisation, *Industrial newspapers. (1949), London.*

5 **Larry Thomus:** Coal Geology, Second Edition, John Wiley Sons Ltd., 2013.

6 **Colin R. Ward** (Edited): Coal Geology and Coal Technology, *Black Well Scientific Publications, 1984.*

7 **Samir Sarkar:** Fuels and Combustion, *Orient Longman, New Delhi, 1974.*

8 **Wilfrid Francis:** Fuels and fuel Technology: A summarized manual, *Pergmon Press, Oxford, London, 1965.*

9 **Robert T. Haslam and Robert P. Russell:** Fuels and their combustion, First edition, *McGrawhill Book Company, Inc. Newyork, 1926.*

10 **Sharma, S.P., Chander Mohan:** Fuels and Combustion, *Tata Mc Graw Hill Publishing Co. Ltd., New Delhi, 1987.*

11 **Chaki, N.R.:** A practical efficient use of Indian coals, *Mrs. Kamala Chaki, C/5, Vidyasagar Niketan, Salt Lake City, Calcutta, 1977.*

12 **Anubhuti Ranjan Prasad:** Coal Industry of India, *Ashish Publishing House, 8/81, Punjabi Bagh, New Delhi, 1986.*

13 **Charles Kernot:** The Coal industry, *Woodhead Publishing Limited, Cambridge, England, 2000.*

14 **The Coal Resource** – A comprehensive overview of coal, *World coal Institute.*

15 **Energy Statistics–2013:** Central statistics office, National statistical organization, Ministry of Statistics and Programme Implementation, *Government of India, New Delhi.*

16 **Coal & Lignite Resources in India:** Plan, Technology and Challenges for 2012–17, *Ministry of coal, Government of India, New Delhi, 2011.*

17 **Krishnan, M.S:** Classification of coal, *Geological survey of India, Vol.VI, No.3, 1940.*

18 **Forrester, C:** Methods of Analysis of coal in India, *Geological survey of India, Vol.VI, No.3, 1940.*

19 **Vibhuti N. Misra, Reddy, P.S.R and Mohapatra, B.K:** Mineral Characterisation and Processing, *Allied Publishers Pvt Ltd. New Delhi 110064, 2004.*

20 **James, G. Speight:** Handbook of Coal Analysis, *John Wiley & Sons, Inc., 2005.*

21 **Gokhale, K.V.G.K. and Rao, T.C.:** Ore Deposits of India (Their distribution and processing), *Affiliated East West Press Pvt. Ltd., New Delhi, 1983.*

22 **Gaudin A.M.:** Principles of Mineral Dressing, *Tata Mc Graw Hill Publishing Company Ltd., New Delhi, 2010.*

23 **Robert H. Richards., Charles E. Locke:** Textbook of Ore Dressing, *Mc Graw Hill Book Company Inc, New York, 1940.*

24 **Dave Osborne:** The Coal Handbook, Towards cleaner production, Volume I & 2, *Woodhead Publishing Ltd, Cambridge, UK, 2013.*

25 **Subba Rao, D.V:** Coal – Its Beneficiation, *Em Kay Publications, Delhi, 2003.*

26 **Subba Rao, D.V:** Evaluation of washability charactertistics of Talcher coal, *The Indian Mineralogist, Journal of The Mineralogical Society of India, Volume 36, No.1 2002.*

27 **Shirley Cheng Tsai:** Fundamentals of Coal Beneficiation and Utilization, *Coal Science and Technology-2, Elsevier Scientific Publishing Company, Amsterdam, 1982.*

28 **Ernst Prochaska:** Coal Washing, First edition, *McGrawhill Book Company, Inc. Newyork, 1921.*

29 **Mitchell David, R:** Coal Preparation, *American Institute of Mining and Metallurgical Engineers- Seeley W. Mudd series 1950.*

30 **Vanangamudi, M:** Coal Preparation, *Third Short term Refresher course on Classification and Concentration organized by IIME., 1989.*

31 **Rao, T.C.:** Short Term course on Coal Preparation, *Organized by Department of Fuel & Mineral Engineering, ISM, Dhanbad, 1989.*

32 **Konar, B.B., et al:** Coal Preparation, CFRI Golden Jubilee Monograph, *Allied Publishers Limited, 1997.*

33 **Wieslaw S. Blaschke:** New Trends in Coal Preparation Technologies and Equipment, *Gordon and Breach Publishers, 1996.*

34 **Preparation of Coal for the Industry,** *Journal of Mines, Metals & Fuels, Special issue 1964.*

35 **Special number on Research and Industry get together,** *Journal of Mines, Metals & Fuels, June 1975.*

36 **TISCO Silver Jubilee Volume, Volume. 27, 1980:** Upgrading of Indian coking coals.

37 **Special number on coal preparation,** *Journal of Mines, Metals & Fuels, Special issue 1983.*

38 **Sarkar, G.G.:** An Introduction to coal preparation practice, *Oxford & IBH Publishing Co., New Delhi, 1986.*

39 **Osborn, D.G:** Coal Preparation Technology, Vol.1, *Graham & Trotman Limited, London, 1988.*

40 **Sanders, G.J:** The Principles of Coal Preparation, *American Coal Preparation Society, 4th Edition, 2007.*

41 **John Sinclair:** Coal Preparation and Power supply at collieries, *Sir Issac Pitman & Sons Ltd., London, 1962.*

42 **Panda, J.P. and Mittal, R.L.:** Coal Beneficiation – Present Scenario new trend, *The Mining, Geological and Metallurgical Institution of India Transactions – Vol.92, No.1, Sept. 1995.*

43 **Mrig, G.C:** Beneficiation of non-coking coal – Our experience, *Journal of mines, metals and fuels, November 2008.*

44 **Haldar, D.D:** Beneficiation of non-coking coals: Basic concepts and technology routes, *Proceedings of the XI International Seminar onMineral Processing Technology (MPT-2010).*

45 **Liu, Y.A.:** Physical cleaning of Coal, *Marcel Dekker, July 26, 1982.*

46 **Khoury, D.L:** Coal Cleaning Technology, *Noyes Data Corporation Park Ridge, 1981.*

47 **James G. Speight:** The Chemistry and Technology of Coal, Third Edition, *CRC Press, Taylor and Francis group, 2012.*

48 **Bernard Cooper:** The Science and Technology of coal and coal utilization, *Springer, 1984.*

49 **Norbert Berkowitz:** An Introduction to Coal Technology, *Academic Press. Inc., 1979.*

50 **Habetinejad Hamidreza, Jorjani Esmaeil and Sam Abbas:** Evaluation of Mayer curve validity on feed blending at the Zarand coal washery plant, *International Journal of Mining Science and Technology, February 2012.*

51 **Cremer, H.W. and Davis, T:** Chemical Engineering Practice, *Volume.3, Butterworths, London, 1956.*

52 **Richard O. Burt:** Gravity Concentration Technology, *Elsevier Scientific Publishing company, Amsterdam, 1984.*

53 **Subba Rao, D.V:** Mineral Beneficiation – A Concise Basic Course, *A Balkema book, Taylor & Francis, Netherland, 2011.*

54 **Jain, S.K.:** Ore Processing, *Oxford & IBH Publishing Co., New Delhi, 1986.*

55 **Barry, A. Wills. and Tim Napier-Munn:** Mineral Processing Technology, *Elsevier Science & Technology Books, 2006.*

56 **Venkatachalam, S. and Degaleesan, S.N.:** Laboratory experiments in Mineral Engineering, *Oxford & IBH Publishing Co., New Delhi, 1982.*

57 **Riazi, M.R., Rajender Gupta (Editors):** Coal production and processing Technology, CRC Press, Taylor & Francis group, 2016.

58 **Bandopadhyay, P. and Rao, T.C.:** Fine coal treatment in India – Problems and prospects, *Journal of Mines, Metals & fuels, May 1983.*

59 **Mark S Klima, Barbara J Arnold and Peter J Bethell:** Challenges in Fine Coal processing, Dewatering and Disposal, *Society for Mining, Metallurgy, Exploration, Inc.(SME), 2012.*

60 **Nicol, S.K. and Bensley C.N.:** Recent Developments in fine coal Preparation in Australia, Industrial Practice of Fine Coal Processing, *Broken Hill Proprietary Co. Ltd.*

61 **Vanangamudi, M and Rao, T.C:** Dense medium cyclones for coal washing, *Mining Magazine, September, 1991.*

62 **de Korte, G.J:** Dense-medium beneficiation of fine coal revisited, *The Journal of The South African Institute of Mining and Metallurgy, October 2002.*

63 **Nikkam Suresh et al:** Water only cyclones, *ISM, Dhanbad, Mining Magazine, April 1990.*

64 **Janusz S. Laskowski:** Coal Flotation and Fine Coal Utilization, Elsevier Science B.V., 2001.

65 **Reddy, P.S.R. et al:** Flotation column for fine coal beneficiation, *International Journal of Mineral Processing, 1988.*

66 **Narasimhan, K.S. et al:** Column flotation for fine coal recovery in India – A Techno economic assessment, *Regional Research Laboratory, Bhubaneswar.*

67 **Durga Das Haldar:** Role of conditioning in oil agglomeration of middlings, *Ph.D Thesis, Indian School of Mines, Dhanbad, 1987.*

68 **Sarkar, G.G., Konar, B.B. & Sakha, S:** An improved Process for Demineralisation of Coal by Oil Agglomeration, *Journal of the Institution of Engineers (India), A supplement volume 31, No.11, May 1982.*

69 **Sinha, R.K. and Sharma, N.L.:** Mineral Economics, *Oxford & IBH Publishing Co., New Delhi, 1970.*

70 **Potential of Clean Coal Technology in India:** An SME Perspective, *European Business and Technology Centre, European Institute of Asian Studies, September 2013.*

71 **Nikhil Gupta:** Dry deshaling of thermal coals in India, Thesis, *Virginia Polytechnic Institute and State University, Blacksburg, Virginia, 2011.*

72 **Mohantaa, S., Darama, A.B., Chakraborty, S. and Meikap, B.C:** Applicability of the air dense medium fluidized bed separator for cleaning of high-ash Indian thermal coals: An experimental study, *South African Journal of Chemical Engineering, Vol. 16, No. 1.*

73 **Asish Kumar Sahoo:** Dry Beneficiation of High ash non-coking coal using an Air Dense Medium Fluidized Bed, *Thesis, National Institute of Technology, Rourkela, 2009.*

74 **Zhang, B., Akbari, H., Yang, F., Mohanty, M.K. and Hirschi, J:** Performance Optimization of the FGX Dry Separator for Cleaning High-Sulfur Coal, *International Journal of Coal Preparation and Utilization, 2011.*

75 **Pawan Kumar, Rakesh Sah, Vidyadhar Ari and Avimanyu Das:** Dry Beneficiation of coal fines using Air Table, *Proceedings of the XI International Seminar onMineral Processing Technology (MPT-2010).*

76 **Wakeman, R.J and Tarleton, E.S:** Solid/Liquid Separation: Scale up of Industrial Equipment, *Elsevier Ltd., 2005.*

77 **Trevor Sparks:** Solid-Liquid Filtration: A User's Guide to Minimizing Cost and Environmental Impact, Maximizing Quality and Productivity, *Elsevier Ltd., 2012.*

78 **Barbara J.Arnold., Mark S.Klima. and Peter J. Bethell:** Designing the coal preparation plant of the future, *Society for Mining, Metallurgy & Exploration, Inc. 2007.*

79 **Yarar, B. and Dogan, A.M:** Mineral Processing Design, *NATO ASI Series, Martinus Nijhoff Publishers, 1987.*

80 **Subba Rao, D.V.:** Field and Factory report on TISCO Jamadoba Coal Washery, Andhra University, Waltair, 1979.

81 **Chopra, R.K:** Solution Approach to some coal washing issues in India, Workshop on Benchmarking of Coal Washing Technology & Reject management, CMPDI, 14 April, 2012.

82 **Haldar, D.D:** Beneficiation of non-coking coals: Basic concepts and technology routes, *XI International Seminar on Mineral Processing Technology (MPT-2010).*

83 **Administrative College of India, Hyderabad:** EIA Guidance manual for Coal Washeries, *Ministry of Environment & Forests, Govt. of India, 2010.*

84 **de Korte, G.J:** Real-time plant efficiency measurement, *Coaltech-2020, Division of Mining Technology, CSIR, Project, October, 2002.*

85 **Keller, Jr. D.V:** Otisca T-Process, A New Coal Beneficiation Approach for the Preparation of Coal Slurries, *Coal Gasification, Liauifaction, and Conversion to Electricity Conference, University of Pittsburgh, August 1982.*

86 **Raghu Kumar, C:** Analysis of Separation characteristics of fine Particles in Floatex Density Separator, *Doctoral Thesis, Indian School of Mines, 2014.*

87 **Rakgase, K.E:** Applications of Reflux Classifier on SA Coals, *Coaltech Research Association, Annual Colloquium, 31 August 2012.*

88 **Jacobs, J. and de Korte, G.J:** The three-product cyclone: adding value to South African coal processing, *The Journal of The Southern African Institute of Mining and Metallurgy, Volume 113, November 2013.*

89 **Mazumdar, M.K. et al:** Triboelectric separation of coal from mineral impurities, *ESA 1995 Annual Meeting Proceedings.*

90 **Basu ,T.K., Mitra, P.K., Choudhury, S.G., Banerjee, T., Roy, J. and Choudhury, A:** Coal Carbonisation, CFRI Golden Jubilee Monograph, 1997.

91 **Philip J. Wilson and Joseph H.Wells:** Coal, Coke and Coal Chemicals, *Tata Mc Graw Hill, 1960.*

92 **Tupkary, R.H and Tupkary, V.R:** An Introduction to Modern Iron Making, *Khanna Publishers, Delhi, 2005.*

93 **Ahindra Ghosh and Amit Chatterjee:** Iron making and steel making – Theory and practice, *PHI Learning private Limited, New Delhi, Eastern Economy Edition, 2008.*

94 **Amit chatterjee:** Sponge Iron Production by Direct Reduction of Iron Oxide, *PHI Learning private Limited, New Delhi, Eastern Economy Edition, 2010.*

95 **Malti Goel:** Energy Sources and Global Warming, *Allied Publishers Pvt. Ltd., 2005.*

Solutions to problems for practice

6.7.1: *From the sieve analysis of the rod mill product shown in Table 6.7.1, estimate 80% passing size.*

Table 6.7.1 Sieve analysis of rod mill product for problem 6.7.1.

Aperture size of the sieve, microns	Weight fraction retained
1680	0.005
1190	0.075
840	0.075
595	0.085
420	0.110
297	0.144
210	0.125
149	0.103
105	0.078
105 pass	0.200

Solution:

Cumulative weight fractions are calculated from the bottom and tabulated in Table 6.7.1.1.

Table 6.7.1.1 Cumulative sieve analysis of rod mill product for problem 6.7.1.

Aperture size of the sieve, microns	Cumulative weight fraction passing
1680 (retained)	1.000
1680	0.995
1190	0.920
840	0.845
595	0.760
420	0.650
297	0.506
210	0.381
149	0.278
105	0.200

Graph between aperture size and cumulative weight fraction passing is drawn as shown in Figure 6.7.1.1.

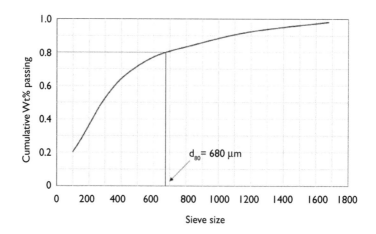

Figure 6.7.1.1 Cumulative plot of rod mill product for problem 6.7.1.

From the graph 80% passing size is 680 microns.

6.7.2: *For the size analysis data of ball mill feed shown in Table 6.7.2, draw frequency plots on linear, semi-log and log-log scales. Also draw cumulative plots on linear and semi-log scales. Obtain Rosin-Rammler and Gates-Gaudin-Schuhmann equations.*

Table 6.7.2 Size analysis data of ball mill feed for problem 6.7.2.

Mesh number	Mesh size microns	Weight% retained
12	1410	2.61
14	1190	9.30
20	840	11.80
28	595	12.89
35	420	9.81
48	297	8.19
65	210	7.74
100	149	5.60
150	105	6.09
200	74	3.88
−200		22.09

Solution:
All necessary calculations are done and shown in Table 6.7.2.1

Table 6.7.2.1 Calculated values for problem 6.7.2.

Mesh number	Mesh size microns	Mean size microns	Wt% retained	Cum. wt% passing W	100 − W	$\dfrac{100}{100-W}$	$\ln\dfrac{100}{100-W}$
12	1410		2.61	97.39	2.61	38.314	3.646
14	1190	1300.0	9.30	88.09	11.91	8.396	2.128
20	840	1015.0	11.80	76.29	23.71	4.218	1.439
28	595	717.5	12.89	63.40	36.60	2.732	1.005
35	420	507.5	9.81	55.59	44.41	2.252	0.812
48	297	358.5	8.19	43.40	56.60	1.767	0.569
65	210	253.5	7.74	37.66	62.34	1.604	0.473
100	149	179.5	5.60	32.06	67.94	1.472	0.387
150	105	127.0	6.09	25.97	74.03	1.351	0.301
200	74	89.5	3.88	22.09	77.91	1.284	0.250
−200		37.0	22.09				

The graphs drawn are shown in Fig. 6.7.2.1 to 6.7.2.7

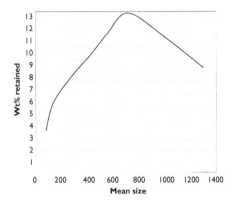

Figure 6.7.2.1 Linear scale frequency plot.

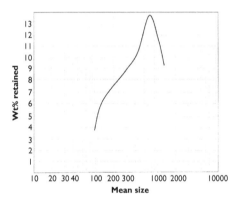

Figure 6.7.2.2 Semi-log frequency plot.

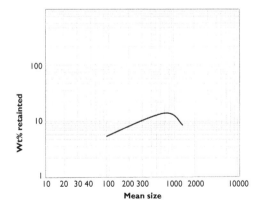

Figure 6.7.2.3 Log-log frequency plot.

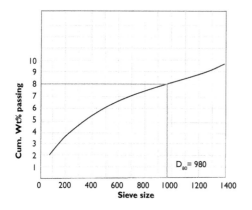

Figure 6.7.2.4 Linear scale cumulative plot.

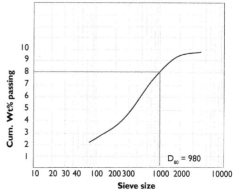

Figure 6.7.2.5 Semi-log cumulative plot.

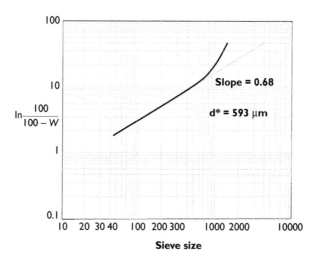

Figure 6.7.2.6 Rosin-Rammler plot.

From the graph   Slope = n = 0.68

$$\ln\frac{100}{100-w} = \ln\frac{100}{100-63.212} = 1.0$$

d* = 593 μm   corresponding to 1.0

Rosin-Rammler Equation is $W = 100 - 100e^{-\left(\frac{d}{593}\right)^{0.68}}$

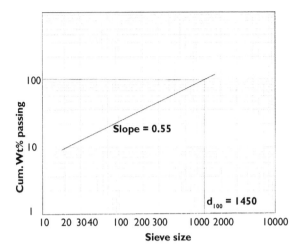

Figure 6.7.2.7 Gates-Gaudin-Schuhmann plot.

From the graph, slope = 0.55 and d_{100} = 1450 microns.

Schuhmann Equation: $W = 100\left(\dfrac{d}{1450}\right)^{0.55}$

7.10.1: *Three samples are taken to determine the proximate analysis of a coal. The following are the observations in a laboratory.*

   a   *First sample is taken in a 25 ml silica crucible of 18.765 gm and weighed as 19.649 gm and used for the determination of moisture present in the coal. The weight of the crucible after heating at 105°C in a hot air oven till constant weight is 19.570 gm.*

   b   *Second sample is taken in a 19.109 gm silica volatile matter crucible and weighed as 20.012 gm. This is kept in a muffle furnace at 925°C for 7 minutes and then weighed as 19.664 gm.*

   c   *Third sample is taken in another 25 ml silica crucible weighing 18.567 gm and kept in a muffle furnace at 750°C till the coal completely burns. The weights of crucible before and after heating are 19.490 gm and 18.945 gm respectively.*

   What is proximate analysis?

Solution:

a Weight of the coal   = 19.649 – 18.765 = 0.884 gm
   Weight of moisture = 19.649 – 19.570 = 0.079 gm

$$\% \text{ moisture} = \frac{0.079}{0.884} \times 100 = 8.94\%$$

b   Weight of the coal   = 20.012 – 19.109 = 0.903 gm
    Weight of volatile matter + moisture = 20.012 – 19.664 = 0.348 gm

$$\% \text{ volatile matter + moisture} = \frac{0.348}{0.903} \times 100 = 38.54\%$$

$$\% \text{ volatile matter} = 38.54 - 8.94 = 29.60\%$$

c   Weight of the coal   = 19.490 – 18.567 = 0.923 gm
    Weight of ash   = 18.945 – 18.567 = 0.378 gm

$$\% \text{ ash} = \frac{0.378}{0.923} \times 100 = 40.95\%$$

$$\% \text{ fixed carbon} = 100 - 8.94 - 29.60 - 40.95 = 20.51\%$$

Proximate analysis of the coal taken is   M = 08.94%
                                            VM = 29.60%
                                            A = 40.95%
                                            FC = 20.51%

7.10.2: *A high volatile bituminous coal has 8% moisture, 34% volatile matter and 46% ash. Calculate fixed carbon percent on dry, d.a.f. and d.m.m.f. bases.*

Solution:
    % fixed carbon = 100 – 8 – 34–46 = 12%

% fixed carbon on dry basis

$$= \frac{C}{100 - M} \times 100 = \frac{12}{100 - 8} \times 100 = 13.04\%$$

% fixed carbon on d.a.f basis

$$= \frac{C}{100 - M - A} \times 100 = \frac{12}{100 - 8 - 46} \times 100 = 26.09\%$$

% fixed carbon on d.m.m.f basis

$$= \frac{C}{100 - M - 1.1A} \times 100 = \frac{12}{100 - 8 - 1.1 \times 46} \times 100 = 28.99\%$$

9.2.1: *Calculate the gross and net calorific value of a coal which analyses: C 74%, H 6%, N 1%, O 9%, S 0.8%, moisture 2.2% and ash 8%.*

Solution:

$$GCV = 80.8\,C + 344\left(H - \frac{O}{8}\right) + 22.2\,S$$

$$= 80.8 \times 74 + 344\left(6 - \frac{9}{8}\right) + 22.2 \times 0.8 = 7674 \text{ Kcal/kg}$$

$$NCV = GCV - 52.83 \times \%H$$
$$= 7674 - 52.83 \times 6 \quad = 7357 \ Kcal/kg$$

$$\frac{NCV}{GCV} = \frac{7357}{7674} = 0.959$$

Thus NCV = 0.959 times GCV in this case.

9.2.2: *The proximate analysis of coal is: Moisture 2.4%, Volatile Matter 29.4%, Fixed Carbon 58%, Ash 9.7% and Sulphur 0.5%. Its gross calorific value is 7650 Kcal/Kg. Calculate proximate analysis and calorific value on*
 a *Moisture free basis* b *Dry ash free basis*

Solution:

a Moisture free basis

$$\% \ Volatile \ matter \ = \frac{V}{100-M} \times 100 = \frac{29.4}{100-2.4} \times 100 = 30.1\%$$

$$\% \ Fixed \ carbon \ \ = \frac{FC}{100-M} \times 100 = \frac{58}{100-2.4} \times 100 = 59.4\%$$

$$\% \ Ash \ \ \ \ \ = \frac{A}{100-M} \times 100 = \frac{9.7}{100-2.4} \times 100 = 9.9\%$$

$$\% \ Sulphur \ \ \ \ = \frac{S}{100-M} \times 100 = \frac{0.5}{100-M} \times 100 = 0.51\%$$

$$Calorific \ value \ \ \ = \frac{GCV}{100-M} \times 100 = \frac{7650}{100-2.4} \times 100 = 7838 \ Kcal/kg$$

b Dry ash free basis

$$\% \ Volatile \ matter \ = \frac{V}{100-M-A} \times 100 = \frac{29.4}{100-2.4-9.7} \times 100 = 33.5\%$$

$$\% \ Fixed \ carbon \ \ = \frac{FC}{100-M-A} \times 100 = \frac{58}{100-2.4-9.7} \times 100 = 66.0\%$$

$$\% \ Sulphur \ \ \ \ = \frac{S}{100-M-A} \times 100 = \frac{0.5}{100-2.4-9.7} \times 100 = 0.57\%$$

$$Calorific \ value \ \ \ = \frac{GCV}{100-M-A} \times 100 = \frac{7650}{100-2.4-9.7} \times 100 = 8703 \ Kcal/kg$$

9.2.3: *The ultimate analysis of bituminous coal (dry basis%) is: C 77, H 5.8, N 1.7, O 4.8, S 2.5 and ash 9. The moisture content is 5%. The gross calorific power is 7650 Kcal/Kg on dry basis. Calculate*

b *Gross calorific value, moist basis*
c *Net calorific value, moist basis*
d *Net calorific value, dry basis*
e *Gross calorific value, dry basis*

Solution:

$$\%C = \frac{C(100-M)}{100} = \frac{77(100-5)}{100} = 73.10\%$$

$$\%H = \frac{H(100-M)}{100} = \frac{5.8(100-5)}{100} = 5.51\%$$

$$\%N = \frac{N(100-M)}{100} = \frac{1.7(100-5)}{100} = 1.61\%$$

$$\%O = \frac{O(100-M)}{100} = \frac{4.8(100-5)}{100} = 4.56\%$$

$$\%S = \frac{S(100-M)}{100} = \frac{2.5(100-5)}{100} = 2.38\%$$

$$\%A = \frac{A(100-M)}{100} = \frac{9(100-5)}{100} = 8.55\%$$

$$\% M = 5.00\%$$

$$\text{GCV on moist basis} = 80.8\ C + 344\left(H - \frac{O}{8}\right) + 22.2\ S$$

$$= 80.8 \times 73.1 + 344\left(5.51 - \frac{4.56}{8}\right) + 22.2 \times 2.38$$

$$= 7658.7\ \text{Kcal/kg}$$

$$\text{NCV on moist basis} = \text{GCV} - 52.83 \times \%H$$

$$= 7658.7 - 52.83 \times 5.51 \qquad = 7367.6\ \text{Kcal/kg}$$

$$\text{NCV on dry basis} = \text{NCV on moist basis} \times \frac{100}{100-M}$$

$$= 7367.6 \times \frac{100}{100-5} \qquad = 7755.4\ \text{Kcal/kg}$$

$$\text{GCV on dry basis} = \text{GCV on moist basis} \times \frac{100}{100-M}$$

$$= 7658.7 \times \frac{100}{100-5} \qquad = 8061.8\ \text{Kcal/kg}$$

$$\text{GCV on dry basis} = 80.8\ C + 344\left(H - \frac{O}{8}\right) + 22.2\ S$$

$$= 80.8 \times 77 + 344\left(5.8 - \frac{4.8}{8}\right) + 22.2 \times 2.5 \qquad = 8065.9\ \text{Kcal/kg}$$

17.9.1: *A screen of 2 mm opening is used to remove coarser size from a coal consists of 80% of –2 mm. If the weight percent of +2 mm material in overflow and underflow products of a screen are 40% and 10% respectively, estimate the effectiveness of the screen.*

Solution:

Fraction of +2 mm material in the feed $\qquad$ = f = 0.2

Fraction of +2 mm material in the overflow $\quad$ = p = 0.4

Fraction of +2 mm material in the underflow $\quad$ = u = 0.1

Efficiency (effectiveness) of the screen = $\eta = \dfrac{p(f-u)(1-u)(p-f)}{f(p-u)^2(1-f)}$

$$= \frac{0.4(0.2-0.1)(1-0.1)(0.4-0.2)}{0.2(0.4-0.1)^2(1-0.2)}$$

$$= 0.5 \Rightarrow 50\%$$

17.9.2: *A coal is being fed to a double deck vibrating screen for separation. The desired product is –40+60 mesh fraction. A 40 mesh and a 60 mesh screens are therefore used. The feed is introduced on the 40 mesh screen. From the following sieve analysis of the feed and the three products shown in Table 17.9.2, calculate the effectiveness of the double deck screen in separating –40+60 mesh fraction.*

Table 17.9.2 Sieve analysis of feed and three products for problem 17.9.2.

Mesh	Feed	Oversize from 40 mesh screen	Oversize from 60 mesh screen	Undersize from 60 mesh screen
–10+20	0.097	0.197	0.026	0.0005
–20+30	0.186	0.389	0.039	0.0009
–30+40	0.258	0.337	0.322	0.0036
–40+60	0.281	0.066	0.526	0.3490
–60+85	0.091	0.005	0.061	0.2990
–85+100	0.087	0.006	0.026	0.3470

Solution:

Fraction of –40+60 mesh material in the feed $\qquad\qquad$ = f = 0.281

Fraction of –40+60 mesh material in middle fraction $\qquad$ = p = 0.526

Fraction of –40+60 mesh material in other fraction $\qquad$ = u = $\dfrac{0.066+0.349}{2}$

$$= 0.2075$$

Efficiency (effectiveness) of the double deck screen in separating the

$-40+60$ mesh material $= \eta = \dfrac{p(f-u)(1-u)(p-f)}{f(p-u)^2(1-f)}$

$$= \frac{0.526(0.281 - 0.2075)(1 - 0.2075)(0.526 - 0.281)}{0.281(0.526 - 0.2075)^2(1 - 0.281)}$$

$$= 0.366 \Leftrightarrow 36.6\%$$

17.9.3: *Coal containing 45% of –0.5 mm coal is screened on 0.5 mm screen at the rate of 700 tons per day. If 280 tons per day of undersize is obtained and it contains no oversize, determine the efficiency of the screen.*

Solution:

Efficiency of the screen = η

$$= \frac{\text{Quantity of undersize material obtained from the screen}}{\text{Quantity of undersize material present in the feed}} \times 100$$

$$= \frac{Uu}{Ff} \times 100 = \frac{280 \times 100}{700 \times 45} \times 100 = 88.89\%$$

19.2.1: *450 gm of coal is taken and prepared a pulp of 500 cc by adding water to it. If the weight of 500 cc pulp is 600 gm, Calculate the density of coal in kg/m^3. Also calculate percent coal in the pulp by weight and by volume.*

Solution:

Weight of water = 600 – 450 = 150 gm
Volume of coal = 500 – 150 = 350 cc

$$\text{Sp.gr of coal} = \frac{\frac{450}{350}}{1} = 1.286$$

Density of coal   = 1.286 × 1000 = 1286 Kg/m³
% coal by weight   = 450/600 = 0.75 ⇒ 75%
% coal by volume   = 350/500 = 0.70 ⇒ 70%

19.2.2: *Calculate the quantity of bromoform and benzene required to prepare 100 cc of solutions of heavy liquids with specific gravities of 1.4, 1.6 and 1.8. The specific gravities of bromoform and benzene are 2.85 and 0.8 respectively.*

Solution:

To prepare 1.4 sp. gr liquid
$\rho_1 = 2.85$; $\rho_2 = 0.8$; $\rho_{so} = 1.4$
Fraction of liquid 1 (bromoform) by volume = C_{v1}
$C_{v1}\rho_1 + (1 - C_{v1})\rho_2 = \rho_{so} \Rightarrow C_{v1} \times 2.85 + (1 - C_{v1}) \times 0.8 = 1.4$
$$\Rightarrow C_{v1} = 0.293$$

Fraction of liquid 2 (benzene) by volume   = 1 – 0.293 = 0.707
Volume of liquid 1 (bromoform)   = 0.293 × 100 = 29.3 cc

Volume of liquid 2 (benzene)	$= 0.707 \times 100 = 70.7$ cc
Weight of liquid 1 (bromoform)	$= 29.3 \times 2.85 = 83.5$ gm
Weight of liquid 2 (benzene)	$= 70.7 \times 0.8 = 56.5$ gm

To prepare 1.6 sp. gr liquid

$\rho_1 = 2.85$; $\rho_2 = 0.8$; $\rho_{so} = 1.6$

Fraction of liquid 1 (bromoform) by volume $= C_{v1}$

$$C_{v1}\rho_1 + (1 - C_{v1})\rho_2 = \rho_{so} \Rightarrow C_{v1} \times 2.85 + (1 - C_{v1}) \times 0.8 = 1.6$$
$$\Rightarrow C_{v1} = 0.39$$

Fraction of liquid 2 (benzene) by volume	$= 1 - 0.39 = 0.61$
Volume of liquid 1 (bromoform)	$= 0.39 \times 100 = 39$ cc
Volume of liquid 2 (benzene)	$= 0.61 \times 100 = 61$ cc
Weight of liquid 1 (bromoform)	$= 39 \times 2.85 = 111.2$ gm
Weight of liquid 2 (benzene)	$= 61 \times 0.8 = 48.8$ gm

To prepare 1.8 sp. gr liquid

$\rho_1 = 2.85$; $\rho_2 = 0.8$; $\rho_{so} = 1.8$

Fraction of liquid 1 (bromoform) by volume $= C_{v1}$

$$C_{v1}\rho_1 + (1 - C_{v1})\rho_2 = \rho_{so} \Rightarrow C_{v1} \times 2.85 + (1 - C_{v1}) \times 0.8 = 1.8$$
$$\Rightarrow C_{v1} = 0.488$$

Fraction of liquid 2 (benzene) by volume	$= 1 - 0.488 = 0.512$
Volume of liquid 1 (bromoform)	$= 0.488 \times 100 = 48.8$ cc
Volume of liquid 2 (benzene)	$= 0.512 \times 100 = 51.2$ cc
Weight of liquid 1 (bromoform)	$= 48.8 \times 2.85 = 139.1$ gm
Weight of liquid 2 (benzene)	$= 51.2 \times 0.8 = 40.9$ gm

19.2.3: *It is required to prepare a pulp of 30% solids by volume with 4.2 litres of water. Determine the weight of solids to be added in kilograms if the specific gravity of solids is 2.65.*

Solution:

$$C_v\rho_g + (1 - C_v)\rho_w = \rho_{sl} \Rightarrow 0.30 \times 2.65 + (1 - 0.30) = 1.495 \text{ gm/cc}$$

Volume of the pulp $= 4.2/0.7 \quad = 6$ litres

Weight of the pulp $= 1.495 \times 6 \quad = 8.97$ kg

$$\frac{C_w}{\rho_p} + \frac{1 - C_w}{\rho_w} = \frac{1}{\rho_{sl}} \Rightarrow \frac{C_w}{2.65} + \frac{1 - C_w}{1} = \frac{1}{1.495} \Rightarrow C_w = 0.532$$

Weight of solids to be added $= 8.97 \times 0.532 = 4.77$ kg

20.10.1: *Float and sink test data of coal of −38+25 mm size is shown in Table 20.10.1. Determine the washability characteristics.*

Table 20.10.1 Float and sink test data for problem 20.10.1.

Specific gravity	Wt% of floats	Floats Ash%
1.40	12.35	15.28
1.50	34.96	22.08
1.60	25.04	33.17
1.70	3.45	42.37
1.80	13.06	48.69
1.90	2.61	53.15
1.90 (sink)	8.53	76.03

Solution:

Cumulative wt% of floats and their ash% and cumulative wt% of sinks and their ash% are calculated and tabulated as shown in Table 20.10.1.1.

Table 20.10.1.1 Float and sink test results for problem 20.10.1.

Specific gravity	Wt% of floats	Floats Ash%	Ash product	Cumulative floats Wt%	Cumulative floats Ash product	Cumulative floats Ash%	Cumulative sinks Wt%	Cumulative sinks Ash product	Cumulative sinks Ash%
1.40	12.35	15.28	188.71	12.35	188.71	15.28	87.65	3171.83	36.19
1.50	34.96	22.08	771.92	47.31	960.63	20.31	52.69	2399.91	45.55
1.60	25.04	33.17	830.58	72.35	1791.21	24.76	27.65	1569.33	56.76
1.70	3.45	42.37	146.18	75.80	1937.39	25.56	24.20	1423.15	58.81
1.80	13.06	48.69	635.89	88.86	2573.28	28.96	11.14	787.26	70.67
1.90	2.61	53.15	138.72	91.47	2712.00	29.65	8.53	648.54	76.03
1.90 (sink)	8.53	76.03	648.54	100.0	3360.54	33.61	—	—	—

Percent ±0.1 near gravity material (NGM) at each specific gravity, cumulative ash percentages with respect to total ash present in the coal and degree of washabilty at each specific gravity by using the expression

$$\frac{\text{Recovery percent of clean coal} \times (\text{Ash\% in raw coal} - \text{Ash\% in clean coal})}{\text{Ash\% in raw coal}}$$

are calculated and tabulated as shown in Table 20.10.1.2.

Table 20.10.1.2 Calculated values of NGM & D.W. for problem 20.10.1.

Sp. gr	Wt%	Cum wt%	NGM	Ash%	Ash product	Ash% w.r.t total ash	Cum Ash% w.r.t total ash	D.W
1.4	12.35	12.35	47.31	15.28	188.71	5.61	5.61	6.74
1.5	34.96	47.31	60.00	22.08	771.92	22.97	28.58	18.72
1.6	25.04	72.35	28.49	33.17	830.58	24.72	53.30	19.05
1.7	3.45	75.80	16.51	42.37	146.18	4.35	57.65	18.16
1.8	13.06	88.86	15.67	48.69	635.89	18.92	76.57	12.29
1.9	2.61	91.47	–	53.15	138.72	4.13	81.70	10.78
1.9 sink	8.53	100.00	–	76.03	648.54	19.30	100.00	–
	100.00				3359.54	100.00		

With these values, washability curves are drawn as shown in Fig. 20.10.1.1.

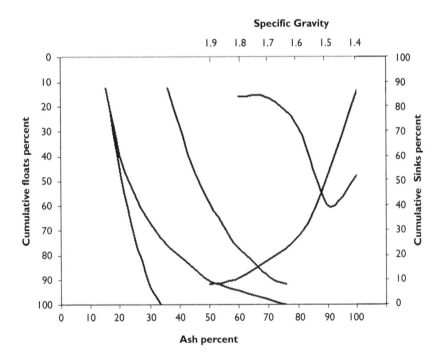

Figure 20.10.1.1 Washability Curves for problem 20.10.1.

Another two graphs, one to determine washability index and another to determine optimum degree of washability, are drawn as shown in Figs. 20.10.1.2 & 20.10.1.3.

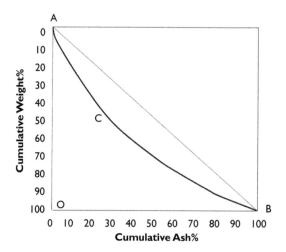

Figure 20.10.1.2 Graph to determine Washability Index for problem 20.10.1.

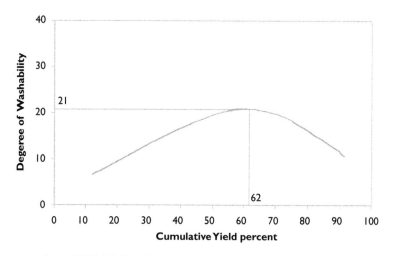

Figure 20.10.1.3 Graph to determine O.D.W. for problem 20.10.1.

From the shape of characteristic curve, it is difficult to wash the coal. The near gravity material at 1.5 and 1.6 specific gravities is more than 25%. Hence the coal is exceedingly difficult to wash as per the BIRD'S classification. At 1.7 specific gravity, the coal is difficult to wash.

The value of Washability Index (WI) obtained from the graph is 26 and the value of Optimum Degree of Washability (ODW) obtained from the graph is 21. The yield corresponding to ODW of 21 is 62% from the graph. From washability curves, ash in clean coal corresponding to this yield is 22, corresponding specific gravity of separation is 1.55, near gravity material (NGM) at this optimum cut point is 47.

Washability number (WN) $= \frac{21}{22} \times 10 = 9.5$

From the values of NGM, WI and WN, it can be concluded that the coal is difficult to wash.

20.10.2: *Washability test data of a coal sample is shown in Table 20.10.2.*

Table 20.10.2 Washability test data for problem 20.10.2.

Sp. gr.	Differential% of floats	Ash% in differential floats
1.30	7.6	5.9
1.40	21.3	12.7
1.50	36.7	21.8
1.60	13.8	30.5
1.70	11.6	39.6
1.80	4.8	48.3
1.80 (sink)	4.2	63.4

Determine the specific gravity at which the separation should be done for the beneficiation of this coal so that the ash content of the clean coal is not more than 17%. What is the expected yield of clean coal corresponding to this separation? Find out the ash percent in refuse and maximum ash of a particle in the yield. Calculate the yield reduction factor.

Solution:
The required values are calculated and tabulated as shown in Table 20.10.2.1.

Table 20.10.2.1 Calculated values for problem 20.10.2.

Sp. gr	Wt%	Ash%	Ash product		Cumulative floats			Cumulative sinks	
				Wt%	Ash product	Ash%	Wt%	Ash product	Ash%
1	2	3	4	5	6	7	8	9	10
1.30	7.6	5.9	44.84	7.6	44.84	5.90	92.4	2448.95	26.50
1.40	21.3	12.7	270.51	28.9	315.35	10.91	71.1	2178.44	30.64
1.50	36.7	21.8	800.06	65.6	1115.41	17.00	34.4	1378.38	40.07
1.60	13.8	30.5	420.90	79.4	1536.31	19.35	20.6	957.48	46.48
1.70	11.6	39.6	459.36	91.0	1995.67	21.93	9.0	498.12	55.35
1.80	4.8	48.3	231.84	95.8	2227.51	23.25	4.2	266.28	63.40
1.80 sink	4.2	63.4	266.28	100.0	2493.79	24.94	–	–	–

From the 8th row of the table, for floats of 17% ash the following are read:

a   Recovery of the clean coal   = 65.6%   (5th column)
b   Ash percent in rejects   = 40.07%   (10th column)
c   Maximum ash in any particle
    in the clean coal product   = 21.8%   (3rd column)
d   Specific gravity of separation = 1.50   (1st column)

Reduction in yield   = 100 – 65.6   = 34.4%
Reduction in ash   = 24.94 – 17.0 = 7.94%

$$\therefore \text{Yield Reduction Factor} = \frac{34.4}{7.94} = 4.33$$

Hence the coal is easy to wash.

20.10.3: *Washability test data of a coal sample is shown in Table 20.10.3.*

Table 20.10.3 Washability test data for problem 20.10.3.

Sp. gr.	Differential% of floats	Ash% in differential floats
1.40	7.5	14.1
1.50	13.1	26.6
1.60	12.6	36.6
1.70	11.8	42.7
1.80	6.8	47.9
1.90	7.2	53.8
2.00	7.0	61.1
2.00 (sink)	34.0	76.3

Determine yield and ash percentages of clean coal and middlings to get clean coal of 30% ash and refuse of 75% ash.

Solution:
Cumulative weight percentages and ash percentages are calculated necessary for drawing M-curve and shown in Table 20.10.3.1.

Table 20.10.3.1 Cumulative percentages for problem 20.10.3.

Sp. gr.	Float		Cum. float	
	Wt%	Ash%	Wt%	Ash%
1.40	7.5	14.1	7.5	14.1
1.50	13.1	26.6	20.6	22.1
1.60	12.6	36.6	33.2	27.6
1.70	11.8	42.7	45.0	31.6
1.80	6.8	47.9	51.8	33.7
1.90	7.2	53.8	59.0	36.2
2.00	7.0	61.1	66.0	38.8
2.00 (sink)	34.0	76.3	100.0	51.5

M-curve is drawn as per the procedure given in article 20.8.1. and yield and ash percentages are determined from M-curve as per the procedure given in article 20.8.2. and shown in Figure 20.10.3.1.

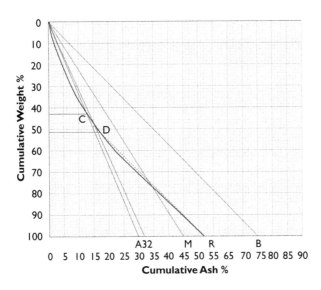

Figure 20.10.3.1 M-curve for problem 20.10.3.

The following results were obtained from the graph:

Yield of clean coal corresponding to point C = 43%
Yield of clean coal and middlings corresponding to point D = 52%
∴ Yield of middlings = 52 − 43 = 9%

Ash% of middlings at M = 45%
Ash% of clean coal and middlings together = 32%
Yield of refuse = 100 − 52 = 48%

22.7.1: *Calculate the terminal settling velocity of shale particle having 2.5 specific gravity and 50 microns in size settling in water.*

Solution:

Density of the shale particle $= \rho_p = 2.5$ gm/cc
Diameter of the shale particle $= d = 50$ microns $= 0.005$ cm
Density of water $= \rho_w = 1.0$ gm/cc
Viscosity of water $= \mu_w = 0.01$ poise

As per Stoke's law $v_m = \dfrac{d^2 g(\rho_p - \rho_w)}{18\mu_w}$

$$= \frac{(0.005)^2 (980)(2.5 - 1.0)}{18(0.01)} = 0.204 \text{ cm/sec}$$

22.7.2: *R.O.M Coal contains coal of specific gravity 1.35 and shale of specific gravity 2.40 has size range of 10 microns to 40 microns. When the ROM coal is classified in a free settling classifier, calculate the size range of coal particles separated and those remain with refuse.*

Solution:

Density of the coal particle $= \rho_{co} = 1.35$ gm/cc
Density of the shale particle $= \rho_{sh} = 2.40$ gm/cc
Density of water $\qquad = \rho_w = 1.0$ gm/cc

Let the diameters of the coal and shale particles be d_{co} and d_{sh}

By Stokes' law, Free settling ratio $= \dfrac{d_{co}}{d_{sh}} = \left(\dfrac{\rho_{sh} - \rho_w}{\rho_{co} - \rho_w} \right)^{1/2} = \left(\dfrac{2.40 - 1.00}{1.35 - 1.00} \right)^{1/2} = 2$

Diameter of the coal particle that settles equally with smallest shale particle
$$= d_{co} = 2 \times d_{sh} = 2 \times 10 = 20 \text{ microns}$$

All the coal particles of size less than 20 microns will get separated.
Size range of coal particles that remain in refuse with shale is 20–40 microns.

22.7.3: *R.O.M Coal contains coal of specific gravity 1.35 and shale of specific gravity 2.40 has size range of 10 microns to 40 microns. Will it be possible to separate all the coal particles under hindered settling conditions where the specific gravity of the pulp is maintained at 1.20?*

Solution:

Density of the coal particle $\quad = \rho_{co} = 1.35$ gm/cc
Density of the shale particle $\quad = \rho_{sh} = 2.40$ gm/cc
Density of the pulp $\qquad\qquad = \rho_{sl} = 1.20$ gm/cc

Let the diameters of the coal and shale particles be d_{co} and d_{sh}

By Newton's law, hindered settling ratio $= \dfrac{d_{co}}{d_{sh}} = \dfrac{\rho_{sh} - \rho_{sl}}{\rho_{co} - \rho_{sl}} = \dfrac{2.40 - 1.20}{1.35 - 1.20} = 6.2$

Diameter of the coal particle that settles equally with smallest shale particle
$$= d_{co} = 6.2 \times d_{sh} = 6.2 \times 10 = 62 \text{ microns}$$

It means that no single coal particle will settle until all the shale particles settle. Hence all the coal particles can be separated.

31.6.1: *Float and sink data of a coal is shown in Table 31.6.1. This coal is washed in three product chance cone employing 1.5 and 1.7 specific gravities. Assuming 100% efficiency, calculate the yield of cleans, middlings and rejects. Also calculate their ash percentages.*

Table 31.6.1 Float and sink data for problem 31.6.1.

Specific gravity	Wt% of coal floated	Ash%
1.40	12.35	15.28
1.50	34.96	22.08
1.60	25.04	33.17
1.70	3.45	42.37
1.80	13.06	48.69
1.90	2.61	53.15
1.90 (sink)	8.53	76.03

Solution:

Clean coal yield at 1.5 specific gravity $= 12.35 + 34.96$ $\qquad = 47.31\%$

Ash% in clean coal $= \dfrac{12.35 \times 15.28 + 34.96 \times 22.08}{47.31}$ $\qquad = 20.31\%$

Middling yield at 1.7 specific gravity $= 25.04 + 3.45$ $\qquad = 28.49\%$

Ash% in middlings $= \dfrac{25.04 \times 33.17 + 3.45 \times 42.37}{28.49}$ $\qquad = 34.28\%$

Rejects at 1.7 specific gravity $= 13.06 + 2.61 + 8.53$ $\qquad = 24.20\%$

Ash% in rejects $= \dfrac{13.06 \times 48.69 + 2.61 \times 53.15 + 8.53 \times 76.03}{24.20}$ $\qquad = 58.81\%$

31.6.2: *When a coal of 31% ash is treated in a froth flotation cell, a froth of 15% ash and a tailing of 55% ash is obtained. Calculate the percent yield of clean coal.*

Solution:

Percent ash in feed $\qquad = f = 31\%$

Percent ash in clean coal $\qquad = c = 15\%$

Percent ash in tailing $\qquad = t = 55\%$

Let the feed to flotation be 100 tons.

$$F = C + T \qquad \Rightarrow 100 = C + T$$
$$Ff = Cc + Tt \qquad \Rightarrow 100 \times 31 = 15C + 55T$$

Solving these two equations gives $C = 60$ tons

$$\therefore \text{Yield percent of clean coal} = \frac{60}{100} \times 100 = 60\%$$

31.6.3: *Raw coal feed to a coal washery has the following float and sink analysis as shown in Table 31.6.3.*

Table 31.6.3 Float and sink analysis of raw coal for problem 31.6.3.

Sp. gr.	Yield%	Ash%
below 1.25	1.5	2.6
+1.25–1.35	25.9	7.3
+1.35–1.45	38.4	20.0
+1.45–1.55	15.2	26.7
+1.55–1.65	7.7	37.1
+1.65–1.75	2.2	43.2
Above 1.75	9.1	57.1

On washing in a plant, a clean coal of 18% ash at an yield of 82% is obtained. Evaluate its performance.

Solution:
All the calculations are shown in the Table 31.6.3.1

Table 31.6.3.1 Calculations for problem 31.6.3.

Sp. gr.	Wt% of coal floated	Ash% in floated coal	Cum. wt% coal floated	Ash product	Cum. Ash product	Cum ash%
1	2	3	4	$5 = 2 \times 3$	6	$7 = 6/4$
1.25	1.5	2.6	1.5	3.90	3.90	2.60
1.35	25.9	7.3	27.4	189.07	192.97	7.04
1.45	38.4	20.0	65.8	768.00	960.97	14.60
1.55	15.2	26.7	81.0	405.84	1366.81	16.81
1.65	7.7	37.1	88.7	285.67	1652.48	18.63
1.75	2.2	43.2	90.9	95.04	1747.52	19.22
1.75 (sink)	9.1	57.1	100.0	519.61	2267.13	22.67

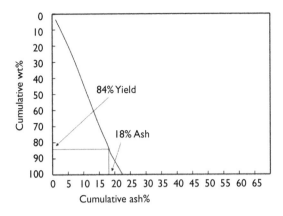

Figure 31.6.3.1 Total floats ash curve for problem 31.6.3.

From Total floats ash curve of Figure 31.6.3.1,

The yield of clean coal of 18% ash = 84%

Performance of the washery = Efficiency of the washery

$$= \frac{\text{Yield actually obtained from the washery}}{\text{Yield to be obtained}} \times 100 = \frac{82}{84} \times 100 = 97.6\%$$

Subject index